A BIBLIOGRAPHY OF
BRITISH INDUSTRIAL RELATIONS
1971–1979

A BIBLIOGRAPHY OF
BRITISH INDUSTRIAL RELATIONS
1971–1979

G. S. BAIN and J. D. BENNETT

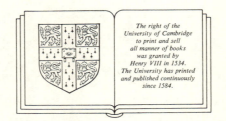

*The right of the
University of Cambridge
to print and sell
all manner of books
was granted by
Henry VIII in 1534.
The University has printed
and published continuously
since 1584.*

CAMBRIDGE UNIVERSITY PRESS

CAMBRIDGE

LONDON   NEW YORK   NEW ROCHELLE

MELBOURNE   SYDNEY

Published by the Press Syndicate of the University of Cambridge
The Pitt Building, Trumpington Street, Cambridge CB2 IRP
32 East 57th Street, New York, NY 10022, USA
10 Stamford Road, Oakleigh, Melbourne 3166, Australia

First published 1985

Printed in Great Britain at the University Press, Cambridge

Library of Congress catalogue card number: 84–7677

British Library cataloguing in publication data

Bain, George Sayers
A bibliography of British industrial relations 1971–1979.
1. Industrial relations – Great Britain – History – 20th century – Bibliography
I. Title   II. Bennett, J. D.

016.331'0941 Z7164.LI
ISBN 0 521 26699 8

TM

SHORT CONTENTS

CONTENTS

Part Four

Employers and their Organisation

Part Five

Labour – Management Relations

Part Six

The Labour Force, Labour Markets, and Conditions of Employment

Part Seven

The State and its Agencies

x   **Contents**

PREFACE

This volume is a supplement to G. S. Bain and G. B. Woolven, *A Bibliography of British Industrial Relations*, which attempted 'to bring together all the secondary source material, except that of an ephemeral or strictly propagandist nature, published in English between 1880 and 1970 on British industrial relations'.[1] The present volume has the same aim for the period 1971 to 1979 inclusive and, as far as possible, it adheres to the principles and methods used by Bain and Woolven. Hence, with a few exceptions noted below, the introduction to their volume also applies to this supplement.

The subject scope of the bibliography remains unaltered. Industrial relations continues to be defined as the study of *all* aspects of job regulation – the process of making and administering the rules that regulate or control employment relationships. Some reviewers of the earlier volume pointed out that this definition reflects a particular approach to the study of industrial relations. It obviously does as, indeed, must any definition of the subject. But although this definition is, as another reviewer noted, 'contentious ... in practice it allows for the inclusion of material from many disciplines and none, and cannot lead to the exclusion of many, if any, items which one would expect to find in such a bibliography'.[2]

The supplement narrows the geographical scope of the bibliography by excluding material relating to Eire after its separation from the United Kingdom in 1922. But it has slightly broadened the categories of material covered by the bibliography. It includes 'consultative documents' published by government departments as well as the more substantial and more discursive articles that now appear in the *Employment Gazette*. It also includes the more substantial articles in several previously excluded journals of a 'practitioner'

nature, such as *Personnel Management*, *Industrial Society*, *Work Study*, and *Industrial and Commercial Training*, especially in areas where literature from 'learned' journals is scanty. Inevitably, new journals have been established since 1970 and some older journals have disappeared, and these changes are reflected in the list of periodical titles given below. Although this list, like that in the earlier volume, conforms to the specifications laid down by the British Standards Institution, some journal titles may now be abbreviated in a different manner because the Institution has amended its specifications.[3]

The supplement includes a few items published before 1971 that were inadvertently omitted from the earlier volume. But it excludes items published before 1971 that have been reprinted after this date, unless the reprint contains new material (e.g. a new introduction to an earlier edition). It also excludes articles from such current awareness bulletins as *Industrial Relations Review and Report* and *European Industrial Relations Review*.

The supplement, like the earlier volume, is comprehensive in nature, but it does not claim to be complete. The publications of official and semi-official organisations have proved particularly difficult to track down, and no doubt some of these as well as other relevant items have been overlooked. We hope readers will draw to our attention any omissions or errors that they detect. These can then be made good in the bibliographic article by John Bennett that now appears annually in the *British Journal of Industrial Relations*.[4]

The subject classification in the supplement differs in two minor respects from that in the earlier volume. First, the attention of writers

---

[1] G. S. Bain and G. B. Woolven, *A Bibliography of British Industrial Relations* (Cambridge: Cambridge University Press, 1979), xiii.

[2] Richard K. Brown, *Sociology*, xiv (February 1980), 153.

[3] See *Recommendations for the Abbreviation of Titles of Periodicals*, BS4148 (London: BSI, 1967); *Specification for the Abbreviation of Titles of Periodicals, Part 1: Principles*, BS4148 (London: BSI, 1970); and *Specification for the Abbreviation of Titles of Periodicals, Part 2: Word-Abbreviation List*, BS4148(2) (London: BSI, 1975).

[4] See *British Journal of Industrial Relations*, xx (November 1982), 377–414; and xxi (July 1983), 234–64.

during the 1970s was directed away from some areas, such as the Poor Laws, and towards others, such as industrial democracy, and the resulting changes in the structure of the literature have demanded that the degree of specificity in the classification be decreased in subject areas such as the former and increased in those such as the latter. Second, since the supplement covers a much shorter period than the earlier volume, the amount of material included is substantially less, and the degree of specificity in some areas of the classification, especially those sub-divided by industry, has been decreased.

In all other respects the arrangement and classification of the bibliography remain unaltered. In particular, within each subject class the entries are arranged chronologically by date of publication. One reviewer of the earlier volume 'would prefer materials to be organised under authors rather than chronologically, avoiding for example an item listing somebody's thesis often separated by other items from the book to which the thesis gave rise'.[5] In our view, however, since an author index is provided, a chronological arrangement provides a useful additional perspective of the literature, enabling the reader to see how the writings on a particular topic have developed over time. Some reviewers of the earlier

volume also bemoaned the absence of a subject index. We cannot deny that an adequate subject index would be useful, but to compile such an index would be an enormous task which, as one reviewer correctly surmised, would be 'beyond the technical, temporal and emotional resources of the bibliographers'.[6] It would also greatly increase the size and the price of an already lengthy and expensive bibliography. In the absence of a subject index, we have tried to assist the reader by providing as much detail in the subject classification and as many cross-references as possible.

The compilation of this supplement was facilitated by a grant from the Nuffield Foundation. The University of Warwick Library supported the project with material and other resources. Howard Gospel, Richard Storey, and Stephen Wood helped by providing references and pointing out omissions. We are most grateful to these institutions and individuals. Our greatest debt is to Annemarie Flanders; she began work on the supplement as a typist but rapidly became sub-editor-in-chief. Those errors and omissions that have evaded even her remain our responsibility.

GEORGE BAIN
JOHN BENNETT

---

[5] P. O'Higgins, *Industrial Law Journal*, VIII (December 1979), 253–4.

[6] Brian Towers, *Industrial Relations Journal*, x (Winter 1979–80), 66–7.

PERIODICAL TITLES
AND ABBREVIATIONS

Account. Bus. Res.	*Accounting and Business Research*
Account. Mag.	*Accountants' Magazine*
Account. Organ. Soc.	*Accounting, Organizations and Society*
Acta Sociol.	*Acta Sociologica*
Adm. Manage.	*Administrative Management*
Adm. Sci. Q.	*Administrative Science Quarterly*
Administration	*Administration* (Dublin)
Advance	*Advance*
Albion	*Albion*
Am. Econ. Rev.	*American Economic Review*
Am. Hist. Rev.	*American History Review*
Am. J. Econ. Sociol.	*American Journal of Economics and Sociology*
Am. J. Sociol.	*American Journal of Sociology*
Am. Polit. Sci. Rev.	*American Political Science Review*
Ann. Am. Acad. Polit. Soc. Sci.	*Annals of the American Academy of Political and Social Science*
Ann. Publ. Coop. Econ.	*Annals of Public and Cooperative Economy*
Appl. Econ.	*Applied Economics*
Appl. Ergonom.	*Applied Ergonomics*
Appl. Stat.	*Applied Statistics*
Arbit. J.	*Arbitration Journal*
Archit. J.	*Architects' Journal*
Archives	*Archives*
Aslib Proc.	*Aslib Proceedings*
Assist. Libr.	*Assistant Librarian*
Aust. Econ. Rev.	*Australian Economic Review*
Ayrshire Collect.	*Ayrshire Collections*
B.A.C.I.E. J.	*B.A.C.I.E. Journal* (British Association for Commercial and Industrial Education)
Banker	*Banker*
Bankers' Mag.	*Bankers' Magazine*
Barclays Bank Rev.	*Barclays Bank Review*
Battle Dist. Hist. Soc. Trans.	*Battle and District Historical Society Transactions*
Beds. Mag.	*Bedfordshire Magazine*
Blackcountryman	*Blackcountryman*
Bookseller	*Bookseller*
Br. Book News	*British Book News*
Br. J. Criminol.	*British Journal of Criminology*
Br. J. Guid. Couns.	*British Journal of Guidance and Counselling*
Br. J. Ind. Relat.	*British Journal of Industrial Relations*
Br. J. Law Soc.	*British Journal of Law and Society*
Br. J. Polit. Sci.	*British Journal of Political Science*
Br. J. Psychol.	*British Journal of Psychology*
Br. J. Soc. Work	*British Journal of Social Work*
Br. J. Sociol.	*British Journal of Sociology*

Br. Psychol. Soc. Bull.	*British Psychological Society Bulletin*
Bris. Glouc. Archaeol. Soc. Trans.	*Bristol and Gloucestershire Archaeological Society Transactions*
Build. Soc. Inst. Q.	*Building Societies Institute Quarterly*
Bull. Econ. Res.	*Bulletin of Economic Research*
Bull. Local Hist. East Midl. Reg.	*Bulletin of Local History: East Midland Region*
Bus. Adm.	*Business Administration*
Bus. Arch.	*Business Archives*
Bus. Econ.	*Business Economics*
Bus. Hist.	*Business History*
Bus. Manage.	*Business Management*
C.B.I. Rev.	*C.B.I. Review* (Confederation of British Industry)
Cake and Cock Horse	*Cake and Cock Horse*
Camb. J. Econ.	*Cambridge Journal of Economics*
Camb. Law J.	*Cambridge Law Journal*
Cap. Cl.	*Capital and Class*
Careers Q.	*Careers Quarterly*
Chief Exec.	*Chief Executive*
Comm. Can. Labour Hist. Bull.	*Committee on Canadian Labour History Bulletin*
Community Dev. J.	*Community Development Journal*
Comp. Stud. Soc. Hist.	*Comparative Studies in Society and History*
Contemp. Rev.	*Contemporary Review*
Coop. Inf.	*Cooperative Information*
Co-partnership	*Co-partnership*
Crim. Law Rev.	*Criminal Law Review*
Cumberland & Westmorland Antiq. Archaeol. Soc. Trans.	*Cumberland and Westmorland Antiquarian and Archaeological Society Transactions*
Curr. Leg. Probl.	*Current Legal Problems*
Dep. Employment Gaz.	*Department of Employment Gazette*
Devon Hist.	*Devon Historian*
Dumfriesshire & Galloway Nat. Hist. Antiq. Soc. Trans.	*Dumfriesshire and Galloway Natural History and Antiquarian Society Transactions*
Durham Res. Rev.	*Durham Research Review*
Durham Univ. J.	*Durham University Journal*
E. London Pap.	*East London Papers*
E. London Rec.	*East London Record*
Econ. Anal. Workers' Manage.	*Economic Analysis and Workers' Management*
Econ. Hist. Rev.	*Economic History Review*
Econ. Humanisme	*Economie et Humanisme*
Econ. J.	*Economic Journal*
Econ. Soc. Rev.	*Economic and Social Review*
Econ. Soc. Tijdschr.	*Economisch en Sociaal Tijdschrift*
Economica	*Economica*
Educ. Train.	*Education and Training*
Employee Relat.	*Employee Relations*
Encounter	*Encounter*
Engl. Hist. Rev.	*English Historical Review*
Essex J.	*Essex Journal*
Eur. Demogr. Inf. Bull.	*European Demographic Information Bulletin*
Eur. J. Mark.	*European Journal of Marketing*
Eur. Train.	*European Training*
Explor. Econ. Hist.	*Explorations in Economic History*
Expos. Times	*Expository Times*
Folklife	*Folklife*
Friends' Hist. Soc. J.	*Friends' Historical Society Journal*
Friends' Q.	*Friends' Quarterly*
Genealogists' Mag.	*Genealogists' Magazine*
Geogr.	*Geography*
Gov. Oppos.	*Government and Opposition*

Greater London Council Intell. Unit Q. Bull.	Greater London Council Intelligence Unit Quarterly Bulletin
Greater London Intell. J.	Greater London Intelligence Journal
Halifax Antiq. Soc. Trans.	Halifax Antiquarian Society Transactions
Harv. Bus. Rev.	Harvard Business Review
Higher Educ. Rev.	Higher Educational Review
Hist. Educ.	History of Education
Hist. J.	Historical Journal
Hist. Soc.	Histoire Sociale
Hist. Stud.	History Studies (Buckland)
Hist. Today	History Today
Hist. Workshop	History Workshop
History	History
Hosp. Health Serv. Rev.	Hospital and Health Services Review
Hum. Relat.	Human Relations
I.M.S. Monit.	I.M.S. Monitor (Institute for Manpower Studies)
Ind. Archaeol.	Industrial Archaeology
Ind. Commer. Train.	Industrial and Commercial Training
Ind. Gerontol.	Industrial Gerontology
Ind. Labor Relat. Rev.	Industrial and Labor Relations Review
Ind. Law J.	Industrial Law Journal
Ind. Law Rev.	Industrial Law Review
Ind. Participation	Industrial Participation
Ind. Relat.	Industrial Relations
Ind. Relat. J.	Industrial Relations Journal
Ind. Soc.	Industrial Society
Ind. Train. Int.	Industrial Training International
Ind. Tutor	Industrial Tutor
Indian J. Ind. Relat.	Indian Journal of Industrial Relations
Indian J. Labour Econ.	Indian Journal of Labour Economics
Inst. Transp. J.	Institute of Transport Journal
Insurg. Sociol.	Insurgent Sociologist
Int. Comp. Law Q.	International and Comparative Law Quarterly
Int. Econ. Rev.	International Economic Review
Int. Inst. Labour Stud. Bull.	International Institute for Labour Studies Bulletin
Int. J. Soc. Econ.	International Journal of Social Economics
Int. Labour Rev.	International Labour Review
Int. Manage.	International Management
Int. Monetary Fund Staff Pap.	International Monetary Fund Staff Papers
Int. Rev. of Soc. Hist.	International Review of Social History
Int. Soc.	International Socialism
Int. Soc. Secur. Rev.	International Social Security Review
Ir. Ancestor	Irish Ancestor
Ir. Arch. Bull.	Irish Archives Bulletin
Irish Hist. Stud.	Irish Historical Studies
J. Agric. Econ.	Journal of Agricultural Economics
J. Br. Stud.	Journal of British Studies
J. Bus. Finance	Journal of Business Finance
J. Bus. Finance Account.	Journal of Business Finance and Accounting
J. Bus. Policy	Journal of Business Policy
J. Common Mark. Stud.	Journal of Common Market Studies
J. Contemp. Hist.	Journal of Contemporary History
J. Econ. Hist.	Journal of Economic History
J. Econ. Issues	Journal of Economic Issues
J. Econ. Stud.	Journal of Economic Studies
J. Educ. Adm. Hist.	Journal of Educational Administration and History
J. Eur. Ind. Train.	Journal of European Industrial Training
J. Eur. Train.	Journal of European Training

J. Gen. Manage.	Journal of General Management
J. Imp. Commonw. Hist.	Journal of Imperial and Commonwealth History
J. Ind. Affairs	Journal of Industrial Affairs
J. Ind. Econ.	Journal of Industrial Economics
J. Ind. Relat.	Journal of Industrial Relations
J. Interdisciplinary Hist.	Journal of Interdisciplinary History
J. Manage. Stud.	Journal of Management Studies
J. Manx Mus.	Journal of the Manx Museum
J. New Zealand Hist.	Journal of New Zealand History
J. Occup. Psychol.	Journal of Occupational Psychology
J. Peasant Stud.	Journal of Peasant Studies
J. Polit. Econ.	Journal of Political Economy
J. Soc. Hist.	Journal of Social History
J. Soc. Policy	Journal of Social Policy
J. South. Afr. Stud.	Journal of Southern African Studies
J. Transp. Hist.	Journal of Transport History
Juridical Rev.	Juridical Review
Labor Hist.	Labor History
Labor Law J.	Labor Law Journal
Labor Stud. J.	Labor Studies Journal
Labour and Soc.	Labour and Society
Labour Hist.	Labour History
Labour Mon.	Labour Monthly
Law Q. Rev.	Law Quarterly Review
Library	Library
Listener	Listener
Llafur	Llafur
Lloyds Bank Rev.	Lloyds Bank Review
Local Gov. Stud.	Local Government Studies
Local Historian	Local Historian
Local History	Local History
Local Pop. Stud.	Local Population Studies
London Bus. School J.	London Business School Journal
Long Range Plann.	Long Range Planning
Manage. Account.	Management Accounting
Manage. Action	Management in Action
Manage. Decis.	Management Decision
Manage. Educ. Dev.	Management Education and Development
Manage. Finance	Managerial Finance
Manage. Objectives	Management by Objectives
Manage. Serv.	Management Services
Manage. Serv. Gov.	Management Services in Government
Manage. Sympos.	Management Symposium
Manchr. Bus. School Rev.	Manchester Business School Review
Manchr. Lit. Philos. Soc. Proc.	Manchester Literary and Philosophical Society Proceedings
Manchr. Sch. Econ. Soc. Stud.	Manchester School of Economic and Social Studies
Manchr. Stat. Soc. Trans.	Manchester Statistical Society Transactions
Manpower J.	Manpower Journal
Mar. Mirror	Mariner's Mirror (Society for Nautical Research)
Marit. Hist.	Maritime History
Marit. Policy Manage.	Maritime Policy and Management
Marit. Stud. Manage.	Maritime Studies and Management
Marx Meml. Libr. Q. Bull.	Marx Memorial Library Quarterly Bulletin
Marxism Today	Marxism Today
Medicoleg. J.	Medico-legal Journal
Midl. Hist.	Midlands History
Mod. Law Rev.	Modern Law Review
Mod. Tramway	Modern Tramway

Mon. Labor Rev.	Monthly Labor Review
Montgomeryshire Collect.	Montgomeryshire Collections
Month	Month
Moor. Wall Street	Moorgate and Wall Street
Mus. J.	Museums Journal
N.E. Group Study Labour Hist. Bull.	North East Group for the Study of Labour History Bulletin
N. Staffs. J. Field Stud.	North Staffordshire Journal of Field Studies
N.W. Labour Hist. Soc. Bull.	North West Labour History Society Bulletin
N. Yorks. County Record Office J.	North Yorkshire County Record Office Journal
Natl. Inst. Econ. Rev.	National Institute Economic Review
Natl. Westminster Bank Q. Rev.	National Westminster Bank Quarterly Review
Nature	Nature
New Blackfriars	New Blackfriars
New Community	New Community
New Humanist	New Humanist
New Law J.	New Law Journal
New Left Rev.	New Left Review
New Sci.	New Scientist
New Soc.	New Society
New Zealand J. Hist.	New Zealand Journal of History
Norfolk Archaeol.	Norfolk Archaeology
Norfolk Ind. Archaeol. Soc. J.	Norfolk Industrial Archaeology Society Journal
North. Hist.	Northern History
Northamps. Past Present	Northamptonshire Past and Present
O & M Bull.	O & M Bulletin
Occup. Psychol.	Occupational Psychology
Occup. Saf. Health	Occupational Safety and Health
Old Motor	Old Motor
Old Wexford Soc. J.	Old Wexford Society Journal
Omega	Omega
Oper. Res. Q.	Operational Research Quarterly
Optima	Optima
Oral Hist.	Oral History
Oxf. Agrar. Stud.	Oxford Agrarian Studies
Oxf. Bull. Econ. Stat.	Oxford Bulletin of Economics and Statistics
Oxf. Econ. Pap.	Oxford Economic Papers
Oxf. Univ. Inst. Econ. Stat. Bull.	Oxford University Institute of Economics and Statistics Bulletin
Oxoniensia	Oxoniensia
P.T.T.I. Stud.	P.T.T.I. Studies (Postal, Telegraph and Telephone International)
Parliamentary Aff.	Parliamentary Affairs
Past & Present	Past & Present
Pensions World	Pensions World
Pers. Manage.	Personnel Management
Pers. Rev.	Personnel Review
Plann.	Planner
Police J.	Police Journal
Polit. Q.	Political Quarterly
Polit. Sci.	Political Science
Polit. Sci. Q.	Political Science Quarterly
Polit. Soc.	Politics and Society
Polit. Stud.	Political Studies
Popul. Stud.	Population Studies
Poverty	Poverty
Prakseologia	Prakseologia
Prod. Eng.	Production Engineer
Public Adm.	Public Administration
Public Finance Account.	Public Finance and Accountancy

Q. J. Econ.	Quarterly Journal of Economics
R & D Manage.	R & D Management
RIBA J.	RIBA Journal
R. Inst. G. B. Proc.	Royal Institute of Great Britain Proceedings
R. Soc. Arts J.	Royal Society of Arts Journal
R. United Services Inst. Def. Stud. J.	Royal United Services Institute for Defence Studies Journal
Race	Race
Race & Class	Race & Class
Race Today	Race Today
Rec. Bucks.	Records of Buckinghamshire
Reg. Stud.	Regional Studies
Relat. Industrielles	Relations Industrielles
Renaissance Mod. Stud.	Renaissance and Modern Studies
Retail Distrib. Manage.	Retail Distribution and Management
Rev. Econ. Stat.	Review of Economics and Statistics
Rev. Econ. Stud.	Review of Economic Studies
Rev. Int. Sci. Adm.	Revue Internationale des Sciences Administratives
Round Table	Round Table
Saothar	Saothar
Scott. Bankers' Mag.	Scottish Bankers' Magazine
Scott. Geogr. Mag.	Scottish Geographical Magazine
Scott. Ind. Hist.	Scottish Industrial History
Scott. J. Polit. Econ.	Scottish Journal of Political Economy
Scott. Labour Hist. Soc. J.	Scottish Labour History Society Journal
Sight & Sound	Sight & Sound
Soc. Econ. Adm.	Social and Economic Administration
Soc. Hist.	Social History
Soc. Study Labour Hist. Bull.	Society for the Study of Labour History Bulletin
Social. Comment.	Socialist Commentary
Social. Reg.	Socialist Register
Sociol. Anal. Theory	Sociological Analysis and Theory
Sociol. Rev.	Sociological Review
Sociol. Work Occup.	Sociology of Work and Occupations
Sociology	Sociology
Sov. Stud.	Soviet Studies
Sri Lanka Labour Gaz.	Sri Lanka Labour Gazette
Stud. Int.	Studio International
Stud. Pers. Psychol.	Studies in Personnel Psychology
Studies	Studies
Suffolk Rev.	Suffolk Review
Surrey Archaeol. Collect.	Surrey Archaeological Collections
Sx. Archaeol. Collect.	Sussex Archaeological Collections
Tex. Hist.	Textile History
Theology	Theology
Thores. Soc. Publ.	Thoresby Society Publications
Three Banks Rev.	Three Banks Review
Town Ctry Plann.	Town and Country Planning
Town Plann. Rev.	Town Planning Review
Trade Union Inf.	Trade Union Information (Dublin)
Train. Off.	Training Officer
Transp. Hist.	Transport History
Twentieth Century	Twentieth Century
Univ. Leuven Inst. Labour Relat. Bull.	University of Leuven Institute of Labour Relations Bulletin
Upper Ards Hist. Soc. J.	Upper Ards Historical Society Journal
Urb. Stud.	Urban Studies
Vic. Stud.	Victorian Studies
Welsh Hist. Rev.	Welsh History Review

Wesley Hist. Soc. Proc.	*Wesley Historical Society Proceedings*
Woolhope Nat. Field Club Trans.	*Woolhope Naturalists Field Club Transactions*
Worcs. Archaeol. Soc. Trans.	*Worcestershire Archaeological Society Transactions*
Work Study	*Work Study*
Work Study Manage. Serv.	*Work Study and Management Services*
Works Manage.	*Works Management*
Yorks. Bull. Econ. Soc. Res.	*Yorkshire Bulletin of Economic and Social Research*

PART ONE

GENERAL

I. BIBLIOGRAPHIES AND GUIDES TO ARCHIVAL AND STATISTICAL SOURCES

This section includes not only general bibliographies on industrial relations but also those which are concerned with a particular aspect of the subject. Surveys of research and opinion are classified with the subject to which they pertain. Statistical sources on a particular subject are to be found with the subject.

1 **Fla**, B. *Safety in Mines Research Establishment bibliography.* London: The Establishment, 1969. viii, 325p.
   Third edition.

2 **Pettman**, Barrie Owen. *An annotated bibliography of labour turnover studies.* Bradford: Institute of Scientific Business, 1970. 38p. (Bibliographical studies 1.)

3 **Bain**, George Sayers and **Woolven**, Gillian Beatrice. 'Labour economics and industrial relations.' Fletcher, John (ed.). *The uses of economic literature.* London: Butterworth, 1971. p. 240–60.

4 **Bain**, George Sayers and **Woolven**, Gillian Beatrice. 'The primary materials of British industrial relations.' *Br. J. Ind. Relat.*, IX, 3 (November 1971), 388–414.

5 **Brighton Reference Library.** *Sussex labour records held in the Brighton Reference Library.* Brighton: B.R.L., 1971.

6 **Harrison**, Royden. 'The arithmetic of labour.' *New Soc.*, XVIII (22 July 1971), 147–9.

7 **Lipsey**, D. *Productivity in distribution: a summary of the literature.* London: National Economic Development Office, 1971. 20, 4p.

8 **McMenamin**, S. 'Board of Guardian records: classifying and cataloguing.' *Ir. Arch. Bull.*, I, 2 (October 1971), 19–33.

9 **National Book League** and **British Association for Commercial and Industrial Education.** *Books for training officers.* London: The Authors, 1971. 48p.

10 **Pettman**, Barrie Owen. *A bibliography on strikes.* Bradford: Institute of Scientific Business, 1971. 40p.

11 **Pettman**, Barrie Owen. *Industrial democracy: Algeria to Zambia: a selected bibliography.* Bradford: Institute of Scientific Business, 1971.

12 **Pettman**, Barrie Owen. *Industrial democracy in general and in Great Britain: a selected bibliography.* Bradford: Institute of Scientific Business, 1971. 90p.

13 **Pettman**, Barrie Owen. *The Industrial Training Act and the work of the Industrial Training Boards: a selected and annotated bibliography.* Bradford: Institute of Scientific Business, 1971. 40p.

14 **Child**, John. 'British publications on work and organization.' *Br. Book News* (December 1972), 1014–18.

15 **Gottschalk**, Andrew W. *Industrial democracy: a select bibliography of the literature since 1960.* Nottingham: University of Nottingham Department of Adult Education, 1972. 33p.

16 **Jones**, M. 'The Swansea project.' *Llafur*, I, 1 (May 1972), 33–4.

17 **Llafur.** 'Bibliography of Welsh labour history.' *Llafur*, I, 1 (May 1972), 16–28.

18 **McDonald**, R. W. 'Sources for Welsh labour history no. 1: the National Library of Wales – part 1.' *Llafur*, I, 1 (May 1972), 27–32.

19 **Manchester Business School Library.** *Industrial democracy.* Manchester: The Library, 1972. 16p. (Bibliographies 16.)

20 **Parker**, Stanley Robert. *Annotated bibliography on leisure, Great Britain.* Prague: European Centre for Leisure and Education, 1972. 57p. (Bibliographical series 5.)

21 **Torrington**, Derek P. 'Sources of information.' Torrington, Derek P. (ed.). *Handbook of industrial relations.* 1972. p. 97–106.

22 **Francis**, Hywel. 'Survey of Miners' Institute and Welfare Hall libraries.' *Llafur*, I, 2 (May 1973), 55–64.

23 **Gottschalk**, Andrew W. *Workplace industrial relations and bargaining behaviour: a behavioural approach: a select bibliography.* Nottingham: University of Nottingham Department of Adult Education, 1973. 36p.

24 **Liverpool City Libraries.** *List of records of the Liverpool Trades Council (formerly the Liverpool Trades' Guardian Association, founded 1848) deposited in Liverpool City Libraries.* Liverpool: Brown, Picton and Hornby Libraries. 1973. 35p.

25 **National Economic Development Office.** *Labour statistics: report of a conference held under the general auspices of the Standing Committee of Statistics Users, 1973, London.* London: N.E.D.O., 1973. v, 141p.

26 **Pettman**, Barrie Owen. *Training for the future and after: a selected and annotated bibliography.* Bradford: Institute of Scientific Business, 1973. 57p. (Bibliographies 6.)

27 **Pettman**, Barrie Owen. *Wastage analysis: a selected international and temporal bibliography.* Hull: Emmasglen, 1973. 89p.

28 **Rule**, John. 'The British fisherman 1840–1914: a bibliographical essay.' *Soc. Study Labour Hist. Bull.*, XXVII (Autumn 1973), 53–63.

29 **Brighton, Hove and District Trades Council**, History Sub-Committee. [Labour history source lists.] Brighton: The Trades Council [1974?]

30 **Institute of Development Studies Library.** *International trade unions: a preliminary check list of publications.* Brighton: I.D.S. Library, 1974. 68p.

31 **University of Nottingham Library**, Department of Manuscripts. *Amalgamated Society of Operative Lacemakers and Auxiliary Workers: records 1888–1973, a list.* Nottingham: The Department, 1974. 15p.

32 **Barlow**, A. C. 'Trade union organisation in Ireland: a review of recent publications.' *Econ. Soc. Rev.*, VII, 1 (October 1975), 87–92.

33 **Barry**, Anthony. 'Survey of sources of information.' Bowey, Angela M. (ed.). *Handbook of salary and wage systems.* 1975. p. 369–76.

34 **Bennett**, John David. *The disclosure of company information: a selected bibliography.* Aberystwyth: Business Information Press, 1975. 21p.

35 **Bishopsgate Institute.** *George Howell collection: index to the correspondence.* London: The Institute, 1975. 29p. Revised edition.

36 **Cooperative Union Library**. *Robert Owen: a checklist of books, pamphlets, press cuttings and MSS in the Library of the ...* Manchester: The Library, 1975. 6p.

37 **Gerrard**, Susan. *A bibliography of Pilkington Brothers Ltd., with particular reference to their strikes.* St Helens: St Helens Borough Council. Libraries, Museum and Arts Department, 1975. Typescript.

38 **Hepple**, Robert Alexander, **Neeson**, Jeannette M. and **O'Higgins**, Paul. *A bibliography of the literature on British and Irish labour law.* London: Mansell, 1975. xxv, 331p.

39 **Hutton**, Joyce and **Hutton**, Bill. 'Understanding numbers.' Coker, E. and Stuttard, G. (eds.). *Industrial studies 1: the key skills.* 1975. p. 125–32.

40 **Institute of Personnel Management**. *I.P.M. bibliography.* London: I.P.M. Information Department, 1974–5. 3p.

41 *Labour relations on large industrial construction sites.* London: Gothard House, 1975.

42 **Neville**, Robert G. and **Benson**, John. 'Labour in the coalfields: a select critical bibliography.' *Soc. Study Labour Hist. Bull.*, XXXI (Autumn 1975), 45–59.

43 **Raine**, John Stanley. *Fringe benefits and company pensions: a selected bibliography.* Aberystwyth: Business Information Press, 1975. 28p.

44 **Raine**, John Stanley. *Sources of information on flexible working hours: a bibliography and directory of manufacturers and information services.* Aberystwyth: Business Information Press, 1975. 11p.

45 **University of Leuven Institute of Labour Relations Bulletin.** 'Labour law and industrial relations: international bibliography. National studies: United Kingdom.' *Univ. Leuven Inst. Labour Relat. Bull.*, VI (1975), 205–10.

46 **Chaloner**, William Henry and **Richardson**, R. C. *British economic and social history: a bibliographic guide.* Manchester: Manchester U.P., 1976. xiv, 130p.

47 **Druker**, Janet. 'The builders' history: notes on sources.' *Soc. Study Labour Hist. Bull.*, XXXII (Spring 1976), 33–7.

48 **Farrant**, Sue. 'Some records of the old Poor Law as sources of local history.' *Local Historian*, XII, 3–4 (November 1976), 136–8.

49 **Francis**, Hywel. 'The origins of the South Wales Miners' Library.' *Hist. Workshop*, II (Autumn 1976), 183–205.

50 **Lowndes**, Richard. 'The Industrial Relations Training Resource Centre.' *Ind. Commer. Train.*, VIII, 5 (May 1976), 203–7.

51 **MacCafferty,** Maine. *Employment relations in the UK.* London: Aslib, 1976. VI, 48p. (Bibliographies 2.)

52 **Pettman**, Barrie Owen. *Strikes: a selected bibliography.* Bradford: MCB Books, 1976. 64, viip.

53 **Rowat**, C. L. *Workers' participation: a bibliographical survey.* London: Rowat Information Services, 1976. 83p.

54 **Smith**, Harold. *Remember 1926: catalogue of an exhibition to commemorate the 50th anniversary of the General Strike.* London: The Compiler, 1976. 8p.

55 **Swann**, Brenda. 'The Public Record Office as a source for labour history.' *Hist. Workshop*, II (Autumn 1976), 96–103.

56 **British Association for Commercial and Industrial Education.** *The BACIE bibliography of publications in the field of education and training in commerce and industry.* London: B.A.C.I.E., 1977. Edited by P. J. C. Perry.

57 **Buxton**, Neil K. and **MacKay**, Donald Iain. *British employment statistics: a guide to sources and methods.* Oxford: Blackwell, 1977. 197p. (Warwick studies in industrial relations.)

58 **Cameron**, Alan. 'The records of the Lace-makers' Society.' *Bull. Local Hist. East Midl. Reg.*, XII (1977), 12–16.

59 **Conway**, Eddie (comp.). *Labour history of Manchester and Salford: a bibliography.* Manchester: Manchester Centre for Marxist Education, 1977. 34p.

60 **Doyle**, Mel. *A trade unionist's guide to sources of information.* London: W.E.A., 1977. 13p.

61 **Druker**, Janet. 'Preserving labour's history.' *Ind. Tutor*, II, 6 (March 1977), 74–6.

62 **Druker**, Janet and **Storey**, Richard A. 'The Modern Records Centre at Warwick and the local historian.' *Local Historian*, XII, 8 (November 1977), 394–400.

63 **Francis**, Hywel. 'The origins of the South Wales Miners' Library.' *Assist. Libr.*, LXX, 12 (December 1977), 186–90.

64 **Harrison**, Royden, **Woolven**, Gillian Beatrice and **Duncan**, Robert. *The Warwick guide to British labour periodicals, 1790–1970: a check list.* London: Harvester P., 1977. 685p.

65 **Irish Labour History Society**. *One hundred and fifty years: union history: [catalogue of an] exhibition of the records of the Irish Bakers, Confectioners and Allied Workers Union to the Irish Labour History Society.* Dublin: Irish Congress of Trade Unions, 1977. 22p.

66 **Nevin**, Donal. 'James Larkin 1876–1947: a bibliography.' *Trade Union Inf.* (Winter 1976–7), 220–2.

67 **Rigney**, P. 'Some records of the Irish T&GWU in the National Library of Ireland.' *Saothar*, III (1977), 14–15.

68 **Storey**, Richard A. 'The Modern Records Centre, University of Warwick Library and Scottish labour history sources.' *Scott. Ind. Hist.*, I, 2 (Spring 1977), 16–19.

69 **Storey**, Richard A. and **Druker**, Janet. *Guide to the Modern Records Centre, University of Warwick Library.* Coventry: The Library, 1977. 152p.

70 **Swift**, John. 'The Bakers' records.' *Saothar*, III (1977), 1–5.

71 **Woolven**, Gillian Beatrice. *Publications of the Independent Labour Party.* Coventry: Society for the Study of Social History, 1977. 38p.

72 **Brake**, Terence. *Work organisation: a bibliography 1970–77.* London: Social Science Research Council, 1978.

73 **Coates**, Christine. *Trade unions and industrial relations.* London: Library Association, 1978. 44p. (Public Libraries Group readers' guides 11.)

74 **Crawford**, John C. *Wanlockhead miners' library: a guide book.* Glasgow: Wanlockhead Museum Trust, 1978. 16p.

75 **Druker**, Janet. 'Women's history and trade union records.' *Soc. Study Labour Hist. Bull.*, XXXVI (Spring 1978), 28–35.

76 **D'Silva**, C. *Unemployment: a survey of the literature.* Preston: Preston Polytechnic, Fylde Coast Study Group, 1978.

77 **Harber**, Julian. 'Labour archives in the Calder Valley.' *Hist. Workshop*, V (Spring 1978), 147–54.

78 **Industrial Relations Training Resource Centre**. *Catalogue of audio-visual training material.* Berkhamsted: I.R.T.R.C., 1978. 112p.

79 **Linkman**, Audrey. 'Manchester Studies Trade Union Project: records of the cotton unions.' *N.W. Labour Hist. Soc. Bull.*, V (1978), 38–44.

80 **MacDougall**, Ian. *A catalogue of some labour records in Scotland, and some Scots records outside Scotland.* Edinburgh: Scottish Labour History Society, 1978. 598p.

81 **Nevin**, Donal (comp.). 'Bibliography on industrial relations in Ireland.' *Trade Union Inf.* (Spring 1978), 19–30.

82 **Pettman**, Barrie Owen. *Industrial democracy: a selected bibliography.* Bradford: M.C.B. Publications, 1978. 95p.

83 **Samuel**, Raphael. 'The Bishopsgate Institute.' *Hist. Workshop*, V (Spring 1978), 168–72.

84 **Storey**, Richard A. 'The development of the Modern Records Centre, University of Warwick Library.' *Archives*, VIII (Spring 1978), 137–42.

85 **Swann**, Brenda and **Turnbull**, Maureen. *Records of interest to social scientists, 1919–1939, employment and unemployment.* London: H.M.S.O., 1978. 590p. (Public Record Office handbooks 18.)

86 **University of Nottingham Library**. *Trade union periodicals: a handlist of material in the trade union collection.* Nottingham: The Library, 1978.
    Second edition.

87 **Woodland**, Christine (comp.) and **Storey**, Richard A. (ed.). *The Taff Vale case: a guide to the ASRS records.* Coventry: University of Warwick Library, 1978. 28p. (Occasional publications 3.)

88 **Bain**, George Sayers and **Woolven**, Gillian Beatrice. *A bibliography of British industrial relations.* Cambridge: Cambridge U.P., 1979. xxiv, 665p.

89 **Bennett**, John David (comp.) and **Storey**, Richard A. (ed.). *Trade union and related records.* Coventry: University of Warwick Library, 1979. 30p. (Occasional publications 5.)

90 **Bland**, Richard. 'Measuring "social class": a discussion of the Registrar-General's classification.' *Sociology*, XIII (May 1979), 283–91.

91 **Brignall**, Stan. *Disclosure of company financial information to employees and trade unions: a bibliography.* Southampton: Business Information Press, 1979. 19p.

92 **Chell**, Elizabeth and **Rowat**, Christine L. *Worker participation: report and bibliography.* Borth: Emerson Rowat Information Services, 1979.

93 **Hyman**, Richard and **Price**, Robert. 'Labour statistics.' Irvine, J. and others (eds.). *Demystifying social statistics.* 1979. p. 222–36.

94 **Irvine**, John, **Miles**, Ian and **Evans**, Jeff

(eds.). *Demystifying social statistics*. London: Pluto, 1979. x, 390p.

95 **Lee**, Clive Howard. *British regional employment statistics, 1841–1971*. Cambridge: Cambridge U.P., 1979. 480p.

96 **O'Connell**, Deirdre (comp.). 'A bibliography of Irish labour history, 1973–77.' *Saothar*, v (1979), 97–108.

97 **Perry**, Derek, **Wahhab**, Rifat and **Owen**, Antonia. *Public information: a directory of information sources for trade unionists and campaign groups*. London: London Labour Library, 1979. [48p.]

98 **Pollock**, Hugh M. 'The Irish Labour History Society Archive.' *Saothar*, v (1979), 54–7.

99 **Walsh**, Ruth M. and **Birkin**, Stanley J. *Job satisfaction and motivation: an annotated bibliography*. London: Greenwood P., 1979. viii, 643p.

100 **Woodland**, Christine (comp.) and **Storey**, Richard A. (ed.). *The Osborne case papers and other records of the Amalgamated Society of Railway Servants*. Coventry: University of Warwick Library, 1979. 48p. (Occasional publications 4.)

See also: 1735.

II. NATURE AND STUDY OF THE SUBJECT

As discussions on the nature of a subject tend to be theoretical, this section, unlike other parts of the bibliography, includes works which are primarily based on foreign experience but which are nevertheless relevant to the study of the subject in Britain.

101 **Allen**, Victor Leonard. 'Analytical methods in studies of trade unionism.' Hughes, G. (ed.). *Men of no property*. 1971. p. 1–10.

102 **Loveridge**, Ray. 'Social science research and the study of industrial relations.' Mitchell, Jeremy and others (eds.). *Social science research and industry*. London: Harrap, 1971. p. 42–50.

103 **Dunlop**, John Thomas. 'Political systems and industrial relations.' *Int. Inst. Labour Stud. Bull.*, IX (1972), 99–116.

104 **Roberts**, Benjamin Charles. 'Affluence and disruption.' Robson, W. A. (ed.). *Men and social sciences*. London: Allen & Unwin, 1972. p. 247–72.

105 **Somers**, Gerald G. 'Centres for teaching and research in industrial relations: a comparative review.' *Int. Inst. Labour Stud. Bull.*, IX (1972), 117–28.

106 **Brehaut**, John. 'Sociological aspects of industrial relations.' *J. Ind. Relat.*, XV, 2 (June 1973), 190–7.

107 **Crossley**, John Rodney. 'A mixed strategy for labour economists.' *Scott. J. Polit. Econ.*, XX (November 1973), 211–38.

108 **Fox**, Alan. 'Industrial relations: a social critique of pluralist ideology.' Child, J. (ed.). *Man and organization*. 1973. p. 185–233.

109 **Gottschalk**, Andrew. 'Industrial relations and the behavioural scientist.' *Pers. Manage.*, v, 2 (February 1973), 32–5.

110 **Hobsbawm**, Eric John Ernest. 'Ideology and labour history.' *Soc. Study Labour Hist. Bull.*, XXVII (Autumn 1973), 32–3.

111 **Marsh**, Arthur Ivor and **Evans**, E. O. *Dictionary of industrial relations*. London: Hutchinson, 1973. 415p.

112 **Shimmin**, Sylvia and **Singh**, R. 'Industrial relations and organizational behaviour: a critical approach.' *Ind. Relat. J.*, IV, 3 (Autumn 1973), 37–42.
Reprinted in Barrett, B. and others (eds.).

Industrial relations and the wider society. 1975.

113 **Smith**, Eric Owen. 'Economics and the study of industrial relations: a survey and some comments.' *Ind. Relat. J.*, IV, 1 (Spring 1973), 50–66.

114 **Turner**, Robert. 'Towards an oral history of labour.' *Soc. Study Labour Hist. Bull.*, XXVII (Autumn 1973), 63–71.

115 **Bain**, George Sayers and **Clegg**, Hugh Armstrong. 'A strategy for industrial relations research in Great Britain.' *Br. J. Ind. Relat.*, XII, 1 (March 1974), 91–113.

116 **Hill**, Stephen R. and **Thurley**, Keith. 'Sociology and industrial relations.' *Br. J. Ind. Relat.*, XII, 2 (July 1974), 147–70.

117 **Laffer**, Kingsley. 'Is industrial relations an academic discipline?' *J. Ind. Relat.*, XVII (March 1974), 62–73.

118 **Clegg**, Hugh Armstrong. 'Pluralism in industrial relations.' *Br. J. Ind. Relat.*, XIII, 3 (November 1975), 309–16.

119 **Eldridge**, John E. T. 'Panaceas and pragmatism in industrial relations.' *Ind. Relat. J.*, VI, 1 (Spring 1975), 4–13.

120 **Fox**, Alan. 'Collective bargaining, Flanders and the Webbs.' *Br. J. Ind. Relat.*, XIII, 2 (July 1975), 151–74.

121 **Kahn-Freund**, Sir Otto. *Law and labour: an ambivalent relationship*. London: Imperial College, 1975. 11p.
Third Joan Woodward memorial lecture.

122 **Molhuysen**, P. C. 'The academic respectability of industrial relations and labour economics.' *J. Ind. Relat.*, XVII, 1 (March 1975), 97–9.

123 **Webb**, Beatrice. *Our partnership*. Cambridge: Cambridge U.P., 1975. liv, 544p.
First published 1948. Reprinted with a new introduction by George Feaver.

124 **Fatchett**, Derek John. 'Trends and developments in industrial relations theory.' *Ind. Relat. J.*, VII, 1 (Spring 1976), 50–60.

125 **Hammerton**, A. J. 'New trends in the history of working women in Britain.' *Labour Hist.*, XXXI (November 1976), 53–60.

126 **Hill**, Stephen R. 'Organizational behaviour and theoretical models of industrial relations.' Industrial Relations Research Associa-

tion. *Proceedings of the twenty-eighth annual winter meeting, Dallas, December 28–30, 1975. 1976.* p. 47–55.

127 **Horn**, R. V. 'Industrial relations and labour economics.' *J. Ind. Relat.*, XVII, 3 (September 1975), 296–7.

128 **McArthur**, Peter. *A glossary of industrial relations terms.* Berkhamsted: Ashridge Management College, 1976.

129 **Wagner**, A., **Armstrong**, E. G. A., **Goodman**, J. F. B. and **Davis**, J. E. 'The "industrial relations system" concept as a basis for theory in industrial relations.' *Br. J. Ind. Relat.*, XIII, 3 (November 1975), 291–308.

130 **Shepherd**, R. A. 'Personnel research under review.' *Pers. Manage.*, VIII, 9 (September 1976, 28–32.

131 **Turner**, Robert. 'The contribution of oral evidence to labour history.' *Oral Hist.*, IV, 1 (Spring 1976), 23–40.

132 **Collins**, R. G. 'Industrial relations as an occupation.' *Ind. Relat. J.*, VIII, 1 (Spring 1977), 37–49.

133 **Conway**, Eddie. 'Teaching labour history.' *N.W. Labour Hist. Soc. Bull.*, IV (1977), 130–40.

134 **Geare**, Alan J. 'The field of study of industrial relations.' *J. Ind. Relat.*, XIX, 3 (September 1977), 274–85.

135 **Wood**, Stephen J. and **Elliott**, Ruth. 'A critical evaluation of Fox's radicalization of industrial relations theory.' *Sociology*, XI, 1 (January 1977), 105–25.

136 **Blain**, Nicholas. 'Approaches to industrial relations theory: an appraisal and synthesis.' *Labour & Soc.*, III, 2 (April 1978), 199–216.

137 **Brown**, Richard K. 'From Donovan to where? Interpretations of industrial relations in Britain since 1968.' *Br. J. Sociol.*, XXIX (December 1978), 439–61.

138 **Brown**, William Arthur. 'Transforming the miraculous into the natural: current trends in industrial relations research in Britain.' Turkington, D. J. (ed.). *Industrial relations teaching and research in Australia and New Zealand.* Wellington: Victoria University of Wellington. Industrial Relations Centre, 1978. p. 1–23.

139 **Gabriel**, Yiannis. 'Collective bargaining: a critique of the Oxford School.' *Polit. Q.*, XXIX (July–September 1978), 334–48.

140 **Halstead**, John. 'Labour history in Britain.' *Comm. Can. Labour Hist. Bull.*, VI (Autumn 1978), 15–22.

141 **Hyman**, Richard. 'From Donovan to where? Interpretations of industrial relations in Britain since 1968. Comment.' *Br. J. Sociol.*, XXIX (December 1978), 461–3.

142 **Hyman**, Richard. 'Pluralism, procedural consensus and collective bargaining.' *Br. J. Ind. Relat.*, XVI, 1 (March 1978), 16–40.

143 **Nicholson**, Nigel and **Wall**, Toby. 'Psychology's place in industrial relations.' *Pers. Manage.*, X, 5 (May 1978), 22–5.

144 **Parris**, John. 'Using the social sciences to solve practical problems.' *Pers. Manage.*, X, 9 (September 1978), 31–4.

145 **Singh**, Ram. 'Theory and practice in industrial relations.' *Ind. Relat. J.*, IX, 3 (Autumn 1978), 57–64.

146 **Strauss**, George and **Feuille**, Peter. 'Industrial relations research: a critical analysis.' *Ind. Relat.*, XVII, 3 (October 1978), 259–77.

147 **Fox**, Alan. 'A note on industrial relations pluralism.' *Sociology*, XIII, 1 (January 1979), 105–9.

148 **Kirkbride**, Paul. 'Industrial relations theory and research.' *Manage. Decis.*, XVII, 4 (1979), 326–40.

149 **Marsh**, Arthur Ivor. *Concise encyclopedia of industrial relations, with bibliography.* Epping: Gower, 1979. 423p.

A revised version of *Dictionary of industrial relations.* 1973.

150 **Sampson**, Margaret. 'Recent criticisms of labour history in Britain and Australia.' *Labour Hist.*, XXXVI (May 1979), 70–93.

151 **Watson**, Tony J. 'Industrial sociology: theory, research and teaching: some problems and proposals.' *J. Manage. Stud.*, XVI, 2 (May 1979), 117–38.

See also: 152; 307; 348; 413; 526; 722; 2087; 2174; 6161.

III. THE INDUSTRIAL RELATIONS SYSTEM

This section contains works of the following nature: those pertaining to more than one aspect of the industrial relations system, those comparing the British system with systems in other countries, and those concerned with the place of labour in society and similar philosophical questions. See also Part Three, II, A; Part Five, I; Part Five, V, A; and Part Seven, I.

A. GENERAL

152 **Allen**, Victor Leonard. *The sociology of industrial relations: studies in method.* London: Longman, 1971. viii, 282p.

153 **Cooper**, John, *Baron Cooper of Stockton Heath.* 'A trade union view of industrial relations.' *Co-partnership*, DXLVII (November 1971), 26–35.

154 **Kessler**, Sidney and **Weekes**, Brian (eds.). *Conflict at work: reshaping industrial relations: a book of original essays.* London: B.B.C., 1971. 134p.

155 **Management Counsellors International**. *A survey of industrial relations in Britain, 1970.* Brussels: The Authors, 1971. 68p.

156 **Balfour**, William Campbell. *Industrial relations in the Common Market.* London: Routledge & Kegan Paul, 1972. x, 132p.

157 **Bull**, George, **Hobday**, Peter and **Hamway**, John. *Industrial relations: the boardroom view-point.* London: Bodley Head, 1972. 208p.

158 **Clark**, M. and **Tolfree**, P. *Industrial relations.* London: Industrial Society, 1972. 42p. (Notes for managers 11.)
Revised edition.

159 **Clarke**, Ronald Oliver. 'Patterns of European industrial relations.' *Pers. Manage.*, IV, 9 (September 1972), 39–42.

160 **Clegg**, Hugh Armstrong. *The system of industrial relations in Great Britain.* Oxford: Blackwell.
Second edition. 1972. x, 500p.
Third edition. 1976. xiii, 522p.
See also *The changing system of industrial relations in Great Britain.* 1979.

161 **Gunter**, Ray. 'Industrial relations.' *Ind. Participation*, DXLVII (Spring 1972), 5–7.

162 **Hawkins**, Kevin H. *Conflict and change: aspects of industrial relations.* London: Holt, Rinehart & Winston, 1972. xiv, 257p.

163 **Lowndes**, Richard. *Industrial relations: a contemporary survey.* London: Holt, Rinehart & Winston, 1972.

164 **Roberts**, Benjamin Charles. *Future industrial relations: Netherlands, Norway, Sweden and the United Kingdom.* Geneva: International Institute for Labour Studies, 1972. iv, 38p. (Research project on future industrial relations. Document 6.)

165 **Torrington**, Derek P. *Handbook of industrial relations.* Epping: Gower, 1972. xix, 328p.

166 **Wickham**, E. R. 'The social implications of industrial relations.' Torrington, Derek P. (ed.). *Handbook of industrial relations.* 1972. p. 303–11.

167 **Barratt Brown**, Michael and **Coates**, Ken (eds.). *Trade union register: 3.* Nottingham: Spokesman, 1973. 296p.

168 **Cowan**, L. D. 'The impact of Europe on U.K. industrial relations.' *Ind. Commer. Train.*, V, 6 (June 1973), 262–8.

169 **Cuthbert**, Norman H. and **Hawkins**, Kevin H. *Company industrial relations policies: the management of industrial relations in the 1970s.* London: Longman, 1973. xvi, 303p.

170 **Sykes**, Andrew James Macintyre. *Myths of industrial relations.* London: Working Together Campaign, 1973. 10p.

171 **Walsh**, Peter. 'The future of industrial relations.' *Month*, VI (August 1973), 270–3.

172 **Working Together Campaign**. *Industrial relations: what the people think.* London: The Authors, 1973. 21p.

173 **Bagwell**, Philip Sidney. *Industrial relations.* Dublin: Irish University P., 1974, vii, 166p.

174 **Taylor**, Nancy. *The search for the industrial relations panacea.* London: Working Together Campaign, 1974.

175 **Barkin**, Solomon (ed.). *Worker militancy and its consequences 1965–75: new directions in Western industrial relations.* New York: Praeger, 1975. xxxvi, 408p.

176 **Barrett**, Brian, **Rhodes**, Ed and **Beishon**, Ronald John (eds.). *Industrial relations and wider society: aspects of interaction.* London: Collier Macmillan, 1975. x, 466p.

177 **Beesley**, Michael. *Industrial relations in a changing world.* London: Croom Helm, 1975. 154p.

178 **Bryder**, Tom. *Power and responsibility: contending approaches to industrial relations and decision-making in Britain, 1963–1971.* [London]: C. W. K. Gleerup, 1975.

179 **Burgess**, Keith. *The origins of British industrial relations: the nineteenth century experience.* London: Croom Helm, 1975. xiii, 331p.

180 **Craig**, Alton W. J. 'A framework for the analysis of industrial relations systems.' Barrett, B. and others (eds.). *Industrial relations and the wider society.* 1975. p. 8–20.
Paper given at the Third World Congress of the International Industrial Relations Association, 1973.

181 **Downing**, J. D. H. *Some aspects of the presentation of industrial relations and race relations in some major British news media.* 1975. (Ph.D. thesis, University of London.)

182 **Goodman**, John F. B. 'Great Britain: toward the social contract.' Barkin, Solomon (ed.). *Worker militancy and its consequences.* 1975. p. 39–81.

183 **Hyman**, Richard. *Industrial relations: a marxist introduction.* London: Macmillan, 1975. x, 220p.

184 **Smith**, Eric Owen. *British industrial relations.* Loughborough: University of Loughborough. Department of Economics, 1975. (Loughborough papers on recent developments in economic policy and thought 9.)
Second edition. 1976. 55p.

185 **Barrett**, Brian and **Beishon**, John. *Approaches to industrial relations.* Milton Keynes: Open U.P., 1976. 52p. (PT 281 Unit 1.)

186 **Cooper**, Bruce M. and **Bartlett**, A. F. *Industrial relations: a study in conflict.* London: Heinemann, 1976. ix, 310p.

187 **Gennard**, John and the **Open University Industrial Relations Course Team.** *Institutions and the economic environment.* Milton Keynes: Open U.P., 1976. 79p. (PT 281 Unit 5.)

188 **Hawkins**, Kevin H. *British industrial relations 1945–75.* London: Barrie & Jenkins, 1976. 223p.

189 **Hillard**, John. *Institutions and political and legal environments.* Milton Keynes: Open U.P., 1976. 68p. (PT 281 Unit 13.)

190 **Loveridge**, Ray. *Socio-cultural environment: an introduction.* Milton Keynes: Open U.P., 1976. 30p. (PT 281 Unit 8A.)
Bound with Hillard, J. *Political and legal environments.*

191 **Loveridge**, Ray and **Morrish**, Pat. *Institutions and the socio-cultural environment.* Milton Keynes: Open U.P., 1976. 46p. (PT 281 Unit 10.)

192 **Rhodes**, Ed and **Harding**, Andy. *Trends and prospects*. Milton Keynes: Open U.P., 1976. 49p. (PT 281 Unit 16.)
193 **Winchester**, David. *Workers, management and government: institutions and regulatory processes*. Milton Keynes: Open U.P., 1976. 51p. (Open University. Industrial relations unit 2.)
194 **Anthony**, Peter D. *The conduct of industrial relations*. London: Institute of Personnel Management, 1977. vi, 330p.
195 **Barrett**, B. 'Review of industrial relations literature.' *Br. Book News* (January 1977), 6–14.
196 **Central Office of Information.** *Manpower and employment in Britain: industrial relations*. London: H.M.S.O., 1977. 38p. (Reference pamphlet 148.)
197 **Grant**, Ronald M. *Industrial relations*. Manchester: Ginn, 1977. 56p.
     Revised by Maureen Woodhall.
198 **Hunt**, Denis D. *Common sense industrial relations*. Newton Abbot: David & Charles, 1977. 182p.
199 **Jackson**, Michael Peart. *Industrial relations: a textbook*. London: Croom Helm, 1977. 281p.
200 **Whitehead**, Ken. *Industrial relations*. London: Teach Yourself Books, 1977. 223p.
201 **Hawkins**, Kevin H. *The management of industrial relations*. Harmondsworth: Penguin, 1978. 265p.
202 **Thomson**, Andrew William John and **Hunter**, Laurence Colvin. 'Great Britain.' Dunlop, J. T. and Galenson, W. (eds.). *Labour in the twentieth century*. New York: Academic Press, 1978. p. 85–148.
203 **Clegg**, Hugh Armstrong. *The changing system of industrial relations in Great Britain*. Oxford: Blackwell, 1979. xi, 479p.
     A completely rewritten version of *The system of industrial relations in Great Britain*.
204 **Colloquium on Management and Industrial Relations**, 1979, UWIST. *Proceedings of the Colloquium*. Cardiff: U.W.I.S.T., 1979. 227p.
205 **Farnham**, David and **Pimlott**, John. *Understanding industrial relations*. London: Cassell, 1979. xv, 496p.
206 **Kahn-Freund**, Sir Otto. *Labour relations: heritage and adjustment*. Oxford: Oxford U.P., 1979. 102p.
207 **Kelly**, Aidan and **Bourke**, Philip. *Management, labour and consumer*. Dublin: Gill & Macmillan, 1979. 64p.
208 **National Economic Development Office.** *Industrial relations in Great Britain: an introduction for inward investors*. London: N.E.D.O., 1979 31p.
209 **National Economic Development Office.** *Industrial relations in Great Britain: an introduction for inward investors: a summary*. London: N.E.D.O., 1979. 16p.
210 **Poole**, Michael. 'Management and industrial relations: strategic themes and issues.' Colloquium on Management and Industrial Rela-

tions. *Proceedings*. 1979. p.6–21.
211 **Shields**, Peter. 'Putting the future into industrial relations.' *Employee Relat.*, 1, 4 (1979), 13–16.
See also: 81; 678; 749; 1284; 1302; 1508; 1510; 1840.

B. INDUSTRIAL RELATIONS AND THE MEDIA

212 **Clark**, Eric. *The media and industrial relations*. London: Working Together Campaign, [1973?]. [12p.]
213 **Hartmann**, Paul. 'Industrial relations in the news media.' *Ind. Relat. J.*, VI, 4 (Winter 1975–6), 4–18.
214 **Morley**, David. 'Industrial conflict and the mass media.' *Sociol. Rev.*, XXIV, 2 (1976), 245–68.
215 **Philo**, Greg and **Hewitt**, John. 'Trade unions and the media.' *Ind. Relat. J.*, VII, 3 (Autumn 1976), 4–18.
216 **University of Glasgow Media Group.** *Bad news*. Vol. 1. London: Routledge & Kegan Paul, 1976. xvi, 310p.
     Edited by Peter Beharrel and others.
217 **Beckett**, Francis. 'Press and prejudice.' Beharrel, P. and Philo, G. (eds.). *Trade unions and the media*. 1977. p.32–49.
218 **Beharrel**, Peter and **Philo**, Greg (eds.). *Trade unions and the media*. London: Macmillan, 1977. xi, 150p.
219 **Goodman** Andrew. 'Working for television: the experience of censorship and control.' Beharrel, P. and Philo, G. (eds.). *Trade unions and the media*. 1977. p. 73–83.
220 **Griffiths**, Toni. 'The Production of trade union news.' Beharrel, P. and Philo, G. (eds.). *Trade unions and the media*. 1977. p. 60–72.
221 **Marshall**, Tony. 'Trouble at t'millford: farmworkers in the media.' Beharrel, P. and Philo, G. (eds.). *Trade unions and the media*. 1977. p. 50–9.
222 **Murdoch**, Graham and **Golding**, Peter. 'Beyond monopoly: mass communication in an age of conglomerates.' Beharrel, P. and Philo, G. (eds.). *Trade unions and the media*. 1977. p. 93–117.
223 **Philo**, Greg, **Beharrel**, Peter and **Hewitt**, John. 'One-dimensional news: television and the control of explanation.' Beharrel, P. and Philo, G. (eds.). *Trade unions and the media*. 1977. p. 1–22.
224 **Philo**, Greg, **Beharrel**, Peter and **Hewitt**, John. 'Strategies and policies.' Beharrel, P. and Philo, G. (eds.). *Trade unions and the media*. 1977. p. 135–42.
225 **Sapper**, Alan. 'Opening the box: the unions inside television.' Beharrel, P. and Philo, G. (eds.). *Trade unions and the media*. 1977. p. 84–92.
226 **Walton**, Paul and **Davis**, Howard. 'Bad news for trade unionists.' Beharrel, P. and Philo, G.

(eds.). *Trade unions and the media*. 1977. p. 118–37.

227 **Young**, Jock and **Crutchley**, J. Brooke. 'May the first, 1973: a day of predictable madness.' Beharrel, P. and Philo, G. (eds.). *Trade unions and the media*. 1977. p. 23–31.

228 **Edwards**, Paul K. '"The awful truth about strife in our factories": a case study in the production of news.' *Ind. Relat. J.*, x, 1 (Spring 1979), 7–11.

229 **Goodman**, Geoffrey. 'The impact of the media on industrial relations.' *Pers. Manage.*, xi, 10 (October 1979), 44–7.

See also: 2142.

PART TWO

EMPLOYEES: INDUSTRIAL ATTITUDES AND BEHAVIOUR

The memoirs and autobiographies of workers have generally been classified at Part Six, IV, A, 1–2 because they are primarily concerned with describing conditions of work. But they also contain material on workers' attitudes and behaviour.

I. GENERAL

This section includes general material on industrial sociology and industrial psychology (but see Part One, II for material on the contribution of sociology and psychology to the study of industrial relations), as well as on such subjects as work and leisure, the meaning of work, orientations to work, and the sociology of particular occupations. General material on social relationships at work is also included here; but material on the more formal aspects of work group organisation is classified at Part Three, II, F, 8; and that on work structuring and job design is classified at Part Two, V. Material dealing with the attitudes of supervisors towards their work is classified at Part Four, II, C. See also Part Six, II, A.

230 **Westergaard**, John H. 'The rediscovery of the cash nexus: some recent interpretations of trends in British class structure.' *Social. Reg.* (1970), 111–38.

231 **Bell**, Colin. 'Occupational career, family cycle and extended family relations.' *Hum. Relat.*, XXIV (December 1971), 463–75.

232 **Craft**, Maurice and **Craft**, Alma. 'The interprofessional perspectives of teachers and social workers: a pilot inquiry.' *Durham Res. Rev.*, VI (Spring 1971), 523–30.

233 **The Edinburgh Group.** 'Behavioural science in British industry.' *Pers. Manage.*, III, 9 (September 1971), 28–30.

234 **Eldridge**, John Eric Thomas. *Sociology and industrial life.* London: Michael Joseph, 1971. viii, 230p.

235 **Feldman**, Maurice P. *Psychology in the industrial environment.* London: Butterworth, 1971. viii, 128p.

236 **Goldthorpe**, John H. 'Daniel on orientations to work: a final comment.' *J. Manage. Stud.*, VIII (1971), 226–73.

237 **Hall**, Kenneth and **Miller**, Isobel. 'Industrial attitudes to skills dilution.' *Br. J. Ind. Relat.*, IX, 1 (March 1971), 1–20.

238 **Halsbury**, Hardinge Stanley Giffard, 1st Earl. 'Men at work: the next fifty years.' *Occup. Psych.*, XLV (1971), 163–5, 197–8.

239 **Parker**, Stanley R. *The future of work and leisure.* London: Paladin, 1971. 160p.

240 **Parker**, S. R. 'A sociological portrait: occupation.' *New Soc.*, XVIII (21 October 1971), 766–8.

241 **Payne**, Roy L., **Pheysey**, Diana C. and **Pugh**, D. S. 'Organization structure, organizational climate and group structure: an exploratory study of their relationships in two British manufacturing companies.' *Occup. Psychol.*, XLV (1971), 45–55.

242 **Salaman**, Graeme. 'Some sociological determinants of occupational communities.' *Sociol. Rev.*, XIX, 1 (February 1971), 53–77.

243 **Salaman**, Graeme. 'Two occupational communities: examples of a remarkable convergence of work and non-work.' *Sociol. Rev.*, XIX, 3 (August 1971), 389–407.

244 **Sheldrake**, P. F. 'Orientations towards work among computer programmers.' *Sociology*, V, 2 (May 1971), 209–24.

245 **Shimmin**, Sylvia. 'Behaviour in organisations: problems and perspectives.' *Occup. Psychol.*, XLV (1971), 13–26.

246 **Stephenson**, Geoffrey M. 'Intergroup relations and negotiating behaviour.' Warr, P. (ed.). *Psychology at work.* 1971. p. 347–73.

247 **Super**, Donald Edwin and **Bohn**, Martin J. *Occupational psychology.* London: Tavistock, 1971. ix, 209p.

248 **Thoms**, David C. 'Work and its definition.' *Sociol. Rev.*, XIX, 4 (November 1971), 543–55.

249 **Trist**, Eric. 'Critique of scientific management in terms of socio-technical theory.' *Prakseologia*, XXXIX–XL (1971), 159–74.
Reprinted in Weir, M. (ed.). *Job satisfaction.* 1976. p. 81–90.

250 **Turner**, Barry A. *Exploring the industrial subculture.* London: Macmillan, 1971. ix, 202p.

251 **Warr**, Peter Bryan. 'Judgements about people at work.' Warr, P. (ed.). *Psychology at work*. 1971. p. 208–31.

252 **Warr**, Peter Bryan (ed.). *Psychology at work*. Harmondsworth: Penguin, 1971. 460p.
Second edition. 1978. 448p.

253 **Williams**, A., **Roger**, T. and **Blackler**, Frank H. M. 'Motives and behaviour at work'. Warr, P. (ed.). *Psychology at work*. 1971. p. 304–21.

254 **Willmott**, Peter. 'Family, work and leisure conflicts among male employees: some preliminary findings.' *Hum. Relat.*, xxiv (1971), 575–84.

255 **Argyle**, Michael. 'Group dynamics.' *New Soc.*, xxii (2 November 1972), 283–4.

256 **Argyle**, Michael. 'Persons and work.' *New Soc.*, xxii (16 November 1972), 408–9.

257 **Argyle**, Michael. 'Social skills: the experience of work.' *New Soc.*, xxii (9 November 1972), 342–3.

258 **Argyle**, Michael. *Social psychology of work*. Harmondsworth: Penguin, 1972. xi, 291p.

259 **Argyle**, Michael. 'Working in groups.' *New Soc.*, xxii (26 October 1972), 220–1.

260 **Argyris**, Chris. *The applicability of organisational sociology*. Cambridge: Cambridge U.P., 1972. ix, 138p.

261 **Bain**, George Sayers and **Price**, Robert. 'Who is a white collar employee?' *Br. J. Ind. Relat.*, x, 3 (November 1972), 325–39.

262 **Bass**, Bernard Morris and **Barrett**, Gerald V. *Man, work and organizations: an introduction to industrial and organizational psychology*. London: Allyn & Bacon, 1972.

263 **Beynon**, Huw and **Blackburn**, Robert Martin. *Perceptions of work: variations within a factory*. Cambridge: Cambridge U.P., 1972. 179p.

264 **Child**, John and **Mansfield**, Roger. 'Technology, size and organization structure.' *Sociology*, vi, 3 (September 1972), 369–93.

265 **Cooper**, Robert. 'Man, task and technology: three variables in search of a future.' *Hum. Relat.*, xxv (April 1972), 131–57.

266 **Corlett**, Esmond Nigel. *People and work*. Birmingham: University of Birmingham, 1972. 12p.
Inaugural lecture.

267 **Cotgrove**, Stephen and **Vamplew**, Clive. 'Technology, class, and politics: the case of the process workers.' *Sociology*, vi, 2 (May 1972), 169–85.

268 **Daniel**, William Wentworth. 'What interests a worker?' *New Soc.*, xix (23 March 1972), 583–6.

269 **Dubrin**, Andrew J. *The practice of managerial psychology: concepts and methods for manager and organization development*. London: Pergamon P., 1972. xv, 326p.

270 **Gorman**, Liam and **Molloy**, Eddie. *People, jobs and organizations*. Dublin: Irish Productivity Centre, 1972.

271 **Gottschalk**, A.W. 'Lessons from the behavioural sciences.' Torrington, Derek P. (ed.), *Handbook of industrial relations*. 1972. p. 285–301.

272 **Jacobson**, D. 'Fatigue-producing factors and pre-retirement attitudes.' *Occup. Psychol.*, iv (1972), 193–200.

273 **Kelsall**, R. K., **Poole**, A. and **Kuhn**, A. *Graduates: the sociology of an elite*. London: Methuen, 1972. 284p.

274 **Kemeny**, Paul James. 'The affluent worker project: some criticisms and a derivative study.' *Sociol. Rev.*, xx, 3 (August 1972), 373–89.

275 **Keohane**, J. 'Methods for surveying employee attitudes.' *Occup. Psychol.*, xlv, 3–4 (1972), 217–31.

276 **Newby**, Howard. 'Agricultural workers in the class structure.' *Sociol. Rev.*, xx, 3 (August 1972), 413–39.

277 **Scase**, Richard. '"Industrial man": a reassessment with English and Swedish data.' *Br. J. Sociol.*, xxiii, 2 (June 1972), 204–20.

278 **Sofer**, Cyril. *Organizations in theory and practice*. London: Heinemann, 1972. xxviii, 419p.

279 **Wedderburn**, Dorothy. 'What determines shopfloor behaviour?' *New Soc.*, xxi (20 July 1972), 128–30.

280 **Williamson**, D.T.N. 'The anachronistic factory.' *Royal Society Proceedings*, cccxxxi, Section A (1972), 139–60.
Reprinted in Weir, M. (ed.). *Job satisfaction*. 1976. p. 160–9.

281 **Bell**, Colin and **Newby**, Howard. 'The sources of variation in agricultural workers' images of society.' *Sociol. Rev.*, xxi, 2 (May 1973), 229–53.

282 **Beynon**, Huw. *Working for Ford*. Harmondsworth: Allen Lane, 1973. 328p.
Another edition. London: E.P. Publishing, 1975.

283 **Bowen**, Donald D. and **Siegel**, Jacob P. 'Process and performance: a longitudinal study of the reactions of small task groups to periodic performance feedback.' *Hum. Relat.*, xxvi (August 1973), 433–48.

284 **Brown**, Richard. 'Sources of objectives in work and employment.' Child, J. (ed.). *Man and organization*. 1973. p. 17–38.

285 **Child**, John (ed.). *Man and organization: the search for explanation and social relevance*. London: Allen & Unwin, 1973. 261p.

286 **Chivers**, T.S. 'The proletarianization of a service worker.' *Sociol. Rev.*, xxi, 4 (November 1973), 633–56.

287 **Daniel**, William Wentworth. 'Understanding employee behaviour in its context: illustrations from productivity bargaining.' Child, J. (ed.). *Man and Organization*. 1973. p. 39–62.

288 **Davies**, Celia, **Dawson**, Sandra and **Francis**, Arthur. 'Technology and other variables: some current approaches in organization theory.' Warner, M. (ed.). *Sociology of the workplace*. 1973. p. 149–63.

289 **Eldridge**, John E.T. 'Sociological imagination and industrial life.' Warner, M. (ed.).

Sociology of the workplace. 1973. p. 274–86.

290 **Gottschalk**, Andrew. 'Industrial relations and the behavioural scientist.' *Pers. Manage.,* v, 2 (February 1973), 32–4.

291 **Gowler**, Dan and **Legge**, Karen. 'Perceptions, the principle of cumulation and the supply of labour.' Warner, M. (ed.). *Sociology of the workplace.* 1973. p. 116–48.

292 **Guest**, David and **Williams**, Roger. 'How home affects work.' *New Soc.,* XXIII (18 January 1973), 114–17.

293 **Hopper**, Earl and **Pearce**, Adam. 'Relative deprivation, occupational status and occupational "situs": the theoretical and empirical application of a neglected concept.' Warner, M. (ed.). *Sociology of the workplace.* 1973. p. 211–55.

294 **Jones**, Marjorie Caton. 'Some mental attitudes.' Parkinson, C.N. (ed.). *Industrial disruption.* 1973. p. 77–91.

295 **Macbeath**, Innis. *Cloth cap and after.* London: Allen & Unwin, 1973. 225p.

296 **Macbeath**, Innis. *Personal attitude to work and leadership.* London: Working Together Campaign, 1973. 12p.

297 **Mann**, Michael. *Consciousness and action among the Western working class.* London: Macmillan, 1973. 80p.

298 **Mansfield**, Roger. 'Career and individual strategies.' Child, J. (ed.). *Man and organization.* 1973. p. 107–32.

299 **Mars**, Gerald. 'Chance, punters and the fiddle: institutionalized pilferage in a hotel dining room.' Warner, M. (ed.). *Sociology of the workplace.* 1973. p. 200–10.

300 **Negandhi**, Anant R. and **Reimann**, Bernard C. 'Task environment, decentralization and organizational effectiveness.' *Hum. Relat.,* XXVI (April 1973), 203–14.

301 **Pfeffer**, Jeffrey. 'Canonical analysis of the relationship between an organization's environment and managerial attitudes toward subordinates and workers.' *Hum. Relat.,* XXVI, 3 (May–June 1973), 325–37.

302 **Sills**, Patrick A. *The behavioural sciences: techniques of application.* London: I.P.M., 1973. 45p.

303 **Singleton**, W. T., **Fox**, J. G., and **Whitfield**, D. *Measurement of man at work: an appraisal of physiological and psychological criteria in man–machine systems.* London: Taylor & Francis, 1973. xiii, 267p.

304 **Toynbee**, Polly. *Working life.* Harmondsworth: Penguin, 1973. 153p.

305 **Warner**, Malcolm (ed.). *Sociology of the workplace: an inter-disciplinary approach.* London: Allen & Unwin, 1973. 291p.

306 **Weir**, David. *Men and work in modern Britain.* London: Fontana, 1973. 443p.

307 **Ackroyd**, Stephen. 'Economic rationality and the relevance of Weberian sociology to industrial relations.' *Br. J. Ind. Relat.,* XII, 2 (July 1974), 236–48.

308 **Anderson**, Nels. *Man's work and leisure.* Leiden: Brill, 1974. x, 146p.

309 **Bechhofer**, Frank, **Elliott**, Brian, **Rushforth**, Monica and **Bland**, Richard. 'Small shopkeepers: matters of money and meaning.' *Sociol. Rev.,* XXII, 4 (November 1974), 465–82.

310 **Bell**, Clifford R. *Men at work.* London: Allen & Unwin, 1974. 119p. (Advances in psychology 4.)

311 **Bocock**, R. *Ritual in industrial society: a sociological analysis of rituals in modern England.* 1974. (Ph.D. thesis, University of Brunel.)

312 **Carter**, Ian. 'Agricultural workers in the class structure: a critical note.' *Sociol. Rev.,* XXII, 2 (May 1974), 271–9.

313 **Clayre**, Alasdair. *Work and play: ideas and experience of work and leisure.* London: Weidenfeld & Nicolson, 1974. 261p.

314 **Edwards**, Elwyn and **Lees**, Frank Pearson (eds.). *The human operator in process control.* London: Taylor & Francis, 1974. xxii, 480p.

315 **Eldridge**, John Eric Thomas and **Crombie**, A.D. *A sociology of organisations.* London: Allen & Unwin, 1974. 218p.

316 **Fox**, Alan. *Beyond contract: work, power and trust relations.* London: Faber, 1974. 408p.

317 **Fox**, Alan. 'Work and contract in low-trust society.' *New Soc.,* XXVIII (18 April 1974), 123–5.

318 **Goldthorpe**, John H. and **Hope**, K. *The social grading of occupations.* Oxford: Clarendon, 1974. viii, 188p.

319 **Hann**, P. 'Chaos pays off.' *Ind. Soc.,* LVI, 1–2 (January–February 1974), 16–18.

320 **Hill**, Stephen R. 'Norms, groups and power: the sociology of workplace industrial relations.' *Br. J. Ind. Relat.,* XII, 2 (July 1974), 213–35.

321 **Lansbury**, Russell. 'Careers, work and leisure among the new professionals.' *Sociol. Rev.,* XXII, 3 (August 1974), 385–400.

322 **Moore**, Michael. 'Demonstrating the rationality of an occupation: the depiction of their occupation by "progressive clergymen".' *Sociology,* VIII (January 1974), 111–23.

323 **Nichols**, Theo. 'Labourism and class consciousness: the class ideology of some Northern foremen.' *Sociol. Rev.,* XXII, 4 (November 1974), 483–502.

324 **Poole**, Michael J. F. 'The origins of trade unionists' values: some theoretical inferences.' *Sociol. Anal. Theory,* IV, 3 (October 1974), 47–74.

325 **Rowbottom**, R., **Hey**, A. and **Billis**, D. *Social services departments: developing problems of work and organization.* London: Heinemann, 1974. xiii, 298p.

326 **Salaman**, Graeme. *Community and occupation: an exploration of work-leisure relationships.* Cambridge: Cambridge U.P., 1974. 136p.

327 **Batstone**, Eric V. 'Deference and the ethos of small-town capitalism.' Bulmer, M. (ed.). *Working class images of society.* 1975. p. 116–30.

328 **Carvell**, Fred J. *Human relations in business.* London: Macmillan, 1975. viii, 408p. Second edition.

329 **Davies**, David Roy and **Shackleton**, Vivian John. *Psychology and work.* London: Methuen, 1975. 144p.

330 **Dunkerley**, D. *Occupations and society.* London: Routledge & Kegan Paul, 1975. vi, 87p.

331 **Esland**, Geoff and **Salaman**, Graeme. 'Towards a sociology of work.' Esland, G. and others (eds.). *People and work.* 1975. p. 15–32.

332 **Esland**, Geoff, **Salaman**, Graeme and **Speakman**, Mary-Anne (eds.). *People and work.* Edinburgh: Holmes MacDougall in association with the Open University P., 1975. 344p.

333 **Fineman**, Stephen. 'The work preference questionnaire.' *J. Occup. Psychol.*, XLVIII, 1 (1975), 11–31.

334 **Hyman**, Richard and **Brough**, Ian. *Social values and industrial relations: a study of fairness and equality.* Oxford: Blackwell, 1975. x, 277p. (Warwick studies in industrial relations.)

335 **Levin**, E. *Work and leisure.* 1975. (Ph.D. thesis, University of Glasgow.)

336 **Long**, Joyce Ruth. 'Attitude to work: local authority personnel responses'. *Local Gov. Stud.*, v, 3 (July 1975), 13–25.

337 **Lupton**, Tom. 'Best fit in the design of organizations.' *Pers. Rev.*, v, 1 (Winter 1975), 15–21.

338 **McCormick**, Ernest James and **Tiffin**, Joseph. *Industrial psychology.* London: Allen & Unwin, 1975. xii, 625p. Sixth edition.

339 **Mackenzie**, Gavin. 'World images and the world of work.' Esland, G. and others (eds.). *People and work.* 1975. p. 170–85.

340 **Newby**, Howard. 'Defence and the agricultural worker.' *Sociol. Rev.*, XXIII, 1 (February 1975), 51–60.

341 **Nichols**, Theo. 'The "socialism" of management: some comments on the new "human relations".' *Sociol. Rev.*, XXIII, 2 (May 1975), 245–65.

342 **Parker**, S. R. 'Sociology of leisure: progress and problems.' *Br. J. Sociol.*, XXVI, 1 (March 1975), 91–101.

343 **Robb**, R.M.E. *Some aspects of time allocation: the work – nonwork choice.* 1975. (Ph.D. thesis, University of Essex.)

344 **Rose**, Michael. *Industrial behaviour: theoretical development since Taylor.* London: Allen Lane, 1975. 304p.

345 **Vickerman**, R. W. *Economics of leisure and recreation.* London: Macmillan, 1975. xii, 229.

346 **Warr**, Peter Bryan and **Wall**, Toby. *Work and well-being.* Harmondsworth: Penguin, 1975. 220p.

347 **Williams**, R. S., **Morea**, P. G. and **Ives**, J. M. 'The significance of work: an empirical study.' *J. Occup. Psychol.*, XLVIII (1975), 45–51.

348 **Ackroyd**, Stephen. 'Sociological theory and the human relations school.' *Sociol. Work Occup.*, III, 4 (November 1976), 379–410.

349 **Bowen**, Peter. *Social control in industrial organisations: industrial relations and industrial sociology: a strategic and occupational study of British steelmaking.* London: Routledge & Kegan Paul, 1976. xii, 270p.

350 **Bowey**, Angela M. *The sociology of organisations.* London: Hodder & Stoughton, 1976. 228p.

351 **Brown**, A. J. *Clerical and manual workers' self and other images.* 1976. (Ph.D. thesis, University of Warwick.)

352 **Carby**, Keith and **Thakur**, Manab. *Transactional analysis at work.* London: I.P.M., 1976. 100p.

353 **Cook**, F.G., **Clark**, S.C., **Roberts**, K. and **Semeonoff**, Elizabeth. 'White and blue collar workers' attitude to unionism.' *Ind. Relat. J.*, VI, 4 (Winter 1975–6), 47–58.

354 **Crossick**, Geoffrey J. *Social structure and working class behaviour: Kentish London, 1840–1880.* 1976. (Ph.D. thesis, Birkbeck College, University of London.)

355 **Donaldson**, L. and **Lynn**, R. 'Conflict resolution process: the two-factor theory and an industrial case.' *Pers. Rev.*, v, 2 (Spring 1976), 21–8.

356 **Heller**, Frank Alex. 'Towards a practical psychology of work.' *J. Occup. Psychol.*, XLIX, 1 (1976), 45–54.

357 **Lansbury**, Russell. 'Work attitudes among management specialists.' *J. Manage. Stud.*, XIII, 1 (February 1976), 32–48.

358 **Leary**, Malcolm. 'The process of influencing in I.R.' *Manage. Decis.*, XIV, 5 (1976), 261–73.

359 **Loveridge**, Ray. *Socio-cultural environment: an introduction.* Milton Keynes: Open U.P., 1976. 30p. (Open University. Industrial relations unit 8a.)

360 **Loveridge**, Ray. *Socio-cultural effects on regulation.* Milton Keynes: Open U.P., 1976. 52p. (PT 281 Unit 11.)

361 **Murrell**, Hywel. *Men and machines.* London: Methuen, 1976. 144p.

362 **Whelan**, C. T. 'Orientations to work: some theoretical and methodological problems.' *Br. J. Ind. Relat.*, XIV, 2 (July 1976), 142–58.

363 **Anthony**, Peter D. *The ideology of work.* London: Tavistock, 1977. viii, 340p.

364 **Boot**, R.L., **Cowling**, A.G. and **Stanworth**, M.J.K. *Behavioural science for managers.* London: Arnold, 1977. viii, 232p.

365 **Cox**, Mary and **Cox**, Charles. 'Alienation in the workplace: a transactional analysis approach.' Ottaway, R. (ed.). *Humanising the workplace.* 1977. p. 101–22.

366 **Dearden**, G. *Construction craft apprentices: a study of their attitudes towards employment, work and training.* 1977. (M.Sc. thesis, University of Salford.)

367 **George**, K. D., **McNabb**, R. and **Storey**, John. 'The size of the work unit and labour market behaviour.' *Br. J. Ind. Relat.*, XV, 2 (July 1977), 265–78.

368 **Humphries**, J. 'Class struggle and the persistence of the working-class family.' *Camb. J. Econ.*, I, 3 (September 1977), 241–58.

369 **Langrish**, John. 'Technological determinism.' Ottaway, R. (ed.). *Humanising the workplace*. 1977. p. 25–43.

370 **Jones**, Jack. *The human face of labour*. London: B.B.C., 1977.
Richard Dimbleby lecture.

371 **Milutinovich**, Jugoslav S. 'Black – white differences in job satisfaction, group cohesiveness and leadership style.' *Hum. Relat.*, XXX (December 1977), 1079–87.

372 **National Economic Development Committee**, Economic Development Committee for the Foundry Industry. *Foundrymen's views: an attitude survey in the ferrous foundries industry.* London: N.E.D.C., 1977.

373 **National Economic Development Office**, Manpower and Industrial Relations Division. *Machine tools: the employees' view of the industry.* London: N.E.D.O., 1977. iv, 47p.

374 **Newby**, Howard. *The deferential worker: a study of farm workers in East Anglia*. Harmondsworth: Allen Lane, 1977. 462p.

375 **Newby**, Howard. 'Paternalism and capitalism.' Scase, R. (ed.). *Industrial society*. 1977. p. 59–73.

376 **Pearcey**, D. 'Work groups in the clothing industry.' *B.A.C.I.E. J.*, XXXI (February 1977), 26–8.

377 **Pridham**, Karen F. 'Towards an adequate theory of stress resolution in work groups.' *Hum. Relat.*, XXX (September 1977), 787–801.

378 **Roberts**, K., **Cook**, F.G., **Clark**, S.C. and **Semeonoff**, Elizabeth. *The fragmentary class structure*. London: Heinemann, 1977. viii, 200p.

379 **Scase**, Richard (ed.). *Industrial society: class, cleavage and control*. London: Allen & Unwin, 1977. 221p.

380 **Welford**, A. T. 'Psychological research on age and work.' *J. Occup. Psychol.*, XLIX, 3 (1977), 139–53.

381 **Abrams**, Philip. 'Where have all the workers gone? The meaning of work.' *Encounter*, LI (December 1978), 57–8, 60–4.

382 **Barker**, Dave. 'What TA can do for you.' *Pers. Manage.*, X, 5 (May 1978), 36–9.

383 **Bennett**, Roger D. 'Orientation to work and organizational analysis.' *J. Manage. Stud.*, XV (May 1978), 187–210.

384 **Coombs**, Rod. 'Labour and monopoly capital.' *New Left Rev.*, CVII (January–February 1978), 79–96.

385 **Hearn**, Francis. *Domination, legitimation, and resistance: the incorporation of the nineteenth century English working class*. Greenwood: Greenwood Press, 1978. ix, 309p.

386 **Kumar**, Krishan. *Prophecy and progress: the sociology of industrial and post-industrial society*. London: Allen Lane, 1978. 416p.

387 **Legge**, Karen. 'Work in prison: the process of inversion.' *Br. J. Criminol.*, XVIII (January 1978), 6–22.

388 **Ribeaux**, Peter and **Poppleton**, Stephen E. *Psychology and work: an introduction*. London: Macmillan, 1978. xvi, 362p.

389 **Roadburg**, A. *An enquiry into meanings of work and leisure: the case of professional and amateur football players and gardeners*. 1978. (Ph.D. thesis, University of Edinburgh.)

390 **Rodger**, Leslie W. 'The games business people play: some explorations in management behaviour and executive action.' *Scott. Bankers' Mag.*, LXX (August 1978), 111–20; LXXI (November 1978), 159–63.

391 **Smith**, Peter. 'Coming to terms with job crises.' *Pers. Manage.*, X, 1 (January 1978), 32–5.

392 **Wellin**, Mike. 'T.A. in the workplace.' *Pers. Manage.*, X, 7 (July 1978), 37–41.

393 **Clarke**, John. 'Capital and culture: the post-war working class revisited.' Clarke, J. and others (eds.). *Working-class culture*. 1979. p. 238–53.

394 **Clarke**, John, **Critcher**, Chas and **Johnson**, Richard (eds.). *Working-class culture: studies in history and theory*. London: Hutchinson, 1979. 301p.

395 **Corlett**, E. N. 'Isolation and curiosity as sources of work attitudes.' Sell, R.G. and Shipley, P. (eds.). *Satisfactions in work design*. 1979. p 51–6.

396 **Cox**, T. and **Mackay**, C.J. 'The impact of repetitive work.' Sell, R.G. and Shipley, P. (eds.). *Satisfactions in work design*. 1979. p. 101–12.

397 **Critcher**, Chas. 'Sociology, cultural studies and the post-war working class.' Clarke, J. and others (eds.). *Working class culture*. 1979. p. 13–40.

398 **Davis**, Howard H. *Beyond class images: explorations in the structure of social consciousness*. London: Croom Helm, 1979. 213p.

399 **Dickson**, John W. and **Buchholz**, R. A. 'Beliefs about work.' *J. Manage. Stud.*, XVI (May 1979), 235–51.

400 **Handy**, C. 'The shape of organisations to come.' *Pers. Manage.*, XI, 6 (June 1979), 24–6.

401 **Hobsbawm**, Eric John Ernest. 'Inside every worker there is a syndicalist trying to get out.' *New Soc.*, XLVIII (5 April 1979), 8–10.

402 **Hughes**, James J. and **Brinkley**, Ian. 'Attitudes and expectations of Skill Centre trainees towards trade unions and trade union membership.' *Br. J. Ind. Relat.*, XVII, 1 (March 1979), 64–9.

403 **Johnson**, Richard. 'Culture and the historians.' Clarke, J. and others (eds.). *Working-class culture*. 1979. p. 41–71.

404 **Johnson**, Richard. 'Three problematics: elements of a theory of working-class culture.' Clarke, J. and others (eds.). *Working-class culture*. 1979. p. 201–37.

405 **Kakabadse**, Andrew P. 'Organization structure and attitudes to work.' *Manage. Decis.*, XVII, 2 (1979), 189–201.

406 **Newman**, Otto. 'The newly acquisitive

affluent worker?' *Sociology*, XIII, I (January 1979), 35–46.

407 **Oldham**, Greg R. and **Miller**, Howard E. 'The effect of significant other's job complexity on employee reactions to work.' *Hum. Relat.*, XXXII (March 1979), 247–60.

408 **Paul**, L. 'Sixteen-year-olds' image of work.' *Pers. Rev.*, VIII (Winter 1979), 10–13.

409 **Saunders**, Ken. 'The hospital porter.' *Employee Relat.*, I, 4 (1979), 30–2.

410 **Schumacher**, E.F. *Good work*. London: Abacus, 1979. xi, 147p.

411 **Shipley**, Patricia. 'A study of quality of life and work in a professional group.' Sell, R.G. and Shipley, P. (eds.). *Satisfactions in work design*. 1979. p. 121–32.

412 **Stephenson**, Geoffrey Michael and **Brotherton**, Christopher J. (eds.). *Industrial relations: a*

social psychological approach. Chichester: Wiley, 1979. xii, 412p.

413 **Walker**, Kenneth F. 'Psychology and industrial relations: a general perspective.' Stephenson, G. and Brotherton, C. (eds.). *Industrial relations: a social psychological approach*. 1979. p. 5–31.

414 **Willis**, Paul. 'Shop-floor culture, masculinity and the wage form.' Clarke, J. and others (eds.). *Working-class culture*. 1979. p. 185–98.

See also: 14; 23; 112; 121; 190; 191; 523; 529; 543; 547; 641; 668; 822; 973; 990; 993; 1006; 1037; 1041; 1043; 1044; 1052; 1056; 1464; 1495; 1497; 1508; 1520; 1561; 1563; 1579; 1593; 1699; 1768; 1783; 1881; 1947; 2137; 2167; 2181; 2614; 2615; 2635; 2645; 2646; 2654; 2656; 3387; 3483; 3496; 3515; 3536; 3537; 3624; 3847; 4049; 4908; 4982; 5213; 5532; 5798.

II. MOTIVATION AND MORALE

This section includes the more sociological and psychological literature on such subjects as job satisfaction, incentives to work, and restriction of output. Many of the general works in Part Two, I also contain material on these topics. See Part Five, II for the literature dealing with trade union restrictions on output and Part Six, III, F for literature on wage incentives.

415 **Blackler**, Frank H. M. and **Williams**, A. Roger T. 'People's motives at work.' Warr, P. (ed.). *Psychology at work*. 1971. p. 283–303.

416 **Brown**, R. G. S. 'Fulton and morale.' *Public Adm.*, XLIX, 2 (Summer 1971), 185–95.

417 **Dowling**, William Francis and **Sayles**, Leonard Robert. *How managers motivate: the imperatives of supervision*. London: McGraw-Hill, 1971. 436p.

418 **Fielding**, B. 'Job evaluation and employee motivation.' *Work Study Manage. Serv..*, IX, 11 (November 1971), 705–8.

419 **Haller**, Max and **Rosenmayr**, Leopold. 'The pluridimensionality of work commitment: a study of young married women.' *Hum. Relat.*, XXIV (December 1971), 501–18.

420 **Safilios-Rothschild**, Constantina. 'Towards the conceptualization and measurement of work commitment.' *Hum. Relat.*, XXIV (December 1971), 489–93.

421 **Advisory Panel on Hospital Administration.** 'Staff morale and the organisation.' *Hosp. Health Serv. Rev.*, LXVIII, 6 (June 1972), 188–91. (Hospital Administration Panel papers 2.)

422 **Charles-Edwards**, D. 'Work and motivation.' *Work Study Manage. Serv.*, X, 5 (May 1972), 258–61.

423 **Ditton**, Jason. 'Absent at work: or how to manage monotony.' *New Soc.*, XXII (21 December 1972), 679–81.

424 **Lawrence**, Allan C. 'Individual differences in work motivation.' *Hum. Relat.*, XXV (September 1972), 327–35.

425 **Mumford**, Enid. 'Job satisfaction: a method of analysis.' *Pers. Rev.*, I, 3 (Summer 1972), 48–57.

426 **Mumford**, Enid. *Job satisfaction: a study of computer specialists*. London: Longman, 1972. 242p.

427 **Neal**, *Sir* Leonard Francis. 'Future trends in industrial relations.' *Occup. Psychol.*, XLV, 3–4 (1972), 167–72.

428 **Weir**, David. 'Satisfactions in white-collar work.' Butterworth, E. and Weir, D. (eds.). *Social problems of modern Britain*. London: Fontana, 1972. p. 374–83.

429 **Wilson**, Glenn D., **Tunstall**, Olive A. and **Eysenck**, H. J. 'Measurement of motivation in predicting industrial performance: a study of apprentice gas fitters.' *Occup. Psychol.*, XLVI (1972), 15–24.

430 **Abell**, Peter and **Mathew**, David. 'The task analysis framework in organizational analysis.' Warner, M. (ed.). *Sociology of the workplace*. 1973. p. 164–76.

431 **Cooper**, Robert. 'How jobs motivate.' *Pers. Rev.*, II, 2 (Spring 1973), 4–11. Reprinted in Weir, M. (ed.). *Job satisfaction*. 1976. p. 138–46.

432 **Cooper**, Robert. 'Task characteristics and intrinsic motivation.' *Hum. Relat.*, XXVI (1973), 387–413.

433 **Cross**, Denys. 'The worker opinion survey: a measure of shopfloor satisfaction.' *Occup. Psych.*, XLVII, 3–4 (1973), 193–208.

434 **Engel**, Gloria V. 'Social factors affecting work satisfaction of the physician's assistant: a preliminary report.' Halmos, P. (ed.). *Professionalisation and social change*. 1973. p. 245–62.

435 **Nettelbeck**, T. 'A note on knowledge of results as an incentive to production among vocational rehabilitees.' *Occup. Psych.*, XLVII (1973), 63–5.

436 **Reynolds**, M. 'Ownership in work.' *Manage. Educ. Dev.*, XI (August 1973), 86–94.

437 **Robertson**, K. B. 'Job satisfaction in the Civil Service.' *Manage. Serv. Gov.*, XXVIII, 3 (August 1973), 133–9.

438 **Wild**, Ray. 'Manpower planning and job satisfaction.' *Manage. Decis.*, XI (Spring 1973), 11–19.

439 **Wild**, Ray. 'Work needs of female workers: the influence of biographical and personal variables.' *Br. J. Ind. Relat.*, XI, 2 (July 1973), 297–9.

440 **Williamson**, D. T. N. 'The anachronistic factory.' *Pers. Rev.*, III, 3 (Autumn 1973), 26–37.

441 **Blake**, Jenny. 'Experiments in job satisfaction.' *Pers. Manage.*, VI, 1 (January 1974), 32–3.

442 **Brandis**, J. 'Managing and motivating by objectives in practice.' *Manage. Objectives*, IV, 1 (1974), 11–19.

443 **Cooper**, Robert. *Job motivation and job design.* London: I.P.M., 1974. 140p.

444 **Court**, J. L. 'Incentives and the motivation of workers and management.' *Work Study Manage. Serv.*, 4 (April 1974), 214–16.

445 **Gowler**, Dan. 'Values, contracts and job satisfaction.' *Pers. Rev.*, IV, 4 (Autumn 1974), 4–14.

446 **Iles**, D. J. *The disincentive effects of income taxation on work effort.* 1973–4. (M.Sc. thesis, University of Bath.)

447 **Lasko**, Roger. 'A comment on analysis of an index of industrial morale.' *Br. J. Ind. Relat.*, XII, 1 (March 1974), 114–16.

448 **Lupton**, Tom. 'Size and morale.' *Manage. Serv. Gov.*, XXIX, 4 (November 1974), 188–98.

449 **Paul**, R. J. 'Role clarity and satisfaction.' *J. Manage. Stud.*, XI, 3 (October 1974), 233–45.

450 **Pencavel**, John H. 'Analysis of an index of industrial morale.' *Br. J. Ind. Relat.*, XII, 1 (March 1974), 48–55.

451 **Reynolds**, P. M. 'Management practice and the politics of motivation.' *Manage. Decis.*, XII, 3 (1974), 139–44.

452 **Solem**, Allen R. 'On structure and process in work motivation.' *Hum. Relat.*, XXVII (October 1974), 779–920.

453 **Davies**, D. 'Peculiar problems of the British Civil Service.' *Nature*, CCLV, 5506 (22 May 1975), 293–6.

454 **Davies**, E. C. 'The problem of frustration.' *Work Study Manage. Serv.*, XI, 9 (September 1975), 328–32.

455 **Gill**, H. S. 'Handling redundancy and how to maintain morale.' *Pers. Manage.*, VII, 3 (March 1975), 34–7.

456 **Payne**, Roy. 'A-type work for A-type people.' *Pers. Manage.*, VII, 12 (December 1975), 22–4.

457 **Pencavel**, John H. 'A rejoinder on industrial morale.' *Br. J. Ind. Relat.*, XIII, 2 (July 1975), 266–8.

458 **Whitfield**, P. R. *Creativity in industry.* Harmondsworth: Penguin, 1975. 217p.

459 **Bromage**, N. and **Graves**, D. 'Motivation of secretaries and typists.' *Ind. Commer. Train.*, VIII, 9 (September 1976), 347–51.

460 **Clay**, M. 'The sacrificial multitude.' *Management in Action*, V (July 1973), 4–5; V (August 1973), 4–5; V (September 1973), 4–5; VI (October 1973), 6–7; VI (November 1973), 4–5.

461 **Graham**, Kenneth. 'Union attitudes to job satisfaction.' Weir, M. (ed.). *Job satisfaction.* 1976. p. 265.

462 **Groves**, D. L. 'Planning: satisfaction and productivity.' *Long Range Plann.*, IX, 4 (August 1976), 52–7.

463 **Guest,** David. 'Motivation after Maslow.' *Pers. Manage.*, VIII, 3 (March 1976), 29–32.

464 **McDavid**, Ian. 'Improving job satisfaction in an office.' Weir, M. (ed.). *Job satisfaction.* 1976. p. 210–4.

465 **Oldham**, Greg R. 'Job characteristics and internal motivation: the moderating effect of interpersonal and individual variables.' *Hum. Relat.*, XXIX (June 1976), 559–69.

466 **Ramsden**, P. J. 'Individual motivation in management.' *J. Gen. Manage.*, III (Winter 1975–1976), 52–66.

467 **Weir**, Mary (ed.). *Job satisfaction: challenge and response in modern Britain.* London: Fontana/Collins, 1976. 288p.

468 **Ditton**, Jason. 'Alibis and aliases: some notes on the motives of fiddling bread salesmen.' *Sociology*, XI, 2 (May 1977), 233–55.

469 **Evered**, Roger D. 'Personal scenarios: an empirical study of their relation to individual performance and to organizational activism.' *Hum. Relat.*, XXX (November 1977), 1057–69.

470 **Gardner**, Godfrey. 'The higher-order needs of London bus crews: a two-factor analysis.' *Hum. Relat.*, XXX (September 1977), 767–85.

471 **Blanchard**, Ian. 'Labour productivity and work psychology in the English mining industry, 1400–1600.' *Econ. Hist. Rev.*, XXXI, 1 (February 1978), 1–24.

472 **Chalmers**, Brian. 'Employment and the meeting of human needs.' *Manage. Decis.*, XVI, 6 (1978), 300–5.

473 **Hartston**, W. and **Mottram**, R. 'Brainpower, motivation and the elements of success.' *Pers. Manage.*, X, 8 (August 1978), 30–2.

474 **Kakabadse**, Andrew P. and **Worral**, Richard. 'Job satisfaction and organizational structure: a comparative study of nine social service departments.' *Br. J. Soc. Work*, VIII (Spring 1978), 51–70.

475 **Maimon**, Zvi and **Ronen**, Simiha. 'Measures of job facets satisfaction as predictors of the tendency to leave or the tendency to stay with an organization.' *Hum. Relat.*, XXXI (December 1978), 1019–30.

476 **Mason**, A. *Worker motivation in building.* London: Institute of Building, 1978. 36p. (Occasional papers 19.)

477 **Passey**, R.D.C. 'Award schemes for employee inventors.' *Pers. Manage.*, X, 2 (February 1978), 27–30.

478 **Arvey**, Richard D. and **Dewhirst**, H. Dud-

ley. 'Relationships between diversity of interests, age, job satisfaction and job performance.' *J. Occup. Psychol.*, LII (1979), 17–23.

479 **Cooper**, Cary L. and **Torrington**, Derek P. 'Strategies for relieving stress at work.' *Pers. Manage.*, XI, 6 (June 1979), 28–31.

480 **Cope**, D. 'Understanding the concept of job satisfaction.' Sell, R. G. and Shipley. P. (eds.). *Satisfactions in work design.* 1979. p.57–64.

481 **Crawley**, R. and **Spurgeon**, P. 'Computer assistance and the air traffic controller's job satisfaction.' Sell, R. G. and Shipley, P. (eds.). *Satisfactions in work design.* 1979. p. 169–78.

482 **Lindon**, L. D. 'An experimental investigation of the effect of different reference points on expressed job satisfaction.' Sell, R. G. and Shipley, P. (eds.). *Satisfactions in work design.* 1979. p. 65–74.

483 **Singleton**, W. T. 'Some conceptual and operational doubts about job satisfaction.' Sell, R. G. and Shipley, P. (eds.). *Satisfactions in work design.* 1979. p. 9–16.

484 **Stansfield**, R. G. 'Typing pools: a study in satisfactions in work.' Sell, R. G. and Shipley, P. (eds.). *Satisfactions in work design.* 1979. p. 89–95.

See also: 253; 355; 500; 543; 558; 596; 636; 664; 667; 1007; 1433; 1884; 4749; 4906.

III. ABSENTEEISM

See also Part Six, II, E, 5; Part Six, IV, D; and Part Seven, VII, B, 2–3.

485 **Deady**, E. 'Absence contained.' *Ind. Soc.*, LIII, 12 (December 1971), 14–15.

486 **Jones**, Richard Merfyn. *Absenteeism.* London: Department of Employment, 1971. v, 49p.

487 **Martin**, J. 'Absence in a light engineering factory.' *Occup. Psychol.*, XLV, 2 (1971), 77–89.

488 **Moody**, David. 'Absence minded.' *Pers. Manage.*, III, 11 (November 1971), 28–31.

489 **Chadwick-Jones**, John K., **Brown**, G. A. and **Nicholson**, Nigel. 'A-type and B-type absence: empirical trends for women employees.' *Occup. Psychol.*, XLVII, 1–2 (1973), 75–80.

490 **Kearns**, J. L. 'Out of sight: absenteeism.' *Ind. Soc.*, LV, 9 (September 1973), 13–15.

491 **Raven**, R. E. 'Absenteeism.' *Work Study*, XXII, 1 (January 1973), 44–50.

492 **Almond**, J. M. 'The management of absenteeism.' *Prod. Eng.*, LIV, 12 (December 1975), 650–54.

493 **Austin**, R. *Financial commitments, leisure and elective absenteeism.* 1975. (M.Sc. thesis, University of Keele.)

494 **Behrend**, Hilde. 'New approach to the analysis of absences from work.' *Ind. Relat. J.*, V, 4 (Winter 1974–5), 4–21.

495 **Clark**, Jill. *Time out? A study of absenteeism among nurses.* London: Royal College of Nursing and National Council of Nurses of the United Kingdom, 1975. 68p.

496 **Income Data Services.** *Absence.* London: I.D.S., 1975. 18p. (I.D.S. study 111.)

497 **King**, M. J. W. *A study of absence among shopfloor employees in the Glasgow plant of the Caterpillar Tractor Company Limited.* 1975. (M. Phil. thesis, University of Edinburgh.)

498 **O'Muircheartaigh**, Colin A. *Absenteeism in Irish industry.* Dublin: Irish Productivity Centre, 1975. 164p.

499 **Behrend**, Hilde and **Pocock**, S. 'Absence and the individual: a six-year study in one organisation.' *Int. Labour Rev.*, CXIV, 3 (November 1976), 311–27.

500 **Nicholson**, Nigel. *Industrial absence as an indication of motivation and job satisfaction: a study of contrasting technologies in the North of England and South Wales.* 1976. (Ph.D. thesis, University of Wales, Cardiff.)

501 **Nicholson**, Nigel. 'Management sanctions and absence control.' *Hum. Relat.*, XXIX (February 1976), 139–51.

502 **Nicholson**, Nigel and **Goodge**, P. M. 'Factors in female absenteeism.' *J. Manage. Stud.*, XII, 3 (October 1976), 234–54.

503 **Nicholson**, Nigel. 'Absence behaviour and attendance motivators.' *J. Manage. Stud.*, XIV, 3 (October 1977), 231–52.

504 **Behrend**, Hilde. *How to monitor absence from work: from headcount to computer.* London: I.P.M., 1978.

505 **Dennett**, Barrie. 'How to minimise malingering.' *Pers. Manage.*, X, 5 (May 1978), 30–32.

506 **Incomes Data Services.** *Absenteeism.* London: I.D.S., 1978. 24p. (I.D.S. study 169.)

507 **Nicholson**, Nigel, **Jackson**, Paul and **Howes**, Gillian. 'Shiftwork and absence: an analysis of temporal trends.' *J. Occup. Psychol.*, LI (June 1978), 127–37.

508 **Edwards**, Paul K. 'Attachment to work and absence behaviour.' *Hum. Relat.*, XXXII (December 1979), 1065–80.

509 **Edwards**, Paul K. and **Scullion**, Hugh. 'Does sick pay encourage absenteeism?' *Pers. Manage.*, XI, 7 (July 1979), 32–5.

510 **Jonson**, L. C. 'Social accounting for absenteeism and personnel turnover.' *Account., Organ. Soc.*, III, 3–4 (1979), 261–8.

See also: 4532; 4597; 5761; 7079.

IV. ATTITUDES TOWARDS INNOVATION AND CHANGE

Many of the general works in Part Two, I also discuss workers' attitudes to innovation and change. The voluminous literature on the nature and extent of automation is not included here. See also Part Five, II; and Part Six, II, D, 3.

511 **Lupton**, Tom. 'Organizational change: "top-down" or "bottom-up" management?' *Pers. Rev.*, I, 3 (Autumn 1971), 22–8.

512 **Mumford**, Enid. *Systems design for people.* Manchester: National Computing Centre, 1971. 52p.

513 **Teire**, John and **Varney**, David. 'Social values and technological change.' *Manage. Decis.*, IX, 2 (Summer 1971), 179–87.

514 **Wainwright**, David. 'The human side of mergers.' *Ind. Soc.*, LIV, 12 (December 1972), 7–9.

515 **Wedderburn**, Dorothy and **Crompton**, Rosemary. *Workers' attitudes and technology.* Cambridge: Cambridge U.P., 1972. 176p.

516 **Barrett**, Peter Francis. *Human implications of mergers and takeovers.* London: I.P.M., 1973. 128p.

517 **Connolly**, D. J. 'Social repercussions of new cargo handling methods in the Port of London.' *Int. Labour Rev.*, CV, 6 (June 1972), 543–68.

518 **Gorman**, Liam and **Mullan**, C. 'Human aspects of the management of technological change.' *J. Manage. Stud.*, X, 1 (February 1973), 48–61.

519 **Halmos**, P. *Professionalism and social change.* Newcastle-under-Lyme: Keele University, 1973. i, 338p. (Sociological review monographs 20.)

520 **Johns**, E. A. *The sociology of industrial change.* London: Pergamon, 1973. x, 173p.

521 **Peach**, Len. 'The responsible management of technological change.' *Pers. Manage.*, V, 8 (August 1973), 18–21.

522 **Thurley**, Keith E. 'Computers and supervisors.' Warner, M. (ed.), *Sociology of the workplace.* 1973. p. 177–200.

523 **Vamplew**, Clive. 'Automated process workers: work attitudes and behaviour.' *Br. J. Ind. Relat.*, XI, 3 (November 1973), 415–30.

524 **Edwards**, G. A. B. 'Group technology: answer to a social problem.' *Pers. Manage.*, VI, 3 (March 1974), 35–9.

525 **Jones**, T. Ken. *The human face of change: social responsibility and rationalization at British Steel.* London: I.P.M., 1974. 71p.

526 **Margerison**, Charles J. 'Industrial relations and organization development.' *Ind. Relat. J.*, V, 3 (Autumn 1974), 18–26.

527 **Sneath**, F. 'Keeping up with organizational change.' *Pers. Manage.*, VI, 10 (October 1974), 45–7.

528 **Civil Service Department** and **Civil Service National Whitley Council.** *Civil ser-vants and change.* London: H.M.S.O., 1975. 42p.

529 **Miller**, Eric J. 'Socio-technical systems in weaving 1953–1970: a follow-up study.' *Hum. Relat.*, XXVIII (May 1975), 349–86.

530 **Nash**, Al. 'Hospital technology: prescription for peace?' *Pers. Manage.*, VII, 3 (March 1975), 24–7.

531 **Seal**, V. A. 'Product change on the shop-floor.' *Pers. Rev.*, V, 4 (Autumn 1975), 51–6.

532 **Abbott**, Lewis F. *Social aspects of innovation and industrial technology: a survey of research.* London: H.M.S.O., 1976. v, 130p. (Department of Industry, C.F.I.T. papers 1.)

533 **Biddle**, Derek and **Hutton**, Geoffrey. 'Toward a tolerance theory of worker adaptation.' *Hum. Relat.*, XXIX (September 1976), 833–62.

534 **Lowndes**, Richard 'Technological innovation: capital and labour.' *Ind. Commer. Train.*, VIII, 8 (August 1976), 318–29.

535 **Shye**, Samuel and **Elizur**, Dov. 'Worries about deprivation of job rewards following computerization: a partial order scalogram analysis.' *Hum. Relat.*, XXIX (January 1976), 63–71.

536 **Weltz**, Friedrich and **Schmidt**, Gerd. *Introduction of new technologies, employment policies and industrial relations.* Munich: Anglo-German Foundation for the Study of Industrial Society, 1976. 20p.

537 **Lindquist**, M. G. 'A systems approach to organizational change.' *Pers. Rev.*, VII (Summer 1977), 5–8.

538 **Ottaway**, Richard N. 'An apology for change.' Ottaway, R. (ed.). *Humanising the workplace.* 1977. p. 13–24.

539 **Randolph**, W. Alan and **Finch**, Frederic E. 'The relationship between organization technology and the direction and frequency dimensions of task communications.' *Hum. Relat.*, XXX (December 1977), 1131–45.

540 **Shirley**, Robert C. 'The human side of mergers.' *Long Range Plann.*, X, 1 (February 1977), 35–9.

541 **Warmington**, Allan, **Lupton**, Tom and **Gribbon**, Cecily. *Organizational behaviour and performance: an open systems approach to change.* London: Macmillan, 1977. ix, 258p.

542 **Brown**, David and **Harrison**, Michael J. *A sociology of industrialisation: an introduction.* London: Macmillan, 1978. 200p.

543 **Gallie**, Duncan. *In search of the new working class: automation and social integration within the capitalist enterprise.* Cambridge: Cambridge U.P., 1978. viii, 348p. (Cambridge studies in sociology 9.)

544 **Jacobs**, Eric. *The approach to industrial change: a comparative study of workplace industrial relations and manpower policies in British and West German enterprises.* Munich: Anglo-German Founda-

tion for the study of Industrial Society, 1978. Vol. 1. *The British experience.*

545 **Jacobs**, Eric. *The approach to industrial change in Britain and Germany: a comparative study of workplace industrial relations and manpower policies in British and West German enterprises.* Munich: Anglo-German Foundation for the Study of Industrial Society, 1978.

546 **Miller**, J. A. 'Contingency theory, values and change.' *Hum. Relat.*, XXXI, 10 (October 1978), 885–904.

547 **Berg**, Maxine (ed.). *Technology and toil in nineteenth century Britain: documents.* London: CSE Books, 1979. 240p.

548 **Fowler**, Alan G. 'The manpower implications of organic change.' *Pers. Manage.*, XI, 5 (May 1979), 35–9, 48.

549 **Harland**, Peter. 'New technologies: the hu-man dimension.' Washington, Derek (ed.). *Technological change and the future of work.* 1979. p. 25–38.

550 **Mills**, B. E. 'Microprocessors: their impact on work and participation.' *Ind. Participation*, DLXVI (1979), 15–19.

551 **Mumford**, Enid. 'Human values and the introduction of technical change.' *Manch. Bus. School Rev.*, III, 2 (1979), 13–17.

552 **Taylor**, Linda King. 'The implementation of change.' *Ind. Participation*, DLXX (Autumn 1979), 21–4.

553 **Washington**, Derek (ed.). *Technological change and the future of work: proceedings of a conference, University of Sussex, 1979.* Redhill: South East Forum, 1979.

See also: 685; 757; 759; 1008; 1448; 1476; 1518; 1631; 1767; 3455.

V. WORK STRUCTURING AND JOB DESIGN

This section includes material on such topics as job enrichment, job enlargement, the humanization of work, autonomous work groups, and the quality of working life. The technical literature on ergonomics is excluded. Material describing conditions of work in industry is classified at Part Six, IV. See also Part Five, VI, D, 1.

554 **Binsted**, Douglas. 'Job enrichment.' *Co-partnership*, DXLVI (November 1971), 63–4.

555 **Butteriss**, Margaret. *Job enrichment and employee participation: a study.* London: I.P.M., 1971. 71p.

556 **Dickson**, John W. 'What's in a job?' *Pers. Manage.*, III, 6 (June 1971), 39–40.

557 **Little**, Alan and **Warr**, Peter Bryan. 'Who's afraid of job enrichment?' *Pers. Manage.*, III, 2 (February 1971), 34–7.
Reprinted in Weir, M. (ed.). *Job Satisfaction.* 1976. p. 175–9.

558 **Paul**, W. J. and **Robertson**, K. B. 'Job enrichment and employee motivation.' *Co-partnership*, DXLIV (April 1971), 12–17.

559 **Starbuck**, William H. (ed.). *Organizational growth and development: selected readings.* Harmondsworth: Penguin, 1971. 383p.

560 **White**, David. 'Desk life.' *New Soc.*, XVI (25 March 1971), 477–9.

561 **Wilson**, A. T. M. 'Considerations affecting the design of a new establishment.' Bartholomew, D. J. and Morris, B. R. (eds.). *Aspects of manpower planning.* 1971. p. 109–25.

562 **Daniel**, William Wentworth and **McIntosh**, Neil. *Right to manage? A study of leadership and reform in employee relations.* London: Macdonald, 1972. 217p.
A Political and Economic Planning report.

563 **Industrial and Commercial Training.** 'Not for bread alone.' *Ind. Comm. Train.*, IV, 3 (March 1972), 129–32.

564 **Plant**, R. 'Releasing supervisory potential.' *Eur. Train.*, 1 (Spring 1972), 34–42.

565 **Birchall**, David W. and **Wild**, Ray. 'Group working.' *Work Study Manage. Serv.*, XI, 10 (October 1973), 702–7.
Reprinted in Weir, M. (ed.). *Job satisfaction.* 1976. p. 150–60.

566 **Birchall**, David W. and **Wild**, Ray. 'Job restructuring amongst blue-collar workers.' *Pers. Rev.*, III, 2 (Spring 1973), 40–54.

567 **Butera**, F. 'Advances in work organization.' *Work Study*, XXII, 10 (October 1973), 9–20.

568 **Cherns**, Albert B. 'Better working lives: a social scientist's view.' *Occup. Psychol.*, XLVII (1973), 23–8.

569 **Chichester-Clark**, Robin. 'On the quality of working life.' *Pers. Manage.*, V, 11 (November 1973), 26–9.
Reprinted in Weir, M. (ed.). *Job satisfaction.* 1976. p. 26–31.

570 **Dickson**, John W. 'The physical correlates of variety in work.' *Hum. Relat.*, XXVI, 6 (June 1973), 715–33.

571 **Hallam**, P. A. 'An experiment with group working.' *Work Study Manage. Serv.*, X, 4 (April 1973), 240–4.
Reprinted in Weir, M. (ed.). *Job satisfaction.* 1976. p. 193–201.

572 **Jackson**, Peter. 'Better working lives: an organisational consultant's view.' *Occup. Psychol.*, XLVII (1973), 29–31.

573 **Kempner**, T. and **Wild**, Ray. 'Job design and productivity.' *J. Manage. Stud.*, X, 1 (February 1973), 64–83.

574 **Leich**, D. N. 'Experience in advances in work organization.' *Work Study*, XXII, 8 (August 1973), 21–30.

575 **Mills**, S. 'Job design.' *Pers. Rev.*, III, 2 (Spring 1973), 68–72.

576 **Mumford**, Enid. 'Designing systems for job satisfaction.' *Omega*, I, 4 (1973), 493–8.
Reprinted in Weir, M. (ed.). *Job satisfaction.* 1976. p. 170–5.

577 **Owen**, Trevor. 'Advances in work organization.' *Work Study*, XXII, 7 (July 1973), 21–7.

578 **Sirota**, D. 'Production and service personnel

and job enrichment.' *Work Study*, XXII, 1 (January 1973), 9–15.

579 **Walsh**, William. 'Job enrichment in a public utility.' *Ind. Participation*, DLIII (Autumn – Winter 1973), 19–23.

580 **Walsh**, William. 'Job enrichment in the office.' *Work Study*, XXII, 6 (June 1973), 28–31.

581 **Warr**, Peter Bryan. 'Better working lives: a university psychologist's view.' *Occup. Psychol.*, XLVII (1973), 15–22.

582 **Wild**, Ray and **Birchall**, David W. 'Means and ends in job restructuring.' *Pers. Rev.*, III, 3 (Autumn 1973), 18–23.

583 **Wilson**, N. A. B. *On the quality of working life.* London: H.M.S.O., 1973. v, 52p. (Department of Employment, Manpower papers 7.)

584 **Birchall**, David W. and **Wild**, Ray. 'Autonomous work groups.' *J. Gen. Manage.*, 1, 4 (Autumn 1974), 36–43.

585 **Blair**, Jon. 'Three studies in improving clerical work.' *Pers. Manage.*, VI, 2 (February 1974), 34–7.

586 **Edwards**, Elwyn and **Lees**, Frank P. (eds.). *The human operator in process control.* London: Taylor & Francis, 1974. 480p.

587 **Hughes**, John and **Gregory**, Denis L. 'Richer jobs for workers?' *New Soc.*, XXVII (14 February 1974), 386–7.
Reprinted in Weir, M. (ed.). *Job satisfaction.* 1976. p. 251–7.

588 **Marsh**, John. 'Humanizing work.' *R. Soc. Arts J.*, CXXII (March 1974), 203–13.

589 **Mumford**, Enid. 'Computer systems and work design.' *Pers. Rev.*, IV, 1 (Spring 1974), 40–9.

590 **Noordhof**, Dick. 'Work structuring and consultation at Philips.' *Ind. Participation*, DLV (Summer 1974), 3–7.

591 **Pym**, Denis. 'Better working lives: a personal view.' *Occup. Psychol.*, XLVII, 1–2 (1974), 33–6.

592 **Walsh**, William. 'Reviewing job enrichment.' *Work Study Manage. Serv.*, X, 5 (May 1974), 282–6.

593 **Whitaker**, D. 'Effect of group technology on the shop-floor.' *Prod. Eng.*, LIII, 6 (June 1974), 193–4.

594 **Wild**, Ray. 'Group working in mass production.' *Prod. Eng.*, LII, 12 (December 1973), 457–61; LIII, 1 (January 1974), 31–5.

595 **Wild**, Ray. 'Job restructuring and work organization.' *Manage. Decis.*, XII, 3 (1974), 117–26.

596 **Baker**, Sally H. and **Hansen**, Richard A. 'Job design and worker satisfaction: a challenge to assumptions.' *J. Occup. Psychol.*, XLVIII, 2 (June 1975), 79–91.

597 **Birchall**, David W. 'Job design.' Bowey, Angela M. (ed.). *Handbook of salary and wage systems.* 1975. p. 29–40.

598 **Birchall**, David W. *Job design: a planning and implementation guide for managers.* London: Gower, 1975. xiv, 141p.

599 **Blackler**, Frank H. M. and **Brown**, G. A. 'The impending crisis in job redesign.' *J. Occup. Psychol.*, XLVIII, 3 (September 1975), 185–93.

600 **Buckingham**, Graeme Lovell, **Jeffrey**, Robert George and **Thorne**, Bruce Alan. *Job enrichment and organizational change: a study in participation at Gallaher Ltd.* London: Gower, 1975. x, 161p.

601 **Cherns**, Albert B. 'Perspectives on the quality of working life.' *J. Occup. Psychol.*, XLVIII, 3 (1975), 155–67.

602 **Department of Employment**, Tripartite Steering Group on Job Satisfaction. *Making work more satisfying: increasing opportunities for people to derive greater satisfaction from their jobs through changes in job design and work organisation.* London: H.M.S.O., 1975, 27p.
Chairman: J. Fraser.

603 **Donaldson**, Lex. 'Job enlargement: a multi-dimensional process.' *Hum. Relat.*, XXVIII (September 1975), 593–610.

604 **National Economic Development Committee**, Economic Development Committee for Mechanical Engineering. *Why group technology?* London: N.E.D.C., 1975.

605 **Painter**, C. W. and **Codd**, F. A. 'Reconciliation of customer service with labour efficiency.' *Prod. Eng.*, LIV, 4 (April 1975), 242–7.

606 **Spink**, Peter. 'Some comments on the quality of working life.' *J. Occup. Psychol.*, XLVIII, 3 (September 1975), 179–84.

607 **Taylor**, James C. 'The human side of work: the socio-technical approach to work system design.' *Pers. Rev.*, IV, 3 (Summer 1975), 17–22.

608 **Wild**, Ray and **Birchall**, David W. 'Job structuring and work organization.' *J. Occup. Psychol.*, XLVIII, 3 (September 1975), 169–77.

609 **Blake**, Jenny and **Ross**, Shirley. 'Some experiences with autonomous work groups.' Weir, M. (ed.). *Job satisfaction.* 1976. p. 185–93.

610 **Carby**, Keith. *Job redesign in practice.* London: I.P.M., 1976. 67p.

611 **Dar-El**, M. and **Young**, L. F. 'Supportive approaches to worker–staff partnership.' *Pers. Rev.*, V, 2 (Spring 1976), 5–11.

612 **Delamotte**, Yves. 'Working conditions and government policy: some Western European approaches.' *Int. Labour Rev.*, CXIV, 2 (September–October 1976), 139–54.

613 **Garnier**, T. and **Wellens**, John. 'Humanized management at Kalamazoo.' *Ind. Commer. Train.*, VIII, 7 (July 1976), 260–9.

614 **Hines**, John. 'Work groups under stress.' *Ind. Soc.*, LVIII, 5 (September–October 1976), 17–18.

615 **Klein**, Lisl. *New forms of work organisation.* Cambridge: Cambridge U.P., 1976. viii, 106p.

616 **McCormick**, Ernest James. *Human factors in*

engineering and work design. London: McGraw-Hill, 1976. xi, 491p.
Fourth edition.

617 **Mumford**, Enid. 'Strategy for the redesign of work.' *Pers. Rev.*, v, 2 (Spring 1976), 33–9.

618 **Mumford**, Enid. 'Towards the democratic design of work systems.' *Pers. Manage.*, VIII, 9 (September 1976), 32–5.

619 **National Economic Development Office.** *Industrial restructuring: some management aspects.* London: N.E.D.O., 1976. (Discussion paper 4.)

620 **Rose**, E. 'Work control in industrial society.' *Ind. Relat. J.*, VII, 3 (Autumn 1976), 20–30.

621 **Sheppard**, H. L. 'Task enrichment, wage levels and worker attitudes.' *J. Manage. Stud.*, XIII, 1 (February 1976), 49–60.

622 **Wild**, Ray. 'The nature and context of job restructuring in the engineering industries of Europe.' Weir, M. (ed.). *Job satisfaction.* 1976. p. 275–9.

623 **Cooley**, Michael J. E. 'Taylor in the office.' Ottaway, R. (ed.). *Humanising the workplace.* 1977. p. 65–77.

624 **Department of Employment Gazette.** 'Work organisation and attitudes in garage workshops: replanning for the 1980s.' *Dep. Employment Gaz.*, LXXXV, 9 (September 1977), 951–3.

625 **Dickson**, Paul. *Work revolution.* London: Allen & Unwin, 1977. x, 378p.
Foreword by Jack Jones.

626 **Exley**, M. 'Job satisfaction in H.M. Customs and Excise.' *Pers. Rev.*, VII (Summer 1977), 12–20.

627 **Hunter**, J. and **Crampton**, D. B. 'Job satisfaction: bridging the information gap.' *Manage. Serv. Gov.*, XXXII (August 1977), 134–43.

628 **Jessup**, Gilbert. 'The case for shop floor participation.' *Dep. Employment Gaz.*, LXXXV, 6 (June 1977), 575–7.

629 **Lupton**, Tom. 'Efficiency and the quality of worklife.' *Manchr. Bus. School Rev.*, II, 2 (1977), 16–24.

630 **Ottaway**, Richard N. (ed.). *Humanising the workplace: new proposals and perspectives.* London: Croom Helm, 1977. 175p.

631 **Ream**, Betty. 'Job restructuring.' *Ind. Soc.*, LIX, 4 (July–August 1977), 9–10.

632 **Rosow**, Jerome M. 'The quality of working life and productivity: the double pay-off.' *Ind. Participation*, DLXII (Autumn 1977), 9–12.

633 **Rowbottom**, Ralph and **Billis**, David. 'The stratification of work and organizational design.' *Hum. Relat.*, XXX (January 1977), 53–76.

634 **Schumacher**, C. 'Structuring work.' *Ind. Participation*, DLX (1977), 6–18.

635 **Taylor**, James C. 'Experiments in work design.' *Pers. Rev.*, VII, 1 (Summer 1977), 21–2; VII, 2 (Autumn 1977), 21.

636 **Taylor**, James C. 'Job satisfaction and the quality of working life.' *J. Occup. Psychol.*, L (December 1977), 243–52.

637 **Watson**, J. N. 'New management attitudes to the humanisation of work.' Ottaway, R. (ed.). *Humanising the workplace.* 1977. p. 135–48.

638 **Weir**, Mary. 'Are computer systems and humanised work compatible?' Ottaway, R. (ed.) *Humanising the workplace.* 1977. p. 44–64.

639 **Wilson**, Alex Thomson Macbeth. *Development of new forms of work organisation in the United Kingdom: four illustrative examples and some general points.* Geneva: International Institute for Labour Studies, 1977. 132p.

640 **Bailey**, J. 'Moulding work to people.' *Ind. Soc.*, LIX, 3 (May–June 1978), 13–14.

641 **Bennett**, Roger D. 'Orientation to work and job-work design.' *Manage. Decis.*, XVI, 6 (1978), 338–49.

642 **Birchall**, David W. 'Group working in biscuit manufacture.' *Pers. Rev.*, VIII (Spring 1978), 40–9.

643 **Birchall**, David W. 'The Work Research Group approach to redesigning jobs.' Birchall, D. and Morris, B. (eds.). *The practice of job design and work organisation.* 1978. p. 78–92.

644 **Birchall**, David W. 'Work system design: deciding between alternatives.' *Manage. Decis.*, XVI, 6 (1978), 321–30.

645 **Birchall**, David W. and **Morris**, Barbara (eds.). *The practice of job design and work organisation: ideas and issues.* Henley-on-Thames: Administrative Staff College Work Research Group, 1978. 92p.

646 **Blackler**, Frank H. and **Brown**, G. A. *Job redesign and management control: studies in British Leyland and Volvo.* London: Saxon House, 1978. 146p.

647 **Carnall**, Colin A. 'Implementation and evaluation.' Birchall, D. and Morris, B. (eds.). *The practice of job design and work organisation.* 1978. p. 65–77.

648 **Gregory**, Denis L. (ed.). *Work organization: Swedish experience and British context.* London: SSRC, 1978. x, 270p.
Papers from a conference at Imperial College, London, 1974.

649 **Hengen**, William K. 'Change processes within organisations.' Birchall, D. and Morris, B. (eds.). *The practice of job design and work organisation.* 1978. p. 16–33.

650 **Hengen**, William K. 'Working with groups.' Birchall, D. and Morris, B. (eds.). *The practice of job design and work organisation.* 1978. p. 47–64.

651 **Hull**, Daryll. *The shop stewards' guide to work organisation.* Nottingham: Spokesman, 1978. 130p.

652 **McLean**, A. J. and **Sims**, D. B. P. 'This theoretical poverty of job enrichment.' *Pers. Rev.*, VII (Spring 1978), 5–10.

653 **Social Science Research Council.** *Research needs in work organization: a working party report to the Management and Industrial Relations Committee.* London: SSRC, 1978. 96p.

654 **Wedley**, William C. 'Diagnosing work ailments.' Birchall, D. and Morris, B. (eds.).

The practice of job design and work organisation. 1978. p. 34–46.

655 **Wild**, Ray. 'Dimensions and stages of job design.' Birchall, D. and Morris, B. (eds.). *The practice of job design and work organisation.* 1978. p. 5–15.

656 **Birchall**, David W. 'A workshop for restructuring jobs.' *Pers. Manage.*, XI, 11 (November 1979), 37–41.

657 **Buchanan**, David A. *The development of job design theories and techniques.* London: Saxon House, 1979.

658 **Clegg**, Chris W. 'The process of job redesign: signposts from a theoretical orphanage?' *Hum. Relat.*, XXXII (December 1979), 999–1022.

659 **Cooper**, Cary L. 'Improving the quality of working life.' *Employee Relat.*, I, 4 (1979), 17–18.

660 **Dale**, B. G. 'Social aspects of group technology.' *Work Study*, XXVIII, 10 (October 1979), 19–24.

661 **Incomes Data Services.** *Changes in work organisation.* London: I.D.S., 1979. 18p. (I.D.S. study 203.)

662 **Handy**, Charles. 'The shape of organisations to come.' *Pers. Manage.*, XI, 6 (June 1979), 24–7.

663 **Hayes**, C. 'Job and skills in the melting pot.' *Pers. Manage.*, XI, 8 (August 1979), 36–40.

664 **Klein**, Lisl. 'Some problems of theory and method.' Sell, R. G. and Shipley, P. (eds.). *Satisfactions in work design.* 1979. p. 17–22.

665 **Morley**, Ian E. 'Job enrichment, job enlargement, and participation in work.' Stephenson, G. and Brotherton, C. (eds.). *Industrial relations: a social psychological approach.* 1979. p. 259–84.

666 **Mumford**, Enid and **Weir**, Mary. *Computer systems in work design: the ETHICS method: effective technical and human implementation of computer systems: a work design exercise book for individuals and groups.* London: Associated Business Press, 1979.

667 **Orpen**, Christopher. 'The effects of job enrichment on employee satisfaction, motivation, involvement and performance: a field experiment.' *Hum. Relat.*, XXXII (March 1979), 189–217.

668 **Pleasance**, E. J. and **Saldanka**, F. G. J. 'Work research.' *Manage. Serv. Gov.*, 2 (May 1979), 103–9.

669 **Pym**, Denis. 'Work is good, employment is bad.' *Employee Relat.*, I, 1 (1979), 16–18.

670 **Ross**, Kirsty and **Screeton**, Jeffrey. 'Introducing autonomous work groups in Philips.' Guest, David and Knight, Kenneth (eds.). *Putting participation into practice.* 1979. 96–113.

671 **Searle**, David. 'Team organisation in a construction firm.' Guest, David and Knight, Kenneth (eds.). *Putting participation into practice.* 1979. p. 114–31.

672 **Sell**, Reginald George. 'Job design in action: the perspective of the practitioner.' Sell, R. G. and Shipley, P. (eds.). *Satisfactions in work design.* 1979. p. 1–8.

673 **Sell**, Reginald George and **Shipley**, Patricia (eds.). *Satisfactions in work design: ergonomics and other approaches.* London: Taylor & Francis, 1979. xiv, 202p.

674 **White**, G. C. 'Job design and individual differences.' Sell, R. G. and Shipley, P. (eds.). *Satisfactions in work design.* 1979. p. 75–80.

See also: 72; 325; 355; 411; 443; 460; 461; 464; 467; 470; 524; 938; 1802; 2445; 2572; 2576; 2577; 2614; 2615; 2635; 2645; 2646; 2654; 2656; 2722; 2746; 2748; 5801.

PART THREE

EMPLOYEE ORGANISATION

The concept of a 'trade union' is taken here in its widest sense to cover all organisations of employees which try by any means to influence and regulate the terms and conditions of employment of their members. More specifically, the literature on manual unions, white-collar unions, professional unions and associations, and staff associations as well as friendly societies, craft guilds, and livery companies is included.

I. CRAFT GUILDS, LIVERY COMPANIES, AND FRIENDLY SOCIETIES

See also Part Three, II, F, 5; Part Four, I; Part Six, II, B, 3, a; and Part Seven, VII, B.

675 *Friendly societies 1798–1839.* New York: Arno Press, 1972. (British labour struggles: contemporary pamphlets 1727–1850.)

676 **Russell**, Rex Charles. *Friendly societies in the Caistor, Binbrook and Brigg areas in the nineteenth century; Oddfellows, Foresters, Driads, Rechabites, Free Gardeners, interment societies.* Barton-on-Humber: Nettleton Workers' Educational Association, 1975. 17p.

677 **Doyle**, Mel. 'The Dublin guilds and journeymen's clubs.' *Saothar*, III (1977), 6–14.

See also: 1204.

II. TRADE UNIONS AND PROFESSIONAL ASSOCIATIONS

See also Part Five; and Part Seven, V. Many of the works in Part Six, IV on conditions of employment also contain material on trade unionism.

A. GENERAL

This section includes the more general discussions and analyses of trade unionism as opposed to the general historical studies which appear in Part Three, II, B, and the more specialised works on union growth, structure, government, and administration which appear in Part Three, II, F. See also Part One, III; Part Five, I; and Part Seven, I.

678 **Flanders**, Allan. 'Great Britain.' Galenson, W. (ed.). *Comparative labor movements.* New York: Russell & Russell, 1952. p. 1–103.

679 **Bescoby**, John H. 'A combination of strength.' *Pers. Manage.*, III, 6 (June 1971), 28–32.

680 **Cook**, F. G. *The concept of ideology and its application to the study of trade unions.* [1971?]. (M.A. thesis, University of Liverpool.)

681 **Feather**, Victor. *The essence of trade unionism: a background book.* London: Bodley Head, 1971. 127p.
New edition.

682 **Leeson**, Robert Arthur. *United we stand: an illustrated account of trade union emblems.* London: Adams & Dart, 1971. 72p.

683 **Lees-Smith**, H. B. *Encyclopaedia of the labour movement.* London: Caxton.
Vol. 1. 1971. 321p.
Vol. 2. 1971. 319p.
Vol. 3. 1971. 336p.
Reprint of 1928 edition.

684 **Millard**, Patricia. *Trade associations and professional bodies of the United Kingdom.* London: Pergamon, 1971. xii, 469p.
Fifth edition.

685 **Mortimer**, James Edward. *Trade unions and technological change.* Oxford: OUP, 1971. vii, 108p.

686 **Roberts**, Benjamin Charles. *Trade unions: the challenge before them.* London: Industrial Education and Research Foundation, 1971. 16p.

687 **Bauman**, Zygmunt. *Between class and elite: the evolution of the British labour movement: a sociological study.* Manchester: Manchester U.P., 1972. xiii, 334p.

688 **Levinson**, Charles. *International trade unionism.* London: Allen & Unwin, 1972. 402p.

689 **McCarthy**, William Edward John (ed.).

Trade unions: selected readings. Harmondsworth: Penguin, 1972. 416p.

690 **Murphy**, John Thomas. *Preparing for power: a critical study of the history of the British working-class movement.* London: Pluto, 1972. 296p.
With a new introduction by James Hinton.

691 **Sturmthal**, Adolf. *Comparative labor movements: ideological roots and institutional development.* Belmont, Ca.: Wadsworth, 1972. vi, 176p.

692 **Trades Union Congress**. *Workers and the environment: report of a T.U.C. conference held at Congress House on July 6, 1972.* London: T.U.C., 1972. 57p.

693 **Williamson**, Hugh. *The trade unions.* London: Heinemann.
Second edition. 1972. viii, 136p.
Third edition. 1975. viii, 138p.
Fourth edition. 1977. viii, 140p.
Fifth edition. 1979. viii, 142p.

694 **Barbash**, Jack. 'Consumption values of trade unions.' *J. Econ. Issues*, VII, 2 (June 1973), 289–301.

695 **Cole**, George Douglas Howard. *The world of labour.* London: Harvester, 1973. XL, 443p.
Fourth edition.
First published, 1919.
New edition edited with an introduction and notes by John Lovell.

696 **Gorman**, John. *Banner bright: an illustrated history of the banners of the British trade union movement.* London: Allen Lane, 1973. 184p.

697 **Harrod**, J. 'British and continental trade unions: some differences and common economic problems.' *Annals Publ. Coop. Econ.*, XLIV, 2 (April–June 1973), 147–58.

698 **Howell**, George. *Trade unionism new and old.* Greenwood: Harvester, 1973. LV, xv, 282p.
Reprint of fourth revised edition. 1907.
Edited with introduction and notes by F. M. Leventhal.

699 **Hughes**, John and **Pollins**, Harold (eds.). *Trade unions in Great Britain.* Newton Abbot: David & Charles, 1973. 264p.

700 **Jacobs**, Eric. *European trade unionism.* London: Croom Helm, 1973. 180p.

701 **Banks**, Joseph Ambrose. *Trade unionism.* London: Collier-Macmillan, 1974. vi, 138p.

702 **Basnett**, David. *Trade union responsibilities.* London: Foundation for Business Responsibilities, 1974. 6p.

703 **Ham**, Tom. *The trade unions and working together.* London: Working Together Campaign, 1974. 8p.

704 **Hobhouse**, Leonard Trelawney. *The labour movement.* London: Harvester, 1974. 159, xxxp.
Text reprinted from third edition 1912, with an introduction and notes by Philip P. Poirier.

705 **Hooberman**, Ben. *An introduction to British trade unions.* Harmondsworth: Penguin, 1974.
149p.

706 **Lane**, Tony. *The union makes us strong: the British working class, its trade unionism and politics.* London: Arrow, 1974. 320p.

707 **Stewart**, Margaret. *Trade unions in Europe.* Epping: Gower, 1974. XX, 220p.
See especially Chapter 13: 'United Kingdom.' p. 167–94.

708 **Williams**, M. *Directory of trade unions in the European Economic Community, 1974.* London: Graham Trotman Dudley, 1974. 112p.
See Chapter 6: 'Great Britain.' p. 51–74.

709 **Eaton**, John, **Barratt Brown**, Michael and **Coates**, Ken. *Economic strategy for the labour movement: an alternative.* Nottingham: Institute for Workers' Control, 1975. 24p. (Spokesman pamphlets 47.)

710 **Hyman**, Richard and **Fryer**, Robert H. 'Trade unions: sociology and political economy.' McKinlay, J. (ed.). *Processing people.* 1975. p. 160–3, 182–91.
Reprinted in Clarke, T. and Clements, L. (eds.). *Trade unions under capitalism.* 1977. p. 152–74.

711 **Jones**, Jack. *A world to win.* London: Birkbeck College, 1975. 14p.

712 **Kendall**, Walter. *The labour movement in Europe.* London: Allen Lane, 1975. xxi, 456p.
See especially Chapter 7: 'Britain.' p. 180–208.

713 **Taylor**, Robert. 'One kind of working class power.' *New Soc.*, XXXII, 664 (26 June 1975), p. 773–5.

714 **Brittan**, Samuel. 'The political economy of British union monopoly.' *Three Banks Rev.*, CXI (September 1976), 3–32.

715 **Clegg**, Hugh Armstrong. *Trade unionism under collective bargaining: a theory based on comparisons of six countries.* Oxford: Blackwell, 1976. xi, 121p. (Warwick studies in industrial relations.)

716 **Frow**, Eddie and **Frow**, Ruth. 'Trade union emblems.' *N. W. Labour Hist. Soc. Bull.*, III (1976), 23–31.

717 **Harrison**, Margaret and **Blain**, Brian. 'Towards a trade union policy on the arts.' *Stud. Int.*, CXCI (March–April 1976), 173–6.

718 **Milligan**, Stephen. *The new barons: union power in the 1970s.* London: Temple Smith, 1976. 254p.

719 **Warburton**, David. 'Trade unions: a role in society.' *Natl. Westminster Bank Q. Rev.* (February 1976), 19–30.

720 **Worsthorne**, Peregrine. 'Of strong unions in weak societies: thoughts on a ruinous contradiction.' *Encounter*, XLVI (January 1976), 22–8.

721 **Backhouse**, Roger. 'Library services to trade unions: ignored or forgotten?' *Assist. Libr.*, LXX, 12 (December 1977), 182–5.

722 **Bornat**, J. 'Home and work: a new context for trade union history.' *Oral Hist.*, V, 2 (Autumn 1977), 101–23.

723 **Briggs**, Asa and **Saville**, John (eds.). *Essays*

in labour history 1918–1939. London: Croom Helm, 1977. 292p.

724 **Central Office of Information**. *Manpower and employment in Britain: trade unions*. London: H.M.S.O., 1977. ii, 30p. (Reference pamphlet 128.)

725 **Clarke**, Tom and **Clements**, Laurie (eds.). *Trade unions under capitalism*. London: Harvester and Fontana, 1977. 413p.

726 **Clements**, Laurie. 'Reference groups and trade union consciousness.' Clarke, T. and Clements, L. (eds.). *Trade unions under capitalism*. 1977. 309–32.

727 **Ward**, Jim. 'The role of poetry and song in British trade unions.' *Marx Meml. Libr. Q. Bull.*, LXXXI (January–March 1977), 21–2.

728 **Radice**, Giles. *The industrial democrats: trade unions in an uncertain world*. London: Allen & Unwin, 1978. 241p.

729 **Taylor**, Robert. *The fifth estate: trade unions in the modern world*. London: Routledge & Kegan Paul, 1978. xvi, 368p.

730 **Wheeler**, Robert F. 'Organized sport and organized labour: the workers' sports movement.' *J. Contemp. Hist.*, XIII, 2 (April 1978), 191–210.

731 **Coldrick**, A. P. and **Jones**, Philip. *The international directory of the trade union movement*. London: Macmillan, 1979. xiv, 1365p.

732 **Currie**, Robert. *Industrial politics*. Oxford: Clarendon P., 1979. vii, 294p.

733 **Department of Manpower Services for Northern Ireland**, Industrial Relations Division. *Directory of principal organisations of employers and workers in Northern Ireland*. Belfast: H.M.S.O., 1979. 46p.
Twentieth edition.

734 **Hyman**, Richard. 'British trade unionism in the 70's.' *Stud. Polit. Econ.*, I, I (Spring 1979), 93–112.

735 **Macbeath**, Innis. *Votes, virtues and vices: trade union power*. London: Associated Business Press, 1979. 197p.

736 **Marchington**, Mick. 'The issue of union power.' *Employee Relat.*, I, 4 (1979), 3–7.

737 **Marengo**, Franco Damaso. *The code of British trade union behaviour*. London: Saxon, 1979, x, 200p.

738 **Peel**, J. A. 'Can trade unions cope with change?' *Manchr. Bus. School Rev.*, III, I (1979), 6–7.

739 **Wessex Study Group**. *Our trade unions*. Wessex Study Group, 1979. 19p.

See also: 61; 86; 110; 114; 131; 295; 324; 402; 1123; 1304; 1307; 1338; 1393; 1465; 1680; 1744; 1874; 3382; 4461; 5966.

B. CHRONOLOGICAL STUDIES

This section contains general historical studies of trade unionism and works dealing with particular historical periods. In addition, it includes more specialised material on such subjects as the Tolpuddle Martyrs, Luddism, 'New Unionism', William Collison and the National Free Labour Association, the Labour Aristocracy, and the Triple Alliance. Historical aspects of the legal regulation of trade unions, especially works concerned with the Combination Acts, are classified in Part Seven, V; material on Robert Owen and works on Owenism are classified in Part Five, VI, A; Guild Socialism and Syndicalism are classified in Part Five, VI, B; material on historical aspects of the shop stewards' movement is classified at Part Three, II, F, 8; material on the regulation of labour during the two World Wars is contained in Part Seven, IV, C; material on the National Minority Movement is classified at Part Three, II, H; and historical studies of industrial conflict are classified at Part Five, V, A – C. See also Part Three, II, G – K; and Part Five, I.

740 **Bagwell**, Philip Sidney. 'The Triple Industrial Alliance, 1913–1922.' Briggs, A. and Saville, J. (eds.). *Essays in labour history, 1886–1923*. 1971. p. 96–128.

741 **Briggs**, Asa and **Saville**, John (eds.). *Essays in labour history, 1886–1923*. London: Macmillan, 1971. vii, 360p.

742 **Jones**, E. J. '"Scotch cattle" and early trade unionism in Wales.' Hughes, G. (ed.). *Men of no property*. 1971. p. 11–19.

743 **Jones**, Olive. 'The Scotch cattle.' Hughes, G. (ed.). *Men of no property*. 1971. p. 20–4.

744 **Pelling**, Henry. *A history of trade unionism*. London: Macmillan, 1971. 312p.
Second edition.
Third edition. 1976. xiii, 326p.

745 **Phillips**, Gordon A. 'The triple industrial alliance in 1914.' *Econ. Hist. Rev.*, XXIV (February 1971), 55–67.

746 **Renshaw**, Patrick. 'Black Friday 1921.' *Hist. Today*, XXI (June 1971), 416–25.

747 **Williams**, L. J. 'The New Unionism in South Wales, 1889–92.' Hughes, G. (ed.). *Men of no property*. 1971. p. 33–50.

748 **Fyrth**, Hubert Jim. *Men and masters*. London: Ginn, 1972. 144p.

749 *Labour problems before the industrial revolution 1727–1745*. New York: Arno, 1972. (British labour struggles: contemporary pamphlets 1727–1850.)

750 *The Luddites 1812–1839*. New York: Arno, 1972. (British labour struggles: contemporary pamphlets 1727–1850.)

751 **Marlow**, Joyce. *The Tolpuddle martyrs*. London: Deutsch, 1972. 320p.

752 **Musson**, Albert Edward. *British trade unions, 1800–1875*. London: Macmillan, 1972. 80p.

753 **Porter**, Jeffrey Harvey (ed.). *Provincial labour history*. Exeter: University of Exeter, 1972. 73p.

754 *Rebirth of the trade union movement: five pamphlets 1838–1847*. New York: Arno, 1972. (British labour struggles: contemporary pamphlets 1727–1850.)

755 **Robertson**, Norman and **Sams**, K. I. (eds.).

British trade unionism: select documents. Oxford: Blackwell, 1972. xxviii, 607p. 2v.

756 **Rooke**, Patrick. *The trade union movement.* London: Wayland, 1972. 128p.

757 **Shellard**, P. *Men and machines, 1717–1896.* London: Evans, 1972. 66p.

758 **Smith**, S. R. 'The Apprentices' Parliament of 1647.' *Hist. Today*, XXII (1972), 576–82.

759 *The spread of machinery 1793–1806.* New York: Arno, 1972. (British labour struggles: contemporary pamphlets 1727–1850.)

760 **Thomis**, Malcolm Ian (ed.). *Luddism in Nottinghamshire.* Chichester: Phillimore, 1972. 86p.

761 *Trade unions in the early 1830s: seven pamphlets 1831–1837.* New York: Arno, 1972. (British labour struggles: contemporary pamphlets 1727–1850.)

762 **Tufnell**, Edward Carlton. *Character, object and effects of trades' unions with some remarks on the law concerning them.* New York: Arno, 1972. (British labour struggles: contemporary pamphlets 1727–1850.)
First published in 1834.

763 **Bean**, Ron. 'Aspects of "new" unionism in Liverpool, 1889–91.' Hikins, H. (ed.). *Building the union.* 1973. p. 99–118.

764 **Cowie**, Leonard Wallace. *The trade unions: 1750 to the present day.* London: Nelson, 1973. 48p.

765 **Liversidge**, Douglas. *Luddites: machine-breakers of the early nineteenth century.* London: Franklin Watts, 1973. 96p.

766 **Morton**, A. L. and **Tate**, G. *The British labour movement 1770–1920: a history.* London: Lawrence & Wishart, 1973. 314p.

767 *Trade unions in the Victorian age: debates on the issue from 19th century critical journals.* London: Gregg International, 1973. 4v.
With an introduction by G.W. Crompton.

768 **Brown**, Kenneth D. *Essays in anti-labour history: responses to the rise of labour in Britain.* New York: Archon, 1974. viii, 409p.

769 **Firth**, M. M. and **Hopkinson**, A. W. *The Tolpuddle martyrs.* London: E.P. Publishing, 1974. 141p.

770 **Fraser**, William Hamish. *Trade unions and society: the struggle for acceptance 1850–1880.* London: Allen & Unwin, 1974. 292p.

771 **Musson**, Albert Edward. *Trade union and social history.* London: Frank Cass, 1974. ix, 211p.

772 **Harvey**, John Hooper. *Mediaeval craftsmen.* London: Batsford, 1975.

773 **Hutt**, Allen. *British trade unionism: a short history.* London: Lawrence & Wishart, 1975. 265p.
Sixth edition.
With concluding chapter by John Gollan.

774 **Jones**, Gareth Stedman. 'Class struggle and the Industrial Revolution.' *New Left Rev.*, XC (March–April 1975), 35–69.

775 **Longmate**, Norman. *Milestones in working class history.* London: B.B.C., 1975. 159p.

776 **Woolaston**, G. 'Richard Jefferies: thoughts on the labour question.' *Notes and Queries*, n.s. XX, 3 (March 1975), 118–19.

777 **Wrigley**, Christopher J. *Lloyd George and the labour movement (with particular reference to the years 1914–1922).* 1975. (Ph.D. thesis, Birkbeck College, University of London.)

778 **Alderman**, Geoffrey. 'The National Free Labour Association: a case study of organized strike breaking in the late 19th and early 20th centuries.' *Int. Rev. of Soc. Hist.*, XXI, 3 (1976), 309–36.

779 **Crossick**, Geoffrey J. 'An artisan elite in Victorian England.' *New Soc.*, XXXVIII (23–30 December 1976), 610–3.

780 **Donnelly**, F. K. 'Ideology and early English working-class history: Edward Thompson and his critics.' *Soc. Hist.*, II (May 1976), 219–38.

781 **Hogenkamp**, Bert. 'The use of film by the Workers' Movement in Great Britain 1929–1939.' *Sight and Sound*, XLV (Spring 1976), 68–76.

782 **Humphries**, Barbara. *The Tolpuddle Martyrs: victims of the rich man's law.* London: World Books, 1979. 14p.

783 **Jones**, Derek C. 'British economic thought on association of labourers 1848–1974.' *Annals Publ. Coop. Econ.*, LXIX, 1 (1976), 1–32.

784 **Kynaston**, David. *King Labour: the British working class, 1850–1914.* London: Allen & Unwin, 1976. 184p.

785 **Price**, Richard N. 'The making of working class history.' *Vic. Stud.*, XX, 1 (Autumn 1976), 69–74.

786 **Tijn**, T. van. 'A contribution to the scientific study of the history of trade unions.' *Int. Rev. of Soc. Hist.*, XXI (1976), 212–39.

787 **Wrigley**, Christopher J. *David Lloyd George and the British labour movement.* Greenwood: Harvester, 1976. 298p.

788 **Briggs**, Asa and **Saville**, John (eds.). *Essays in labour history, 1918–1939.* London: Croom Helm, 1977. 292p.

789 **Lovell**, John. *British trade unions 1875–1933.* London: Macmillan, 1977. 75p.

790 **Lovell**, John. 'The T.U.C. Special Industrial Committee, January–April 1926.' Briggs, A. and Saville, J. (eds.). *Essays in labour history, 1918–1939.* 1977. p. 36–56.

791 **Savage**, Katharine. *The story of British trade unions.* London: Kestrel, 1977. 143p.

792 **Vernon**, Sally. 'Trouble up at t'mill: the rise and decline of the factory play in the 1830s and 1840s.' *Vic. Stud.*, XX, 2 (Winter 1977), 117–39.

793 **Crossick**, Geoffrey J. *An artisan elite in Victorian society.* London: Croom Helm, 1978. 244p.

794 **Lovell**, John. 'The new unions.' *Soc. Study Labour Hist. Bull.*, XXXVI (Spring 1978), 15–17.

795 **Moorhouse**, H. F. 'The marxist theory of

the labour aristocracy.' *Soc. Hist.*, III, 1 (January 1978), 61–82.

796 **Pollins**, Harold. 'Trade unions.' Williams, T. I. (ed.). *A history of technology.* Oxford: O.U.P.
Vol. 6. *The twentieth century, c1900 to c1950.* 1978. p. 93–112.

797 **Shepherd**, M. A. 'The origins and incidence of the term Labour Aristocracy'. *Soc. Study Labour Hist. Bull.*, XXXVII (Autumn 1978), 51–67.

798 **Taylor**, Robert. *The fifth estate: Britain's unions in the seventies.* London: Routledge & Kegan Paul, 1978. 368p.

799 **Browne**, Harry. *The rise of British trade unions 1825–1914.* London: Longman, 1979. v, 154p.

800 **Leeson**, Robert Arthur. *Travelling brothers: the six centuries' road from craft fellowship to trade unionism.* London: Allen & Unwin, 1979. 348p.

801 **Wrigley**, Christopher J. (ed.). *The British labour movement in the decade after the First World War.* Loughborough: Loughborough University, Department of Economics, 1979. iii, 54p.

See also: 101; 126; 150; 179; 547; 818; 819; 826; 919; 1031; 1032; 1090; 1116; 1189; 1237; 1692; 1704; 1762; 1971; 2059; 2074; 2075; 2095; 2154; 2217; 2330; 2341; 2352; 4455; 6822; 6841.

C. REGIONAL STUDIES

This section includes works which focus on a particular town, county, or region. Regional works relating to a specific industry are classified with that industry in Part Three, II, D. Regional studies of trade union participation in strikes and other forms of industrial conflict are classified at Part Five, V. See also Part Three, II, F, 3.

802 **Hughes**, Goronwy Alun (ed.). *Men of no property: historical studies of Welsh trade unions.* Caerwys: Gwasg Gwenffowd, 1971. viii, 93p.

803 **Hughes**, Goronwy Alun. 'The need for research'. Hughes, G. (ed.). *Men of no property.* 1971. p. vi – viii.

804 **Mandrell**, T. R. *The structure and organization of London trades, wages and prices and the organization of labour, 1793–1815.* [1971?]. (M.Litt. thesis, University of Cambridge.)

805 **Boyd**, A. *The rise of the Irish trade unions 1729–1970.* Tralee: Anvil Books, 1972. 155p.

806 **Porter**, Jeffrey Harvey. 'Labour history in Devon and Cornwall.' Porter, J. (ed.). *Provincial labour history.* 1972. p. 1–4.

807 **Porter**, Jeffrey Harvey (ed.). *Provincial labour history.* Exeter: University of Exeter, 1972. 73p.

808 **Williams**, G. A. 'Merthyr 1831: Lord Melbourne and the trade unions.' *Llafur*, 1 (1972), 3–15.

809 **Young**, James D. 'Images of rural "idiocy" and labour movements.' *Soc. Study Labour Hist. Bull.*, XXIV (Spring 1972), 34–7.

810 **Hikins**, Harold R. (ed.). *Building the union: studies on the growth of the workers' movement, Merseyside, 1756–1967, to celebrate the 125th anniversary of the Liverpool Trades Council.* Liverpool: Toulouse P., 1973. 198p.

811 **Lane**, Tony. 'Some Merseyside militants of the 1930's.' Hikins, H. (ed.). *Building the union.* 1973. p. 153–77.

812 **McCarthy**, Charles. 'Civil strife and the growth of trade union unity: the case of Ireland.' *Gov. Oppos.*, VIII, 4 (1973), 407–31.

813 **McCarthy**, Charles. *The decade of upheaval: Irish trade unions in the nineteen sixties.* Dublin: Institute of Public Administration, 1973. 263p.

814 **Stead**, Peter. 'The Welsh working class.' *Llafur*, I, 2 (May 1973), 42–54.

815 **Carr**, Alan. *The Belfast labour movement.* Belfast: Athol. Part 1. *1885–93.* 1974. 49p.

816 **Workers' Association.** *What's wrong with Ulster trade unionism? An exposure of anti-partitionist manoeuvre and disruption in the trade union leadership.* Belfast: Workers' Association, 1974. 27p.

817 **Todd**, Nigel. 'The labour movement in North Lancashire, 1890–1910.' *N. W. Labour Hist. Soc. Bull.*, II (1975), 1–15.

818 **Crossick**, Geoffrey J. 'The labour aristocracy and its values: a study of mid-Victorian Kentish London.' *Vic. Stud.*, XIX, 3 (March 1976), 301–28.

819 **Gray**, Robert Q. *The labour aristocracy in Victorian Edinburgh.* Oxford: O.U.P., 1976. 230p.

820 **Pollard**, Sidney and **Holmes**, Colin (eds.). *Essays in the economic and social history of South Yorkshire.* Sheffield: South Yorkshire County Council, 1976. 308p.

821 **Barnsby**, George. *The working-class movement in the Black Country 1750–1867.* Birmingham: Integrated Publishing Services, 1977. 233p.

822 **Baxter**, J. L. *The origins of the social war in South Yorkshire: a study of capitalist evolution and labour class realization in one industrial region, c. 1750–1855.* 1977. (Ph.D. thesis, University of Sheffield.)

823 **Carlton**, F. *'A substantial and sterling friend to the labouring man': the Kent and Sussex Labourers' Union, 1872–1895.* 1977. (M.Phil. thesis, University of Sussex.)

824 **McCarthy**, Charles. *Trade unions in Ireland, 1894–1960.* Dublin: Institute of Public Administration, 1977. 671p.

825 **McCord**, Norman. *Essays in Tyneside labour history.* Newcastle-upon-Tyne: Newcastle-upon-Tyne Polytechnic, Department of Humanities, 1977. iii, 197p.

826 **Patterson**, Henry. 'The new unionism and Belfast.' *Soc. Study Labour Hist. Bull.*, XXXV (Autumn 1977), 7–9.

827 **Porter**, Jeffrey Harvey. 'Devon labour history.' *Devon Hist.*, XV (October 1977), 39–61.

828 **Arts Council of Ireland.** *Marching workers: an exhibition of Irish trade banners and regalia at the Ulster Museum, Belfast and the Douglas Hyde Gallery, Dublin, 1978, compiled by Belinda Lofts.* Dublin: The Council, 1978. 92p.

829 **Haden**, H. Jack. 'The brick-makers' battle.' *Blackcountryman*, XI (Spring 1978), 24.

830 **MacDougall**, Ian (ed.). *Essays in Scottish labour history: a tribute to W. H. Marwick.* Edinburgh: Donald, 1978. xvi, 265p.

831 **Prothero**, Iorweth J. 'London trade unionism in the 1830's and 1840's.' *Soc. Study Labour Hist. Bull.*, XXXVI (Spring 1978), 10–13.

832 **Samuel**, Raphael. 'The London labour movement.' *Soc. Study Labour Hist. Bull.*, XXXVI (Spring 1978), 13–15.

833 **Shipley**, Stan. 'London journeymen, 1810–1830.' *Soc. Study Labour Hist. Bull.*, XXXVI (Spring 1978), 9–10.

834 **Young**, James D. *The rousing of the Scottish working class.* London: Croom Helm, 1979. 242p.

See also: 16; 17; 18; 22; 24; 32; 59; 63; 67; 68; 70; 77; 80; 96; 98; 742; 743; 747; 753; 760; 835; 847; 848; 849; 850; 853; 854; 855; 866; 900; 1121; 1197; 1226; 1229; 1235; 1239; 1245; 1251; 1254; 1292; 1294; 1303; 1410; 1413; 1415; 1761; 1971; 2059; 2116; 2143; 2184; 2191; 2202; 2260; 2261; 2263; 2341.

D. STUDIES OF PARTICULAR OCCUPATIONS AND INDUSTRIES

Material relating to specific unions is classified with that industry or occupational group in which most of their membership is located. See also Part Three, II, F. In particular, see Part Three, F, 7 for material on the leaders of individual unions. See also Part Five, IV; Part Five, V, C; Part Six, III, D; and Part Six, IV, A, 2.

1. Agriculture, Forestry, and Fishing

835 **Williams**, J. Roose. 'Ap ffarmwr.' Hughes, G. (ed.). *Men of no property.* 1971. p. 86–7.

836 **Arnold**, Rollo. 'English rural unionism and Taranaki immigration, 1871–1876.' *New Zealand J. Hist.*, VI (April 1972), 20–41.

837 **Horn**, Pamela L. R. 'The Warwickshire Agricultural and General Workers' Union 1893–97.' *Midl. Hist.*, I (1971–2), 23–6.

838 *The rising of the agricultural labourers 1830–1831.* New York: Arno, 1972. (British labour struggles: contemporary pamphlets 1727–1850.)

839 **Maynard**, Joan (ed.). *A hundred years of farmworkers' struggle.* Nottingham: Institute for Workers' Control, 1974. 23p. (I.W.C. pamphlets 44.)

840 **Maynard**, Joan. 'The way forward for farmworkers.' Maynard, J. (ed.). *A hundred years of farmworkers' struggle.* 1974. p. 3–5.

841 **Newby**, Howard. 'Agricultural trade unionism and structural change.' Maynard, J. (ed.). *A hundred years of farmworkers' struggle.* 1974. p. 6–10.

842 **Czerkawska**, Catherine Lucy. *Fisherfolk of Carrick: a history of the fishing industry in South Ayrshire.* Glasgow: Molendinar Press, 1975. 59p.

843 **Fenoaltea**, Stefano. 'Authority, efficiency, and agricultural organization in medieval England and beyond: a hypothesis.' *J. Econ. Hist.*, XXXV, 4 (December 1975), 693–718.

844 **Horn**, Pamela L. R. 'Agricultural trade unionism in Buckinghamshire 1872–85.' *Rec. Bucks.*, XX, 1 (1975), 76–86.

845 **Clark**, Samuel. 'The importance of agrarian classes: agrarian class structure and collective action in nineteenth century Ireland.' *Br. J. Sociol.*, XXIX, 1 (March 1978), 22–40.

846 **Robertson**, Barbara W. 'The Scottish farm servant and his union: from encapsulation to integration.' MacDougall, I. (ed.). *Essays in Scottish labour history.* 1978. p. 90–114.

See also: 1221; 1234; 1255; 4447.

2. Mining and Quarrying

847 **Garside**, W. Richard. 'The Durham miners between the wars.' Dewdney, J. C. (ed.). *Durham County and City with Deeside.* Durham: British Association for the Advancement of Science, 1970. p. 307–12.

848 **Bell**, Idris C. 'The Tinplate Workers' Union.' Hughes, G. (ed.). *Men of no property.* 1971. p. 25–32.

849 **Evans**, D.D. 'The relationship between the N.U.M. and the structure of the coal-mining industry.' Hughes, G. (ed.). *Men of no property.* 1971. p. 73–9.

850 **Evans**, E. W. 'Mabon and trade unionism in the South Wales coalfield.' Hughes, G. (ed.). *Men of no property.* 1971. p. 51–9.

851 **Fynes**, R. *Miners of Northumberland and Durham: a history of their social and political progress.* Newcastle-upon-Tyne: S. R. Publishers, 1971. xi, 302p.

852 **Garside**, W. Richard. *The Durham miners, 1919–1960.* London: Allen & Unwin, 1971. 544p.

853 **Griffiths**, James. 'The Miners' Union in the anthracite coalfield.' Hughes, G. (ed.). *Men of no property.* 1971. p. 60–7.

854 **Paynter**, William. 'The "Fed."' Hughes, G. (ed.). *Men of no property.* 1971. p. 68–72.

855 **MacFarlane**, James. 'Denaby Main: a South Yorkshire mining village.' *Soc. Study Labour Hist. Bull.*, XXV (1972), 82–100; XXVI (1973), 39–42.
Reprinted in Benson, J. and Neville, R. (eds.). *Studies in the Yorkshire coal industry.* 1976. p. 109–44.

856 **Challinor**, Raymond. *The Lancashire and Cheshire miners.* Newcastle-upon-Tyne: Frank Graham, 1972. 320p.

857 **Davison**, Jack. *Northumberland miners 1919– 1939.* Blyth: N.U.M., Northumberland Area, 1973. 13, 289p.

858 **Jones**, Richard Merfyn. 'The slate quarry-men of North Wales and the problem of Welsh nationality.' *Soc. Study Labour Hist. Bull.*, xxvii (Autumn 1973), 7–10.

859 **Moyes**, William A. *Banner parade: a selection of lodge banners of the Durham Miners' Associa-tion on exhibition at the D.L.I. Museum and Arts Centre, 1973.* Newcastle-upon-Tyne: Frank Graham, 1973. 24p.

860 **Smith**, D. 'The struggle against company unionism in the South Wales coalfield, 1926–1939.' *Welsh Hist. Rev.*, vi (1972–3), 354–78.

861 **Gwynned Archives Service.** *Chwareli a chwarelwyr: a booklet to accompany an exhibition prepared to celebrate the centenary of the founding of the North Wales Quarrymen's Union.* Gwyn-ned Archives Service, 1974.
     Text in Welsh and English.

862 **Moyes**, William A. *The banner book: a study of the banners of the lodges of the Durham Miners' Association.* Newcastle-upon-Tyne: Frank Graham, 1974. 159p.

863 **Arnot**, Robin Page. *South Wales miners: a history of the South Wales Miners' Federation, 1914–26.* Cardiff: Cymric Federation Press, 1975. xv, 356p.

864 **Jones**, Richard Merfyn. *The trade union and political activities of the North Wales slate quarrymen in relation to their social and working conditions.* 1975. (Ph.D. thesis, University of Warwick.)

865 **Potts**, A. and **Wade**, E. *Stand true: North-umberland Colliery Mechanics Association: NUM, 1875–1975.* Blyth: N.U.M., 1975. 36p.

866 **Benson**, John and **Neville**, Robert G. (eds.). *Studies in the Yorkshire coal industry.* Manchester: Manchester University P., 1976. 180p.

867 **Burton**, Anthony. *The miners.* London: Andre Deutsch, 1976. 175p.

868 **Campbell**, Alan B. *Honourable men and de-graded slaves: a social history of trade unionism in the Lanarkshire coalfield, 1775–1874, with par-ticular reference to the Coatbridge and Larkhall districts.* 1976. (Ph.D. thesis, University of Warwick.)

869 **MacFarlane**, James. '"One association – the Yorkshire Miners' Association": the Denaby Main lock-out of 1885.' Pollard, S. and Holmes, C. (eds.). *Essays in the economic and social history of South Yorkshire.* 1976. p. 74–88.

870 **Neville**, Robert G. *The Yorkshire miners in camera.* Hendon Publishing, 1976. [44]p.

871 **Purdon**, Gavin. *Cotia pit: the story of the Harraton colliery miners.* Durham: Durham Record Office, 1976.

872 **Thompson**, E. P. 'On history, sociology and historical relevance.' *Br. J. Sociol.*, xxvii, 3 (September 1976), 387–402.
     Review article.

873 **Didsbury**, Brian. 'Cheshire saltworkers.' Samuel, R. (ed.). *Miners, quarrymen and salt-workers.* 1977. p. 137–203.

874 **Douglass**, Dave. 'The Durham pitman.' Samuel, R. (ed.). *Miners, quarrymen and salt-workers.* 1977. p. 205–95.

875 **Douglass**, Dave. 'Pit talk in County Durham.' Samuel, R. (ed.). *Miners, quarry-men and saltworkers.* 1977. p. 297–348.

876 **Griffin**, A. R. and **Griffin**, C. P. 'The non-political trade union movement.' Briggs, A. and Saville, J. (eds.). *Essays in labour history, 1918–1939.* 1977. p. 133–62.

877 **Jones**, Merfyn. 'Y, chwarelwyr: the slate quarrymen of North Wales.' Samuel, R. (ed.). *Miners, quarrymen and saltworkers.* 1977. p. 99–135.

878 **Samuel**, Raphael. 'Mineral workers.' Samuel, R. (ed.). *Miners, quarrymen and saltworkers.* 1977. p. 1–97.

879 **Samuel**, Raphael (ed.). *Miners, quarrymen and saltworkers.* London: Routledge & Kegan Paul, 1977. xvi, 363p.

880 **Wilson**, G. M. *The miners of the West of Scotland and their trade unions, 1842–74.* 1977. (Ph.D. thesis, University of Glasgow.)

881 **Campbell**, Alan B. 'Honourable men and degraded slaves: a comparative study of trade unionism in two Lanarkshire mining communities, c. 1830–1974.' Harrison, R. (ed.). *Independency collier.* 1978. p. 75–113.

882 **Campbell**, Alan B. and **Reid**, Fred. 'The independent collier in Scotland.' Harrison, R. (ed.). *Independent collier.* 1978. p. 54–74.

883 **Fisher**, Chris. *Free miners and colliers: custom, the crown and trade unionism in the Forest of Dean, 1788–1886.* 1978. (Ph.D. thesis, University of Warwick.)

884 **Fisher**, Chris. 'The free miners of the Forest of Dean, 1800–1841.' Harrison, R. (ed.). *Independent collier.* 1978. p. 17–53.

885 **Fisher**, Chris and **Smethurst**, John. '"War on the law of supply and demand": the Amalgamated Association of Miners and the Forest of Dean colliers, 1869–1875.' Harrison, R. (ed.). *Independent collier.* 1978. p. 114–55.

886 **Fisher**, Chris and **Spaven**, Pat. 'Edward Rymer and "the moral workman": the dilemma of the radical miner under "Mac-Donaldism".' Harrison, R. (ed.). *Independent collier.* 1978. p. 232–71.

887 **Harrison**, Royden (ed.). *Independent collier: the coal miner as archetypal proletarian reconsi-dered.* London: Harvester, 1978. 276p.

888 **Lloyd**, Albert Lancaster. *Come all ye bold miners: ballads and songs of the coalfields.* Lon-don: Lawrence & Wishart, 1978. 143p.
     Revised edition.

889 **MacFarlane**, James. 'Counter-offensive for a South Yorkshire mining community.' Har-

rison, R. (ed.). *Independent collier.* 1978. p. 180–200.

890 **Reid**, Fred. 'Alexander MacDonald and the crisis of the independent collier, 1872–1974.' Harrison, R. (ed.). *Independent collier.* 1978. p. 156–79.

891 **Smethurst**, John B. *Lancashire and the Miners' Association of Great Britain and Ireland, 1842–1848.* Eccles: Eccles & District Local History Society, 1978. 31p.

892 **Spaven**, Pat. 'Main gates of protest: contrasts in rank and file activity among South Yorkshire miners, 1858–1894.' Harrison, R. (ed.). *Independent collier.* 1978. p. 201–31.

893 **Arnot**, Robin Page. *The miners: one union, one industry: a history of the National Union of Mineworkers, 1939–46.* London: Allen & Unwin, 1979. xvi, 212p.

894 **Campbell**, Alan B. *The Lanarkshire miners: a social history of their trade unions, 1775–1974.* Edinburgh: Donald, 1979. 354p.

895 **Howells**, Kim. *A view from below: tradition, experience and nationalisation in the South Wales coalfield, 1937–1957.* 1979. 2 v. (Ph.D. thesis, University of Warwick.)

See also: 16; 22; 42; 49; 63; 74; 179; 1163; 1202; 1204; 1231; 1240; 1243; 1246; 1248; 1252; 1413; 1872; 1935; 2289; 2459.

3. Manufacturing Industries

896 **Bookseller**. 'Trade unions and the publishing industry.' *Bookseller* (27 February 1971), 1400–4.

897 **Burchill**, Frank and **Sweeney**, Jim. *A History of trade unionism in the North Staffordshire textile industry.* Newcastle-under-Lyme: University of Keele, Department of Adult Education, 1971. 143p.

898 **Carew**, A. *Rank and file movements and workers' control in the British engineering industry, 1850–1969.* 1970–71. (M.Phil. thesis, University of Sussex.)

899 **Gilding**, Bob. *The Journeymen Coopers of East London: workers' control in an old London trade.* London: History Workshop, 1971. iv, 86p. (History Workshop pamphlets 40.)

900 **Griffiths**, Arthur. 'B.I.S.A.K.T.A. in North Wales.' Hughes, G. (ed.). *Men of no property.* 1971. p. 88–93.

901 **Serjeant**, W. R. 'An early trade union episode at Ramsey.' *J. Manx Mus.*, VII (1971), 177–81.

902 **Bookseller**. 'Unions in publishing: survey of editorial and production staffs.' *Bookseller* (28 October 1972), 2220–1.

903 *The framework knitters and handloom weavers: their attempts to keep up wages 1820–1845.* New York: Arno, 1972. (British labour struggles: contemporary pamphlets 1727–1850.)

904 **Searby**, Peter. *Weavers and freemen in Coventry, 1820–1861: social and political traditionalism in an early Victorian town.* 1972. (Ph.D. thesis, University of Warwick.)

905 **Speirs**, Malcolm. *One hundred years of a small trade union: a history of the Card Setting Machine Tenters' Society.* Cleckheaton: Card Setting Machine Tenters' Society, 1972. 88p.

906 **Verma**, Pramod Chandra. 'Multiple unionism: a study of trade unionism in the British chemical industry.' *Indian J. Ind. Relat.*, VII, 4 (April 1972), 549–68.

907 **Fowler**, Alan G. 'Twentieth century trade clubs: a study in cotton trade unionism.' *Tex. Hist.*, IV (October 1973), 84–93.

908 **Mortimer**, James Edward. *The history of the Boilermakers' Society.* London: Allen & Unwin.
Vol. 1. *1834–1906.* 1973. 228p.

909 **Wright**, Helena. 'The uncommon mill girls of Lowell.' *Hist. Today*, XXIII (January 1973), 10–19.

910 **Bowen**, Peter, **Shaw**, Monica and **Smith**, Robin. 'The steelworker and work control: a sociological analysis and industrial relations case study.' *Br. J. Ind. Relat.*, XII, 2 (July 1974), 249–67.

911 **Brassay**, Z. G. *The cotton spinners in Glasgow and the West of Scotland, c. 1790–1840: a study in early industrial relations.* 1974. (M.Litt. thesis, University of Strathclyde.)

912 **Tuckett**, Angela. *The blacksmiths' history: what smithy workers gave trade unionism.* London: Lawrence & Wishart, 1974. 418p.

913 **Carpenter**, J.H. *The Amalgamated Society of Engineers, Worcester Branch: the study of a Victorian trades union.* London: Amalgamated Union of Engineering Workers, 1975. 12p.

914 **Dougan**, David. *The shipwrights: the history of the Shipconstructors' and Shipwrights' Association, 1882–1963.* Newcastle upon Tyne: Frank Graham, 1975. 341p.

915 **Dougan**, David. 'The shipwrights: the history of the Ship Constructors' and Shipwrights' Association 1882–1963.' *N. E. Group Study Labour Hist. Bull.*, IX (October 1975), 18–19.

916 **Carroll**, K. L. 'Quaker weavers at Newport, Ireland, 1720–40.' *Friends' Hist. Soc. J.*, LIV (1976), 15–27.

917 **Fowler**, Alan G. *A short history of the Lancashire packing case makers.* Manchester: Lancashire Box Packing Case and General Woodworkers Society, 1976. 28p.

918 **Gurnham**, Richard. *A history of the trade union movement in the hosiery and knitwear industry, 1776–1976: the history of the National Union of Hosiery and Knitwear Workers, its evolution and its predecessors.* Leicester: National Union of Hosiery and Knitwear Workers, 1976. xiii, 197p.

919 **Matsumura**, Takao. *The flint glass makers in the classic age of the labour aristocracy, 1850–1880, with special reference to Stourbridge.* 1976. (Ph.D. thesis, University of Warwick.)

920 **Price**, J. H. 'Trouble at the Falcon.' *Mod. Tramway*, XXXIX, 463 (July 1976), 219–25.

921 **Shipley**, Stan. 'The libraries of the Alliance Cabinet Makers' Association in 1879.' *Hist. Workshop*, I (Spring 1976), 180–4.

922 **Smethurst**, John B. 'The Manchester banner makers.' *N. W. Labour Hist. Soc. Bull.*, III (1976), 17–28.

923 **Walker**, William M. *Dundee's jute and flax workers, 1885–1923*. 1976. (Ph.D. thesis, University of Dundee.)

924 **Burchill**, Frank and **Ross**, Richard. *History of the Pottery, Ceramics and Allied Trades Union*. Hanley: Ceramic and Allied Trades Union, 1977. 292p.

925 **Clarke**, J. F. 'Engineering workers on Tyneside.' McCord, N. (ed.). *Essays in Tyneside labour history*. 1977. p. 88–108.

926 **Clarke**, J. F. 'Workers in the Tyneside shipyards.' McCord, N. (ed.). *Essays in Tyneside labour history*. 1977. p. 109–31.

927 **Cuca**, James R. 'Industrial change and the progress of labor in the English cotton industry.' *Int. Rev. of Soc. Hist.*, XXII, 2 (1977), 241–55.

928 **Holt**, James. 'Trade unionism in the British and U.S. steel industries, 1882–1912: a comparative study.' *Labor Hist.*, XVIII, I (Winter 1977), 5–35.

929 **Waters**, Mavis. 'Craft consciousness in a government enterprise: Medway dockyardmen, 1860–1906.' *Oral Hist.*, V, I (Spring 1977), 51–62.

930 **Barnes**, June C. F. 'The trade union and radical activities of the Carlisle handloom weavers.' *Cumberland & Westmorland Antiq. Archaeol. Soc. Trans.*, LXXVIII (1978), 149–61.

931 **Bennet**, D. 'The silvermakers of Limerick.' *Ir. Ancestor*, X, 2 (1978), 99–107.

932 **Exell**, Arthur. 'Morris motors in the 1930s (part I).' *Hist. Workshop*, VI (Autumn 1978), 52–78.

933 **Murray**, Norman. *The Scottish handloom weavers: 1790–1850: a social history*. Edinburgh: Donald, 1978. 269p.

934 **White**, Joseph L. *The limits of trade union militancy: the Lancashire textile workers, 1910–1914*. Westport, Connecticut: Greenwood, 1978. 258p.

935 **Department of Employment**. *Report of the Committee of Inquiry into Certain Trade Union Recruitment Activities*. London: H.M.S.O., 1979. vi, 82p. (Cmnd. 7706.) Chairman: Andrew Leggatt

936 **Edelstein**, J. David. 'Trade unions in British producers' cooperatives.' *Ind. Relat.*, XVIII, 3 (Fall 1979), 358–63.

937 **Walker**, William M. *Juteopolis: Dundee and its textile workers, 1885–1923*. Edinburgh: Scottish Academic Press, 1979. 561p.

See also: 31; 58; 65; 70; 79; 179; 969; 1013; 1033; 1051; 1052; 1130; 1131; 1132; 1175; 1238; 1247; 1249; 1267.

4. Construction

938 **Lamb**, Dave. *The Lump: an heretical analysis*. Lancaster: Solidarity, 1974. 24p. (Solidarity pamphlets.)

939 **Mordsley**, B. I. 'Some problems of the "lump".' *Mod. Law Rev.*, XXXVIII (September 1975), 504–17.

940 **Viles**, D. B. *The building trade workers of London, 1835–1860*. 1975. (M.Phil. thesis, Bedford College, University of London.)

941 **Austrin**, Terry B. 'A divided workforce: casual workers in the building trade and union membership.' *New Soc.*, XXXVII (15 July 1976), 115–16.

942 **Latham**, Peter. *Rank and file movements in building, 1910–20*. London: Communist Party of Great Britain History Group, 1977. 28p.

943 **Wood**, Leslie W. *A union to build: the story of UCATT*. London: Lawrence & Wishart, 1979. 208p.

See also: 47; 179; 1200; 1982.

5. Transport, Communications, and Distribution

See part Seven, V for material on the Taff Vale case, and Part Five, VI, A for material on co-operative production.

944 **Alderman**, Geoffrey. 'The railway companies and the growth of trade unionism in the late nineteenth and early twentieth century.' *Hist. J.*, XIV (1971), 129–52.

945 **Bean**, R. 'Working conditions, labour agitation and the origins of unionism on the Liverpool Tramways.' *Transp. Hist.*, V (July 1972), 173–93.

946 **Hill**, Stephen R. 'Dockers and their work.' *New Soc.*, XXI (17 August 1972), 338–40.

947 **Jones**, T. S. *The Associated Society of Locomotive Engineers and Firemen and communications*. 1972. (M.A. thesis, University of Warwick.)

948 **Rowe**, D. J. 'A trade union of the north-east coast seamen in 1825.' *Econ. Hist. Rev.*, n.s., XXV (1972), 81–98.

949 **Brown**, R. *Waterfront organization in Hull 1870–1900*. Hull: University of Hull, 1973. 103p.

950 **Jones**, Stephen. 'Community and organization: early seamen's trade unionism on the north-east coast, 1768–1844.' *Marit. Hist.*, III (1973), 35–66.

951 **Whitaker**, Wilfred Barnett. *Victorian and Edwardian shopworkers: the struggle to obtain better conditions and a half-holiday*. Newton Abbott: David & Charles, 1973. 222p.

952 **Moran**, Michael J. *The determination of goals in a trade union: a case study of the British Union of Post Office Workers*. 1974. (Ph.D. thesis, University of Essex.)

953 **Moran**, Michael J. *Union of Post Office Workers: a study in political sociology*. London: Macmillan, 1974. 184p.

954 **Rose**, E. 'On the nature of work and union involvement: a study of London busmen.' *Ind. Relat. J.*, v, 2 (Summer 1974), 27–36.

955 **Taplin**, Eric L. *Liverpool dockers and seamen, 1870–1890*. Hull: University of Hull, 1974. viii, 96p. (University of Hull occasional papers in economic and social history 6.)

956 **Carter**, J. P. H. 'Contributions, badges and the Liverpool carters.' *N. W. Labour Hist. Soc. Bull.*, II (1975), 17–21.

957 **Hanson**, Harry. *The canal boatmen 1760–1914*. Manchester: Manchester University Press, 1975. xii, 244p.

958 **Bealey**, Frank. *The Post Office Engineering Union: the history of the Post Office Engineers, 1870–1970*. London: Bachman & Turner, 1976. 432p.

959 **McKenna**, Frank. 'Victorian railway workers.' *Hist. Workshop*, 1 (Spring 1976), 26–73.

960 **Royal Commission on the Press.** *A report on industrial relations in the national newspaper industry*. London: H.M.S.O., 1976. xiv, 342p. Chairman: Oliver MacGregor.

961 **Daunton**, M. J. 'The Cardiff Coal Trimmers' Union, 1884–1914.' *Marit. Hist.*, v, 1 (Spring 1977), 51–67.

962 **Keogh**, Dermot. 'Michael O'Sehane and the organisation of linen drapers' assistants.' *Saothar*, III (1977), 33–43.

963 **Daunton**, M. J. 'The Cardiff Coal-Trimmers' Union, 1888–1914.' *Llafur*, II, 3 (Summer 1978), 10–23.

964 **Daunton**, M. J. 'Jack ashore: seamen in Cardiff before 1914.' *Welsh Hist. Rev.*, IX, 2 (December 1978), 176–203.

965 **Richardson**, *Sir* William. *A union of many trades: the history of USDAW*. Manchester: USDAW, 1979. 388p.

See also: 1154; 1197; 1251; 2003; 2006.

6. White-Collar and Professional

In addition to including works on white-collar and professional unions, this section also includes material on the process of professionalisation and the status of professions.

a. GENERAL

966 **Morrell**, K. and **Smith**, J. 'The white-collar split.' *Ind. Soc.*, LIII, 8 (August 1971), 7–10.

967 **Wainwright**, D. 'Smoothing the path for white collar unions.' *Pers. Manage.*, III, 5 (May 1971), 18–22.

968 **Bowen**, Peter and **Shaw**, Monica. 'Collar colour and the unions.' *New Soc.*, XXI (27 July 1972), 180, 182–3.

969 **Bowen**, Peter and **Shaw**, Monica. 'Patterns of white-collar unionization in the steel industry.' *Ind. Relat. J.*, III, 2 (Summer 1972), 8–34.

970 **Elliot**, P. *Sociology of the professions*. London: Macmillan, 1972. x, 180p.

971 **Howard**, Carol A. *White collar unions: a review*. London: Institute of Personnel Management, 1972. 118p. (Institute of Personnel Management. Information reports, new series 11.)

972 **Johnson**, T. J. *Professions and power*. London: Macmillan, 1972. 96p.

973 **Loveridge**, Ray. 'Occupational change and the development of interest groups among white-collar workers in the U.K.: a long-term model.' *Br. J. Ind. Relat.*, x, 3 (November 1972), 340–65.

974 **Bain**, George Sayers, **Coates**, David and **Ellis**, Valerie. *Social stratification and trade unionism: a critique*. London: Heinemann, 1973. vi, 174p.

975 **Bennett**, William S. and **Hokenstad**, Merl C. 'Full-time people workers and conceptions of the professional.' Halmos, P. (ed.). *Professionalisation and social change*. 1973. p. 21–46.

976 **Bocock**, Jean. 'The politics of white collar unionisation.' *Polit. Q.*, XLIV, 3 (July–September 1973), 294–303.

977 **Elliott**, Philip. 'Professional ideology and social situation.' *Sociol. Rev.*, XXI, 2 (May 1973), 211–28.
Extracts from this article were reprinted in Esland, G. and others (eds.). *People and work*. 1975. p. 275–86.

978 **Goldner**, Fred H., **Ference**, Thomas P. and **Ritti**, R. Richard. 'Priests and laity: a profession in transition.' Halmos, P. (ed.). *Professionalisation and social change*. 1973. p. 119–38.

979 **Halmos**, Paul (ed.). *Professionalisation and social change*. Newcastle-under-Lyme: University of Keele, 1973. 338p. (Sociological Review monograph 20.)

980 **Haug**, Marie R. 'Deprofessionalization: an alternative hypothesis for the future.' Halmos, P. (ed.). *Professionalisation and social change*. 1973. p. 195–212.

981 **Heraud**, Brian J. 'Professionalism, radicalism and social change.' Halmos, P. (ed.). *Professionalisation and social change*. 1973. p. 85–102.

982 **Illich**, Ivan. 'The professions as a form of imperialism.' *New Soc.*, XXV (13 September 1973), 633–5.

983 **Industrial Society.** *Development and recognition of white collar unions: union profiles and company case studies*. London: The Society, 1973. 59p. (Surveys and reports 180.)

984 **Industrial Society.** 'Updating the white-collar image.' *Ind. Soc.*, LV, 3 (March 1973), 7–10.

985 **Katan**, Joseph. 'The attitudes of professionals towards the employment of indigenous non-professionals in human service organizations.' Halmos, P. (ed.). *Professionalisation and social change*. 1973. p. 229–44.

986 **Leonard**, Peter. 'Professionalization, community action and the growth of social service bureaucracies.' Halmos, P. (ed.).

Professionalisation and social change. 1973. p. 103–18.

987   **Lumley**, Roger. *White-collar unionism in Britain: a survey of the present position.* London: Methuen, 1973. 160p.

988   **McKinlay**, John B. 'On the professional regulation of change.' Halmos, P. (ed.). *Professionalisation and social change.* 1973. p. 61–84.

989   **Montague**, Joel B. and **Miller**, Ronald J. 'The new professionalism in sociology.' Halmos, P. (ed.). *Professionalisation and social change.* 1973. p. 139–58.

990   **Oppenheimer**, Martin. 'The proletarianization of the professional.' Halmos, P. (ed.). *Professionalisation and social change.* 1973. p. 213–28.

991   **Taylor**, Robert. 'Deskmen's unions.' *New Soc.*, xxiii (8 March 1973), 536–7.

992   **Tegner**, Bill. *White-collar unions.* London: Industrial Society, 1973. 34p. (Notes for managers 23.)

993   **Bowen**, Peter, **Elsy**, V. E. and **Shaw**, Monica P. 'Attachment of white-collar workers to trade unions.' *Pers. Rev.*, iii, 3 (Summer 1974), 22–32.

994   **Lansbury**, Russell. 'Professionalism and unionization among management services specialists.' *Br. J. Ind. Relat.*, xii, 2 (July 1974), 292–302.

995   **Prandy**, Kenneth, **Stewart**, A. and **Blackburn**, Robin M. 'Concepts and measures: the example of unionateness.' *Sociology*, viii (September 1974), 427–46.

996   **Adams**, Roy Joseph. *Growth of white-collar unionism in Britain and Sweden: a comparative investigation.* Madison: Wisconsin University. Industrial Relations Research Institute, 1975. 63p.

997   **Adams**, Roy Joseph. 'Recognition of white-collar worker unions.' *Br. J. Ind. Relat.*, xiii, 1 (March 1975), 102–6.

998   **Dickens**, Linda. 'Staff associations and the Industrial Relations Act: the effect on union growth.' *Ind. Relat. J.*, vi, 3 (Autumn 1975), 29–41.

999   **Williams**, Michael E. 'Professions.' *New Blackfriars*, lvi (December 1975), 559–61.

1000 **Crompton**, Rosemary. 'Approaches to the study of white collar unionism.' *Sociology*, x, 3 (September 1976), 407–26.

1001 **Thakur**, Manab and **Naylor**, Michael. *White collar unions.* London: Institute of Personnel Management, 1976. 88p. (Information reports 22.)

1002 **Carpenter**, Michael J. 'The new managerialism and professionalism in nursing.' *Health and the division of labour: proceedings of a Conference on Sociology, Health and Illness, London 1976.* London: Croom Helm, 1977. p. 165–93.

1003 **Johnson**, Terence. 'The professions in the class structure.' Scase, R. (ed.). *Industrial society.* 1977. p. 93–110.

1004 **Joseph**, M. *The nature of the professions: a sociological analysis of professional power, socialisation and ideologies.* 1977. (B.Phil. thesis, Open University.)

1005 **Banks**, J. A. 'A comment on Rosemary Crompton's "Approaches to the study of white collar unionism".' *Sociology*, xii, 1 (January 1978), 141–2.

1006 **Cook**, Frederick G., **Clark**, Stanley C., **Roberts**, Kenneth and **Semeonoff**, Elizabeth. 'Are white-collar trade unionists different?' *Sociol. Work Occup.*, v, 2 (May 1978), 235–46.

1007 **Kelly**, Aidan. 'Job satisfaction and the unionization of the white-collar employee.' *Studies*, lxvii, 267 (Autumn 1978), 143–63.

1008 **Kelly**, Aidan. 'The unionisation of the white-collar employee and attitudes towards change in the office.' *Administration*, xxvi, 1 (Spring 1978), 77–94.

1009 **Blyton**, Paul. 'When "them" are part of "us": some implications of organizing a single trade union.' Colloquium on Management and Industrial Relations, 1979. *Proceedings.* p. 81–100.

1010 **Crompton**, Rosemary. 'Trade unionism and the insurance clerk.' *Sociology*, xiii, 3 (September 1979), 403–26.

1011 **Jenkins**, Clive and **Sherman**, Barrie. *White-collar unionism: the rebellious salariat.* London: Routledge & Kegan Paul, 1979. ix, 174p.

1012 **Marsh**, R. and **Pedler**, Malcolm. 'Unionizing the white-collar workers.' *Employee Relat.*, i, 2 (1979), 2–6.

See also: 261; 319; 351; 353; 378; 1093; 1128; 1139; 1173; 2018.

b. PARTICULAR OCCUPATIONS AND INDUSTRIES

1013 **Bowen**, Peter and **Shaw**, Monica. 'Patterns of white-collar unionization in the steel industry.' *Ind. Relat. J.*, iii, 2 (Summer 1972), 8–34.

1014 **Coates**, R. D. *Teachers' unions and interest group politics: a study in the behaviour of organised teachers in England and Wales.* Cambridge: Cambridge U.P., 1972. xiii, 138p.

1015 **Davies**, Celia. 'Professionals in organisations: some preliminary observations on hospital consultants.' *Sociol. Rev.*, xx, 4 (November 1972), 553–67.

1016 **Dickens**, Linda. 'U.K.A.P.E.: a study of a professional union.' *Ind. Relat. J.*, iii, 3 (Autumn 1972), 2–16.

1017 **Gosden**, Peter Henry John Heather. *The evolution of a profession: a study of the contribution of teachers' associations to the development of school teaching as a professional occupation.* Oxford: Blackwell, 1972. 372p.

1018 **Mandle**, W. F. 'The professional cricketer in England in the nineteenth century.' *Labour Hist.*, xxiii (November 1972), 1–16.

1019 **Roberts**, Benjamin Charles, **Loveridge**,

Ray, **Gennard**, John and **Eason**, J. V. *Reluctant militants: a study of industrial technicians.* London: Heinemann, 1972. 342p. (London School of Economics and Political Science industrial relations series.)

1020 **Biochemical Society.** *Biochemists in industry.* London: The Society, 1973. ix, 58p. (Special publications 2.)
Proceedings of a Colloquium, Nottingham, 1972.

1021 **Insurance Institute of Manchester.** *Centenary 1973: 1873–1973.* Manchester: The Institute, 1973. 41p.

1022 **Lawrence**, Susanne. 'Battle of the banks.' *Pers. Manag.*, V, 11 (November 1973), 33–5.

1023 **Taylor**, George. 'Unionising the foreign banks.' *Banker*, CXXIII (November 1973), 1291, 1293, 1295.

1024 **Farnham**, D. 'Association of Teachers in Technical Institutions: a case study of the origins, formation and growth of a white collar organization.' *Int. Rev. of Soc. Hist.*, XIX, 3 (1974), 377–95.

1025 **Hamilton**, Robert. 'Social work: an aspiring profession and its difficulties.' *Br. J. Soc. Work*, IV (Autumn 1974), 333–42.

1026 **Blume**, Stuart S. and **Chennells**, Elizabeth. 'Professional civil servants.' *Public Adm.*, LIII, 2 (Summer 1975), 111–31.

1027 **Council of Engineering Institutions.** *Professional engineers and trade unions.* London: The Council, 1975. 12p.

1028 **Department of Health and Social Security.** *Report of the Committee of Inquiry into the Regulation of the Medical Profession.* London: H.M.S.O., 1975. 200p. (Cmnd. 6018.)
Chairman: A. W. Merrison.

1029 **Gospel**, Howard F. and **Cameron**, Alastair. 'Trade unions on campus.' *New Soc.*, XXXIV (16 October 1975), 141–3.

1030 **Green**, Stephen. 'Professional bureaucratic conflict: the case of the medical profession in the National Health Service.' *Sociol. Rev.*, XXIII (February 1975), 121–41.

1031 **Anderson**, Gregory L. *Victorian clerks.* Manchester: Manchester U.P., 1976. 145p.

1032 **Anderson**, Gregory L. 'Victorian clerks and voluntary associations in Liverpool and Manchester.' *North. Hist.*, XII (1976), 202–19.

1033 **Bamber**, Greg J. 'Trade unions for managers?' *Pers. Rev.*, V, 4 (Autumn 1976), 36–41.

1034 **Chanan**, Michael. *Labour power in the British film industry.* London: British Film Institute, 1976. 57p.

1035 **Dickens**, Linda. 'Fighting for the professional engineer.' *Pers. Manage.*, VIII, 5 (May 1976), 18–22.

1036 **Johnson**, A. G. 'The manager: employer or employee?' *Pers. Manage.*, VIII, 11 (November 1976), 20–23.

1037 **Lansbury**, Russell. 'Career orientations and unionization among technical specialists.' *J. Ind. Relat.*, XVIII, 1 (March 1976), 1–16.

1038 **MacLeod**, E. K. *Politics, professionalisation and the organisation of scientists: the Association of Scientific Workers, 1917–1942.* 1976. (D.Phil. thesis, University of Sussex.)

1039 **Purcell**, John. 'Managers and union membership.' *R & D Manage.*, VI, 3 (1976), 97–103.

1040 **Watson**, H. B. *Organizational bases of professional status: a comparative study of the engineering profession.* 1976. (Ph.D. thesis, London School of Economics.)

1041 **Weir**, David. 'Radical managerialism: middle managers' perceptions of collective bargaining.' *Br. J. Ind. Relat.*, XIV, 3 (November 1976), 324–38.

1042 **Anderson**, Gregory L. 'The social economy of late-Victorian clerks.' Crossick, G. (ed.). *The lower middle class in Britain 1870–1914.* London: Croom Helm, 1977. p. 113–33.

1043 **Atkinson**, Paul, **Reid**, Margaret and **Sheldrake**, Peter. 'Medical mystique.' *Sociol. Work Occup.*, IV, 3 (August 1977), 243–80.

1044 **Bellaby**, Paul and **Oribabor**, Patrick. 'The growth of trade union consciousness among general hospital nurses viewed as a response to proletarianisation.' *Sociol Rev.*, XXV (November 1977), 801–22.

1045 **Christian**, H. *The development of trade unionism and professionalism among British journalists: a sociological inquiry.* 1977. (Ph.D. thesis, London School of Economics.)

1046 **Donnison**, Jean. *Midwives and medical men: a history of inter-professional rivalries and women's rights.* London: Heinemann, 1977. 250p.

1047 **Howie**, Will. *Trade unions and the professional engineer.* London: Telford, 1977. 76p.

1048 **Jones**, K. L. *The growth and development of white collar trade unionism in the British steel industry.* 1977. (Ph.D. thesis, London School of Economics.)

1049 **Parry**, Noel and **Parry**, José. 'Professionalism and unionism: some aspects of class conflict in the National Health Service.' *Sociol. Rev.*, XXV (November 1977), 823–41.

1050 **Price**, B. 'Who speaks for the manager?' *Pers. Manage.*, IX, 11 (November 1977), 27–32.

1051 **Senior**, Michael Edward. *Management attitudes and their effect on white collar union development: a study from the fibreboard packing case industry.* 1977. (M.Phil. thesis, University of Warwick.)

1052 **Shaw**, M. P. *The Cinderellas of industry: the occupational and trade union identity of clerical workers.* 1977. (M.Phil. thesis, University of Durham.)

1053 **Siebert**, W. S. 'Occupational licensing: the Merrison report on the regulation of the medical profession.' *Br. J. Ind. Relat.*, XV, 1 (March 1977), 29–38.

1054 **Swabe**, A. I. *The Association of Teachers in Technical Institutions, 1904–45: white collar unionism among professional people.* 1977.

(M.Phil. thesis, London School of Economics.)

1055 **Engleman**, Stephen R. 'Occupational licensing: the Merrison report on the regulation of the medical profession: a comment.' *Br. J. Ind. Relat.*, XVI, 1 (March 1978), 106.

1056 **Lansbury**, Russell D. *Professionals and management: a study of behaviour in organizations.* St Lucia, Queensland: Queensland U.P., 1978. xv, 201p.

1057 **Navarro**, Vicente. *Class struggle, the state and medicine: an historical and contemporary analysis of the medical sector in Great Britain.* Oxford: Martin Robertson, 1978. xviii, 156p.

1058 **Purcell**, John. 'Computer staff and industrial relations.' *Pers. Rev.*, VII, 1 (Winter 1978), 31–9.

1059 **Seglow**, Peter. *Trade unionism in television: a case study in the development of white collar militancy.* London: Saxon House, 1978. 287p.

1060 **Siebert**, W. S. 'Occupational licensing: the Merrison report on the regulation of the medical profession: a reply.' *Br. J. Ind. Relat.*, XVI, 1 (March 1978), 107.

1061 **Dimmock**, Stuart. 'Dilemmas of medical representation: a view.' Bosanquet, N. (ed.). *Industrial relations in the N.H.S.* 1979. p. 199–220.

1062 **Dyson**, Roger and **Spary**, Katherine. 'Professional associations.' Bosanquet, N. (ed.). *Industrial relations in the N.H.S.* 1979. p. 145–76.

1063 **Frost**, Paul. 'Approaches to management unionism.' Colloquium on Management and Industrial Relations, 1979. *Proceedings.* p. 101–20.

1064 **Mercer**, J. *Aspects of professionalisation in professions supplementary to medicine.* 1979. (Ph.D. thesis, Institute of Education, University of London.)

1065 **Poole**, Michael and **Blyton**, Paul. 'The industrial relations of managers: a comment.' Colloquium on Management and Industrial Relations, 1979. *Proceedings.* p. 148–51.

1066 **Simpson**, David. 'The industrial relations of managers.' Colloquium on Management and Industrial Relations, 1979. *Proceedings.* p. 122–47.

See also: 994; 1045.

7. Public Administration

This section includes material on unionism in national and local government. See also Part Three, II, D, 2, 3, 5, and 6.

1067 **Headey**, B. 'The Civil Service as an elite in Britain and Germany.' *Rev. Int. Sci. Adm.*, XXXVIII, 1 (1972), 41–8.

1068 **Fryer**, Robert H., **Fairclough**, Andy and **Manson**, Tom B. *Organisation and change in the National Union of Public Employees: a report prepared for the Special National Conference on Reorganisation.* Coventry: University of Warwick Department of Sociology, 1974. 66p.

1069 **Edwards**, Kathleen Louisa. *The story of the Civil Service Union.* London: Allen & Unwin, 1975. 95p.

1070 **Reiner**, Robert. *The blue-coated worker: a sociological study of police unionism.* 1976. (Ph.D. thesis, University of Bristol.)

1071 **Neill**, C. G. E. *The practice of trade unionism by principal local government officials.* 1978. (Ph.D. thesis, University of Leeds.)

1072 **Reiner**, Robert. *The blue-coated worker: a sociological study of police unionism.* Cambridge: Cambridge U.P., 1978. 295p.

1073 **Dann**, K. G. F. 'Unions and the Armed Forces.' *R. United Services Inst. Def. Stud. J.*, CXXIV (March 1979), 72–4.

1074 **Home Office**, Committee of Inquiry on the Police. *The structure and role of police staff associations.* London: H.M.S.O., 1979. x, 122p. (Report 3.)
Chairman: Lord Edmund-Davies.

See also: 1026; 1049; 1142; 1154; 2042.

E. STUDIES OF PARTICULAR GROUPS

1. Ethnic Groups

See also Part Six, II, D, 7; Part Six, II, E, 2; Part Six, IV, A, 3, c; and Part Seven, III, A, 1.

1075 **Runnymede Industrial Unit.** *The trade union movement and discrimination: a collection of essays based on papers given at a conference convened by Ruskin College, Oxford in 1970.* London: The Unit, 1971. 24p.

1076 **Brooks**, Dennis and **Singh**, Karamjit. 'Race relations, industrial relations and pluralism.' *New Community*, 1 (Summer 1972), 277–81.

1077 **Meth**, Monty. *Brothers to all men? A report on trade union actions and attitudes on race relations.* London: Runnymede Industrial Unit, 1972. 84p.

1078 **Race Today.** 'Towards racial justice: black workers and trade unions.' *Race Today*, V, 8 (August 1973), 235–46.

1079 **New Community.** 'Migrants, work and the law: trade unions and immigrant workers.' *New Community*, IV (Winter 1974 – Spring 1975), 19–36.

1080 **Runnymede Trust.** 'Trade unions and immigrant workers.' *New Community*, IV (Winter 1974 – Spring 1975), 19–36.

1081 **Race Today.** 'Grunwick gates: the entry to unionisation.' *Race Today*, IX, 4 (June–July 1977), 76–8.

1082 **Race Today.** 'The Grunwick strike: the trades unions fail to deliver.' *Race Today*, IX, 3 (April–May 1977), 52–4.

1083 **Miles**, Robert and **Phizacklea**, Ann. 'The TUC and black workers.' *Br. J. Ind. Relat.*, XVI, 2 (July 1978), 195–207.

2. Women

See also Part Six, II, C, 4; Part Six, II, D, 7; Part Six, III, E; Part Six, IV, A, 3, a; Part Seven, II, C; and Part Seven, IV, D.

1084 **General and Municipal Workers' Union.** *Equal rights for women: report to the annual Congress, 1972.* Esher: G.M.W.U., 1972. 10p.

1085 **O'Brien**, J. *Women's liberation in labour history: a case study from Nottingham.* Nottingham: Bertrand Russell Peace Foundation, 1972. 15p.

1086 **Ramelson**, M. *Petticoat rebellion: a century of struggle for women's rights.* London: Lawrence & Wishart, 1972. 208p.

1087 **Lewenhak**, Sheila. 'The lesser trade union organization of women than of men.' *Soc. Study Labour Hist. Bull.*, XXVI (Spring 1973), 19–22.

1088 **Lewenhak**, Sheila. 'Women in the leadership of the Scottish Trades Union Congress, 1897–1970.' *Scott. Labour Hist. Soc. J.*, VII (July 1973), 3–23.

1089 **Strachey**, R. *Cause: a short history of the women's movement in Great Britain.* London: Cedric Chivers, 1974. 429p.

1090 **Auchmuty**, Rosemary. 'Spinsters and trade unions in Victorian Britain.' *Labour Hist.*, XXIX (1975), 109–22.

1091 **Frow**, Ruth and **Frow**, Eddie. 'Women workers in Manchester.' *Labour Mon.*, LIV (December 1975), 561–2.

1092 **Hunt**, Judith. *Organising women workers.* London: Workers' Educational Association, 1975. 35p. (Studies for trade unionists 1, 3.)

1093 **Godwin**, Anne. 'Early years in the trade unions.' Middleton, L. (ed.). *Women in the labour movement.* 1977. p. 94–112.

1094 **Lewenhak**, Sheila. *Women and trade unions: an outline history of women in the British trade union movement.* London: Benn, 1977. 308p.

1095 **McCarthy**, Margaret. 'Women in trade unions.' Middleton, L. (ed.). *Women in the labour movement.* 1977. p. 161–74.

1096 **Middleton**, Lucy. *Women in the labour movement: the British experience.* London: Croom Helm, 1977. 221p.

1097 **Solden**, Norbert C. *Women in British trade unions 1874–1976.* Dublin: Gill & Macmillan, 1978. 226p.

1098 **Liddington**, Jill. 'Women cotton workers and the suffrage campaign: the radical suffragists in Lancashire 1893–1914.' Burman, Sandra (ed.). *Fit work for women.* London: Croom Helm, 1979. p. 98–111.

1099 **Purcell**, Kate. 'Militancy and acquiescence amongst women workers.' Burman, Sandra (ed.). *Fit work for women.* London: Croom Helm, 1979. p. 112–33.
See also: 75; 1236; 2439.

3. The Unemployed

Material on workers' sit-ins is classified at Part Five, V. See also Part Six, II, D; Part Six, IV, A, 3, d; Part Seven, II, D, 4; and Part Seven, VII, B, 1.

1100 **Gould**, Tony. 'Out of work: the activist.' *New Soc.*, XVII (20 May 1971), 856–8.

1101 **Gould**, Tony and **Kenyon**, Joe. *Stories from the dole queue.* London: Temple Smith, 1972. 192p.

1102 **Hayburn**, P. 'The police and the hunger marchers.' *Int. Rev. of Soc. Hist.*, XVII (1972), 1–27.

1103 **McLachlan**, Hugh V. 'The right to work.' *Contemp. Rev.*, CCXXII (June 1973), 31–4.

1104 **Imperial Typewriters Union Action Committee.** *Why Imperial Typewriters must not close: a preliminary social audit.* Nottingham: Institute for Workers' Control, 1975. 16p. (I.W.C. pamphlets 46.)

1105 **Jenkins**, Mick. 'Some unemployed struggles in the thirties.' *Marxism Today*, XIX, 3 (March 1975), 76–85.

1106 **Bede Gallery**, Jarrow. *Jarrow march 1936.* Jarrow: The Gallery, 1976. 104p.
Exhibition organised by the Gallery. Text by David Dougan; photographic interpretations by Irene Reddish.

1107 **Hannington**, Walter. *Unemployed struggles 1919–1936: my life and struggles amongst the unemployed.* London: Lawrence & Wishart, 1977. 328p.
First published 1936. Reprinted with a new introduction by Will Paynter.

1108 **Harvey**, A. D. 'Mass unemployment: the ultra-left's lost opportunity.' *Contemp. Rev.*, CCXXX (April 1977), 191–5.

1109 **Jull**, C. *The working class, unemployment and the stage: an examination of working class attitudes towards, and action in promoting, measures to deal with the problem of unemployment in Britain and America, 1870–1914.* 1977. (M.A. thesis, University of Sussex.)

1110 **Red Notes.** *The little red blue book: fighting the layoffs at Fords.* London: Red Notes, 1978. (Red Notes pamphlets.)

1111 **Edwards**, Bert. 'Organising the unemployed in the 1920s.' Craig, G. and others (eds.). *Jobs and community action.* 1979. p. 27–33.

F. GROWTH, STRUCTURE, GOVERNMENT, AND ADMINISTRATION

See also Part Seven, V.

1. General

See also Part Three, II, A.

1112 **Edelstein**, J. David and **Warner**, Malcolm. 'On measuring and explaining union democracy: a reply to Dr. Martin's critique.' *Sociology*, V, 3 (September 1971), 398–400.

1113 **Gretton**, John. 'Academic help.' *New Soc.*, XVIII (9 December 1971). 1145–6.

1114 **Gretton**, John. 'How are trade unions reshaping themselves?' *New Soc.*, XVII (4 March 1971), 348–51.

1115 **Hyman**, Richard. *Marxism and the sociology of trade unionism.* London: Pluto, 1971. 53p.

1116 **Hyman**, Richard. *The Workers' Union.* Oxford: Clarendon, 1971. xii, 231p.

1117 **Lawrence**, Susanne. 'Background to bargaining.' *Pers. Manage.*, III, 8 (August 1971), 26–9.

1118 **Martin**, Roderick. 'Edelstein, Warner and Cooke on union democracy.' *Sociology*, V, 2 (May 1971), 243–4.

1119 **Bain**, George Sayers and **Price**, Robert J. 'Union growth and employment trends in the U.K.; 1964–1970.' *Br. J. Ind. Relat.*, X, 3 (November 1972), 366–81.

1120 **Fleming**, Richard. *Problems of trade union democracy.* Nottingham: Institute of Workers' Control, 1972. 14p. (IWC pamphlets 21.)

1121 **Hillery**, Brian J. P. *Trade union structure and organisation in the Republic of Ireland.* 1971–2. (Ph.D. thesis, National University of Ireland, Dublin.)

1122 **Institute for Workers' Control.** *Trade unions and rising prices.* Nottingham: The Institute. 1972. 23p.

1123 **Prothero**, Iorweth J. 'The Beacon: the first trade union newspaper?' *Soc. Study Labour Hist. Bull.*, XXIV (Spring 1972), 33–4.

1124 **Simpson**, D. H. 'An analysis of the size of trade unions.' *Br. J. Ind. Relat.*, X, 3 (November 1972), 382–92.

1125 **Warner**, Malcolm. 'Organizational profile of the small trade union: a composite case study.' *Ind. Relat. J.*, III, 4 (Winter 1972), 51–64.

1126 **Warner**, Malcolm. 'Trade unions and organizational theory: preliminary analysis of union environment, structure and performance.' *J. Ind. Relat.*, XIV, 1 (March 1972), 47–62.

1127 **Burkitt**, Brian. 'The calculation of the degree of unionization.' *Br. J. Ind. Relat.*, XI, 3 (November 1973), 449–58.

1128 **Child**, John, **Loveridge**, Ray and **Warner**, Malcolm. 'Towards an organizational study of trade unions.' *Sociology*, VII, 1 (January 1973), 71–91.

1129 **Fletcher**, Richard. 'Trade union democracy: the case of the AUEW rule book.' Barratt Brown, M. (ed.). *Trade union register 3.* 1973. p. 125–49.

1130 **Hughes**, John. 'Patterns of trade union growth.' Barratt Brown, M. (ed.). *Trade union register 3.* 1973. p. 47–59.

1131 **Industrial Research and Information Services.** *A.U.E.W. (E.) postal ballots.* London: The Services, 1973. 24p.

1132 **Roberts**, Ivor. 'Trade union membership trends in seven Western European countries 1950–1968.' *Ind. Rel. J.*, IV, 2 (Summer 1973), 45–56.

1133 **Wigham**, Eric Leonard. *Participation in the trade unions.* London: Working Together Campaign, 1973. 12p.

1134 **Burkitt**, Brian and **Bowers**, David. 'The degree of unionization, 1948–1968.' *Bull. Econ. Res.*, XXVI, 1 (May 1974), 79–100.

1135 **Donaldson**, Lex and **Warner**, Malcolm. 'Bureaucratic and electoral control in occupational interest associations.' *Sociology*, VII (January 1974), 47–57.

1136 **Donaldson**, Lex and **Warner**, Malcolm. 'Structure of organizations in occupational interest associations.' *Hum. Relat.*, XXVII (1974), 721–38.

1137 **Latta**, Geoff and **Lewis**, Roy. 'Trade union legal services.' *Br. J. Ind. Relat.*, XII, 1 (March 1974), 56–70.

1138 **Mortimer**, James Edward. 'Patterns in trade union membership.' *Pers. Manage.*, VI, 6 (June 1974), 20–4.

1139 **Adams**, Roy Joseph. 'The recognition of white collar unions.' *Br. J. Ind. Relat.*, XIII, 1 (March 1975), 102–6.

1140 **Boraston**, Ian, **Clegg**, Hugh Armstrong and **Rimmer**, Malcolm. *Workplace and union: a study of local relationships in fourteen unions.* London: Heinemann, 1975. viii, 199p. (Warwick studies in industrial relations.)

1141 **Edelstein**, J. David and **Warner**, Malcolm. *Comparative union democracy: organisation and opposition in British and American unions.* London: Allen & Unwin, 1975. viii, 378p.

1142 **Fryer**, Robert H., **Fairclough**, Andy J. and **Manson**, Tom B. 'Democracy in the trade unions.' *Pers. Manage.*, VII, 4 (April 1975), 20–3, 39.

1143 **Hillery**, Brian J. P., **Kelly**, Aidan and **Marsh**, Arthur Ivor. *Trade union organisation in Ireland.* Dublin: Irish Productivity Centre, 1975. 196p.

1144 **Abbott**, Stephen. *How to bring democracy and participation to the trade unions.* London: Aims for Freedom & Enterprise, 1976. 12p.

1145 **Bain**, George Sayers and **Elsheikh**, Farouk. *Union growth and the business cycle: an econometric analysis.* Oxford: Blackwell, 1976. xv, 155p. (Warwick studies in industrial relations.)

1146 **Carew**, Anthony. *Democracy and government in European trade unions.* London: Allen & Unwin, 1976. 244p.

1147 **Cockburn**, Claud. *Union power: the growth and challenge in perspective.* London: Kimber, 1976. 206p.

1148 **Forester**, Tom. 'How democratic are the unions?' *New Soc.*, XXXVI (13 May 1976), 343–5.

1149 **Price**, Robert J. and **Bain**, George Sayers. 'Union growth revisited: 1948–1974 in perspective.' *Br. J. Ind. Relat.*, XIV, 3 (November 1976), 339–55.

1150 **Robertson**, N. and **Sams**, K. I. 'The role of the full-time union officer.' *Econ. Soc. Rev.*, VIII, 1 (October 1976), 23–42.

1151 **Taylor**, Robert. 'How democratic are the

trade unions?' *Polit. Q.*, XVII, 1 (January–March 1976), 29–38.

1152 **Adams**, Roy J. 'Bain's theory of white collar union growth: a conceptual critique.' *Br. J. Ind. Relat.*, XV, 3 (November 1977), 317–21.

1153 **Armstrong**, K. J., **Bowers**, D. and **Burkitt**, B. 'The measurement of trade union bargaining power.' *Br. J. Ind. Relat.*, XV, 1 (March 1977), 91–100.

1154 **Bealey**, Frank. 'The political system of the POEU.' *Br. J. Ind. Relat.*, XV, 3 (November 1977), 374–95.

1155 **Burkitt**, Brian and **Bowers**, David. 'The degree of unionization 1948–68: a reply.' *Bull. Econ. Res.*, XXIX, 1 (May 1977), 54–6.

1156 **Mayhew**, K. 'The degree of unionisation, 1948–1968: a comment.' *Bull. Econ. Res.*, XXIX, 1 (May 1977), 51–3.

1157 **North East Trade Union Studies Information Unit.** *A guide to the Unit.* Newcastle-upon-Tyne: The Unit, 1977. 13p.

1158 **Ramaswamy**, E. A. 'The participatory dimension of trade union democracy: a comparative sociological view.' *Sociology*, XI, 3 (September 1977), 465–80.

1159 **Rice**, Mick. 'The state of the unions.' Ottaway, R. (ed.). *Humanising the workplace.* 1977. p. 158–71.

1160 **Richardson**, Ray. 'Trade union growth: review article.' *Br. J. Ind. Relat.*, XV, 2 (July 1977), 279–82.

1161 **Adeney**, Martin. 'Ballots: a secret weapon.' *Listener*, C (19 March 1978), 774–5.

1162 **Burkitt**, B. and **Bowers**, D. 'The determination of the rate of change of unionization in the United Kingdom: 1924–1966.' *Appl. Econ.*, X (1978), 161–72.

1163 **Egan**, David. 'The Unofficial Reform Committee and the miners' next step.' *Llafur*, II, 3 (Summer 1978), 64–80.

1164 **Elsheikh**, Farouk and **Bain**, George Sayers. 'Trade union growth: a reply.' *Br. J. Ind. Relat.*, XVI, 1 (March 1978), 99–102.

1165 **England**, Joe and **Anderson**, Geoff. 'Trade union structure: is it moving with the times?' *Pers. Manage.*, X, 2 (February 1978), 22–6.

1166 **Hemingway**, John. *Conflict and democracy: studies in trade union government.* Oxford: Clarendon, 1978. 184p.

1167 **Pedersen**, Peder J. 'Union growth and the business cycle: a note on the Bain–Elsheikh model.' *Br. J. Ind. Relat.*, XVI, 3 (November 1978), 373–7.

1168 **Richardson**, Ray. 'Trade union growth: a rejoinder.' *Br. J. Ind. Relat.*, XVI, 1 (March 1978), 103–5.

1169 **Undy**, Roger. 'The devolution of bargaining levels and responsibilities in the Transport and General Workers' Union 1965–75.' *Ind. Relat. J.*, IX, 3 (Autumn 1978), 44–56.

1170 **Aims for Freedom and Enterprise.** *The Woodward case: banned for life: the price of union participation.* London: The Authors, 1979. 4p.

1171 **Bain**, George Sayers and **Elsheikh**, Farouk. 'The determination of the rate of change of unionization in the U.K.: a comment and further analysis.' *Appl. Econ.*, XI (1979), 451–63.

1172 **Bain**, George Sayers and **Elsheikh**, Farouk. 'An inter-industry analysis of unionisation in Britain.' *Br. J. Ind. Relat.*, XVII, 2 (July 1979), 137–57.

1173 **Crompton**, Rosemary. 'The growth of white collar unionism: insurance as a case study.' *Sociology*, XIII, 1 (January 1979), 103–4.

1174 **Fletcher**, Richard. *Trade union rules.* London: Arrow Books in association with the Society of Industrial Tutors, 1979. 117p. (Trade union industrial studies.)

1175 **Undy**, Roger. 'The electoral influence of the opposition party in the AUEW Engineering Section 1960–75.' *Br. J. Ind. Relat.*, XVII, 1 (March 1979), 19–33.

See also: 710; 886; 944; 952; 953; 954; 973; 996; 997; 998; 1000; 1010; 1068; 1200; 1250.

2. Federations

Material on the Triple Alliance is classified at Part Three, II, B.

1176 **Industrial Research and Information Services.** *The TUC 1868–1972.* London: The Authors, 1972. 36p.

1177 **Taylor**, Robert. 'The TUC: a study in influence.' *New Soc.*, XXV (9 August 1973), 327–30.

1178 **Trades Union Congress.** *Case for the unions.* London: The Authors, 1973. 25p.

1179 **Roberts**, Benjamin Charles and **Liebhaberg**, Bruno. 'European trade union confederation: influence of regionalism, detente and multinationals.' *Br. J. Ind. Relat.*, XIV, 3 (November 1976), 261–73.

1180 **Winchester**, David. 'Power and influence in the T.U.C.: a quest for control.' Purcell, J. and Smith, R. (eds.). *The control of work.* 1979. p. 100–32.

See also: 692; 790; 1083; 1232; 5818.

3. Trades Councils

1181 **Clarke**, J. F. and **McDermott**, T. P. *The Newcastle and District Trades Council, 1873–1973: a centenary history.* Newcastle-upon-Tyne: Frank Graham, 1973. 70p.

1182 **Large**, David and **Whitfield**, Robert. *The Bristol Trades Council 1873–1973.* Bristol: Bristol Branch of the Historical Association, 1973. 36p.

1183 **Durr**, Andy (ed.). *A history of Brighton Trades Council and labour movement, 1890–1970.* Brighton: Brighton, Hove & District Trades Council, 1974. 80p.

1184 **Burke**, Barry. *Rebels with a cause: the history of Hackney Trades Council, 1900–1975.* Hackney:

Hackney Trades Council and Hackney Workers' Educational Association, 1975. 87p.

1185 **Frow**, Eddie and **Frow**, Ruth. *To make that future – now! A history of the Manchester and Salford Trades Council.* Didsbury: Morten, 1979. 176p.

1186 **Taplin**, Eric L. 'Liverpool Trades Council, 1880–1914.' *N.W. Labour Hist. Soc. Bull.*, III (1976), 12–16.

1187 **Clinton**, Alan. *The trade union rank and file: trades councils in Britain 1900–40.* Manchester: Manchester University Press, 1977. x, 262p.

1188 **Fidler**, G. C. 'The Liverpool Trades Council and technical education in the era of the technical instruction committee.' *Hist. Educ.*, VI, 3 (October 1977), 209–22.

1189 **Fraser**, W. Hamish. 'Trades councils in the labour movement in nineteenth century Scotland.' MacDougall, I. (ed.). *Essays in Scottish labour history.* 1978. p. 1–28.

1190 **Liddell**, P. H. *The role of the trades council in the political and industrial life of Glasgow, 1858–1976.* 1978. (M.Sc. thesis, University of Strathclyde.)

1191 **Russell**, Dave. *Southwark Trades Council: a short history, 1903–1978.* London: Southwark Trades Council, 1978. 72p.

See also: 1091.

4. Mergers, Amalgamations, and Inter-Union Relations

Material on the Triple Alliance is classified at Part Three, II, B.

1192 **Mortimer**, James Edward. 'Bridlington and the Act.' *Pers. Manage.*, IV, 4 (April 1972) 18–22.

1193 **Trades Union Congress.** *Disputes procedure.* London: The Authors, 1972. 12p.

1194 **Buchanan**, R. T. 'Merger waves in British Unionism.' *Ind. Relat. J.*, V, 2 (Summer 1974,) 37–45.

1195 **Kay**, Maurice. 'The settlement of membership disputes in trade unions.' Carby-Hall, J. R. (ed.). *Studies in labour law. 1976.* p. 160–201.

1196 **Trades Union Congress.** *Disputes procedures and principles.* London: The Authors, 1976. 26p.

1197 **Daunton**, M. J. 'Inter-union relations on the waterfront: Cardiff 1888–1914.' *Int. Rev. of Soc. Hist.*, XXII, 3 (1977), 350–78.

1198 **Kalis**, Peter J. 'The adjudication of inter-union membership disputes: the T.U.C. Disputes Committee revisited.' *Ind. Law J.*, VI, 1 (March 1977), 19–34.

1199 **Kalis**, Peter J. 'The effectiveness and utility of the Disputes Committee of the Trades Union Congress.' *Br. J. Ind. Relat.*, XVI, 1 (March 1978), 41–51.

1200 **England**, Joe. 'How UCATT revised its rules: an anatomy of organisational change.' *Br. J. Ind. Relat.*, XVII, 1 (March 1979), 1–18.

See also: 906; 1799; 2327; 6814.

5. Finances and Benefits

See also Part Three, I; and Part Seven, V.

1201 **Latta**, Geoff. 'Trade union finances.' *Br. J. Ind. Relat.*, X, 3 (November 1972), 392–411.

1202 **Benson**, John. 'English coal miners' trade union accident funds, 1850–1900.' *Econ. Hist. Rev.*, XXVIII, 3 (August 1975), 401–12.

1203 **Hanson**, C. G. 'Craft unions, welfare benefits, and the case for trade union law reform, 1867–75.' *Econ. Hist. Rev.*, XXVIII, 2 (May 1975), 243–59.

1204 **Benson**, John. 'The records of the West Riding of Yorkshire Miners' Permanent Relief Fund Friendly Society.' *Soc. Study Labour Hist. Bull.*, XXXIII (Autumn 1976), 37–8.

1205 **Hanson**, C. G. 'Craft unions, welfare benefits, and the case for trade union law reform, 1867–75: a reply.' *Econ. Hist. Rev.*, XXIX, 4 (October 1976), 631–5.

1206 **Musson**, Albert Edward. 'Craft unions, welfare benefits, and the case for trade union law reform, 1867–75: a comment.' *Econ. Hist. Rev.*, XXIX, 4 (October 1976), 626–30.

1207 **Thane**, Pat. 'Craft unions, welfare benefits, and the case for trade union law reform, 1867–75: a comment.' *Econ. Hist. Rev.*, XXIX, 4 (October 1976), 617–25.

See also: 956; 6822.

6. Closed Shop and Check-Off

See also Part Seven, V.

1208 **Commission on Industrial Relations.** *Approved closed shop agreement: British Shipping Federation/National Union of Seamen.* London: H.M.S.O., 1972. VI, 32p. (Report 30.)

1209 **Cowan**, L. D. 'The case of the conscientious objector.' *Pers. Manage.*, VI, 5 (May 1972), 26–8.

1210 **Commission on Industrial Relations.** *Approved closed shop in theatre, independent television and films.* London: H.M.S.O., 1973. VI, 62p. (Report 40.)

1211 **Beloff**, Nora. *Freedom under Foot: the battle over the closed shop in British journalism.* London: Temple Smith, 1976. 143p.

1212 **Bourn**, Colin J. 'The closed shop in practice.' *Pers. Manage.*, IX, 5 (May 1977), 28–31, 37.

1213 **Burton**, John. 'Are trade unions a public good/bad? The economics of the closed shop.' Institute of Economic Affairs. *Trade unions: public goods or public bads?* 1978. p. 41–52.

1214 **McKeown**, Andrew. 'Hands off the closed shop.' *Month*, XI (January 1978), 16–19.

1215 **Ricketts**, Martin. 'Is efficiency more important than justice and equity?' Institute of Economic Affairs. *Trade unions: public goods or public bads?* 1978. p. 53–5.

1216 **Weekes**, Brian. 'Collective rights and individual liberty.' *Pers. Manage.*, IX, 8 (August 1978), 18–21.

1217 **Yarrow**, George. 'Trade unions and economic welfare.' Institute of Economic Affairs. *Trade unions: public goods or public bads?* 1978. p. 55–7.

1218 **Gennard**, John, **Dunn**, Stephen and **Wright**, Michael. 'The content of British closed shop agreements.' *Dep. Employment Gaz.*, LXXXVII, 11 (November 1979), 1088–92.

1219 **Hart**, Moira. 'Why the bosses love the closed shop.' *New Soc.*, XXV (15 February 1979), 352–4.

1220 **McIlroy**, John. 'The closed shop: conflict or consensus? Part 1.' *Employee Relat.*, 1, 4 (1979), 22–5.

See also: 6825; 6829; 6831.

7. Leadership and Leaders

This section does not include works on Labour politicians unless they were also prominent in the trade union movement.

1221 **Horn**, Pamela L. R. *Joseph Arch (1826–1919): the farm workers' leader.* Kineton: Roundwood Press, 1971. 262p.

1222 **Bellamy**, Joyce Margaret and **Saville**, John (eds.). *Dictionary of labour biography.* London: Macmillan, 1972–9. 5 v.

1223 **Morris**, R. J. 'The rise of James Kitson: trades union and Mechanics Institution, Leeds 1826–1851.' *Thores. Soc. Publ.*, LIII (1972), 179–200.

1224 **Paynter**, William. *My generation.* London: Allen & Unwin, 1972. 172p.

1225 **Taylor**, B., *Baron* Taylor. *Uphill all the way: a miner's struggle.* London: Sidgwick & Jackson, 1972. 200p.

1226 **Barker**, B. 'Anatomy of reformism: the social and political ideas of the labour leadership in Yorkshire.' *Int. Rev. of Soc. Hist.*, XVIII (1973), 1–27.

1227 **Brown**, G. 'Tom Mann and Jack Tanner and international revolutionary syndicalism, 1910–1920.' *Soc. Study Labour Hist. Bull.*, XXVII (Autumn 1973), 19–22.

1228 **Cannon**, *Lady* Olga and **Anderson**, John Richard Lane. *The road from Wigan pier: a biography of Les Cannon.* London: Gollancz, 1973. 332p.

1229 **Cowe**, B. 'The making of a Clydeside communist.' *Marxism Today*, XVII (1973), 112–16.
Jimmy Reid.

1230 **Geering**, K. *George White, a nineteenth century workers' leader and the Kirkdale phenomenon.* 1973. (M.A. thesis, University of Sussex.)

1231 **MacFarlane**, J. 'J.T.E. (Eddie) Collins: socialist and miners' leader.' *Soc. Study Labour Hist. Bull.*, XXVI (Spring 1973), 39–42.

1232 **Silver**, Eric. *Victor Feather, T.U.C.* London: Gollancz, 1973. 226p.

1233 **Smith**, F. B. *Radical artisan: William James Linton 1812–1897.* Manchester: Manchester University Press, 1973. 254p.

1234 **Smith**, J. H. *Joe Duncan, the Scottish Farm Servants and British agriculture.* Edinburgh: University of Edinburgh, 1973. XIV, 254p.

1235 **Stead**, P. 'Working class leadership in South Wales 1900–1920.' *Welsh Hist. Rev.*, VI (1972–3), 329–53.

1236 **Goldman**, Harold. *Emma Paterson: she led women into a man's world.* London: Lawrence & Wishart, 1974. 127p.

1237 **Radice**, Giles and **Radice**, Lisanne. *Will Thorne: constructive militant: a study in new unionism and new politics.* London: Allen & Unwin, 1974. 134p.

1238 **Bagley**, J. J. *Lancashire diarists: three centuries of Lancashire lives.* Manchester: Phillimore, 1975. 210p.
Includes the diary of John O'Neil, President of the Clitheroe Power Loom Workers.

1239 **Carney**, Jack. *Convict no. 50945: Jim Larkin, Irish labour leader.* Cork: Cork Workers Club, 1975. 19p. (Historical reprints 12.)

1240 **Scargill**, Arthur. 'The new unionism.' *New Left Rev.*, XCII (July–August 1975), 3–33.

1241 **Kirby**. R. G. and **Musson**, Albert Edward. *The voice of the people: John Doherty, 1798–1854: trade unionist, radical and factory reformer.* Manchester: Manchester University Press, 1976. 474p.

1242 **Reid**, Jimmy. *Reflections of a Clyde-built man.* London: Souvenir Press, 1976. viii, 166p.

1243 **Smith**, Robin. 'Sir William Lawther, 1889–1976: obituary article.' *N.E. Group Study Labour Hist. Bull.*, X (October 1976), 27–33.

1244 **Levenson**, S. *James Connolly.* London: Quartet, 1977. 349p.

1245 **Morgan**, Austen. 'James Connolly in Belfast, 1910–14.' *Soc. Study Labour Hist. Bull.*, XXXV (Autumn 1977), 9–11.

1246 **Davies**, Paul. 'The making of A. J. Cook.' *Llafur*, II, 3 (Summer 1978), 43–63.

1247 **Gallacher**, William. *Revolt on the Clyde.* London: Lawrence & Wishart, 1978. ix, 301p.
New edition with an introduction by Michael McGahey.

1248 **Hopkin**, Deian. 'A. J. Cook in 1916–18.' *Llafur*, II, 3 (Summer 1978), 81–8.

1249 **McKibbon**, R. I. 'Arthur Henderson as labour leader.' *Int. Rev. of Soc. Hist.*, XXIII, 1 (1978), 79–101.

1250 **Sherman**, Alfred. *The newest pofession.* London: Aims for Freedom & Enterprise, 1978. 16p.

1251 **Taplin**, Eric L. 'James Larkin, Liverpool and the National Union of Dock Labourers:

the apprenticeship of a revolutionary.' *Saothar*, IV (1978), 1–7.

1252 **Williams**, J. Roose. *Quarryman's champion: the life and activities of William John Parry of Coetmor*. Denbigh: Gee, 1978. 258p.

1253 **Goodman**, Geoffrey. *The awkward warrior: Frank Cousins, his life and times*. London: Davis-Poynter, 1979. xxi, 616p.

1254 **Greaves**, C. D. *James Connolly and trade unionism*. Dublin: Irish Transport & General Workers' Union, 1979. 42p.

1255 **Scotland**, Nigel A. D. 'Zacharias Walker (1843–1900): Norfolk radical and agricultural trade unionist.' *Norfolk Archaeol.*, XXXVII (1979), 212–15.

See also: 66; 132; 890; 1088; 1093; 1150; 1269; 1271; 2352.

8. Shop Stewards and Workshop Organisation

See also Part Three, II, B; Part Three, II, F, 1; Part Five, II and Part Five, VI, B. Material on the more informal aspect of work group organisation is classified at Part Two, I and V. Material on shop steward training is classified at Part Three, II, K and Part Six, II, B, 3, b, iv.

1256 **Goodman**, John Francis Bradshaw. 'The role of the shop steward.' Kessler, S. and Weekes, B. (eds.). *Conflict at work*. 1971. p. 53–74.

1257 **Kessler**, Sydney. 'Shop steward recognition.' *Pers. Manage.*, III, 7 (July 1971), 16–19.

1258 **Trades Union Congress.** *Facilities for shop stewards: a statement of policy*. London: The Authors, 1971. 11p.

1259 **Warren**, A. 'The role of the shop steward in industrial relations.' *Ind. Relat. J.*, II, 3 (Autumn 1971), 52–60.

1260 **Cousins**, Jim. 'The non-militant shop steward.' *New Soc.*, XIX (3 February 1972), 226–8.

1261 **Gallacher**, William and **Campbell**, John R. *Direct action: an outline of workshop and social organisation*. London: Pluto, 1972. 32p. First published in 1919. This edition with a new introduction by Alastair Hatchett.

1262 **Murphy**, John Thomas. *The workers' committee: an outline of its principles and structure*. London: Pluto, 1972. 26p. First published in 1971. This edition with a new introduction by James Hinton.

1263 **Murray**, J. 'The role of the shop steward in industry.' Torrington, Derek P. (ed.). *Handbook of industrial relations*. 1972. p. 269–82.

1264 **Evans**, Edward Owen. 'Cheap at twice the price? Shop stewards and workshop relations in engineering.' Warner, M. (ed.). *Sociology of the workplace*. 1973. p. 82–115.

1265 **Goodman**, John Francis Bradshaw and **Whittingham**, Terence George. *Shop stewards*. London: Pan, 1973. 286p.

Revised and expanded edition of *Shop stewards in British industry*, 1969.

1266 **Hinton**, James. *The first shop stewards' movement*. London: Allen & Unwin, 1973. 352p.

1267 **Marsh**, Arthur Ivor, **Evans**, Edward Owen and **Garcia**, P. 'Trade union workshop organization and facilities in engineering.' Marsh, A. (ed.). *Managers and shop stewards*. 1973. p. 121–34.

1268 **New Left Review.** 'Politics and the shop floor: interview with four shop stewards from a car factory.' *New Left Rev.*, LXXX (July–August 1976), 28–42.

1269 **Pedler**, Malcolm J. 'Shop stewards as leaders.' *Ind. Relat. J.*, IV, 4 (Winter 1973), 43–60.

1270 **Nicholson**, Nigel. *Role stress, role strain and role performance: an empirical study of the shop steward in the engineering industry*. London: Medical Research Council Social and Applied Psychology Unit, 1974.

1271 **Poole**, Michael J. F. 'Towards a sociology of shop stewards.' *Sociol. Rev.*, XXII, 1 (February 1974), 57–82.

1272 **Appleby**, Ken. 'The rank and file movement yesterday and today.' *Int. Soc.* (November 1975), 10–15.

1273 **Higgins**, Jim. 'Democracy at the top?' *Spectator*, 7686 (18 October 1975), 496.

1274 **Incomes Data Services.** *Shop stewards' facilities*. London: The Authors, 1975. 16p. (I.D.S. study 97.)

1275 **Topham**, Tony. 'Approaches to work-place organization in industrial relations.' Coker, E. and Stuttard, G. (eds.). *Industrial studies 1: the key skills*. 1975. p. 75–99

1276 **Friedman**, Henry. *Multi-plant working and trade union organisation*. London: Workers' Educational Association, 1976. 21p. (Studies for trade unionists 218.)

1277 **Macbeath**, Innis. 'Dichotomies of the shop steward.' *Pers. Manage.*, VIII, 8 (August 1976), 18–21.

1278 **Nicholson**, Nigel. 'The role of the shop steward.' *Ind. Relat. J.*, VII, 1 (Spring 1976), 15–26.

1279 **Poole**, Michael J. F. 'Workplace labour relations.' *Ind. Relat. J.*, VII, 3 (Autumn 1976), 31–43.

1280 **Shafto**, T.A.C. *An enquiry into the work and problems of shop stewards in selected establishments of the West Midlands, with special reference to differing expectations on their roles and to the development and implications of shop steward factory organisation*. 1976. (Ph.D. thesis, University of London.)

1281 **Batstone**, Eric, **Boraston**, Ian and **Frenkel**, Stephen. *Shop stewards in action: the organization of workplace conflict and accommodation*. Oxford: Blackwell, 1977. xx, 316p. (Warwick studies in industrial relations.)

1282 **Brown**, William Arthur, **Ebsworth**, Robert and **Terry**, Michael. 'Factors shaping shop steward organisation in Britain.' *Br. J. Ind. Relat.*, XVI, 2 (July 1978), 139–59.

1283 **Buchanan**, R. T. 'The shop steward movement, 1935–47.' *Scott. Labour Hist. Soc. J.*, XII (February 1978), 34–55.

1284 **Fox**, Alan. *Socialism and shop floor power: the British predicament.* London: Fabian Society, 1978. 20p. (Fabian research series 338.)

1285 **Fryer**, Robert H., **Fairclough**, Andrew J. and **Manson**, Tom B. 'Facilities for female shop stewards: the Employment Protection Act and collective agreements.' *Br. J. Ind. Relat.*, XVI, 2 (July 1978), 160–74.

1286 **Partridge**, B. E. 'The activities of shop stewards.' *Ind. Relat. J.*, VIII, 4 (Winter 1977–8), 28–42.

1287 **Wittingslow**, G. E. 'Workers' perception of the shop stewards and their functions: indications of two factors which affect the performance of stewards.' *J. Ind. Affairs*, V,2 (Spring 1978), 34–7.

1288 **Hyman**,Richard. 'The politics of workplace trade unionism: recent tendencies and some problems for theory.' *Cap. Cl.*, VIII (Summer 1979), 54–67.

1289 **Terry**, Michael. 'The emergence of a lay elite? Some recent changes in shop steward organisation.' *Sociologie du Travail*, XXI (1979), 380–96.

See also: 23; 279; 282; 318; 811; 898; 942; 1159; 1392; 1393; 1394; 1396; 1398; 1400; 1411; 1414; 1599; 1788; 1849; 1852; 1881; 1893; 1896; 2669; 2690; 2755; 5316; 5744; 5756; 5758; 6810.

G. POLITICAL ACTION AND THE LABOUR PARTY

This section generally excludes works on the Labour Party which are not concerned with the relationship between it and the trade union movement. See also Part Three, II, A–B; Part Five, VI, A–B; and Part Seven, V.

1290 **Hindess**, Barry. *The decline of working class politics.* London: MacGibbon & Kee, 1971. 191p.

1291 **Leventhal**, Fred M. *Respectable radical: George Howell and Victorian working class politics.* London: Weidenfeld & Nicolson, 1971. xv, 276p.

1292 **McLean**, I. S. *The labour movement in Clydeside politics, 1914–22.* 1971. (D.Phil. thesis, University of Oxford.)

1293 **McPherson**, E. *The trade union as a local pressure group.* 1971. (M.A. thesis, University of Liverpool.)

1294 **Parry**, Cyril. 'Trade unions and politics in north-west Wales, 1870–1914.' Hughes, G. (ed.). *Men of no property.* 1971. p. 80–5.

1295 **Prothero**, I. J. 'London chartism and the trades.' *Econ. Hist. Rev.*, XXIV, 2 (1971), 202–17.

1296 **Quinn**, E. *Trade unions and incomes policy: a study in the attitudes and behaviour of a pressure group.* [1971?]. (M.Sc. thesis, University of Strathclyde.)

1297 **Adelman**, Paul. *The rise of the Labour Party 1800–1945.* London: Longman, 1972. vi, 137p.

1298 **Barbash**, Jack and **Barbash**, Kate. 'United Kingdom: in transition.' *Trade unions and national economic policy.* Baltimore: John Hopkins, 1972. p. 111–44.

1299 **Muller**, William D. 'Trade union M.P.s and parliamentary specialization.' *Polit. Stud.*, XX (September 1972), 317–24.

1300 **Tomison**, Maureen. *The English sickness: the rise of trade union political power.* London: Tom Stacey, 1972. 256p.

1301 **Finer**, S. E. 'The political power of organized labour.' *Gov. Oppos.*, VIII (Autumn 1973), 391–406.

1302 **Heffer**, Eric S. *The class struggle in Parliament: a socialist view of industrial relations.* London: Gollancz, 1973. 350p.

1303 **Jones**, Gareth Stedman. 'Working-class culture and working-class politics in London 1870–1900: notes on the remaking of a working class.' *Soc. Study Labour Hist. Bull.*, XXVII (Autumn 1973), 29–30.

1304 **May**, Timothy C. and **Moran**, Michael J. 'Trade unions as pressure groups.' *New Soc.*, XXV, 570 (6 September 1973), 570–3.

1305 **Muller**, William D. 'Union–M.P. conflict: an overview.' *Parliamentary Aff.*, XXVI (Summer 1973), 336–55.

1306 **Pountney**, Ernie. *For the socialist cause: the class struggle in the times of my forebears and myself.* London: Lawrence & Wishart, 1973. 80p.

1307 **Richter**, Irving. *Political purpose in trade unions.* London: Allen & Unwin, 1973. 258p.

1308 **Simpson**, Bill. *Labour: the unions and the Party: a study of trade unions and the British labour movement.* London: Allen & Unwin, 1973. 256p.

1309 **Minkin**, Lewis. 'The British Labour Party and the trade unions: crisis and compact.' *Ind. Labor Relat. Rev.*, XXVIII, 1 (October 1974), 7–37.

1310 **Stewart**, Margaret. *Protest or power? A study of the Labour Party.* London: Allen & Unwin, 1974. 133p.
See especially Chapter V: 'Trade unions and the Party'.

1311 **Finer**, S. E. 'The unions and power.' *New Soc.*, XXXI (6 February 1975), 329–30.

1312 **Joyce**, Patrick. 'The factory politics of Lancashire in the later 19th century.' *Hist. J.*, XVIII, 3 (1975), 525–53.

1313 **Maehl**, William H. 'The north-eastern miners' struggle for the franchise 1872–4.' *Int. Rev. of Soc. Hist.*, XX, 2 (1975), 198–219.

1314 **May**, Timothy C. *Trade unions and pressure group politics.* Lexington: Heath, 1975. vii, 148p.

1315 **Beackon**, Steven. 'Labour Party politics and the working class.' *Br. J. Polit. Sci.*, VI, 2 (April 1976), 231–8.

1316 **Farnham**, David. 'The labour alliance: reality or myth?' *Parliamentary Aff.*, XXIX (Winter 1976), 37–46.

1317 **Mitchell**, Arthur. *Labour in Irish politics, 1890–1930: the Irish labour movement in an age of revolution.* Dublin: Irish Academic Press, 1976. 317p.

1318 **Taylor**, Robert. 'The uneasy alliance: Labour and the unions.' *Pol. Q.*, XLVII (October–December 1976), 398–407.

1319 **Callott**, M. 'The organisation of political support for labour in the North of England: the work of Margaret Gibb, 1929–57.' *N.E. Group Study Labour Hist. Bull.*, XI (1977), 13–27.

1320 **Gilmore**, G. *Labour and the Republican movement.* Dublin: Repsol, 1977. 15p.

1321 **Lane**, J., **Loughton**, Alf and **Wicks**, Harry. *This was our heyday.* London: Battersea Labour Party, 1977. 16p.
    Bound with Groves, Reg. *The General Strike in Battersea.*

1322 **Marshall**, C. R. *Levels of industrial militancy and the political radicalization of the Durham miners, 1885–1914.* 1977. (M.A. thesis, University of Durham.)

1323 **Muller**, William D. *The 'kept men'? The first century of trade union representation in the British House of Commons, 1874–1975.* London: Harvester Press, 1977. xx, 283p.

1324 **Scase**, Richard. *Social democracy in capitalist society: working class politics in Britain and Sweden.* London: Croom Helm, 1977. 104p.

1325 **Behrens**, Robert. 'Blinkers for the cart-horse: the Conservative Party and the trade unions, 1974–1978.' *Pol. Q.*, XLIX (October–December 1978), 457–66.

1326 **Carr**, F. W. *Engineering workers and the rise of Labour in Coventry 1914–1939.* 1978. (Ph.D. thesis, University of Warwick.)

1327 **Gill**, Ken. 'Unions, governments and party politics.' *Pers. Manage.*, X, 10 (October 1978), 42–4, 55

1328 **McCord**, Norman. 'The role of history.' Institute of Economic Affairs. *Trade unions: public goods or public bads?* 1978. p. 17–18.

1329 **Martin**, David E. 'The instruments of the people?: The Parliamentary Labour Party in 1906.' Martin, D. and Rubinstein, D. (eds.). *Ideology and the labour movement.* 1978. 125–46.

1330 **Martin**, David E. and **Rubinstein**, David (eds.). *Ideology and the labour movement: essays presented to John Saville.* London: Croom Helm, 1978. 276p.

1331 **Minkin**, Lewis. *The Labour Party conference: a study in the politics of intra-party democracy.* Manchester: Manchester U.P., 1978. xv, 448p.

1332 **Minkin**, Lewis. 'The party connection: divergence and convergence in the British labour movement.' *Gov. Oppos.*, XIII (Autumn 1978), 458–84.

1333 **Morgan**, Austen. *Politics, the labour movement and the working class in Belfast, 1905–23.* 1978. (Ph.D. thesis, Queen's University, Belfast.)

1334 **Peacock**, Alan. 'Trade unions and economic policy.' Institute of Economic Affairs. *Trade unions: public goods or public bads?* 1978. p. 119–25.

1335 **Prothero**, Iorweth J. *Artisans and politics in early nineteenth century London.* Folkestone: Dawson, 1978. 336p.

1336 **Rubinstein**, David. 'The Independent Labour Party and the Yorkshire Miners: the Barnsley by-election of 1897.' *Int. Rev. of Soc. Hist.*, XXIII, 1 (1978), 102–34.

1337 **Trodd**, G. N. *Political change and the working class in Blackburn and Burnley, 1880–1914.* 1978. (Ph.D. thesis, University of Lancaster.)

1338 **Burton**, John. *The Trojan horse.* Leesbury, Va.: Adam Smith Institute, 1979. 72p.

1339 **Moran**, Michael J. 'The Conservative Party and the trade unions since 1974.' *Pol. Stud.*, XXVII, 1 (1979), 38–53.

1340 **Moran**, Michael J. *Trade unions and politics: past patterns, future problems.* Hull: University of Hull, Department of Politics, 1979. ii, 20p. (Hull papers in politics 4.)

1341 **Taylor**, Ann and **Fyrth**, Hubert Jim. *Political action.* London: Arrow, 1979. 121p. (Trade union industrial studies.)

See also: 71; 690; 732; 735; 777; 787; 864; 876; 886; 904; 976; 1038; 1226; 1284; 2122; 2255; 4294; 6696; 6712; 6878.

H. TRADE UNIONISM AND COMMUNISM

This section generally excludes works on Communism which are not specifically concerned with the relationship between it and the trade union movement. See also Part Three, II, A – B; and Part Five, VI, B.

1342 **Bor**, M. H. *The Socialist League and the labour movement (1932 to 1937).* [1971?] (M.A. thesis, University of Wales, Bangor.)

1343 **Holton**, Robert J. *Syndicalism and its impact in Britain, with particular reference to Merseyside, 1910–1914.* [1971?] (D.Phil. thesis, University of Sussex.)

1344 **Barratt Brown**, Michael. *From labourism to socialism: the political economy of labour in the 1970's.* Nottingham: Spokesman, 1972. 252p.

1345 **Ferris**, Paul. *New militants: crisis in the trade unions.* Harmondsworth: Penguin, 1972. 112p.

1346 **Hyman**, Richard. 'Communist industrial policy in the 1920s.' *Int. Soc.*, LIII (October–December 1972), 14–22.

1347 **Aims of Industry.** *Reds under the bed.* London: The Authors, 1974. 12p.

1348 **Economic League**. *The agitators: extremist activities in British industry.* London: The League, 1974. 75p. (Service to industry series 3.)

1349 **Trory**, Ernie. *Between the wars: recollections of a communist organiser.* Brighton: Crabtree Press, 1974. 159p.

1350 **Challinor**, Raymond. 'Memories of a militant.' *N. E. Group Study Labour Hist. Bull.*, IX (October 1975), 34–42.

1351 **Croucher**, Richard. 'The Coventry branch of the Minority Movement.' *Soc. Study Labour Hist. Bull.*, XXX (Spring 1975), 37–41.

1352 **Egan**, David. 'The Swansea conference of the British council of soldiers' and workers' delegates, July 1917: reactions to the Russian revolution of February 1917 and the anti-war movement in South Wales.' *Llafur*, I, 4 (Summer 1975), 12–37.

1353 **Frow**, Eddie and **Frow**, Ruth. *Frank Bright: miner, Marxist and Communist organiser, 1891–1944.* Manchester: North West History Group of the Communist Party, [1975?]. 9p.

1354 **Hinton**, James and **Hyman**, Richard. *Trade unions and revolution: the industrial politics of the early British Communist Party.* London: Pluto, 1975. 78p.

1355 **Croucher**, Richard. *Communist politics and shop stewards in engineering, 1935–46.* 1977. (Ph.D. thesis, University of Warwick.)

1356 **Englander**, David. *The diary of Fred Knee.* Nottingham: Society for the Study of Labour History, 1977. 122p.

1357 **MacIntyre**, Stuart. 'British labour, marxism and working class apathy in the nineteen-twenties.' *Hist. J.*, XX, 2 (June 1977), 479–96.

1358 **McShane**, Harry and **Smith**, Joan. *Harry McShane: no mean fighter.* London: Pluto, 1977. 282p.

1359 **Nassibian**, A. *Attitudes on Clydeside to the Russian Revolution, 1917–1924.* 1978. (M.Litt. thesis, University of Strathclyde.)

1360 **Rabinovitch**, Victor. *British Marxist socialism and trade unionism: the attitudes, experiences and activities of the Social-Democratic Federation, 1884–1901.* 1978. (D.Phil. thesis, University of Sussex.)

1361 **Davies**, R. S. W. 'The Liverpool Labour Party and the Liverpool working class, 1900–39.' *N. W. Labour Hist. Soc. Bull.*, VI (1979–80), 2–14.

See also: 1229; 2206; 2212; 2222; 2230.

I. TRADE UNIONISM AND RELIGION

1362 **McMullan**, G. *The development of clerical trade unionism in the North of Ireland during the twentieth century.* [1971?] (Ph.D. thesis, Queen's University, Belfast.)

1363 **Moore**, Robert. *Religion and the Durham miners.* Durham: Wesley Historical Society, 1973. 8p. (Wesley Historical Society, North East Branch occasional publications 2.)

1364 **Moore**, Robert. *Pit-men, preachers and politics: the effects of Methodism in a Durham mining community.* Cambridge: Cambridge U.P., 1974. xi, 292p.

1365 **Taylor**, Robert. 'Shopfloor Ulster.' *New Soc.*, XXVIII (23 May 1974), 433–4.

1366 **Brown**, Kenneth D. 'Non-conformity and the British labour movement.' *J. Soc. Hist.*, IX (Winter 1975), 113–20.

1367 **Gurden**, Helen. *Trade unionism, education and religion: aspects of the social history of Warwickshire agricultural labourers in the 1870's.* 1975. (M.Phil. thesis, University of Warwick.)

1368 **Gurden**, Helen. 'Primitive methodism and agricultural trade unionism in Warwickshire, 1872–5.' *Soc. Study Labour Hist. Bull.*, XXXIII (Autumn 1976), 4–6.

1369 **Scotland**, Nigel A. D. 'Methodism and the "revolt of the field" in East Anglia, 1892–96.' *Wesley Hist. Soc. Proc.*, XLI, I (February 1977), 2–11; 2 (June 1977), 39–42.

See also: 1543; 2405.

J. TRADE UNIONISM AND INTERNATIONAL AFFAIRS

See also Part Three, II, B.

1370 **Beever**, Colin. 'Europe, the unions and social policy.' *New Community*, I, I (October 1971), 43–6.

1371 **Sweet**, Colin. *The White Paper answered.* London: British Peace Committee, for Trade Unions against the Common Market, 1971. 14p.

1372 **Trades Union Congress.** *Britain and the E.E.C.: report of the T.U.C. General Council to the 103rd annual trades union congress.* London: T.U.C., 1971. 23p.

1373 **Harrod**, J. *Trade union foreign policy: a study of British and American trade union activities in Jamaica.* London: Macmillan, 1972. 485p.

1374 **Levinson**, Charles. *International trade unionism.* London: Allen & Unwin, 1972. 402p.

1375 **Radice**, Giles (ed.). *International industrial relations.* London: Industrial Society, 1972. 20p.

1376 **Industrial Research and Information Services.** *Trade unions and the E.E.C.* London: The Authors, 1973. 35p.

1377 **Taylor**, Robert. 'Playing hard to get: British trade unions and the European Common Market.' *New Soc.*, XXIV (17 May 1973), 369–70.

1378 **Young**, James D. 'Changing images of American democracy and the Scottish labour movement.' *Int. Rev. of Soc. Hist.*, XVIII (1973), 69–89.

1379 **Willatt**, Norris. *Multinational unions.* London: Financial Times, 1974. 141p.

1380 **Cork Workers' Club.** *Irish labour and its*

international relations in the era of the Second International and the Bolshevik revolution. Cork: The Authors, [1975?]. 56p.

1381 **Gupta**, Partha Sarathi. *Imperialism and the British labour movement 1914–1964.* London: Macmillan, 1975. xviii, 454p.

1382 **Keserich**, Charles. 'The British Labour press and Italian fascism 1922–5.' *J. Contemp. Hist.*, x, 4 (October 1975), 579–90.

1383 **Calhoun**, Daniel Fairchild. *The United Front: the TUC and the Russians, 1923–28.* Cambridge: Cambridge U.P., 1976. 450p.

1384 **Revolutionary Communist Group**. *Ireland: British labour and British imperialism.* London: The Authors, 1976. 33p.

1385 **Hirsch**, Fred and **Fletcher**, Richard. *The CIA and the labour movement.* Nottingham: Spokesman, 1977. 71p.

1386 **Lovell**, John. 'The Irish and the London dockers.' *Soc. Study Labour Hist. Bull.*, xxxv (Autumn 1977), 16–18.

1387 **Sekules**, E. *The Miners' International Federation, 1945–1967: a case study of international trade unionism.* 1977. (M.Phil. thesis, London School of Economics.)

1388 **Drake**, P. D. *Labour and Spain: British Labour's response to the Spanish Civil War, with particular reference to the Labour movement in Birmingham.* 1977–8. (M.Litt. thesis, University of Birmingham.)

1389 **Malament**, Barbara. 'British labour and Roosevelt's New Deal: the response of the left and the unions.' *J. Br. Stud.*, xvii, 2 (Spring 1978), 136–67.

1390 **Northrup**, Herbert R. and **Rowan**, Richard L. 'Multinational unionism.' *Ind. Relat. J.*, ix, 1 (Spring 1978), 27–36.

1391 **Steinberg**, David A. 'The workers' sport internationals 1920–28.' *J. Contemp. Hist.*, xiii (April 1978), 233–51.

1392 **Thomson**, Don and **Larson**, Rodney. *Where were you, brother? An account of trade union imperialism.* London: War on Want, 1978. 138p.

See Also: 30; 688; 1428; 1749; 2206.

K. TRADE UNION EDUCATION

This section is concerned with the education of trade unionists by trade unions or other organisations. It is not concerned with workers' education more broadly defined or with adult education. Hence material relating to such bodies as the Workers' Educational Association has generally been excluded. See also Part Six, II, B, 3, b, iv; and Part Six, IV, D, 2.

1393 **Warren**, A. 'The aims and methods of the education and training of shop stewards: a case study.' *Ind. Relat. J.*, ii, 1 (Spring 1971), 35–53.

1394 **Sutherland**, J. R. S. (ed.). *Shop stewards training: trade union symposium.* Solihull: A. J. Parkinson, 1972. 28p.

1395 **Trades Union Congress**. *Training full-time officers.* London: T. U. C., 1972 50p.

1396 **Withnall**, A. 'Education and training for shop stewards: a reassessment.' *Ind. Relat. J.*, iii, 1 (Spring 1972), 40–50.

1397 **Brown**, William Arthur and **Lawson**, M. 'The training of trade union officers.' *Br. J. Ind. Relat.*, xi, 3 (November 1973), 431–48.

1398 **Corfield**, Alan John. *Shop stewards' and representatives' training: teaching manual.* London: W.E.A., 1973.
Revised edition.

1399 **Silver**, H. 'Education and the labour movement: a critical review of the literature.' *Hist. Educ.*, ii, 2 (June 1973), 173–202.

1400 **Pedler**, Malcolm J. 'Training implications of the shop steward's leadership role.' *Ind. Relat. J.*, v, 1 (Spring 1974), 57–70.

1401 **British Broadcasting Corporation**. *Trade union studies: a course for active trade unionists.* London: BBC, 1975. 80p.

1402 **Coker**, Ed. 'On being a trade union student.' Coker, E. and Stuttard, G. (eds.). *Industrial studies 1: the key skills.* 1975. p. 13–35.

1403 **Coker**, Ed and **Stuttard**, Charles Geoffrey (eds.). *Industrial studies 1: the key skills.* London: Arrow, 1975. 168p.

1404 **Hedderwick**, Karl. *Statistics for bargainers.* London: Hutchinson/Arrow, 1975. 96p. (Trade union industrial studies.)

1405 **Houlton**, Bob. *The activists' handbook: a guide to organizing and communication.* London: Hutchinson/Arrow, 1975. 82p. (Trade union industrial studies.)

1406 **Hutton**, Joyce and **Hutton**, Bill. *Calculating.* London: Hutchinson/Arrow, 1975. 92p. (Trade union industrial studies.)

1407 **Stuttard**, Charles Geoffrey. *Learning from industrial relations.* London: Longman, 1975. viii, 147p.

1408 **Stuttard**, Charles Geoffrey. 'Studying together in an industrial context.' Coker, E. and Stuttard, G. (eds.). *Industrial studies 1: the key skills.* 1975. p. 37–50.

1409 **Topham**, Tony. *The organized worker.* London: Hutchinson/Arrow, 1975, 96p. (Trade union industrial studies.)

1410 **Lewis**, Richard. 'The South Wales miners and the Ruskin College strike of 1909.' *Llafur*, ii, 1 (Spring 1976), 57–72.

1411 **Lover**, J. G. 'Shop steward training: conflicting objectives and needs.' *Ind. Relat. J.*, vii, 1 (Spring 1976), 27–39.

1412 **Macbeath**, Innis. 'Putting over the paradox of shop stewardship.' *Pers. Manage.*, viii, 8 (August 1976), 18–21.

1413 **Neville**, Robert G. 'The Yorkshire miners and education, 1881–1930.' *J. Educ. Adm. Hist.*, viii, 2 (July 1976), 30–7.

1414 **Sawbridge**, D. and **Keithley**, G. R. 'Industrial relations training for shop stewards: training without objectives.' *Manage. Decis.*, xiv, 3 (1976), 148–60.

1415 **Yorke**, Paul. *Ruskin College, 1899–1909: education and the working class.* Oxford: Ruskin College, 1977. 41p.

1416 **Millar**, J. P. M. *The Labour College Movement.* London: National Council of Labour Colleges [1979?]. iv, 301p.

'Despite having made a major contribution to the preparation of this work, Dr. Lowe has chosen to withdraw his name as joint author.'

1417 **Roberts**, Higdon C. 'Steward training in Great Britain: a view from the Midlands.' *Labor Stud. J.*, IV, 1 (1979), 3–21.

See also: 1754; 3811; 3821.

PART FOUR

EMPLOYERS AND THEIR ORGANISATION

I. EMPLOYERS' ASSOCIATIONS

This section includes material on those employers' associations which perform industrial relations functions. Works relating to employers' associations which are exclusively concerned with 'trade' matters are generally excluded. See also Part Three, I.

1418 **Grant**, Wyn P. and **Marsh**, D. 'The Confederation of British Industry.' *Pol. Stud.*, XIX, 4 (1971), 403–15.

1419 **Jukes**, Martin. *The role of the industrial federation in the 1970's*. London: Industrial, Educational and Research Foundation [1971?]. 9p.

1420 **Commission of Inquiry into Industrial and Commercial Representation**. *Report by the Chairman, Lord Devlin*. London: Association of British Chambers of Commerce and the Confederation of British Industry, 1972. 127p.

1421 **Commission on Industrial Relations.** *Employers' organisations and industrial relations.* London: H.M.S.O., 1972. 74p. (CIR study 1.)

1422 **Blank**, Stephen. *Industry and government in Britain: the Federation of British Industries in politics 1945–1965.* Lexington: Health, 1973. xiii, 256p.

1423 **Grant**, Wyn P. 'British employers' associations and the enlarged Community.' *J. Common Mark. Stud.*, XI, 4 (June 1973), 276–86.

1424 **Griffin**, Alan Ramsay and **Griffin**, C. P. 'The role of coal owners' associations in the East Midlands in the nineteenth century.' *Renaissance Mod. Stud.*, XVII (1973), 95–121.

1425 **Wigham**, Eric Leonard. *Power to manage: a history of the Engineering Employers' Federation.* London: Macmillan, 1973. x, 326p.

1426 **Gospel**, Howard F. *Employers' organizations: their growth and function in the British system of industrial relations in the period 1918–1939.* 1975. (Ph.D. thesis, London School of Economics.)

1427 **Bean**, Ron. 'Employers' associations in the Port of Liverpool, 1890–1914.' *Int. Rev. of Soc. Hist.*, XXI, 3 (1976), 358–82.

1428 **Jackson**, Peter J. and **Sisson**, Keith. 'Employers' confederations in Sweden and the U.K. and the significance of industrial infrastructure.' *Br. J. Ind. Relat.*, XIV, 3 (November 1976), 306–23.

1429 **Williams**, L. J. 'The coalowners of South Wales 1873–80: problems of unity.' *Welsh Hist. Rev.*, VIII (June 1976), 75–93.

1430 **Grant**, Wyn P. and **Marsh**, David. *The Confederation of British Industry.* London: Hodder & Stoughton, 1977. vii, 226p.

1431 **Sisson**, Keith. 'Why employers' organisations are important.' *Econ. Humanisme*, XXXVI, 4 (July–August 1977), 65–73. See also: 733; 768; 1680; 1759; 1786.

II. PERSONNEL MANAGEMENT

A. GENERAL

This section includes general works on the development of personnel administration as an explicit management function; business leadership; and ideologies of employers, particularly those aspects which relate to the management of employees. Material on such technical aspects of personnel management as interviewing, selection, and testing techniques has generally been excluded; these topics are covered by the Institute of Personnel Management, *I.P.M. Bibliography* (London: I.P.M., 1974 onwards). More general works on manpower planning at firm and industry level have been classified at Part Six, II, B. Business histories have generally been excluded. Some of the general works in Part One, III; Part Three, II, A; Part Five, I; and Part Five, V, A also contain material on employer attitudes towards labour. See also Part Five, VI, A, C, and D for employers' views on joint consultation and industrial democracy. Material on attitudes to work, behaviour at work, the effect of work on attitudes and behaviour, and work organisation is included in Part Two. See also Part Six, IV, C.

1432 **Armstrong**, Sir William. *Personnel management in the Civil Service: a speech . . . to the Institute of Personnel Management.* London: H.M.S.O., 1971. 28p.

1433 **Bevan**, G. 'Motivating junior personnel specialists.' *Pers. Manage.*, III, 12 (December 1971), 33–4.

1434 **Brown**, Pamela. 'The computer and personnel management.' *Pers. Manage.*, III, 9 (September 1971), 24–7.

1435 **Cooke**, P. J. D. 'Inflation and personnel: how do they relate?' *Pers. Manage.*, III, 10 (October 1971), 22–5.

1436 **Domach**, M. 'Personnel planning and information systems.' *Long Range Plann.*, IV (December 1971), 12–16.

1437 **Fraser**, John Munro. *Introduction to personnel management.* London: Nelson, 1971. x, 198p.

1438 **Gordon**, Jon and **Swann**, Humphrey. 'People at work.' *Pers. Manage.*, III, 3 (March 1971), 18–22.

1439 **Hill**, Paul. *Towards a new philosophy of management: the company development programme of Shell UK Limited.* Epping: Gower, 1971. xiv, 255p.

1440 **Lyons**, Terry P. *The personnel function in a changing environment.* London: Pitman, 1971. xii, 224p.

1441 **McFarland**, Dalton Edward (ed.). *Personnel management: selected readings.* Harmondsworth: Penguin, 1971. 407p.

1442 **Marsh**, Arthur Ivor. 'Staffing of industrial relations management in the engineering industry.' *Ind. Relat. J.*, II, 2 (Summer 1971). 14–23.

1443 **Myers**, Charles A. 'The changing role of the personnel manager.' *Pers. Rev.*, I, 1 (Autumn 1971), 12–19.

1444 **Nuttall**, John. 'Towards saner personnel systems.' *Pers. Manage.*, III, 2 (February 1971), 30–2.

1445 **Springall**, Joan. *Personnel records and the computer: a survey.* London: Institute of Personnel Management and Industrial Society, 1971. 44p.

1446 **Stokes**, R. 'A company fit to live in.' *Pers. Manage.*, III, 8 (August 1971), 33–5.

1447 **Thomason**, George Frederick. *The management of industrial relations: an inaugural lecture.* Cardiff: University College, 1971. 54p.

1448 **Wilcock**, Stephen. 'Personnel strategy and organization development: a case study.' *Manage. Decis.*, IX (Spring 1971), 39–45.

1449 **Wood**, B. 'Staffing problems in the reorganization of local government.' *Public Adm.*, XLVIII (Autumn 1971), 279–89.

1450 **Appleyard**, John. 'Towards a European view.' *Pers. Manage.*, IV, 12 (December 1972), 22–5.

1451 **Bennett**, Roger D., **Dawson**, R. O. and **Maule**, P. G. 'Putting research to work.' *Pers. Manage.*, IV, 3 (March 1972), 23–5.

1452 **Bourn**, Colin J. 'Is money the answer to labour problems?' *Pers. Manage.*, IV, 3 (March 1972), 16–20.

1453 **Cherns**, Albert B. 'Personnel management and the social sciences.' *Pers. Rev.*, I, 2 (Spring 1972), 4–10.

1454 **Chruden**, H. J. and **Sherman**, A.W. *Personnel practices of American companies in Europe.* New York: American Management Association, 1972. ix, 148p.

1455 **Coates**, Jack. 'European integration and the personnel manager.' *Pers. Rev.*, I, 4 (Autumn 1972), 4–12.

1456 **Foster**, J. G. and **Staples**, F. W. 'A study in staff relations.' *Pers. Manage.*, IV, 3 (March 1972), 34–6.

1457 **Hopwood**, Anthony George. 'The relationship between accounting and personnel management.' *Pers. Rev.*, II, 1 (Spring 1972), 40–7.

1458 **Lansbury**, Russell. 'Managing the professional.' *Pers. Manage.*, IV, 4 (April 1972), 24–7.

1459 **Howells**, George William. *Executive aspects of man management.* London: Pitman, 1972. xiv, 173p.

1460 **Kean**, J. 'Management by consent.' *Ind. Soc.*, LIV, 1 (January 1972), 7–8; LIV, 2 (February 1972), 10–11.

1461 **Lawrence**, Kenneth Charles. *Personnel management.* London: Hutchinson, 1972. 78p.

1462 **Lawrence**, Susanne. 'Personnel in small firms.' *Pers. Manage.*, IV, 9 (September 1972), 24–8.

1463 **Lee**, Jack. *The contribution of the personnel manager.* London: Working Together Campaign, 1972. 14p.

1464 **Lupton**, Tom. *Industrial behaviour and personnel management.* London: Institute of Personnel Management, 1972. 50p.

1465 **Lyons**, R. 'Working with the union.' Torrington, Derek P. (ed.). *Handbook of industrial relations.* 1972. p. 255–67.

1466 **Marks**, Winifred Rose. *Preparing an employee handbook.* London: Institute of Personnel Management, 1972. viii, 53p.

1467 **Millard**, Graham. *Personnel management in hospitals.* London: Institute of Personnel Management, 1972. 122p.

1468 **Neal**, Sir Leonard Francis. 'Management responsibility.' Torrington, Derek P. (ed.). *Handbook of industrial relations.* 1972. p. 109–20.

1469 **Peach**, Len. 'Personnel management: art or science?' *Pers. Manage.*, IV, 1 (January 1972), 26–9.

1470 **Singer**, Edwin J. and **Ramsden**, J. *Human resources: obtaining results from people at work.* London: McGraw-Hill, 1972. v, 197p.

1471 **Thomas**, John M. and **Bennis**, Warren G. (eds.). *Management of change and conflict: selected readings.* Harmondsworth: Penguin, 1972. 507p.

1472 **Thomas**, Raymond E. *Challenge and opportunity: the employer's role in a changing environment.* London: Working Together Campaign, 1972. 12p.

1473 **Torrington**, Derek Peter. *Face to face: techniques for handling the personal encounter at work.* Epping: Gower, 1972. 95p.

1474 **Torrington**, Derek Peter. 'Management and industrial relations.' Torrington, Derek P. (ed.). *Handbook of industrial relations.* 1972. p. 3–10.

1475 **Torrington**, Derek Peter. 'Personnel management and the Code of Practice.' Torrington, Derek P. (ed.). *Handbook of industrial relations.* 1972. p. 49–63.

1476 **Wilson**, A. C. B. 'Human and organization problems in corporate planning.' *Long Range Plann.*, v, 1 (March 1972), 67–71.

1477 **Wishart**, D. 'Computers in personnel management.' *Pers. Rev.*, II, 1 (Spring 1972), 48–55.

1478 **Barber**, David. *Basic personnel procedures: guidance on setting up a personnel department.* London: Institute of Personnel Management, 1973. 52p.

1479 **Commission on Industrial Relations**. *Role of management in industrial relations.* London: H.M.S.O., 1973. v, 40p. (Report 34.)

1480 **Cooper**, K. R. 'Personnel management: freedom and control.' *Manage. Serv. Gov.*, XXVIII, 4 (November 1973), 117–81.

1481 **Cuthbert**, Norman H. 'Industrial relations and the development of company policies.' Cuthbert, N. and Hawkins, K. (eds.). *Company industrial relations policies.* 1973. p. 1–33.

1482 **Cyriax**, Oliver (ed.). *Who's who in personnel administration and industrial relations.* Epping: Gower, 1973. 518p.

1483 **Fletcher**, Colin. 'The end of management.' Child, J. (ed.). *Man and organization.* 1973. 135–57.

1484 **Garnett**, John. *Work challenge.* London: Industrial Society, 1973. 96p.

1485 **Garnett**, John. *Policies towards people: the Sir Frederic Hooper Essay award, 1973.* London: Foundation for Business Responsibilities, [1973].

1486 **George**, Pat. *Redundancy counselling.* London: Industrial Society, 1973.

1487 **Grant**, Jean Valerie and **Smith**, Geoffrey John. *Personnel administration and industrial relations.* London: Longman, 1973. x, 337p.

1488 **Hebden**, H. J. 'Controlling and evaluating personnel strategy: the approach of Massey-Ferguson.' Cuthbert, N. and Hawkins, K. (eds.). *Company industrial relations policies.* 1973. p. 247–69.

1489 **Hopps**, R. L. 'Long-range planning for personnel.' *Build. Soc. Inst. Q.*, XXVII, 3 (July 1973), 157–64.

1490 **Incomes Data Services**. *Personnel aspects of V.A.T.* London: I.D.S., 1973. 16p. (Study 60.)

1491 **Jenkins**, Clive. 'Is personnel still underpowered?' *Pers. Manage.*, v, 6 (June 1973), 34–5.

1492 **Laing**, Hector. *United Biscuits: an approach to human relations.* London: United Biscuits, 1973. 12p.

1493 **Marsh**, John. 'To make working and living more acceptable.' *Ind. Participation*, DLII (Summer 1973), 22–5.

1494 **Miner**, John Burnham and **Miner**, Mary Green. *Personnel and industrial relations: a managerial approach.* London: Macmillan, 1973. xii, 595p.
Second edition.

1495 **Molander**, Christopher F. 'Organisational development and industrial relations.' Cuthbert, N. and Hawkins, K. (eds.). *Company industrial relations policies.* 1973. p. 134–44.

1496 **Norton**, A. and **Long**, Joyce. 'Lessons for personnel in local government.' *Pers. Manage.*, v, 9 (September 1973), 34–8.

1497 **Parkinson**, Cyril Northcote. 'Managerial attitudes.' Parkinson, C. N. (ed.). *Industrial disruption.* 1973. p. 156–69.

1498 **Personnel Management**. 'The largest personnel department of them all.' *Pers. Manage.*, v, 6 (June 1973), 18–22.

1499 **Poole**, Michael J. F. 'A back seat for personnel.' *Pers. Manage.*, v, 5 (May 1973), 38–41.

1500 **Roff**, H. E. 'Developments of a decade.' *Pers. Manage.*, v, 6 (June 1973), 23–5.

1501 **Sidney**, E., **Brown**, M. and **Argyle**, Michael. *Skills with people: a guide for managers.* London: Hutchinson, 1973. 232p.

1502 **Womack**, Bob, **Handel**, John and **Cuming**, Maurice. 'Personnel management in the public service.' *Pers. Manage.*, v, 2 (February 1973), 22–5.

1503 **Zentner, P.** 'Inside insurance.' *Ind. Soc.*, LV, 5 (May 1973), 10–12.
Concerns personnel management in the insurance industry.

1504 **Appleby**, Robert. 'Management and the people who do the work.' *Prod. Eng.*, LII, 12 (December 1973), 441–6; LIII, 1 (January 1974), 19–25.

1505 **Boella**, M. J. *Personnel management in the hotel and catering industry.* London: Barrie & Jenkins, 1974. xiv, 167p.

1506 **Crane**, Donald P. *Personnel management: a situational approach.* London: Wadsworth, 1974. 242p.

1507 **Eccles**, A. J. 'Serving two masters in the modern organization.' *Manage. Decis.*, XII, 5 (1974), 288–98.

1508 **Fox**, Alan. *Man mismanagement.* London: Hutchinson, 1974. 178p.

1509 **Gardner**, J. J. and **Gillespie**, L. R. 'Personnel management in Northern Ireland.' *Pers. Manage.*, VI, 11 (November 1974), 24–8.

1510 **Hague**, Hawdon (ed.). *Human and industrial relations: a working handbook.* London: Kluwer-Hamp, 1974. 3 v.
Loose leaf service.

1511 **Heesom**, A. J. 'Entrepreneurial paternalism: the third Lord Londonderry (1778–1854) and the coal trade.' *Durham Univ. J.*, LXVI (June 1974), 238–56.

1512 **Holland**, B. J. 'Accountability for staff management.' *Manage. Serv. Gov.*, XXIX, 2 (May 1974), 85–90.

1513 **Institute of Manpower Studies**. *The management of professionals*. London: The Institute, 1974. 27p.

1514 **Lang**, D. 'Project control comes to personnel.' *Pers. Manage.*, VI, 5 (May 1974), 27–30.

1515 **Mackechnie**, Geoffrey. *Labour relations policies within the firm*. Dublin: Irish Productivity Centre, 1974. (Human sciences in industry studies 10.)

1516 **Naylor**, Rachel and **Torrington**, Derek Peter (eds.). *Administration of personnel policies*. Epping: Gower, 1974. xxii, 519p.

1517 **Sadler**, P. 'Personnel policy in a changing society.' *Pers. Manage.*, VI, 4 (April 1974), 26–9.

1518 **Taylor**, Linda King. 'Management of change: an example from local government.' *Ind. Commer. Train.*, VI, 1 (January 1974), 16–21.

1519 **Torrington**, Derek Peter (ed.). *Encyclopaedia of personnel management*. London: Gower, 1974. x, 474p.

1520 **Baker**, R. and **Wood**, G. 'Benefits of being small.' *Pers. Manage.*, VII, 2 (February 1975), 29–31.

1521 **Campion**, Michael. 'Personnel management goes to school.' *Pers. Manage.*, VII, 7 (July 1975), 22–5, 37.

1522 **Farnham**, David and **Peacock**, A. 'Raising I. R. on the council agenda.' *Pers. Manage.*, VII, 12 (December 1975), 25–9.

1523 **Fowler**, Alan G. *Personnel management in local government*. London: Institute of Personnel Management, 1975. 319p.

1524 **Henstridge**, John. 'Personnel management: a framework for analysis.' *Pers. Rev.*, IV, 1 (Winter 1975), 47–53.

1525 **Legge**, Karen. 'The personnel specialist's dilemma.' *Ind. Relat. J.*, VI, 3 (Autumn 1975), 51–65.

1526 **Mayhew**, R. J. 'Personnel management on the campus.' *Pers. Manage.*, VII, 6 (June 1975), 29–33.

1527 **Miller**, Harry. *Management and the working environment*. London: Hutchinson Benham, 1975. 139p.

1528 **Musgrave**, T. 'The practice of personnel management.' *Public Finance Account.*, II, 5 (May 1975), 148–52.

1529 **Peach**, Len. 'Personnel management by objectives.' *Pers. Manage.*, VII, 3 (March 1975), 20–3, 39.

1530 **Prentice**, Gordon. 'Managing a scattered workforce.' *Pers. Manage.*, VII, 4 (April 1975), 30–3.

1531 **Randall**, F. E. 'Personnel record information system for management.' *Manage. Serv. Gov.*, XXX, 3 (August 1975), 121–9.

1532 **Stewart**, R. 'Classifying different types of managerial jobs.' *Pers. Rev.*, IV, 2 (Spring 1975), 25–30.

1533 **Thomason**, George F. *Textbook of personnel management*. London: Institute of Personnel Management, 1975. 472p.
Second edition, 1976. 536p.
Third edition, 1978. 594p.

1534 **Yarmie**, A. H. *The captains of industry in mid-Victorian Britain: a study of their social, industrial and political attitudes towards labour*. 1975. (Ph.D. thesis, King's College, University of London.)

1535 **Allen**, Victor Leonard. 'Marxism and the personnel manager.' *Pers. Manage.*, VIII, 12 (December 1976), 18–22.

1536 **Brearley**, Arthur. *The control of staff-related overhead*. London: Macmillan, 1976. x, 181p.

1537 **Cuthbert**, Norman H. and **Whitaker**, A. 'Industrial relations: a matter of policy.' *Pers. Manage.*, VIII, 8 (August 1976), 29–33.

1538 **Downs**, P. 'Challenge at Woolworth's.' *Ind. Soc.*, LVIII, 6 (November–December 1976), 5–6.

1539 **Elliott**, C. K. and **Margerison**, Charles J. 'The personnel manager and his subordinates.' *Pers. Rev.*, V, 3 (Summer 1976), 49–51.

1540 **Gray**, Jerry L. (ed.). *The Glacier Project: concepts and critiques – selected readings on the Glacier theories of organization and management*. London: Heinemann, 1976. xv, 452p.

1541 **Honey**, P. 'On the trail of the personnel professional.' *Pers. Manage.*, VIII, 4 (April 1976), 33–5.

1542 **Owen**, Trevor. 'Getting the best out of Europe.' *Pers. Manage.*, VIII, 2 (February 1976), 16–20.

1543 **Prentice**, Gordon. 'The message is the mission.' *Pers. Manage.*, VIII, 3 (March 1976), 33–6.

1544 **Sieff**, Sir Marcus. 'Freedom to lead.' *Ind. Soc.*, LVIII, 1 (January–February 1976), 4–5.

1545 **Stewart**, R. 'Patterns of work and the dictates of time.' *Pers. Manage.*, VIII, 6 (June 1976), 25–8.

1546 **Whittaker**, D. J. 'Power and accountability in business: the role of management: experiment at Leyland.' *Month*, IX (July 1976), 238–42.

1547 **Bamforth**, J. M. 'What future for the personnel function?' *Pers. Manage.*, IX, 12 (December 1977), 22–5.

1548 **Grant**, Jeanne Valerie and **Smith**, Geoffrey John. *Personnel administration and industrial relations*. London: Longman.
Second edition, 1977. 318p.

1549 **Hesmondhaigh**, S. 'Personnel in the arts.' *Pers. Manage.*, IX, 4 (April 1977), 22–7.

1550 **Kilcourse**, Tom. 'What line managers need to know about IR.' *Pers. Manage.*, IX, 5 (May 1977), 32–5.

1551 **Legge**, Karen. 'Contingency theory and the personnel function.' *Pers. Manage.*, IX, 8 (August 1977), 22–5.

1552 **Purcell**, John and **Earl**, M. J. 'Control systems and industrial relations.' *Ind. Relat.*, VIII, 2 (Summer 1977), 41–54.

1553 **Watson**, Tony J. *The personnel management occupation: a study in the sociology of work and employment.* 1976–7. (Ph.D. thesis, University of Nottingham.)

1554 **Watson**, Tony J. *The personnel managers: a study in the sociology of work and employment.* London: Routledge & Kegan Paul, 1977. xvi, 246p.

1555 **Wellens**, John. 'The human aspect of management.' *Ind. Commer. Train.*, IX, 9 (September 1977), 366; IX, 10 (October 1977), 404; IX, 11 (November 1977), 446.

1556 **Colclough**, Julia A. 'Personnel management 1984: a day in the life of 169401815.' *Pers. Manage.*, X, 11 (November 1978), 28–31.

1557 **Cuming**, Maurice William. *Personnel management in the National Health Service.* London: Heinemann, 1978. ix, 270p.

1558 **Finnie**, John. 'Personnel Management 1984: the dilemmas remain.' *Pers. Manage.*, X, 11 (November 1978), 24–7.

1559 **Gill**, John. 'Managing a merger: the acquisition and the aftermath.' *Pers. Manage.*, X, 1 (January 1978), 14–17.

1560 **Gill**, Roger. 'Personnel: the production manager's fairy godmother.' *Pers. Manage.*, X, 3 (March 1978), 30–3.

1561 **Kelly**, John E. 'Understanding Taylorism: some comments.' *Br. J. Sociol.*, XXIX (June 1978), 203–7.

1562 **Legge**, Karen. *Power, innovation and problem solving in personnel management.* London: McGraw-Hill, 1978. xiii, 151p.

1563 **Littler**, Craig J. 'Understanding Taylorism.' *Br. J. Sociol.*, XXIX (June 1978), 185–202.

1564 **Long**, Roland. 'Personnel management 1984: Old Long's almanac.' *Pers. Manage.*, X, 11 (November 1978), 32–3.

1565 **Margerison**, Charles J. *Influencing organizational change: the role of the personnel specialist.* London: Institute of Personnel Management, 1978. 219p.

1566 **Anstey**, Edgar. 'Interviewing; how should it develop?' *J. Ind. Affairs.*, VII, 1 (Autumn 1979), 16–20.

1567 **Armstrong**, Michael. *Case studies in personnel management.* London: Kogan Page, 1979. 206p.

1568 **Barber**, David. *The practice of personnel management.* London: Institute of Personnel Management, 1979. 92p.
Second edition.

1569 **de Swart**, J. M. M. 'Personnel planning: a strategic view.' *Long Range Plann.*, XII, 3 (June 1979), 8–15.

1570 **Dyer**, Barbara. *Personnel systems and records.* Epping: Gower, 1979. 216p.
Third edition.

1571 **Edwards**, Brian. 'Managers and industrial relations.' Bosanquet, N. (ed.). *Industrial relations in the N. H. S.* 1979. p. 125–44.

1572 **Fowler**, Alan G. 'Making the most of management services: a local government view.' *Pers. Manage.*, XI, 2 (February 1979), 30–3.

1573 **Gammon**, G. and **Young**, D. 'Personnel management in the Ministry of Defence.' *Public Adm.*, LVI, 3 (Autumn 1979), 271–85.

1574 **Greenlaw**, Paul Stephen and **Biggs**, William D. *Modern personnel management.* London: Saunders, 1979. 665p.

1575 **Henry**, S. 'Controlling the hidden economy.' *Employee Relat.*, I, 3 (1979), 17–22.

1576 **Owen**, Trevor. *The manager and industrial relations.* London: Pergamon, 1979. xi, 186p.

1577 **Purcell**, John. 'A strategy for management control in industrial relations.' Purcell, J. and Smith, R. (eds.). *The control of work.* 1979. p. 27–58.

1578 **Smith**, Robin. 'The maximisation of control in industrial relations systems.' Purcell J. and Smith, R. (eds.). *The control of work.* 1979. p. 1–26.

1579 **Swinburne**, Penny. 'Psychology and the personnel manager: is a little knowledge a dangerous thing?' *Pers. Manage.*, XI, 5 (May 1979), 40–3.

1580 **Torrington**, Derek Peter. 'Personnel management and the invasion of privacy.' *Pers. Manage.*, XI, 4 (April 1979), 33–6.

1581 **Torrington**, Derek Peter and **Chapman**, John. *Personnel management.* London: Prentice-Hall, 1979. 500p.

See also: 40; 130; 132; 140; 157; 165; 169; 201; 249; 860; 1051; 1685; 1704; 1724; 1755; 1781; 1861; 1874; 2091; 2114; 2180; 2542; 2585; 3045; 3119; 3128; 3144; 3153; 3155; 3201; 4608; 5757.

B. COMMUNICATIONS IN INDUSTRY

This section includes the literature dealing with communications as an aspect of personnel management. The literature is primarily normative in nature and is generally concerned with arguing the need for better communications in industry and pointing out how this can be achieved. Much of the basic sociological and psychological research listed in Part Two also contains material on communications in industry. Material on company reports for employees is included here, but that on the disclosure of information for the purposes of collective bargaining is classified at Part Five, III.

1582 **Beishon**, Ronald John and **Zorkoczy**, Peter. *The human component.* Milton Keynes: Open U.P., 1971. 45, 43p. (Open University Technology Foundation Course. Unit 2.)

1583 **Engineering Employers' Federation.** *Improving communications: an E.E.F. guide.* London: The Federation, 1971. 31p.

1584 **Garnett**, John. *The manager's responsibility for*

communication. London: Industrial Society. Fourth edition, 1971. 34p. Fifth edition, 1976. 36p.

1585 **Miller**, *Sir* Bernard. 'Communication and consultation.' *Co-partnership*, DXLIV (July 1971), 9–14.

1586 **Jeffrey**, R. H. and **Howarth**, C. 'Communications structure.' Torrington, Derek P. (ed.). *Handbook of industrial relations.* 1972. p. 141–58.

1587 **Brown**, Robert Douglas. *Company newspapers and effective communication in industry.* London: Working Together Campaign, [1973]. 11p.

1588 **Fletcher**, J. A. 'The push and pull of communication.' Fletcher, J. and others (eds.). *A programme for working together.* 1973. p. 3–8.

1589 **Gordon-Brown**, Ian, **Armstrong**, J. R. and **Allen**, A. 'The Lucas suggestion scheme.' *Ind. Participation*, DLII (Summer 1973), 26–9.

1590 **Hibbert**, V. 'Only a suggestion.' *Ind. Soc.*, LV, 2 (February 1973), 11–14.

1591 **Pensions World**. 'Communicating the pension scheme.' *Pensions World*, II, 2 (September–October 1973), 339–44.

1592 **Smith**, P. I. S. *Job involvement and communications.* London: Business Books, 1973. x, 126p.

1593 **Anderson**, M. F. 'Employee attitude surveys.' *Ind. Commer. Train.*, V, 1 (January 1974), 34–7.

1594 **Weinstein**, K. 'Programming communication.' *Ind. Soc.*, LVI, 5 (May 1974), 6–9.

1595 **Confederation of British Industry.** *Provision of information to employees: guidelines for action.* London: C.B.I., 1975. 25p.

1596 **Emery**, R. *Staff communication in libraries.* London: Clive Bingley, 1975. 213p.

1597 **Finniston**, *Sir* Montague. 'Information communication and management.' *Aslib Proc.*, XXVII, 8 (August 1975), 346–9.

1598 **Garnett**, John. 'Effective communication in a participative era.' *Prod. Eng.*, LIV, 6 (June 1975), 350–2.

1599 **Houlton**, Bob. 'Considering communications.' Coker, E. and Stuttard, G. (eds.). *Industrial studies 1: the key skills.* 1975. p. 51–74.

1600 **Taylor**, A. H. 'The presentation of financial information to employees.' *Manage. Finance*, I, 1 (1975), 14–23.

1601 **Wellens**, John. 'Training in the economic facts of life.' *Ind. Commer. Train.*, VII, 4 (April 1975), 134–6.

1602 **Brandon**, Michael. 'Communicating along the right lines.' *Pers. Manage.*, VIII, 10 (October 1976), 37–40.

1603 **Cooper**, A. 'Providing information: what, how and to whom?' *Ind. Participation*, DLXV (Autumn 1976), 18–21.

1604 **Hopps**, R. 'Communication at NatWest.' *Ind. Soc.*, LVIII, 1 (January–February 1976), 7–9.

1605 **Irvine**, J. S. 'Improving pensions communications.' *Ind. Commer. Train.*, VIII, 2 (February 1976), 79–81.

1606 **Olsen**, Kristine. 'Suggestion schemes seventies style.' *Pers. Manage.*, VIII, 4 (April 1976), 36–9.

1607 **Smith**, G. 'Attitudes and communication.' *Ind. Commer. Train.*, VIII, 10 (October 1976), 387–90.

1608 **Taylor**, A. H. 'Presenting financial information to employees.' *Manage. Finance*, II, 1 (1976), 13–18.

1609 **Brewster**, Chris J. and **Connock**, Steve L. 'The interactive skills of industrial relations.' *Ind. Commer. Train.*, IX, 9 (September 1977), 377–81.

1610 **Confederation of British Industry**. *Communication with people at work.* London: C.B.I., 1977. 32p.

1611 **Everard**, K. B. 'Business education for workers.' *Ind. Commer. Train.*, IX, 8 (August 1977), 313–17.

1612 **Keyworth**, R. 'Communicating complex information.' *Ind. Commer. Train.*, IX, 11 (November 1977), 455–61.

1613 **Knight**, K. 'The employee survey: handle with care.' *J. Gen. Manage.*, IV (Winter 1976–7), 41–9.

1614 **Palmer**, R. 'A participative approach to attitude surveys.' *Pers. Manage.*, IX, 12 (December 1977), 26–8.

1615 **Parkinson**, Cyril Northcote and **Rowe**, Nigel. *Communicate: Parkinson's formula for business survival.* London: Prentice-Hall, 1977. xiii, 205p.

1616 **Rosenfeld**, Peter. 'Training trade unionists for today and tomorrow.' *Pers. Manage.*, IX, 6 (June 1977), 37–41.

1617 **Wellens**, John and **Douglass**, S. 'An experiment in communication at I.C.I.' *Ind. Commer. Train.*, IX, 7 (July 1977), 271–8.

1618 **Fletcher**, Clive A. 'Management/subordinate communication.' *Pers. Rev.*, VIII (Winter 1978), 59–62.

1619 **James**, C. M. 'Employee reports.' *C.B.I. Rev.* (Winter 1977–8), 11–19.

1620 **Unwin**, A. 'Communicating financial information.' *Ind. Commer. Train.*, X, 9 (September 1978), 363; X, 10 (October 1978), 416; X, 11 (November 1978), 461; X, 12 (December 1978), 502.

1621 **Wellens**, John. 'Economics for workers.' *Ind. Commer. Train.*, X, 3 (March 1978), 112–17.

1622 **ApSimon**, H. G. 'The forms of authority.' *Ind. Participation*, DLXXVIII (Summer 1979), 12–15.

1623 **Barrable**, Colin. 'Employee reports: the small company.' *Ind. Soc.*, LXI, 3 (May–June 1979), 3–4.

1624 **Cassell**, M. 'The employee report.' *Works Manage.*, XXX, 3 (March 1979), 66–8.

1625 **Dobbins**, Richard and **Pettman**, Barrie Owen. 'GKN Steelstock Ltd: designing an employee information system.' *Employee Relat.*, I, 2 (1979), 22–8.

1626 **Fanning**, David. 'Employment reports: an appraisal.' *Employee Relat.*, I, 4 (1979), 8–12.

1627 **Unwin**, A. 'Communicating company information.' *Ind. Commer. Train.*, XI, I (January 1979), 24; XI, 2 (February 1979), 72.

1628 **Unwin**, A. 'Communicating company information.' *Ind. Commer. Train.*, XI, 3 (March 1979), 119–22.

1629 **Wilson**, Brian. 'Creating and sharing wealth.' *Employee Relat.*, I, I (1979), 7–10; I, 2 (1979), 7–11.

1630 **Wright**, D. 'Why communicate?' *Ind. Commer. Train.*, XI, 4 (April 1979), 143–5.

C. SUPERVISION OF EMPLOYEES

See also Part Six, II, B, 3, b, iii.

1631 **Jackson**, P. *The supervisor and technological change: a study of the role of the supervisor in the port transport industry.* London: National Ports Council, 1970. 18p. (Training research occasional papers 1.)

1632 **Donovan**, Anthony F. *Management of supervisors.* London: Macmillan, 1971. 165p.

1633 **Dunkerley,** David. *Task and structural characteristics of foreman roles.* [1971?]. (Ph.D. thesis, University of Wales, Cardiff.)

1634 **Harris**, A. J. *Staff inspection in an engineering design department of the Civil Service.* 1971. (M.Sc. thesis, University of Bath.)

1635 **Hawkins**, Kevin H. and **Molander**, Christopher F. 'Supervisors out in the cold.' *Pers. Manage.*, III, 4 (April 1971), 37–41.

1636 **Russell**, Lawrence. *ABC of supervision.* London: Pitman, 1972. 88p.

1637 **Thurley**, Keith Ernest. 'Change and the role of the supervisor.' *Pers. Manage.*, IV, 10 (October 1972), 30–3.

1638 **Bowey**, Angela M. 'The changing status of the supervisor.' *Br. J. Ind. Relat.*, XI, 3 (November 1973), 393–414.

1639 **Foxen**, Trevor. 'First line – last priority.'

Ind. Soc., LV, 3 (March 1973), 10–12.

1640 **Hill**, Stephen R. 'Supervisory roles and the man in the middle: dock foreman.' *Br. J. Sociol.*, XXIV (June 1973), 305–21.

1641 **Robertson**, A. 'Daywork supervision.' *Ind. Soc.*, LV, 12 (December 1973), 15–17.

1642 **Thurley**, Keith Ernest and **Wirdenius**, Hans. *Supervision: a reappraisal.* London: Heinemann, 1973. 238p.

1643 **Weir**, Mary and **Mills**, S. 'The supervisor as a change catalyst.' *Ind. Relat. J.*, IV, 4 (Winter 1973–4), 61–9.

1644 **Child**, John. 'The industrial supervisor.' Esland, G. and others (eds.). *People and work.* 1975. p. 70–87.

1645 **Clarke**, Joe F. 'The foreman – a neglected figure in the history of industrial relations?' *N.E. Group Study Labour Hist. Bull.*, IX (October 1975), 20–33.

1646 **Dunkerley**, David. *The foreman: aspects of task and structure.* London: Routledge & Kegan Paul, 1975. viii, 192p.

1647 **Institute of Personnel Management.** *Profile of a supervisor.* London: The Institute, 1975. 21p. (Information reports 17.)

1648 **Pfeffer**, Jeffrey and **Salancik**, Gerald R. 'Determinants of supervisory behaviour: a role set analysis.' *Hum. Relat.*, XXVIII (March 1975), 139–54.

1649 **Walsh**, B. 'Improving first line supervision.' *Work Study*, XII, 4 (April 1976), 8–12.

1650 **Cox**, M. F. *General foremen's labour strategy in the building industry.* 1977–8. (M.Sc. thesis, University of Birmingham.)

1651 **Toye**, Janet. *Supervisors in industry: a survey of research and opinion.* London: Industrial Training Research Unit, 1978. 47p.

1652 **Welch**, Barry. 'Keeping the discipliners in line.' *Pers. Manage.*, X, 8 (August 1978), 21–4.

1653 **Williamson**, Derek A. 'Perceptions of staff supervision in the probation service.' *Br. J. Soc. Work*, VIII (Spring 1978), 27–43.

See also: 301; 323; 357; 564; 2002; 2006; 6495.

LABOUR–MANAGEMENT RELATIONS

I. GENERAL

This section contains works concerned with general aspects of the relationship between workers and employers as distinct from works on the industrial relations system in general, which are to be found in Part One, III. Also included here is material on national and industry-wide bargaining, and labour relations in multi-national companies. General material on the recognition of trade unions by employers is also included here; but that on recognition disputes is classified at Part Five, V,C. See Part Three, II, J for material on the international aspects of trade unionism; Part Five, II for material on plant and company bargaining; and Part Seven, VI for the more legalistic material on union recognition. See also Part Three, II, A–B; Part Five, V, A; Part Five, VI, D, I; and Part Seven, I.

1654 **Flanders**, Allan. 'The changing character of collective bargaining.' *Dep. Employment Gaz.*, LXXVII, 12 (December 1967), 1100–5.

1655 **Banks**, Robert Frederick. 'British collective bargaining: the challenge of the 1970's.' *Relat. Industrielles*, XXVI, 3 (August 1971), 642–91.

1656 **Cliff**, Tony. 'The class struggle in Britain.' Harris, Nigel and Palmer, John (eds.). *World crisis*. London: Hutchinson, 1971. p. 225–50.

1657 **Cooper**, Neville. *How to change the course of industrial relations*. London: Top Management Partnership, 1971. 19p.

1658 **Gennard**, John and **Steuer**, M. D. 'The industrial relations of foreign-owned subsidiaries.' *Br. J. Ind. Relat.*, IX, 2 (July 1971), 143–59.

1659 **Kennet**, W. *Sovereignty and multinational companies*. London: Fabian Society, 1971. 28p. (Fabian tracts 409.)

1660 **Lea**, David. 'The international company and trade union interests.' *J. Bus. Policy*, I, 4 (Summer 1971), 30–9.
Reprinted in Cuthbert, N. and Hawkins, K. (eds.). *Company industrial relations*. 1973. p. 270–82.

1661 **Lea**, David. 'Multinational companies and trade union interests.' Dunning, J.H. (ed.). *The multinational enterprise*. London: Allen & Unwin, 1971. p. 147–63.

1662 **McCarthy**, William Edward John. 'Changing bargaining structures.' Kessler, S. and Weekes, B. (eds.). *Conflict at work*. 1971. p. 83–93.

1663 **Phelps Brown**, Sir Ernest Henry. *Collective bargaining reconsidered*. London: Athlone, 1971. 17p.

1664 **Scanlon**, Hugh. *Workers' control and the transitional company*. Nottingham: Institute for Workers' Control, 1971. 8p. (Pamphlet series 22.)

1665 **Thomson**, G. M. *Cost of living indexation agreements in wage bargaining, with special reference to Great Britain since 1945.* [1971?] (M.A. thesis, University of Manchester.)

1666 **Trades Union Congress.** *Good industrial relations*. London: T.U.C., 1971. 29p.

1667 **Armstrong**, Eric George Abbott. 'Collective bargaining.' Torrington, Derek P. (ed). *Handbook of industrial relations*. 1972. p. 11–27.

1668 **Brandt**, Floyd Stanley. *The process of negotiation: strategy and tactics in industrial relations*. London: Industrial and Commercial Techniques, 1972. 158p.

1669 **Fyrth**, Hubert Jim. *Men and masters*. London: Ginn, 1972. 144p.

1670 **Gennard**, John. *Multinational corporations and British labour: a review of attitudes and responses*. London: British–North American Committee, 1972. vii, 53p.

1671 **Gunther**, K. *Collective bargaining and the challenge of new technology*. Geneva: I.L.O., 1972. ii, 71p.

1672 **Incomes Data Services.** *Quarterly review of settlements*. London: I.D.S., 1972. 16p. (Study 21.)

1673 **Incomes Data Services.** *Quarterly review of settlements*. London: I.D.S., 1972. 16p. (Study 27.)

1674 **Incomes Data Services.** *Quarterly review of settlements*. London: I.D.S., 1972. 16p. (Study 33.)

1675 **Incomes Data Services.** *Quarterly review of settlements.* London: I.D.S., 1972. 16p. (Study 39.)

1676 **Industrial Society.** *Model procedure agreements.* London: The Society, 1972. 39p. (Model management documents 1.)

1677 **Lewis**, Roy. 'Realities of recognition.' *Pers. Manage.*, IV, 7 (July 1972), 26–8.

1678 **Lewis**, Roy and **Latta**, Geoff. 'Bargaining units and bargaining agents.' *Br. J. Ind. Relat.*, X, 1 (March 1972), 84–106.

1679 **Marlow Association.** *Marlow charter of industrial relations and responsibilities.* Reading: The Association, 1972. 22p.

1680 **Naylor**, Rachel. 'The conduct of negotiations: a viewpoint.' Torrington, Derek P. (ed.). *Handbook of industrial relations.* 1972. p. 239–52.

1681 **Naylor**, Rachel. 'Employers' associations and trade unions.' Torrington, Derek P. (ed.). *Handbook of industrial relations.* 1972. p. 81–95.

1682 **Neal**, *Sir* Leonard Francis. *Reforming relationships in industry.* Edinburgh: Scottish Academic Press, 1972. 11p.

1683 **O'Brien**, *Sir* Richard. 'Points of procedure.' *Pers. Manage.*, IV, 8 (August 1972), 23–5.

1684 **Phelps Brown**, *Sir* Ernest Henry. 'Inflation, collective bargaining and public opinion.' *Polit. Q.*, XLIII (October–December 1972), 448–58.

1685 **Roberts**, Benjamin Charles. 'Factors influencing the organisation and style of management and their effect on the pattern of industrial relations in multi-national corporations.' Günter, Hans (ed.). *Transnational industrial relations.* London: Macmillan, 1972. p. 109–32.

1686 **Roberts**, Benjamin Charles and **Rothwell**, S. 'Recent trends in collective bargaining in the United Kingdom.' *Int. Labour Rev.*, CVI, 6 (December 1972), 543–71.

1687 **Stephens**, B. 'The numbers game in collective bargaining.' *Pers. Manage.*, IV, 9 (September 1972), 32–5.

1688 **United States**, Congress, House Committee on Education and Labor. *Labor–management relations in Europe: results of a field investigation conducted by the Special Subcommittee on Labor.* Washington, D.C.: U.S.G.P.O., 1972. vi, 506p.

1689 **Warner**, Malcolm and **Turner**, Louis. 'Trade unions and the multinational firm.' *J. Ind. Relat.*, XIV, 2 (June 1972), 143–71.

1690 **Williams**, Roy and **Siethoff**, Hellmuth J. 'Industrial relations in an organisational perspective.' *Pers. Manage.*, IV, 5 (May 1972), 29–31.

1691 **Aikin**, Olga. *The disclosure of information.* London: Working Together Campaign, [1973]. 12p.

1692 **Charles**, Rodger. *Development of industrial relations in Britain, 1911–1939: studies in the evolution of collective bargaining at national and industry level.* London: Hutchinson, 1973. 340p.

1693 **Commission on Industrial Relations.** *Communications and collective bargaining.* London: H.M.S.O., 1973. v, 30p. (Report 39.)

1694 **Flanders**, Allan. 'Measured daywork and collective bargaining.' *Br. J. Ind. Relat.*, XI, 3 (November 1973), 368–92.

1695 **Forsyth**, David J. C. 'Foreign-owned firms and labour relations.' *Br. J. Ind. Relat.*, XI, 1 (March 1973), 20–8.

1696 **Goodman**, John Francis Bradshaw and **Thomson**, G. M. 'Cost of living indexation agreements in post-war British collective bargaining.' *Br. J. Ind. Relat.*, XI, 2 (July 1973), 181–210.

1697 **Gospel**, Howard F. 'An approach to a theory of the firm in industrial relations.' *Br. J. Ind. Relat.*, XI, 2 (July 1973), 211–28.

1698 **Goss**, John and **Goodman**, M. *Collective bargaining in Western Europe.* London: Institute of Personnel Management, 1973. 119p. (Information reports 13.)

See especially chapter on the U.K. p. 98–108.

1699 **Gottschalk**, Andrew W. 'A behavioural analysis of bargaining.' Warner, M. (ed.). *Sociology of the workplace.* 1973. p. 36–81.

1700 **Incomes Data Services.** *Quarterly review of settlements.* London: I.D.S., 1973. 12p. (Study 46.)

1701 **Incomes Data Services.** *Quarterly review of settlements.* London: I.D.S., 1973. 12p. (Study 51.)

1702 **Macbeath**, Innis. *European approach to worker–management relationships.* New York: British–North American Committee, 1973. ix, 92p.

1703 **McCarthy**, William Edward John and **Collier**, A. S. *Coming to terms with trade unions: six case studies in collective bargaining strategy.* London: Institute of Personnel Management, 1973. 164p.

1704 **McDonald**, G. W. and **Gospel**, Howard F. 'The Mond–Turner talks 1927–1933: a study in industrial co-operation.' *Hist. J.*, XVI (December 1973), 807–29.

1705 **Molander**, Christopher F. 'Organizational development and industrial relations.' *Pers. Rev.*, III, 4 (Winter 1973), 26–33.

1706 **Phelps Brown**, *Sir* Ernest Henry. 'New wine in old bottles: reflections on the changed working of collective bargaining in Great Britain.' *Br. J. Ind. Relat.*, XI, 3 (November 1973), 329–37.

Reprinted in Barrett, B. and others (eds.). *Industrial relations and the wider society.* 1975. p. 120–8.

1707 **Roberts**, Benjamin Charles. 'Multinational collective bargaining: a European prospect?' *Br. J. Ind. Relat.*, XI, 1 (March 1973), 1–19.

1708 **Shadforth**, A. T. 'Future developments in collective bargaining: a managerial view.'

Cuthbert, N. and Hawkins, K. (eds.). *Company industrial relations policies.* 1973. p. 283–90

1709 **Taylor**, Robert. 'Multinationals and their workers.' *New Soc.*, xxiv (14 June 1973), 613–5.

1710 **Trades Union Congress.** *Economic policy and collective bargaining in 1973: report of special Trades Union Congress.* London: T.U.C., 1973. 109p.

1711 **Warr**, Peter Bryan. *Psychology and collective bargaining.* London: Hutchinson, 1973. xii, 224p.

1712 **Brown**, William Arthur. 'Conspiracy, collective bargaining and co-determination.' *Scott. J. Polit. Econ.*, xxi (1974), 309–15.

1713 **Commission on Industrial Relations.** *Employee relations in the smaller firm: a practical guide for employers.* London: H.M.S.O., 1974. iv, 27p.

1714 **Commission on Industrial Relations.** *Industrial relations in multi-plant undertakings.* London: H.M.S.O., 1974. v, 66p. (Report 85.)

1715 **Commission on Industrial Relations.** *Trade union recognition: C.I.R. experience.* London: H.M.S.O., 1974. iv, 90p. (Study 5.)

1716 **Dempsey**, P. J. R. 'Strategy and tactics in collective bargaining.' *Pers. Manage.*, vi, 4 (April 1974), 22–6.

1717 **Department of Industry.** *Handbook of collective agreements and procedures.* London: The Department, 1974.

1718 **Neal**, *Sir* Leonard Francis. 'The next decade in industrial relations.' *Long Range Plann.*, vii, 4 (August 1974), 7–11.

1719 **Phelps Brown**, *Sir* Ernest Henry. 'Wage determination: final reflections on the conference.' *Indian J. Labour Econ.*, xvii, 1–2 (April–July 1974), 25–30.

1720 **Ramsay**, J. C. and **Hill**, J. M. *Collective agreements: a guide to their drafting.* London: Institute of Personnel Management, 1974. 56p.

1721 **Roberts**, Benjamin Charles. 'The challenge to traditional methods of determining pay.' *Ind. J. Labour Econ.*, xvii, 1–2 (April–July 1974), 1–24.

1722 **Roberts**, Benjamin Charles and **May**, Jonathan. 'The responses of multinational enterprises to international trade union pressures.' *Br. J. Ind. Relat.*, xii, 3 (November 1974), 403–16.

1723 **Ulman**, Lloyd. 'Connective bargaining and competitive bargaining.' *Scott. J. Polit. Econ.*, xxi, 2 (June 1974), 97–109.

1724 **Winkler**, J. T. 'The ghost at the bargaining table: directors and industrial relations.' *Br. J. Ind. Relat.*, xii, 2 (July 1974), 191–212.

1725 **Addison**, John T. 'The role of comparability in wage determination.' *Br. J. Ind. Relat.*, xiii, 3 (November 1975), 388–95.

1726 **Atkinson**, Gerald G. M. *Effective negotiator: a practical guide to the strategies and tactics of*

conflict bargaining. London: Quest, 1975. viii, 176p.

1727 **Bowey**, Angela M. and **Eccles**, A. J. 'Relativities, national job evaluation and collective bargaining.' *J. Manage. Stud.*, xii, 1 (February 1975), 83–94.

1728 **Bracegirdle**, Cyril. 'A grass roots view of industrial relations.' *Contemp. Rev.*, ccxxvii (September 1975), 157–60.

1729 **Bryder**, Tom. *Power and responsibility: contending approaches to industrial relations and decision-making in Britain, 1963–1971.* London: CWK Gleerup, 1975. 186p.

1730 **Buckingham**, G. L. 'Collective bargaining.' Bowey, Angela M. (ed.). *Handbook of salary and wage systems.* 1975. p. 93–104.

1731 **Castle**, C. H. A. F. 'Multinationals and trade unions.' *Month*, viii (May 1975), 132–5.

1732 **Edwards**, Christine and **Harper**, D. G. 'Bargaining at the trade union-management interface.' Abell, Peter (ed.). *Organizations as bargaining and influence systems.* London: Heinemann, 1975. p. 41–71.

1733 **Gill**, H. S., **Pedler**, Malcolm J. and **Shipton**, J. 'Organization development and the trade unions.' *Pers. Rev.*, iv, 2 (Spring 1975), 11–14.

1734 **Hann**, P. 'Dockland disclosure.' *Ind. Soc.*, lvii, 3 (May–June 1975), 7–9.

1735 **Hedderwick**, Karl. *Statistics of bargainers.* London: Hutchinson, 1975. 96p. (Trade union industrial studies.)

1736 **Hutt**, W. H. *The theory of collective bargaining 1930–1975.* London: Institute of Economic Affairs, 1975. xix, 140p.

1737 **Kessler**, Sydney and **Palmer**, Gill. 'Reconsidering recognition.' *Pers. Manage.*, vii, 7 (July 1975), 18–21, 37.

1738 **Singleton**, Norman. *Industrial relations procedures.* London: H.M.S.O., 1975. iii, 85p. (Department of Employment manpower papers 14.)

1739 **Smith**, I. G. 'Sensitivity bargaining: an alternative to conflict.' *Pers. Rev.*, iv, 2 (Spring 1975), 17–23.

1740 **Stamp**, Maxwell. 'The abuse of collective bargaining.' *Moor. Wall Street* (Spring 1975), 5–16.

1741 **Atherton**, John. 'Reality, hope and collective bargaining.' *Theology*, lxxix (May 1976), 138–43.

1742 **Atkinson**, Gerald G. M. 'Bargaining: the rules of the game.' *Pers. Manage.*, vii, 2 (February 1976), 21–5.

1743 **Bradbury**, Paul. 'The changing balance: industry and the worker.' *C.B.I. Rev.* (Spring 1976), 5–10.

1744 **Brown**, William Arthur. 'From strikes to participation: a sociologist's eye view.' *Pers. Manage.*, viii, 6 (June 1976), 29–31.

1745 **Chapple**, Frank. *The responsibility of trade unions and managers.* London: Foundation for Business Responsibilities, 1976. 5p.

1746 **Coker**, Ed. 'Bargaining in practice and theory.' Coker, E. and Stuttard, G. (eds.). *Industrial studies 2*. 1976. p. 43–67.

1747 **Coker**, Ed and **Stuttard**, Geoffrey (eds.). *Industrial studies 2: the bargaining context*. London: Arrow, 1976. 282p. (Trade union industrial studies.)

1748 **Elliott**, Robert F. and **Steele**, R. 'The importance of national wage agreements.' *Br. J. Ind. Relat.*, XIV, 1 (March 1976), 43–55.

1749 **Gennard**, John. *Multinationals: industrial relations and the trade union response*. Nottingham: Universities of Leeds and Nottingham in association with the Institute of Personnel Management, 1976. v, 34p.

1750 **Gowan**, Doug. 'The bargaining system.' Coker, E. and Stuttard, G. (eds.). *Industrial studies 2*. 1976. p. 139–59.

1751 **Jayne**, Terry. 'Bargaining with recognition.' *Pers. Manage.*, VIII, 10 (October 1976), 21–5.

1752 **McIlroy**, John. 'Bargaining for rights.' Coker, E. and Stuttard, G. (eds.). *Industrial studies 2*. 1976. p. 211–45.

1753 **Mortimer**, James Edward. 'The government and collective bargaining.' Coker, E. and Stuttard, G. (eds.). *Industrial studies 2*. 1976. p. 188–208.

1754 **Pedler**, Mike. 'Learning to negotiate.' Coker, E. and Stuttard, G. (eds.). *Industrial studies 2*. 1976. p. 89–138.

1755 **Sieff**, *Sir* Marcus. 'Co-operation or confrontation.' *R. Inst. G.B. Proc.*, XLIX (1976), 1–16.

1756 **Stuttard**, Geoffrey. 'The bargaining context.' Coker, E. and Stuttard, G. (eds.). *Industrial studies 2*. 1976. p. 13–18.

1757 **Tegner**, Bill. 'Grievance procedures.' *Ind. Soc.*, LVIII, 5 (September–October 1976), 14.

1758 **Thomson**, Andrew William John and **Murray**, V. V. *Grievance procedures*. London: Saxon, 1976. 193p.

1759 **Confederation of British Industry.** *The future of pay determination: a discussion document*. London: C.B.I., 1977. 56p.

1760 **Foley**, Bernard J. and **Maunders**, Keith. *Accounting information disclosure and collective bargaining*. London: Macmillan, 1977. x, 210p.

1761 **Friedman**, Andrew L. *Industry and labour: class struggle at work and monopoly capitalism*. London: Macmillan, 1977. xii, 313p.

1762 **Garside**, William Redvers. 'Management and men: aspects of British industrial relations in the inter-war period.' Supple, B. (ed.). *Essays in British business history*. Oxford: O.U.P., 1977. p. 244–67.

1763 **Incomes Data Services.** *Structure of agreements: six contrasting company agreements*. London: I.D.S., 1977. (Study 147.)

1764 **Institute of Personnel Management.** National Committee on Employee Relations. *Trade union recognition*. London: I.P.M., 1977. 68p.

1765 **Jenkins**, Clive and **Sherman**, Barrie. *Collective bargaining: what you always wanted to know about trade unions and never dared to ask*. London: Routledge & Kegan Paul, 1977. 156p.

1766 **Keenoy**, T. *Industrial relations: power and conflict*. 1977. (D.Phil. thesis, University of Oxford.)

1767 **Millward**, Neil and **McQueeney**, John. 'The industrial relations effects of mergers and takeovers.' *Dep. Employment Gaz.*, LXXV, 9 (September 1977), 944–6.

1768 **Morley**, Ian E. and **Stephenson**, Geoffrey M. *The social psychology of bargaining*. London: Allen & Unwin, 1977. 317p.

1769 **Roberts**, Benjamin Charles and **Liebhaberg**, B. 'International regulation of multinational enterprises.' *Br. J. Ind. Relat.*, XV, 3 (November 1977), 356–73.

1770 **Sisson**, Keith. *Negotiating in practice: role-playing for managers and shop stewards*. London: Institute of Personnel Management, 1977. 64p.

1771 **Stephenson**, Geoffrey M., **Kniveton**, Bromley K. and **Morley**, Ian E. 'Interaction analysis of an industrial wage negotiation.' *J. Occup. Psychol.*, L (December 1977), 231–41.

1772 **Storey**, John. 'Collective bargaining and management prerogatives.' *Ind. Relat. J.*, VII, 4 (Winter 1976–7), 40–55.

1773 **Vann**, Neil. *Negotiating planning agreements*. London: W.E.A., 1977. 22p. (Studies for trade unionists III, 9.)

1774 **Brown**, William Arthur and **Terry**, Michael. 'The changing nature of national wage agreements.' *Scott. J. Polit. Econ.*, XXV (June 1978), 119–33.

1775 **Brown**, William Arthur and **Terry**, Michael. 'The future of collective bargaining.' *New Soc.*, XXXVII (23 March 1978), 659–60.

1776 **Cummings**, Colin. 'The future of wage bargaining as a trade unionist sees it.' *Month*, XI (July 1978), 221–4.

1777 **Farnham**, David. 'Sixty years of Whitleyism.' *Pers. Manage.*, X, 7 (July 1978), 29–32.

1778 **Ferns**, Harry. 'Conditions for the future of collective bargaining.' Institute of Economic Affairs. *Trade unions: public goods or public bads?* 1978. p. 112–3.

1779 **Gibson**, Chris. 'Centralised wage bargaining and industrial relations: The Irish experience.' *Pers. Manage.*, X, 9 (September 1978), 22–6.

1780 **Incomes Data Services.** *The right to be recognised*. London: I.D.S., 1978. 74p. (Handbook 11.)

1781 **Purcell**, John. 'Management control through collective bargaining.' *Manchr. Bus. School Rev.*, XII, 3 (1978), 17–23.

1782 **Sloane**, P. J.'Collective bargaining: analysis of conflict and proposed reforms.' Institute of Economic Affairs. *Trade unions: public goods or public bads?* 1978. p. 30–3.

1783 **Stephenson**, Geoffrey M. and **Kniveton**, Bromley K. 'Interpersonal and interparty exchange: an experimental study of the effect of seating position on the outcome of negotiations between teams representing parties in dispute.' *Hum. Relat.*, XXXI (June 1978), 555–66.

1784 **Tinsley Park Employee Relations Project.** *Developing employee relations.* London: Saxon House, 1978. 216p.

1785 **Coates**, J. 'Multinational enterprises, industrial relations and codes of conduct: the employer's point of view.' *Univ. Leuven Inst. Labour Relat. Bull.*, X (1979), 107–12.

1786 **Confederation of British Industry.** *Pay: the choice ahead: CBI proposals for reforming pay determination.* London: C.B.I., 1979. 28p.

1787 **Farr**, Robert M. 'The relevance of experimental gaming studies to industrial relations.' Stephenson, G. and Brotherton, C. (eds.). *Industrial relations: a social psychological approach.* 1979. p. 95–110.

1788 **George**, Mike and **Elliott**, David. 'The Lucas Aerospace workers campaign.' *Employee Relat.*, I, 1 (1979), 24–8.

1789 **Hawkins**, Kevin H. *A handbook of industrial relations practice.* London: Kogan Page, 1979. 251p.

1790 **Hawkins**, Kevin. 'The institution of collective bargaining.' Stephenson, G. and Brotherton, C. (eds.). *Industrial relations: a social psychological approach.* 1979. p. 157–80.

1791 **Hepple**, Robert Alexander. 'Trends in collective bargaining: Great Britain.' *Univ. Leuven Inst. Labour Relat. Bull.*, X (1979), 379–84.

1792 **Kahn-Freund**, Sir Otto. *Labour relations: heritage and adjustment.* Oxford: O.U.P., 1979. 102p.

1793 **Morley**, Ian E. 'Behavioural studies of industrial bargaining.' Stephenson, G. and Brotherton, C. (eds.). *Industrial relations: a social psychological approach.* 1979. p. 211–36.

1794 **Nicholson**, Nigel. 'Industrial relations climate.' *Pers. Rev.*, IX, 3 (Summer 1979), 20–5.

1795 **Purcell**, John and **Smith**, Robin (eds.). *The control of work.* London: Macmillan, 1979. xiv, 184p.

1796 **Robinson**, D. 'Trade union recognition.' *Pers. Manage.*, XI, 8 (August 1979), 29–35.
See also: 23; 33; 120; 134; 135; 141; 246; 360; 688; 694; 715; 1169; 1257; 1258; 1379; 1390; 1426; 1454; 1465; 1471; 1481; 1508; 1534; 1552; 1577; 1578; 1609; 1821; 1976; 2003; 2032; 2178; 4619; 4627; 4647; 4650; 4673; 4708; 6029; 6048; 6136; 6616; 6690.

II. PLANT AND COMPANY BARGAINING, PRODUCTIVITY BARGAINING, AND LABOUR UTILISATION

The more sociological and psychological literature on restriction of output is classified at Part Two, I, II, and IV. The literature on work organisation and productivity is classified at Part Two, V; that on Luddism at Part Three, II, B; and that on the relationship between effort and remuneration at Part Six, III, F. See also Part Three, II, F, 8; Part Six, II, B; and Part Six, II, D, 3.

1797 **Urwin**, Harry. *Plant and productivity bargaining.* London: Transport & General Workers' Union, 1970. 19p.
Second edition.

1798 **Allard**, R., **Keal**, J. E., **Mount**, H. W., **Samuel**, P. J., **Smith**, G. R. and **Swannack**, A. R. *Productivity measurement: a symposium for the seventies.* London: Institute of Personnel Management, 1971. 50p.

1799 **Armstrong**, Eric George Abbott. 'Management and multi-unionism.' Kessler, S. and Weekes, B. (eds.). *Conflict at work.* 1971. p. 31–52.

1800 **Beston**, Jack. 'Joint regulation at the workplace.' *Co-partnership*, CCXLVI (November 1971), 50–5.

1801 **Cooper**, F. R. 'Bargaining for efficiency.' *Pers. Manage.*, III, 12 (December 1971), 24–7.

1802 **Cotgrove**, Stephen Frederick, **Dunham**, Jack and **Vamplew**, Clive. *The nylon spinners: a case study in productivity bargaining and job enlargement.* London: Allen & Unwin, 1971. 151p.

1803 **Daniel**, William Wentworth. 'Productivity bargaining and orientation to work: a rejoinder to Goldthorpe.' *J. Manage. Stud.*, VIII, 3 (October 1971), 329–35.

1804 **Delamotte**, Yves. *The social partners face the problems of productivity and employment: a study in comparative industrial relations.* Paris: Organisation for Economic Cooperation and Development, 1971. 202p.
See especially Chapter I: 'The Fawley agreements'. p. 9–22.

1805 **Edwards**, Ronald Stanley and **Roberts**, R. D.V. *Status, productivity and pay: a major experiment: a study of the electricity supply industry's agreements and their outcome, 1961–1971.* London: Macmillan, 1971. 456p.

1806 **Gupta**, S. and **Steedman**, Ian. 'An input – output study of labour productivity in the British economy.' *Oxf. Univ. Inst. Econ. Stat. Bull.*, XXXIII, 1 (February 1971), 21–34.

1807 **Hawkins**, Kevin H. 'Company bargaining: problems and prospects.' *Br. J. Ind. Relat.*, IX, 2 (July 1971), 198–213.

1808 **Hawkins**, Kevin H. *Current trends in collective bargaining in British industry, with special reference to productivity bargaining.* 1971. (B.Litt. thesis, University of Oxford.)

1809 **Hawkins**, Kevin H. 'Productivity bargaining: a reassessment.' *Ind. Relat. J.*, II, 1 (Spring 1971), 10–34.
Reprinted in Cuthbert, N. and Hawkins, K. (eds.). *Company industrial relations policies.* 1973. p. 173–205.

1810 **McDavid**, I. S. 'Productivity agreements: past, present and future.' *Work Study Manage. Serv.*, IX, 8 (August 1971), 511–17.

1811 **McMahon**, P. 'A trade union view on incentives and productivity agreements.' *Work Study Manage. Serv.*, IX, 11 (November 1971), 695–700.

1812 **O'Brien**, Richard. 'Plant procedures and agreements: a case study.' Kessler, S. and Weekes, B. (eds.). *Conflict at work.* 1971, p. 75–82.

1813 **Parker**, Peter Anthony Lawrence, **Hawes**, William Robert and **Lumb**, A. L. *The reform of collective bargaining at plant and company level.* London: H.M.S.O., 1971. viii, 115p. (Department of Employment manpower papers 5.)
Study directed by W. E. J. McCarthy. Research consultant G. S. Bain.

1814 **Parker**, Stanley Robert and **Scott**, M. H. 'Developing models of workplace industrial relations.' *Br. J. Ind. Relat.*, IX, 2 (July 1971), 214–24.

1815 **Priest**, Arthur. *Lecture notes on ten years of productivity bargaining in the electricity supply industry.* London: Electricity Council, 1971. 65p.

1816 **Ramsay**, J. C. 'Negotiating in a multi-plant company.' *Ind. Relat. J.*, II, 2 (Summer 1971), 42–8.

1817 **Richbell**, S. M. *A study of implementation problems in a productivity bargain.* 1971. (M.Sc. thesis, University of Wales, Cardiff.)

1818 **Roberts**, R. *An investigation into workshop relations at the Saunders Valve Co. during a period of change.* 1971. (M.Sc. thesis, University of Bath.)

1819 **Smith**, Eric Owen. *Productivity bargaining.* 1971. (Ph.D. thesis, University of Loughborough.)

1820 **Smith**, Eric Owen. *Productivity bargaining: a case study in the steel industry.* London: Pan, 1971. xvi, 428p.

1821 **Smith**, Ian G. 'Productivity agreements and productivity: an appraisal and a possible approach to productivity measurement at the plant and firm level.' *Ind. Relat. J.*, II, 4 (Winter 1971), 68–80.

1822 **Steuer**, M. D., **Gennard**, John and **Caves**, R. E. 'Industrial relations, labour disputes and labour utilization in foreign-owned firms in the United Kingdom.' Dunning, J. H. (ed.). *The multinational enterprise.* London: Allen & Unwin, 1971. 89–146.

1823 **Towers**, Brian and **Whittingham**, Terence George. 'Productivity bargaining in the United Kingdom: an overview.' *J. Ind. Relat.*, XIII, 3 (September 1971), 251–73.

1824 **White**, P. J. *Productivity bargaining in the Scottish gas industry.* 1971. (M.Sc. thesis, University of Strathclyde.)

1825 **Work Study**. 'Productivity agreements.' *Work Study*, VII, 8 (August 1971), 43–9.

1826 **Brown**, William Arthur. 'A consideration of "custom and practice".' *Br. J. Ind. Relat.*, X, 1 (March 1972), 42–61.

1827 **Delamotte**, Yves. 'British productivity agreements, German rationalisation agreements and French employment security agreements.' *Int. Inst. Labour Stud. Bull.*, IX (1972), 30–44.

1828 **Evans**, Erick Wyn. 'The rise and fall of productivity bargaining.' *Moor. Wall Street* (Autumn 1972), 63–72.

1829 **Kennedy**, G. *Productivity bargaining: a case study of a petroleum refinery, 1964–71.* 1972. (M.Sc. thesis, University of Strathclyde.)

1830 **McKersie**, Robert B., **Hunter**, Laurence Colvin and **Sengenberger**, Werner. *Productivity bargaining: the British and American experience.* Washington, D.C.: United States Government Printing Office, 1972. iv, 19p.

1831 **Norman**, Richard Gordon and **Bahiri**, S. *Productivity measurement and incentives.* London: Butterworth, 1972. 181p.

1832 **Parker**, Stanley Robert. 'Models for workplace bargaining.' *Pers. Manage.*, IV, 2 (February 1972), 30–3.

1833 **Torrington**, Derek Peter. 'Plant agreements.' Torrington, Derek P. (ed.). *Handbook of industrial relations.* 1972. p. 121–39.

1834 **Towers**, Brian, **Whittingham**, Terence George and **Gottschalk**, A. W. *Bargaining for change.* London: Allen & Unwin, 1972. 279p.

1835 **Whittingham**, Terence George and **Towers**, Brian. 'Bargaining for change.' *Ind. Relat. J.*, III, 1 (Spring 1972), 64–8.

1836 **Brown**, William Arthur. *Piecework bargaining.* London: Heinemann, 1973. 176p. (Warwick studies in industrial relations.)

1837 **Commission on Industrial Relations.** *Industrial relations at establishment level: a statistical survey.* London: H.M.S.O., 1973. vii, 75p. (Study 2.)

1838 **Daniel**, William Wentworth. *Incomes policy and collective bargaining at the workplace.* London: Political and Economic Planning, 1973. 73p. (P. E. P. broadsheets XXXIX, 541.)

1839 **De Jong**, J. R. 'Productivity in the E. E. C.' *Work Study*, IX, 2 (February 1973), 9–16.

1840 **Dore**, Ronald Philip. *British factory – Japanese factory: the origins of national diversity in industrial relations.* London: Allen & Unwin, 1973. 432p.

1841 **Ferm**, R. S. 'Whatever happened to common sense?' *Ind. Participation*, DLI (Spring 1973), 17–20.

1842 **George**, Kenneth D. and **Ward**, Terry.

'Productivity growth in the retail trade.' *Oxf. Univ. Inst. Econ. Stat. Bull.*, XXXV (February 1973), 31–47.

1843 **Goodrich**, Carter Lyman. *The frontier of control: a study in British workshop politics.* London: Pluto, 1973. xli, 284p.
First published 1920.
Reprinted with a new foreword and additional notes by Richard Hyman.

1844 **Gordon**, B. 'Management approaches to industrial relations in the firm: a regional study.' *J. Ind. Relat.*, XV, 4 (December 1973), 348–59.

1845 **Htun-Aye**, M. 'Taking another look at manpower utilisation.' *Ind. Participation*, DLIII (Autumn 1973), 29–30.

1846 **Jones**, Jack and **Swinden**, A. 'Changing roles in collective bargaining.' *Pers. Manage.*, V, 1 (January 1973), 26–8.

1847 **Kelly**, Aidan and **Hillery**, Brian J. P. 'Bargaining for productivity.' *Studies*, LXII (Autumn – Winter 1973), 221–32.

1848 **McKersie**, Robert B. and **Hunter**, Laurence Colvin. *Pay, productivity and collective bargaining.* London: Macmillan, 1973. xvii, 389p.

1849 **Marsh**, Arthur Ivor (ed.). *Managers and shop stewards: shop floor revolution?* London: Institute of Personnel Management, 1973. 174p.

1850 **Marsh**, Arthur Ivor. 'Managers, shop stewards and the Industrial Relations Act: the search for a new system.' Marsh, A. (ed.). *Managers and shop stewards.* 1973. p. 155–74.

1851 **Mitchell**, William and **Corbett**, Alan R. *Employee relations within the factory.* London: Macmillan, 1973. 135p.

1852 **Parker**, Stanley Robert. 'Research into workplace industrial relations: progress and prospects.' Warner, M. (ed.). *Sociology of the workplace.* 1973. p. 19–35.

1853 **Smith**, Ian G. *Measurement of productivity: a systems approach in the context of productivity agreements.* Epping: Gower, 1973. vii, 167p.

1854 **Taylor**, Robert. 'Poor relations.' *New Soc.*, XXIV, 552 (3 May 1973), 248.

1855 **Wood**, G. 'How do you rate in the manpower productivity league?' *Ind. Commer. Train.*, V, 8 (August 1973), 369–72.

1856 **Addison**, John Thomas. 'Productivity bargaining: the externalities question.' *Scott. J. Polit. Econ.*, XXI, 2 (June 1974), 123–42.

1857 **Bell**, Joseph Denis Milburn. 'The administrative aspects of the introduction of productivity payment schemes in the Electricity Supply Industry.' *Public Adm.*, LII (Autumn 1974), 341–9.

1858 **Bescoby**, John H. and **Potts**, A. 'Productivity agreements in Tyneside shiprepair 1969–72.' *Durham Univ. J.*, LXVI (March 1974), 185–202.

1859 **Brown**, William Arthur. 'Productive of change.' *New Soc.*, XXX (14 November 1974), 420–1.

1860 **The Collier**. *The great productivity trick.*

London: The Collier, 1974. 14p.

1861 **Henderson**, Joan and **Johnson**, Bert. 'Labour relations in the smaller firm.' *Pers. Manage.*, VI, 12 (December 1974), 28–31.

1862 **Lawrence**, Susanne. 'Productivity bargaining: resurrection or reprieve?' *Pers. Manage.*, VI, 1 (January 1974), 29–31.

1863 **McCarthy**, William Edward John. 'Relationships at the place of work.' *Work Study*, X, 4 (November 1974), 39–45.

1864 **Addison**, John Thomas. 'Whatever happened to productivity bargaining?' *Manage. Decis.*, XIII, 5 (1975), 337–47.

1865 **Brown**, William Arthur and **Sisson**, Keith. 'The use of comparisons in workplace wage determination.' *Br. J. Ind. Relat.*, XIII, 1 (March 1975), 23–53.

1866 **Dufty**, Norman F. *Changes in labour – management relations in the enterprise.* Paris: Organisation for Economic Cooperation and Development, 1975. 125p.

1867 **Gill**, C. 'Industrial relations in a multi-plant organization: some considerations.' *Ind. Relat. J.*, V, 4 (Winter 1974–5), 22–35.

1868 **National Economic Development Committee**, Economic Development Committee for the Clothing Industry. *Unlocking productivity potential.* London: N.E.D.C., 1975.

1869 **Parker**, Stanley Robert. *Workplace industrial relations 1973: an enquiry carried out on behalf of the Department of Employment.* London: H.M.S.O., 1975. xv, 150p.

1870 **Roeber**, Joe. *Social change at work: the I.C.I. weekly staff agreement.* London: Duckworth, 1975. xxiv, 342p.

1871 **Thomson**, Andrew William John and **Hunter**, Laurence Colvin. 'Level of bargaining in a multi-plant company.' *Ind. Relat. J.*, VI, 2 (Summer 1975), 23–40.

1872 **Walters**, Rhodri. 'Labour productivity in the South Wales steam-coal industry 1870–1914.' *Econ. Hist. Rev.*, XXVIII, 2 (May 1975), 280–303.

1873 **Wilders**, M. G. and **Parker**, Stanley Robert. 'Changes in workplace industrial relations 1966–72.' *Br. J. Ind. Relat.*, XIII, 1 (March 1975), 14–22.

1874 **Aldridge**, Alan. *Power, authority and restrictive practices: a sociological essay on industrial relations.* Oxford: Blackwell, 1976. 135p.

1875 **Batstone**, Eric, **Boraston**, Ian and **Frenkel**, Stephen. 'Principles in work-place bargaining.' Coker, E. and Stuttard, G. (eds.). *Industrial studies 2.* 1976. p. 19–40.

1876 **Briscoe**, Geoffrey. 'Recent productivity trends in the U.K. service sector.' *Oxf. Bull. Econ. Stat.*, XXXVIII, 4 (November 1976), 265–80.

1877 **Catherwood**, Sir Frederick. 'Shop floor power.' *Prod. Eng.*, LV, 6 (June 1976), 297–301.

1878 **Daniel**, William Wentworth. *Wage determination in industry.* London: Political and Economic Planning, 1976. xi, 132p.

1879 **National Economic Development Committee**, Economic Development Committee for the Distributive Trades. *The measurement of labour efficiency in retail stores.* London: N.E.D.C., 1976.

1880 **Smith**, G. 'Understanding productivity.' *Ind. Commer. Train.*, VIII, 12 (December 1976), 485–9.

1881 **Nichols**, Theo and **Beynon**, Huw. *Living with capitalism: class relations and the modern factory.* London: Routledge & Kegan Paul, 1977. ix, 204p.

1882 **Nightingale**, Martyn. *The sociology of productivity bargaining.* 1977. (Ph.D. thesis, University of Bristol.)

1883 **Terry**, Michael. 'The inevitable growth of informality.' *Br. J. Ind. Relat.*, XV, 1 (March 1977), 76–90.

1884 **Blanchard**, Ian. 'Labour productivity and work psychology in the English mining industry, 1400–1600.' *Econ. Hist. Rev.*, XXXI, 1 (1978), 1–24.

1885 **Fisher**, John. *Productivity bargaining.* London: Workers' Educational Association, 1978. 28p. (Studies for trade unionists, IV, 14.)

1886 **Incomes Data Services**. *Productivity bargaining.* London: I.D.S., 1978. 20p. (Study 162.)

1887 **Industrial Facts and Forecasting.** *Workplace industrial relations in manufacturing industry 1978: key results [of a survey conducted by I.F.F. for the Industrial Relations Research Unit of the Social Science Research Council].* London: I.F.F., 1978. 13p.

1888 **Jones**, G. Llywelyn. 'Productivity bargaining revisited.' *Pers. Manage.*, X, 1 (January 1978), 18–21.

1889 **National Economic Development Committee**, Economic Development Committee for Food and Drink Manufacture. *Productivity growth in the U.K. food and drink manufactur-*

ing industry. London: N.E.D.C., 1978.

1890 **National Economic Development Committee**, Sector Working Party for Food and Drink Machinery. *A participative approach to productivity improvement.* London: N.E.D.C., 1978.

1891 **Stolliday**, I. and **Attwood**, M. 'Financial inducements and productivity bargaining.' *Ind. Commer. Train.*, X, 3 (June 1978), 231–6.

1892 **Wood**, Duncan. 'Productivity bargaining: phase III progress and prospects for phase IV.' *Pers. Manage.*, X, 6 (June 1978), 26–9.

1893 **Beynon**, Huw and **Wainwright**, Hilary. *The workers' report on Vickers.* London: Pluto, 1979. 208p.

1894 **Incomes Data Services.** *Productivity schemes.* London: I.D.S., 1979, 18p. (Study 186.)

1895 **Lindop**, E. 'Workplace bargaining: the end of an era.' *Ind. Relat. J.*, X, 1 (Spring 1979), 12–21.

1896 **Marchington**, Mick. 'Shop-floor control and industrial relations.' Purcell, J. and Smith, R. (eds.). *The control of work.* 1979. p. 133–55.

1897 **National Economic Development Committee**, Sector Working Party for Heating, Ventilating, Air Conditioning and Refrigeration Equipment. *A participative approach to efficiency improvement.* London: N.E.D.C., 1979.

1898 **Purcell**, John. 'Attempts to reform workplace industrial relations.' *Ind. Relat. J.*, X, 2 (Summer 1979), 4–22.

1899 **Wood**, Duncan and **Turton**, David (eds.). *White collar productivity schemes: pay increases without price rises: papers given at a conference.* London: Oyez, 1979. 48p.

See also: 23; 93; 268; 287; 318; 471; 573; 685; 732; 757; 759; 1273; 1276; 1515; 1609; 1635; 1966; 2500; 3148; 3593; 3959; 4894; 6632.

III. DISCLOSURE OF INFORMATION FOR COLLECTIVE BARGAINING

The literature on the disclosure of information for collective bargaining tends not to draw a sharp distinction between the legal and non-legal aspects of the subject, and hence it has all been classified here. Material on company reports to employees and communications in industry generally is classified at Part Four, II, B. See also Part Five, VI, D, 1; and Part Seven, VI.

1900 **Basnett**, David. 'Disclosure of information: a union view.' Kessler, S. and Weekes, B. (eds.). *Conflict at work.* 1971. p. 115–23.

1901 **Robertson**, E. J. 'Disclosure of information: a management view.' Kessler, S. and Weekes, B. (eds.). *Conflict at work.* 1971. p. 105–14.

1902 **Incomes Data Services.** *Disclosure of information.* London: I.D.S., 1972. 16p. (Study 34.)

1903 **Robertson**, D. 'Disclosure disclosed.' *Ind.*

Soc., LIV, 11 (November 1972), 22–4.

1904 **Scouller**, Alan. 'The disclosure of information in collective bargaining.' *Pers. Manage.*, IV, 11 (November 1972), 22–5.

1905 **Beever**, Colin. 'How much should an employer tell? Disclosure of financial information to trade unions.' *New Soc.*, XXIII (15 February 1973), 385–6.

1906 **Smith**, Robin and **Manley**, P. S. 'Company information and the development of collective bargaining.' *Three Banks Rev.*, XCIX (September 1973), 27–48.

1907 **Maunders**, Keith and **Foley**, Bernard J. 'Accounting information, employees and collective bargaining.' *J. Bus. Finance Account.*, I, 1 (Spring 1974), 109–27.

1908 **Smith**, G. 'Participation through information disclosure.' *Ind. Commer. Train.*, VI, 8 (August 1974), 350–3.

1909 **Watson**, Tom. 'The accountant's role in

industrial relations: an outsider's view.' *Accountant's Magazine*, LXXVIII, 3 (March 1974), 118–30.

1910 **Confederation of British Industry.** *Provision of information by multinational enterprises in the U.K.* London: C.B.I., 1975. 25p.

1911 **Hird**, Christopher. *Your employer's profits.* London: Pluto, 1975. 200p. (Workers' handbook 2.)

1912 **Scouller**, Alan. 'All you need to know about disclosure.' *Pers. Manage.*, VII, 8 (August 1975), 25–8.

1913 **Wellens**, John. 'Information disclosure.' *Ind. Commer. Train.*, VII, 5 (May 1975), 179–84.

1914 **Gospel**, Howard F. 'Disclosure of information to trade unions.' *Ind. Law J.*, V, 4 (December 1976), 223–36.

1915 **Marsh**, Arthur Ivor and **Rosewell**, R. 'A question of disclosure.' *Ind. Relat. J.*, VII, 2 (Summer 1976), 4–16.

1916 **Barratt Brown**, Michael and **Coates**, Ken. *Accountability and industrial democracy.* Nottingham: Institute for Workers' Control, 1977. 13p. (I.W.C. pamphlets 50.)

1917 **Department of Employment Gazette**. 'Taking some of the guesswork out of industrial relations: disclosure of information.' *Dep. Employment Gaz.*, LXXXV, 8 (August 1977), 799–800, 807.

1918 **Incomes Data Services.** *Disclosure of information.* London: I.D.S., 1977 (Study 149.)

1919 **Jones**, D. M. C. 'The path to disclosure.' *Manage. Decis.*, IV (1977), 410–9.

1920 **Smith**, Robin. 'Disclosure of information: can Britain learn from Belgium?' *Pers. Manage.*, IX, 7 (July 1977), 20–4.

1921 **Barratt Brown**, Michael. 'Profits and losses and the social audit.' Coates, Ken (ed.). *The right to useful work.* 1978. p. 25–60.

1922 **Cuthbert**, Norman H. and **Whitacker**, A. 'Disclosure of information and collective bargaining.' *J. Bus. Finance Account.*, IV, 3 (1978), 373–8.

1923 **Gospel**, Howard F. 'The disclosure of information to trade unions: approaches and problems.' *Ind. Relat. J.*, IX, 3 (Autumn 1978), 18–26.

1924 **Department of Trade.** *Company accounting and disclosure: a consultative document.* London: H.M.S.O., 1979. vi, 94p. (Cmnd. 7654.)

1925 **Hancock**, P. J. 'Disclosure of financial information to employees.' *Employee Relat.*, I, 2 (1979), 19–21.

1926 **Robinson**, Derek. 'Capital plans for company assets.' *Pers. Manage.*, XI, 4 (April 1979), 41–4.

1927 **Wilders**, M. G. 'The disclosure of financial and related information.' *J. Gen. Manage.*, VII (Autumn 1979), 12–22.

1928 **Wilson**, B. 'The added value approach.' *Employee Relat.*, I, 1 (1979), 7; I, 2 (1979), 7.

See also: 1595; 1600; 1601; 1608; 1611; 1616; 1619; 1621; 1629.

IV. COLLECTIVE BARGAINING IN PARTICULAR OCCUPATIONS AND INDUSTRIES

See also Part Three, II, D; Part Five, V, C; Part Five, VI, D, 1; Part Six, III, D; and Part Six, IV, A, 2.

A. AGRICULTURE, FORESTRY, FISHING, MINING, AND QUARRYING

1929 **Industrial Research and Information Services.** *Democracy at work in mining.* London: The Services, 1971. 32p.

1930 **Bullock**, Jim. *Them and us.* London: Souvenir Press, 1972. 254p.

1931 **Griffin**, Alan Ramsay. 'Consultation and conciliation in the mining industry: the need for a new approach.' *Ind. Relat. J.*, III, 3 (Autumn 1972), 29–48.

1932 **Gidwell**, D. I. *Industrial relations and the wages structure in the coal mining industry.* 1975. (M.Sc. thesis, University of Wales, Cardiff.)

1933 **Mee**, Graham. 'Employer – employee relationships in the Industrial Revolution: the Fitzwilliam Collieries.' Pollard, S. and Holmes, C. (eds.). *Essays in the economic and social history of South Yorkshire.* 1976. p. 46–58.

1934 **Rhodes**, E. *The changing face of coal: a case study of industrial relations in the coal mining*

industry. Milton Keynes: Open U.P., 1976. 83p.

1935 **Edwards**, Christine. 'Measuring union power: a comparison of two methods applied to the study of local union power in the coal industry.' *Br. J. Ind. Relat.*, XVI, 1 (March 1978), 1–15.

1936 **Handy**, L. J. *Wage policy in the coalmining industry since nationalisation: a case study of national wage bargaining.* 1978. (Ph.D. thesis, University of Cambridge.)

1937 **Spaven**, Patrick John. *Accommodating the miners: a comparative study of industrial relations and community involvement in some South Yorkshire coalmining townships, 1855–1894.* 1978. 2 v. (Ph.D. thesis, University of Warwick.)

1938 **McCormick**, Brian Joseph. *Industrial relations in the coal industry.* London: Macmillan, 1979. xi, 263p.

See also: 1424; 1429; 1511; 1732; 1860; 1872.

B. MANUFACTURING, CONSTRUCTION, GAS, ELECTRICITY, AND WATER

1939 **Brown**, William Arthur. 'Piecework wage determination in Coventry.' *Scott. J. Polit. Econ.*, XVIII, 1 (February 1971), 1–30.

1940 **Commission on Industrial Relations.** *Clayton Dewandre Company Limited.* London: H.M.S.O., 1971. v, 48p. (Report 15. Cmnd. 4640.)

1941 **Commission on Industrial Relations.** *Shipbuilding and shiprepairing.* London: H.M.S.O., 1971. x, 189p. (Report 22. Cmnd. 4756.)

1942 **Commission on Industrial Relations.** *Standard Telephones and Cables Limited.* London: H.M.S.O., 1971. iv, 47p. (Report 14. Cmnd. 4598.)

1943 **Derber**, Milton. 'Labor – management relations in the metalworking industries of three countries.' *J. Ind. Relat.*, XIII, 1 (March 1971), 1–29.

1944 **Dyson**, R. F. *The development of collective bargaining in the cotton spinning industry, 1893–1914.* 1971. (Ph.D. thesis, University of Leeds.)

1945 **Marsh**, Arthur Ivor, **Evans**, Edward Owen and **Garcia**, Paul. *Workplace industrial relations in engineering.* London: Kogan Page, 1971. 22, 223p. (Engineering Employers' Federation research series.)

1946 **Barker**, Colin. *The power game.* London: Pluto, 1972. 92p.

1947 **Brown**, R. K., **Brannen**, P., **Cousins**, J. M. and **Samphier**, M. L. 'The contours of solidarity: social stratification and industrial relations in shipbuilding.' *Br. J. Ind. Relat.*, x, 1 (March 1972), 12–41.

1948 **Commission on Industrial Relations.** *Alcan Smelter site.* London: H.M.S.O., 1972. v, 73p. (Report 29.)

1949 **Commission on Industrial Relations.** *Engelhard Industries Limited.* London: H.M.S.O., 1972. c, 28p. (Report 26.)

1950 **Commission on Industrial Relations.** *The hotel and catering industry. Part II: industrial catering.* London: H.M.S.O., 1972. v, 37p. (Report 27.)

1951 **Commission on Industrial Relations.** *John Bamber Engineering Ltd.* London: H.M.S.O., 1972. v, 15p. (Report 28.)

1952 **Counter Information Services.** *General Electric Company Limited.* London: The Services, 1972. 36p. (Anti-reports 2.)

1953 **Hyman**, Richard. *Disputes procedure in action: a study of the engineering disputes procedures in Coventry.* London: Heinemann, 1972. (Warwick studies in industrial relations.)

1954 **Liddle**, R. J. and **McCarthy**, William Edward John. 'Third party intervention in the exhibition contracting industry: a case study in bargaining reform.' *Ind. Relat. J.*, III, 4 (Winter 1972), 5–23.

1955 **Lowry**, Pat. 'The B.L.M.C. agreement: a model procedure.' *Pers. Manage.*, IV, 6 (June 1972), 39–40.

1956 **Mallaber**, Ted. 'Unionisation without tears.' *Ind. Soc.*, LIV, 4 (April 1972), 10–11. Union recognition at I.C.I.

1957 **Verma**, Pramod Chandra. 'Industrial relations in the British chemical industry: a case study.' *Indian J. Ind. Relat.*, VIII, 1 (July 1972), 67–81.

1958 **Wearne**, Stephen Hugh (ed.). *Problems and policy in industrial relations on industrial sites: a report of discussions in seminars and working parties held in Manchester in 1971.* Manchester: University of Manchester Institute of Science and Technology, 1972.

1959 **Bayley**, L. G. *Building: teamwork or conflict.* London: George Godwin, 1973. viii, 120p.

1960 **Commission on Industrial Relations.** *Recognition of white-collar unions in engineering and chemicals.* London: H.M.S.O., 1973. ii, 75p. (Study 3.)

1961 **Commission on Industrial Relations.** *Walter Alexander and Company (Coachbuilders) Limited.* London: H.M.S.O., 1973. v, 47p. (Report 45.)

1962 **Kingsford**, P. W. *Builders and building workers.* London: Arnold, 1973. 242p.

1963 **Verma**, Pramod Chandra. 'Collective bargaining in the British chemical industry: a case study.' *Indian J. Ind. Relat.*, VIII, 4 (April 1973), 513–26.

1964 **Commission on Industrial Relations.** *Imperial Chemical Industries Limited.* London: H.M.S.O., 1974, vii, 102p. (Report 88.)

1965 **Pafford**, Elizabeth R. and **Pafford**, John Henry Pyle. *Employer and employed: Ford, Ayrton and Co. Ltd., Silk Spinners [and] Worker participation, Leeds and Low Bentham, 1870–1970.* Edington: Pasold Research Fund, 1974. 77p. (Pasold occasional papers 2.)

1966 **Rhys**, D. G. 'Employment, efficiency and labour relations in the British motor industry.' *Ind. Relat. J.*, v, 2 (Summer 1974), 4–26.

1967 **Advisory Conciliation and Arbitration Service.** *Electricity supply industry: report of an inquiry into the negotiating and representative arrangements for managerial and higher executive grades.* London: A.C.A.S., 1975. 26p. (Report 4.)

1968 **Bell**, Joseph Denis Milburn. 'Development of industrial relations in nationalized industries in postwar Britain.' *Br. J. Ind. Relat.*, XIII, 1 (March 1975), 1–13.

1969 **Jennings**, John and **Brown**, Penny. *The boxmakers: a brief history of the paper box industry, the Wages Council and the struggle for trade union recognition.* London: Society of Graphical and Allied Trades, 1975. 36p.

1970 **Lowry**, Pat. 'British Leyland's industrial relations.' *Prod. Eng.*, LIV, 12 (December 1975), 631–7.

1971 **Rowlands**, Marie Bernadette. *Masters and men in the West Midlands metalware trade before the industrial revolution.* Manchester: Manchester U.P., 1975. x, 198p.

1972 **Sisson**, Keith. *Industrial relations in Fleet Street: a study in pay structure.* Oxford: Blackwell, 1975. xvi, 185p. (Warwick studies in industrial relations.)

1973 **Barnes**, R. 'Appeals procedure at Glacier Metal.' *Ind. Commer. Train.*, VIII, 10 (October 1976), 383–6.

1974 **Derber**, Milton. 'Strategic factors in industrial relations systems: the metalworking industry.' *Labour & Soc.*, I, 1 (January 1976), 18–28.

1975 **Nichols**, Theo and **Armstrong**, P. *Workers divided*. Glasgow: Fontana/Collins, 1976. 221p.

1976 **Northrup**, Herbert R. and **Rowan**, Richard L. 'Multinational bargaining approaches in the Western European flat glass industry.' *Ind. Labor Relat. Rev.*, XXX, 1 (October 1976), 32–46.

1977 **Rhodes**, Ed. *Press, papers and print: a case study of industrial relations in the national newspaper industry*. Milton Keynes: Open U.P., 1976. 112p. (PT 281 Unit 4.)

1978 **Taylor**, Eric. *The better temper: a commemorative history of the Midland Iron and Steel Wages Board, 1876–1976*. London: Iron & Steel Trades Confederation, 1976. 38p.

1979 **Goodman**, John Francis Bradshaw, **Armstrong**, Eric George Abbott, **Davis**, J. E. and **Wagner**, A. 'Focus on footwear: formula for conflict but a pattern of peace.' *Pers. Manage.*, IX, 6 (June 1977), 22–6.

1980 **Goodman**, John Francis Bradshaw, **Armstrong**, Eric George Abbott, **Davis**, J. E. and **Wagner**, A. *Rule-making and industrial peace: industrial relations in the footwear industry*. London: Croom Helm, 1977. 213p.

1981 **Wilkinson**, Frank. 'Collective bargaining in the steel industry in the 1920s.' Briggs, A. and Saville, J. (eds.). *Essays in labour history 1918–1939*. 1977. p. 102–32.

1982 **Austrin**, Terry B. *Industrial relations in the construction industry: some sociological considerations on wage contracts and trade unionism (1914–1973)*. 1978. (Ph.D. thesis, University of Bristol).

1983 **Gill**, C., **Morris**, R. and **Eaton**, J. *Industrial relations in the chemical industry*. London: Saxon, 1978. 256p.

1984 **Chorley**, E. 'Consultative councils in the Lowman Engineering Group.' *Ind. Participation*, DLXXVI (Summer 1979), 16–22.

See also: 41; 910; 1267; 1425; 1802; 1815; 1820; 1824; 1829; 1857; 1858; 1870; 1881; 2762.

C. TRANSPORT, COMMUNICATIONS, AND DISTRIBUTION

1985 **Commission on Industrial Relations.** *The hotel and catering industry. Part I: hotels and restaurants*. London: H.M.S.O., 1971. iv, 71p. (Report 23. Cmnd. 4789.)

1986 **Jensen**, Vernon H. *Decasualization and modernization of dock work in London*. Ithaca, N.Y.: New York State School of Industrial &

Labor Relations, 1971. vi, 101p. (I.L.R. paperback 9.)

1987 **Thomson**, Andrew William John. 'Collective bargaining under incomes legislation: the case of Britain's buses.' *Ind. Labor Relat. Rev.*, XIV, 3 (April 1971), 389–406.

1988 **Blain**, Alexander Nicholas John. *Pilots and management: industrial relations in the U.K. airlines*. London: Allen & Unwin, 1972. 372p.

1989 **Hawkins**, Kevin H. 'Brewer – licensee relations: a case study in the growth of collective bargaining and white collar militancy.' *Ind. Relat. J.*, III, 1 (Spring 1972), 23–39.

Reprinted in Cuthbert, N. and Hawkins, K. (eds.). *Company industrial relations policies.* 1973. p. 112–53.

1990 **Jones**, C. D. 'The use of comparability in salary bargaining: the evidence from British Railways 1960–1968.' *Bull. Econ. Res.*, XXIV, 2 (November 1972), 98–110.

1991 **Macbeath**, Innis. 'What's really happening in the docks?' *New Humanist*, LXXXVIII (1972), 153–5.

1992 **Mellish**, Michael. *The docks after Devlin: a study of the effects of the recommendations of the Devlin committee on industrial relations in the London docks*. London: Heinemann, 1972. 146p. (Warwick studies in industrial relations.)

1993 **Nicholson**, Brian and **Greendale**, Walt. *Docks III: a national strategy*. Nottingham: Institute for Workers' Control, 1972. 9p. (I.W.C. pamphlets 32.)

1994 **Wilson**, David F. *Dockers: the impact of industrial change*. London: Fontana/Collins, 1972. 336p.

1995 **Close**, Tony. 'Talking shop.' *Ind. Soc.*, LV, 4 (April 1973), 8–19.

1996 **Fuchs**, John. 'Strategic factors in industrial relations in shipping.' *Int. Inst. Labour Stud. Bull.*, II (1973), 25–34.

1997 **Jackson**, Michael Peart. *Labour relations on the docks*. Farnborough: Saxon, 1973. ix, 146p.

1998 **McConville**, James. 'Collective bargaining in the shipping industry.' *Marit. Stud. Manage.*, I (1973) 74–97.

1999 **Commission on Industrial Relations.** *Retail distribution*. London: H.M.S.O., 1974. xi, 190p. (Report 89.)

2000 **Joint Special Committee on the Ports Industry.** *Final report*. London: The Committee, 1974. 16p.

Joint chairmen: Lord Aldington and Jack Jones.

2001 **Wallace**, J. *An examination of the principal methods and problems of wage determination in the retail distributive trades in the United Kingdom*. 1973–4. (M.Sc. thesis, University of Bath.)

2002 **Hill**, Stephen R. *A comparative occupational analysis of dock foremen and dock workers in the port of London*. 1975. (Ph.D. thesis, London School of Economics.)

2003 **Rowan**, Richard L. and **Northrup**, Herbert R. 'Multinational bargaining in the telecommunications industry.' *Br. J. Ind. Relat.*, XIII, 2 (July 1975), 257–62.

2004 **Bate**, S. P. *Workers' participation in industrial rule-making processes: a theoretical analysis and empirical investigation of a sample of employees in the Port of London.* 1976. (Ph.D. thesis, London School of Economics.)

2005 **Fairhurst**, D. W. and **Bean**, Ron. 'Industrial relations in municipal passenger transport.' *Ind. Relat. J.*, VII, 2 (Summer 1976), 60–62.

2006 **Hill**, Stephen R. *The dockers: class and tradition in London:* London: Heinemann, 1976. 252p.

2007 **Kinahan**, J. 'Maritime industrial relations: concepts and consequences.' *Marit. Policy Manage.*, IV (1976), 97–105.

2008 **McLean**, A. J. *A case study of wage determination in two cooperative stores.* 1975–6. (M.Sc. thesis, University of Bath.)

2009 **Advisory Conciliation and Arbitration Service.** *Industrial relations in the provincial newspaper and periodical industries.* London: H.M.S.O., 1977. x, 158p. (Cmnd. 6810–2. Royal Commission on the Press research series 2.)

2010 **Advisory Conciliation and Arbitration Service.** *Industrial relations in the national newspaper industry: a report to the Royal Commission on the Press.* London: A.C.A.S., 1977. xiv, 342p. (A.C.A.S. report 5.)

2011 **Advisory Conciliation and Arbitration Service.** *Scottish and Newcastle Breweries Limited: report of an inquiry into industrial relations in the transport activities of the Company's North East Region.* London: A.C.A.S., 1977. 48p. (A.C.A.S. report 9.)

2012 **Fuke**, H. *Japanese and British telecommunications systems: a comparative industrial relations analysis.* 1977. (M.Litt. thesis, University of Glasgow.)

2013 **McConville**, James. *Strategic factors in industrial relations systems: the shipping industry in the United Kingdom.* Geneva: International Institute for Labour Studies, 1977. 87p. (Research series 26.)

2014 **Weighell**, Sid. 'Industrial relations in the railway industry.' *Inst. Transp. J.*, XXXVII, 9 (March 1977), 255–9.

2015 **Underwood**, David. 'Industrial relations in the shipping industry.' *Pers. Manage.*, X, 3 (March 1978), 22–6.

See also: 1427; 1842.

D. WHITE-COLLAR, PROFESSIONAL, PUBLIC ADMINISTRATION, AND MISCELLANEOUS SERVICES

2016 **Bain**, George Sayers. 'Management and white-collar unionism.' Kessler, S. and Weekes, B. (eds.). *Conflict at work.* 1971. p. 15–30.

Reprinted in Cuthbert, N. and Hawkins, K. (eds.) *Company industrial relations policies.* 1973. p. 95–111.

2017 **Commission on Industrial Relations.** *Commercial Union Assurance Company Limited.* London: H.M.S.O., 1971. iv, 31p. (Report 16. Cmnd. 4642.)

2018 **Edinburgh Study Group.** 'Smoothing the path for white collar unions.' *Pers. Manage.*, III, 5 (May 1975), 18–22.

2019 **Hilton**, Irene M. 'Suffrage in medicine.' *Contemp. Rev.*, CCXVIII (March 1971), 130–1.

2020 **Levinson**, Harold Myer. *Collective bargaining by British local authority employees.* Ann Arbor: University of Michigan, Institute of Labour and Industrial Relations, 1971. v, 80p.

2021 **Loveridge**, Ray. *Collective bargaining by national employees in the United Kingdom.* Ann Arbor: University of Michigan, Institute of Labor and Industrial Relations, 1971. vii, 357p.

2022 **Pratt**, T. H. 'Revolution in the city.' *Pers. Manage.*, III, 3 (March 1971), 31–3.

2023 **Fraser**, R. A. and **Bell**, D. J. 'Facing up to staff representation.' *Pers. Manage.*, V, 3 (March 1973), 28–30.

2024 **Kelf-Cohen**, R. *British nationalisation 1945–1973.* London: Macmillan, 1973. xi, 288p.

2025 **Lewis**, R. *The new service society.* London: Longman, 1973. 179p.

2026 **Parris**, H. *Staff relations in the Civil Service: fifty years of Whitleyism.* London: Allen & Unwin, 1973. 204p.

2027 **Pettigrew**, Andrew M. 'Occupational specialization as an emergent process.' *Sociol. Rev.*, XXI, 2 (May 1973), 255–78.

Extracts reprinted in Esland, G. and others (eds.). *People and work.* 1975. p. 258–74.

2028 **Commission on Industrial Relations.** *Building societies.* London: H.M.S.O., 1974. v, 54p. (Report 86.)

2029 **Williams**, Sir Leslie. 'Industrial relations in the Civil Service.' *Manage. Serv. Gov.*, XXIX, 4 (November 1974), 176–88.

2030 **Dimmock**, Stuart and **Farnham**, David. 'Working with Whitley in today's N.H.S.' *Pers. Manage.*, VII, 1 (January 1975), 35–8.

2031 **Hopps**, R. L. 'The responsibilities of banks to their staff.' *J. Gen. Manage.*, III, 3 (Autumn 1975), 20–31.

2032 **Rowan**, Richard L. and **Northrup**, Herbert R. 'Multinational bargaining in the telecommunications industry.' *Br. J. Ind. Relat.*, XIII, 2 (July 1975), 257–62.

2033 **Berridge**, John. *A suitable case for treatment: a case study of industrial relations in the National Health Service.* Milton Keynes: Open U.P., 1976. 74p. (PT 281 Unit 9.)

2034 **McCarthy**, William Edward John. *Making Whitley work: a review of the operation of the National Health Service Whitley Council system.* London: Department of Health and Social Security, 1976. iv, 144p.

2035 **Mars**, Gerald and **Mitchell**, Peter. *Room for reform? A case study of industrial relations in the hotel industry.* Milton Keynes: Open U.P., 1976. 40p. (PT 282 Unit 6.)

2036 **Morriss**, R. A. 'Labour relations in the royal dockyards, 1801–5.' *Mar. Mirror*, LXII, 4 (November 1976), 337–46.

2037 **Scott**, R. 'Facing the realities of office unions.' *J. Gen. Manage.*, IV, 3 (Autumn 1976), 72–4.

2038 **White**, I. H. B. 'Academic involvement.' *Ind. Soc.*, LVIII, 2 (March–April 1976), 9–10.

2039 **Advisory Conciliation and Arbitration Service.** *Committee of inquiry into industrial relations in the London Fire Service.* London: A.C.A.S., 1977. 215p. (Report 8.)

2040 **Marsh**, R. S. *The recognition process in white collar trade unionism.* 1977. (M. Phil. thesis, Council for National Academic Awards.)

2041 **National Economic Development Committee.** Economic Development Committee for the Hotels and Catering Industry. *Employment policy and industrial relations in the hotels and catering industry.* London: N.E.D.C., 1977.

2042 **Somerton**, Michael. *Trade unions and industrial relations in local government.* London: Workers' Educational Association, 1977. 32p. (Studies for trade unionists III, 11.)

2043 **Farnham**, David. 'Sixty years of Whitleyism.' *Pers. Manage.*, X, 7 (July 1978), 29–32.

2044 **Jones**, P. 'Industrial relations in the public sector.' *Pers. Manage.*, X, 2 (February 1978), 38–42.

2045 **Thomson**, Andrew William John and **Beaumont**, Philip B. *Public sector bargaining: a study of relative gain.* London: Saxon House, 1978. 206p.

2046 **Bosanquet**, Nicholas (ed.). *Industrial relations in the N.H.S.: the search for a system.* London: King Edward's Hospital Fund for London, 1979. 253p.

2047 **Bosanquet**, Nicholas. 'Reform plans and priorities.' Bosanquet, N. (ed.). *Industrial relations in the N.H.S.* 1979. p. 222–9.

2048 **Bosanquet**, Nicholas. 'The search for a system.' Bosanquet, N. (ed.). *Industrial relations in the N.H.S.* 1979. p. 1–22.

2049 **Dyson**, Roger. 'Consultation and negotiation.' Bosanquet, N. (ed.). *Industrial relations in the N.H.S.* 1979. p. 73–96.

2050 **Hancock**, Christine. 'Special industrial relations problems in nursing.' Bosanquet, N. (ed.). *Industrial relations in the N.H.S.* 1979. p. 177–88.

2051 **Vulliamy**, Daniel L. and **Moore**, Roger. *Whitleyism and health: the NHS and its industrial relations.* London: Workers' Educational Association, 1979. 32p. (Studies for trade unionists V, 19.)

2052 **West**, Christopher and **Goodman**, Trevor. 'Disputes procedures and grievance procedures.' Bosanquet, N. (ed.). *Industrial relations in the N.H.S.* 1979. p. 55–72.

See also: 984; 997; 1139; 1456; 1571; 1899; 1967; 1968; 1989; 6127.

V. INDUSTRIAL CONFLICT

See also Part Five, I. Many of the works in Part Three, II, A–E also contain material on industrial conflict. Works on private conciliation and arbitration are listed here, but material on conciliation and arbitration by the state and that on the law relating to industrial conflict is included in Part Seven, VI.

A. GENERAL

Some of the general works in Part One, III also contain material on industrial conflict. See also Part Seven, VI.

2053 **Fore**, Mark. *Strategy for industrial struggle.* Bromley: Solidarity, 1971. 28p. (Solidarity pamphlets 37.)

2054 **Frow**, Ruth, **Frow**, Eddie and **Katanka**, Michael (eds.). *Strikes: a documentary history.* London: Charles Knight, 1971. xxx, 227p.

2055 **Industrial Participation Association.** *Resolving industrial conflicts.* London: The Association, 1971. 22p.

2056 **Jackson**, Michael Peart. *A critical assessment of the Ministry of Labour's method of analysing the causes of stoppages – with special reference to major stoppages – in the port, transport and coal mining industries between 1963 and 1966 (inc.).*

[1971?] (M.A. thesis, University of Hull.)

2057 **Munby**, Lionel Maxwell (ed.). *The Luddites and other essays.* London: Katanka, 1971. 281p.

2058 **Oxnam**, D. W. 'Issues in industrial conflict: an international comparison.' *J. Ind. Relat.*, XIII, 2 (June 1971), 130–7.

2059 *The Sheffield outrages.* Bath: Adams & Dart, 1971. 488p.
With a new introduction by Sidney Pollard.

2060 **Taylor**, L. and **Walton**, P. 'Industrial sabotage: motives and meanings.' Cohen, S. (ed.). *Images of deviance.* 1971. p. 219–45.
Reprinted in Barrett, B. and others (eds.). *Industrial relations and the wider society.* 1975. p. 348–58.

2061 **Whittingham**, T. G. and **Towers**, Brian. 'Strikes and the economy.' *Natl. Westminster Bank Q. Rev.* (November 1971), 33–42.
Reprinted in Butterworth, E. and Weir, D. (eds.). *Social problems of modern Britain.* London: Fontana, 1972. p. 349–56; and in Evans, E. and Creigh, S. (eds.). *Industrial conflict in Britain.* 1977. p. 77–88.

2062 **Durcan**, James W. and **McCarthy**, William Edward John. 'What is happening to strikes?' *New Soc.*, XXII (2 November 1972), 267–9.

2063 **Eccles**, Anthony J. 'The hunt for homo obstreperans.' *Pers. Rev.*, I, 2 (Spring 1972), 56–9.

2064 **Eldridge**, John Eric Thomas. *Industrial disputes: essays in the sociology of industrial relations*. London: Routledge & Kegan Paul, 1972. x, 277p.

2065 **Fox**, Alan. 'Coming to terms with conflict.' *Pers. Manage.*, V, 6 (June 1972), 20–3.

2066 **Gretton**, John. 'To sit or not to sit?' *New Soc.*, XX (15 June 1972), 564–6.

2067 **Hyman**, Richard. *Strikes*. London: Fontana. First edition. 1972. 184p. Revised edition. 1977. 218p.

2068 **Jackson**, Dudley and **Turner**, Herbert A. 'Inflation, stratoinflation and social conflict.' Jackson, D. and others. *Do trade unions cause inflation?* 1972. p. 11–62.

2069 **Jackson**, Dudley, **Turner**, Herbert A. and **Wilkinson**, Frank. *Do trade unions cause inflation? Two studies with a theoretical introduction and policy conclusion*. Cambridge: Cambridge U.P., 1972. viii, 128p. (Cambridge University. Department of Applied Economics. Occasional papers 36.)
Second edition. 1975. xviii, 126p.

2070 **Jackson**, Michael Peart. 'The Department of Employment's method of classifying the cause of stoppages.' *Br. J. Ind. Relat.*, X, 3 (November 1972), 445–7.

2071 **Knight**, K. G. 'Strikes and wage inflation in British manufacturing industry 1950–1968.' *Oxf. Univ. Inst. Econ. Stat. Bull.*, XXXIV, 3 (August 1972), 281–94.

2072 *Labour disputes in the early days of the industrial revolution 1758–1780*. New York: Arno Press, 1972. (British labour struggles: contemporary pamphlets 1727–1850.)

2073 **Leeson**, Robert Arthur. *Strike: a live history, 1887–1971*. London: Allen & Unwin, 1972. 246p.

2074 **McCord**, Norman. 'The nine hours strike of 1871 in Northern England.' *Soc. Study Labour Hist. Bull.*, XXIV (Spring 1972), 12–13.

2075 **Rimmer**, Malcolm. *Race and industrial conflict: a study in a group of midland foundries*. London: Heinemann, 1972. 74p. (Warwick studies in industrial relations.)

2076 **Sykes**, Andrew James Macintyre. *The resolution of conflict*. London: Working Together Campaign, 1972. 10p.

2077 **Wilkinson**, Frank and **Turner**, Herbert A. 'The wage – tax spiral and labour militancy.' Jackson, D. and others. *Do trade unions cause inflation?* 1972. p. 63–103.

2078 **Beever**, Colin. 'Sitting it out.' *Ind. Soc.*, LV, 5 (May 1973), 13–16.

2079 **Bishop**, Terry. 'When workers take control.' *Pers. Manage.*, V, 3 (March 1973), 24–8.

2080 **Coates**, Ken. 'Converting the unions to socialism.' Barratt Brown, M. and Coates,

K. (eds.). *Trade union register: 3*. 1973. p. 9–43.

2081 **Eldridge**, John E. T. 'Industrial conflict: some problems of theory and method.' Child, J. (ed.). *Man and organization*. 1973. p. 158–84.

2082 **Evans**, Erick Wyn and **Galambos**, P. 'Work stoppages in the United Kingdom 1965–70: a quantitative study.' *Bull. Econ. Res.*, XXV, 1 (May 1973), 22–42.
Reprinted in Evans, E. W. and Creigh, S. (eds.). *Industrial conflict in Britain*. 1977. p. 31–57.

2083 **Fisher**, M. *Measurement of labour disputes and their economic effects*. Paris: O.E.C.D., 1973. 239p.

2084 **Fletcher**, J. A., **Towers**, J. Maxwell, **Trussler**, May and **Wallis**, Linda. *A programme for working together: winning papers*. London: Working Together Campaign, 1973. 23p.

2085 **Forward**, N. S. 'Revision of the Department of Employment's classification for the causes of stoppages.' *Br. J. Ind. Relat.*, XI, 1 (March 1973), 143–5.

2086 **Howell**, Ralph. 'State-aided strikes.' *Spectator* (17 March 1973), 343–4.

2087 **Hyman**, Richard. 'Industrial conflict and the political economy of the sixties and prospects for the seventies.' *Social. Reg.* (1973), 101–53.

2088 **Hyman**, Richard. 'Living with strikes.' *New Soc.*, XXVI (25 October 1973), 204–6.

2089 **Jones**, Marjorie Caton. 'Trouble-free trades.' Parkinson, C. N. (ed.). *Industrial disruption*. 1973. p. 112–23.

2090 **Marsh**, Arthur Ivor. 'The causes of conflict.' Parkinson, C. N. (ed.). *Industrial disruption*. 1973. p. 64–76.

2091 **Marsh**, Arthur Ivor. 'Company policy.' Parkinson, C. N. (ed.). *Industrial disruption*. 1973. p. 145–55.

2092 **Parkinson**, Cyril Northcote (ed.). *Industrial disruption*. London: Leviathan House, 1973. xiv, 181p.

2093 **Shelton**, W. J. *English hunger and industrial disorder: a study of social conflict during the first decade of George III's reign*. London: Macmillan, 1973. 226p.

2094 **Silver**, Michael. 'Recent British strike trends: a factual analysis.' *Br. J. Ind. Relat.*, XI, 1 (March 1973), 66–104.
Reprinted in Evans, E. W. and Creigh, S. (eds.). *Industrial conflict in Britain*. 1977. p. 89–130.

2095 **Towers**, J. Maxwell. 'The territorial imperative and working together.' Fletcher, J. and others. *A programme for working together*. 1973. p. 11–18.

2096 **Trussler**, May. 'Caught in the crossfire.' Fletcher, J. and others. *A programme for working together*. 1973. p. 19.

2097 **Vessey**, S. C. 'Understanding workers on strike.' *Police Journal*, XLVI (October 1973), 321–37.

2098 **Wallis**, Linda. 'Working together for a better Britain.' Fletcher, J. and others. *A programme for working together.* 1973. p. 21–3.

2099 **Warner**, Malcolm. 'Industrial conflict revisited.' Warner, M. (ed.). *Sociology of the workplace.* 1973. p. 256–73.

2100 **Bean**, R. and **Peel**, D. A. 'A quantitative analysis of wage strikes in four U.K. industries, 1962–1970.' *J. Econ. Stud.*, I, 2 (November 1974), 88–97.

2101 **Bryant**, Richard. 'Linking community and industrial action.' *Community Dev. J.*, IX (January 1974), 213–35.

2102 **Durcan**, James W. and **McCarthy**, William Edward John. 'State subsidy theory of strikes: an examination of statistical data for the period 1956–1970.' *Br. J. Ind. Relat.*, XII, I (March 1974), 26–47.

2103 **Gennard**, John and **Lasko**, Roger. 'Supplementary benefit and strikers.' *Br. J. Ind. Relat.*, XII, I (March 1974), 1–25.

2104 **Hunter**, Laurence Colvin. 'The state subsidy theory of strikes: a reconsideration.' *Br. J. Ind. Relat.*, XII, 3 (November 1974), 438–44.

2105 **Ingham**, Geoffrey K. *Strikes and industrial conflict: Britain and Scandinavia.* London: Macmillan, 1974. 95p. (Studies in sociology.)

2106 **Institute for the Study of Conflict.** *Sources of conflict in British industry: report of a study group, London, November 1973 – February 1974.* London: The Institute, 1974. 39p.

2107 **Preston**, R. H. (ed.). *Industrial conflicts and their place in modern society: an international symposium.* London: S.C.M. Press, 1974.

2108 **Sapsford**, D. R. *The U.K.'s industrial disputes (1893–1971): a study in the economics of industrial unrest.* 1974. (M.Phil. thesis, University of Leicester.)

2109 **Stearns**, Peter N. 'Measuring the evolution of strike movements.' *Int. Rev. of Soc. Hist.*, XIX, I (1974), 1–27.

2110 **Armstrong**, Eric George Abbott. 'An anatomy of strikes: some basic incisions.' Preston, R. (ed.). *Perspectives on strikes.* 1975. p. 8–31.

2111 **Bean**, Ron. 'Relationship between strikes and "unorganized" conflict in manufacturing industries.' *Br. J. Ind. Relat.*, XIII, I (March 1975), 98–101.

2112 **Blacklaws**, Allan F. 'Strikes as a problem to management.' Preston, R. (ed.). *Perspectives on strikes.* 1975. p. 32–43.

2113 **Cordingley**, Brian L. 'Strikes as seen by an industrial chaplain.' Preston, R. (ed.). *Perspectives on strikes.* 1975. p. 82–93.

2114 **Creigh**, S. W. *Work stoppages in the Humberside sub-region, 1960–1971.* 1975. (M.Sc. thesis, University of Hull.)

2115 **Dahrendorf**, Ralf. *Conflict and contract: industrial relations and the political community in times of crisis.* Liverpool: Liverpool U.P., 1975. 18p.
Second Leverhulme memorial lecture.

2116 **Fulcher**, James. 'Industrial conflict in Britain and Sweden: critical note.' *Sociology*, IX, 3 (September 1975), 476–84.

2117 **Gennard**, John and **Lasko**, Roger. 'The individual and the strike.' *Br. J. Ind. Relat.*, XIII, 3 (November 1975), 346–70.

2118 **Hemingway**, John and **Keyser**, William. *Who's in charge? Worker sit-ins in Britain today: a Metra Oxford study.* Oxford: Metra Consulting Group, 1975. 67p.

2119 **Hickling**, M. A. *Labour disputes and unemployment insurance benefits in Canada and England.* Don Mills, Ontario: C.C.H. Canadian, 1975.

2120 **Jackson**, Dudley and **Turner**, Herbert A. 'Inflation, stratoinflation and social conflict.' Jackson, D. and others. *Do trade unions cause inflation?* 1975. p. 11–62.

2121 **Jeuda**, Diana. 'The role of strikes in trade union strategy.' Preston, R. (ed.). *Perspectives on strikes.* 1975. p. 45–65.

2122 **Johnston**, Ernie. *Industrial action.* London: Arrow, 1975. 86p.

2123 **Keiser**, Jack and **Kelly**, Kevin T. 'Human causes and effects of strikes.' Preston, R. (ed.). *Perspectives on strikes.* 1975. p. 66–81.

2124 **Lasko**, Roger. 'The payment of supplementary benefit for strikers' dependants: misconception and misrepresentation.' *Mod. Law Rev.*, XXXVIII (January 1975), 31–8.

2125 **Margerison**, Charles J. and **Leary**, Malcolm. 'Crisis mediation.' *Manage. Decis.*, XIII, 4 (1975), 216–29.

2126 **Margerison**, Charles J. and **Leary**, Malcolm. 'Identifying opportunities for mediation.' *Manage. Decis.*, XIII, 4 (1975), 258–87.

2127 **Margerison**, Charles J. and **Leary**, Malcolm. 'Industrial mediation.' *Manage. Decis.*, XIII, 4 (1975), 195–214.

2128 **Margerison**, Charles J. and **Leary**, Malcolm. *Managing industrial conflicts: the mediator's role.* London: Resource Development Associates, 1975. 94p.

2129 **Margerison**, Charles J. and **Leary**, Malcolm. 'The mediator in action.' *Manage. Decis.*, XIII, 4 (1975), 230–57.

2130 **Preston**, R. H. (ed.). *Perspectives on strikes.* Manchester: SCM Press, 1975. 149p.

2131 **Sapsford**, D. R. 'A time series analysis of U.K. industrial disputes.' *Ind. Relat.*, XIV, 2 (May 1975), 242–9.

2132 **Shorey**, John C. *A quantitative analysis of strike activity in the United Kingdom, with reference to the time pattern and to inter-industry differences.* 1975. (Ph.D thesis, London School of Economics.)

2133 **Shorey**, John C. 'Size of the work unit and strike incidence.' *J. Ind. Econ.*, XXIII, 3 (March 1975), 175–88.

2134 **Smith**, Michael. 'Power and conflict in society.' Preston, R. (ed.). *Perspectives on strikes.* 1975. p. 114–28.

2135 **Taylor**, Michael H. 'Evaluating strikes.'

Preston, R. (ed). *Perspectives on strikes.* 1975. p. 129–49.

2136 **Wilkinson**, Frank and **Turner**, Herbert A. 'The wage–tax spiral and labour militancy.' Jackson, D. and others. *Do trade unions cause inflation?* 1975. p. 63–103.

2137 **Bean**, Ron. 'Industrial reactions.' Coker, E. and Stuttard, G. (eds.). *Industrial studies 2.* 1976. p. 68–88.

2138 **Bentley**, Stuart. 'Industrial conflict, strikes and black workers: problems of research methodology.' *New Community,* v (Summer 1976), 127–38.

2139 **Cooper**, Bruce Michael and **Bartlett**, A. F. *Industrial relations: a study in conflict.* London: Heinemann, 1976. ix, 310p.

2140 **De Smours**, Luigi Dusmet. 'Power and accountability in business: the areas of confrontation: a philosophical approach.' *Month,* ix (July 1976), 225–30.

2141 **Institute of Personnel Management.** *Sit-ins and work-ins.* London: The Institute, 1976. 39p.

2142 **Morley**, David. 'Industrial conflict and the mass media.' *Sociol. Rev.,* xxiv (May 1976), 245–68.

2143 **North-East Trade Union Studies Information Unit.** *Workers' occupations and the North-East experience.* Newcastle-upon-Tyne: The Unit, 1976.

2144 **O'Brien**, Richard. 'Causes of industrial peace.' *Ind. Participation,* DLXIII (Spring 1976), 3–10.

2145 **Shorey**, John C. 'Inter-industry analysis of strike frequency.' *Economica,* XLIII, 172 (November 1976), 349–65.

2146 **Thomas**, C. 'Strategy for a sit-in.' *Pers. Manage.,* viii, 1 (January 1976), 33–6.

2147 **Baldry**, C. J. *A sociological examination of the causes of British inter-industrial strike patterns, 1950–1969.* 1977. (Ph.D. thesis, University of Durham.)

2148 **Bennison**, B. R. 'Strikes: a break-even analysis.' *Pers. Manage.,* ix, 2 (February 1977), 22–31.

2149 **Brown**, Geoff. *Sabotage: a study in industrial conflict.* Nottingham: Spokesman, 1977. xiii, 396p.

2150 **Edwards**, Paul K. 'A critique of the Kerr–Siegel hypothesis of strikes and the isolated mass: a study of the falsification of sociological knowledge.' *Sociol. Rev.,* xxv (August 1977), 551–74.

2151 **Evans**, Erick Wyn and **Creigh**, S. W. (eds.). *Industrial conflict in Britain.* London: Cass, 1977. 292p.

2152 **Gennard**, John. *Financing strikers.* London: Macmillan, 1977. 184p.

2153 **Greenwood**, John. *Worker sit-ins and job protection: case studies of union intervention.* Epping: Gower, 1977. ix, 121p.

2154 **Howkins**, Alun. 'Edwardian Liberalism and industrial unrest: a class view of the decline of liberalism.' *Hist. Workshop,* IV (Autumn 1977), 143–61.

2155 **Kassalow**, Everett M. 'Industrial conflict and consensus in the United States and Western Europe: a comparative analysis.' Industrial Relations Research Association. *Proceedings of the thirtieth annual winter meeting, New York, December 28–30, 1977.* p. 113–22.

2156 **Milne**, Maurice. 'Strikes and strike breaking in North-East England, 1815–44: the attitude of the local press.' *Int. Rev. of Soc. Hist.,* xxii, 2 (1977), 226–40.

2157 **Personnel Management.** 'Strikes: a break-even analysis.' *Pers. Manage.,* ix, 2 (February 1977), 22–9.

2158 **Shorey**, John C. 'Time series analysis of strike frequency.' *Br. J. Ind. Relat.,* xv, 1 (March 1977), 63–75.

2159 **Turner**, Herbert Arthur, **Roberts**, Geoffrey and **Roberts**, David. *Management characteristics and labour conflict: a study of managerial organisation, attitudes and industrial relations.* Cambridge: Cambridge U.P., 1977. viii, 80p.

2160 **Batstone**, Eric, **Boraston**, Ian and **Frenkel**, Stephen. *The social organisation of strikes.* Oxford: Blackwell, 1978. 236p. (Warwick studies in industrial relations.)

2161 **Crouch**, Colin. 'The intensification of industrial conflict in the United Kingdom.' Crouch, Colin and Pizzorno, Alessandro (eds.). *The resurgence of class conflict in Western Europe since 1968.* London: Macmillan. Vol. 1. *National studies.* 1978. p. 191–256.

2162 **Daly**, S. *Cork, a city in crisis: a history of labour conflict and social misery, 1870–1872.* Cork: Tower Books, 1978. xvii, 336p.

2163 **Hay**, Greg. 'The whys and wherefores of private arbitration.' *Pers. Manage.,* x, 9 (September 1978), 35–8.

2164 **Hyman**, Richard. 'Occupational structure, collective organisation and industrial militancy.' Crouch, Colin and Pizzorno, Alessandro (eds.). *The resurgence of class conflict in Western Europe since 1968.* London: Macmillan. Vol. 2. *Comparative analyses.* 1978 p. 35–70.

2165 **McKay**, S. *Some disciplinary penalties against strikers.* 1978. (Ph.D thesis, University of Cambridge.)

2166 **Martin**, Roderick. 'The effects of recent changes in industrial conflict on the internal politics of trade unions: Britain and Germany.' Crouch, C. and Pizzorno, A. (eds.). *The resurgence of class conflict in Western Europe since 1968.* London: Macmillan. Vol. 2. *Comparative analyses.* 1978. p. 101–26.

2167 **Porter**, Marilyn. Consciousness and second-hand experience: wives and husbands in industrial action.' *Sociol. Rev.,* xxvi (May 1978), 263–82.

2168 **Sapsford**, D. 'Employer resistance and strikes: a contradiction resolved.' *Scott. J.*

Polit. Econ., xxv (November 1978), 311–15.

2169 **Smith**, C. T. B., **Clifton**, Richard, **Makeham**, Peter, **Creigh**, S. W. and **Burn**, R. V. *Strikes in Britain: a research study of industrial stoppages in the United Kingdom.* London: Department of Employment, 1978. 180p. (Manpower papers 15.)

2170 **Wray**, Ian. 'The Mersey bug.' *New Soc.*, xxxi (27 April 1978), 202–3.

2171 **Batstone**, Eric. 'The organization of conflict.' Stephenson, G. and Brotherton, C. (eds.). *Industrial relations: a social psychological approach.* 1979. p. 55–74.

2172 **Chermesh**, R. 'Strikes: the issue of social responsibility.' *Br. J. Ind. Relat.*, xvii, 3 (November 1979), 337–46.

2173 **Cronin**, James E. *Industrial conflict in modern Britain.* London: Croom Helm, 1979. 242p.

2174 **Edwards**, Paul K. 'Methodological issues in quantitative strike analysis: a comment.' *Ind. Relat.*, xviii (1979), 117–9.

2175 **Edwards**, Paul K. 'The "social" determination of strike activity: an explication and critique.' *J. Ind. Relat.*, xxi (1979), 198–216.

2176 **Edwards**, Paul K. 'Strikes and unorganised conflict: some further considerations.' *Br. J. Ind. Relat.*, xiii, 1 (March 1979), 95–8.

2177 **Mayhew**, K. 'Economists and strikes.' *Oxf. Bull. Econ. Stat.*, xli (February 1979), 1–19.

2178 **Millward**, Neil. 'The strike record of foreign-owned manufacturing plants in Great Britain.' *Br. J. Ind. Relat.*, xvii, 1 (March 1979), 99–104.

2179 **Montague**, Ken. *Going on strike.* London: Rank and File, 1979. 24p. (Rank and file handbooks 10.)

2180 **Sheane**, D. 'When and how to intervene in conflict.' *Pers. Manage.*, xi, 11 (November 1979), 32–5.

2181 **Skinner**, Martin R. 'The social psychology of intergroup conflict.' Stephenson, G. and Brotherton, C. (eds.). *Industrial relations: a social psychological approach.* 1979. p. 75–93.

2182 **Willis**, John. 'ITV strike notebook.' *Listener*, cii (18 October 1979), 515–6.

2183 **Wrigley**, Christopher J. '1919: the critical year.' Wrigley, C. (ed.). *The British labour movement in the decade after the First World War.* 1979. p. 1–19.

See also: 10; 52; 228; 294; 778; 1739; 1744; 1782; 2312; 4634; 6841; 6878; 6921; 6937; 7064.

B. GENERAL STRIKES

See also Part Three, II, B; and Part Five, VI, B.

2184 **McCarthy**, Terry. *Labour v. Sinn Fein: the Dublin General Strike 1913–14.* London: National Museum of Labour History, [1971]. 20p.

2185 **Scheps**, A. E. *Trade unions and Government, 1925–7, with particular reference to the General Strike.* 1971. (D.Phil. thesis, University of Oxford.)

2186 **Farman**, Christopher. *The General Strike, May 1926.* London: Rupert Hart-Davis, 1972. xi, 305p.

2187 **Mather**, F. C. 'The general strike of 1842: a study of leadership, organisation and the threat of revolution during the Plug Plot disturbances.' Porter, J. (ed.). *Provincial labour history.* 1972. p. 5–27.

2188 **Usherwood**, Stephen. 'The B.B.C. and the General Strike.' *Hist. Today*, xxii (December 1972), 858–65.

2189 **Williams**, A. R. 'The General Strike in Gloucestershire.' *Bris. Glouc. Archaeol. Soc. Trans.*, xci (1972), 207–13.

2190 **Wyncoll**, P. 'The General Strike in Nottingham.' *Marxism Today*, xvi (1972), 172–80.

2191 **Moran**, William. 'The Dublin lockout–1913.' *Soc. Study Labour Hist. Bull.*, xxvii (Autumn 1973), 10–16.

2192 **Morris**, Margaret. *British general strike 1926.* London: Historical Association, 1973. 40p. (Historical Association. General series 82.)

2193 **Bean**, Ron. 'The general strike in Merseyside.' *N.W. Labour Hist. Soc. Bull.*, 1 (1974), 6–10.

2194 **Carter**, Paul and **Carter**, Carol. *The miners of Kilsyth in the 1926 general strike and lockout.* London: Communist Party of Great Britain History Group, 1974. 26p. (Our history pamphlets 58.)

2195 **Frow**, Eddie and **Frow**, Ruth. 'The general strike in Manchester.' *N.W. Labour Hist. Soc. Bull.*, 1 (1974), 1–5.

2196 *Glasgow 1919: the story of the 40 hours strike.* Glasgow: Molendinar Press, [1974]. With an introduction by Harry McShane.

2197 **Mather**, F. C. 'The general strike of 1842: a study of leadership, organisation and the threat of revolution during the Plug Plot disturbances.' Quinault, R. and Stevenson, J. (eds.). *Popular protest and public order.* London: Allen & Unwin, 1974. p. 115–40.

2198 **Workers' Association.** *The Ulster general strike: strike bulletins of the Workers' Association.* Belfast: Workers' Association, 1974. [23]p.

2199 **Arnot**, Robin Page. *The General Strike May 1926: its origin and history.* Wakefield: E. P. Publishing, 1975. 245p. First published 1926. Reprinted with a new introduction by Lord Feather.

2200 **Carr**, Bill. 'Memories of the General Strike.' *Marxism Today*, xix, 5 (May 1975), 146–52.

2201 **Clarke**, Joe F. 'The General Strike on Tyneside.' *N.E. Group Study Labour Hist. Bull.*, ix (October 1975), 4–6.

2202 **Fisk**, Robert. *The point of no return: the strike which broke the British in Ulster.* London: Deutsch, 1975. 266p.

2203 **Renshaw**, Patrick. *The general strike.* London: Eyre Methuen, 1975. 301p.

2204 **Renshaw**, Patrick. *Nine days in May: the General Strike.* London: Eyre Methuen, 1975. 128p.

2205 **Trory**, Ernie. *Brighton and the General Strike.* Brighton: Crabtree, 1975. 32p.

2206 **Trory**, Ernie. *Soviet trade unions and the General Strike.* Brighton: Crabtree, 1975. 48p.

2207 **Attfield**, John and **Lee**, John. 'Deptford and Lewisham.' Skelley, J. (ed.). *The General Strike, 1926.* 1976. p. 261–82.

2208 **Barnsby**, George. 'The Black Country.' Skelley, J. (ed.). *The General Strike, 1926.* 1976. p. 193–207.

2209 **Barnsby**, George. *The General Strike in the Black Country.* Wolverhampton: Wolverhampton, Bilston and District Trades Council, 1976. [18]p.

2210 **Carr**, Bill. 'From the Yorkshire coalfield.' Skelley, J. (ed.). *The General Strike, 1926.* 1976. p. 340–51.

2211 **Carr**, Bill. 'Memories of the General Strike.' *N.E. Group Study Labour Hist. Bull.*, x (October 1976), 14–21.

2212 **Carter**, Paul. 'The West of Scotland.' Skelley, J. (ed.). *The General Strike, 1926.* 1976. p. 111–39.

2213 **Cohen**, Jack. 'Marxism versus reformism in the General Strike.' *Marxism Today*, xx, 5 (May 1976), 156–62.

2214 **Davies**, Bob. 'From St. Helens.' Skelley. J. (ed.). *The General Strike, 1926.* 1976. p. 330–9.

2215 **Davies**, Trevor. *Bolton, May 1926: a review of the General Strike as it affected Bolton and district.* Bolton: Bolton Trades Council, 1976. 19p.

2216 **Durr**, Andy. *Who were the guilty? General Strike, Brighton, May 1926.* Brighton: Labour History Press, 1976. 40p.

2217 **Foster**, John. 'British imperialism and the labour aristocracy.' Skelley, J. (ed.). *The General Strike, 1926.* 1976. p. 3–57.

2218 **Foster**, John. 'The state and ruling class during the General Strike.' *Marxism Today*, xx, 5 (May 1976), 136–48.

2219 **Francis**, Hywel. 'South Wales.' Skelley, J. (ed.). *The General Strike, 1926.* 1976. p. 232–59.

2220 **Frow**, Edmund and **Frow**, Ruth. 'Manchester diary.' Skelley, J. (ed.). *The General Strike, 1926.* 1976. p. 160–72.

2221 **Green**, Horace. 'Newcastle: the other side.' *N.E. Group Study Labour Hist. Bull.*, x (October 1976), 21–4.

2222 **Hallas**, Duncan. 'The Communist Party and the General Strike.' *Int. Soc.*, LXXXVIII (May 1976), 16–24.

2223 **Hastings**, R. P. 'Birmingham.' Skelley, J. (ed.). *The General Strike, 1926.* 1976. p. 208–31.

2224 **Hatvany**, D. 'The General Strike in Aberdeen.' *Scott. Labour Hist. Soc. J.*, x (June 1976), 3–20.

2225 **Jacobs**, Julie. 'From Hackney.' Skelley, J. (ed.). *The General Strike, 1926.* 1976. p. 360–7.

2226 **Jaques**, Martin. 'Consequences of the General Strike.' Skelley, J. (ed.). *The General Strike, 1926,* 1976. p. 375–404.

2227 **Jenkins**, Mick. 'The Councils of Action as a form of struggle: Britain, home of the General Strike.' *Marxism Today*, xx, 5 (May 1976), 148–54.

2228 **Kee**, Robert. *General Strike report.* Leeds: Yorkshire Television, 1976. 56p.

2229 **Kerrigan**, Peter. 'From Glasgow.' Skelley, J. (ed.). *The General Strike, 1926.* 1976. p. 315–29.

2230 **Klugmann**, James. 'Marxism, reformism and the General Strike.' Skelley, J. (ed.). *The General Strike, 1926.* 1976. p. 58–107.

2231 **Large**, Marion, **Bulgin**, D., **Drake**, P., **Eyton**, W., **Milsom**, R. and **Pitt**, A. *The nine days in Birmingham: the General Strike 4–12 May 1926.* Birmingham: Birmingham Public Libraries, Social Services Department, 1976. 43p.
With a preface by Lord Feather.

2232 **MacDougall**, Ian. 'Edinburgh.' Skelley, J. (ed.). *The General Strike, 1926.* 1976. p. 140–59.

2233 **McLean**, John. *The 1926 General Strike in Lanarkshire.* London: Communist Party of Great Britain History Group, 1976. 26p. (Our history pamphlets 65.)

2234 **Morris**, Margaret. *The General Strike.* Harmondsworth: Penguin, 1976. 479p.

2235 **Morris**, R. W. 'The General Strike.' *N.E. Group Study Labour Hist. Bull.*, x (October 1976), 2–13.

2236 **Muckle**, William. 'Cramlington.' *N.E. Group Study Labour Hist. Bull.*, x (October 1976), 12–13.

2237 **Newitt**, Ned. *The General Strike in Leicester.* Leicester: Gadfly Designs, 1976. 14p.

2238 **Noel**, Gerrard Eyre. *The great lock-out of 1926.* London: Constable, 1976. 239p.

2239 **Phillips**, Gordon Ashton. *The General Strike: The politics of industrial conflict.* London: Weidenfeld & Nicolson, 1976. 388p. (Radical men, movements and ideas.)

2240 **Skelley**, Jeffrey (ed.). *The General Strike, 1926.* London: Lawrence & Wishart, 1976. xiv, 412p.

2241 **Trotsky**, Leon, **Grant**, Ted and **Taafe**, Peter. *General Strike 1926: articles ...* London: Militant, 1976. 59p.

2242 **Tuckett**, Angela. 'Swindon.' Skelley, J. (ed.). *The General Strike, 1926.* 1976. p. 283–311.

2243 **Union Place Community Resources Centre.** *Nine days 1926: the General Strike in Southwark.* London: The Centre, 1976. 52p.

2244 **Watson**, Harry. 'An incident on the River Thames.' Skelley, J. (ed.). *The General Strike, 1926.* 1976. p. 368–71.

2245 **Wicks**, Harry. *The General Strike.* London: Workers' League, 1976. 28p.

2246 **Wilson**, David A. 'From Bradford.' Skelley, J. (ed.). *The General Strike, 1926.* 1976. p. 352–9.

2247 **Wilson**, David A. 'The General Strike and backlash.' *New Left Rev.*, XCVII (May–June 1976), 54–69.

2248 **Wyncoll**, Peter. 'The East Midlands.' Skelley, J. (ed.). *The General Strike, 1926.* 1976. p. 173-92.

2249 **Barton**, David and **Gasse**, Ian. *Newark and the General Strike.* Newark: The Authors, 1977. 8p.

2250 **Griffin**, C. P. 'The Leicestershire miners and the mining dispute of 1926.' *Int. Rev. of Soc. Hist.*, XXII, 3 (1977), 299-312.

2251 **Groves**, Reg, **Lane**, Jimmy, **Loughton**, Alf and **Wicks**, Harry. *The general strike in Battersea 1926: a reassessment.* London: Battersea Labour Party, 1977. 16p.
Bound with Lane, J. and others. *This was our heyday.*

2252 **Jones**, Richard Merfyn. 'A note on 1926 in North Wales.' *Llafur*, II, 2 (Spring 1977), 59-64.

2253 **Kibblewhite**, Elizabeth and **Rigby**, Andrew. *Aberdeen in the General Strike.* Aberdeen: Aberdeen People's Press, 1977. 33p.

2254 **McHugh**, J. 'The Belfast labour dispute and riots of 1907.' *N.W. Labour Hist. Soc. Bull.*, IV (1977), 92-129.

2255 **Phillips**, G. A. 'The Labour Party and the general strike.' *Llafur*, II, 2 (Spring 1977), 44-58.

2256 **Society for the Study of Welsh Labour History.** '1926 remembered and revealed: extracts from tape-recordings of a conference.' *Llafur*, II, 2 (Spring 1977), 9-30.

2257 **Williams**, R. 'The social significance of 1926.' *Llafur*, II, 2 (Spring 1977), 5-8.

2258 **Box**, Angela. 'The effects of the 1926 General Strike in the Midlands.' *Blackcountryman*, XI (Summer 1978), 24-5.

2259 **Frank**, David. 'Two documents on the British General Strike, 1926.' *Comm. Can. Labour Hist. Bull.*, V (Spring 1978), 8-11.

2260 **Keogh**, Dermot. 'William Martin Murphy and the origins of the 1913 lock-out.' *Saothar*, IV (1978), 15-35.

2261 **MacDougall**, Ian. 'Some aspects of the 1926 General Strike in Scotland.' MacDougall, I. (ed.). *Essays in Scottish labour history.* 1978. p. 170-206.

2262 **Moran**, William. '1913, Jim Larkin and the British labour movement.' *Saothar*, IV (1978), 35-49.

2263 **Morris**, Margaret. 'The General Strike in retrospect.' Wrigley, C. (ed.). *The British labour movement in the decade after the First World War.* 1979. p. 20-35.

See also: 54.

C. PARTICULAR OCCUPATIONS AND INDUSTRIES

See also Part Three, II, D; Part Five, IV; Part Five, V, B; Part Six, III, D; Part Six, IV, A, 2; and Part Seven, VI.

1. Agriculture, Forestry, Fishing, Mining, and Quarrying

See also Part Five, V, B.

2264 **Haden**, H. Jack. 'The 1921 coal strike: a bid for nationalisation that failed.' *Blackcountryman*, IV (Autumn 1971), 20-8.

2265 *The aftermath of the 'last labourers' revolt': fourteen pamphlets, 1830-1831.* New York: Arno, 1972. (British labour struggles: contemporary pamphlets 1727-1850.)

2266 **Barratt Brown**, Michael. *What really happened to the coal industry: the background to the miners' strike.* Nottingham: Institute for Workers' Control, 1972. (IWC pamphlets 31.)

2267 **Department of Employment.** *Report of the Court of Inquiry into a Dispute between the National Coal Board and the National Union of Mineworkers.* London: H.M.S.O., 1972. iv, 16p. (Cmnd. 4903.)
Chairman: Lord Wilberforce.

2268 *Labour disputes in the mines 1831-1844.* New York: Arno, 1972. (British labour struggles: contemporary pamphlets 1727-1850.)

2269 **Ravensdale**, J. R. 'The 1913 china clay strike and the Workers' Union.' Porter, J. (ed.). *Provincial labour history.* 1972. p. 53-73.

2270 **Thompson**, Edward Palmer. 'A special case.' *New Soc.*, XIX (24 February 1972), 402-4.

2271 **Williams**, J. E. 'The miners' lockout of 1893.' *Soc. Study Labour Hist. Bull.*, XXIV (Spring 1972), 13-16.

2272 **Winchester**, David. 'The British coal mine strike of 1972.' *Mon. Labor Rev.*, XCV, 10 (October 1972), 30-6.

2273 **Bryant**, Richard. 'Professionals in the firing line.' *Br. J. Soc. Work*, III (Summer 1973), 161-74.
Impact of the 1972 miners' strike on social services.

2274 **Dunbabin**, John Paul Delacour. *Rural discontent in nineteenth century Britain.* London: Faber, 1974. 320p.

2275 **Fieldhouse**, R. 'Strike action.' Maynard, J. (ed.). *A hundred years of farmworkers' struggle.* 1974. p. 18-21.

2276 **Butler**, R. J. 'Relative deprivation and power: a switched replication design using time series data of strike rates in American and British coal mining.' *Hum. Relat.*, XXIX (July 1976), 623-4.

2277 **Jones**, David. 'Thomas Campbell Foster and the rural labourer: incendiarism in East Anglia in the 1840s.' *Soc. Hist.*, I (January 1976), 5-43.

2278 **Neville**, Robert G. 'In the wake of Taff Vale: the Densby and Cadeby miners' strike and conspiracy case, 1902-06.' Benson, J. and Neville, R. (eds.). *Studies in the Yorkshire coal industry.* 1976. p. 145-62.

2279 **Neville**, Robert G. 'The Yorkshire miners and the 1893 lockout: the Featherstone "massacre".' *Int. Rev. of Soc. Hist.*, XXI, 3 (1976), 337–57.

2280 **Short**, George. 'The miners fight on.' *Marxism Today*, XX, 5 (May 1976), 163–8.

2281 **Ulman**, Lloyd. 'Runaway unionism: the British coal strike, the social contract, and the economics of militancy.' *Round Table*, CCLXII (April 1976), 161–72.

2282 **Edwards**, P. J. and **Marshall**, J. 'Sources of conflict and community in the trawling industries of Hull and Grimsby between the Wars.' *Oral Hist.*, V, 1 (Spring 1977), 97–121.

2283 **Garside**, W. Richard. 'Wage determination and the Miners' lockout of 1892.' McCord, N. (ed.). *Essays in Tyneside labour history.* 1977. p. 132–53.

2284 **Howkins**, Alun. 'Structural conflict and the farmworker: Norfolk 1900–1920.' *J. Peasant Stud.*, IV, 3 (April 1977), 217–29.

2285 **Jeremy**, P. 'Life on circular 703: the crisis of destitution in the S. Wales coalfield during the lock-out of 1926.' *Llafur*, II, 2 (Spring 1977), 65–75.

2286 **Barclay**, Martin. 'The slaves of the lamp: the Aberdare Miners' strike, 1910.' *Llafur*, II, 3 (Summer 1978), 24–42.

2287 **Lynch**, Lisa. 'Strike frequency in British coal mining 1950–1974.' *Br. J. Ind. Relat.*, XVI, 1 (March 1978), 95–8.

2288 **Walsh**, K. *A comparative sociological study of political and industrial militancy among coalminers in selected British coalfields, 1890–1914.* 1978. (M.Phil. thesis, University of Kent.)

2289 **Hughes**, Kevin. 'Only one way to learn.' MacFarlane, J. (ed.). *Essays from the Yorkshire coalfield.* 1979. p. 86–8.

2290 **Roberts,** Robert. 'The big strike.' MacFarlane, J. (ed.). *Essays from the Yorkshire coalfield.* 1979. p. 4–6.

See also: 2250.

2. Manufacturing Industries, Construction, Gas, Electricity, and Water

See also Part Five, V, B.

2291 **Abrines**, Sam. 'The Clyde's fight for jobs.' *New Soc.*, XVIII (12 August 1971), 287–9.

2292 **Allen**, E., **Clarke**, J. F., **McCord**, Norman and **Rowe**, D. J. *The North-East engineers' strikes of 1871: the Nine Hours' League.* Newcastle-upon-Tyne: Frank Graham, 1971. 196p.

2293 **Arnison**, Jim. *The million pound strike.* London: Lawrence & Wishart, 1971. 85p.

2294 **Department of Employment.** *Report of the Court of Inquiry into a Dispute between the Parties Represented on the National Joint Council for the Electricity Supply Industry.* London: H.M.S.O., 1971. iv, 54p. (Cmnd. 4594.) Chairman: Lord Wilberforce.

2295 **Department of Employment.** *Report of the inquiry into the causes of dispute between Amalgamated Union of Engineering Workers and Transport and General Workers Union and Fine Tubes Ltd.* London: H.M.S.O., 1971. 36p. Chairman: A.D. Campbell.

2296 **Eaton**, John, **Hughes**, John and **Coates**, Ken. *U.C.S.: workers' control: the real defence against unemployment is attack.* Nottingham: Institute for Workers' Control, 1971. (IWC pamphlets 25.)

2297 **Lane**, Tony and **Roberts**, Kenneth. *Strike at Pilkingtons.* London: Collins/Fontana, 1971. 266p.

2298 **Buchan**, Alasdair. *The right to work: the story of the Upper Clyde confrontation.* London: Calder & Boyars, 1972. 160p.

2299 **Burgess**, Keith. 'The 1852 lockout in the British engineering industry.' *Soc. Study Labour Hist. Bull.*, XXIV (Spring 1972), 7–21.

2300 **Burgess**, Keith. 'Trade union policy and the 1852 lockout in the British engineering industry.' *Int. Rev. of Soc. Hist.*, XVII (1972), 645–60.

2301 **Fleet**, Kenneth. *Whatever happened at U.C.S.?* Nottingham: Institute for Workers' Control, 1972. 26p. (IWC pamphlets 28.)

2302 **Institute for Workers' Control.** *U.C.S.: the social audit: a special report by the IWC.* Nottingham: The Institute, 1972. 16p. (IWC pamphlet 26.)

2303 **Mathews**, John. *Ford strike: the workers' story.* London: Panther, 1972. 208p.

2304 **Palmer**, R. E. 'The funny rigs of good and tender-hearted masters in the happy town of Kidderminster, anno 1828: an account of a strike of carpet weavers.' *Worcs. Archaeol. Soc. Trans.*, III (1970–2), 105–13.

2305 **Thompson**, Willie and **Hart**, Finlay. *The UCS work-in.* London: Lawrence & Wishart, 1972. 95p. Foreword by Jimmy Reid.

2306 **Alexander**, Kenneth John Wilson. 'A work-in re-assessed.' *New Soc.*, XXV (20 September 1973), 707–8.

2307 **Chadwick**, Graham. 'The Manchester engineering sit-ins, 1972.' Barratt Brown, M. and Coates, K. (eds.). *Trade union register: 3.* 1973. p. 113–24.

2308 **Hopkins**, Eric. 'An anatomy of strikes in the glass industry, 1850–1914.' *Midl. Hist.*, II (1973), 21–31.

2309 **International Socialists.** *Pickets on trial: defend North Wales 24.* London: The Authors, 1973. 12p.

2310 **Johns**, Stephen. *Reformism on the Clyde.* London: Socialist Labour League, 1973. 128p.

2311 **McGill**, Jack. *Crisis on the Clyde: the story of Upper Clyde Shipbuilders.* London: Davis-Poynter, 1973. 143p.

2312 **Melton**, Vicki Lynne. *Trade unionism and the Sheffield outrages.* Sheffield: Sheffield City Museum, 1973. 4p.

2313 **Arnison**, Jim. *The Shrewsbury three: strikes, pickets and 'conspiracy'.* London: Lawrence & Wishart, 1974. 84p.

2314 **Beck**, Tony. *Fine Tubes strike*. London: Stage 1, 1974. 128p.

2315 **Clarke**, Tom. *Sit-in at Fisher-Bendix*. Nottingham: Institute for Workers' Control, [1974]. [26]p.

2316 **Hendrick**, H. 'The Leeds gas strike 1890.' *Thores. Soc. Publ.*, LIV (1974), 78–98.

2317 **Jenkins**, Mick. *Time and motion strike – Manchester 1934–7: the wiredrawers' struggle against the Bedaux system at Richard Johnson's*. London: Communist Party of Great Britain History Group, 1974. 300p. (Our history pamphlets 60.)

2318 **McLean**, Ian. 'Popular protest and public order: Red Clydeside, 1915–1919.' Quinault, R. and Stevenson, J. (eds.). *Popular protest and public order*. London: Allen & Unwin, 1974. p. 215–42.

2319 **White**, P. J. 'Gasworkers' strike 1972–3: an analysis of causes.' *Ind. Relat. J.*, V, 1 (Spring 1974), 27–37.

2320 **Advisory Conciliation and Arbitration Service.** *Court of inquiry into a dispute between the National Union of Blastfurnacemen and the British Steel Corporation*. London: A.C.A.S., 1975. 52p. (Report 3.)

2321 **Advisory Conciliation and Arbitration Service.** *Panel of investigation: dispute between British Leyland Cowley and AUEW and TGWU concerning mechanical rectifiers*. London: A.C.A.S., 1975. iv, 40p. (Report 1.)

2322 **Bean**, Ron. 'The relationship between strikes and "unorganized" conflict in manufacturing industries.' *Br. J. Ind. Relat.*, XIII, 1 (March 1975), 98–101.

2323 **Cole**, W. J. 'Financing of the individual striker: a case study in the building industry.' *Br. J. Ind. Relat.*, XIII, 1 (March 1975), 94–7.

2324 **Croucher**, Richard. 'The North East Engineers' strike of 1908.' *N.E. Group Study Labour Hist. Bull.*, IX (October 1975), 43–56.

2325 **Pearce**, Cyril. *The Manningham Mills strike, Bradford, December 1890–April 1891*. Hull: University of Hull, 1975. 85p. (University of Hull occasional papers in economic and social history 7.)

2326 **Price**, Richard N. 'The other face of respectability: violence in the Manchester brickmaking trade 1859–1870.' *Past & Present*, LXVI (February 1975), 110–32.

2327 **Robertson**, Paul L. 'Demarcation disputes in British shipbuilding before 1914.' *Int. Rev. of Soc. Hist.*, XX, 2 (1975), 220–35.

2328 **Todd**, Nigel. 'Trade unions and the engineering industry dispute at Barrow-in-Furness 1897–8.' *Int. Rev. of Soc. Hist.*, XX, 1 (1975), 33–47.

2329 **Bullen**, Andrew. 'The calling of the 1932 cotton strike.' *N.W. Labour Hist. Soc. Bull.*, III (1976), 7–11.

2330 **Parssinen**, T. M. and **Prothero**, I. J. 'The London tailors' strike of 1834 and the collapse of the Grand National Consolidated Trades Union: a police spy's report.' *Int. Rev. of Soc. Hist.*, XXII, 1 (1977), 65–107.

2331 **Popps**, James. 'The engineers and the lock-out of 1897.' *Halifax Antiq. Soc. Trans.* (1976), 47–69.

2332 **Race and Class.** 'Grunwick.' *Race and Class*, XIX, 1 (Summer 1977), 69–72.

2333 **Searby**, Peter. *Crisis in Coventry, 1858–1863: ribbon factory, free trade, and strike*. Coventry: University of Warwick Open Studies and Coventry Branch of the Historical Association, 1977. (Coventry and North Warwickshire history pamphlets 10.)

2334 **Warren**, Des. *Shrewsbury: whose conspiracy? The need for an enquiry*. London: The Author, [1977]. [20]p.

2335 **Barratt Brown**, Michael. 'Upper Clyde Shipbuilders.' Coates, Ken (ed.). *The right to useful work*. 1978. p. 61–77.

2336 **Bullen**, Andrew. 'Watching and besetting: the Burnley police and the more looms disputes, 1931–32.' *N.W. Labour Hist. Soc. Bull.*, V (1978), 1–10.

2337 **Dromey**, Jack and **Taylor**, Graham. *Grunwick: the workers' story*. London: Lawrence & Wishart, 1978. 207p.

2338 **Murphy**, P. J. 'The origins of the 1852 lock-out in the British engineering industry reconsidered.' *Int. Rev. of Soc. Hist.*, XXIII, 2 (1978), 242–66.

2339 **Race and Class.** 'Grunwick (2).' *Race and Class*, XIX, 3 (Winter 1978), 289–94.

2340 **Whitehorn**, Katharine. *Whose news?* London: Liberal Publication Department, 1978. 16p. (Unservile state papers 23.)

2341 **Wilson**, Gordon M. 'The strike policy of the miners of the West of Scotland, 1842–74.' MacDougall, I. (ed.). *Essays in Scottish labour history*. 1978. p. 29–64.

See also: 37; 2442; 2451; 6207.

3. Transport, Communications, and Distribution

See also Part Five, V, B.

2342 **Darby**, D. J. 'The banks and the postal strike.' *Bankers' Mag.*, CXXVIII, 9 (September 1971), 127–30.

2343 **General Post Office.** *Report of a committee appointed by the Post Office and Union of Post Office Workers to enquire into the circumstances of a dispute arising out of the Union's claim for pay increases and shortening of incremental scales*. London: H.M.S.O., 1971. 72p.

Chairman: *Sir* Henry Hardman.

2344 **Jacobs**, Joe. *Sorting out the postal strike*. Bromley: Solidarity, 1971. 9p. (Solidarity pamphlets 36.)

2345 **Weal**, John. *The Post Office workers v. the state: the great 1971 Post Office strike*. London: International Marxist Group, 1971. 31p.

2346 **Hikins**, Harold R. 'Liverpool dockers,

1967.' Hikins, H. (ed.). *Building the union.* 1973. p. 181–8.

2347 **Taplin**, Eric L. 'The Liverpool tramwaymen's agitation of 1889.' Hikins, H. (ed.). *Building the union.* 1973. p. 55–73.

2348 **Topham**, Tony. 'The attack on the dockers.' Barratt Brown, M. and Coates, K. (eds.). *Trade union register: 3.* 1973. p. 219–32.

2349 **Perry**, Nick. 'Conflict on board ship: an interpretation.' *Sociol. Rev.*, XXII, 4 (November 1974), 557–80.

2350 **Wasp**, David and **Davis**, Alan. *The great dock strike, 1889.* London: Longman, 1974. 112p.

2351 **Advisory Conciliation and Arbitration Service.** *Panel of investigation: difficulties affecting London docks.* London: H.M.S.O., 1975. vi, 34p. (Report 2.)

2352 **Patterson**, Henry. 'James Larkin and the Belfast Dockers' and Carters' strike of 1907.' *Saothar*, IV (1978), 8–14.

2353 **Wailey**, Tony. 'Seamen's strike, Liverpool, 1966.' *Hist. Workshop*, V (Spring 1978), 111–2.

2354 **Bartlett**, Gerald. *What happened at the Economist's Bookshop: a story of human and industrial relations in a small enterprise.* London: Hurst, 1979. 31p.

2355 **Department of Employment.** *Report of a Court of Inquiry into a trade dispute at Dyce Airport, Aberdeen, between Bristow Helicopters Ltd. and members of the British Air Line Pilots Association.* London: H.M.S.O., 1979. 54p. (Cmnd. 6951.)
Chairman: R. H. McDonald.

See also: 945.

4. White-Collar, Professional, Public Administration, and Miscellaneous Services

2356 **Burke**, Vincent. *Teachers in turmoil.* Harmondsworth: Penguin, 1971. 192p.

2357 **Williams**, J. E. 'The Leeds Corporation strike in 1913.' Briggs, A. and Saville, J. (eds.). *Essays in labour history, 1886–1923.* 1971. p. 70–95.

2358 **Gregory**, R. G. *Ring your own bloody bell.*

Market Drayton: Private Print, 1972. 68p.

2359 **Lawrence**, Susanne. 'Marching militancy in the public service.' *Pers. Manage.*, V, 3 (March 1973), 34–7.

2360 **Marsh**, Arthur Ivor. 'Public action.' Parkinson, C. N. (ed.). *Industrial disruption.* 1973. p. 134–44.

2361 **Eaton**, Jack. 'The stable lads' strike of 1975.' *Br. J. Ind. Relat.*, XIV, 2 (July 1976), 174–85.

2362 **Department of Employment.** *Report of the Court of Inquiry into a dispute between Grunwick Processing Laboratories Limited and members of the Association of Professional, Executive, Clerical and Computer Staff.* London: H.M.S.O., 1977. 25p. (Cmnd. 6922.)
Chairman: Lord Scarman.

2363 **Rogaly** Joy. *Grunwick.* Harmondsworth: Penguin, 1977. 199p.

2364 **Ward**, George. *Fort Grunwick.* London: Temple Smith, 1977. 123p.

2365 **Hounslow Hospital Occupation Committee, Elizabeth Garrett Anderson Joint Shop Stewards Committee, Plaistow Maternity Action Committee** and **Save St. Nicholas Hospital Campaign.** *Keeping hospitals open: work-ins at E.G.A., Hounslow and Plaistow hospitals.* London: The Authors, 1978. 24p.

2366 **Phizacklea**, Anne Marie and **Miles**, Robert. 'The strike at Grunwick.' *New Community*, VI (Summer 1978), 268–78.

2367 **Sellwood**, Arthur Victor. *Police strike – 1919.* London: W. H. Allen, 1978. 214p.

2368 **Turner**, Jill. 'Behind Liverpool's social work strike.' *New Soc.*, XXXIII (26 October 1978), 207–8.

2369 **Button**, J. H. 'Industrial action: a learning experience.' *Hosp. Health Serv. Rev.*, LI, 6 (June 1979), 198–201.

2370 **Hince**, Kevin. 'The university teacher strikes – or almost!' *Vestes*, XXII (1979), 8–35.

2371 **Townshend**, Charles. 'The Irish railway strike of 1920: industrial action and civil resistance in the struggle for independence.' *Irish Hist. Stud.*, XXI, 83 (March 1979), 265–82.

See also: 1060; 1498; 1989; 2273.

VI. INDUSTRIAL DEMOCRACY

The more general literature on industrial democracy and worker participation in decision-making is classified at Part Five, VI, D, 1.

A. CO-OPERATIVE PRODUCTION AND CO-PARTNERSHIP

Some of the general works in Part Four, II, A also contain material on employer attitudes to co-operative production and co-partnership. Material on Robert Owen and Owenism is classified here, but see also general chronological studies in Part Three, II, B.

2372 **Butt**, John. 'Robert Owen and trade unionism.' Cole, M. and others. *Robert Owen.* 1971. p. 15–19.

2373 **Butt**, John. 'Robert Owen at New Lanark.' *Co-partnership*, DXLIII (January 1971), 14–17.

2374 **Butt**, John, **Donnaghie**, I. and **Hume**, J.R. 'Robert Owen of New Lanark, 1771–1858.' *Ind. Archaeol.*, VIII (May 1971), 186–93.

2375 **Cole**, Margaret. 'Owen's mind and methods.' Pollard, S. and Salt, J. (eds.). *Robert Owen, prophet of the poor.* 1971. p. 188–213.

2376 **Cole**, Margaret. 'Robert Owen until after New Lanark.' Cole, M. and others. *Robert Owen.* 1971. p. 4–14.

2377 **Cole**, Margaret Isabel, **Butt**, John, **Watkins**, William P. and **Harrison**, John. *Robert Owen: industrialist, reformer, visionary, 1771–1858.* London: Robert Owen Bicentenary Association, 1971. 32p.

2378 **Garnett**, R. G. 'Robert Owen and the community experiments.' Pollard, S. and Salt, J. (eds.). *Robert Owen, prophet of the poor.* 1971. p. 39–64.

2379 **Harrison**, Brian. 'Robert Owen's crusade.' *New Soc.,* XVII (13 May 1971), 812–4.

2380 **Harrison**, John. 'Robert Owen and the communities.' Cole, M. and others. *Robert Owen.* 1971. p. 27–32.

2381 **Harrison**, J. F. C. 'A new view of Mr. Owen.' Pollard, S. and Salt, J. (eds.). *Robert Owen, prophet of the poor.* 1971. p. 1–12.

2382 **Harrison**, J. F. C. 'Robert Owen: the quest for the new moral world.' *Montgomeryshire Collect.,* LXII, 1 (1971), 1–9.

2383 **Laird**, J. A. *The Clarion movement: a study of a Socialist attempt to implement the co-operative commonwealth in England, 1891–1914.* 1971. (M.A. thesis, University of Manchester.)

2384 **Oliver**, W. H. 'Owen in 1817: the millenialist moment.' Pollard, S. and Salt, J. (eds.). *Robert Owen, prophet of the poor.* 1971. p. 166–87.

2385 **Pollard**, Sidney and **Salt**, John (eds.). *Robert Owen, prophet of the poor: essays in honour of the two hundredth anniversary of his birth.* London: Macmillan, 1971. xi, 318p.

2386 **Robert Owen Bi-Centenary Summer School, 1971.** *Robert Owen and his relevance to our times: addresses contributed to the …* Manchester: Cooperative Union Education Department, 1971. 63p. (Cooperative College papers 14.)

2387 **Robertson**, A. J. 'Robert Owen, cotton spinner: New Lanark, 1800–25.' Pollard, S. and Salt, J. (eds.). *Robert Owen, prophet of the poor.* 1971. p. 145–66.

2388 **Saville**, John. 'J.E. Smith and the Owenite movement, 1833–4.' Pollard, S. and Salt, J. (eds.). *Robert Owen, prophet of the poor.* 1971. p. 115–44.

2389 **Silver**, Harold. 'Owen's reputation as an educationist.' Pollard, S. and Salt, J. (eds.). *Robert Owen, prophet of the poor.* 1971. p. 65–83.

2390 **Tsuzuki**, Chushichi. 'Robert Owen and revolutionary politics.' Pollard, S. and Salt, J. (eds.). *Robert Owen, prophet of the poor.* 1971. p. 13–38.

2391 **Watkins**, William P. 'Robert Owen and the cooperative movement.' Cole, M. and others. *Robert Owen.* 1971. p. 20–6.

2392 **Yeo**, Eileen. 'Robert Owen and radical culture.' Pollard, S. and Salt, J. (eds.). *Robert Owen, prophet of the poor.* 1971. p. 84–114.

2393 *Cooperation and the working class: theoretical contributions 1827–1834.* New York: Arno, 1972. (British labour struggles: contemporary pamphlets 1727–1850.)

2394 *Cooperative communities: plans and descriptions 1825–1847.* New York: Arno, 1972. (British labour struggles: contemporary pamphlets 1727–1850.)

2395 **Derrick**, Paul. 'A lesson from Robert Owen.' *Twentieth Century,* CLXXIX, 1049 (1972), 48–50.

2396 **Garnett**, Ronald George. *Cooperation and the Owenite socialist communities in Britain 1825–45.* Manchester: Manchester U.P., 1972. xii, 272p.

2397 *Motherwell and Orbiston: the first Owenite attempts at cooperative communities 1822–1825.* New York: Arno, 1972. (British labour struggles: contemporary pamphlets 1727–1850.)

2398 *Owenism and the working class 1821–1834.* New York: Arno, 1972. (British labour struggles: contemporary pamphlets 1727–1850.)

2399 *Robert Owen at New Lanark 1824–1838.* New York: Arno, 1972. (British labour struggles: contemporary pamphlets 1727–1850.)

2400 **Baxter**, Robert. *Co-operative democracy in industry: a discussion pamphlet.* Manchester: Cooperative Union, 1973. 15p.

2401 **Butt**, John. 'Robert Owen of New Lanark: his critique of British society.' Butt, J. and Clarke, I.F. (eds.). *The Victorians and social protest.* Newton Abbot: David & Charles, 1973. p. 13–32.

2402 **Garnett**, Ronald George. *William Pare (1805–1873): a cooperator and social reformer.* Manchester: Cooperative Union Education Department, 1973. 56p. (Cooperative College papers 16.)

2403 **Rose**, R.B. 'John Finch, 1784–1857: a Liverpool disciple of Robert Owen.' Hikins, H. (ed.). *Building the union.* 1973. p. 31–52.

2404 **Tann**, J. 'The Whitby Union Mill Company—a case of early cooperative production.' *Bus. Arch.,* XXXIX (1973), 32–8.

2405 **Backstrom**, Philip N. *Christian socialism and cooperation in Victorian England: Edward Vansittart Neale and the cooperative movement.* London: Croom Helm, 1974. 238p.

2406 **Norton Villiers Triumph Ltd.** *Meriden: historical summary 1972–1974.* Coventry: The Authors, 1974. iii, 37p.

2407 **Saxena**, K. K. *Evolution of cooperative thought.* Bombay: Somaiya Publications, 1974. x, 159p.

2408 **Bader**, Ernest. *Economics and the living spirit; or what can we learn from the Scott Bader Commonwealth?* Bomere Heath: Wrekin Trust, 1975. 24p.

2409 **Faherty**, Ray. 'The memoir of Thomas Martin Wheeler, Owenite and Chartist.' *Soc. Study Labour Hist. Bull.,* XXX (Spring 1975), 11–13.

2410 **Herd**, William Leslie. *New Lanark.* Crowborough: P.V. Publications, 1975. 24p. Third edition.

2411 **Keyworth**, Stan. 'Worker co-operatives and

their dividends for management.' *Pers. Manage.*, VII, 10 (October 1975), 24–7.

2412 **Morley**, J. A. E. 'Agricultural cooperatives in the United Kingdom.' *Coop. Inf.*, LI, 2 (1975), 3–20.

2413 **Morley**, J. A. E. *British agricultural cooperatives.* London: Hutchinson, 1975. 168p.

2414 **Williams**, M. Worthington. 'Sound as a bell.' *Old Motor*, IX, 2 (November 1975), 150–7.

2415 **Williams**, T. Ceiriog. *Robert Owen.* Swansea: Hughes a'i Fab, 1975. 43p.

2416 **Benn**, Tony. 'The industrial context.' Coates, K. (ed.). *The new worker cooperatives.* 1976. p. 71–87.

2417 **Coates**, Ken. 'A crossroads?' Coates, K. (ed.). *The new worker cooperatives.* 1976. p. 216–9.

2418 **Coates**, Ken (ed.). *The new worker cooperatives.* Nottingham: Spokesman, 1976. 230p.

2419 **Coates**, Ken. 'Some questions and some arguments.' Coates, K. (ed.). *The new worker cooperatives.* 1976. p. 11–33.

2420 **Eccles**, Tony. 'Kirkby manufacturing and engineering.' Coates, K. (ed.). *The new worker cooperatives.* 1976. p. 141–69.

2421 **Fleet**, Ken. 'Triumph Meriden.' Coates, K. (ed.). *The new worker cooperatives.* 1976. p. 88–108.

2422 **Fletcher**, Richard. 'Worker coops and the Cooperative Movement.' Coates, K. (ed.). *The new worker cooperatives.* 1976. p. 173–215.

2423 **Jones**, Derek C. 'British producer cooperatives.' Coates, K. (ed.). *The new worker cooperatives.* 1976. p. 34–68.

2424 **Mackie**, Alister. 'The Scottish Daily News.' Coates, K. (ed.). *The new worker cooperatives.* 1976. p. 109–40.

2425 **Yeabsley**, J. *Sharing decisions: aspects of cooperatives.* 1976. (Ph.D. thesis, University of Essex.)

2426 **Derrick**, Paul. 'Industrial democracy and cooperative ownership.' *Ind. Participation*, DLXII (Autumn 1977), 13–22.

2427 **Jones**, Derek C. and **Backus**, D. K. 'British producer cooperatives in the footwear industry: an empirical evaluation of the theory of financing.' *Econ. J.*, LXXXVII (1977), 488–510.

2428 **Parkyn**, B. 'The Scott Bader Commonwealth.' *Ind. Commer. Train.*, IX, 2 (February 1977), 70–2.

2429 **Bradley**, K. *Worker control as a state managerial device: a study of the Scottish Daily News worker cooperative.* 1978. (Ph.D. thesis, University of Essex.)

2430 **Bruce-Gardyne**, Jock. *Meriden: odyssey of a lame duck.* London: Centre for Policy Studies, 1978. 67p.

2431 **Derrick**, Paul. 'Prospects for industrial cooperatives.' *Month*, XI (July 1978), 225–7.

2432 **Hoe**, Susanna. *The man who gave his company away: a biography of Ernest Bader, founder of the Scott Bader Commonwealth.* London: Heine-

mann, 1978. 242p.
Foreword by E.F. Schumacher.

2433 **Jones**, Derek C. 'Producer cooperatives in industrialized Western economies: an overview.' *Annals Publ. Coop. Econ.*, II (1978), 149–61.

2434 **Oakeshott**, Robert. 'Industrial cooperatives: the middle way.' *Lloyds Bank Rev.*, CXXVII (January 1978), 44–58.

2435 **Allan**, J. Murray. *New Lanark village.* Edinburgh: Jordanhill College of Education, 1979. 40p.

2436 **Clayre**, Alasdair. 'The political economy of third sector enterprises.' Burns, T. and others (eds.). *Work and power.* 1979. p. 357–68.

2437 **Cooke**, A. J. 'Robert Owen and the Stanley Mills.' *Bus. Hist.*, XXI (January 1979), 107–11.

2438 **Eccles**, Tony. 'Control in the democratised enterprise: the case of K.M.E.' Purcell, J. and Smith, R. (eds.). *The control of work.* 1979. p. 156–77.

2439 **Wajcman**, J. *Fakenham enterprises: the rise and fall of a women's coop.* 1979. (Ph.D. thesis, University of Cambridge.)

2440 **Young**, Michael and **Rigge**, Marianne. 'A manifesto for coops.' *New Soc.*, XXXIV (26 April 1979), 192–3.

See also: 36; 936; 2566; 6153.

B. GUILD SOCIALISM, SYNDICALISM, AND WORKERS' CONTROL

Material on workers' sit-ins is classified at Part Five, V, A and C. See also Part Three, II, B; Part Three, II, F, 8; Part Three, II, G–H; and Part Five, V, B.

2441 **Cole**, Margaret. 'Guild socialism and the Labour Research Department.' Briggs, A. and Saville, J. (eds.). *Essays in labour history, 1886–1923.* 1971. p. 260–83.

2442 **Matthews**, Frank. 'The building guilds.' Briggs, A. and Saville, J. (eds.). *Essays in labour history, 1886–1923.* 1971. p. 284–331.

2443 **Roberts**, Ernie. *The Industrial Relations Act! Unemployment! The solution is workers' control.* Nottingham: Bertrand Russell Peace Foundation, 1971. 14p. (Spokesman pamphlets 19.)

2444 **Barratt Brown**, Michael and **Coates**, Ken. *Workers' control in the nationalised industries.* Nottingham: Bertrand Russell Peace Foundation, 1972. 12p. (Spokesman pamphlets 26.)

2445 **Coates**, Ken. *Quality of life and workers' control.* Nottingham: Bertrand Russell Peace Foundation, 1972. 15p. (Spokesman pamphlets 27.)

2446 **Cole**, George Douglas Howard. *Self-government in industry.* London: Hutchinson, 1972. xxxv, 273p.

First published in 1917. Reprinted with an introduction by J.G. Corina.

2447 **Eaton**, John. *The new society: planning and workers' control.* Nottingham: Institute for Workers' Control, 1972. 16p. (I.W.C. pamphlets 33).

2448 **Fleet**, Kenneth. 'Workers' control.' *New Blackfriars*, LIII (November 1972), 502–11.

2449 *The Rational system 1837–1841.* New York: Arno Press, 1972. (British labour struggles: contemporary pamphlets 1727–1850.)

2450 **Solidarity**. *Workers' councils and the economics of a self-managed society.* London: Solidarity, 1972. (Solidarity pamphlets 40.)

2451 **Spencer**, Bruce. 'Case for workers' take-over: G.E.C. and U.C.S.' *Polit. Q.*, XLIII, 4 (October–December 1972), 425–36.

2452 **Barratt Brown**, Michael and **Holland**, Stuart. *Public ownership and democracy.* Nottingham: Institute for Workers' Control, 1973. 8p. (I.W.C. pamphlets 38.)

2453 **Coates**, Ken and **Topham**, Tony. *Catching up with the times: how far the TUC got the message about workers' control.* Nottingham: Institute for Workers' Control, 1973. 20p. (I.W.C. pamphlets 37.)

2454 **Holton**, Bob. 'Syndicalism and labour on Merseyside, 1906–14.' Hikins, H. (ed.). *Building the union.* 1973. p. 121–50.

2455 **Kendall**, Walter. *State ownership, workers' control and socialism.* Nottingham: Institute for Workers' Control, 1973. 14p. (I.W.C. pamphlets 35.)

2456 **National Conference on Workers' Control, 1973**. *Workers' control: how far can the structure meet our demands?* Nottingham: Institute for Workers' Control, 1973. 15p. (I.W.C. pamphlets 36.)

2457 **Roberts**, Ernie. *Workers' control.* London: Allen & Unwin, 1973. 308p.

2458 **Bristol Aircraft Workers' Study Group**. *A new approach to public ownership.* Nottingham: Institute for Workers' Control, 1974. 32p. (I.W.C. pamphlets 43.)

2459 **Coates**, Ken. *Democracy in the mines: some documents of the controversy on mines nationalisation up to the time of the Sankey Commission.* Nottingham: Spokesman Books, 1974. 128p. (Bertrand Russell Peace Foundation. Documents in social history 2.)

2460 **Hill**, Mike. *The feasibility of worker self management.* Brighton: Smoothie, 1974. 26p.

2461 **Hyman**, Richard. 'Workers' control and revolutionary theory: an appraisal of the publications of the Institute for Workers' Control.' *Social. Reg.* (1974), 241–78.

2462 **Scanlon**, Hugh. 'The poverty of expectation.' *J. Gen. Manage.*, I, 3 (Summer 1974), 15–22.

2463 **Varley**, Eric. *The case for workers' control in the mining industry.* Nottingham: Institute for Workers' Control, 1974. 8p. (I.W.C. pamphlets 40.)

2464 **Barker**, Rodney. 'Guild socialism revisited?'

Polit. Q., XLVI (July–September 1975), 246–54.

2465 **Morgan**, Kenneth O. 'Socialism and syndicalism: the Welsh miners' debate 1912.' *Soc. Study Labour Hist. Bull.*, XXX (Spring 1975), 22–37.

2466 **Hinton**, James. 'Workers' control and the historians: a new economism: a rejoinder.' *New Left Rev.*, XCVII (May–June 1976), 100–4.

2467 **Holton**, Robert J. *British syndicalism, 1900–1914: myths and realities.* London: Pluto, 1976. 240p.

2468 **Monds**, Jean. 'Workers' control and the historians: a new economism.' *New Left Rev.*, XCVII (May–June 1976), 81–100.

2469 **Shackleton**, J. N. 'Is workers' self-management the answer?' *Natl. Westminster Bank Q. Rev.* (February 1976), 15–57.

2470 **Wright**, Anthony. 'From Fabianism to Guild Socialism: the early political thought of G. D. H. Cole.' *Soc. Study Labour Hist. Bull.*, XXXII (Spring 1976), 23–5.

2471 **Benn**, Anthony Wedgwood. *Industry, technology and democracy.* Nottingham: Institute for Workers' Control, 1978. 17p. (I.W.C. pamphlets 60.)

2472 **Bodington**, Steve and **Coates**, Ken. 'Corporate planning, workers' control and employment.' Coates, K. (ed.). *The right to useful work.* 1978. p. 263–87.

2473 **Cooley**, Mike, **Scargill**, Arthur and **Wise**, Audrey. *A debate on workers' control: edited contributions by the principal speakers ... at the IWC's tenth birthday conference, 1978.* Nottingham: Institute for Workers' Control, 1978. 11p.

2474 **Matthews**, Frank. 'The ladder of becoming: A. R. Orage, A.J. Plenty and the origins of Guild Socialism in England.' Martin, D. and Rubinstein, D. (eds.). *Ideology and the labour movement.* 1978. p. 147–66.

2475 **Woodhouse**, M. G. 'Mines for the nation or mines for the miners?' *Llafur*, II, 3 (Summer 1978), 92–109.

2476 **Hobsbawm**, Eric John Ernest. 'Inside every worker there is a syndicalist trying to get out.' *New Soc.*, XLVIII (5 April 1979), 8–10.

See also: 732; 1227; 1788; 2528.

C. PROFIT–SHARING AND EMPLOYEE SHARE OWNERSHIP

The more sociological and psychological material on motivation and incentives is classified at Part Two, II; and material on wage payment systems and incentives at Part Six, III, F.

2477 **Church**, Roy A. 'Profit-sharing and labour relations in England in the nineteenth century.' *Int. Rev. of Soc. Hist.*, XVI, 1 (1971), 2–16.

2478 **Bell**, D. Wallace. 'Employees savings trust.' *Ind. Participation*, DL (Winter 1972), 15–19.

2479 **Copeman**, George Henry and **Rumble**, Tony. *Capital as an incentive*. London: Leviathan House, 1972. 221p.

2480 **Morton**, C. P. 'Profit sharing for industry.' *J. Bus. Finance*, IV, 2 (Summer 1972), 47–53.

2481 **Bell**, D. Wallace. 'Budget proposals: share savings schemes for all employees.' *Ind. Participation*, DLI (Spring 1973), 14–15.

2482 **Bell**, D. Wallace. *Financial participation: wages, profit sharing and employee shareholding*. London: Industrial Participation Association, 1973. 84p.

2483 **Cavaghan**, R. L. 'Employee attitudes to profit sharing: a research report.' *Ind. Participation*, DLIII (Autumn–Winter 1973), 15–18.

2484 **Murray**, Ian. *Workers' shares and savings*. London: Working Together Campaign, [1973?]. 9p.

2485 **Vinson**, Nigel. 'Participation in profit.' *Ind. Soc.*, LV, 8 (August 1973), 14–17.

2486 **Copeman**, George Henry. *Employee share participation in nationalised and other enterprises*. London: Aims of Industry, 1974. 18p.

2487 **Incomes Data Services.** *Savings related share schemes part 1*. London: I.D.S., 1974. 19p. (I.D.S. study 70.)

2488 **Incomes Data Services.** *Savings related share schemes part 2*. London: I.D.S., 1974. 20p. (I.D.S. study 76.)

2489 **Wellens**, John. 'Employee participation through shareholding.' *Ind. Commer. Train.*, VI, 10 (October 1974), 459–63.

2490 **Bell**, D. Wallace. *Employee shareholding trusts*. London: Industrial Participation Association, 1975. 22p.

2491 **Copeman**, George Henry. *Employee share ownership and industrial stability*. London: Institute of Personnel Management, 1975. 204p.

2492 **Copeman**, George Henry. 'Employee participation in capital growth.' *Manage. Decis.*, XIV, 2 (1976), 71–102.

2493 **Miller**, *Sir* Bernard. 'Partnership not participation.' *Ind. Participation*, DLIX (Spring 1976), 12–21.

2494 **Pollard**, Sidney and **Turner**, Robert. Profit sharing and autocracy.' *Bus. Hist.*, XVIII, 1 (January 1976), 4–34.

2495 **Bell**, D. Wallace. 'Profit sharing and employee shareholding.' *Ind. Participation*, DLXI (Summer 1977), 9–12.

2496 **Copeman**, George Henry. 'Share and reward schemes.' *Pers. Manage.*, IX, 1 (January 1977), 34–7.

2497 **Franklin**, John. 'Company-wide savings-related share schemes.' *Ind. Participation*, DLX (Winter 1977), 20–22.

2498 **Incomes Data Services**. *Profit sharing 1: descriptions of 57 schemes*. London: I.D.S., 1977. (I.D.S. study 160.)

2499 **Wellens**, John. 'Employee funds.' *Ind. Commer. Train.*, IX, 5 (May 1977), 183–6.

2500 **Bell**, D. Wallace. 'Profit sharing and productivity plans: case study.' *Ind. Participation*, DLXIII (Winter 1977–8), 3–9.

2501 **Confederation of British Industry.** *Financial participation in companies: an introductory booklet*. London: C.B.I., 1978. 36p.

2502 **Crockatt**, J. L. 'Employee shareholding in the Johnson Group: case study.' *Ind. Participation*, DLXIII (Winter 1977–8), 30–6.

2503 **Crockatt**, J. L. and **Nightingale**, N. J. 'Employee shareholding case histories.' *Ind. Participation*, DLXIII (Winter 1977–8), 30–42.

2504 **Franklin**, John. 'Introducing employee shareholding.' *Ind. Participation*, DLXIII (Winter 1977–8), 25–9.

2505 **Incomes Data Services.** *Profit sharing 2*. London: I.D.S., 1978. 20p. (I.D.S. study 163.)

2506 **Nightingale**, N. J. 'Employee share option scheme in Rowntree Mackintosh Ltd.: case study.' *Ind. Participation*, DLXIII (Winter 1977–8), 37–43.

2507 **Wilson**, Donald. 'Profit sharing and employee shareholding in ICI.' *Ind. Participation*, DLXIII (Winter 1977–8), 10–17.

2508 **Wilson**, Donald and **Davies**, T. J. 'Profit-sharing case histories.' *Ind. Participation*, DLXIII (Winter 1977–8), 10–24.

2509 **Bailey**, Ron and **Ross**, Brian. 'Profit sharing at the Midland.' *Pers. Manage.*, XI, 3 (March 1979), 37–9.

2510 **Copeman**, George Henry. 'Profit sharing in perspective.' *Pers. Manage.*, XI, 1 (January 1979), 36–8.

2511 **Incomes Data Services**. *Profit sharing schemes*. London: I.D.S., 1979. 17p. (I.D.S. study 204.)

2512 **Morse**, Geoffrey and **Williams**, David. *Profit sharing: legal aspects of employee share schemes*. London: Sweet & Maxwell, 1979. 222p.

D. WORKER PARTICIPATION

Some of the works in Part Four, II, A – B also contain material on employer attitudes towards joint consultation and worker participation in decision-making. Material on job enrichment, autonomous work groups, and other forms of direct employee participation in decision-making is classified at Part Two, V; that on worker participation in the administration of pension schemes is classified at Part Six, IV, C, 2; that on worker participation in the administration of health and safety is classified at Part Six, IV, D, 3; and that on trade union participation in national socio-economic planning is classified at Part Seven, I.

1. General

2513 **Henderson**, Joan. *A practical guide to joint consultation*. London: Industrial Society, 1970. 26p. (Notes for managers 9.)

2514 **Henderson**, Joan and **Fatchett**, D. *Some examples of effective consultative committees.* London: Industrial Society, 1970. 41p.

2515 **Philp**, A. J. 'The use of working parties in industrial relations.' *Ind. Relat. J.*, I, 2 (September 1970), 23–32.

2516 **Schregle**, Johannes. 'Forms of participation in management.' *Ind. Relat.*, IX, 2 (February 1970), 117–22.

2517 **Appleyard**, J. R. and **Coates**, J. A. G. *Workers' participation in Western Europe.* London: Institute of Personnel Management, 1971. 103p. (Institute of Personnel Management. Information reports 10.)

2518 **Axton**, Ken. 'Involvement: a personal view.' *Co-partnership*, DXLIII (January 1971), 32–3.

2519 **Coates**, Ken. *Essays on industrial democracy.* Nottingham: Bertrand Russell Peace Foundation, 1971. 64p.

2520 **Hespe**, George W. A. and **Little**, Alan J. 'Some aspects of employee participation.' Warr, P. (ed.). *Psychology at work.* 1971. p. 322–47.

2521 **Shephard**, G. C. 'Effective participation.' *Co-partnership*, DXLIV (July 1971), 30–3.

2522 **Swanborough**, J. F. 'Planning and participation.' *J. Bus. Policy*, I, 4 (Summer 1971), 60–3.

2523 **Thomason**, George F. *Experiments in participation.* London: Institute of Personnel Management, 1971. 54p.

2524 **Vinson**, Nigel. 'Involvement in the smaller unit.' *Co-partnership*, CCXLVI (November 1971), 56–7.

2525 **Best**, Robert D. 'Sharing power and responsibility (S.P.R.) in small scale industry.' *Friends' Q.*, XVII (July 1972), 324–32.

2526 **Clarke**, Ronald Oliver and **Fatchett**, Derek John. 'Workers' participation in management in Great Britain.' *Int. Inst. Labour Stud. Bull.*, IX (1972), 173–207.

2527 **Clarke**, Ronald Oliver, **Fatchett**, Derek John and **Roberts**, Benjamin Charles. *Workers' participation in management in Britain.* London: Heinemann Educational, 1972. 214p. (London School of Economics and Political Science industrial relations series.)

2528 **Coates**, Ken and **Topham**, Tony. *New unionism: the case for workers' control.* London: Peter Owen, 1972. 250p.

2529 **Davies**, John. 'Interdependence.' *Ind. Participation*, DXLIX (Autumn 1972), 3–5.

2530 **Fletcher**, Ted. 'From joint control to joint regulation.' *Ind. Participation*, DIL (Spring 1972), 9–11.

2531 **Fogarty**, Michael Patrick. 'Company and corporation reform and worker participation: the state of the debate.' *Br. J. Ind. Relat.*, X, 1 (March 1972), 1–11.

2532 **Friedrichs**, Hans. 'European trends in personnel and participation: personnel and social policies.' *Ind. Participation*, DXLVIII (Summer 1972), 5–6.

2533 **Gordon-Brown**, Ian. *Participation in industry: an introductory guide.* London: Industrial Co-partnership Association, 1972. 56p.

2534 **Hespe**, George and **Gordon-Brown**, Ian. 'Do employees want participation?' *Ind. Participation*, DXLVII (Spring 1972), 12–13.

2535 **Huddleston**, John. 'Industrial democracy.' *Parliamentary Aff.*, XXV (Summer 1972), 224–33.

2536 **Ireson**, P. 'The open road to industrial democracy.' *Ind. Soc.*, LIV, 1 (January 1972), 13–14.

2537 **Neal**, *Sir* Leonard Francis. 'The advance of participation.' *Ind. Participation*, DXLVIII (Summer 1972), 3–5.

2538 **Peacock**, L. 'Participation pays.' *Ind. Soc.*, LIV, 9 (September 1972), 17–20.

2539 **Pearce**, A. W. 'Employee participation: involvement or negotiation?' *Ind. Participation*, DXLIX (Autumn 1972), 7–12.

2540 **Society of Industrial Tutors.** *Teaching industrial relations: industrial democracy and industrial relations: a report.* Barnet: The Society, 1972. 28p.

2541 **Vinson**, Nigel. *Towards a common purpose in industry: involvement in the smaller unit.* London: Working Together Campaign, 1972. 14p.

2542 **Walker**, Kenneth. 'European trends in personnel and participation: employee participation in management.' *Ind. Participation*, DXLVIII (Summer 1972), 7–8.

2543 **Balfour**, Campbell. *Participation.* London: Croom Helm, 1973. 217p.

2544 **Bier**, T. 'Participation or profits?' *Ind. Soc.*, LV, 1 (January 1973), 9–10.

2545 **Bond-Williams**, N. I. 'Participation in practice.' *Ind. Soc.*, LV, 7 (July 1973), 8–10.

2546 **Bow Group.** *Employee participation in British companies: an examination of all levels of employee participation in industry.* London: Bow Group, 1973. 44p.

2547 **Brooks**, E. 'Worker participation: the fundamental issues.' *Ind. Commer. Train.*, V, 9 (September 1973), 411–18.

2548 **Fairweather**, Ronald G. 'A car assembler comments.' *Ind. Participation*, DLII (Summer 1973), 15–18.

2549 **Feather**, Victor. 'Trade unions and industrial democracy.' *Ind. Participation*, DLII (Summer 1973), 5–6.

2550 **Ferm**, R. S. 'Whatever happened to common sense?' *Ind. Participation*, DLI (Spring 1973), 17–19.

2551 **Laing**, *Sir* Hector. 'Working together effectively.' *Ind. Participation*, DLIII (Autumn–Winter 1973), 73–81.

2552 **McKinnon**, Robert. *Renewal of purpose.* London: Working Together Campaign, [1973]. 12p.

2553 **Norman**, G. 'Industrial democracy in banking.' *Bankers' Mag.*, CCXVI, 1557 (December 1973), 235–6.

2554 **O'Mahony**, David. 'The participatory economy.' *Studies*, LXII (Spring 1973), 35–50.

2555   **Pocock**, Pamela. 'Participation in Preston.' *Pers. Manage.*, v, 12 (December 1973), 31–4.

2556   **Reynolds**, J. 'Employee participation: a trade union view.' Cuthbert, N. and Hawkins, K. (eds.). *Company industrial relations policies*. 1973. p. 147–56.

2557   **Taylor**, Linda King. 'Participation without patronising.' *Ind. Commer. Train.*, v, 5 (May 1973), 211–15.

2558   **Taylor**, Mike. 'Creating a health workers' democracy.' Barratt Brown, M. and Coates, K. (eds.). *Trade union register: 3*. 1973. p. 162–98.

2559   **Trades Union Congress**. *Industrial democracy: interim report by the T.U.C. General Council*. London: T.U.C., 1973. 46p.

2560   **Aims of Industry**. *Guide to industrial participation: essential steps, essential research*. London: The Authors, 1974. 12p.

2561   **Allan**, David R. *Socialising the company*. London: Fabian Society, 1974. 48p. (Young Fabian pamphlets 37.)

2562   **Bell**, D. Wallace. 'The participation debate.' *Ind. Participation*, DLV (Summer 1974), 9–12.

2563   **Bennett**, P. W. 'Participation in planning.' *J. Gen. Manage.*, 1, 4 (Autumn 1974), 12–16.

2564   **Berry**, Alan P. *Worker participation: the European experience*. Coventry: Coventry & District Engineering Employers' Association, 1974. 146p.

2565   **Blanpain**, Roger. 'The influence of labour on management decision-making: a comparative legal survey.' *Ind. Law J.*, III (March 1974), 5–19.

2566   **Bray**, Jeremy and **Falk**, Nicholas. *Towards a worker managed economy*. London: Fabian Society, 1974. 25p. (Fabian tracts 430.)

2567   **Business International**. *Industrial democracy in Europe: the challenge and management responses*. Geneva: The Authors, 1974. 170p.

2568   **Commission on Industrial Relations**. *Worker participation and collective bargaining in Europe*. London: H.M.S.O., 1974. iii, 176p. (C.I.R. Studies 4.)

2569   **Confederation of British Industry**. *Employee participation: CBI's contribution to the debate*. London: C.B.I., 1974. 12p.

2570   **Engineering Employers' Federation**. *Employee participation*. London: The Federation, 1974. 12p.

2571   **Flunder**, D. *Practical policies for participation: a guide to action by management, unions and government*. London: Industrial Society, 1974. 32p.

2572   **Guest**, David and **Fatchett**, Derek John. *Worker participation: individual control and performance*. London: Institute of Personnel Management, 1974. 252p.

2573   **Hann**, P. 'Glacier stays cool.' *Ind. Soc.*, LVI (November–December 1974), 4–6.

2574   **Horner**, J. *Studies in industrial democracy*. London: Gollancz, 1974. 256p.

2575   **Industrial Society**. *Practical policies for participation: a guide to action by management, unions and government*. London: The Society. 1974. 32p.

2576   **Jenkins**, David. *Job power: blue and white collar democracy*. London: Heinemann, 1974. viii, 375p.

2577   **Johnson**, R. J. 'Problem resolution and change through participative group effort.' *J. Manage Stud.*, XI, 2 (May 1974), 129–42.

2578   **Levinson**, C. *Industry's democratic revolution*. London: Allen & Unwin, 1974. 350p.
    See especially Chapters 9 and 10 on the United Kingdom. p. 231–67.

2579   **Mills**, Brian. 'CMG (Computer Management Group).' *Ind. Participation*, DLV (Summer 1974), 15–19.

2580   **Neal**, *Sir* Leonard Francis. 'Making shop floor participation work.' *J. Gen. Manage.*, 1, 4 (Autumn 1974), 44–50.

2581   **Prentice**, Gordon. 'Participation at Fry's.' *Pers. Manage.*, VI, 5 (May 1974), 35–8.

2582   **Radice**, Giles. *Working power: policies for industrial democracy*. London: Fabian Society, 1974. ii, 21p. (Fabian tracts 431.)

2583   **Smith**, G. 'Participation in action at Fry's.' *Ind. Commer. Train.*, VI, 11 (November 1974), 504–7.

2584   **Social Policy Research**. *Workers participation in Britain*. London: Financial Times, 1974. 138p.
    An S.P.R. study in collaboration with John Crossley Wood.

2585   **Taylor**, Linda King. 'Management of change.' *Ind. Commer. Train.*, VI, 4 (April 1974), 178–84.

2586   **Towers**, Brian. 'Worker participation in management: an appraisal and some comments.' *Ind. Relat. J.*, IV, 4 (Winter 1973–4), 4–22.

2587   **Trades Union Congress**. *Industrial democracy: a statement of policy by the … Congress*. London: T.U.C., 1974. 45p.

2588   **Vaughan**, Christopher. 'Industrial democracy at the TUC.' *Month*, VII (November 1974), 774–6.

2589   **Wood**, John C. *Worker participation in Britain*. London: Financial Times, 1974. 144p.

2590   **Adams**, Kenneth. 'The interdependence of participation.' *Ind. Participation*, DLVIII (Summer 1975), 3–5.

2591   **Alexander**, Kenneth John Wilson, **Robertson**, Eddie and **Scanlon**, Hugh. *Worker participation: papers delivered at a symposium at the University of Keele, 1975*. Newcastle-under-Lyne: University of Keele, 1975. [403]p.

2592   **Association of British Chambers of Commerce**. *Employee participation: a policy study by chambers of commerce of moves towards industrial democracy*. London: A.B.C.C., 1975. 28p.

2593   **Bate**, S.P. and **Mangham**, I.L. *The design and implementation of processes of worker participation*. Bath: University of Bath Centre for the Study of Organizational Change and Development, 1975. 44p.

2594 **Bell**, D. Wallace. *Participation in productivity.* London: I.P.A., 1975. 18p. (Industrial Participation Association. IPA participation case studies 1/75.)

2595 **Bell**, D. Wallace. *Responsibility on the shop floor.* London: I.P.A., 1975. 14p. (Industrial Participation Association. IPA participation case studies 2/75.)

2596 **Benn**, Anthony Wedgwood. *Industrial democracy: Tony Benn at the I.W.C. debate.* Nottingham: Institute for Workers' Control, 1975. 22p. (I.W.C. pamphlet 45.)

2597 **British Institute of Management**. *Employee participation: a management view: report of a BIM working party.* London: B.I.M., 1975. 46p.

2598 **British Railways Board**. *Arrangements for participation by employees.* London: The Board, 1975. 5p.

2599 **Brown**, Wilfred Banks Duncan. *Participation.* Bradford: MCB Books, 1975. 40p.

2600 **Chemical Industries Association**. *Code of practice on communication and consultation.* London: The Association, 1975. 14p.

2601 **Coldrick**, Percy. 'Trade unions and industrial democracy.' *Ind. Participation*, DLVI (Winter 1974–5), 3–7.

2602 **Congdon**, Tim. 'The economics of industrial democracy.' *New Soc.*, XXXIV (30 October 1975), 255–7.

2603 **Coveney**, A. 'Olsen's democracy.' *Ind. Soc.*, LVII, 6 (November–December 1975), 11–13.

2604 **Fogarty**, Michael Patrick. *Company responsibility and participation: a new agenda.* London: Political and Economic Planning, 1975. iv, 116p. (P.E.P. broadsheets 554).

2605 **Fogarty**, Michael Patrick. *Work and industrial relations in the European Community.* London: Political and Economic Planning, 1975. 43p. (P.E.P. European series 24.)

2606 **Gilbertson**, Geoffrey. *Power-sharing in industry: a pattern for the future.* London: Church Information Office, 1975. 19p.

2607 **Gordon-Brown**, Ian. *C.M.G.: participation in a professional firm.* London: Industrial Participation Association, 1975. 20p. (Industrial Participation Association. IPA participation case studies 3/75.)

2608 **Goyder**, George. *The responsible worker.* London: Hutchinson, 1975. 144p.

2609 **Hollenweger**, W. J. 'Efficiency and human values: a theological action–research report on co-decision in industry.' *Expository Times*, LXXXVI (May 1975), 228–32.

2610 **Incomes Data Services**. *Worker participation.* London: I.D.S., 1975. 21p. (I.D.S. study 104.)

2611 **Industrial Research and Information Services**. *Industrial democracy.* London: The Authors, 1975. 47p.

2612 **Lessem**, R. 'Guidelines for industrial democracy.' *J. Gen. Manage.*, III, 1 (Winter 1975), 66–79.

2613 **Lischeron**, J. A. *Workers' participation in organisational decision-making.* 1975. (Ph.D. thesis, University of Sheffield.)

2614 **Lischeron**, J.A. and **Wall**, Toby D. 'Attitudes towards participation among local authority employees.' *Hum. Relat.*, XXVIII (August 1975), 499–517.

2615 **Lischeron**, J. A. and **Wall**, Toby D. 'Employee participation: an experimental field study.' *Hum. Relat.*, XXVIII (December 1975), 863–84.

2616 **Macbeath**, Innis. *Power sharing in industry: a practical guide to employee participation in company operations.* London: Gower, 1975. xvii, 180p.

2617 **Morgan**, D.H.J. 'Autonomy and negotiation in an industrial setting.' *Sociol. Work Occup.*, II, 3 (August 1975), 203–26.

2618 **Norman**, D. 'Participation at Norprint.' *Ind. Soc.*, LVII, 5 (September–October 1975), 6–7.

2619 **Poole**, Michael J. F. *Workers' participation in industry.* London: Routledge & Kegan Paul, 1975. x, 198p.

2620 **Ramsay**, Harvie. 'Firms and football teams.' *Br. J. Ind. Relat.*, XIII, 3 (November 1975), 396–400.

2621 **Revans**, R. W. 'Participation in what?' *Ind. Participation*, DLVI (Winter 1974–5), 12–13.

2622 **Roberts**, Benjamin Charles. 'Employee participation: trends and issues.' Basagni, F. and Sauzey, F. (eds.). *Employee participation and company reform.* Paris: Atlantic Institute for International Affairs, 1975. p. 9–20.

2623 **Shutt**, Harry (ed.). *Worker participation in West Germany, Sweden, Yugoslavia and the United Kingdom.* London: Economist Intelligence Unit, 1975. 48p. (Quarterly Economic Review specials 20.)

2624 **Simitis**, S. 'Workers' participation in the enterprise: transcending company law?' *Mod. Law Rev.*, XXXVIII (January 1975), 1–22.

2625 **Trades Union Congress**. *Industrial democracy.* London: T.U.C., 1975. 45p.

2626 **Webster**, Bryan. 'Participation: power shift or power sharing?' *Pers. Manage.*, VII, 11 (November 1975), 20–3.

2627 **Wellens**, John. *Worker participation: a practical policy.* Guilsborough: Wellens Publishing, 1975. 133p.

2628 **Wellens**, John and **Brown**, M. L. 'Levels of participation.' *Ind. Commer. Train.*, VII, 3 (March 1975), 93–8.

2629 **White**, Michael. 'Participation by preference.' *Pers. Manage.*, VII, 5 (May 1975), 24–7.

2630 **Archbold**, S. 'Dimensions of participation.' *J. Gen. Manage.*, IV (Spring 1976), 52–66.

2631 **Bateson**, P. L. *Workers' participation in management–a European Community context and beyond.* 1976. (LL.M. thesis, Queen's University, Belfast.)

2632 **Bedingham**, D. 'Training for participation.' *Ind. Soc.*, LVIII, 3 (May–June 1976), 15–17.

2633 **Birchall**, David W., **Wild**, Ray and **Carnall**, Colin. 'Redesigning a way to worker participation.' *Pers. Manage*, VIII, 8 (August 1976), 26–8.

2634 **Broad**, Geoffrey and **Beishon**, John. *Participation, management and control: concepts and case studies in worker participation*. Milton Keynes: Open U.P., 1976. 54p. (PT 281 Unit 15.)

2635 **Child**, John. 'Participation, organization and social cohesion.' *Hum. Relat.*, XXIX (May 1976), 429–51.

2636 **Clinton**, Geoffrey S. 'Financial control in an age of participation.' *J. Ind. Affairs*, III, 2 (Spring 1976), 181–4.

2637 **Confederation of British Industry**. *Involving people: CBI proposals for employee participation*. London: C.B.I., 1976. 15p.

2638 **Confederation of British Industry**. *Practical employee participation in smaller firms*. London: C.B.I., 1976. 17p.

2639 **Department of Employment Gazette**. 'Industrial democracy in Western Europe.' *Dep. Employment Gaz.*, LXXXIV, 9 (September 1976), 969–75.

2640 **Doyle**, Mel. *What kind of industrial democracy?* London: Workers' Educational Association, 1976. 23p. (Studies for trade unionists II, 7.)

2641 **Fogarty**, Michael Patrick. 'The place of managers in industrial democracy.' *Br. J. Ind. Relat.*, XIV, 2 (July 1976), 119–27.

2642 **Foy**, Nancy and **Gadon**, Herman. 'Worker participation: contrasts in three countries.' *Harv. Bus. Rev.*, LIV, 3 (May–June 1976), 71–83.

2643 **Handy**, Charles (ed.). *Management by consent*. London: London University Institute of Education, 1976. 10p. (Occasional paper 1.) Based on a seminar, 1973.

2644 **Harrison**, Roger. *Workers' participation in Western Europe 1976*. London: Institute of Personnel Management, 1976. 89p.
   Ireland: p. 47–9.
   U.K.:p. 77–80.

2645 **Hespe**, George and **Wall**, Toby. 'The demand for participation among employees.' *Hum. Relat.*, XXIX (May 1976), 411–28.

2646 **Hilgendorf**, E. Linden and **Irving**, Barrie L. 'Workers' experience of participation: the case of British Rail.' *Hum. Relat.*, XXIX (May 1976), 471–505.

2647 **Labour Research Department**. *Industrial democracy: a trade unionist's guide*. London: The Department, 1976. 39p.

2648 **Long**, Joyce Ruth. *Employee participation and local government: a discussion document*. London: Society of Local Authority Chief Executives, 1976. iii, 72p.

2649 **Macbeath**, Innis. 'The state of participation in Britain.' *London Bus. School J.*, III (Spring 1976), 19–24.

2650 **National Consumer Council**. *Industrial democracy and consumer democracy: seven reasons the TUC is wrong*. London: H.M.S.O., 1976. 6p.

2651 **Nottinghamshire Chamber of Commerce and Industry**. *A report on employee participation*. Nottingham: The Chamber, 1976. 23p.

2652 **One Nation Group of M.P.s**. *One nation at work*. London: Conservative Political Centre, 1976. 23p.

2653 **Ottaway**, Richard N. 'A change strategy for worker participation.' *Pers. Rev.*, V, 1 (Winter 1976), 13–18.

2654 **Ramsay**, Harvie. 'Participation: the shop floor view.' *Br. J. Ind. Relat.*, XIV, 2 (July 1976), 128–41.

2655 **Ramsay**, Harvie. 'Who wants participation?' *New Soc.*, XXXVII (30 September 1976), 694–6.

2656 **Richbell**, Suzanne. 'Participation and perception of control.' *Pers. Rev.*, V, 2 (Spring 1976).

2657 **Schregle**, Johannes. 'Workers' participation in decisions within undertakings.' *Int. Labour Rev.*, CXIII, 1 (January–February 1976), 1–15.

2658 **Sharp**, Elizabeth B. *Democracy in industry*. London: Industrial Society, 1976. 38p.

2659 **Sorge**, Arndt. 'Evolution of industrial democracy in the countries of the European Community.' *Br. J. Ind. Relat.*, XIV, 3 (November 1976), 274–94.

2660 **Tavernier**, G. 'Workers dispense corporate charity.' *Int. Manage.*, XXXI, 9 (September 1976), 25–6.

2661 **Taylor**, Linda King. 'Creating an interest in work through participation.' *Ind. Participation*, DLXV (Autumn 1976), 8–14.

2662 **Taylor**, Linda King. 'Creating an interest in work through participation.' *R. Soc. Arts J.*, CXXXIV (June 1976), 380–90.

2663 **Warner**, Malcolm. 'Further thoughts on experiments in industrial democracy and self-management.' *Hum. Relat.*, XXIX (May 1976), 401–10.

2664 **Whalen**, Geoffrey. 'Participation in Leyland cars: the story so far.' *Pers. Manage.*, VIII, 10 (October 1976), 33–6.

2665 **Williams**, Alan, **Kessler**, Sid and **Langson**, John. 'Participative practices in European banks.' *Ind. Relat. J.*, VII, 4 (Winter 1976–7), 21–38.

2666 **Wood**, Norma. 'Improving decision-making in a construction firm.' *Dep. Employment Gaz.*, LXXXIV, 10 (October 1976), 1079–82.

2667 **Aldrich**, J. 'Participation and the nature of the firm.' Heathfield, D. (ed.). *The economics of co-determination*. 1977. p. 122–34.

2668 **Brewer**, Richard W. 'Employee participation: doing what comes naturally.' *Pers. Manage.*, V, 3 (March 1977), 34–8.

2669 **British Broadcasting Corporation**. *Democracy at work: a book for active trade unionists*. London: B.B.C., 1977. 184p.

2670 **British Institute of Management**. *Employee participation: the way ahead, incorporating a guide to participative practice*. London: The Institute, 1977. 10p.

2671 **Carr**, Robert, *Lord*. 'Creative participation in industry.' *Prod. Eng.*, LVI (July–August 1977), 20–5.

2672 **Chiplin**, Brian, **Coyne**, John, **Sirc**, Ljubo, **Wood**, John B. and **Harris**, Ralph. *Can workers manage?* London: Institute of Economic Affairs, 1977. 112p. (Hobart papers 77.)

2673 **Clarke**, Tom. 'Industrial democracy: the institutionalised suppression of industrial conflict?' Clarke, T. and Clements, L. (eds.). *Trade unions under capitalism*. 1977. 351–82.

2674 **Coates**, Ken. *Beyond wage slavery*. Nottingham: Spokesman, 1977. xi, 170p.

2675 **Cockcroft**, Laurence. 'Democrats at the mill.' *New Soc.*, XL (14 April 1977), 64–5.

2676 **Davies**, Mostyn D. 'Sharing-in and sharing-out.' *Theology*, LXXX (March 1977), 91–5.

2677 **Dickson**, John W. 'The adoption of industrial democracy.' *Pers. Rev.*, VII (Autumn 1977), 15–19.

2678 **Farrar**, J. A. 'Participation and design.' *Chart. Mech. Engineer* (October 1977), 73–5.

2679 **Fogarty**, Michael Patrick and **Nicholson**, Sir David. 'Participation and the boardroom.' *Manage. Sympos.* (1977), 5–18.

2680 **Gordon-Brown**, Ian. 'The messiah syndrome: the forgotten factor in participation.' *Ind. Participation*, DLXII (Autumn 1977), 5–8.

2681 **Hawkins**, C. J. 'Some effects of worker participation and the distribution of income.' Heathfield, D. (ed.). *The economics of co-determination*. 1977. p. 36–45.

2682 **Heathfield**, David Frederick (ed.). *The economics of co-determination*. London: Macmillan, 1977. xiii, 154p.

2683 **Hebden**, John E. and **Shaw**, Graham H. *Pathways to participation*. London: Associated Business Programmes, 1977. 267p.

2684 **Incomes Data Services**, *The machinery of industrial democracy*. London: I.D.S., 1977. 66p. (I.D.S. handbooks 8.)

2685 **Ingham**, A. 'Participation and risk.' Heathfield, D. (ed.). *The economics of co-determination*. 1977. p. 135–50.

2686 **Jones**, Derek C. 'Worker participation in management in Britain: evaluation, current developments, and prospects.' Garson, D. G. (ed.). *Worker self-management in industry: the West European experience*. New York: Praeger, 1977. p. 97–151.

2687 **Long**, Joyce Ruth. 'Employee participation and local government.' *Ind. Participation*, DLX (1977), 28–33.

2688 **Loveridge**, Ray. 'Employee participation.' *Pers. Manage.*, IX, 2 (February 1977), 41–5.

2689 **Machin**, Maurice. 'Wolverhampton Industrial Engines Ltd.' *Ind. Participation*, DLXII (Autumn 1977), 26–9.

2690 **Myers**, Charles A. 'Participation: factors for success.' *Ind. Participation*, DLXII (Autumn 1977), 30–2.

2691 **Passingham**, Bernie and **Connor**, Danny. *Ford shop stewards on industrial democracy*. Nottingham: Institute for Workers' Control, 1977. 21p. (I.W.C. pamphlet 54.)

2692 **Pearce**, I. F. 'Participation and income distribution.' Heathfield, D. (ed.). *The economics of co-determination*. 1977. p. 26–35.

2693 **Pipkorn**, Jörn. 'Employee participation in the European company.' *Univ. Leuven Inst. Labour Relat. Bull.*, VIII (1977), 23–44.

2694 **Ramsay**, Harvie. 'Cycles of control: worker participation in sociological and historical perspective.' *Sociology*, XI, 3 (September 1977), 481–506.

2695 **Roberts**, Ernie. 'Democratising the workplace.' Ottaway, R. (ed.). *Humanising the workplace*. 1977. 149–57.

2696 **Smith**, Cyril. *Industrial participation*. London: McGraw-Hill, 1977. viii, 174p.

2697 **Ward**, Benjamin. 'The firm in Illyria: market syndicalism.' Heathfield, D. (ed.). *The economics of co-determination*. 1977. 1–25.

2698 **Warner**, Malcolm and **Peccei**, R. 'Management autonomy and worker participation in multinational companies.' *Pers. Rev.*, II, 3 (Autumn 1977), 7–13.

2699 **Wellens**, John. 'The organic approach to employee participation.' *Ind. Commer. Train.*, IX, 12 (December 1977), 500–4.

2700 **Batstone**, Eric. 'Management and industrial democracy'. International Conference on Industrial Democracy. *Industrial democracy: international views*. 1978. pp. 211–38.

2701 **Brenton**, Maria. 'Worker participation and the social service agency.' *Br. J. Soc. Work*, VIII (Autumn 1978), 289–300.

2702 **Brewer**, Richard W. 'Personnel's role in participation.' *Pers. Manage.*, X, 9 (September 1978), 27–30.

2703 **Clegg**, Chris W., **Nicholson**, Nigel, **Ursell**, Gill, **Blyton**, Paul R. and **Wall**, Toby D. 'Managers' attitudes towards industrial democracy.' *Ind. Relat. J.*, IX, 3 (Autumn 1978), 7–17.

2704 **Clegg**, Hugh Armstrong. 'Industrial democracy and trade union structure.' International Conference on Industrial Democracy. *Industrial democracy: international views*. 1978. p. 245–58.

2705 **Clifton**, Richard. *The economic implications of industrial democracy*. London: Department of Employment Research and Planning Division, 1978. 27p.

2706 **Coates**, Ken. 'Ashfield: how participation turned sour.' Coates, K. (ed.). *The right to useful work*. 1978. p. 132–67.

2707 **Cooley**, Mike. 'Design, technology and production for social needs.' Coates, K. (ed.). *The right to useful work*. 1978. p. 195–211.

2708 **Crispo**, John. *Industrial democracy in Western Europe: a North American perspective*. Toronto:

McGraw-Hill, 1978. 181p.

2709 **Eagle**, F. H. and **West**, A. 'Opening moves in participation.' *Ind. Commer. Train.*, x, 5 (May 1978), 188–95.

2710 **Elliott**, John. *Conflict or cooperation? The growth of industrial democracy.* London: Kogan Page, 1978. xiv, 306p.
Preface by Lord Bullock.

2711 **Fox**, Alan. 'Corporatism and industrial democracy: the social origins of present forms and methods in Britain and Germany.' International Conference on Industrial Democracy. *Industrial democracy: international views.* 1978. p. 1–54.

2712 **International Conference on Industrial Democracy, Adelaide, 1978**. *Proceedings of the ...* Sydney: C.C.H. Australia, 1978. ix, 705p.
See especially 'Industrial democracy in the U.K.' p. 101–36.

2713 **International Conference on Industrial Democracy, Cambridge, 1977**. *Industrial democracy: international views.* Coventry: Social Science Research Council Industrial Relations Research Unit, 1978. 305p.

2714 **Jain**, H. C. 'Information, training and participation.' *Ind. Relat. J.*, ix, 1 (Spring 1978), 48–60.

2715 **Lucas Aerospace Combine Shop Stewards' Committee.** 'The Lucas plan.' Coates, K. (ed.). *The right to useful work.* 1978. p. 212–32.

2716 **Mills**, L. 'The role of unions in strategic planning.' *Long Range Plann.*, xi, 5 (October 1978), 78–82.

2717 **National Economic Development Committee**. Economic Development Committee for Food and Drink Manufacture. *Investment and employment: an approach to improving performance.* London: N.E.D.C., 1978.

2718 **Nicholson**, Nigel. 'Can consultation work?' *Pers. Manage.*, x, 11 (November 1978), 42–6.

2719 **Pace**, David E. and **Hunter**, John. *Direct participation in action: the new bureaucracy.* London: Saxon House, 1978. vii, 118p.

2720 **Parkyn**, B. 'Democracy, accountability and participation.' *Ind. Commer. Train.*, x, 8 (August 1978), 318–21.

2721 **Ponsford**, N. R. and **Carpenter**, P. J. 'Employee involvement and participation.' *Pers. Rev.*, vii (Spring 1978), 11–17.

2722 **Smith**, A. *Towards a reconsideration of 'work participation' as an increasing part of the social order in modern Britain.* 1977–8. (M.Soc.Sc. thesis, University of Birmingham.)

2723 **Somerton**, Michael. *Industrial democracy in local government: the documentary record.* Nottingham: Institute for Workers' Control, 1978. 15p. (I.W.C. pamphlets 59.)

2724 **Suckling**, J. 'A note on the theory of the labour managed firm: the price discriminating labour managed monopolist.' *Bull. Econ. Res.*, xxx (May 1978), 39–44.

2725 **Vickers' National Combine Committee of Shop Stewards.** 'Building a Chieftain tank and the alternative.' Coates, K. (ed.). *The right to useful work.* 1978. p. 233–61.

2726 **Wainwright**, David. 'Launching into participation.' *Pers. Manage.*, x, 12 (December 1978), 28–34.

2727 **Wilson**, William. *Towards industrial democracy in Britain.* Manchester: University of Manchester Department of Adult and Higher Education, 1978. 46p. (Manchester monographs 10.)

2728 **Abell**, Peter. 'Hierarchy and democratic authority.' Burns, T. and others (eds.). *Work and power.* 1979. p. 141–72.

2729 **Adams**, Rex. *Training for participation.* London: Associated Business Press, 1979. xiv, 234p.

2730 **Batstone**, Eric V. 'Systems of domination, accommodation and industrial democracy.' Burns, T. and others (eds.). *Work and power.* 1979. p. 249–74.

2731 **Bell**, D. Wallace. *Industrial participation.* London: Pitman for the Industrial Participation Association, 1979. 239p.

2732 **Benson**, John B. 'Briefing groups and the development of employee participation.' Guest, D. and Knight, K. (eds.). *Putting participation into practice.* 1979. p. 80–95.

2733 **British Institute of Management**. *Why participation? A BIM code of practice on employee participation.* London: The Institute, 1979. 17p.

2734 **Burns**, Tom R., **Karlsson**, Lars Erik and **Rus**, Veljko (eds.). *Work and power: the liberation of work and the control of political power.* London: Sage, 1979. 391p.

2735 **Chadwick**, David. 'Participation through joint consultation.' *Employee Relat.*, 1, 3 (1979), 9–12.

2736 **Cooper**, N. J. 'Involving people in Standard Telephones and Cables.' *Ind. Participation*, DLXXVI (Summer 1979), 2–4.

2737 **Dalton**, Sir Alan. 'Involving middle managers in participation.' *Ind. Participation*, DLXVI (1979), 3–7.

2738 **Damodaran**, Leela. 'Managerial learning needs for effective employee participation.' Sell, R. G. and Shipley, P. (eds.). *Satisfaction in work design.* 1979. p. 161–8.

2739 **Davis**, John. 'Training for participation.' Guest, D. and Knight, K. (eds.). *Putting participation into practice.* 1979. p. 287–305.

2740 **DeVille**, H. G. and **Boyd**, Sir John. 'The realities of involvement at work.' *Ind. Participation*, DLXXIX (Autumn 1979), 3–10.

2741 **Dickson**, J. W. 'Values and rationales for participation.' *Pers. Rev.*, iv, 1 (Spring 1979), 5–13.

2742 **Fatchett**, Derek. 'The form of participation.' Stephenson, G. and Brotherton, C. (eds.). *Industrial relations: a social psychological approach.* 1979. p. 241–57.

2743 **Gregory**, Denis. 'Trade union perspectives on participation.' Guest, D. and Knight, K.

(eds.). *Putting participation into practice.* 1979. p. 249–66.

2744 **Guest**, David. 'A framework for participation.' Guest, D. and Knight, K. (eds.). *Putting participation into practice.* 1979. p. 19–39.

2745 **Guest**, David. 'The future of worker participation.' Guest, D. and Knight, K. (eds.). *Putting participation into practice.* 1979. p. 306–14.

2746 **Guest**, David. 'Participation at shop-floor level.' Guest, D. and Knight, K. (eds.). *Putting participation into practice.* 1979. p. 59–79.

2747 **Guest**, David. 'Participation: why the interest?' Guest, D. and Knight, K. (eds.). *Putting participation into practice.* 1979. p. 5–18.

2748 **Guest**, David. 'Plant-level participation.' Guest, D. and Knight, K. (eds.). *Putting participation into practice.* 1979. p. 137–49.

2749 **Guest**, David and **Knight**, Kenneth (eds.). *Putting participation into practice.* Epping: Gower, 1979. 333p.

2750 **Hepple**, Robert A. 'Workers' participation in management: Great Britain.' *Univ. Leuven Inst. Labour Relat. Bull.,* x (1979), 295–300.

2751 **Institute for Workers' Control**, Motors Group. *A workers' inquiry into the motor industry.* London: C.S.E. Books, 1979. 102p.

2752 **Jenkins**, David. 'Forces and failures in industrial democracy.' *Manchr. Bus. School Rev.,* III, 1 (1979), 11–18.

2753 **Knight**, Kenneth. 'Implications for management.' Guest, D. and Knight, K. (eds.). *Putting participation into practice.* 1979. p. 233–48.

2754 **Knight**, Kenneth. 'Introducing participation.' Guest, D. and Knight, K. (eds.). *Putting participation into practice.* 1979. p. 267–86.

2755 **Lucas Aerospace Combine Shop Stewards' Committee.** *Democracy versus the circumlocation office.* Nottingham: Institute for Workers' Control, 1979. 15p.

2756 **Marchington**, Mick P. and **Loveridge**, Ray. 'Non-participation: the management view?' *J. Manage. Stud.,* XVI (May 1979), 171–84.

2757 **Parker**, Lee D. 'Participation in budget planning.' *Account. Bus. Res.,* IX, 34 (Spring 1979), 123–37.

2758 **Parker**, Sir Peter. *Industry and democracy: is corporatism inevitable?* London: Socialist Commentary, 1979. 19p.
Seventh Rita Hinden memorial lecture.

2759 **Poole**, Michael. 'Industrial democracy: a comparative analysis.' *Ind. Relat.,* XVIII, 3 (Fall 1979), 262–72.

2760 **Poole**, Michael. 'Industrial democracy and management: an explanatory and critical perspective.' Colloquium on Management and Industrial Relations, 1979. *Proceedings.* 1979. p. 117–222.

2761 **Reilly**, Peter A. *Participation, democracy and control: forms of employee involvement.* London: British Institute of Management, 1979. 52p.

2762 **Richards**, Geoffrey. 'Developing participation in a chemical works.' Guest, D. and Knight, K. (eds.). *Putting participation into practice.* 1979. p. 150–73.

2763 **Roach**, J. 'Participation at English China Clays.' *Ind. Participation,* DLXV (1979), 4–9.

2764 **Roberts**, Benjamin Charles. 'United Kingdom.' Roberts, B. C. (ed.). *Towards industrial democracy: Europe, Japan and the United States.* London: Croom Helm, 1979. p. 164–89.

2765 **Tinkler**, D. C. 'Developing industrial democracy.' *Manchr. Bus. School Rev.* (Summer 1979), 16–20.

2766 **Wall**, Toby D. and **Clegg**, Chris W. 'Who wants participation?' Guest, D. and Knight, K. (eds.). *Putting participation into practice.* 1979. p. 40–53.

2767 **Williams**, Derek. 'Multi-level participation at Cadbury-Schweppes.' Guest, D. and Knight, K. (eds.). *Putting participation into practice.* 1979. p. 192–205.

See also: 11; 12; 15; 19; 53; 94; 550; 562; 590; 625; 646; 728; 1483; 1598; 1621; 1712; 1773; 1890; 1897; 1931; 1965; 2004; 2049; 2117; 4959.

2. Worker Representation on Boards of Directors

Material on the Bullock Report (1977) and on the White Paper *Industrial Democracy* (1978) is classified here. All the evidence submitted to the Bullock Committee plus a good deal of the associated material, much of which is unpublished, has been deposited in the Modern Records Centre, University of Warwick Library. Only the more important published material is listed here.

2768 **Jones**, Ken. 'Employee involvement in management: the B.S.C. employee director experiment.' *Co-partnership,* DXLVI (November 1971), 49–50.

2769 **Jones**, Ken. 'Involvement in decision making.' *Co-partnership,* DXLIII (January 1971), 23–31.

2770 **Jones**, Ken. 'Resolving industrial conflict.' *Co-partnership,* DXLVI (November 1971), 49–68.

2771 **Brannen**, Peter. 'The employee director experiment.' *Ind. Participation,* DXLIX (Autumn 1972), 24–5.

2772 **Fogg**, Donald. 'The employee director experiment: a shop steward's point of view.' *Ind. Participation,* DXLIX (Autumn 1972), 26–8.

2773 **Bloomfield**, B. 'Participation on the board.' *Ind. Soc.,* LV, 9 (September 1973), 7–9.

2774 **Cassidy**, Bryan. *Workers on the board: a study in employee participation.* London: Conservative Political Centre, 1973, 24p.

2775 **Engineering Employers' Federation.** *E.E.C. proposals on company law and two-tier* *boards: a report.* London: The Federation, 1973. 16p.

2776 **Goss**, John. *Industrial relations and moves towards industrial democracy in Ireland.* Brighton: University of Sussex, 1973. 30p. (Centre for Contemporary European Studies research papers 4.)

2777 **Industrial Participation Association.** *Employee directors and supervisory boards.* London: The Association, 1973. 16p.

2778 **Industrial Participation Association.** *Works councils, employee directors, supervisory boards: a guide to the debate.* London: The Association, 1973. 32p. (I.P.A. study papers 2.)

2779 **Jones**, D. D. 'Codetermination and worker participation: two tier boards and industrial relations.' *Ind. Commer. Train.*, v, 11 (November 1973), 504–10.

2780 **Mortimer**, James Edward. 'Participation and the German experience.' *Pers. Manage.*, v, 9 (September 1973), 28–30.

2781 **Roberts**, I. L. 'Works constitution acts and industrial relations in West Germany: implications for the United Kingdom.' *Br. J. Ind. Relat.*, xi, 3 (November 1973), 338–67.

2782 **Council of Europe.** *Report on participation by employees in the decision-making process within the enterprise.* Strasbourg: The Council, 1974. 58p.

2783 **Warner**, Malcolm. 'Participative decision-making in a consultative committee context.' *Relat. Industrielles*, xxix, 2 (1974), 272–88.

2784 **Davies**, Paul Lyndon. 'Employee representation on company boards and participation in corporate planning.' *Mod. Law Rev.*, xxxviii (May 1975), 254–73.

2785 **Department of Manpower Services.** *Industrial democracy: a discussion paper on worker participation in Harland & Wolff.* Belfast: H.M.S.O., 1975. 16p.

2786 **European Communities.** *Employee participation and company structure in the European Community.* Luxembourg: European Communities, 1975. 188p.

2787 **House of Lords Select Committee on the European Communities.** *Draft fifth directive on company law: two-tier boards and worker participation with minutes of evidence.* London: H.M.S.O., 1975. 66p.

2788 **Batstone**, Eric. 'Industrial democracy and worker representation at board level: a review of the European experience.' Batstone, Eric and Davies, P. L. *Industrial democracy: European experience.* 1976. p. 9–48.

2789 **Batstone**, Eric and **Davies**, Paul Lyndon. *Industrial democracy: European experience: two research reports.* London: H.M.S.O. for the Industrial Democracy Committee, 1976. 87p.

2790 **Brannen**, Peter, **Batstone**, Eric, **Fatchett**, Derek and **White**, Philip. *The worker directors: a sociology of participation.* London: Hutch-inson, 1976. 278p.

2791 **British and Irish Communist Organisation.** *Workers' control now: evidence to the Committee of Inquiry on Industrial Democracy.* London: B. & I.C.O., 1976. [15]p.

2792 **Davies**, Paul Lyndon. 'European experience with worker representation on the board.' Batstone, E. and Davies, P. L. *Industrial democracy: European experience.* 1976. p. 51–88.

2793 **Drinkwater**, A. *Industrial democracy: company views and the Bullock Committee.* Henley: Administrative Staff College, 1976. 129p.

2794 **Duerr**, C. 'Two-tier board at Bonser.' *Ind. Soc.*, lviii, 5 (September–October 1976), 6–7.

2795 **Fabian Society.** *Workers in the boardroom.* London: The Society, 1976. 19p. (Fabian tracts 441.)

2796 **Fogarty**, Michael P. 'Participation and the boardroom.' Institute of Management Consultants and Management Consultants Association. *Company boards tomorrow.* 1976. p. 5–12.

2797 **Foy**, Nancy. 'Workers on the board: the voices of experience.' Institute of Management Consultants and Management Consultants Association. *Company boards tomorrow.* 1976. p. 27–36.

2798 **General Council of British Shipping.** *Evidence submitted by the ... to the Industrial Democracy Committee.* London: The Council, 1976. 10p.

2799 **Gordon-Brown**, Ian, **Vinson**, Nigel and **Bell**, D. Wallace. *Industrial democracy 1976: the state of play.* London: Industrial Participation Association, 1976. 45p. (I.P.A. study papers 4.)

2800 **Industrial Participation Association.** *Industrial democracy: the way forward: evidence of the ... Association to the Committee of Inquiry on Industrial Democracy.* London: I.P.A., 1976. 55p.

2801 **Institute of Management Consultants** and **Management Consultants Association.** *Company boards tomorrow.* London: The Authors, 1976. 48p. (Management symposium 2.)

2802 **Institute of Personnel Management.** *Industrial democracy: evidence from the IPM to the Committee of Inquiry.* London: The Institute, 1976. 63p.

2803 **National Consumer Council.** *Industrial democracy and consumer democracy: seven reasons the TUC is wrong.* London: H.M.S.O., 1976. 6p.

2804 **Stokes**, Ronald. 'Power to the people: a challenge for industry.' *Pers. Manage.*, viii, 5 (May 1976), 14–17.

2805 **Bain**, George Sayers. 'Bullock: a reply to the critics.' *Social. Comment.*, xxxvi, 4 (April 1977), 3–5.

2806 **Bain**, George Sayers. 'In defence of Bullock's basic thinking.' *Pers. Manage.*, ix, 5 (May 1977), 25–7.

2807 **Bell**, J. D. M. 'Industrial democracy in the nationalised industries.' Benedictus, Roger and others (eds.). *Industrial democracy: the implications of the Bullock Report.* 1977. p. 3.1–3.16.

2808 **Benedictus**, Roger, **Bourn**, Colin and **Neal**, Alan C. (eds.). *Industrial democracy: the implications of the Bullock Report: proceedings of a conference held at the University of Leicester, 1977.* Leicester: University of Leicester Department of Adult Education, 1977.

2809 **British Steel Corporation Employee Directors.** *Worker directors speak.* Epping: Gower, 1977. 114p.
Prefaced by Joan Bank and Ken Jones.

2810 **Chell**, L. 'What do worker directors do?' *Ind. Soc.*, LIX, 6 (November–December 1977), 6–7.

2811 **Chiplin**, Brian and **Coyne**, John. 'Property rights and industrial democracy.' Chiplin, B. and others. *Can workers manage?* 1977. p. 13–48.

2812 **City Company Law Committee.** *A reply to Bullock.* London: The Committee, 1977. 30p.

2813 **Clegg**, Hugh Armstrong. 'The Bullock Report and European experience.' Benedictus, Roger and others (eds.). *Industrial democracy: the implications of the Bullock Report.* 1977. p. 5.1–5.13.

2814 **Coates**, Ken and **Topham**, Tony. *The shop steward's guide to the Bullock report.* Nottingham: Spokesman, 1977. 127p.

2815 **Confederation of British Industry.** *In place of Bullock.* London: C.B.I., 1977. 40p.

2816 **Denton**, Geoffrey. *Beyond Bullock: economic implications of worker participation in control and ownership of industry.* London: Federal Trust for Education and Research, 1977. 25p.

2817 **Department of Trade**, Committee of Inquiry on Industrial Democracy. *Report of the ... Committee.* London: H.M.S.O., 1977. ix, 205p. (Cmnd. 6706.)
Chairman: Lord Bullock.

2818 **Edmonds**, John. 'The Bullock Committee's Report and collective bargaining.' Benedictus, Roger and others (eds.). *Industrial democracy: the implications of the Bullock Report.* 1977. p. 4.1–4.12.

2819 **Farnham**, David and **Pimlott**, John. 'Who wants Bullock?' *New Soc.*, XXXIX (3 March 1977), 451–2.

2820 **Fatchett**, Derek John. *Industrial democracy: prospects after Bullock.* Nottingham: Universities of Nottingham and Leeds, 1977. 38p. (Occasional papers in industrial relations 2.)

2821 **Hanson**, Charles. 'The Bullock Report and the West German system of co-determination.' *Three Banks Rev.*, CXVI (December 1977), 30–51.

2822 **Harris**, Ralph. 'Bullock's basic blunder.' Chiplin, Brian and others. *Can workers manage?* 1977. p. 97–106.

2823 **Harrison**, Roger. 'The European experience and what Bullock left out.' *Pers. Manage.*, IX, 6 (June 1977), 27–9.

2824 **Henderson**, Joan. *A guide to the Bullock Report.* London: Industrial Society, 1977. 28p.

2825 **Incomes Data Services.** *The machinery of industrial democracy.* London: I.D.S., 1977. 66p. (I.D.S. handbooks 8.)

2826 **Industrial Relations Services.** *The Bullock report: special supplement.* London: The Services, 1977. 16p.

2827 **Jones**, Derek C. 'The Bullock report.' *Econ. Anal. Workers' Manage.*, XI (1977), 245–79.

2828 **Jones**, Ken. 'Worker directors at the British Steel Corporation.' *Labour and Soc.*, II, 4 (1977), 425–39.

2829 **Lea**, David. 'The Bullock Committee's Report and the T.U.C. view.' Benedictus, Roger and others (eds.). *Industrial democracy: the implications of the Bullock Report.* 1977. p. 7.1–7.11.

2830 **Lowry**, Pat. 'The Bullock Committee's report and management.' Benedictus, Roger and others (eds.). *Industrial democracy: the implications of the Bullock Report.* 1977. p. 2.1–2.11.

2831 **Murray**, Lionel. 'Trades Union Congress, Blackpool 1977: composite motion 10 on industrial democracy.' *Ind. Participation*, DLXII (Autumn 1977), 23–5.

2832 **North London Workers' Control Group.** *Bullock A–Z: a guide to the report of the Committee of Inquiry on Industrial Democracy.* London: The Authors, 1977. 46p.

2833 **Roberts**, Benjamin Charles. 'Participation by agreement.' *Lloyds Bank Rev.*, CXXV (July 1977), 12–23.

2834 **Schmitthoff**, Clive. 'The Bullock Committee and the E.E.C.' Benedictus, Roger and others (eds.). *Industrial democracy: the implications of the Bullock Report.* 1977. p. 6.1–6.13.

2835 **Scottish Council (Development and Industry)**, Committee on Industrial and Social Conditions. *Towards industrial democracy: a code of practice: some practical guidelines on employee participation.* Edinburgh: The Council, 1977. 12p.

2836 **Scottish Council (Development and Industry)**, Committee on Industrial and Social Conditions. *Towards industrial democracy: policy position paper: a view on employee participation in Scotland.* Edinburgh: The Council, 1977. 8p.

2837 **Sirc**, Ljubo. 'Workers' management under public and private ownership.' Chiplin, Brian and others. *Can workers manage?* 1977. p. 49–86.

2838 **Thomson**, Andrew W. J. 'New focus on industrial democracy in Britain.' *Ann. Am. Acad. Polit. Soc. Sci.*, CDXXXI (May 1977), 32–43.

2839 **Trades Union Congress.** *Industrial democracy: a statement of policy ... with the supplementary note of evidence submitted to the Bullock Committee* of Inquiry on Industrial Democracy. London: T.U.C., 1977. 49p.

2840 **Trades Union Congress.** T.U.C. guide to the Bullock report on industrial democracy. London: T.U.C., 1977. 23p.

2841 **Wedderburn**, K. W. 'Industrial democracy and company law.' Benedictus, Roger and others (eds.). Industrial democracy: the implications of the Bullock Report. 1977. p. 1.1–1.20.

2842 **Wellens**, John. 'The Bullock Report.' Ind. Commer. Train., IX, 3 (March 1977), 93–100.

2843 **Wood**, John B. 'Employee participation and consumer sovereignty: the real lesson of Germany.' Chiplin, Brian and others. Can workers manage? 1977. p. 87–96.

2844 **Bank**, John. 'Worker directors and role conflict.' London Bus. School J., 1 (Spring 1978), 21–4.

2845 **Black**, Errol. 'The politics of industrial democracy in Britain: reflections on the report of the Committee of Inquiry on Industrial Democracy.' Insurg. Sociol., VIII, 2–3 (Fall 1978), 206–15.

2846 **Department of Employment Gazette.** 'Industrial democracy: no longer a question of "if" but "when and how".' Dep. Employment Gaz., LXXXVI, 7 (July 1978), 795–7.

2847 **Industrial Relations Services.** Industrial democracy white paper: a statutory umbrella for flexible arrangements. London: The Services, 1978. 12p.

2848 **Prime Minister's Office.** Industrial democracy. London: H.M.S.O., 1978. ii, 18p. (Cmnd. 7231.)

2849 **Ream**, Betty. A guide to the white paper on industrial democracy. London: Industrial Society, 1978. 24p.

2850 **Shackleton**, J. R. 'The Bullock report: European contrasts.' J. Ind. Affairs, V, 2 (Spring 1978), 26–33.

2851 **Bescoby**, John H. and **Hanson**, C. G. 'The employee–director aspect of industrial democracy.' Durham Univ. J., LXXII (December 1979), 71–8.

2852 **Chell**, L. 'Worker directors in action.' Ind. Soc., LXI, 2 (March–April 1979), 7–9.

2853 **Guest**, David. 'Participation at company level.' Guest, David and Knight, Kenneth (eds.). Putting participation into practice. 1979. p. 179–91.

2854 **Institute of Directors.** The responsibilities and contribution of non-executive directors on the boards of U.K. companies. London: Booz Allen & Hamilton, 1979. 25p.

2855 **Jones**, Ken. 'The process of change in the worker director scheme in the British Steel Corporation.' Guest, David and Knight, Kenneth (eds.). Putting participation into practice. 1979. p. 206–32.

2856 **Knight**, Ian B. Company organisation and worker participation: a survey of attitudes and practices in industrial democracy with special emphasis on the prospects for employee directors. London: Office of Population Censuses and Surveys Social Survey Division, 1979. 158p.

See also: 1724; 2517; 2531; 2559; 2564; 2565; 2567; 2582; 2623; 2624; 2625; 2631; 2637; 2650; 2659; 2703; 2711; 2764.

PART SIX

THE LABOUR FORCE, LABOUR MARKETS, AND CONDITIONS OF EMPLOYMENT

The literature in this part of the bibliography has been particularly difficult to classify as most of it deals with more than one subject. The more general literature has been classified in Part Six, I; Part Six, III, A; and Part Six, IV, A, 1, and these sections should be consulted in conjunction with each other. But there is also considerable overlap with sections Part Six, III, B–E, and Part Six, IV, A, 2–3, and hence these sections should be consulted together.

I. GENERAL

This section contains general works dealing with more than one aspect of the labour market. In particular, it includes general works which are primarily concerned with analysing the interrelationships between such factors as unemployment, wages, and prices. But material on wages and prices which is primarily of a descriptive nature is classified at Part Six, III, A and B–D. See also Part Six, II, B, 1; Part Six, II, C, 1; Part Six, II, D, 1; Part Six, III, A; Part Six, IV, A, 1; and Part Seven, IV, A.

2857 **Braun**, A. R. 'Wages in the United Kingdom: has there been a shift in the Phillips curve?' *Int. Monetary Fund Staff Pap.*, XVIII, 1 (March 1971), 136–82.

2858 **Brown**, *Lord* Wilfred. *Inflation and a possible solution.* London: The Author, 1971. 15p.

2859 **Fisher**, Malcolm Robertson. *The economic analysis of labour.* London: Weidenfeld & Nicolson, 1971. 303p.

2860 **Godfrey**, Leslie. 'The Phillips curve: incomes policy and trade union effects.' Johnson, H. G. and Nobay, A. R. (eds.). *The current inflation.* London: Macmillan, 1971. p. 99–124.

2861 **Laidler**, David. 'The Phillips curve, expectations and incomes policy.' Johnson, H. G. and Nobay, A. R. (eds.) *The current inflation.* London: Macmillan, 1971. p. 75–98.

2862 **MacKay**, Donald Iain, **Brack**, John, **Boddy**, D., **Diack**, J. A. and **Jones**, N. *Labour markets under different employment conditions.* London: Allen & Unwin, 1971. 433p. (Glasgow University social and economic studies 22.)

2863 **Moreh**, J. 'Human capital and economic growth: United Kingdom 1951–1961.' *Econ. Soc. Rev.*, III, 1 (October 1971), 73–93.

2864 **Peston**, Maurice. 'The micro-economics of the Phillips curve.' Johnson, H. G. and Nobay, A. R. (eds.). *The current inflation.* London: Macmillan, 1971. p. 125–42.

2865 **Phelps**, Edmund Strother (ed.). *Microeconomic foundations of employment and inflation theory.* London: Macmillan, 1971. viii, 434p.

2866 **Reilly**, N. M. P. *The relation of real wages to the employment of labour and resources in an industrially developed economy.* [1971?]. (Ph.D. thesis, University of London.)

2867 **Rothschild**, K. W. 'The Phillips curve and all that.' *Scott. J. Polit. Econ.*, XVIII, 3 (November 1971), 245–80.

2868 **Smart**, M. W. *The determination of labour market areas in Great Britain.* [1971?]. (M.Phil. thesis, London School of Economics.)

2869 **Taylor**, J. *Unemployment and wage inflation in Britain and the USA: a post-war study.* [1971?]. (Ph.D. thesis, University of Lancaster.)

2870 **Thirlwall**, A. P. 'The valuation of labour in surplus labour economies: a synoptic view.' *Scott. J. Polit. Econ.*, XVIII (November 1971), 299–314.

2871 **Thomas**, R. L. and **Stoney**, P. J. M. 'Unemployment dispersion as a determinant of wage inflation in the U.K. 1925–66.' *Manchr. Sch. Econ. Soc. Stud.*, XXXIX, 2 (June 1971), 83–116.

2872 **Uehara**, N. *Comparative analysis of prices, wages and labour market structures in Britain and Japan.* [1971?] (M.Litt. thesis, University of Glasgow.)

2873 **Bain**, George Sayers, **Bacon**, R. and **Pimlott**, J. 'The economic environment.' Halsey A. H. (ed.). *Trends in British society since 1900.* London: Macmillan, 1972. p. 64–96.

2874 **Bain**, George Sayers, **Bacon**, R. and **Pimlott**, J. 'The labour force.' Halsey. A. H. (ed.). *Trends in British society since 1900.* London: Macmillan, 1972. p. 97–128.

2875 **Brothwell**, J. F. 'An alternative explanation

of the Phillips curve relationship.' *Bull. Econ. Res.*, XXIV (November 1972), 57–64.

2876 **Burns**, Michael E. 'Regional Phillips curves: a further note.' *Oxf. Bull. Econ. Stat.*, XXXIV, 3 (August 1972), 295–307.

2877 **Corina**, John A. *Labour market economics: a short survey of recent theory.* London: Heinemann, 1972. 81p.

2878 **King**, John Edward. *Labour economics.* London: Macmillan, 1972. 79p.

2879 **Marin**, A. 'The Phillips curve (born 1958–died?).' *Three Banks Rev.*, XCVI (December 1972), 28–42.

2880 **Meade**, James Edward. *Wages and prices in a mixed economy.* London: Institute of Economic Affairs, 1972. 36. (Occasional papers 35.)

2881 **Metcalf**, David and **Richardson**, Ray. 'Labour.' Prest, A. R. and Coppock, D. J. (eds.). *The U.K.: a manual of applied economics.* London: Weidenfeld & Nicolson.
    Fourth edition. 1972. p. 200–68.
    Fifth edition. 1974. p. 218–66.
    Sixth edition. 1976. p. 238–95.
    Seventh edition. 1978. p. 223–84.

2882 **Mukherjee**, Santosh. *Making labour markets work: a comparison of the UK and Swedish systems.* London: Political and Economic Planning, 1972. x, 153p. (P.E.P. broadsheets 532.)

2883 **Mulvey**, C. and **Trevithick**, J. A. 'Trade unions and wage inflation.' *Econ. Soc. Rev.*, IV, 2 (December 1972), 209–29.

2884 **Parkin**, Michael. 'The UK evidence on the causes of inflation.' Haberler, G., Parkin, M. and Smith, Henry. *Inflation and the unions.* 1972. p. 63–78.

2885 **Pratten**, Clifford F. 'How higher wages can cause unemployment.' *Lloyds Bank Rev.*, CIII (January 1972), 12–24.

2886 **Vanderkamp**, J. 'Wage adjustment, productivity and price change expectations.' *Rev. Econ. Stud.*, XXXIX, 117 (January 1972), 61–72.

2887 **Archibald**, G. C., **Kemmis**, Robyn and **Perkins**, J. W. 'Excess demand for labour, unemployment and the Phillips curve: a theoretical and empirical study.' Laidler, D.E.W. and Purdy, D.L. (eds.). *Inflation and labour markets.* 1973. p. 109–63.

2888 **Bacon**, Robert William. 'The Phillips curve: another forerunner.' *Economica*, XL (August 1973), 314–5.

2889 **Bosanquet**, Nicholas and **Doeringer**, Peter B. 'Is there a dual labour market in Great Britain?' *Econ. J.*, LXXXIII, 330 (June 1973), 421–35.

2890 **Brechling**, F.P.R. 'Wage inflation and the structure of regional unemployment.' Laidler, D.E.W. and Purdy, D.L. (eds.). *Inflation and labour markets.* 1973 p. 197–226.

2891 **Gee**, Kenneth P. *The wage–employment tradeoff.* London: Aims of Industry, 1973. 12p.

2892 **Godfrey**, Leslie and **Taylor**, Jim. 'Earnings changes in the United Kingdom 1954–1970: excess labour supply, exported inflation and union influence.' *Oxf. Univ. Inst. Econ. Stat. Bull.*, XXXV, 3 (August 1973), 197–216.

2893 **Hughes**, John. 'Trends in profits and productivity, 1971–2.' Barratt Brown, M. and Coates, K. (eds.). *Trade union register: 3.* 1973. p. 98–106.

2894 **Institute of Manpower Studies.** 'General picture: survey of the British labour market.' *I.M.S. Monit.*, II, 3 (October 1973), 85–98.

2895 **Krimpas**, George Elias. *Labour input measurement and the theory of the labour market.* 1973. (Ph.D. thesis, University of Brunel.)

2896 **Laidler**, David E. W. and **Purdy**, L. (eds.). *Inflation and labour markets.* Manchester: Manchester U.P., 1973. xii, 258p.

2897 **Phelps Brown**, Ernest Henry. 'Levels and movements of industrial productivity and real wages internationally compared 1860–1970.' *Econ. J.*, LXXXIII, 329 (March 1973), 58–71.

2898 **Robinson**, Derek. 'Future trends in the labour market.' Cuthbert, N. and Hawkins, K. (eds.). *Company industrial relations policies.* 1973. p. 157–72.

2899 **Sharot**, T. 'Unemployment dispersion as a determinant of wage inflation in the U.K. 1925–66: a note.' *Manchr. Sch. Econ. Soc. Stud.*, XLI, 2 (June 1973), 225–8.

2900 **Thomas**, R. L. 'Unemployment dispersion as a determinant of wage inflation in the U.K. 1925–1966: a rejoinder.' *Manchr. Sch. Econ. Soc. Stud.*, XLI, 2 (June 1973), 229–33.

2901 **Thomas**, R. L. 'Wage inflation in the U.K.: a multi-market approach.' Laidler, D.E.W. and Purdy, D. L. (eds.). *Inflation and labour markets.* 1973. p. 227–53.

2902 **Wilkinson**, R. K. and **Burkitt**, Brian. 'Wage determination and trade unions.' *Scott. J. Polit. Econ.*, XX, 2 (June 1973), 107–21.

2903 **Wolfstetter**, E. 'Surplus labour, synchronised labour costs and Marx's labour theory of value.' *Econ. J.*, LXXXIII (September 1973), 787–809.

2904 **Grossman**, H. I. 'Cyclical pattern of unemployment and wage inflation.' *Economica*, XLI, 164 (November 1974), 403–13.

2905 **Latham**, R. W. and **Peel**, D. A. 'The wage variable and the Phillips curve.' *Scott. J. Polit. Econ.*, XXI (November 1974), 289–93.

2906 **McCallum**, B. T. 'Wage rate changes and the excess demand for labour: an alternative formulation.' *Economica*, XLI, 163 (August 1974), 269–77.

2907 **MacKay**, Donald Iain and **Hart**, R. A. 'Wage inflation and the Phillips relationship.' *Manchr. Sch. Econ. Soc. Stud.*, XLII, 2 (June 1974), 136–61.

2908 **Rowley**, J. C. R. and **Wilton**, D. A. 'Sensitivity of quarterly models of wage determination to aggregation assumptions.' *Q. J. Econ.*, LXXXVIII, 4 (November 1974), 671–80.

2909 **Taylor**, J. *Unemployment and wage inflation with special reference to Britain and the U.S.A.* London: Longman, 1974. xi, 120p.

2910 **Wachter**, Michael L. 'A new approach to the equilibrium labour force.' *Economica*, XLI, 161 (February 1974), 35–51.

2911 **Webb**, A. E. *Unemployment, vacancies and the rate of change of earnings: a regional analysis.* Cambridge: Cambridge U.P., 1974. 49p. (National Institute of Economic and Social Research regional papers 3.)

2912 **Appleton**, J. D. S. *Labour economics.* London: Macdonald & Evans.
First edition. 1975. x, 238p.
Second edition. 1979. ix, 222p.

2913 **Bacon**, Robert William and **Eltis**, Walter Alfred. 'The implications for inflation, employment and growth of a fall in the share of output that is marketed.' *Oxf. Univ. Inst. Econ. Stat. Bull.*, XXXV (November 1975), 269–95.

2914 **Dawson**, Alistair. 'A new test of the inflation–unemployment relationship.' *J. Ind. Affairs*, III, 1 (December 1975), 141–4.

2915 **Department of Employment Gazette.** 'The changing structure of the labour force.' *Dep. Employment Gaz.*, LXXXIII, 10 (October 1975), 982–5.

2916 **Friedman**, Milton. *Unemployment versus inflation? An evaluation of the Phillips curve.* London: Institute of Economic Affairs, 1975. 48p. (Occasional papers 44.)
With a British commentary by David E.W. Laidler.

2917 **Holden**, K. and **Peel**, D. A. 'A Monte Carlo study of the Phillips curve with errors in variables.' *Oxf. Univ. Inst. Econ. Stat. Bull.*, XXXVII (May 1975), 155–7.

2918 **Krimpas**, George Elias. *Labour input and the theory of the labour market.* London: Duckworth, 1975. xvi, 288p.

2919 **Meade**, James E. *The intelligent radical's guide to economic policy: the mixed economy.* London: Allen & Unwin, 1975. 160p.

2920 **Phipps**, Anthony J. 'The relationship between output and employment in British manufacturing industry.' *Oxf. Univ. Inst. Econ. Stat. Bull.*, XXXVII, 1 (Feburary 1975), 49–65.

2921 **Bacon**, Robert William and **Eltis**, Walter Alfred. *Britain's economic problem: too few producers.* London: Macmillan.
First edition. 1976. xiii, 194p.
Second edition. 1978. xv, 255p.

2922 **Burchill**, Frank. *Economic factors and regulatory processes.* Milton Keynes: Open U.P., 1976. 40p. (PT 281 Unit 7.)

2923 **Henneberry**, Barbara and **Witte**, James G. 'The unemployment–inflation dilemma in macroeconomics: some contradictory aspects of contemporary theory and policy.' *Scott. J. Polit. Econ.*, XXIII (February 1976), 17–36.

2924 **Hines**, A. G. 'The micro-economic foundations of employment and inflation theory: bad old wine in elegant new bottles.' Worswick, G. (ed.). *The concept and measurement of involuntary unemployment.* 1976. p. 58–79.

2925 **Jay**, Peter. *Employment, inflation and politics.* London: Institute of Economic Affairs, 1976. 36p. (Occasional papers 46.)
Sixth Wincott memorial lecture.

2926 **Peel**, D. A. and **Sheriff**, T. D. 'Unemployment and inflation in the U.K. 1893–1938.' *Ind. Relat.*, XV, 3 (October 1976), 324–7.

2927 **Pissarides**, Christopher A. *Labour market adjustment: micro-economic foundations of short-run neoclassical and Keynesian dynamics.* Cambridge: Cambridge U.P., 1976. xi, 258p.

2928 **Pratten**, Clifford F. *Labour productivity differentials within international companies.* Cambridge: Cambridge U.P., 1976. xiii, 118p. (University of Cambridge Department of Applied Economics occasional papers 50.)

2929 **Reece**, William S. 'Aggregate excess labour demand and the rate of change of nominal wages.' *Manchr. Sch. Econ. Soc. Stud.*, XLIV (December 1976), 359–73.

2930 **Thomas**, R. Barry. 'Labour market adjustments.' *Ind. Relat. J.*, VII, 3 (Autumn 1976), 44–58.

2931 **Briscoe**, Geoffrey and **Roberts**, Colin J. 'Structural breaks in employment functions.' *Manchr. Sch. Econ. Soc. Stud.*, XLV, 1 (March 1977), 1–15.

2932 **Butler**, Francis. 'Pay and hours: how satisfied are you?' *Dep. Employment Gaz.*, LXXXV, 9 (September 1977), 906–15.

2933 **Greer**, Douglas F. and **Rhoades**, Stephen A. 'A test of the reserve labour hypothesis.' *Econ. J.*, LXXXVII (June 1977), 290–9.

2934 **Kahn**, Richard and **Posner**, Michael. 'Inflation, unemployment and growth.' *Natl. Westminster Bank Q. Rev.* (November 1977), 28–37.

2935 **Mulvey**, Charles and **Gregory**, Mary. 'The Hines wage inflation model.' *Manchr. Sch. Econ. Soc. Stud.*, XLV, 1 (March 1977), 29–40.

2936 **Thomas**, R. L. 'Unionization and the Phillips curve: time series evidence from seven industrial countries.' *Appl. Econ.*, IX (1977), 33–49.

2937 **Anderson**, Malcolm. 'Power and inflation.' Hirsch, F. and Goldthorpe, J. (eds.). *The political economy of inflation.* 1978. p. 240–62.

2938 **Brittan**, Samuel. 'Inflation and democracy.' Hirsch, F. and Goldthorpe, J. (eds.). *The political economy of inflation.* 1978. p. 161–85.

2939 **Corden**, Werner Max. 'Keynes and the others: wage and price rigidities in macroeconomic models.' *Oxf. Econ. Pap.*, XXX (July 1978), 159–80.

2940 **Fisher**, Malcolm R. 'Wage differentials and

created employment.' Addison, J. T. and others. *Job creation – or destruction?* 1978. p. 41–54.

2941 **Goldthorpe**, John H. 'The current inflation: towards a sociological account.' Hirsch, F. and Goldthorpe, J. (eds.). *The political economy of inflation.* 1978. p. 186–213.

2942 **Hirsch**, Fred and **Goldthorpe**, John H. (eds.). *The political economy of inflation.* Oxford: Martin Robertson, 1978. xi, 307p.

2943 **Hunter**, Laurence Colvin and **Beaumont**, Philip B. *Labour shortages and manpower policy.* London: H.M.S.O. for the Manpower Services Commission, 1978. 108p. (Manpower study 2.)

2944 **Moss**, Scott J. 'Two views on the role of the labour market in inflationary recession: a diagrammatic exposition.' *J. Ind. Affairs*, VI, 1 (Autumn 1978), 7–11.

2945 **Mulvey**, Charles. *The economic analysis of trade unions.* Oxford: Martin Robertson, 1978. viii, 159p. (Glasgow social and economic research studies 5.)

2946 **Pissarides**, Christopher A. 'The role of relative wages and excess demand in the sectoral flow of labour.' *Rev. Econ. Stud.*, XLV (October 1978), 453–67.

2947 **Rosen**, Sherwin. 'Substitution and division of labour.' *Economica*, XLV (August 1978), 235–50.

2948 **Rowley**, Charles K. 'The economics and politics of extortion.' Institute of Economic Affairs. *Trade unions: public goods or public bads?* 1978. p. 90–3.

2949 **Whiting**, E. 'The economics of modes of employment.' *Pers. Rev.*, III, 4 (Winter 1978), 40–52.

2950 **Wragg**, Richard and **Robertson**, James. 'Britain's industrial performance since the war: trends in employment, productivity, output, labour costs and prices by industry: 1950–73.' *Dep. Employment Gaz.*, LXXXVI, 5 (May 1978), 512–9.

2951 **Addison**, John T. and **Siebert**, W. S. *The market for labor: an analytical treatment.* New York: Goodyear, 1979. xi, 500p.

2952 **Blackburn**, Robert Martin and **Mann**, Michael. *The working class in the labour market.* London: Macmillan, 1979. x, 369p.

2953 **Burkitt**, Brian. *Trade unions and the economy.* London: Macmillan, 1979. 144p.

2954 **Davies**, R. J. 'Economic activity, incomes policy and strikes: a quantitative analysis.' *Br. J. Ind. Relat.*, XVIII, 2 (July 1979), 205–23.

2955 **Fallick**, J. L. 'Pay policy and labour supply: some neglected considerations.' *Natl. Westminster Bank Q. Rev.* (February 1979), 7–18.

2956 **Ferguson**, B. L. and **Gupta**, Kanhaya L. 'On the dynamics of inflation and unemployment in a quantity theory framework.' *Economica*, XLVI (February 1979), 51–9.

2957 **Fidgett**, T. and **Moir**, C. B. *A guide to sources of local labour market information.* London: Engineering Industry Training Board, 1979. 76p. (E.I.T.B. Reference Report 5/79.)

2958 **Horne**, Jocelyn. 'The effect of devaluation on the balance of payments and the labour market: United Kingdom, 1967.' *Economica*, XLVI (February 1979), 11–25.

2959 **Wales**, T. J. and **Woodland**, A. D. 'Labour supply and progressive taxes.' *Rev. Econ. Stud.*, XLVI (January 1979), 83–95.

See also: 25; 107; 113; 187; 369; 694; 709; 1145; 1171; 1696; 1701; 2061; 3517; 3906; 4013; 4038; 4198; 4311; 4572; 4573; 4579; 4608; 4658; 4660; 4779; 5069; 6208; 6394; 6405; 6587; 6597; 6598; 6604; 6629; 6681; 6693; 6701; 6722; 7013.

II. THE LABOUR FORCE

A. ENTRY INTO EMPLOYMENT

Some of the general works in part Two, I contain material on attitudes towards choice of occupation and problems arising on entry into employment. See also Part Six, II, C, 5.

1. General

This section contains general references on the problems arising in the transition from school to work. More specific material on vocational choice is contained in Part Six, II, A, 2. See also Part Seven, II, D, 1–2.

2960 **Cotterill**, T. 'In at the deep end.' *Ind. Soc.*, LIII, 10 (October 1971), 22–5.

2961 **Harris**, Evelyn Marjorie. *How to get a job: a practical guide for young people.* London: Institute of Personnel Management, 1971. 32p. (Practical Handbooks 4.)

2962 **Mansfield**, Roger. 'Career development in the first year at work: a study of graduates entering two large firms.' *Occup. Psychol.*, XLV, 2 (1971), 139–49.

2963 **Perks**, M. 'We hope you'll enjoy working for us.' *Pers. Manage.*, III, 8 (August 1971), 36–7.

2964 **Gormley**, Richard and **Wallis-Jones**, Mary. 'First jobs.' *New Soc.*, XXI (20 July 1972), 133–4.

2965 **Gwilliam**, A. 'By way of introduction.' *Ind. Soc.*, LIV, 5 (May 1972), 19–20.

2966 **McLeod**, E. 'Starting work.' *Ind. Soc.*, LIV, 3 (March 1972), 14–18.

2967 **Ritchie**, J., **Frost**, C. and **Dight**, S. *Employment of art college leavers.* London: H.M.S.O., 1972. xvii, 287p.

2968 **Ashton**, D. N. 'Transition from school to work: notes on the development of different frames of reference among young male workers.' *Sociol. Rev.*, XXI, 1 (February 1973), 101–25.

Reprinted in Esland, G. and others (eds.). *People and work.* 1975. p. 147–57.

2969 **Lee**, D. J. 'The regional factor in the further education and employment of male school-leavers.' *Sociology*, VII, 3 (September 1973), 429–36.

2970 **Thomas**, C. J. *Wage earner.* London: Bell, 1973. 46p.
Teaching aid.

2971 **Thomas**, R. and **Wetherell**, D. *Looking forward to work: a report on the first stage of a follow-up survey of fifteen and sixteen year old boy school-leavers.* London: H.M.S.O., 1974. xxi, 435p.

2972 **Allen**, Sheila and **Smith**, Christopher R. 'Minority group experience of the transition from education to work.' Brannen, P. (ed.). *Entering the world of work.* 1975. p. 71–90.

2973 **Ashton**, D. N. 'From school to work: some problems of adjustment experienced by young male workers.' Brannen, P. (ed.). *Entering the world of work.* 1975. p. 53–70.

2974 **Brannen**, Peter (ed.). *Entering the world of work: some sociological perspectives.* London: H.M.S.O., 1975. iv, 128p.

2975 **Brannen**, Peter. 'Industrial and economic change and the entry into work: an overview.' Brannen, P. (ed.). *Entering the world of work.* 1975. p. 113–29.

2976 **Carter**, Michael P. 'Teenage workers: a second chance at 18?' Brannen, P. (ed.). *Entering the world of work.* 1975. p. 91–112.

2977 **Glickman**, M. J. A. 'Education and work: an anthropological view of the transition process.' Brannen, P. (ed.). *Entering the world of work.* 1975. p. 27–52.

2978 **Gray**, H. L. 'On starting a new job.' *J. Occup. Psychol.*, XLVIII, 1 (1975), 33–7.

2979 **MacCormick**, K. J. *Becoming technologists: a study of the recruitment and adjustment of graduate scientists and engineers to industrial employment.* 1975. (Ph.D. thesis, University of Edinburgh.)

2980 **Stewart**, Valerie. 'About induction and induction training.' *Ind. Train. Int.*, X, 7 (July–August 1975), 220–2.

2981 **Department of Employment Gazette.** 'Young people leaving school.' *Dep. Employment Gaz.*, LXXXIV, 5 (May 1976), 455–60.

2982 **Harris**, Evelyn Marjorie. *How to get a job.* London: Institute of Personnel Management, 1976. 119p.

2983 **Moor**, Christine H. *From school to work: effective counselling and guidance.* London: Sage, 1976. 191p.

2984 **Broadfoot**, P. H. 'Assessment of school-leavers.' *Ind. Commer. Train.*, IX, 1 (January 1977), 20–3.

2985 **Fowler**, Bridget, **Littlewood**, Barbara and **Madigan**, Ruth. 'Immigrant school leavers and the search for work: a study of Glas-

gow's Asians.' *Sociology*, XI (January 1977), 65–85.

2986 **Jenner**, A. E. 'The industrial image.' *B.A.C.I.E. J.*, XXXI, 9 (September 1977), 135–9.

2987 **Mathews**, David. *The relevance of school learning experience to performance in industry.* London: Engineering Industry Training Board, 1977. 132p. (E.I.T.B. research reports 6.)
Edited by Elizabeth Orna.

2988 **Reubens**, Beatrice G. *Bridges to work: international comparisons of transition services.* Oxford: Martin Robertson, 1977. xii, 276p.

2989 **Simon**, Martin. *Youth into industry: a study of young people's attitudes to work in a large Midlands factory.* London: National Youth Bureau, 1977. 69p.

2990 **Brooks**, Dennis and **Singh**, Karamjit. *Aspirations versus opportunities: Asian and white school leavers in the Midlands.* Walsall: Walsall Council for Community Relations, 1978. 87p.

2991 **Crowley**, Tony. *Starting a job.* Cambridge: Hobsons Press, 1978.
Fourth edition. 32p.

2992 **Department of Manpower Services (Northern Ireland).** *Opportunities at sixteen: report of a study group.* Belfast: H.M.S.O., 1978. vi, 110p.
Chairman: Derek Birley.

2993 **Industrial Training Research Unit.** *Jobs and numeracy for school-leavers: a local survey.* London: The Unit, 1979. 43p.

2. Vocational Choice

See also Part Seven, II, D, 1.

2994 **Ashley**, B.J., **Cohen**, H., **McIntyre**, D. and **Slatter**, R. 'A sociological analysis of students' reasons for becoming teachers: further notes.' *Sociol. Rev.*, XIX, 3 (August 1971), 421–6.

2995 **Central Youth Employment Executive.** *Art and design.* London: H.M.S.O., 1971. 92p. (Choice of careers booklet 103.)
Third edition.

2996 **Central Youth Employment Executive.** *Choosing your career.* London: H.M.S.O., 1971. 10p. (Choice of careers booklet 1.)

2997 **Central Youth Employment Executive.** *Engineering draughtsman.* London: H.M.S.O., 1971. 28p. (Choice of careers booklet 60.)
Third edition.

2998 **Central Youth Employment Executive.** *Journalism.* London: H.M.S.O., 1971. 40p. (Choice of careers booklet 83.)
Fourth edition.

2999 **Central Youth Employment Executive.** *Library, information and archive work.* London: H.M.S.O., 1971. 38p. (Choice of careers booklet 4.)
Seventh edition.

3000 **Central Youth Employment Executive.**

Ophthalmic optician and dispensing optician. London: H.M.S.O., 1971. 24p. (Choice of careers booklet 74.)
Fourth edition.

3001 **Central Youth Employment Executive.** *Opportunities in the professions, industry and commerce.* London: H.M.S.O., 1971. 432p.
Ninth edition.

3002 **Central Youth Employment Executive.** *Orthoptist.* London: H.M.S.O., 1971. 16p. (Choice of careers booklet 69.)
Fourth edition.

3003 **Central Youth Employment Executive.** *Retailing.* London: H.M.S.O., 1971. 28p. (Choice of careers booklet 75.)
Fourth edition.

3004 **Central Youth Employment Executive.** *Speech therapist.* London: H.M.S.O., 1971. 28p. (Choice of careers booklet 51.)
Fifth edition.

3005 **Coxon**, Anthony P. M. 'Occupational attributes: constructs and structure.' *Sociology*, V, 3 (September 1971), 335–54.

3006 **Hilton**, J. *The employment expectations and aspirations of white and coloured school-leavers in the Manchester area.* 1971. (M.A. thesis, University of Manchester.)

3007 **Lancashire**, Ruth D. 'Occupational choice theory and occupational guidance practice.' Warr, P. (ed.). *Psychology at work.* 1971. p. 194–207.

3008 **March**, P. and **Smith**, M. *18 + choice.* London: Careers Research and Advisory Centre, 1971. 181p.

3009 **O'Connor**, E. *Some aspects of vocational development in Irish male adolescents.* 1971. (M.Sc. thesis, Queen's University, Belfast.)

3010 **Reeb**, M. 'Similarity, prestige and desirability of jobs as seen by counsellors and 14 year old boys.' *Occup. Psychol.*, XLV (1971), 233–42.

3011 **Timperley**, Stuart R. and **Gregory**, Alison M. 'Some factors affecting the career choice and career perceptions of sixth form school leavers.' *Sociol. Rev.*, XIX (February 1971), 95–114.

3012 **Wolpe**, A. M. *Factors affecting the choice of engineering as a profession among women.* 1971. (M.Sc. thesis, University of Bradford.)

3013 **Cotgrove**, Stephen Frederick and **Fuller**, Mary. 'Occupational socialization and choice: the effects of sandwich courses.' *Sociology*, VI, 1 (January 1972), 59–70.

3014 **Department of Employment.** *Architecture and landscape architecture.* London: H.M.S.O., 1972. 48p. (Choice of careers booklet 16.)
Sixth edition.

3015 **Department of Employment.** *Banking and the Stock Exchange.* London: H.M.S.O., 1972. 32p. (Choice of careers booklet 67.)
Sixth edition.

3016 **Department of Employment.** *Company secretary.* London: H.M.S.O. (Choice of careers booklet 29.)

Fifth edition. 1972. 16p.
Sixth edition. 1973. 16p.

3017 **Department of Employment.** *Dentistry.* London: H.M.S.O., 1972. 40p. (Choice of careers booklet 96.)
Fourth edition.

3018 **Department of Employment.** *Electrician.* London: H.M.S.O., 1972. 28p. (Choice of careers booklet 79.)
Second edition.

3019 **Department of Employment.** *Footwear and leather-goods manufacture.* London: H.M.S.O., 1972. 60p. (Choice of careers booklet 3.)
Third edition.

3020 **Department of Employment.** *Hotels and catering.* London: H.M.S.O., 1972. 52p. (Choice of careers booklet 23.)
Second edition.

3021 **Department of Employment.** *Medicine and surgery.* London: H.M.S.O., 1972. 32p. (Choice of careers booklet 108.)
Fourth edition.

3022 **Department of Employment.** *Medical laboratory technician.* London: H.M.S.O., 1972. 44p. (Choice of careers booklet 57.)
Sixth edition.

3023 **Department of Employment.** *Occupational therapist.* London: H.M.S.O., 1972. 12p. (Choice of careers booklet 53.)
Second edition.

3024 **Department of Employment.** *Radiographer.* London: H.M.S.O., 1972. 20p. (Choice of careers booklet 41.)
Sixth edition.

3025 **Central Youth Employment Executive.** *Radio and television servicing.* London: H.M.S.O., 1973. 28p. (Choice of careers booklet 66.)
Fifth edition.

3026 **Department of Education and Science.** *Careers education in secondary schools.* London: H.M.S.O., 1973. iii, 87p.

3027 **Department of Employment.** *Accountant.* London: H.M.S.O., 1973. 28p. (Choice of careers booklet 59.)
Fifth edition.

3028 **Department of Employment.** *Engineering bench and machine work for boys and girls.* London: H.M.S.O., 1973. 52p. (Choice of careers booklet 22.)

3029 **Department of Employment.** *Home economics and institutional management.* London: H.M.S.O., 1973. 40p. (Choice of careers booklet 13.)

3030 **Department of Employment.** *Library, information and archive work.* London: H.M.S.O., 1973. 36p. (Choice of careers booklet 4.)

3031 **Department of Employment.** *Mathematical, statistical and computer work.* London: H.M.S.O., 1973. 44p. (Choice of careers booklet 109.)

3032 **Department of Employment.** *Metal working, welding and cutting.* London: H.M.S.O.,

1973. 44p. (Choice of careers booklet 39.)

3033 **Department of Employment.** *Office work.* London: H.M.S.O., 1973. 15p. (Choice of careers booklet 65.)

3034 **Department of Employment.** *Photography.* London: H.M.S.O., 1973. 60p. (Choice of careers booklet 115.)

3035 **Department of Employment.** *Wood working crafts.* London: H.M.S.O., 1973. 32p. (Choice of careers booklet 25.)

3036 **Hayes**, John. 'Work experience and the perception of occupations.' *Occup. Psychol.*, XLVII (1973), 121–9.

3037 **Pettigrew**, Andrew M. 'Occupational specialization as an emergent process.' *Sociol. Rev.*, XXI (May 1973), 225–78.

3038 **Watts**, A. G. 'Career influences on students' educational choices.' Greenaway, H. and Williams, G. (eds.). *Patterns of change in graduate employment.* 1973. p. 59–66.

3039 **Banks**, J. A. 'The vocational orientations of sociology graduates.' *Sociology*, VIII, 2 (May 1974), p. 297–304.

3040 **Central Youth Employment Executive.** *Clothing manufacture and needlecraft.* London: H.M.S.O., 1974. 55p. (Choice of careers series 106.) Second edition.

3041 **Central Youth Employment Executive.** *Dietitian.* London: H.M.S.O., 1974. 15p. (Choice of careers booklet 42.)

3042 **Central Youth Employment Executive.** *Journalism.* London: H.M.S.O., 1974. 40p. (Choice of careers booklet 83.) Fifth edition.

3043 **Council of Europe.** *Vocational information and guidance for young people.* Strasbourg: The Council, 1974. i, 79, 3p.

3044 **Thomas**, Brenda and **Madigan**, C. 'Strategy and job choice after redundancy: a case study in the aircraft industry.' *Sociol. Rev.*, XXII, 1 (February 1974), 83–102.

3045 **Timperley**, Stuart R. *Personnel planning and occupational choice.* London: Allen & Unwin, 1974. 236p.

3046 **Employment Service Agency**, Careers and Occupational Information Centre. *Choice of careers: agriculture and horticulture.* London: H.M.S.O., 1975. 48p. Fifth edition.

3047 **Employment Service Agency**, Careers and Occupational Information Centre. *Choice of careers: animal care and veterinary science.* London: H.M.S.O., 1975. 64p. Fourth edition.

3048 **Employment Service Agency**, Careers and Occupational Information Centre. *Choice of careers: building and civil engineering contracting.* London: H.M.S.O., 1975. 48p. Third edition.

3049 **Employment Service Agency**, Careers and Occupational Information Centre. *Choice of careers: civil air transport.* London: H.M.S.O., 1975. 60p.

Second edition.

3050 **Employment Service Agency**, Careers and Occupational Information Centre. *Choice of careers: food science and technology.* London: H.M.S.O., 1975. 44p.

3051 **Employment Service Agency**, Careers and Occupational Information Centre. *Choice of careers: furniture manufacture.* London: H.M.S.O., 1975. 24p. Fourth edition.

3052 **Employment Service Agency**, Careers and Occupational Information Centre. *Choice of careers: hairdressing and beauty culture.* London: H.M.S.O., 1975. 32p. Third edition.

3053 **Employment Service Agency**, Careers and Occupational Information Centre. *Choice of careers: laboratory technicians and assistants.* London: H.M.S.O., 1975. 56p. Second edition.

3054 **Employment Service Agency**, Careers and Occupational Information Centre. *Choice of careers: law.* London: H.M.S.O., 1975. 44p. Fifth edition.

3055 **Employment Service Agency**, Careers and Occupational Information Centre. *Choice of careers: merchant navy officers.* London: H.M.S.O., 1975. 48p. Fifth edition.

3056 **Employment Service Agency**, Careers and Occupational Information Centre. *Choice of careers: nursing for men and women.* London: H.M.S.O., 1975. 48p. Fifth edition.

3057 **Employment Service Agency**, Careers and Occupational Information Centre. *Choice of careers: police.* London: H.M.S.O., 1975. 56p. Fourth edition.

3058 **Employment Service Agency**, Careers and Occupational Information Centre. *Choice of careers: scientist.* London: H.M.S.O., 1975. 56p. Third edition.

3059 **Employment Service Agency**, Careers and Occupational Information Centre. *Women's services.* London: H.M.S.O., 1975. 52p. Fifth edition.

3060 **MacDonald**, E. *Why a secretary?* London: British Productivity Council, 1975. v, 37p.

3061 **Miller**, Ruth. *Careers for girls.* Harmondsworth: Penguin, 1975. 477p. Fourth edition.

3062 **National Computing Centre.** *Working with computers: a guide to jobs and careers.* London: N.C.C. Publications, 1975. 80p.

3063 **Roberts**, Kenneth. 'The developmental theory of occupational choice: a critique and an alternative.' Esland, G. and others (eds.). *People and work.* 1975. p. 134–46.

3064 **Rowland**, V. L. 'Migrants, work and the law: race, class and occupational choice.'

New Community, IV (Winter – Spring 1974–75), 46–54.

3065 **Segal**, A. *Careers encyclopaedia.* London, Cassell, 1975. xiv, 815p.
Eighth edition.

3066 **Smith**, Cyril S. 'Entry, location and commitment of young workers in the labour force: a review of sociological thinking.' Brannen, P. (ed.). *Entering the world of work.* 1975. p. 5–26.

3067 **Central Office of Information**. Reference Division. *Manpower and employment in Britain: occupations and conditions of work.* London: H.M.S.O., 1976. iv, 64p. (Reference pamphlet 139.)

3068 **Employment Service Agency**, Careers and Occupational Information Centre. *Choice of careers: art and design.* London: H.M.S.O., 1976. 80p.

3069 **Employment Service Agency**, Careers and Occupational Information Centre. *Choice of careers: forestry.* London: H.M.S.O., 1976. 28p.

3070 **Employment Service Agency**, Careers and Occupational Information Centre. *Choice of careers: road and rail.* London: H.M.S.O., 1976. 44p.

3071 **Employment Service Agency**, Careers and Occupational Information Centre. *Choice of careers: social workers.* London: H.M.S.O., 1976. 48p.

3072 **Employment Service Agency**, Careers and Occupational Information Centre. *Choice of careers: surveying and auctioneering, valuation and estate agency.* London: H.M.S.O., 1976. 52p.

3073 **Employment Service Agency**, Careers and Occupational Information Centre. *Choice of careers: young men in the ranks.* London: H.M.S.O., 1976. 60p.

3074 **Department of Employment Gazette.** 'Career attitudes of undergraduates: men in their final year.' *Dep. Employment Gaz.*, LXXXV, 10 (October 1977), 1083–92.

3075 **Employment Service Agency**, Careers and Occupational Information Centre. *Choice of careers: choosing your career.* London: H.M.S.O., 1977. 36p.

3076 **Employment Service Agency**, Careers and Occupational Information Centre. *Choice of careers: home economics.* London: H.M.S.O., 1977. 32p.

3077 **Employment Service Agency**, Careers and Occupational Information Centre. *Choice of careers: medical laboratory sciences.* London: H.M.S.O., 1977. 40p.

3078 **Employment Service Agency**, Careers and Occupational Information Centre. *Choice of careers: professional engineers.* London: H.M.S.O., 1977. 36p.

3079 **Employment Service Agency**, Careers and Occupational Information Centre. *Choice of careers: the remedial professions.* London: H.M.S.O., 1977. 40p.

3080 **Keenay**, G. A., **Morgan**, R. W. and **Ray**, K. H. 'Career planning in a hierarchy.' *Pers. Rev.*, VI, 4 (Autumn 1977), 43–50.

3081 **Chapman**, Hubert. *A village upbringing: as preparation for entry to the teaching profession.* n.p.: The Author, 1978. 96p.

3082 **Curran**, James and **Stanworth**, John. 'Job choice and the manual worker: where the theories break down.' *Pers. Manage.*, X, 9 (September 1978), 41–5.

3083 **Employment Service Agency**, Careers and Occupational Information Centre. *Choice of careers: accountancy.* London: H.M.S.O., 1978. 32p.

3084 **Employment Service Agency**, Careers and Occupational Information Centre. *Choice of careers: advertising and public relations.* London: H.M.S.O., 1978. 40p.

3085 **Employment Service Agency**, Careers and Occupational Information Centre. *Choice of careers: architecture and landscape architecture.* London: H.M.S.O., 1978. 44p.

3086 **Employment Service Agency**, Careers and Occupational Information Centre. *Choice of careers: dietetics.* London: H.M.S.O., 1978. 28p.

3087 **Hoult**, P. P. and **Smith**, M. C. 'Age and sex differences in the number and variety of vocational choices, preferences and aspirations.' *J. Occup. Psychol.*, LI (June 1978), 119–25.

3088 **Kelley**, Jonathan. 'Wealth and family background in the occupational career: theory and cross-cultural data.' *Br. J. Sociol.*, XXIX (March 1978), 94–109.

3089 **Miller**, Ruth. *Equal opportunities: a careers guide for women and men.* Harmondsworth: Penguin, 1978. xxxii, 476p.
Revised edition.

3090 **Employment Service Agency**, Careers and Occupational Information Centre. *Choice of careers: animal care and veterinary science.* London: H.M.S.O., 1979. 64p.

3091 **Employment Service Agency**, Careers and Occupational Information Centre. *Choice of careers: civil air transport.* London: H.M.S.O., 1979. 60p.

3092 **Employment Service Agency**, Careers and Occupational Information Centre. *Choice of careers: law.* London: H.M.S.O., 1979. 40p.

3093 **Employment Service Agency**, Careers and Occupational Information Centre. *Choice of careers: mathematical, statistical and computer work.* London: H.M.S.O., 1979. 48p.

3094 **Employment Service Agency**, Careers and Occupational Information Centre. *Choice of careers: medical laboratory services.* London: H.M.S.O., 1979. 40p.

3095 **Employment Service Agency**, Careers and Occupational Information Centre. *Choice of careers: the scientist.* London:

H.M.S.O., 1979. 52p.

3096 **Herriott**, Peter and **Ecob**, Russell. 'Occupational choice and expectancy-value theory: testing some modifications.' *J. Occup. Psychol.*, LII (December 1979), 311–24.

3097 **Taylor**, Robert. 'Career orientations and intra-occupational choice: a survey of engineering students.' *J. Occup. Psychol.*, LII (1979), 41–52.

See also: 4538.

B. MANPOWER PLANNING AT FIRM AND INDUSTRY LEVEL

This section includes material dealing with manpower planning by employers; material on the government as employer in this context is also classified here. Material on the state as a regulator of manpower for the economy as a whole is classified at Part Seven, II. Material dealing with redundancy in particular firms is classified at Part Six, II, D. See also Part Four, II, A.

1. General

See also Part Five, II; Part Six, II, B, 2; Part Six, II, E, 4; and Part Six, II, E, 5.

3098 **Allen**, Keith R. and **Cameron**, Keith G. 'Manpower costing in action.' *Pers. Manage.*, III, 2 (February 1971), 26–9.

3099 **Al-Nuami**, A. T. O. *Micro models as an aid to manpower planning.* 1971. (Ph.D. thesis, University of London.)

3100 **Armitage**, P. 'Education planning and manpower needs.' Bartholomew, D. J. and Morris, B. R. (eds.). *Aspects of manpower planning.* 1971. p. 31–44.

3101 **Bartholomew**, David John. 'The statistical approach to manpower planning.' *Statistician*, xx (1971), 3–26.
Partly reprinted in Bartholomew, D. J. (ed.). *Manpower planning.* 1976. p. 67–90.

3102 **Bartholomew**, David John and **Morris**, B. R. (eds.). *Aspects of manpower planning: a volume of papers published for the Manpower Society.* London: English Universities Press, 1971. x, 130p.

3103 **Bartholomew**, David John and **Smith**, A. R. (eds.). *Manpower and management science.* London: Heath, 1971.

3104 **Boydell**, T. H. 'Basic manpower planning.' *B.A.C.I.E. J.*, xxv, 9 (September 1971), 70–80.

3105 **Brown**, A. J. 'The supply of labour to the firm.' *J. Manage. Stud.*, VIII, 3 (October 1971), 280–91.

3106 **Clark**, P. and **Morris**, T. 'Work for all seasons.' *Ind. Soc.*, LIII, 11 (November 1971), 12–14.

3107 **Dun and Bradstreet Ltd**. *Managing your manpower.* Foulsham: The Authors, 1971. 176p.

3108 **Forbes**, A. F. 'Non-parametric methods of estimating the survivor function.' *Statistician*, xx (1971), 27–52.

3109 **Frost**, K. J. *An investigation into manpower planning in the engineering industry at company level and the development of a framework for such planning.* 1971. (M.Sc. thesis, University of Salford.)

3110 **Hunt**, *Sir* Joseph. *Manpower as an asset in a growth economy.* London: British Association for Commercial and Industrial Education, 1971. 10p.

3111 **Jackman**, R. *Manpower aspects of takeover in three builders' merchants' companies in the South East.* 1971. (M.Sc. thesis, University of Bath.)

3112 **Lawrence**, Susanne. 'Putting people on the balance sheet.' *Pers. Manage.*, III, 1 (January 1971), 30–3.

3113 **Layard**, Peter Richard Grenville, **Sargan**, J. D., **Ager**, M. E. and **Jones**, D. J. *Qualified manpower and economic performance: an inter-plant study in the electrical engineering industry.* Harmondsworth: Allen Lane, 1971. 267p.

3114 **Leicester**, C. S. 'An econometric model for national manpower planning.' Bartholomew, D. J. and Morris, B. R. (eds.). *Aspects of manpower planning.* 1971. p. 5–17.

3115 **Price**, P. C. 'Mathematical models of staff structure evolution.' Bartholomew, D. J. and Morris, B. R. (eds.). *Aspects of manpower planning.* 1971. p. 98–108.

3116 **Shipp**, P. J. *Manpower planning in the Scottish National Health Service.* London: Tavistock Institute of Human Relations, 1971. 33p.

3117 **Smith**, A. R. 'Developments in manpower planning.' *Pers. Rev.*, 1 (1971), 44–54.
Partly reprinted as 'The philosophy of manpower planning' in Bartholomew, D. J. (ed.). *Manpower planning.* 1976. p. 19–25.

3118 **Smith**, A. R. (ed.). *Models of manpower systems.* London: English Universities Press, 1971.

3119 **Stainer**, Gareth. *Manpower planning: the management of human resources.* London: Heinemann, 1971. 244p.

3120 **Stainsby**, P. *Manpower planning within the shipbuilding industry.* 1971. (M.Sc. thesis, University of Strathclyde.)

3121 **Willings**, David. 'What jobs are worth.' *New Soc.*, XVII (18 March 1971), 435–7.

3122 **Wilson**, A. T. M. 'Basic assumptions in manpower planning: some trends, difficulties and possibilities.' Bartholomew, D. J. and Smith, A. R. (eds.). *Manpower and management science.* 1971.
Reprinted in Bartholomew, D. J. (ed.). *Manpower planning.* 1976. p. 49–64.

3123 **Young**, A. 'Demographic and ecological models for manpower planning.' Bartholomew, D. J. and Morris, B. R. (eds.). *Aspects of manpower planning.* 1971. p. 75–97.

3124 **Allen**, Keith R. 'Manpower planning for a company viewpoint.' *B.A.C.I.E. J.*, xxv, 3 (March 1972), 27–35.

3125 **Armitage**, P. H. and **Smith**, C. S. 'Controllability: an example.' *Higher Educ. Rev.*, v (1972), 55–66.
Reprinted in Bartholomew, D. J. (ed.). *Manpower planning*. 1976. p. 300–18.

3126 **Boehm**, K. H., **Farrard**, M. and **McKee**, T. J. *Introduction to I.M.S.S.O.C.* London: Institute of Manpower Studies, 1972.
Partly reprinted in Bartholomew, D. J. (ed.). *Manpower planning*. 1976. p. 130–41.
Institute of Manpower Studies System of Occupational Classification.

3127 **Bryant**, D. T. 'Recent developments in manpower research.' *Pers. Rev.*, II, 3 (Summer 1972), 14–30.

3128 **Dorling**, Jenny (comp.). *Company practices in manpower planning*. London: Institute of Personnel Management, 1972. 134p.

3129 **Laslett**, R. E. *A survey of mathematical methods of estimating the supply of and demand for manpower*. London: Engineering Industry Training Board, 1972. 48p. (E.I.T.B. occasional papers 1.)

3130 **Morgan**, Terry, **Nixon**, Ken and **Wallum**, Peter. 'Conspicuous by their absence: manpower planning and training research.' *Pers. Manage.*, IV, 6 (June 1972), 28–32.

3131 **O'Brien**, Richard. 'A company employment policy.' *C.B.I. Rev.* (March 1972), 8–16.

3132 **Ollerenshaw**, *Dame* Kathleen. 'Manpower planning: the threat or spur to education.' *B.A.C.I.E. J.*, xxv, 6 (June 1972), 66–75.
Based on the B.A.C.I.E. Willis Jackson lecture, 1971.

3133 **Perry**, B. J. 'Information work and workers in the coming decade: manpower requirements and training.' *Aslib Proc.*, XXIV, 10 (October 1972), 556–77.

3134 **Skolnik**, M. L. and **Smith**, C. S. 'Selecting an optimal set of manpower requirements when skill substitution is possible.' *Br. J. Ind. Relat.*, x, 2 (July 1972), 256–69.

3135 **Timperley**, Stuart R. 'Towards a behavioural view of manpower planning.' *Pers. Rev.*, II, 3 (Summer 1972), 4–11.

3136 **Bosworth**, Derek I. and **Evans**, G. 'Manpower forecasting techniques: a user's guide.' *Pers. Rev.*, III, 3 (Autumn 1973), 4–16.

3137 **Brandt**, Floyd Stanley. *Manpower planning for organisational development*. London: Industrial and Commercial Techniques, 1973. 83p.

3138 **British Association for Commercial and Industrial Education**. *Planning your manpower: an aid to a year's training for small units*. London: B.A.C.I.E., 1973. 46p.

3139 **Cannon**, J. A. 'Introducing manpower plans.' *Pers. Rev.*, III, 2 (Summer 1973), 28–36.

3140 **Coleman**, Bruce P. 'Corporate strategy and manpower planning.' Cuthbert, N. and Hawkins, K. (eds.). *Company industrial relations policies*. 1973. p. 227–37.

3141 **Cripps**, Francis and **Tarling**, Roger. 'Is labour really scarce?' *New Soc.*, XXVI (22 November 1973), 461–2.

3142 **Cullingford**, G. and **Scott**, D. 'Optimality and manpower planning.' *Pers. Rev.*, III, 2 (Summer 1973), 38–47.

3143 **Gill**, W. 'Manpower planning in the smaller company.' *Pers. Manage.*, v, 10 (October 1973), 39–41, 43.

3144 **Glautier**, M. W. E. and **Underdown**, B. 'Problems and prospects of accounting for human assets.' *Manage. Account.*, LI, 3 (March 1973), 98–102.

3145 **Hopes**, R. F. A. 'Some statistical aspects of manpower planning in the Civil Service.' *Omega*, I (1973), 165–80.
Reprinted in Bartholomew, D. J. (ed.). *Manpower planning*. 1976. p. 190–210.

3146 **Jones**, D. M. C. 'Accounting for human assets.' *Manage. Decis.*, XI, 3 (1973), 183–94.

3147 **Lawrence**, John. 'Manpower and personnel models in Britain.' *Pers. Rev.*, III, 2 (Summer 1973), 4–25.

3148 **Pilkington**, *Sir* Harry. *Manpower, modernisation and productivity*. London: British Association for Commercial and Industrial Education, 1973. 8p.

3149 **Robinson**, David F. 'Progress in human asset accounting.' *Pers. Manage.*, v, 3 (March 1973), 31–3.

3150 **Thomas**, R. B. 'On the definition of "shortages" in administered labour markets.' *Manchr. Sch. Econ. Soc. Stud.*, XLI, 2 (June 1973), 141–67.

3151 **Wilkinson**, G. C. G. and **Mace**, J. D. 'Manpower forecasting and qualified engineers.' Greenaway, H. and Williams, G. (eds.). *Patterns of change in graduate employment*. 1973. p. 123–40.

3152 **Ashdown**, P. L., **Boyd**, D. G., **Cruden**, S., **Sheldon**, J. D. and **Venner**, B. G. 'Manpower planning in the Forestry Commission.' *Pers. Rev.*, III, 4 (Autumn 1974), 26–33.

3153 **Bell**, D. J. *Planning corporate manpower*. London: Longmans, 1974. 179p.

3154 **Bosworth**, Derek L., **Evans**, Graham J. and **Lindley**, Robert M. 'Mechanistic manpower models.' Wabe, J. (ed.). *Problems in manpower forecasting*. 1974. p. 61–84.

3155 **Bowey**, Angela M. *A guide to manpower planning*. London: Macmillan, 1974. xiii, 84p.

3156 **Brand**, A. Martin, **Van der Merwe**, R. and **Borhoff**, A. B. 'The measurement of investment in human resources.' *Pers. Rev.*, III, 2 (Spring 1974), 26–35.

3157 **Cannon**, James A. 'A further comment on human resource accounting.' *Pers. Rev.*, III, 4 (Autumn 1974), 38–41.

3158 **Cannon**, James A. 'Human resource

accounting: a critical comment.' *Pers. Rev.*, III, 3 (Summer 1974), 14–20.

3159 **Evans**, Graham J. and **Wabe**, J. Stuart. 'Testing a demand explanation of the R. A. S. model.' Wabe, J. (ed.). *Problems in manpower forecasting*. 1974. p. 85–96.

3160 **Flamholtz**, E. 'Human resource accounting.' *J. Manage. Stud.*, XI, 1 (February 1974), 44–61.

3161 **Graham**, H. T. *Human resources management*. London: Macdonald & Evans, 1974. x, 261p.

3162 **Kiker**, B. F. 'Nicholson on human capital.' *Scott. J. Polit. Econ.*, XXI, 2 (June 1974), 171–6.

3163 **Moss**, A. 'The company approach to industry manpower forecasting.' *Pers. Rev.*, III, 2 (Spring 1974), 8–25.

3164 **Owen**, Trevor. *The place of manpower planning in management*. London: Civil Service College, 1974.

3165 **Randall**, F. E. 'Manpower planning and the management accountant.' *Manage. Account.*, III, 10 (November 1974), 294–8.

3166 **Robinson**, David F. 'Human asset accounting.' *Long Range Plann.*, VII, 1 (February 1974), 58–60.

3167 **Venning**, M. 'Manpower studies for industrial sectors.' *Long Range Plann.*, VII, 3 (June 1974), 27–33.

3168 **Wabe**, J. Stuart. 'Issues in manpower forecasting.' Wabe, J. (ed.). *Problems in manpower forecasting*. 1974. p. 1–16.

3169 **Wabe**, J. Stuart. 'Practical difficulties in a manpower forecasting exercise.' Wabe, J. (ed.). *Problems in manpower forecasting*. 1974. p. 17–60.

3170 **Wabe**, J. Stuart (ed.). *Problems in manpower forecasting*. London: Saxon House, 1974. xviii, 287p.

3171 **Wabe**, John Stuart, **Bosworth**, Derek L., **Evans**, Graham J., **Lindley**, Robert Michael and **Roberts**, Colin J. *Manpower forecasting for the engineering industry*. London: Engineering Industry Training Board, 1974. 62p. (Occasional papers 4.)

3172 **Barnes**, *Sir* Denis. 'The Manpower Services Commission and company manpower policies.' Lawrence, J. (ed.). *Company manpower planning in perspective*. 1975. p. 11–18.

3173 **Blaug**, Mark. 'The uses and abuses of manpower planning.' *New Soc.*, XXXIII (31 July 1975), 247–8.

3174 **Bramham**, John T. *Practical manpower planning*. London: Institute of Personnel Management, 1975. 200p.

3175 **Cowan**, L. D. 'Practical problems of manpower planning.' Lawrence, J. (ed.). *Company manpower planning in perspective*. 1975. p. 69–80.

3176 **Department of Employment Gazette.** 'Manpower planning in road transport.' *Dep. Employment Gaz.*, LXXXIII, 7 (July 1975), 627–30.

3177 **Dobbins**, Richard and **Trussell**, Peter. 'The valuation of human resources.' *Manage. Decis.*, XIII, 3 (1975), 155–69.

3178 **Forbes**, A. F., **Morgan**, R. W. and **Rowntree**, J. A. 'Manpower planning models in use in the Civil Service Department.' *Pers. Rev.*, IV, 3 (Summer 1975), 23–5.

3179 **Gambling**, T. E. 'Human resource accounting.' *Moor. Wall Street* (Spring 1975), 39–48.

3180 **Helps**, Ian G. *Forecasting manpower: a critical review of mathematical and other models for forecasting changes in employment and productivity at national and sectoral level*. 1975. (M.Phil. thesis, Queen Mary College, University of London.)

3181 **Hopps**, Ralph L. 'Manpower planning in the commercial sector.' Lawrence, J. (ed.). *Company manpower planning in perspective*. 1975. p. 39–60.

3182 **Howard**, R. J. 'Making sense of manpower planning.' *Pers. Manage.*, VII, 10 (October 1975), 37–9.

3183 **Keenay**, G. A. *Manpower planning in large organisations: a statistical approach*. 1975. (Ph.D. thesis, University of Cambridge.)

3184 **Lawrence**, John (ed.). *Company manpower planning in perspective*. London: Institute of Personnel Management, 1975. 88p.

3185 **Lawrence**, John. 'Epilogue: the critical future of manpower planning.' Lawrence, J. (ed.). *Company manpower planning in perspective*. 1975. p. 81–8.

3186 **Lawrence**, John. 'Prologue: the disillusion of manpower planning.' Lawrence, J. (ed.). *Company manpower planning in perspective*. 1975. p. 7–10.

3187 **Linklater**, Peter S. 'Manpower planning in an industrial company: some experience.' Lawrence, J. (ed.). *Company manpower planning in perspective*. 1975. p. 61–8.

3188 **Mottram**, Roger D. 'Management of human resources.' *Ind. Commer. Train.*, VII, 7 (July 1975), 267–77.

3189 **National Economic Development Committee**, Economic Development Committee for the Hotels and Catering Industry. *Manpower policy in the hotels and restaurant industry: research findings*. London: N.E.D.C., 1975.

3190 **National Economic Development Committee**, Economic Development Committee for the Hotels and Catering Industry. *Manpower policy in the hotels and restaurant industry: summary and recommendations*. London: N.E.D.C., 1975.

3191 **Sawtell**, R. A. and **Sweeting**, P. 'Practical guide to company manpower planning.' *Pers. Rev.*, IV, 4 (Autumn 1975), 33–40.

3192 **Sisson**, Keith. 'Fleet Street's manpower dilemma.' *New Soc.*, XXXIV (2 October 1975), 12–14.

3193 **Stewart**, Andrew M. 'Appraisal of employee potential.' Bowey, Angela M. (ed.). *Handbook of salary and wage systems*. 1975. p. 131–48.

3194 **Thakur**, Manab. *Manpower planning in action.* London: Institute of Personnel Management, 1975. 113p. (Information reports 19.)

3195 **Wright**, Rowland S. 'Manpower policies and company objectives.' Lawrence, J. (ed.). *Company manpower planning in perspective.* 1975. p. 19–38.

3196 **Bartholomew**, David John (ed.). *Manpower planning: selected readings.* Harmondsworth: Penguin, 1976. 335p.

3197 **Bell**, David J. 'Making more of manpower information.' *Pers. Manage.*, VIII, 9 (September 1976), 24–7.

3198 **Bell**, David J. 'Manpower in corporate planning.' *Long Range Plann.*, IX, 2 (April 1976), 31–7.

3199 **Bosworth**, Derek L. 'The technology of production and manpower planning.' *J. Ind. Affairs*, IV, 1 (Autumn 1976), 1–7.

3200 **Department of Employment Gazette.** 'Manpower supply planning: getting started.' *Dep. Employment Gaz.*, LXXXIV, 1 (January 1976), 9–12.

3201 **Inbucon Ltd.** *Managing human resources.* London: Heinemann, 1976. 179p.

3202 **Morris**, J. R. S. 'The use of manpower in industry.' *R. Soc. Arts. J.*, CXXIV (May 1976), 323–33.

3203 **Parker**, E. G. *An investigation of the role of the manpower function in facilitating the process of change toward becoming a multinational enterprise.* 1975–6. (M.Sc. thesis, University of Bath.)

3204 **Pettman**, Barrie Owen and **Tavernier**, Gerard. *Manpower planning workbook.* Epping: Gower, 1976. 127p.

3205 **Purkiss**, Clive. 'Manpower planning literature: manpower demand.' *Dep. Employment Gaz.*, LXXXIV, 7 (July 1976), 722–6.

3206 **Redfern**, P. *Input–output analysis and its application to education and manpower planning.* London: H.M.S.O., 1976. 26p. (Civil Service College occasional paper 5.)

3207 **Smith**, A. R. 'Some views on manpower planning.' Bartholomew, D. J. (ed.). *Manpower planning.* 1976. p. 35–48.

3208 **Timperley**, Stuart R. 'Understanding behaviour: a priority for manpower planners.' *Pers. Manage.*, VIII, 10 (October 1976), 30–2.

3209 **Trussell**, P. and **Dobbins**, R. 'Human resource accounting.' *Manage. Finance*, II, 1 (1976), 60–72.

3210 **Allen**, Roger. 'Manpower research: a key to the future.' *Pers. Manage.*, IX, 2 (February 1977), 16–20.

3211 **Bartholomew**, D. J. 'Manpower planning literature: statistical techniques of manpower analysis.' *Dep. Employment Gaz.*, LXXXV, 10 (October 1977), 1093–6.

3212 **Bowey**, Angela M. 'Corporate manpower planning.' *Manage. Decis.*, V (1977), 421–69.

3213 **Farmer**, Marilyn and **Smith**, Peter. 'A practical approach to equal opportunity.' *Pers. Manage.*, IX, 3 (March 1977), 10–16.

3214 **Incomes Data Services.** *Manpower informa-* tion. London: I.D.S., 1977. 24p. (I.D.S. study 154.)

3215 **Moreh**, J. 'Investment in human capital over time.' *Manchr. Sch. Econ. Soc. Stud.*, XLV, 2 (June 1977), 141–61.

3216 **National Economic Development Committee**, Economic Development Committee for Agriculture. *Agriculture into the 1980s: manpower.* London: N.E.D.C., 1977.

3217 **National Economic Development Office.** *A Study of U.K. nationalised industries: manpower and pay trends.* London: N.E.D.O., 1977. (Background paper 4.)

3218 **Smith**, A. R. *Manpower planning in the Civil Service.* London: H.M.S.O., 1977. viii, 292p. (Civil Service Department civil service study 3.)

3219 **Stewart**, Andrew. 'Behavioural science and manpower planning.' *Dep. Employment Gaz.*, LXXXV, 7 (July 1977), 704–10.

3220 **Thomas**, Barry and **Deaton**, David. *Labour shortage and economic analysis: a study of occupational labour markets.* Oxford: Blackwell, 1977. xvi, 264p. (Warwick studies in industrial relations.)

3221 **Allen**, Keith R., **Cannon**, Jim, **Carby**, Keith and **Johnston**, Neil. 'Personnel planning: the key to future business success.' *Pers. Manage.*, X, 10 (October 1978), 50–3.

3222 **Anstey**, Edgar. *An introduction to selection interviewing.* London: H.M.S.O. for the Civil Service Department Working Party on the Selection of Specialists, 1978. ii, 40p.

3223 **Fyfe**, John and **McCloud**, Andrew. 'Manpower planning in companies: general lessons from a number of case studies.' *Dep. Employment Gaz.*, LXXXVI, 5 (May 1978), 540–3.

3224 **Hughes**, James J. 'Training for what?' *Ind. Relat. J.*, IX, 3 (Autumn 1978), 27–33.

3225 **National Economic Development Committee**, Sector Working Party for Knitting. *Manpower and productivity.* London: N.E.D.C., 1978.

3226 **National Economic Development Committee**, Sector Working Party on Fluid Power Equipment. *Manpower issues in the fluid power industry.* London: N.E.D.C., 1978.

3227 **National Economic Development Office.** *Case studies in company manpower planning: a joint MSC/NEDO report.* London: N.E.D.O., 1978. 64p.

3228 **Swann**, H. V. 'Human resource accounting: some aspects which require psychologists' attention.' *J. Occup. Psychol.*, LI, 4 (December 1978), 301–14.

3229 **Bartholomew**, David John and **Forbes**, Andrew F. *Statistical techniques for manpower planning.* Chichester: Wiley, 1979. xiii, 288p.

3230 **Hartley**, Keith. 'The industrial strategy and manpower policy: some puzzles.' *Manage. Decis.*, XVII, 3 (1979), 256–64.

3231 **McConville**, James. 'Changing patterns of manpower and management in the U.K.

shipping industry.' *Marit. Policy Manage.*, VII (1979), 39-47.

3232 **National Economic Development Committee**, Sector Working Party on Plastics Processing. *The plastics industry's view of manpower and efficiency.* London: N.E.D.C., 1979.

3233 **Ripley**, A. R. 'Manpower planning for distribution.' *Retail Distrib. Manage.*, VII, 1 (January-February 1979), 61-3.
See also: 438.

2. Recruitment, Selection, and Placement

This section includes the general literature dealing with the problem of recruiting, selecting, and placing staff in industry. The more specialist literature dealing exclusively with the techniques of recruitment, selection, and placement has generally been excluded. It is extremely difficult to separate the literature dealing with managerial training from that concerned with the recruitment, selection, and placement of managers, and hence the literature pertaining to the latter subjects has been classified at Part Six, II, B, 3, b, iii. See also Part Six, II, B, 3.

a. GENERAL

3234 **Allen**, Keith R. 'Controlling the costs of recruitment.' *Pers. Manage.*, III, 12 (December 1971), 28-30.

3235 **Currer-Briggs**, Noel, **Kennett**, Brian and **Paterson**, Jane. *Handwriting analysis in business: the use of graphology in personnel selection.* London: Associated Business Programmes, 1971. 107p.

3236 **Drenth**, Pieter J.D. 'Theory and methods of selection.' Warr, P. (ed.). *Psychology at work.* 1971. p. 169-93.

3237 **Ray**, Maurice Edward. *Practical job advertising.* London: Institute of Personnel Management, 1971. 67p.

3238 **Salaman**, Graeme. 'A sociology of appraisal.' *Ind. Commer. Train.*, III, 8 (August 1971), 384-7.

3239 **Adamson**, H. 'Married to her work.' *Ind. Soc.*, LIV, 8 (August 1972), 10-11.

3240 **Fry**, J. M. 'Job advertising: attracting the candidate.' *Build. Soc. Inst. Q.*, XXVI, 1 (January 1972), 13-19.

3241 **Lawrence**, Susanne. 'Selecting the medium for your message.' *Pers. Manage.*, IV, 3 (March 1972), 38-40.

3242 **Morea**, P. C. *Guidance, selection and training: ideas and applications.* London: Routledge & Kegan Paul, 1972. XVIII, 361p.

3243 **Morton**, G. 'Are written references really necessary?' *Ind. Soc.*, LIV, 6 (June 1972), 10-11.

3244 **O'Reilly**, A. P. 'Interviewing and the company image.' *Pers. Manage.*, IV, 4 (April 1972), 35-7.

3245 **Cameron**, K. and **Allen**, K. 'Applications

are invited.' *Ind. Soc.*, LV, 5 (May 1973), 19-21.

3246 **Finnigan**, John. *The right people in the right jobs.* London: Business Books, 1973. XII, 131p.

3247 **Fletcher**, Clive A. 'Interview style and the effectiveness of appraisal.' *Occup. Psychol.*, XLVII (1973), 225-30.

3248 **Fletcher**, Clive A. 'Job appraisal reviews.' *Manage. Serv. Gov.*, XXVIII, 4 (November 1973), 188-95.

3249 **Gill**, Deirdre, **Ungerson**, Bernard and **Thakur**, Manab. *Performance appraisal in perspective: a survey of current practice.* London: Institute of Personnel Management, 1973. 109p.

3250 **Morgan**, Terry. 'Recent insights into the selection interview.' *Pers. Rev.*, III, 4 (Winter 1973), 3-12.

3251 **Parsons**, H. 'A case for appraisal.' *Ind. Soc.*, IV, 10 (October 1973), 19-21.

3252 **Plumbley**, Philip Rodney. 'What not to say in a job ad.' *Pers. Manage.*, V, 8 (August 1973), 32-6.

3253 **Pym**, Denis. 'The politics and ritual of appraisals.' *Occup. Psychol.*, XLVII (1973), 231-5.

3254 **Rackham**, Neil. 'Recent thoughts on evaluation.' *Ind. Commer. Train.*, V, 10 (October 1973), 454-61.

3255 **Salaman**, Graeme. 'Improving the appraisal interview.' *Ind. Commer. Train.*, V, 6 (June 1973), 284-7.

3256 **Silverman**, David and **Jones**, Jill. 'Getting in: the managed accomplishment of correct selection outcomes.' Child, J. (ed.). *Man and organization.* 1973. p. 63-106.

3257 **Braithwaite**, Roderick and **Pollock**, J. 'Analyzing response to recruitment advertising.' *Pers. Manage.*, VI, 12 (December 1974), 25-7.

3258 **Hibbert**, V. 'Search and employ.' *Ind. Soc.*, LVI, 5 (May 1974), 9-10.

3259 **Marriott**, D. 'A sociologist looks at induction.' *Pers. Rev.*, III, 4 (Winter 1974), 4-9.

3260 **Plumbley**, Philip Rodney. *Recruitment and selection.* London: Institute of Personnel Management.
New edition. 1974. 211p.
Third edition. 1976. 213p.

3261 **Beveridge**, W. E. *Interview in staff appraisal.* London: Allen & Unwin, 1975. 132p.

3262 **Dobinson**, C. H. 'Integrating selection and placement.' *Ind. Commer. Train.*, VII, 7 (July 1975), 284-5.

3263 **Holdsworth**, Roger. 'Selection tips for small firm managers.' *Pers. Manage.*, VII, 3 (March 1975), 31-3.

3264 **Humphreys**, E. 'The reference game.' *Ind. Soc.*, LVII, 2 (March-April 1973), 225-30.

3265 **Jessup**, Gilbert and **Jessup**, Helen. *Selection and assessment at work.* London: Methuen, 1975. 143p.

3266 **Keenan**, A. and **Wedderburn**, A. A. I.

'Effects of the non-verbal behaviour of interviewers on candidates' impressions.' *J. Occup. Psychol.*, XLVIII (1975), 129–32.

3267 **Killcross**, M. C. and **Bates**, W. T. G. *Selecting the younger trainee.* London: H.M.S.O., 1975. v, 26p. (Training Services Agency. Training information papers 8.)

3268 **Putt**, H. B. 'The recruiting of graduates.' *Public Finance Account.*, II, 3 (April 1975), 123–5.

3269 **Bartholomew**, D. J., **Hopes**, R. G. A. and **Smith**, A. R. 'Manpower planning in the face of uncertainty.' *Pers. Rev.*, V, 3 (Summer 1976), 5–17.

3270 **Courtis**, John. *Cost effective recruitment.* London: Institute of Personnel Management, 1976. 92p.

3271 **Fletcher**, Clive A. and **Williams**, Richard. 'The influence of performance feedback in appraisal interviews.' *J. Occup. Psychol.*, XLIX (June 1976), 75–83.

3272 **Margerison**, Charles J. and **Hibbert**, Vicky. 'A constructive approach to appraisal.' *Pers. Manage.*, VIII, 7 (July 1976), 30–4.

3273 **Stewart**, Andrew and **Stewart**, Valerie. 'Selection and appraisal: the pick of recent research.' *Pers. Manage.*, VIII, 1 (January 1976), 20–4.

3274 **Bayne**, R. 'Can selection interviewing be improved?' *J. Occup. Psychol.*, L, 3 (1977), 161–7.

3275 **Braddick**, W. A. G. and **Smith**, P. J. *The design of appraisal systems.* Berkhamstead: Ashridge Management College, 1977. 27p.

3276 **Courtis**, John. 'Cost-effective recruitment.' *Ind. Soc.*, LIX, 2 (March–April 1977), 6–7.

3277 **Gill**, Deirdre. 'Towards more open performance appraisal.' *Pers. Manage.*, IX, 12 (December 1977), 31–4.

3278 **Jeffery**, R. 'Taking the guesswork out of selection.' *Pers. Manage.*, IX, 10 (October 1977), 40–2.

3279 **Mauger**, W. E. 'Computer job-matching.' *Manage. Serv. Gov.*, XXXII (November 1977), 182–91.

3280 **Parkinson**, R. 'Recipe for a realistic appraisal system.' *Pers. Manage*, IX, 11 (November 1977), 37–40.

3281 **Pearn**, Michael A. *Selecting and training coloured workers.* London: H.M.S.O., 1977. iv, 48p. (Training Services Agency. Training information paper 9.)

3282 **Personnel Management**. 'Effective management of the joining-up process.' *Pers. Manage.*, IX, 2 (February 1977), 34–8.

3283 **Downs**, Sylvia, **Farr**, Robert M. and **Colbeck**, Logan. 'Self-appraisal: a convergence of selection and guidance.' *J. Occup. Psychol.*, LI (September 1978), 271–8.

3284 **Institute of Personnel Management**, Joint Standing Committee on Discrimination. *Towards fairer selection: a code for non-discrimination.* London: The Institute, 1978. 58p.

3285 **Kilcourse**, Rita. 'Trainability testing as an aid to selection.' *Pers. Manage.*, X, 5 (May 1978), 33–6.

3286 **Leicester**, Colin. 'Recruitment in the '80s: reaching the market and reducing the risks.' *Pers. Manage.*, X, 4 (April 1978), 28–31.

3287 **Matteson**, Michael T. 'An alternative approach to using biographical data for predicting job success.' *J. Occup. Psychol.*, LI (June 1978), 155–62.

3288 **Sherratt**, R. 'Recruiting on radio.' *Campaign* (April 1978), 55–6.

3289 **Smith**, David. 'Selection and the decision-making process.' *Manage. Decis.*, XVI, 1 (1978), 23–31.

3290 **Watts**, Martin. 'Screening, inter-firm exploitation and job search.' *Scott. J. Polit. Econ.*, XXV (June 1978), 187–200.

3291 **Braithwaite**, Roderick and **Schofield**, Philip. *How to recruit.* London: British Institute of Management, 1979. 56p.

3292 **Curran**, J. and **Stanworth**, J. 'Self selection and the small firm worker: a critique and an alternative view.' *Sociology*, XIII, 3 (September 1979), 427–44.

3293 **Forbes**, R. 'The selection interview.' *Pers. Manage.*, XI, 7 (July 1979), 36–9.

3294 **Higham**, Martin. *The ABC of interviewing.* London: Institute of Personnel Management, 1979. 208p.

3295 **Keenan**, A. 'Initial graduate recruitment interviews.' *Pers. Rev.*, IV, 1 (Winter 1979), 14–9.

3296 **Nemeroff**, Wayne F. and **Wexley**, Kenneth N. 'An exploitation of the relationship between feedback interview characteristics and interview outcomes as perceived by managers and subordinates.' *J. Occup. Psychol.*, LII (1979), 25–34.

3297 **Rugman**, Nigel. 'Rooting out recruits: headhunting versus standard search.' *Pers. Manage.*, XI, 6 (June 1979), 42–4.
See also: 3675; 3750; 4522.

b. PARTICULAR OCCUPATIONS AND INDUSTRIES

3298 **Anstey**, Edgar. 'The Civil Service Administrative Class: extended interview selection procedure.' *Occup. Psychol.*, XLV (1971), 199–208.

3299 **Anstey**, Edgar. 'The Civil Service Administrative Class: a follow-up of post-war entrants.' *Occup. Psychol.*, XLV (1971), 27–43.

3300 **Chiew**, Tiang Kee. *A study of manpower requirements for an electrical instrumentation contractor.* 1971. (M. Sc. thesis, University of Strathclyde.)

3301 **Gardner**, K. E. *Selection, training and career development of naval officers: a long-term follow-up using multi-variate techniques.* [1971?]. (Ph.D. thesis, City University.)

3302 **Lynch**, J. J. 'Manpower planning from an

industry viewpoint.' *B.A.C.I.E. J.*, xxv, 4 (December 1971), 117–25.

3303 **Purkiss**, C. J. and **Richardson**, J. Z. 'Planning recruitment and training levels in the steel industry.' Bartholomew, D. J. and Morris, B. R. (eds.). *Aspects of manpower planning.* 1971. p. 65–74.

3304 **Working Group on Biological Manpower** and **Council for Scientific Policy.** *Report of the Working Group on Biological Manpower.* London: The Authors, 1971. vii, 137p.

3305 **Blakiston**, M. P. F. 'Employing business graduates at Ford.' *Pers. Manage.*, IV, I (January 1972), 23–5.

3306 **Higham**, T. M. 'Graduate selection.' *Occup. Psychol.*, XLV, 3–4 (1972), 209–15.

3307 **Jevons**, F. R. and **Turner**, H. D. *What kinds of graduates do we need?* Oxford: Oxford U.P., 1972. vi, 120p.

3308 **Kingston**, N. and **Wolfe**, P. D. *Graduates in industry.* London: British Institute of Management, 1972. 25p. (Management survey reports 14.)

3309 **Lillico**, T. M. *Managerial communication.* London: Pergamon Press, 1972. xii, 160p.

3310 **Mansfield**, Roger 'Inducting graduates into industry.' *Manage. Decis.*, X, 2 (Summer 1972), 117–24.

3311 **National Economic Development Committee**, Economic Development Committee for the Electronics Industry. *The electronics industry and the schools: report of the Sub-Committee on Electronics and the Schools to the Electronics EDC Working Group on Scientific and Technological Manpower.* London: N.E.D.O., 1972. xi, 43p.

3312 **Pulle**, S. *Employment policies in the hosiery industry, with particular reference to the position of immigrant workers.* London: Runnymede Industrial Unit, 1972. 30p.

3313 **Thomas**, Ray. 'How London's industrial selection scheme works.' *Town Ctry Plann.*, XL (May 1972), 272–4.

3314 **Anstey**, Edgar. 'Comments on Gardner and Williams: 25 year follow-up of naval officer selection procedure.' *Occup. Psychol.*, XLVII (1973), 163–6.

3315 **Broome**, E. M. 'Library manpower planning.' *Aslib Proc.*, XXV, 11 (November 1973), 400–14.

3316 **Doyle**, P. 'The recruitment and selection of effective salesmen.' *Manage. Decis.*, XI (Spring 1973), 64–8.

3317 **Gardner**, K. E. and **Williams**, A. P. O. 'A twenty-five year follow-up of an extended interview selection procedure in the Royal Navy.' *Occup. Psychol.*, XLVII (1973), 1–13, 149–61.

3318 **Hagger**, A. 'Recruiting school mums.' *Ind. Commer. Train.*, V, 6 (June 1973), 296–7.

3319 **Jones**, D. 'North Sea oil: manpower and training implications.' *Ind. Commer. Train.*, V, 12 (December 1973), 556–61.

3320 **Jones**, R. C., **Morrison**, S. R. and **White-**

man, R. P. 'Planning a bank's manpower resources.' *Oper. Res. Q.*, XXIV, 3 (September 1973), 365–74.

3321 **Law**, G. M. 'Manpower planning in building societies.' *Build. Soc. Inst. Q.*, XXVII, I (January 1973), 9–13.

3322 **National Federation of Building Trades Employers.** *Recruitment, education and training for site management in the building industry.* London: Institute of Building, 1973. 41p.

3323 **Hotel and Catering Industry Training Board.** *Recommendations for the employment, selection and training of training officers.* London: The Board, [1974?]. 18p.

3324 **National Economic Development Committee**, Economic Development Committee for the Distributive Trades. *Manpower and pay in retail distribution.* London: N.E.D.C., 1974.

3325 **Roman**, E. *Recruitment and selection of typists and secretaries.* London: Business Books, 1974. x, 211p.

3326 **Chemical and Allied Products Industry Training Board.** *Survey of career patterns and training needs of engineers, scientists and technologists in the chemical and allied products industry.* London: The Board, 1975. 36p.

3327 **Department of Employment Gazette.** 'Manpower planning in road transport.' *Dep. Employment Gaz.*, LXXXIII, 7 (July 1975), 627–30.

3328 **National Economic Development Committee**, Economic Development Committee for the Hotels and Catering Industry. *Manpower policy in the hotels and restaurant industry: research findings.* London: N.E.D.C., 1975.

3329 **Pryke**, R. W. S. and **Dodgson**, J. S. *The rail problem.* Oxford: Martin Robertson, 1975. x, 294p.

3330 **Sims**, A. *Group selection schemes in the printing industry: a study of predictors and processes.* 1975. (M.Phil. thesis, Birkbeck College, University of London.)

3331 **Wraith**, R. *Appraisal for staff development: a public sector study.* London: Royal Institute of Public Administration, 1975. 89p.

3332 **Barnett**, P. M. *A study of the manpower implications involved in locating a nuclear power station in a rural, isolated area.* 1975–6. (M.Sc. thesis, University of Bath.)

3333 **Deaton**, David. 'The racial mix of London transport recruits.' *New Community*, V (Autumn 1976), 316–9.

3334 **Dulewicz**, S. V. 'Job appraisal reviews three years on.' *Manage. Serv. Gov.*, XXXI, 3 (August 1976), 134–43.

3335 **Kendal**, R. J. 'Selecting the right people.' *Aslib Proc.*, XXVIII, 11–12 (November–December 1976), 370–5.

3336 **Ray**, Keith. 'Local authority manpower planning.' *Local Gov. Stud.*, II, 2 (April 1976), 53–68.

3337 **Ray**, Keith. 'A model for the promotion of professional and administrative staff in a local authority.' *Local Gov. Stud.*, II, 4 (October 1976), 39–50.

3338 **Sheriff**, Peta. *Career patterns in the Higher Civil Service*. London: H.M.S.O., 1976. iv, 74p. (Civil Service Department civil service study 2.)

3339 **Anstey**, Edgar. 'B.S.R.D.: a valedictory message.' *Manage. Serv. Gov.*,, XXXII, 1 (February 1977), 26–34.
    Behavioural Service Research Division of the Civil Service Department.

3340 **Anstey**, Edgar. 'A 30 year follow-up to the CSSB procedure.' *J. Occup. Psychol.*, LXXX, 3 (1977), 149–59.
    Civil Service Selection Boards.

3341 **Bacon**, C. C. *A study of attitudes to the employment of graduates*. 1977. (M.A. thesis, University of Wales.)

3342 **Pearn**, Michael A. 'Recruiting guards for the London Underground.' *B.A.C.I.E. J.*, XXXI, 11 (November 1977), 178–9.

3343 **Shaw**, Ian. 'Selecting for social work.' *Br. J. Soc. Work*, VII (Spring 1977), 55–72.

3344 **Subranamian**, S. 'Engineering manpower planning in an airline.' *Long Range Plann.*, X (August 1977), 56–60.

3345 **Hampton**, K. B. 'Selecting tomorrow's managers: art or science?' *R. Soc. Arts J.*, CXXVI (April 1978), 265–78.

3346 **Keenan**, Anthony. 'Interviewers' feelings about graduate interviewees.' *J. Occup. Psychol.*, L, 4 (1978), 275–83.

3347 **Keenan**, Anthony. 'Interviewing for graduate recruitment.' *Pers. Manage.*, X, 2 (February 1978), 31–5.

3348 **Still**, Michael. 'The technicalities of recruiting technicians.' *Pers. Manage.*, X, 12 (December 1978), 44–8.

3349 **Williams**, Richard S. *Evaluation study of job appraisal reviews in the Department of the Environment*. London: Civil Service Department, Personnel Management Research Branch, 1978.

3350 **Hanley**, J. E. *The rhetoric of police recruit selections*. 1979. (M.Phil. thesis, University of York.)

3351 **Lyons**, Terry P. 'Personnel policy and manpower planning in banking.' *Long Range Plann.*, X (October 1979), 2–7.

3352 **Mars**, Gerald, **Bryant**, Don and **Mitchell**, Peter. *Manpower problems in the hotel and catering industry*. London: Saxon House, 1979. 168p.

3353 **National Economic Development Committee**, Sector Working Party on the Paper and Board Industry. *Recruitment and training in the paper and board industry*. London: N.E.D.C., 1979.

3354 **Phillips**, A. 'Selection of staff for management services.' *Manage. Serv. Gov.*, XXXIV (August 1979), 151–5.

3355 **Rugman**, Nigel. 'Rooting out recruits: headhunting versus standard search.' *Pers. Manage.*, XI, 6 (June 1979), 42–4.

3356 **Schofield**, P. 'Graduate guides as recruitment bait.' *Pers. Manage.*, XI, 12 (December 1979), 38–41.

3357 **Stewart**, Valerie and **Stewart**, Andrew. 'How to spot the high fliers.' *Pers. Manage.*, XI, 9 (September 1979), 28–35.

See also: 2979; 3081; 3121; 3171; 3369; 3375; 3545; 3603; 4012; 4044; 4492; 5238.

3. Industrial Training and Retraining

This section includes works dealing with training provided by private employers or by the state in its role as an employer. Many popular management journals also contain material on training, but it has generally not been included here. Much of this material can be found in P. J. C. Perry (ed.), *The BACIE Bibliography of Publications in the Field of Education and Training in Commerce and Industry* (London: British Association for Commercial and Industrial Education, 1977). Works dealing with industrial training provided by the state for society as a whole are classified at Part Seven, II, E. It is very difficult to separate material on the training of the disabled from that on other employment problems they face, and hence it has been excluded from this section and classified at Part Six, II, C, 7. Material on education as contrasted to industrial training has generally been excluded but material relating to the provision of education for working children is classified at Part Six, IV, A, 3, b. Material on the training of training officers is excluded. Many of the references classified in Part Six, II, C, 3–6 also contain material on training. See also Part Three, II, K; and Part Six, II, B, 2.

a. APPRENTICESHIP

See also Part Three, I; and Part Six, II, B, 3, b, i–ii.

3358 **Singer**, Edwin J. and **Macdonald**, I. D. *Is apprenticeship outdated?* London: Institute of Personnel Management, 1970. 36p.

3359 **Engineering Industry Training Board.** *The analysis and training of certain engineering craft occupations*. London: The Board, 1971. 59p.

3360 **Lee**, D. J. 'Very small firms and the training of engineering craftsmen: some recent findings.' *Br. J. Ind. Relat.*, X, 2 (July 1972), 240–55.

3361 **Industrial Training Authority.** *Apprenticeship: a new approach: discussion document*. Dublin: The Authority, 1973. 52p.

3362 **Robinson**, C. H. 'Apprentice contract: recent developments in craft training in France.' *Ind. Commer. Train.*, V, 11 (November 1976), 528–31.

3363 **Bramham**, John T. 'A closer look at craft apprenticeships.' *Pers. Manage.*, VI, 3 (March 1974), 32–5.

3364 **Venables**, Edith. *Apprentices out of their time: a follow-up study.* London: Faber, 1974. 199p.

3365 **Woodward**, N. 'Feasibility of evaluating apprentice training: a case study.' *J. Eur. Train.*, III, 3 (1974), 226–36.

3366 **Department of Employment Gazette.** 'Apprenticeship and after: agriculture.' *Dep. Employment Gaz.*, LXXXIII, 7 (July 1975), 623–6.

3367 **Department of Employment Gazette.** 'Recent trends in apprenticeship training.' *Dep. Employment Gaz.*, LXXXIII, 11 (November 1975), 1115–7.

3368 **Moslen**, K. I. D. 'Masters and men.' *Library*, XXX, 2 (June 1975), 81–94.

3369 **Ryrie**, Alexander C. *Socialisation into a trade: a study of craft apprentices.* 1975. (M.Litt. thesis, University of Glasgow.)

3370 **Smith**, M. C. and **Downs**, Sylvia. 'Trainability assessment for apprentice selection in shipbuilding.' *J. Occup. Psychol.*, XLVIII (1975), 39–43.

3371 **Woodward**, N. 'Costing the tradesman's entrance.' *Pers. Manage.*, VII, 11 (November 1975), 23–5.

3372 **Woodward**, N. 'Economic evaluation of apprentice training.' *Ind. Relat. J.*, VI, 1 (Spring 1975), 2–3, 31–41.

3373 **Woodward**, N. and **Anderson**, T. 'Profitability appraisal of apprenticeships.' *Br. J. Ind. Relat.*, XIII, 2 (July 1975), 245–56.

3374 **Industrial and Commercial Training.** 'The case of the disappearing engineering craftsmen.' *Ind. Commer. Train.*, VIII, 5 (May 1976), 182–5.

3375 **Mottram**, Roger D. *Selecting apprentices: some problems and implications for selection and training: a follow-up study in the electricity supply industry.* London: Industrial Training Research Unit, 1976. 24p.

3376 **Ryrie**, Alexander C. 'Employers and apprenticeship.' *Br. J. Ind. Relat.*, XIV, 1 (March 1976), 89–91.

3377 **Lane**, Joan. *Apprenticeship in Warwickshire, 1700–1834.* 1976–7. (Ph.D. thesis, University of Birmingham.)

3378 **Thomas**, E. G. 'The old Poor Law and maritime apprenticeship.' *Mar. Mirror*, LXIII, 2 (May 1977), 153–61.

3379 **Hitch**, G. J. 'The numerical abilities of industrial trainee apprentices.' *J. Occup. Psychol.*, LI (June 1978), 163–76.

3380 **Parkin**, N. 'Are apprenticeships outmoded or undervalued?' *Pers. Manage.*, X, 5 (May 1978), 22–6.

3381 **Singh**, D. *Becoming a craftsman: the process of incorporation into a private enterprise production organisation.* 1978. (Ph.D. thesis, University of Bristol.)

3382 **Lee**, D. J. 'Craft unions and the force of tradition: the case of apprenticeship.' *Br. J. Ind. Relat.*, XVII, 1 (March 1979), 34–49.

See also: 237; 366; 4492; 6409.

b. TRAINING AND DEVELOPMENT

i. General

3383 **Downs**, Sylvia. 'Predicting training potential.' *Pers. Manage.*, II, 9 (September 1970), 26–8.

3384 **Balogh**, Thomas and **Streeton**, Paul P. 'The coefficient of ignorance.' Wykstra, R. (ed.). *Human capital formation and manpower development.* 1971. p. 205–15.

3385 **Boydell**, T. H. *A guide to the identification of training needs.* London: British Association for Commercial and Industrial Education, 1971. 32p.
    Second edition. 1976. 43p.

3386 **Cook**, Stephen. 'Training and the small firm.' *Pers. Manage.*, III, 2 (February 1971), 40–1.

3387 **Daniel**, William Wentworth. 'Productivity training and orientation to work.' *J. Manage. Stud.*, VIII, 3 (October 1971), 329–34.

3388 **Debenham**, A. I. S. 'Assignment and simulation: two techniques of training.' *B.A.C.I.E. J.*, XXV, 2 (June 1971), 44–8.

3389 **Department of Employment.** *Glossary of training terms.* London: H.M.S.O., 1971. iii, 43p.
    Second edition.

3390 **Downs**, Sylvia. 'Mistakes in learning: effects on the older trainee.' *Ind. Commer. Train.*, III, 11 (November 1971), 542–4.

3391 **Francis**, Madeleine. 'The training she deserves.' *Pers. Manage.*, III, 6 (June 1971), 20–7.

3392 **Grieg**, F. W. and **Scott**, W. M. 'Northern Ireland: training and its place in the economy.' *Pers. Manage.*, III, 7 (July 1971), 21–4.

3393 **Hall**, Kenneth. *Industrial retraining and labour skills.* 1971. (Ph.D. thesis, Heriot-Watt University.)

3394 **Iron and Steel Industry Training Board.** *Forecasting and planning training loads.* London: The Board, 1971. 8p.

3395 **Mancini**, P. V. *Economics of training.* 1971. (M.Phil. thesis, University of York.)

3396 **Pettman**, Barrie Owen. 'An incentive to train.' *Pers. Manage.*, III, 9 (September 1971), 31–4.

3397 **Rackham**, Neil. 'The search for new methods in interactive skills training.' *Ind. Commer. Train.*, III, 4 (April 1971), 173–82.

3398 **Tavernier**, Gerard. *Industrial training systems and records.* Epping: Gower, 1971. 111p.

3399 **Trades Union Congress.** *Unions, the T.U.C. and industrial training: report of a second conference of trade union members of industrial training boards.* London: T.U.C., 1971. 29p.

3400 **Turner**, R. 'Industrial training: past, present and future.' *Pers. Manage.*, III, 12 (December 1971), 21–3.

3401 **Wood**, R. W. J. 'Assessment of training.' *Ind. Commer. Train.*, III, 8 (August 1971), 380–3.

3402 **Wykstra**, Ronald A. (ed.). *Human capital formation and manpower development.* London: Collier-Macmillan, 1971. xxvi, 502p.

3403 **Adamson**, Campbell and **Graham**, K. 'Training for the future.' *B.A.C.I.E. J.*, xxv, 6 (June 1972), 59–65.

3404 **Belbin**, Eunice and **Belbin**, Raymond Meredith. *Problems in adult retraining.* London: Heinemann, 1972. xv, 208p.

3405 **Belbin**, Eunice and **Belbin**, Raymond Meredith. 'Problems in adult retraining.' *Ind. Commer. Train.*, iv, 11 (November 1972), 516–23.

3406 **Briggs**, Terry. 'Experiments in discovery learning.' *Pers. Manage.*, iv, 9 (September 1972), 29–31.

3407 **Carr**, Robert. 'Training for the future: the government's proposals.' *B.A.C.I.E. J.*, xxv, 3 (March 1972), 9–14.

3408 **Chichester-Clark**, Robin. 'Training for the future.' *B.A.C.I.E. J.*, xxv, 12 (December 1972), 126–44.

3409 **Confederation of British Industry.** *Training for the future: C.B.I. statement of comment.* London: C.B.I., 1972. 5p.

3410 **Cotgrove**, Stephen Frederick and **Johnson**, P. *Training role studies.* Bath: University of Bath. School of Humanities and Social Sciences, for the Hotel and Catering Industry Training Board, 1972. 186, 35p.

3411 **Daley**, P. and **McGivern**, C. 'Training.' *Ind. Commer. Train.*, iv, 1 (January 1972), 26–33.

3412 **Department of Employment.** *Training for the future: a plan for discussion.* London: H.M.S.O., 1972. 79p.

3413 **Furniture and Timber Industry Training Board.** *Training needs analysis: identifying company training needs.* London: The Board, 1972. 20p. (Training notes 7.)

3414 **Gane**, Christopher P. *Managing the training function using instructional technology and systems concepts.* London: Allen & Unwin, 1972. 183p.

3415 **Gode**, W. *Training your staff.* London: Industrial Society, 1972. 40p. (Industrial Society. Notes for managers 3.)

3416 **Hartley**, K. 'The economics of training: theory and evidence.' *Eur. Train.*, i, 2 (Summer 1972), 159–70.

3417 **Hughes**, James J. 'Industrial training and the small firm.' *J. Bus. Policy*, iii, 2 (Winter 1972), 55–61.

3418 *Industrial training: the future: report of the BACIE Conference, 1972.* London: British Association for Commercial and Industrial Education, 1972. 40p.

3419 **Jones**, J. A. G. 'Towards a classification of benefits of training: the results of some cost benefit studies.' *Eur. Train.*, i, 3 (Winter 1972), 212–21.

3420 **Kenney**, J. P. J. and **Donnelly**, E. L. *Manpower training and development.* London: Harrap, 1972. 222p.

3421 **Lewis**, Paul. 'Adverse attitudes and their effect on training.' *Pers. Manage.*, iv, 11 (November 1972), 35–8.

3422 **Lowthian**, G. H. *Trade unions and training for the future: report of a conference in April 1972 of trade union members of industrial training boards.* London: T.U.C., 1972. 51p.

3423 **Murie**, Alan. 'Into training.' *New Soc.*, xix (3 February 1972), 235–6.

3424 **Musgrove**, F. 'Industry's doubts about the sandwich course.' *Durham Res. Rev.*, vi (Spring 1972), 609–16.

3425 **Page**, Graham Terry. *The guide to training and the future.* London: Kogan Page, 1972. 64p.

3426 **Perrigo**, A. E. B. 'Training needs of small firms.' *Ind. Commer. Train.*, iv, 10 (October 1972), 472–4.

3427 **Pheysey**, D. C. 'Off-course considerations in training.' *Pers. Manage.*, iv, 12 (December 1972), 26–9.

3428 **Prentice**, J. 'Training; faith or proof?' *Ind. Train. Int.*, vii, 4 (April 1972), 124–5.

3429 **Randell**, Gerard Anthony, **Packard**, P. M. A., **Shaw**, R. L. and **Slater**, A. J. *Staff appraisal.* London: Institute of Personnel Management, 1972. 79p.

3430 **Singer**, Edwin J. 'The way forward for industrial training.' *Pers. Manage.*, iv, 5 (May 1972), 22–5, 38–36.

3431 **Stephen**, David. 'Vocational training and immigrants.' Van Houte, H. and Melgert, W. (eds.). *Foreigners in our community.* 1972. p. 135–8.

3432 **Stewart**, J. G. 'Further education: the needs of industry.' *Pers. Manage.*, iv, 7 (July 1972), 32–4.

3433 **Trades Union Congress.** *Training for the future: the trade union view.* London: T.U.C., 1972. 24p.

3434 **Wall**, A. 'DMS training on the premises.' *Bus. Admin.* (May 1972), 75–6.

3435 **Wellens**, John. 'Nellie comes into her own.' *Ind. Commer. Train.*, iv, 9 (September 1972), 420–35.

3436 **Wellens**, John. 'Operation Vulcan: training in physical skills.' *Ind. Commer. Train.*, iv, 7 (July 1972), 318–24.

3437 **Wellens**, John. 'Operation Vulcan: training in physical skills: aspects of the instructor's job.' *Ind. Commer. Train.*, iv, 3 (March 1972), 118–27.

3438 **Wellens**, John. 'Training for the future: a question of objectives.' *Ind. Commer. Train.*, iv, 4 (April 1972), 159–65.

3439 **Wellens**, John, **Williams**, J. and **Stewart**, J. G. 'Training for the future.' *Ind. Commer. Train.*, iv, 3 (March 1972), 107–16.

3440 **Wellman**, D. D. 'O & M thoughts on training.' *O & M Bull.*, xxvii, 4 (November 1972), 189–95.

3441 **Young**, D. R. W. and **Findlater**, J. K. 'Training and industrial relations: a broader perspective.' *Ind. Relat. J.*, iii, 1 (Spring 1972), 3–22.

3442 **Barratt**, A. M. and **Lucas**, C. B. 'Programmed learning in the small firm.' *Ind. Commer. Train.*, v, 3 (March 1973), 130–3.

3443 **Dalziel**, S. 'What do we mean by training standards?' *Ind. Train. Int.*, VIII, 2 (February 1973), 48–50.

3444 **Gill**, H. S. and **Tranfield**, D. R. 'Organization development and the management of training.' *Pers. Manage.*, v, 4 (April 1973), 34–5, 37.

3445 **Hall**, Kenneth and **Denholm**, Christine. 'Retraining in retrospect.' *Pers. Manage.*, v, 8 (August 1973), 28–31, 37.

3446 **Leary**, Malcolm and **Pedler**, Malcolm. 'Training strategies for industrial relations change.' *Ind. Train. Int.*, VIII, 5 (May 1973), 150–7.

3447 **Moorby**, E. T. 'The manager as coach.' *Pers. Manage.*, v, 11 (November 1973), 30–2.

3448 **Moreton**, T. 'The future of the training profession: an economist's view.' *Train. Off.*, IX, 7 (July 1973), 191–5.

3449 **National Council for Educational Technology.** *Some examples of innovative activity in industrial training.* London: The Council, 1973. 29p.

3450 **O'Reilly**, A. P. 'What value job analysis in training?' *Pers. Rev.*, III, 2 (Summer 1973), 50–60.

3451 **Pettman**, Barrie Owen (ed.). *Training and retraining, a basis for the future: a report of a conference.* London: Transcripta Books, 1973. 135p.

3452 **Pettman**, Barrie Owen. 'Training progress 1964–1971.' Pettman, B. (ed.). *Training and retraining.* 1973. p. 11–28.

3453 **Pettman**, Barrie Owen. 'Training to meet the needs of firms and industries.' Pettman, B. (ed.). *Training and retraining.* 1973. p. 33–44.

3454 **Stickland**, C. R. 'More O & M thoughts on training.' *Manage. Serv. Gov.*, XXVIII, 4 (November 1973), 210–6.

3455 **Sweeney**, J. A. 'Training for technological change.' *B.A.C.I.E. J.*, XXVII, (June 1973), 30–4.

3456 **Taylor**, B. and **Lewis**, P. 'Informal learning, training and industrial relations.' *Eur. Train.*, II, 2 (1973), 160–80.

3457 **Wellens**, John. 'Operation Vulcan: the broad view of improving total performance.' *Ind. Commer. Train.*, v, 6 (June 1973), 279–83.

3458 **Woodward**, N. 'Break-even points and off-the-job training: some estimates.' *Eur. Train.*, II, 3 (1973), 239–50.

3459 **Battersby**, D. L. N. 'Developing a packaged training system.' *B.A.C.I.E. J.*, XXVIII (May–June 1974), 60–2.

3460 **Cadbury**, G. A. H. and **Newton**, L. S. 'Management by agreement: its impact on training.' *B.A.C.I.E. J.*, XXVIII, 1 (January 1974), 8–12.

3461 **Colquhoun**, J. C. 'Identifying training and development needs.' *Ind. Commer. Train.*, VI, 8 (August 1974), 355–7.

3462 **Council of Europe**, Ad hoc Conference on the Education of Migrants, 1974, Strasbourg. *Problems relating to the education and training of migrants, both adults and adolescents, and to the schooling of migrants' children: country reports.* Strasbourg: The Council, 1974. 277p.

3463 **Davies**, G. 'Ergonomics and training.' *Train. Off.*, x, 9 (September 1974), 256–63.

3464 **Dyar**, D. A. and **Giles**, W. J. *Improving skills in working with people: interaction analysis.* London: H.M.S.O., 1974. v, 38p. (Training Services Agency training paper 7.)

3465 **Everard**, K. B. 'Mutual monitoring.' *Ind. Commer. Train.*, VI, 7 (July 1974), 304–8.

3466 **Hamblin**, Anthony Crandell. *Evaluation and control of training.* London: McGraw-Hill, 1974. viii, 208p.

3467 **James**, M. and **Drake**, P. 'Improvement in systems performance.' *Ind. Commer. Train.*, VI, 8 (August 1974), 359–63.

3468 **Jones**, J. A. G. and **Anderson**, W. T. 'Progress in evaluation.' *Ind. Commer. Train.*, VI, 3 (March 1974), 107–10.

3469 **Morrison**, Lionel. 'Training for black youth.' *New Soc.*, XXVIII (13 June 1974), 638–9.

3470 **Pettman**, Barrie Owen. 'Industrial training in Great Britain.' *Int. J. Soc. Econ.*, I, I (1974), 63–83.

3471 **Pettman**, Barrie Owen. 'Training decisions.' *J. Eur. Train.*, III, 2 (1974), 120–7.

3472 **Prescott**, B. D. 'The management of training.' *Ind. Commer. Train.*, VI, 12 (December 1974), 556–60.

3473 **Wainwright**, G. and **Bloomfield**, B. 'What about the workers?' *Ind. Soc.*, LVI, 6 (November–December 1974), 13–15.

3474 **Walker**, H. 'Training and employment: the new pattern.' *B.A.C.I.E. J.*, XXVIII, 9 (September 1974), 100–14.

3475 **Wellens**, John. *Training in physical skills.* London: Business Books, 1974. xii, 194p.

3476 **Woolrich**, A. E. 'Problems as training opportunities.' *Ind. Commer. Train.*, VI, 9 (September 1974), 411–13.

3477 **Boydell**, T. H. 'Approaches to training needs.' *B.A.C.I.E. J.*, XXIX, 10 (October 1975), 143–7.

3478 **Conference on Research in the Field of Further Education, 1973, Uxbridge.** *Learning and earning: aspects of day-release in further education.* London: N.F.E.R. Publishing Co., 1975. 111p.

3479 **Greensmith**, D. S. 'Tomorrow's people: training for a changing world.' *B.A.C.I.E. J.*, XXIX, 2 (February 1975), 25–7.

3480 **Harrison**, K. and **Cooper**, Cary Lynn. 'Design and training issues in human relations groups.' *J. Eur. Train.*, IV, 3 (1975), 117–33.

3481 **Holland**, Geoffrey. 'Training for the nation:

the grand design.' *Pers. Manage.*, VII, 10 (October 1975), 33–6.

3482 **Incomes Data Services.** *Training: policies and practice.* London: I.D.S., 1975. 22p. (I.D.S. study 106.)

3483 **Keith**, I. and **Wilson**, B. 'The use of organization theory in training.' *Ind. Commer. Train.*, VII, 3 (March 1975), 99–105.

3484 **Killcross**, M. C. and **Bates**, W. T. C. *Selecting the younger trainee.* London: H.M.S.O., 1975. 32p. (Training Services Agency training paper 8.)

3485 **Moorby**, E. T. 'Coaching in context.' *Pers. Manage.*, VII, 3 (March 1975), 28–30.

3486 **Newsham**, Dorothy B. and **Fisher**, Jeanne M. *What's in a style? Measuring the effectiveness of instruction.* London: Industrial Training Research Unit, 1975. 9p.

3487 **Pearn**, Michael A. *CRAMP: a guide to training decisions: user's manual.* London: Industrial Training Research Unit.
    First edition. 1975. ii, 33p.
    Revised edition. 1977. 43p.

3488 **Prescott**, B. D. 'The trouble-shooting approach to training.' *Ind. Commer. Train.*, VII, 1 (January 1975), 32–5.

3489 **Prout**, J. 'The learning discovery.' *Ind. Soc.*, LVII, 2 (March–April 1975), 14–16.

3490 **Richardson**, K. G. 'Training development with limited resources.' *Ind. Commer. Train.*, VII, 9 (September 1975), 369–72.

3491 **Roberts**, J. and **Stone**, M. 'Cost effectiveness: the training officer's life-line.' *Pers. Manage.*, VII, 9 (September 1975), 27–30.

3492 **Smith**, Peter B. and **Wilison**, Michael J. 'The use of group training methods in multi-racial settings.' *New Community*, IV (Summer 1975), 218–31.

3493 **Stammers**, Robert B. and **Patrick**, John. *The psychology of training.* London: Methuen, 1975. 144p.

3494 **Swaisland**, A. E. H. 'Training and development for the small firm.' *Pers. Manage.*, VII, 4 (April 1975), 34–7.

3495 **Training Services Agency.** *Training opportunities for women.* London: The Agency, 1975. 40p.

3496 **Bowles**, D. *The psychological cost of small group training.* 1976. (Ph.D. thesis, University of Manchester Institute of Science and Technology.)

3497 **Campbell**, Malcolm and **Wille**, Edgar. 'Training on E.E.C. money.' *Pers. Manage.*, VIII, 3 (March 1976), 26–8.

3498 **Chowdhury**, S. A. *Non-formal education and employment: a comparative study.* 1976. (Ph.D. thesis, University of Manchester.)

3499 **Colquhoun**, J. C. 'Enlisting management support for training.' *Ind. Commer. Train.*, VIII, 8 (August 1976), 310–12.

3500 **Higgs**, Malcolm. 'The training package: what's in it for you.' *Pers. Manage.*, VIII, 1 (January 1976), 30–2.

3501 **Lewis**, Chris, **Edgerton**, Nick and **Parkinson**, Bob. 'Interview training.' *Pers. Manage.*, VIII, 5 (May 1976), 29–33.

3502 **Lowndes**, Richard. 'Training for the small business.' *Ind. Commer. Train.*, VIII, 1 (January 1976), 8–10.

3503 **Milutinovich**, J. S. and **Battjer**, B. R. 'A systems approach to training.' *Ind. Commer. Train.*, VIII, 7 (July 1976), 276–81.

3504 **Nettelbeck**, T. and **Kirby**, N. H. 'A comparison of part and whole training methods with mentally retarded workers.' *J. Occup. Psychol.*, XLIX (June 1976), 115–20.

3505 **Newsham**, Dorothy B. *Choose an effective style: a self-instructional approach to the teaching of skills.* London: Industrial Training Research Unit, 1976. 26p.

3506 **Phillis**, R. W. 'Training for the shopfloor.' *Pers. Manage.*, VIII, 4 (April 1976), 40–3.

3507 **Roberts**, Ian. 'The use of process simulators.' *Ind. Train. Int.*, XI, 10 (October 1976), 293–5; XI, 11 (November 1976), 318–20.

3508 **Seear**, Beatrice Nancy. *Training: the fulcrum of change.* London: British Association for Commercial and Industrial Education, 1976. 8p.

3509 **Seear**, Beatrice Nancy. 'Training: the fulcrum of change.' *B.A.C.I.E. J.*, XXX, 7 (July 1976), 122–5.

3510 **Singer**, Edwin J. 'Training: a personal testimony.' *Ind. Comm. Train.*, VIII, 10 (October 1976), 395–7.

3511 **Smith**, Graham W. 'The powerful role of the training officer.' *Ind. Train. Int.*, XI, 9 (September 1976), 272–3.

3512 **Smithers**, A. *Sandwich courses: an integrated education?* London: National Foundation for Educational Research, 1976. 180p.

3513 **Stammers**, Robert B. *Part and whole practice in the design of training.* 1976. (Ph.D. thesis, University of Hull.)

3514 **Thomson**, W. O. and **Savage**, G. G. 'Responsibility towards the young trainee.' *Hosp. Health Serv. Rev.*, LXXII, 1 (January 1976), 13–15.

3515 **Cooper**, Cary L. 'Adverse and growthful effects of experiential learning groups: the role of the trainer, participant and group characteristics.' *Hum. Relat.*, XXX (December 1977), 1103–29.

3516 **Downs**, Sylvia. *Trainability testing: a practical approach to selection.* London: H.M.S.O., 1977. iv, 34p. (Training Services Agency training paper 11.)

3517 **James**, M. J. 'The internal labour market and training.' *Ind. Commer. Train.*, IX, 10 (October 1977), 429–34.

3518 **Seymour**, W. D. 'Analytical training.' *Ind. Commer. Train.*, IX, 8 (August 1977), 323–5.

3519 **Tracey**, W. R. 'Training evaluation: another perspective.' *Pers. Manage.*, IX, 3 (March 1977), 28–31.

3520 **Venna**, Y. 'Training needs and targets.' *J. Eur. Ind. Train.*, I, 4 (1977), 22–6.

3521 **Walker**, James, **Fletcher**, Clive, **Williams**, Richard and **Taylor**, Keith. 'Performance appraisal: an open or shut case?' *Pers. Rev.*, VI, 1 (Winter 1977), 38–42.

3522 **Allner**, D. and **Teire**, J. 'Experiential learning.' *J. Eur. Ind. Train.*, II, 1 (1978), 4–10.

3523 **Central Office of Information.** *Manpower and employment in Britain: industrial training.* London: H.M.S.O., 1978. ii, 34p. (Reference pamphlet 153.)

3524 **Cunday**, B. E. 'Psychological approaches to skill acquisition.' *Educ. Train.*, XX, 10 (October 1978), 283–4.

3525 **Getley**, R. 'Notes on training methods.' *Ind. Commer. Train.*, X, 7 (July 1978), 280–1.

3526 **Gibb**, A. A. *A developmental appraisal, from the management viewpoint, of the use of cost-benefit analysis in in-company training situations.* 1978. (Ph.D. thesis, University of Durham.)

3527 **Hart**, S. J. S. 'Determining training priorities.' *J. Eur. Ind. Train.*, II, 1 (1978), 12–15.

3528 **Makeham**, P. 'An approach to financing training: compensatory funding.' *Bull. Econ. Res.*, XXX (November 1978), 82–91.

3529 **Marshall**, J. 'The training manager's role in stress management.' *J. Eur. Ind. Train.*, II, 5 (1978), 7–11.

3530 **Orr**, *Sir* David. 'Training as an investment.' *B.A.C.I.E. J.*, XXXII, 12 (December 1978), 187–9.

3531 **Smith**, Mike. 'Using repertory grids to evaluate training.' *Pers. Manage.*, X, 2 (February 1978), 36–8.

3532 **Wellens**, John. 'The politics of training.' *Ind. Commer. Train.*, X, 1 (January 1978), 22–7.

3533 **Wellens**, John. 'Replying to the unions.' *Ind. Commer. Train.*, X, 7 (July 1978), 272–8.

3534 **Ziderman**, Adrian. *Manpower training: theory and policy.* London: Macmillan, 1978. 90p.

3535 **Bennett**, Roger D. 'Using research in training.' *J. Eur. Ind. Train.*, III, 5 (1979), 1–31.

3536 **Fowler**, C. J. H. and **Wilding**, John. 'Differential effects of noise and incentives on learning.' *Br. J. Psychol.*, LXX (February 1979), 149–53.

3537 **Hay**, Greg. 'Servicing the small firm: a transformation in group training.' *Pers. Manage.*, XI, 3 (March 1979), 32–4.

3538 **Industrial Training Research Unit.** *The A – Z study: differences between improvers and non-improvers among young unskilled workers.* London: The Unit, 1979. 28p.

3539 **O'Brien**, J. and **Gubbay**, D. 'Training to integrate the multi-racial workforce.' *Pers. Manage.*, XI, 1 (January 1979), 20–23.

3540 **Reddy**, Y. R. K. 'Cost-benefit analysis of training.' *Long Range Plann.*, XII (December 1979), 50–55.

3541 **Robertson**, I. 'Applying psychological research to training practice.' *J. Eur. Ind. Train.*, II, 7 (1979), 17–20.

3542 **Wellens**, John. 'The choices ahead.' *Ind. Commer. Train.*, XI, 4 (April 1979), 136; XI, 5 (May 1979), 189.

3543 **Wellens**, John. 'Total training: the training of the eighties.' *Ind. Commer. Train.*, XI, 9 (September 1979), 371–8.

3544 **Wellens**, John. 'Training: the choices ahead.' *Ind. Commer. Train.*, XI, 2 (February 1979), 49; XI, 3 (March 1979), 95.

See also: 9; 26; 50; 56; 78; 2980; 3130; 4522; 5398; 5496.

ii. *Particular Occupations and Industries*

3545 **Cotton and Allied Textiles Industry Training Board.** *Guide to induction training.* Manchester: The Board, 1970. 17p.

3546 **Morgan**, R. G. T. *A study of the work of industrial training officers.* London: Air Transport and Travel Industry Training Board, 1970. xii, 245p.

3547 **Oakley**, K. and **Richmond**, W. *A systematic approach to commercial and clerical training.* London: Pergamon, 1970. viii, 110p.

3548 **Perry**, H. A. 'A new training plan in Britain's construction industry.' *Mon. Labor. Rev.*, XCIII, 2 (February 1970), 27–31.

3549 **Williams**, E. H. *Training for retailing.* London: Macdonald, 1970. xi, 188p.

3550 **Barnett**, D. C. 'Forecasting for the road ahead.' *Pers. Manage.*, III, 6 (June 1971), 34–6.
　　Forecasting training needs.

3551 **Belgrave**, R. 'Training in Europe.' *Ind. Soc.*, LIII, 12 (December 1971), 10–12.

3552 **Birch**, J. A. *An investigation into the cause of wastage during nurse training.* 1971. (M.Ed. thesis, University of Newcastle upon Tyne.)

3553 **Breishin**, G. N. *The training of supermarket staff: a practical case study in a voluntary group.* 1971. (M.Sc. thesis, University of Manchester Institute of Science and Technology.)

3554 **Congdon**, R. A. *The training of office workers within further education: a study of some economic aspects.* 1971. (M.A. thesis, University of Keele.)

3555 **Cottis**, J. 'Training for the Youth Employment Service.' *Careers Q.*, XXIII, 2 (Spring 1971), 13–21.

3556 **Elgood**, C. 'Introduction to decision-making for graduate entrants.' *Ind. Commer. Train.*, III, 9 (September 1971), 431; III, 10 (October 1971), 474.

3557 **Engineering Industry Training Board.** *The training of technicians.* London: The Board, 1971. 52p.

3558 **Hanage**, R. P. *Some effects of 'Coverdale' training on production staff.* 1971. (M.Com. thesis, University of Birmingham.)

3559 **Jones**, L. H. and **Powrie**, P. J. 'Instruction by correspondence course.' *Ind. Commer. Train.*, III, 10 (October 1971), 463–5.

National Ports Council scheme for dockers.

3560 **Keeling**, Desmond. 'The development of central training in the Civil Service.' *Public Adm.*, IL (Spring 1971), 51–71.

3561 **Langham-Brown**, J. B. 'Training for fault diagnosis.' *B.A.C.I.E. J.*, xxv, 1 (March 1971), 9–14.
Royal Navy.

3562 **Morrison**, T. I. *Some effects of the new chemistry syllabuses upon industrial trainees in Scotland.* 1971. (M.Sc. thesis, University of Glasgow.)

3563 **Parkin**, L. 'Training problems in dispersed units.' *Ind. Commer. Train.*, III, 12 (December 1971), 551–4.
Grocers' Institute module training.

3564 **Pettman**, Barrie Owen. *Attitudes of engineering firms towards off-the-job training facilities.* Bradford: Institute of Scientific Business, 1971. 7, [2]p.

3565 **Pocock**, Pamela. 'Projects in the ports.' *Pers. Manage.*, II, 3 (March 1971), 35–7.

3566 **Polston**, L. M. *The external validation of instructor training courses.* London: London University, Birkbeck College, 1971. 128p.

3567 **Roderick**, G. W. *Scientific and technical training in Liverpool and its relevance to industrial Merseyside, 1870–1914.* 1971. (M.A. thesis University of Liverpool.)

3568 **Rodger**, Alec, **Morgan**, Terry and **Guest**, David. *The industrial training officer: his background and his work.* London: Institute of Personnel Management, 1971. 57p.

3569 **Rose**, D. R. *A study of aspects of the vocational development of engineers in training.* 1971. (M.Phil. thesis, Birkbeck College, University of London.)

3570 **Rubber and Plastics Processing Industry Training Board.** *Training for profit: recommendations for the training of glass reinforced plastics laminators.* Brentford: The Board, 1971. 11p.

3571 **Scottish Technical Education Consultative Council.** *Technician courses and examinations in Scotland.* Edinburgh: The Council, 1971. xii, 97p.

3572 **Smith**, W. W. 'The Thanet scheme: training the mechanical technician engineer.' *Ind. Commer. Train.*, III, 11 (November 1971), 514–17.

3573 **Touche Ross and Company.** *A system documented in accordance with the standards in the Systems Documentation Manual.* Manchester: National Computing Centre, 1971. 347p.
Computer training.

3574 **Wellens**, John and **Charles**, H. 'Getting started in the training business.' *Ind. Commer. Train.*, III, 8 (August 1971), 400–13.

3575 **Wille**, Edgar. *Training for effective use of computers.* London: Institute of Personnel Management, 1971. 73p.

3576 **Belbin**, Raymond Meredith and **Stammers**, D. 'Pacing stress, human adaptation and training in car production.' *Appl. Econ.*, III, 3 (September 1972), 142–6.

3577 **Conference on Human Resources and the Training Plan, 1971, York.** *Report of the conference.* London: Iron and Steel Industry Training Board, 1972. 82p.

3578 **Department of Employment**, Joint Committee of Industrial Training Boards. *The training of computer programmers.* London: H.M.S.O., 1972. 46p.

3579 **Department of Employment**, Joint Industrial Training Boards Committee for Commercial and Administrative Training. *Training for marketing.* London: H.M.S.O., 1972. 96p.
Chairman: B. W. Haining.

3580 **Department of Employment**, Joint Industrial Training Boards Committee for Commercial and Administrative Training. *Training for purchasing and supply.* London: H.M.S.O., 1972. 56p.
Chairman: F. Metcalfe.

3581 **Department of Employment**, Joint Industrial Training Boards Committee for Commercial and Administrative Training, Distribution and Transport Sub-Committee. *Training for transport and physical distribution.* London: H.M.S.O., 1972. 39p.

3582 **Department of Health and Social Security.** *Adult training centres.* London: H.M.S.O., 1972. 24p. (Local authority building note 5.)

3583 **Downs**, Sylvia. *Trainability assessments: fork truck operators.* Cambridge: University College, London, Industrial Training Research Unit (Cambridge), 1972. 12p.

3584 **Johnson**, P. S. 'Cost effectiveness of training: a case study operator training.' *Ind. Relat. J.*, III, 4 (Winter 1972), 24–9.

3585 **Keeling**, Desmond. 'Central training in the Civil Service.' *Public Adm.*, L, 1 (Spring 1972), 1–17.

3586 **Lewis**, Paul. 'Relations between trainers and managements.' *Ind. Relat. J.*, III, 2 (Summer 1972), 35–42.

3587 **Margerison**, Charles J. 'The training manager as internal consultant.' *Eur. Train.*, I, 2 (Summer 1972), 177–87.

3588 **Morris**, G. W., **Beak**, E. J. and **Dennington**, D. 'On-the-job training using modular methods: an example from the meat industry.' *Ind. Commer. Train.*, IV, 9 (September 1972), 425–36.

3589 **Powrie**, P. J. 'Training in the British port industry.' *Econ. Soc. Tijdschr.*, XXVI, 1 (February 1972), 43–54.

3590 **Savage**, R. Douglass and **Stewart**, Ronald R. 'Personality and the success of card punch operators in training.' *Br. J. Psychol.*, LXIII (August 1972), 445–50.

3591 **Tranfield**, D. R. and **Gill**, H. S. 'The training manager and organization development.' *Eur. Train.*, I, 1 (Spring 1972), 45–53.

3592 **United Nations**, Social Defence Research Institute. *Evaluation and improvement of manpower training programmes in social defence.* Rome: The Institute, 1972. vi, 33p.
Training of police and prison officers.

3593 **Verma**, Pramod Chandra. 'Training, redundancy and productivity: a case study of the chemical industry in Britain.' *Manpower J.*, VII, 4 (January–March 1972), 23–42.

3594 **Wood**, W. B. E. and **Hyde**, G. 'Programmed learning in a process industry.' *Ind. Train. Int.*, VII, 5 (May 1972), 145–8.
Training of seasonal workers in the sugar processing industry.

3595 **Woodcock**, J. A. D. *Cost reduction through operator training and retraining.* London: Kogan Page, 1972. 138p.

3596 **Air Transport and Travel Industry Training Board.** *Training airline sales representatives.* London: The Board, 1973. 32p. (Marketing series 1.)

3597 **Association of Colleges for Further and Higher Education** and **Association of Principals of Technical Institutions.** *Staff development in further education: report of a joint A.C.F.H.E./A.P.T.I. working party 1973.* London: The Authors, 1973. 39p.

3598 **Atkins**, O. F. 'Use of the tachistoscope in clerical training.' *Ind. Commer. Train.*, V, 11 (November 1973), 516–23.

3599 **Beach**, A. J. 'Training electronics technicians: creating the learning environment.' *Ind. Commer. Train.*, V, 2 (February 1973), 90–93.

3600 **British Association for Commercial and Industrial Education.** 'Rationalising clerical courses and examinations.' *B.A.C.I.E. J.*, XXVII, 3 (September 1973), 69–73.

3601 **British Association for Commercial and Industrial Education.** *Training officer's guide to the education system of Great Britain with special reference to education for engineering trainees.* London: The Association, 1973. 24p. (Training manuals 1.)
Fifth edition.

3602 **Collins**, R., **Herbert**, A. J. and **Wise**, A. 'Commercial training and professional qualifications.' *Ind. Train. Int.*, VIII, 4 (April 1973), 113–22.

3603 **Dasgupta**, C. and **Fricke**, P. H. *Selection and training of Indian crews in the British Merchant Navy: a feasibility study.* Cardiff: University of Wales Institute of Science and Technology, 1973. 158p.

3604 **Distributive Industry Training Board.** *About clerical training.* London: The Board, 1973. 36p.

3605 **Downs**, Sylvia. *Trainability assessments: sewing machinists.* Cambridge: University College, London, Industrial Training Research Unit (Cambridge), 1973. 24p.

3606 **Electricity Supply Industry Training Board.** *Training of systems analysts.* London: The Board, 1973. 60p.

3607 **Engineering Industry Training Board.** *Training officers in the engineering industry 1973.* London: Research Planning and Statistics for the Board, 1973. [106]p.

3608 **Farndale**, W. A. J. and **Harding**, G. *Training for hospital laundry staff and proposed staffing structure.* London: Ravenswood, 1973. 34p.

3609 **Johnson**, P. 'The training adviser in industry.' *Pers. Rev.*, III, 3 (Autumn 1973), 54–9.

3610 **Lodge**, D. 'The design of a learning package.' *Ind. Train. Int.*, VIII, 4 (April 1973), 123–7.

3611 **National Coal Board**, Industrial Training Branch. *Underground locomotive driving.* London: The Board, 1973. 73p. (Training manuals 9.)

3612 **Pettman**, Barrie Owen. *Industrial training systems.* Bradford: Institute of Scientific Business, 1973. 22p. (Reports and surveys 7.)

3613 **Road Transport Industry Training Board.** *Training trends: a study of training activity in the road transport industry 1967/68–1971/72.* London: The Board, 1973. 50p.

3614 **Technician Education Council.** *Consultative document on sector and programme committees.* London: The Council, 1973. 18p.

3615 **Westley**, K. 'Application of programmed learning in footwear manufacture.' *Ind. Train. Int.*, VIII, 1 (January 1973), 9–11; VIII, 2 (February 1973), 41–2.

3616 **Central Council for Education and Training in Social Work.** *Social work – people with handicaps need better trained workers: report of a Working Party on Training for Social Work with Handicapped People.* London: The Council, 1974. 68p.

3617 **Chemical and Allied Products Industry Training Board.** *Basic instructional methods, techniques and aids.* London: H.M.S.O., 1974. 43p. (Information papers 14.)

3618 **Chemical and Allied Products Industry Training Board.** *Five year plan 1975–80.* London: The Board, 1974. 27p.

3619 **Department of Health and Social Security.** *Decade of progress: a history of the Training Council for Teachers of the Mentally Handicapped.* London: H.M.S.O., 1974. 37p.

3620 **Electricity Supply Industry Training Board.** *Training of clerical staff.* London: The Board, 1974. 32p.

3621 **Hackett**, P. 'New dimensions of mining education.' *Optima*, XXIV (1974), 129–37.

3622 **Industrial and Commercial Training.** 'Training officers in the engineering industry.' *Ind. Commer. Train.*, VI, 2 (February 1974), 58–61.

3623 **Institution of Civil Engineers, Institution of Municipal Engineers,** and **Institution of Structural Engineers.** *Mid-career training: report and recommendations.* London: The Authors, 1974. iv, 39p.

3624 **Kilmann**, Ralph H. 'The effect of interpersonal values on laboratory training: an empirical investigation.' *Hum. Relat.*, XXVII (March 1974), 247–65.

3625 **Letch**, R. S. 'Training and development of training officers.' *Local Gov. Stud.*, IV, 4 (October 1974), 55–7.

3626 **Morgan**, Terry and **Amos**, R. *Survey of research knowledge and attitudes of training managers and officers in air transport and travel.* London: Air Transport and Travel Industry Training Board, 1974. 42p. (Research reports 74.)

3627 **National Economic Development Committee**, Economic Development Committee for the Distributive Trades. *Career development in retail distribution.* London: N.E.D.C, 1974.

3628 **Robertson**, Paul L. 'Technical education in the British shipbuilding and marine engineering industries, 1863–1914.' *Econ. Hist. Rev.*, XXVII, 1 (1974), 222–35.

3629 **Rutter**, D. 'Planning for the future in coalmining.' *Ind. Commer. Train.*, VI, 3 (March 1974), 119–22.

3630 **Seager**, A. M. 'Training the professional engineer.' *Ind. Commer. Train.*, VI, 12 (December 1974), 567–73.

3631 **Shipbuilding Industry Training Board.** *Identifying training needs: validating training.* London: The Board, 1974. 8p. (Information papers 3.)

3632 **Technician Education Council.** *Policy statement.* London: The Council, 1974. 45p.

3633 **Thornton**, C. L. 'Training of retail sales assistants.' *B.A.C.I.E. J.*, XXVIII (November 1974), 146–7.

3634 **Turner**, S. R. 'Craft training: mental and perceptual skills.' *Ind. Commer. Train.*, VI, 2 (February 1974), 63–6.

3635 **Woolliscroft**, M. 'Evaluation of training at the Hospital Engineering Centre, Falfield.' *Ind. Commer. Train.*, VI, 10 (October 1974), 472–9.

3636 **Birch**, J. A. *To nurse or not to nurse: an investigation into the causes of withdrawal during nurse training.* London: Royal College of Nursing and National Council of Nurses of the United Kingdom, 1975. 97p.

3637 **Central Council for Education and Training in Social Work.** *Day services: an action plan for training: report of the working party on training for employment in day centres providing care, education and occupational opportunities.* London: The Council, 1975. 86p.

3638 **Department of Employment Gazette.** 'Chemical and allied industries career patterns and training needs of engineers, scientists and technologists.' *Dep. Employment Gaz.*, LXXXIII, 10 (October 1975), 986–91.

3639 **Duncan**, K. D. and **Gray**, M. J. 'An evaluation of a fault-finding training course for refinery process operators.' *J. Occup. Psychol.*, XLVIII (1975), 199–218.

3640 **Elsdon**, K. T. *Training for adult education.* Nottingham: University of Nottingham. De-

partment of Adult Education, 1975. 202p.

3641 **Haygarth**, J. *Group training in the construction industry.* 1975. (M.Sc. thesis, University of Salford.)

3642 **Industrial Training Research Unit.** *Trainability assessments: sewing machinists.* London: The Unit, 1975. 27p.

3643 **Lamb**, R. T. *An evaluation of the training of telephonists.* 1975. (M.Phil. thesis, Council for National Academic Awards.)

3644 **Lancaster**, A. *A study of nurse-tutors' opinions on some issues related to nursing education.* 1975. (M.Ed. thesis, University of Edinburgh.)

3645 **Leary**, Malcolm. 'Flower power in industrial relations.' *Ind. Commer. Train.*, VII, 12 (December 1975), 486–9.

Food, Drink and Tobacco Industry Training Board.

3646 **Lidstone**, John. *Training salesmen on the job.* London: Gower, 1975. xiii, 109p.

3647 **Nevard**, L. 'In-service training for the Health Service.' *Manage. Educ. Dev.*, VI, 2 (August 1975), 84–92.

3648 **Paper and Paper Products Industry Training Board.** *Cutting/greasing machine minder.* London: The Board, 1975. iv, 101p. (Training guidelines 4.)

3649 **Pedler**, Malcolm J. and **Thomson**, A. 'Training officer development.' *Ind. Train. Int.*, X, 7 (July–August 1975), 237–8.

3650 **Prentice**, Gordon. 'The training officer: in search of influence.' *Pers. Manage.*, VII, 7 (July 1975), 26–9.

3651 **Road Transport Industry Training Board.** *Manpower 75: a study of manpower and training needs in the road transport industry, 1967–1980.* London: The Board, 1975. iii, 182p.

3652 **Rubber and Plastics Processing Industry Training Board.** *First report of the Study Group on 'The education/training of 16–18 year olds'.* Brentford: The Board, 1975. 10p.

3653 **Rubber and Plastics Processing Industry Training Board.** *Operative: recommendations for the training of operatives.* Brentford: The Board, [1975?].

3654 **Smith**, M. C. *Trainability assessments: electronic assemblers.* London: Industrial Training Research Unit, 1975. 17p.

3655 **Stammers**, Derek and **Belbin**, Raymond Meredith. *Pacing stress, human adaptation and the problem of training on a car production line.* London: Industrial Training Research Unit, 1975. 12p.

3656 **Bolton**, M. 'Research and the training revolution.' *Pers. Manage.*, VIII, 8 (August 1976), 22–5.

3657 **Department of Health and Social Security.** *Manpower and training for the social services: report of the Working Party.* London: H.M.S.O., 1976. iv, 178p.

3658 **Eagle**, F. H. 'Directed private study in the docks.' *B.A.C.I.E. J.*, XXX, 10 (October 1976), 166–8.

3659 **Insurance Industry Training Council.** *Guide to on-the-job training.* London: The Council, 1976. 14p.

3660 **Owen**, G. M. *A study of six courses integrating basic nursing education with health visiting in a single course.* 1976. (M.Phil. thesis, Chelsea College, University of London.)

3661 **Walsh**, William. 'Training for clerical work restructuring.' *Educ. Train.*, XVIII, 10 (October 1976), 289–91.

3662 **Westley**, K. H. and **Richardson**, K. G. 'Technician training for the small firm.' *Ind. Commer. Train.*, VIII, 9 (September 1976), 359–64.

3663 **Wheatley**, D. *Training officer's guide to the education system of Great Britain with special reference to education for engineering trainees.* London: British Association for Commercial and Industrial Education, 1976. 24p. Sixth edition.

3664 **Williams**, H. 'Work study and operator training.' *Manage. Serv.*, I, 8 (August 1976), 2–6.

3665 **Billis**, D. 'Development in the social services.' *Public Adm.*, LV, 2 (Summer 1977), 181–95.

3666 **Downs**, Sylvia and **Roberts**, A. 'Training of train guards.' *J. Occup. Psychol.*, L, 2 (1977), 111–20.

3667 **Drew**, K. *The training of food (bakery) technicians.* 1976–7. (M.Phil. thesis, University of Nottingham.)

3668 **Industrial Training Research Unit.** *Trainability assessments: fork truck operators.* London: The Unit, 1977. 19p.

3669 **Industrial Training Research Unit.** *Using the CRAMP system to design a training programme: a study at London Transport.* London: The Unit, 1977. 31p.

3670 **Lewis**, R. G. *A study of the effectiveness of branch level training in some retail multiples.* 1977. (M.Phil. thesis, University of Leeds.)

3671 **National Economic Development Committee**, Economic Development Committee for International Freight Movement. *Diversity of training in the international transport industry.* London: N.E.D.C., 1977.

3672 **Ryan**, J. F. 'Training to improve salesmen's performance.' *Ind. Commer. Train.*, IX, 1 (January 1977), 24–7.

3673 **Smith**, David. 'Training for government with a human face.' *Ind. Commer. Train.*, IX, 7 (July 1977), 280–87. Civil service.

3674 **Smith**, David. 'Training in the Civil Service.' *Ind. Commer. Train.*, IX, 9 (September 1977), 382–4.

3675 **Taylor**, D. S. and **Wright**, P. L. 'Training auditors in interviewing skills.' *J. Eur. Ind. Train.*, I, 5 (1977), 8–11.

3676 **Wellens**, John. 'Training the trainer.' *Ind. Commer. Train.*, IX, 1 (January 1977), 4–8.

3677 **Clinard**, H. 'The "managing effective relationships" method.' *B.A.C.I.E. J.*, XXXII, 3

(March 1978), 51–4.

3678 **Economist Intelligence Unit.** *Employment and training in the electrical machinery industry in Great Britain.* London: Engineering Industry Training Board, 1978. 62p. (Reference papers 1/78.)

3679 **Ketchley**, P. and **Anderson**, N. 'Clerical skills training.' *J. Eur. Ind. Train.*, II, 3 (1978), 6–8.

3680 **Manpower Services Commission,** Training of Trainers Committee. *Training of trainers.* London: H.M.S.O., 1978. 24p. (Report 1.)

3681 **Radcliff**, P. J. and **Jenkins**, D. 'Training trainers.' *Ind. Commer. Train.*, X, 9 (September 1978), 378–81.

3682 **Steed**, I. C. *A study of the performance and training of sales assistants within a multiple shoe chain.* 1978. (M.Phil. thesis, University of Leeds.)

3683 **Anderson**, N. J. 'An organizational approach to warehouse training.' *Ind. Commer. Train.*, XI, 7 (July 1979), 278–81.

3684 **Ayres**, R. and **Dalziel**, S. 'Training direct trainers.' *B.A.C.I.E. J.*, XXXIII, 5 (May 1979), 82–3.

3685 **Grindley**, K. 'Overcoming the programmer shortage.' *Ind. Commer. Train.*, XI, 8 (August 1979), 318–22.

3686 **Kemp**, Barry. 'A local government experience with experiential training.' *Pers. Manage.*, XI, 6 (June 1979), 37–41.

3687 **Pope**, J. A. 'The education of professional engineers.' *B.A.C.I.E. J.*, XXXIII, 9 (September 1979), 138–43.

3688 **Stevenson**, Ann. *Agricultural education and training in North Humberside: a survey of experience and attitudes.* Hull: University of Hull Department of Geography, 1979. 144p.

See also: 3319; 3322; 3323; 3325; 3369; 3370; 3375; 3394; 3437; 6386.

iii. *Supervisors and Managers*

In addition to containing material on the training of supervisors and managers, this section includes literature dealing with their recruitment, selection, placement, performance and appraisal, and career development. See also Part Four, II, C; Part Six, II, B, 2; and Part Six, II, B, 3, b, iv.

3689 **Aarons**, H. *A contribution to the prediction of the effectiveness of management training courses.* [1971?] (Ph.D. thesis, Birkbeck College, University of London.)

3690 **Anstey**, Edgar, **Handyside**, J., **Dunnette**, M., **Harrell**, T., **MacNeil**, H. and **Mullan**, C. *Assessing managerial potential.* London: Independent Assessment and Research Centre, 1971. 113p.

3691 **Cordery**, M. 'Evaluation of external supervisory courses.' *Ind. Train. Int.*, VI, 7 (July 1971), 198–201.

3692 **Department of Employment.** *Computer*

appreciation courses for managers. London: H.M.S.O., 1971. 27p.

3693 **Department of Employment.** *Survey on management training and development.* London: The Department, 1971. 70p.
   Chairman: A.C. Mumford.

3694 **Fineman**, Stephen and **Warr**, Peter Bryan. 'Managers: their effectiveness and training.' Warr, P. (ed.). *Psychology at work.* 1971. p. 259–82.

3695 **Hague**, Hawdon. 'Defining management training needs.' *Ind. Commer. Train.*, III, 10 (October 1971), 466–70.

3696 **Hogan**, D. J. *A study of the effects of training on supervisory behaviour.* 1971. (M.Phil. thesis, Birkbeck College, University of London.)

3697 **Hurley**, F. G. (ed.). *Training retail managers: a symposium.* London: Institute of Personnel Management, 1971. 64p.

3698 **Mumford**, Alan. *The manager and training.* London: Pitman, 1971. viii, 152p.

3699 **Rackham**, Neil. *Development and evaluation of supervisory training: a report on research conducted in B.O.A.C. under the joint sponsorship of B.O.A.C. and the Air Transport and Travel Industry Training Board.* London: Air Transport and Travel Industry Training Board, 1971. xii, 43p. (Research reports, 1971, 1.)

3700 **Rayfield**, D. A. 'Training by exception.' *Pers. Manage.*, III, 11 (November 1971), 26–7.

3701 **Rubber and Plastics Processing Industry Training Board.** *Training for profit: guide lines for the training of supervisors in the G.R.P. industry: a supplement to the recommendations for supervisor training.* Brentford: The Board, 1971. 23p.

3702 **Walsh**, B. 'Priority for supervision.' *Ind. Commer. Train.*, III, 12 (December 1971), 577–9.

3703 **Belbin**, Eunice and **Toye**, M. 'How managers learn.' *Ind. Commer. Train.*, IV, 7 (July 1972), 344–7.

3704 **Daley**, P. and **McGivern**, C. 'The on-going management situation as the training vehicle.' *Ind. Commer. Train.*, IV, 3 (March 1972), 137–41.

3705 **Deeks**, J. 'Job-specific management training.' *Ind. Commer. Train.*, IV, 4 (April 1972), 176–81.

3706 **Edmonds**, John. 'The thin line between management and development.' *Pers. Manage.*, IV, 8 (August 1972), 31–3.

3707 **Garbutt**, D. 'Management training needs: a typology.' *Manage. Educ. Dev.*, III, 1 (January 1972), 128–37.

3708 **Hague**, Hawdon. 'Meeting management training needs.' *Ind. Commer. Train.*, IV, 2 (February 1972), 89–93.

3709 **Hamblin**, Anthony Crandell. 'Controlling the training process.' *Manage. Educ. Dev.*, III, 2 (August 1972), 92–7.

3710 **Hancock**, C. J. and **Hodge**, H. C. H.

'MBO and training.' *O&M Bull.*, XXVII, 4 (November 1972), 183–8.

3711 **Hayes**, F. C. 'Training for the management of human resources.' *Ind. Commer. Train.*, IV, 8 (August 1972), 370–75.

3712 **Iron and Steel Industry Training Board.** *Recommendations on management training and related guidance material.* London: The Board, 1972. 51p.

3713 **Jackson**, Peter J. and **Thompson**, M. 'Supervisory training and organizational change.' *Manage. Educ. Dev.*, III, 1 (January 1972), 142–8.

3714 **Joint Industrial Training Boards Committee for Commercial and Administrative Training.** *Training for the management of human resources: a report.* London: H.M.S.O., 1972. 48p.
   Chairman: F.C. Hayes.

3715 **Joint Industrial Training Boards Committee for Commercial and Administrative Training**, Purchasing/ Supply Sub-Committee. *Training for purchasing and supply: a report.* London: H.M.S.O., 1972. 55p.

3716 **Joint Industrial Training Boards Committee for Commercial and Administrative Training**, Sales/ Marketing Sub-Committee. *Training for marketing: a report.* London: H.M.S.O., 1972. 93p.

3717 **Lawrence**, Susanne. 'A role for industry in management education.' *Pers. Manage.*, IV, 1 (January 1972), 18–22.

3718 **Leggatt**, Timothy W. *Training of British managers: a study of need and demand.* London: H.M.S.O., for the National Economic Development Office, 1972. ix, 210p.

3719 **Lusher**, B. 'Training the experienced manager.' *Ind. Commer. Train.*, IV, 12 (December 1972), 581–91.

3720 **Pitfield**, M. and **Rees**, F. M. 'Can team teaching aid the integration of management education?' *Manage. Educ. Dev.*, III, 2 (August 1972), 98–106.

3721 **Reid**, J. G. 'Training for work study.' *Ind. Train. Int.* VII, 9 (September 1972), 280–82.

3722 **Revans**, R. W. 'Action learning: a management development programme.' *Pers. Rev.*, II, 3 (Autumn 1972), 36–43.

3723 **Stait**, N. H. 'Management training and the smaller company.' *Ind. Commer. Train.*, IV, 7 (July 1972), 325–30.

3724 **Still**, Michael. 'Determinants of management training policies.' *J. Bus. Policy*, II, 4 (Summer 1972), 62–9.

3725 **Wernham**, R. 'Getting the measure of management training.' *Pers. Manage.*, IV, 3 (March 1972), 28–31.

3726 **Whitelaw**, Matt. *The evaluation of management training: a review.* London: Institute of Personnel Management, 1972. 63p.

3727 **Back**, Ken and **Horner**, Michael. 'Successful schemes for management appraisal.' *Pers. Manage.*, v, 6 (June 1973), 30–33.

3728 **Bourn**, J. B. 'Management training in the Civil Service.' *J. Eur. Train.*, I (1973), 32–40.

3729 **Burgoyne**, J. G. 'Evaluating management development programmes.' *Pers. Rev.*, III, 3 (Autumn 1973), 40–44.

3730 **Francis**, David and **Johnson**, Ronald. 'Training to advise.' *Pers. Manage.*, v, 7 (July 1973), 36–9.
 Services provided by the Food, Drink and Tobacco Industry Training Board.

3731 **Grieg**, F.W. 'Supervisory training re-examined.' *Ind. Train. Int.*, VIII, 3 (March 1973), 81–97.

3732 **Hoole**, A. F. P. 'Group relations training.' *Manage. Serv. Gov.*, XXVIII, 1 (February 1973), 14–17.

3733 **Insurance Industry Training Council.** *Guide to the training of supervisory and managerial staff.* London: The Council, [1973?]. 10p.

3734 **Joint Committee of Industrial Training Boards on the Training of Accountants.** *Training for professional accountants in industry, commerce and public services: a report.* London: H.M.S.O., 1973. ix, 21p.

3735 **Joint Industrial Training Boards Committee for Commercial and Administrative Training.** *Training for data processing management.* London: H.M.S.O., 1973. 60p.

3736 **Joint Industrial Training Boards Committee for Commercial and Administrative Training,** Sub-Committee on Company Secretaryship/Office Management. *Training for company secretaryship.* London: H.M.S.O., 1973. 30p.

3737 **Jones**, J. A. G. 'The costs and benefits of management training.' *Pers. Manage.*, v, 9 (September 1973), 31–4.

3738 **Mills**, B. 'Recent trends in the development of supervisors: a summary of the latest views of the Institute of Supervisory Management.' *Ind. Commer. Train.*, v, 6 (June 1973), 289–92.

3739 **Misselhorn**, H. J. 'Job situation training for supervisors.' *Ind. Commer. Train.*, v, 3 (March 1973), 145–7.

3740 **Morris**, M. and **Honey**, P. 'Practical experiences in evaluating management training.' *Pers. Manage.*, v, 1 (January 1973), 29–33.

3741 **Thurley**, Keith Ernest and **Wirdenius**, Hans. *Approaches to supervisory development.* London: Institute of Personnel Management, 1973. 94p.

3742 **Boland**, B. 'Training for responsibility.' *Ind. Comm. Train.*, VI, 3 (March 1974), 127–39.

3743 **Brown**, F. 'A supervisory skills course for beginners.' *Ind. Commer. Train.*, VI, 12 (December 1974), 574–80.

3744 **Construction Industry Training Board.** *Guide to coaching for management.* London: The Board, 1974. 12p.

3745 **Handy**, Charles. 'Pitfalls of management development.' *Pers. Manage.*, VI, 2 (February 1974), 20–25.

3746 **Hotel, Catering and Institutional Management Association.** *Tomorrow's managers: a consultative report.* London: The Association, 1974. 16p.

3747 **Joint Committee of Industrial Training Boards.** *Training of key personnel in the application of computer controlled systems to industrial processes: a report to the Department of Employment.* London: H.M.S.O., 1974. 35p.

3748 **Prynne**, P. 'The use of management training.' *Ind. Commer. Train.*, VI, 8 (August 1974), 364–7.

3749 **Singer**, Edwin J. *Effective management coaching.* London: Institute of Personnel Management, 1974. 191p.

3750 **Stewart**, Valerie and **Stewart**, A. 'Reviewing appraisal training.' *Ind. Train. Int.*, IX, 4 (April 1974), 114–16.

3751 **Baynes**, M. 'Major variables in the management training process.' *Pers. Rev.*, v, 1 (Winter 1975), 47–53.

3752 **Civil Service Department.** *Guide for new managers.* London: H.M.S.O., 1975. 34p.

3753 **Hague**, Hawdon. 'Coaching.' *Ind. Commer. Train.*, VII, 9 (September 1975), 362–7.

3754 **Joint Industrial Training Boards Committee for Commercial and Administrative Training,** Sub-Committee on Company Secretaryship/Office Management. *Training for office management.* London: H.M.S.O., 1975. 27p.

3755 **Koudra**, M. *Management training: practice and attitudes.* London: British Institute of Management, 1975. 30p. (Management survey reports 24.)

3756 **Mumford**, Alan. 'Management development, with or without the boss.' *Pers. Manage.*, VII, 6 (June 1975), 26–8.

3757 **Smith**, M. and **Ashton**, D. 'Evaluating management training.' *Pers. Rev.*, v, 4 (Autumn 1975), 15–21.

3758 **Woodward**, N. 'Cost – benefit analysis of supervisor training.' *Ind. Relat. J.*, VI, 2 (Summer 1975), 2–3, 41–7.

3759 **Woodward**, N. 'The economic evaluation of supervisor training.' *J. Eur. Train.*, IV, (1975), 134–47.

3760 **Zeira**, Y. 'Planned change through top management training.' *Ind. Relat. J.*, VI, 1 (Spring 1975), 42–52.

3761 **Bamber**, Greg J. and **Leggett**, Colin J. 'Training in administrative skills.' *Ind. Train. Int.*, XI, 10 (October 1976), 286–8.

3762 **Beer**, N. F. and **Swaffin-Smith**, C. 'Rejuvenating the redundant manager.' *Pers. Manage.*, VIII, 12 (December 1976), 26–9.

3763 **Hacon**, Richard. 'A change of course in management training.' *Pers. Manage.*, VIII, 2 (February 1976), 30–33.

3764 **Honey**, Peter. 'On-the-job management

training.' *Ind. Commer. Train.*, VIII, 6 (June 1976), 229–35.

3765 **Hughes**, C. P. 'Supervisory training: one company's experience.' *Ind. Commer. Train.*, VIII, 12 (December 1976), 482–4.

3766 **Jain**, H. C. 'Leadership training.' *J. Eur. Train.*, V (1976), 234–44.

3767 **Stewart**, Andrew and **Stewart**, Valerie. *Tomorrow's men today: the identification and development of management potential.* London: Institute of Personnel Management and Institute of Manpower Studies, 1976. 247p.

3768 **Cooper**, Cary L. 'Management education methods for humanising the workplace.' Ottaway, R. (ed.). *Humanising the workplace.* 1977. p. 123–34.

3769 **Cooper**, Cary L. and **Bowles**, David. *Hurt or helpful? A study of the personnel impact on managers of experiential, small group training programmes.* London: H.M.S.O., 1977. iv, 48p. (Training Services Agency training information paper 10.)

3770 **Oliver**, M.V.L. *Interactive simulation and model building as a method of training in production management.* 1976–7. (M.Sc. thesis, University of Loughborough.)

3771 **Training Services Agency.** *A discussion document on management development.* London: The Agency, 1977. 25p.

3772 **Whitelaw**, Matt. 'Training events and data collection.' *J. Eur. Ind. Train.*, I, 3 (1977), 14–16.

3773 **Austin**, Bruce and **Knibbs**, J. 'Management courses for local government.' *Local Gov. Stud.*, VII, 1 (January 1978), 39–48.

3774 **Barnett**, David. 'Managers in road transport.' *Dep. Employment Gaz.*, LXXXVI, 8 (August 1978), 922–6.

3775 **Binstead**, D. 'A framework for management learning events.' *J. Eur. Ind. Train.*, II, 5 (1978), 25–8.

3776 **Burgess**, R. A. and **Fryer**, B. G. 'The role of the management development practitioner.' *Pers. Rev.*, VIII, 2 (Summer 1978), 35–40.

3777 **Burgoyne**, J. G. and **Stuart**, R. 'Methods of management development.' *Pers. Rev.*, VIII (Winter 1978), 53–8.

3778 **Casey**, D. 'Project training for managers.' *J. Eur. Ind. Train.*, II, 5 (1978), 3–6.

3779 **Davies**, B. 'Developing managers for the eighties.' *Manchr. Bus. School Rev.*, II, 4 (1978), 2–5.

3780 **Fripp**, John. 'Getting long term value from executive appointments.' *Pers. Manage.*, X, 11 (November 1978), 34–7.

3781 **Gorb**, Peter. 'Management development for the small firm.' *Pers. Manage.*, X, 1 (January 1978), 24–7.

3782 **Guerrier**, Yvonne and **Macmillan**, Keith. 'Developing managers in a low-growth organisation.' *Pers. Manage.*, X, 12 (December 1978), 34–8.

3783 **Guerrier**, Yvonne and **Philpot**, Nigel. *The British manager: careers and mobility.* London: British Institute of Management, 1978. 46p. (B.I.M. management survey reports 39.)

3784 **Lawrence**, Peter. 'Executive head-hunting.' *New Soc.*, XXXII (25 May 1978), 416–17.

3785 **McGivern**, C. 'Management succession.' *Manage. Decis.*, XVI, 1 (1978), 32–42.

3786 **Thorley**, Stan. 'Training supervisors and the cascade effect: how it helped hospital hygiene.' *Pers. Manage.*, X, 4 (April 1978), 44–7.

3787 **Williams**, T. A. and **Alford**, T. J. 'Learning to manage learning: increasing organizational capability through the self-education of managers.' *Hum. Relat.*, XXXI (December 1978), 1031–53.

3788 **Bennison**, M. 'A new approach to career management.' *Pers. Manage.*, XI, 10 (October 1979), 58–62.

3789 **Edwards**, Joe. 'Overriding apathy in supervisory training.' *Pers. Manage.*, XI, 5 (May 1979), 44–8.

3790 **Guglielmino**, P. J. and **Carroll**, A. B. 'The hierarchy of management skills: future professional development for mid-level managers.' *Manage. Decis.*, XVII, 4 (1979), 341–5.

3791 **Margerison**, Charles J. 'Action-based selection for top management jobs.' *J. Gen. Manage.*, VII (Summer 1979), 78–82.

3792 **Margerison**, Charles J. 'Highway to managerial success.' *Pers. Manage.*, XI, 8 (August 1979), 24–8.

3793 **Paul**, Nancy. 'Assertiveness without tears: a training programme for executive equality.' *Pers. Manage.*, XI, 4 (April 1979), 37–40.

3794 **Salaman**, Graeme. 'Management development and organization theory.' *J. Eur. Ind. Train.*, II, 7 (1979), 7–11.

3795 **Saynor**, J. and **Ryan**, M. 'Management development: a contextual learning programme.' *J. Eur. Ind. Train.*, III, 6 (1979), 2–6.

3796 **Stewart**, Sandy, **Prandy**, Kenneth and **Blackburn**, Robert. 'Social stratification and careers into management.' Colloquium on Management and Industrial Relations, 1979. *Proceedings.* p. 68–77.

3797 **Thomason**, George. 'Social stratification and careers into management: a critique.' Colloquium on Management and Industrial Relations, 1979 *Proceedings.* p. 78–80.

See also: 3322; 6392.

iv. *Industrial Relations Training*

This section contains the more general material on industrial relations training. Material on the training of shop stewards and trade union officers is classified at Part Three, II, K, and that on safety education and training is classified at Part Six, IV, D, 2.

3798 **British Institute of Management.** *Industrial relations: training for managers: report and recommendations of a BIM working party.* London: The Institute, 1971. v, 28p.

3799 **Lowry**, Pat. 'Industrial relations training: the need for action.' *Pers. Manage.*, III, 10 (October 1971), 29–31.

3800 **Commission on Industrial Relations.** *Industrial relations training.* London: H.M.S.O., 1972. 14p. (Report 33.)

3801 **Kettle**, C. V. 'Training in industrial relations.' Torrington, Derek P. (ed.). *Handbook of industrial relations.* 1972. p. 221–37.

3802 **Knibbs**, John R. and **Henderson**, John. 'Industrial relations and management development.' *Ind. Train. Int.*, VII, 1 (January 1972), 21–4.

3803 **Walsh**, B. 'A one-day course in industrial relations.' *Ind. Commer. Train.*, IV, 5 (May 1972), 242–5.

3804 **Young**, D. and **Talbot**, J. 'Industrial relations training in the company framework.' *Ind. Train. Int.*, VII, 1 (January 1972), 17–20.

3805 **Commission on Industrial Relations.** *Industrial relations training: statistical supplement.* London: H.M.S.O., 1973, viii, 95p. (Report 33A.)

3806 **Dalziel**, S. J. 'A wasted opportunity.' *Pers. Manage.*, V, 2 (February 1973), 28–9.

3807 **Jones**, J. A. G. 'Training for personnel officers in the Health Service.' *Pers. Manage.*, V, 5 (May 1973), 35–7.

3808 **Kenney**, John. 'Developments in training for personnel management.' *Pers. Manage.*, V, 10 (October 1973), 26–8, 44.

3809 **Lawrence**, Susanne. 'Industrial relations training: oases in the desert.' *Pers. Manage.*, V, 7 (July 1973), 26–9.

3810 **Paper and Paper Products Industry Training Board.** *An approach to industrial relations training within a company.* London: The Board, 1973.

3811 **Pedler**, Malcolm J. 'Industrial relations training on the shop floor.' *J. Eur. Train.*, II, 3 (1973), 214–26.

3812 **Personnel Management.** 'The C.I.R. on industrial relations training.' *Pers. Manage.*, V, 2 (February 1973), 26–9.

3813 **Purcell**, John. 'Training for change in industrial relations.' *Ind. Commer. Train.*, V, 3 (March 1973), 134–9.

3814 **Farnham**, David. 'Some aspects on the demand for, and supply of industrial relations courses for managers.' *J. Ind. Affairs*, I, 2 (March 1974), 49–51.

3815 **Kniveton**, Bromley H. 'Industrial negotiating: some training implications.' *Ind. Relat. J.*, V, 3 (Autumn 1974), 27–37.

3816 **Lawrence**, Susanne. 'Personnel management training on the job.' *Pers. Manage.*, VI, 9 (September 1974), 33–6.

3817 **Lawson**, B. and **Bennett**, R. 'Training for personnel management in local government.' *Ind. Commer. Train.*, VI, 4 (April 1974), 160–67.

3818 **Leary**, Malcolm. 'Industrial relations: techniques and methods of training.' *Ind. Commer. Train.*, VI, 5 (May 1974), 226–31.

3819 **Industrial and Commercial Training.** 'Industrial relations training for the smaller company.' *Ind. Commer. Train.*, VII, 12 (December 1975), 513–17.

3820 **National Economic Development Office,** Management Education, Training and Development Committee. *Management training in industrial relations.* London: N.E.D.O., 1975. VII, 39p.

3821 **Rubber and Plastics Processing Industry Training Board.** *Industrial relations training within a company: an approach for trade union representatives.* Brentford: The Board, 1975. 16p.

3822 **Agnew**, W. M. 'Industrial relations in action.' *Ind. Commer. Train.*, VIII, 3 (March 1976), 121–3.

3823 **Bamber**, Greg J. and **Leggett**, Chris. 'Industrial relations training at the Civil Service College: some comments on the Edinburgh Centre.' *Public Adm.*, LIV (Summer 1976), 211–22.

3824 **Kniveton**, Bromley H. 'Negotiation training and social psychology.' *Ind. Relat. J.*, VI, 4 (Winter 1975–76), 59–72.

3825 **Wellens**, John. 'Training in the new legislation.' *Ind. Commer. Train.*, VIII, 11 (November 1976), 436–8.

3826 **Williams**, J. and **Rolfe**, B. 'Training in negotiating skills.' *Educ. Train.*, XVIII, 11–12 (November–December 1976), 297–9.

3827 **Hyett**, K. 'IR training for line managers.' *Ind. Commer. Train.*, IX, 4 (April 1977), 165–9.

3828 **Keenan**, Tony, **Paterson**, Janis and **Craig**, Vic. 'Personnel skills the workshop way.' *Pers. Manage.*, IX, 6 (June 1977), 34–6, 43.

3829 **Kilcourse**, Tom. 'IR training: what line managers need to know.' *Pers. Manage.*, IX, 5 (May 1977), 32–5.

3830 **Knibbs**, John R. 'Negotiating skills training.' *Pers. Rev.*, VI, 1 (Winter 1977), 29–31.

3831 **Marsh**, Arthur Ivor. 'Tailoring IR training to the manager and his needs.' *Pers. Manage.*, IX, 8 (August 1977), 26–7, 35.

3832 **Towers**, M. 'New laws: new managers?' *Ind. Commer. Train.*, IX, 2 (February 1977), 50–57.

3833 **Walton**, Frank. *Industrial relations training: consultation and negotiation.* London: Local Government Training Board, 1977. 28p.

3834 **Wilson**, W. and **Nichol**, J. B. 'Worker education for industrial democracy.' Ottaway, R. (ed.). *Humanising the workplace.* 1977. p. 78–100.

3835 **Barrington**, Harry. 'Developing personnel training for the management trainee.' *Pers.*

Manage., x, 10 (October 1978), 38–41.

3836 **Brewster**, Chris J. and **Connock**, Steve L. 'Feeding company policy into IR training.' *Pers. Manage.*, x, 8 (August 1978), 28–30.

3837 **Kniveton**, Bromley H. and **Towers**, Brian. *Training for negotiating: a guide for management and employee negotiators.* London: Business Books, 1978. 213p.

3838 **Wright**, Samuel. 'Industrial relations training: co-ordinating resources.' *Ind. Commer. Train.*, x, 9 (September 1978), 358–61.

3839 **Brewster**, C. J. and **Connock**, S. L. 'An integrated approach to IR training.' *Ind. Commer. Train.*, xi, 2 (February 1979), 69–71.

3840 **Gore**, T. 'Trade unions: background for trainers.' *Ind. Commer. Train.*, xi, 4 (April 1979), 150–54.

See also: 1271; 1611; 1616; 1739; 2632; 2714; 3446; 3456.

C. THE LEVEL AND STRUCTURE OF EMPLOYMENT

The literature on employment and unemployment overlaps considerably. Hence this section should be consulted in conjunction with Part Six, II, D; Part Six, IV, A, 3, d; and Part Seven, II, A – C.

1. General

In addition to containing general works on the level and structure of employment, this section includes general references on such topics as labour supply and demand; the relationship between employment, output, and productivity; double jobholding; and models for forecasting employment. See also Part Six, II, D, 1.

3841 **Gribble**, I. A. *Labour supply and industrialization: two case studies, Britain and the United States of America to c. 1860.* 1971. (Ph.D. thesis, University of Sheffield.)

3842 **Leicester**, C. S. 'Future manpower requirements of the British economy.' Smith, A. R. (ed.). *Models of manpower systems.* 1971. p. 13–35.
Partly reprinted in Bartholomew, D. J. (ed.). *Manpower planning.* 1976. p. 254–78.

3843 **Richards**, S. F. *A comparative study of manpower in selected industries with similar technologies in India and the United Kingdom.* 1971. (M.Phil. thesis, London School of Economics.)

3844 **Williams**, Roger and **Guest**, David. 'Are the middle classes becoming work shy?' *New Soc.*, xviii (1 July 1971), 9–11.
Reprinted in Weir, M. (ed.). *Job satisfaction.* 1976. p. 120–25.

3845 **Department of Employment**. *Classification of occupations and directory of occupational titles.* London: H.M.S.O., 1972. 3 v.

3846 **Dougherty**, C. R. S. 'Substitution and the structure of the labour force.' *Econ. J.*, LXXXII, 325 (March 1972), 170–82.

3847 **Leicester**, Colin. *Britain 2001 AD: an analysis of economic activity, work and leisure time at the turn of the century.* London: H.M.S.O., 1972. vii, 46p.

3848 **Ross**, Jack C. and **Anderson**, Raoul R. 'Occupational pluralism: expansive strategies in barbering.' *Sociol. Rev.*, xx, 2 (May 1972), 207–27.
Theoretical study of the concept of occupation.

3849 **Yates**, John. 'The second job mystery.' *New Soc.*, xx (25 May 1972), 401–2.

3850 **Godfrey**, Leslie and **Taylor**, Jim. 'Earnings changes in the United Kingdom 1954–70: excess labour supply, expected inflation and union influence.' *Oxf. Univ. Inst. Econ. Stat. Bull.*, xxxv, 3 (August 1973), 197–216.

3851 **Leicester**, Colin. 'Vacancies and the demand for labour.' *I.M.S. Monit.*, II, 3 (October 1973), 105–25.

3852 **Leicester**, Colin and **Hobbs**, Judith. 'Changing patterns in the labour force.' *Pers. Manage.*, v, 5 (May 1973), 24–7.

3853 **Morgan**, Terry. 'The whys and wherefores of occupational classification.' *Pers. Manage.*, v, 4 (April 1973), 22–5, 37.

3854 **Thomas**, R. Barry. 'On the definition of "shortages" in administered labour markets.' *Manchr. Sch. Econ. Soc. Stud.*, XLI (1973), 169–86.

3855 **Bosworth**, Derek L. 'Production functions and skill requirements.' Wabe, J. (ed.). *Problems in manpower forecasting.* 1974. p. 153–96.

3856 **Coxon**, A. P. M. and **Jones**, C. L. 'Problems in the selection of occupational titles.' *Sociol. Rev.*, xxii, 3 (August 1974), 369–84.

3857 **Evans**, Graham J. 'The labour market mechanism and the hoarding of manpower.' Wabe, J. (ed.). *Problems in manpower forecasting.* 1974. p. 97–152.

3858 **Harley**, C. K. 'Skilled labour and the choice of technique in Edwardian industry.' *Explor. Econ. Hist.*, xi, 4 (Summer 1974), 391–414.

3859 **Lindley**, Robert M. 'Manpower movements and the supply of labour.' Wabe, J. (ed.). *Problems in manpower forecasting.* 1974. p. 239–81.

3860 **Napier**, S. 'Moonlighting madness.' *Ind. Soc.*, LVI, 5 (September–October 1974), 9.

3861 **Parikh**, Ashok. 'An analysis of sectoral employment in the U.K.' *Manchr. Sch. Econ. Soc. Stud.*, XLII (December 1974), 340–58.

3862 **Roberts**, Colin J. 'The demand for manpower: employment functions.' Wabe, J. (ed.). *Problems in manpower forecasting.* 1974. p. 197–238.

3863 **Tompson**, B. E. *The changing employment opportunities since 1952 and the implications for the 1980's.* 1973–4. (M.Sc. thesis, University of Bath.)

3864 **Bowers**, John K. 'British activity rates: a survey of research.' *Scott. J. Polit. Econ.*, XXII, 1 (February 1975), 57–90.

3865 **Briscoe**, Geoff and **Peel**, D. A. 'The specification of the short-run employment function: the demand for labour in the U.K. manufacturing sector 1955–1972.' *Oxf. Univ. Inst. Econ. Stat. Bull.*, XXXVII (May 1975), 115–42.

3866 **Central Office of Information.** *Manpower and employment in Britain: occupations and conditions of work.* London: H.M.S.O., 1975. 61p. (Reference pamphlet 139.)

3867 **Department of Employment Gazette.** 'Labour force projections 1976–1991: Great Britain and the regions.' *Dep. Employment Gaz.*, LXXXIII, 12 (December 1975), 1258 –63.

3868 **Department of Employment Gazette.** 'View of occupational employment in 1981.' *Dep. Employment Gaz.*, LXXXIII, 7 (July 1975), 619–22.

3869 **Hall**, Ray. 'Early nineteenth century occupational structures: parish registers as a source of information.' *Local Historian*, X, 1 (May 1975), 340–43.

3870 **Knights**, D. 'Classificatory scheme for occupations.' *Br. J. Sociol.*, XXVI, 3 (September 1975), 294–308.

3871 **McKendrick**, S. 'Inter-industry analysis of labour hoarding in Britain 1953–1972.' *Appl. Econ.*, VII, 2 (June 1975), 101–17.

3872 **Mulvey**, Charles and **Trevithick**, J. A. 'Expectations hypothesis under changing employment conditions.' *J. Econ. Stud.*, II, 1 (May 1975), 67–71.

3873 **Stoneman**, Paul. 'Effect of computers on the demand for labour in the United Kingdom.' *Econ. J.*, LXXXV, 339 (September 1975), 590–606.

3874 **Alden**, Jeremy D. *The extent and nature of double-job holding in Great Britain.* 1976. (Ph.D. thesis, University of Wales Institute of Science and Technology.)

3875 **Department of Employment**, Unit for Manpower Studies. *The changing structure of the labour force: project report.* London: The Unit, 1976.

3876 **Oppenheimer**, P. M. 'Employment, balance of payments and oil in the United Kingdom.' *Three Banks Rev.*, CIX (March 1976), 3–25.

3877 **Slattery**, D. G. *The estimation of full employment output in the Republic of Ireland.* 1976. (Ph.D. thesis, Queen's University, Belfast.)

3878 **Alden**, Jeremy D. 'Double jobholding.' *Ind. Relat. J.*, VIII, 3 (Autumn 1977), 14–33.

3879 **Thomas**, R. Barry and **Deaton**, David. *Labour shortage and economic analysis: a study of occupational labour markets.* Oxford: Blackwell, 1977. 264p. (Warwick studies in industrial relations.)

3880 **Beaumont**, Philip B. 'The duration of registered vacancies: an exploratory exercise.' *Scott. J. Pol. Econ.*, XXV (February 1978), 75–87.

3881 **Central Office of Information.** *Manpower and employment in Britain.* London: H.M.S.O., 1978. ii, 34p.

3882 **Gottmann**, Jean. 'Urbanisation and employment: towards a general theory.' *Town Plann. Rev.*, XLIX (July 1978), 393 –401.

3883 **Harris**, Donald F. and **Taylor**, F. John. *The service sector: its changing role as a source of employment.* London: Centre for Environmental Studies, 1978. 19p. (Research papers 25.)

3884 **Hart**, R. A. 'The short-run demand for workers and hours: a recursive model.' *Rev. Econ. Stud.*, XLV (June 1978), 299–309.

3885 **Hazeldine**, Tim. 'New specifications for employment and hours function.' *Economica*, XLV (May 1978), 179–93.

3886 **Leslie**, Derek G. and **Laing**, Clive. 'The theory and measurement of labour hoarding.' *Scott. J. Polit. Econ.*, XXV (February 1978), 41–56.

3887 **Nickell**, S. J. 'Fixed costs, employment and labour demand over the cycle.' *Economica*, XLV (November 1978), 329–45.

3888 **Peel**, D. A. and **Walker**, Ian. 'Short-run employment functions, excess supply and the speed of adjustment: a note.' *Economica*, XLV (May 1978), 195–202.

3889 **University of Warwick**, Manpower Research Group. *Britain's medium-term employment prospects.* Coventry: University of Warwick, 1978. 128p.

Prepared by Robert M. Lindley, D. P. B. Elias, J. D. Whitley, R. A. Wilson, P. C. Collier, P. A. Dutton, B. A. Harper, and D. J. E. Smith.

3890 **Centre for Alternative Industrial and Technological Systems.** *Energy options and employment.* London: The Centre, 1979. 146p.

3891 **Dean**, Andrew. 'A survey of the current employment situation.' *Manage. Decis.*, XVII, 3 (1979), 241–55.

3892 **Dutton**, Patricia Ann. *The employment effects of mergers: a case study of the GEC, AEI and English Electric mergers.* 1979. (Ph.D. thesis, University of Warwick.)

3893 **Knox**, Frank. *Labour supply in economic development: the future of the large market economies to the year 2000.* London: Saxon House, 1979. vi, 114p.

3894 **Pearce**, David. *Employment and energy future in the UK: an analysis of the CAITS scenario.* Aberdeen: University of Aberdeen, Department of Political Economy, 1979. 62p.

CAITS: Centre for Alternative Industrial and Technological Systems.

3895 **Robinson**, Olive. 'Part-time employment in the EEC: a marginal labour force?' *Three Banks Rev.*, CXXII (June 1979), 61–76.

3896 **Thornton**, P. and **Wheelock**, V. 'What future for employment?' *Employee Relat.*, I, I (1979), 3–6.

3897 **Zabalza**, Antoni. 'A note on the estimation of subjective rates of discount from labour supply functions.' *Economica*, XLVI (May 1979), 197–202.
See also: 85; 291; 1119; 2913; 2959; 3141; 3150; 3898; 3921; 3963; 3971; 3978; 3989; 4019; 4121; 4149; 4198; 5107.

2. Regional Distribution of Employment

For the purposes of this section Wales, Scotland, and Ireland are treated as regions, and material on employment in these areas is generally classified here. See also Part Six, II, D, 5; Part Six, II, E, 4; Part Six, III, C; and Part Seven, II, D, 3.

3898 **Alden**, Jeremy D. 'Double job-holding: a regional analysis of Scotland.' *Scott. J. Polit. Econ.*, XVIII (February 1971), 99–112.

3899 **Beard**, R. 'Changing patterns of employment in the Forest of Dean.' *Geogr.*, LVI (January 1971), 43–6.

3900 **Brownrigg**, M. 'The regional income multipliers: an attempt to complete the model.' *Scott. J. Polit. Econ.*, XVIII, 3 (November 1971), 281–97.

3901 **Deeny**, James. *The Irish worker: a demographic study of the labour force in Ireland.* Dublin: Institute of Public Administration, 1971. 97p.

3902 **McNie**, W. M. *Long run local employment multiplier effects in Great Britain, 1921–51.* 1971. (Ph.D. thesis, University of Cambridge.)

3903 **Ruddy**, Sheila Ann, **Smith**, Barbara Mary Dimond and **Cherry**, Gordon Emanuel. *Employment problems in a country town: study of Bridgnorth, Shropshire.* Birmingham: University of Birmingham Centre for Urban and Regional Studies, 1971. 52p.

3904 **Smith**, P. *Employment linkages in the Coventry sub-region of the West Midlands.* 1971. (Ph.D. thesis, University of Birmingham.)

3905 **Thomas**, W. K. *Industry and employment in metropolitan Kent, 1945–1960.* 1971. (Ph.D. thesis, London School of Economics.)

3906 **Burns**, Michael E. 'Regional Phillips curves: a further note.' *Oxf. Univ. Inst. Econ. Stat. Bull.*, XXXIV (August 1972), 295–307.

3907 **Duggon**, Edward Patrick. *Impact of industrialization on an urban labour market: Birmingham, 1770–1860.* 1972. (Ph.D. thesis, University of Wisconsin.)

3908 **Essex County Council Planning Department.** *Chelmsford study: employment in Chelmsford 1972.* Chelmsford: The Council, 1972. 60p.

3909 **Mortlock**, David. 'Employment changes in Greater London.' *Greater London Council Intell. Unit Q. Bull.*, XX (September 1972), 16–26.

3910 **Moyes**, A. 'Employment change in the North Staffordshire conurbation 1951–1966.' *N. Staffs. J. Field Stud.*, XII (1972), 83–100.

3911 **Chisholm**, Michael and **Oeppen**, Jim. *Changing patterns of employment: regional specialisation and industrial localisation in Britain.* London: Croom Helm, 1973. 127p.

3912 **Randall**, J. N. 'Shift-share analysis as a guide to the employment performance of West Central Scotland.' *Scott. J. Polit. Econ.*, XX (February 1973), 1–26.

3913 **Smith**, Barbara Mary Dimond. *Black Country employment, 1959–70: an analysis based on employment exchange data and incorporating comparisons between inner and outer exchanges between the Black Country and Birmingham and Great Britain.* Birmingham: University of Birmingham Centre for Urban and Regional Studies, 1973. 178p.

3914 **Wagstaff**, H. R. 'Employment multipliers in rural Scotland.' *Scott. J. Polit. Econ.*, XX, 3 (November 1973), 239–61.

3915 **Black**, W. and **Jefferson**, C. W. *Regional employment patterns in Northern Ireland.* Dublin: Economic and Social Research Institute, 1974. (Institute papers 73.)

3916 **Carstairs**, Andrew McLaren. *The Tayside industrial population: the changing character and distribution of the industrial population in the Tayside area 1911–51.* Dundee: Abertay Historical Society, 1974. 115p.

3917 **Henry**, Edmund W. *Irish full employment structures 1968 and 1975.* Dublin: Economic and Social Research Institute, 1974. 109p.

3918 **O'Cleireacain**, Carol Chapman. 'Labour market trends in London and the rest of the South-East.' *Urb. Stud.*, XI (October 1974), 329–39.

3919 **Weeden**, R. *Regional rates of growth of employment: an analysis of variance treatment.* Cambridge: Cambridge U.P., 1974. 48p.

3920 **Black**, W. and **Slattery**, D. G. 'Regional and national variations in employment and unemployment: Northern Ireland, a case study.' *Scott. J. Polit. Econ.*, XXII, 2 (June 1975), 195–205.

3921 **Department of Employment Gazette.** 'Labour force projections 1976–1991: Great Britain and the regions.' *Dep. Employment Gaz.*, LXXXIII, 12 (December 1975), 1258–63.

3922 **Docklands Development Team.** *Work and industry in East London.* London: The Team, 1975. 42p. (Working papers of consultation 2.)

3923 **Flynn**, N. *The structure of employment in new industries in the northern region since 1948.* 1975. (M.A. thesis, University of Newcastle-upon-Tyne.)

3924 **Frost**, M. E. *Regional employment change in Great Britain, 1952–68, with special reference to the influence of government policy on the northern* *region.* 1975. (Ph.D. thesis, London School of Economics.)

3925 **Hodgson**, J. *Changes in the structure of employment in the northern region of England, 1921–71.* 1975. (M.A. thesis, University of Newcastle upon Tyne.)

3926 **Scottish Development Department.** *Forecasting employment for regional reports and structure plans: regional reports advice.* Edinburgh: The Department, 1975. 33p.

3927 **Buck**, T. W. and **Atkins**, M. H. 'Impact of British regional policies on employment growth.' *Oxf. Econ. Pap.*, xxviii, 1 (March 1976), 118–32.

3928 **Christie**, P. S. *Occupations in Portsmouth, 1550–1851.* 1976. (M.Phil. thesis, Council for National Academic Awards.)

3929 **Hall**, David. 'Policy reversal by G. L. C.' *Town Ctry Plann.*, xliv (March 1976), 150–52.
    Employment policy in Greater London.

3930 **Corkindale**, John. 'The decline of employment in metropolitan areas.' *Dep. Employment Gaz.*, lxxxv, 11 (November 1977), 1199–1202.

3931 **Department of Employment Gazette.** 'North Sea oil industry tests Scottish skills.' *Dep. Employment Gaz.*, lxxxv, 3 (March 1977), 220–25.

3932 **Lennon**, G. 'Trades and occupations of Portaferry in the mid 19th century.' *Upper Ards Hist. Soc. J.*, 1 (1977), 26–8.

3933 **Smith**, E. *Short run labour supply: evidence from manufacturing establishments in the North East.* 1977. (M.Phil. thesis, University of Durham.)

3934 **Williams**, L. J. and **Boyns**, T. 'Occupation in Wales, 1851–1971.' *Bull. Econ. Res.*, xxix (November 1977), 71–83.

3935 **Button**, Kenneth J. 'Employment and industrial decline in the inner areas of British cities: the experience of 1962–1977.' *J. Ind. Affairs*, vi, 1 (Autumn 1978), 1–6.

3936 **Dennis**, Robert. 'The decline of manufacturing employment in Greater London: 1966–74.' *Urb. Stud.*, xv (February 1978), 63–73.

3937 **Norris**, G. M. 'Industrial paternalist capitalism and local labour markets.' *Sociology*, xii (September 1978), 469–89.

3938 **Town**, Stephen W. *After the mines: changing employment opportunities in a South Wales valley.* Cardiff: University of Wales Press, 1978. 138p.

3939 **Treble**, J. H. 'The seasonal demand for adult labour in Glasgow, 1890–1914.' *Soc. Hist.*, iii, 2 (January 1978), 43–60.

3940 **Cheshire**, Paul C. 'Inner areas as spatial labour markets: a critique of the inner area studies.' *Urb. Stud.*, xvi (February 1979), 29–43.

3941 **Needham**, Barrie. *Guidelines for a local employment study.* London: Saxon, 1979. 111p.

3942 **Sadler**, Peter G. and **Jarvis**, Richard. *The*

Welsh social accounts, 1968: a labour dimension. Cardiff: Welsh Council, 1979. 38p.

See also: 3943; 3944; 3983; 4034; 4080; 4094; 4123; 4163; 4432; 4493; 4496; 4502; 4503; 4506; 4511; 4514; 4517; 4530.

3. Occupational and Industrial Distribution of Employment

See also Part Six, II, B, 2, b; Part Six, II, B, 3, b, ii – iii; Part Six, II, D, 6; and Part Seven, II, D, 3.

a. AGRICULTURE, FORESTRY, AND FISHING

3943 **National Economic Development Committee**, Economic Development Committee for the Agricultural Industry. *Agricultural manpower in England and Wales.* London: H.M.S.O., 1972. vi, 126p.

3944 **Thomas**, C. 'Agricultural employment in nineteenth-century Wales.' *Welsh Hist. Rev.*, vi (1972), 143–60.

3945 **Tyler**, G. J. 'Factors affecting the size of the labour force and the level of earnings in U.K. agriculture 1948–65.' *Oxf. Agrar. Stud.*, i, 1 (1972), 20–45.

3946 **Bessell**, James Edward. *The younger worker in agriculture: projections to 1980.* London: N.E.D.O., 1973. vii, 50p.

3947 **Gasson**, Ruth. *Mobility of farm workers: a study of the effects of towns and industrial employment on the supply of farm labour.* Cambridge: Cambridge University, Department of Land Economy, 1974. 96p. (Occasional papers 2.)

3948 **Gasson**, Ruth. 'Town expansion and the farm worker.' *Town Ctry Plann.*, xlii (April 1974), 217–22.

3949 **Gasson**, Ruth. 'Turnover and size of labour force on farms.' *J. Agric. Econ.*, xxv, 2 (May 1974), 115–27.

3950 **Dewey**, P. E. 'Agricultural labour supply in England and Wales during the first world war.' *Econ. Hist. Rev.*, xxviii, 1 (February 1975), 100–112.

3951 **Collins**, E. J. T. 'Migrant labour in British agriculture in the nineteenth century.' *Econ. Hist. Rev.*, xxix, 1 (February 1976), 38–59.

3952 **Nunn**, Paul. 'Aristocratic estates and employment in South Yorkshire, 1700–1800.' Pollard, S. and Holmes, C. (eds.). *Essays in the economic and social history of South Yorkshire.* 1976. p. 28–45.

3953 **Folley**, Roger Roland Westwell. *Employment in horticulture: an estimate of the number of people in England and Wales, in total and by region whose present livelihood depends upon the exercise of horticultural skill…* London: Wye College Agricultural Economics Unit, 1978. 42p.

3954 **O'Rourke**, A. D. and **McStay**, T. *Output and employment in the Irish food industry to 1990.*

Dublin: Economic and Social Research Institute, 1979. 150p.
See also: 4140; 4477; 4482; 4496.

b. MINING, MANUFACTURING, AND CONSTRUCTION

3955 **Craven**, T. *An analysis of seasonal and cyclical movements in employment in the British motor vehicle industry over the period 1949–1969.* 1971. (M.B.A. thesis, Queen's University, Belfast.)

3956 **National Economic Development Committee**, Economic Development Committee for the Electronics Industry. *Qualified manpower in the electronics industry: a preliminary report.* London: N.E.D.O., 1971. 44p.

3957 **Bell**, R. M. N. *Changing technology and manpower requirements in the engineering industry.* Brighton: Sussex University Press, 1972. 101p. (Science Policy Research Unit research reports 3.)

3958 **Institute of Building**. *Manpower crisis 1973.* London: The Institute, 1973. 18p.
    Papers presented at the Annual Conference, 1972.

3959 **National Economic Development Office.** *Chemicals manpower in Europe: report of a comparative study of industrial relations manpower productivity in the U.K., France, Germany, and Holland.* London: H.M.S.O., 1973. v, 67p.

3960 **Senker**, Peter and **Huggett**, Charlotte. *Technology and manpower in the UK engineering industry: an interim report 1973.* London: Engineering Industry Training Board, 1973. 44p. (Occasional papers 3.)

3961 **Central Policy Review Staff**. *Future of the British car industry: a report.* London: H.M.S.O., 1975. xvi, 141p.

3962 **Lindley**, Robert Michael. 'Demand for apprentice recruits by the engineering industry 1951–1971.' *Scott. J. Polit. Econ.,* XXII, 1 (February 1975), 1–29.

3963 **Phipps**, Anthony J. 'The relationship between output and employment in British manufacturing industry.' *Oxf. Univ. Inst. Econ. Stat. Bull.,* XXXVII (February 1975), 49–63.

3964 **Plant**, J. J. *A survey of labour availability and requirements on London local authority construction sites.* London: Greater London Council, 1975. 64p.

3965 **Shah**, S. *Immigrants and employment in the clothing industry: the rag trade in London's East End.* London: Runnymede Trust, 1975. 42p.

3966 **Hartley**, Keith and **Corcoran**, William J. 'British aircraft firms and the employment effects of defence contracts.' *Bull. Econ. Res.,* XXVIII (November 1976), 95–103.

3967 **Hogg**, Alexander and **Hutcheson**, A. MacGregor. 'Scotland and offshore oil: the developing impact.' *Scott. Geogr. Mag.,* XCII (September 1976), 75–9.

3968 **Pratten**, Clifford F. and **Atkinson**, A. G. 'The use of manpower in British manufacturing industry.' *Dep. Employment Gaz.,* LXXXIV, 6 (June 1976), 571–6.

3969 **Wright**, S. C. *The fixed quota supply system for craft labour in the general printing industry and its effect on economic growth.* 1975–6. (M.Sc. thesis, University of Bath.)

3970 **Department of Employment Gazette.** 'The declining asset: recent surveys of engineering craftsmen.' *Dep. Employment Gaz.,* LXXXV, 4 (April 1977), 345–52.

3971 **Gatrell**, V. A. C. 'Labour, power and the size of firms in Lancashire cotton in the second quarter of the nineteenth century.' *Econ. Hist. Rev.,* XXX (1977), 95–139.

3972 **Lindley**, Robert Michael. *Modelling a labour market: the case of engineering craftsmen.* 1977. (Ph.D. thesis, University of Warwick.)

3973 **National Economic Development Office**, Committee on the Supply and Utilisation of Skilled Engineering Manpower. *Engineering craftsmen: shortages and related problems.* London: N.E.D.O., 1977. 51p.

3974 **North East Trade Union Studies Information Unit.** *Direct labour: the answer to building chaos: a joint report produced by the TUSIU and Tyne and Wear Resource Centre.* Newcastle upon Tyne: The Unit, 1977.

3975 **Wabe**, John Stuart. *Manpower changes in the engineering industry.* London: Engineering Industry Training Board, 1977. 141p.

3976 **Irvin**, G. W. 'Labour intensive technology and distribution: road construction revisited.' *Oxf. Univ. Inst. Econ. Stat. Bull.,* XL, 1 (February 1978), 37–53.

3977 **National Economic Development Committee**, Sector Working Party for Heating, Ventilating, Air Conditioning and Refrigeration Equipment. *Skill shortages in the H.V.A.C.R. industry.* London: N.E.D.O., 1979.

See also: 4056; 4061; 4123; 4493; 4509; 4530; 4531; 4535.

c. TRANSPORT AND DISTRIBUTION

3978 **Hill**, John Michael Meath. *The seafaring career: a study of the forces affecting joining, serving and leaving the Merchant Navy.* London: Tavistock Institute of Human Relations, 1972. 158p.

3979 **National Economic Development Committee**, Economic Development Committee for the Distributive Trades. *Manpower and pay in retail distribution.* London: N.E.D.O., 1974. 76p.

3980 **Moreby**, D. H. *The human element in shipping.* London: Seatrade Publications, 1975. xi, 214p.

3981 **Department of Employment Gazette.** 'Work patterns in retailing: an approach to information on occupations.' *Dep. Employment Gaz.,* LXXXIV, 5 (May 1976), 461–5.

3982 **Department of Employment Gazette.** 'Coping with labour shortage: bus drivers and draughtsmen.' *Dep. Employment Gaz.*, LXXXV, 1 (January 1977), 8–13.

3983 **Lee**, Joseph. 'Railway labour in Ireland, 1833–1856.' *Saothar*, V (1979), 9–26.

d. WHITE-COLLAR, PROFESSIONAL, AND PUBLIC ADMINISTRATION

3984 **Central Statistical Office.** *Qualified manpower in Great Britain: the 1966 census of population.* London: H.M.S.O., 1971. iii, 52p. (Studies in official statistics 18.)

3985 **Economic Consultants Limited.** *Demand and supply for office workers and the local impact of office development.* London: Location of Offices Bureau, 1971. 144p.

3986 **Mulkay**, M. J. and **Turner**, B. S. 'Over-production of personnel and innovation in three social settings.' *Sociology*, V, 1 (January 1971), 47–61.

3987 **New Scientist.** 'Scientific manpower in Britain and abroad.' *New Sci.*, L, 752 (20 May 1971), 440–62.

3988 **Wroe**, D. C. L. and **Bishop**, H. E. 'Highly qualified manpower in the United Kingdom: relevant official statistics.' Bartholomew, D. J. and Morris, B. R. (eds.). *Aspects of manpower planning.* 1971. p. 18–30.

3989 **Jones**, Richard Merfyn. 'The market for labour and the office staff sector.' *Br. J. Ind. Relat.*, X, 2 (July 1972), 193–205.

3990 **Layton**, C., **Harlow**, C. and **Hoghton**, C. *Ten innovations: an international study on technological development and the use of qualified scientists and engineers in ten industries.* London: Allen & Unwin, 1972. xii, 199p.

3991 **Sheriff**, P. E. 'Outsiders in a closed career.' *Public Adm.*, L, 4 (Winter 1972), 397–417. Mature entrants to the Civil Service.

3992 **Webb**, D. R. 'The employment of 1970 sociology graduates: a preliminary report.' *Sociology*, VI, 3 (September 1972), 433–42.

3993 **Bury**, M. O. 'Graduates in industry.' Greenaway, H. and Williams, G. (eds.). *Patterns of change in graduate employment.* 1973. p. 101–10.

3994 **Department of Trade and Industry.** *Survey of professional scientists 1971.* London: H.M.S.O., 1973. v, 79p. (Studies in technological manpower 4.)

3995 **Greenaway**, Harriet. 'The impact of educational policy.' Greenaway, H. and Williams, G. (eds.). *Patterns of change in graduate employment.* 1973. p. 1–24.

3996 **Greenaway**, Harriet and **Williams**, Gareth. 'Is there a crisis?' Greenaway, H. and Williams, G. (eds.). *Patterns of change in graduate employment.* 1973. p. 155–60.

3997 **Greenaway**, Harriet and **Williams**, Gareth (eds.). *Patterns of change in graduate employment.* London: Society for Research into Higher Education, 1973. 171p. (Research into higher education monographs 19.)

3998 **Johnson**, Terence. 'Imperialism and the professions: notes on the development of professional occupations in Britain's colonies and the new states.' Halmos, P. (ed.). *Professionalization and social change.* 1973. p. 281–310.

3999 **London University**, Careers Advisory Service. *Main areas of graduate employment.* London: London University, 1973. 46p. Second edition.

4000 **Metcalf**, David. 'Pay dispersion, information and returns to search in a professional labour market.' *Rev. Econ. Stud.*, XL, 4 (October 1973), 491–505.

4001 **Robins**, W. G. H. 'Mid-career problems of graduates in industry.' Greenaway, H. and Williams, G. (eds.). *Patterns of change in graduate employment.* 1973. p. 111–22.

4002 **Rudd**, Ernest. 'Graduate study and the market for labour.' Greenaway, H. and Williams, G. (eds.). *Patterns of change in graduate employment.* 1973. p. 67–76.

4003 **Snow**, T. 'Observations on the present crisis.' Greenaway, H. and Williams, G. (eds.). *Patterns of change in graduate employment.* 1973. p. 85–100.

4004 **Webb**, David. 'Some factors associated with the employment of sociology graduates in social work.' *Sociol. Rev.*, XXI, 4 (November 1973), 599–612.

4005 **Whybrew**, E. G. 'Trends in the labour market for highly qualified manpower.' Greenaway, H. and Williams, G. (eds.). *Patterns of change in graduate employment.* 1973. p. 35–40.

4006 **Williams**, Gareth. 'The economics of the graduate labour market.' Greenaway, H. and Williams, G. (eds.). *Patterns of change in graduate employment.* 1973. p. 41–58.

4007 **Williams**, Gareth. 'First employment of university graduates.' Greenaway, H. and Williams, G. (eds.). *Patterns of change in graduate employment.* 1973. p. 25–34.

4008 **Williams**, Gareth. 'Graduate employment in Europe.' Greenaway, H. and Williams, G. (eds.). *Patterns of change in graduate employment.* 1973. p. 141–54.

4009 **Williams**, Gareth. 'Graduates and the labour market.' *Three Banks Rev.*, XCIX (September 1973), 3–26.

4010 **Department of Employment.** *Employment prospects for the highly qualified.* London: H.M.S.O., 1974. iv, 52p.

4011 **Kelly**, T. K. *Employment patterns of graduates from O.N.D. and H.N.D. courses in hotel, catering and institutional management subjects.* London: Hotel and Catering Industry Training Board, 1974. 44p.

4012 **Williams**, Gareth. 'Graduate outlook.' *Pers. Manage.*, VI, 7 (July 1974), 22–5.

4013 **Williams**, Gareth, **Blackstone**, Tessa and **Metcalf**, David. *The academic labour market: economic and social aspects of a profession.* London: Elsevier, 1974. xvi, 566p.

4014 **Department of Education and Science.** *Census of staff in librarianship and information work in the United Kingdom 1972.* London: The Department, 1975. 31p.

4015 **Department of Employment Gazette.** 'Employment prospects for new graduates in 1975.' *Dep. Employment Gaz.*, LXXXIII, 4 (April 1975), 298–302.

4016 **Department of Employment Gazette.** 'Professional engineers and scientists in the engineering industry.' *Dep. Employment Gaz.*, LXXXIII, 4 (April 1975), 291–7.

4017 **Department of Employment Gazette.** 'The role of graduates in industry.' *Dep. Employment Gaz.*, LXXXIII, 1 (January 1975), 6–10.

4018 **Hall**, J. 'Excess demand in the graduate employment cycle.' *Nature*, CCLV, 5506 (22 May 1975), 284–6.

4019 **Mace**, John D. and **Taylor**, S. M. 'Demand for engineers in British industry: some implications for manpower forecasting.' *Br. J. Ind. Relat.*, XIII, 2 (July 1975), 175–93.

4020 **Sadler**, Judy and **Whitworth**, Tony. *Reserves of nurses.* London: H.M.S.O., 1975. 84p. (Office of Population Censuses and Surveys. Social Survey Division report SS483.)

4021 **Silverstone**, Rosalie. 'Just a sec.' *Pers. Manage.*, VII, 6 (June 1975), 35–6.
Survey of secretarial employment in London.

4022 **Smith**, Cyril S. 'The employment of sociologists in research occupations in Britain in 1973.' *Sociology*, IX, 2 (May 1975), 309–16.

4023 **Soothill**, K. 'White collars and black sheep.' *Pers. Manage.*, VII, 7 (July 1975), 30–33.
Employment of white-collar ex-offenders.

4024 **Thomas**, R. Barry. 'The supply of graduates to school teaching.' *Br. J. Ind. Relat.*, XIII, 1 (March 1975), 107–14.

4025 **Turnbull**, P. and **Williams**, G. 'Supply and demand in the labour market for teachers: qualification differentials in teachers' pay.' *Br. J. Ind. Relat.*, XIII, 2 (July 1975), 215–22.

4026 **Venning**, M. *Professional engineers, scientists and technologists in the engineering industry.* London: Engineering Industry Training Board, 1975. 150p. (Research report 4.)

4027 **Bunkell**, H. W. 'An inflated bureaucracy?' *Manage. Serv. Gov.*, XXXI, 4 (November 1976), 184–90.
Manning levels in the Civil Service.

4028 **Central Statistical Office.** *Qualified manpower in Great Britain: 1971 Census of Population.* London: H.M.S.O., 1976. iv, 32p. (Studies in official statistics 29.)

4029 **Daniels** P. W. 'Office employment in new towns.' *Town Plann. Rev.*, XLVII (July 1976), 209–24.

4030 **Department of Employment Gazette.** 'Employment of the highly qualified 1971–1986'. *Dep. Employment Gaz.*, LXXXVI, 5 (May 1976), 531–9.

4031 **Department of Employment Gazette.** 'Flow of new graduates into industry.' *Dep. Employment Gaz.*, LXXXIV, 10 (October 1976), 1075–8.

4032 **Department of Employment Gazette.** 'Manpower in London's public services.' *Dep. Employment Gaz.*, LXXXIV, 1 (January 1976), 3–5.

4033 **Local Authorities Management Services and Computer Committee.** *Staffing of public libraries.* London: H.M.S.O., 1976. 3v.

4034 **O'Reilly**, A. P. *The utilisation of scientific manpower in Ireland.* 1976. (Ph.D. thesis, University of London.)

4035 **Buxton**, A. J. 'Some evidence on the productivity of qualified manpower in Britain.' *Bull. Econ. Res.*, XXIX, 1 (May 1977), 61–8.

4036 **Dean**, T. and **Prior-Wandesforde**, G. W. 'Graduate supply and demand in 1977.' *Dep. Employment Gaz.*, LXXXV, 2 (February 1977), 116–18.

4037 **Department of the Environment**, Local Government Staff Commission for England. *Report of the ... Commission ...* London: H.M.S.O., 1977. vi, 162p.
Chairman: Anthony Greenwood.

4038 **Elliott**, R. F. 'The growth of white collar employment in Great Britain 1951–1971.' *Br. J. Ind Relat.*, XV, 1 (March 1977), 39–44.

4039 **Kemp**, Barry. 'Local government manpower.' *Work Study*, XIII, 7 (July 1977), 21–4.

4040 **Mace**, John D. and **Wilkinson**, G. C. G. 'Are labour markets competitive? A case study of engineers.' *Br. J. Ind. Relat.*, XV, 1 (March 1977), 1.

4041 **Bosworth**, Derek L. and **Wilson**, R. A. 'Some evidence on the productivity of qualified manpower in Britain: a note.' *Bull. Econ. Res.*, XXX (May 1978), 45–9.

4042 **Buxton**, A. J. 'Some evidence on the productivity of qualified manpower in Britain: a reply.' *Bull. Econ. Res.*, XXX (May 1978), 50–53.

4043 **Department of Employment Gazette.** 'The supply of potential engineers.' *Dep. Employment Gaz.*, LXXXVI, 12 (December 1978), 1383–9.

4044 **Mace**, John D. 'Internal labour markets for engineers in British industry.' *Br. J. Ind. Relat.*, XVII, 1 (March 1979), 50–63.

4045 **Parkhouse**, James. *Medical manpower in Britain.* London: Churchill Livingstone, 1979. 144p.

4046 **Zabalza**, Antoni. 'The determinants of

teacher supply.' *Rev. Econ. Stud.*, XLVI (January 1979), 131–47.

4047 **Zabalza**, Antoni, **Turnbull**, Philip and **Williams**, Gareth. *The economics of teacher supply.* Cambridge: Cambridge U.P., 1979. xi, 280p.

See also: 3956; 3957; 3960; 4048; 4055; 4079; 4088; 4090; 4095; 4115; 4169; 4480; 4534; 4539; 4550; 4551; 4557; 4560; 4561; 4562.

4. Female Employment

This section includes material on housework and the domestic labour debate. See also Part Three, II, E, 2; Part Six, II, C, 4; Part Six, II, D, 7; Part Six, III, E; Part Six, IV, A, 3, a; Part Seven, IV, C; and Part Seven, IV, D.

4048 **Civil Service Department.** *The employment of women in the Civil Service: the report of a Departmental Committee.* London: H.M.S.O., 1971. 46p. (Management studies 3.)

4049 **Fuchs**, Riet. 'Different meanings of employment for women.' *Hum. Relat.*, XXIV (December 1971), 495–9.

4050 **Hawthorn**, Geoffrey and **Paddon**, Michael. 'Work, family and fertility: an interpretation of data from four industries.' *Hum. Relat.*, XXIV (December 1971), 611–28.

4051 **Huang**, F.-S. *The role of women workers in the British textile industry, 1780–1850.* 1971. (M.Litt. thesis, University of Cambridge.)

4052 **Khairy**, A. H. F. *The employment of women: evolution, pattern and composition, with special reference to the United Kingdom.* 1971. (B.Phil. thesis, University of St. Andrews.)

4053 **Pinnelli**, Antonella. 'Female labour and fertility in relationship to contrasting social and economic conditions.' *Hum. Relat.*, XXIV (December 1971), 603–10.

4054 **Rapoport**, Rhona and **Rapoport**, Robert. 'Early and later experiences as determinants of adult behaviour: married women's family and career patterns.' *Br. J. Sociol.*, XXII (March 1971), 16–30.

4055 **Fogarty**, Michael Patrick and **Rapoport**,R. *Women and top jobs: the next move.* London: Political & Economic Planning, 1972. 93p. (P.E.P. broadsheet 535.)

4056 **Heather-Bigg**, Ada. 'Women in the nail and chain trade: a Victorian viewpoint.' *Blackcountryman*, V (Summer 1972), 55–8.

4057 **Bridge**, E. 'Women's employment: problems of research.' *Soc. Study Labour Hist. Bull.*, XXVI (Spring 1973), 5–7.

4058 **Hanna**, Max. 'The typecast third.' *New Soc.*, XXIII (1 February 1973), 232–5.

4059 **House of Commons Expenditure Committee.** *Employment of women: 6th report of the ... together with part of the minutes of the evidence taken before the Employment and Social Services Sub-Committee in session 1971–2 and 1972–3, appendices and index.* London: H.M.S.O., 1973. xxxi, 211p.

4060 **Institute of Personnel Management.** *Women and employment: policy statement.* London: I.P.M., 1973. 15p.

4061 **Tolley**, R. S. 'Female employment and local industrial development: a case study of the Coalbrookdale coalfield.' *N. Staffs. J. Field Stud.*, XIII (1973), 67–82.

4062 **Bishop**, Colin. 'The demand for female labour.' *Plann.*, LX (December 1974), 937–42.

4063 **Fogarty**, Michael Patrick and **Rapoport**, R. 'Men and women: the next frontiers.' *Econ. Soc. Rev.*, VI, 1 (October 1974), 5–25.

4064 **Hebron**, C. C. de Winter. 'Jobs for the girls?' *New Soc.*, XXIX (1 August 1974), 290–91.

4065 **King**, J. S. *Women and work: a statistical survey.* London: Department of Employment, 1974. 70p. (Manpower papers 9.)

4066 **Oakley**, Anne. *Sociology of housework.* Oxford: Martin Robertson, 1974. viii, 242p.

4067 **Richards**, Eric. 'Women in the British economy since about 1700: an interpretation.' *History*, LIX (October 1974), 337–57.

4068 **Stewart**, Valerie. *Women in industry.* Brighton: University of Sussex, Institute of Manpower Studies, 1974. 36p.

4069 **Branca**, Patricia. 'A new perspective on women's work: a comparative typology.' *J. Soc. Hist.*, IX, 2 (Winter 1975), 129–53.

4070 **Coulson**, Margaret, **Magas**, Branka and **Wainwright**, Hilary. 'The housewife and her labour under capitalism – a critique.' *New Left Rev.*, LXXXIX (January–February 1975), 59–71.

4071 **Davies**, Ross. *Women and work.* London: Hutchinson, 1975. 191p.

4072 **Department of Employment Gazette.** 'Women and work.' *Dep. Employment Gaz.*, LXXXIII, 1 (January 1975), 10–14.

4073 **Edmond**, Wendy and **Fleming**, Suzie (eds.). *All work and no pay: women, housework and the wages due.* Bristol: Power of Women Institute and Falling Wall Press, 1975. 127p.

4074 **Ferguson**, N. A. 'Women's work: employment opportunities and economic rules 1918–39.' *Albion*, VII (1975), 55–68.

4075 **Gardiner**, Jean. 'Women's domestic labour.' *New Left Rev.*, LXXXIX (January –February 1975), 47–58.

4076 **National Advisory Centre on Careers for Women.** *Returners: some notes for those returning to employment later in life or considering training for a new career.* London: The Centre, 1975. iii, 68p.

4077 **Scott**, Joan W. and **Tilly**, Louise A. 'Women's work and the family in nineteenth-century Europe.' *Comp. Stud. Soc. Hist.*, XVII, 1 (January 1975), 36–64.

4078 **Wainwright**, David. 'Opening the door for the working women.' *Pers. Manage.*, VII, 11 (November 1975), 16–19.

4079 **Walton**, Ronald G. *Women in social work.*

London: Routledge & Kegan Paul, 1975. xvi, 308p.

4080 **Evason**, E. 'Women in Northern Ireland: employment, law and social provision.' *New Community*, v, 1–2 (Summer 1976), 59–63.

4081 **Fonda**, Nickie and **Moss**, Peter (eds.). *Mothers in employment: trends a issues: papers from a conference held at Brunel University, 1976.* Uxbridge: Brunel University, 1976. 141p.

4082 **Fonda**, Nickie and **Moss**, Peter. 'The next five years.' Fonda, N. and Moss, P. (eds.). *Mothers in employment.* 1976. p. 125–41.

4083 **Ginsberg**, Susannah. 'Women, work and conflict.' Fonda, N. and Moss, P. (eds.). *Mothers in employment.* 1976. p. 75–88.

4084 **Green**, Sheila. 'The employer's attitude to working mothers.' Fonda, N. and Moss, P. (eds.). *Mothers in employment.* 1976. p. 89–106.

4085 **Lecoultre**, Denise. 'Family, employment and the allocation of time.' Fonda, N. and Moss, P. (eds.). *Mothers in employment.* 1976. p. 107–24.

4086 **MacDonald**, John Stuart and **MacDonald**, Leatrice D. 'Women at work in Britain and the Third World.' *New Community*, v, 1–2 (Summer 1976), 76–84.

4087 **Moss**, Peter. 'The current situation.' Fonda, N. and Moss, P. (eds.). *Mothers in employment.* 1976. p. 6–38.

4088 **Partington**, Geoffrey. *Women teachers in the twentieth century in England and Wales.* Windsor: NFER Publishing, 1976. 107p.

4089 **Rapoport**, R. and **Rapoport**, R. N. *Dual-career families re-examined: new integrations of work and family.* Oxford: Martin Robertson, 1976. 382p.
Second edition.

4090 **Silverstone**, Rosalie. 'Office work for women: an historical review.' *Bus. Hist.*, XVIII, 1 (January 1976), 98–110.

4091 **Hostettler**, Eve. 'Gourlay Steell and the sexual division of labour.' *Hist. Workshop*, IV (Autumn 1977), 95–100.

4092 **McNabb**, Robert. 'The labour force participation of married women.' *Manchr. Sch. Econ. Soc. Stud.*, XLV, 3 (September 1977), 221–35.

4093 **Summerfield**, Penny. 'Women workers in Britain in the Second World War.' *Cap. Cl.*, 1 (Spring 1977), 27–42.

4094 **Taylor**, Sandra. 'The effect of marriage on job possibilities for women, and the ideology of the home: Nottingham, 1890–1930.' *Oral Hist.*, v, 2 (Autumn 1977), 46–61.

4095 **Wellens**, John. 'Girl technicians for engineering.' *Ind. Commer. Train.*, IX, 3 (March 1977), 104–11.

4096 **Wellens**, John. 'Mothers in employment.' *Ind. Commer. Train.*, IX, 3 (March 1977), 112–16.

4097 **Garnsey**, Elizabeth. 'Women's work and theories of class stratification.' *Sociology*, XII (May 1978), 223–43.

4098 **Hakim**, Catherine. 'Sexual divisions within the labour force: occupational segregation.' *Dep. Employment Gaz.*, LXXXVI, 11 (November 1978), 1264–8, 1278.

4099 **Hunt**, Pauline. 'Cash-transactions and household tasks: domestic behaviour in relation to industrial employment.' *Sociol. Rev.*, XXVI (August 1978), 555–71.

4100 **Miller**, D. 'Working wives.' *Ind. Soc.*, LX, 5 (September–October 1978), 8–16.

4101 **North Tyneside Community Development Project.** *North Shields: women's work.* Newcastle-upon-Tyne: The Project, 1978.

4102 **Smith**, Paul. 'Domestic labour and Marx's theory of value.' Kuhn, A. and Wolpe, A. (eds.). *Feminism and materialism.* 1978. p. 198–219.

4103 **Thorne**, E. S. *The sociology of home economics, with particular reference to the economic status of women.* 1978. (Ph.D. thesis, University of Sheffield.)

4104 **Thrall**, Charles A. 'Who does what: role stereotypy, children's work and continuity between generations in the household division of labour.' *Hum. Relat.*, XXXI (March 1978), 249–65.

4105 **Tilly**, Louise A. and **Scott**, Joan Wallach. *Women, work and family.* London: Holt, Rinehart & Winston, 1978. xiv, 247p.

4106 **Wolpe**, AnnMarie. 'Education and the sexual division of labour.' Kuhn, A. and Wolpe, A. (eds.). *Feminism and materialism.* 1978. p. 290–328.

4107 **Breugel**, Irene. 'Women as a reserve army of labour: a note on recent British experience.' *Feminist Rev.*, III (1979), 12–23.

4108 **Industrial and Commercial Training.** 'A place for women in engineering.' *Ind. Commer. Train.*, XI, 12 (December 1979), 489–95.

4109 **Mackintosh**, Maureen M. 'Domestic labour and the household.' Burman, Sandra (ed.). *Fit work for women.* London: Croom Helm, 1979. 173–91.

4110 **McNally**, Fiona. *Women for hire: a study of the female office worker.* London: Macmillan, 1979. x, 214p.

4111 **Middleton**, Christopher. 'The sexual division of labour in feudal England.' *New Left Rev.*, CXIII/CXIV (January–April 1979), 147–68.

4112 **Moulder**, Cathy and **Sheldon**, Pat. *Back to work: a practical guide for women.* London: Kogan Page, 1979. 247p.

4113 **Pettman**, Barrie Owen. 'Women in work.' *Employee Relat.*, I, 1 (1979), 19–22.

4114 **Rowbotham**, Sheila. 'When Adam delved and Eve span ... who was then the oppressor and oppressed.' *New Soc.*, XXXVI (4 January 1979), 10–12.

4115 **Silverstone**, Rosalie and **Williams**, Allan. 'Recruitment, training, employment and careers of women chartered accountants in

England and Wales.' *Account. Bus. Res.*, IX, 34 (Spring 1979), 105–21.

4116 **Woolley**, Rob. *Gi it sum ommer*. Epwell, Oxon.: The Author, 1979. 34p.
Employment of women in the Black Country.
See also: 125; 4144; 4427; 4432; 4441; 4476.

5. Youth Employment

See also Part Six, II, A; Part Six, II, D, 7; Part Six, IV, A, 3, b; and Part Seven, II, D, 2, b.

4117 **Wild**, Ray. 'Urbanization and the job needs of school leavers.' *J. Manage. Stud.*, VIII, 3 (October 1971), 348–54.

4118 **Schofield**, P. 'Young people at work.' *Pers. Manage.*, IV, 12 (December 1972), 34–6.

4119 **White**, David. 'The young workers.' *New Soc.*, XX (1 June 1972), 457–61.

4120 **Blair**, Jon. 'Opportunity knocks, or does it? Employment problems facing less able school leavers.' *Pers. Manage.*, V, 12 (December 1973), 34–9.

4121 **Institute of Manpower Studies.** 'Effects of the raising of the school leaving age (ROSLA) on labour supply.' *I.M.S. Monit.*, II, 2 (July 1973), 50–61.

4122 **Kinnock**, Neil. 'Youth employment: the political challenge.' *Careers Q.*, XXV, 4 (Autumn 1973), 31–5.

4123 **Horn**, Pamela L. R. 'Child labour in the pillow lace and straw plait trades of Victorian Buckinghamshire and Bedfordshire.' *Hist. J.*, XVII (December 1974), 779–96.

4124 **National Youth Employment Council.** *Unqualified, untrained and unemployed: report of a working party*. London: H.M.S.O., 1975. 96p.
Chairman: R. J. Elles.

4125 **Ashton**, D. N. and **Field**, David. *Young workers*. London: Hutchinson, 1976. 192p.

4126 **Hughes**, John. 'Employ the young.' *New Soc.*, XXXVIII (14 October 1976), 74–5.

4127 **Colledge**, Maureen. 'Young people and work: research into the attitudes and experiences of young people and employers.' *Dep. Employment Gaz.*, LXXXV, 12 (December 1977), 1345–7.

4128 **Colledge**, Maureen, **Llewellyn**, Geoffrey and **Ward**, Vernon. *Young people and work*. London: H.M.S.O. for the Manpower Services Commission, 1978. 80p. (Manpower study 1.)

4129 **Department of Manpower Services,** Northern Ireland. *Opportunities at sixteen: report of a study group*. London: H.M.S.O., 1978. vi, 110p.
Chairman: Derek Birley.

6. Employment of Older Workers

Material on age discrimination and compulsory retirement is classified here. See also Part Six, II, D, 7; Part Six, IV, C, 2; and Part Seven, VII, B, 4.

4130 **Crawford**, Marion. 'Retirement and disengagement.' *Hum. Relat.*, XXIV (June 1971), 255–78.

4131 **Griew**, S. 'Occupational aspects of aging.' Warr, P. (ed.). *Psychology at work*. 1971. p. 146–68.

4132 **Industrial Society** and **Pre-Retirement Association.** *Flexibility: new attitudes to work and retirement: papers presented at a joint conference held 1971*. London: The Society and the Association, 1971. 41p.

4133 **Baylis**, Norman. 'Working on at Rubery Owen.' *Ind. Participation*, DXLVIII (Summer 1972), 20–22.

4134 **Frost**, J. R. 'Getting ready for retirement.' *Pers. Manage.*, IV, 2 (February 1972), 34–6.

4135 **Samaon**, E. *Future perfect: retirement planning and management*. London: Henry Kimpton, 1972. 130p.

4136 **Slater**, Robert. 'Age discrimination in Great Britain.' *Ind. Gerontol.*, XV (Fall 1972), 12–19.

4137 **Wheeler**, Brian and **Andrews**, Peter. 'Cost of an age structure.' *Pers. Manage.*, IV, 4 (April 1972), 32–6.

4138 **Crawford**, Marion P. 'Retirement: a rite de passage.' *Sociol. Rev.*, XXI, 3 (August 1973), 447–61.

4139 **Crawford**, Marion P. 'Retirement rituals: the farewell to work.' *New Soc.*, XXVI (20 December 1973), 711–13.

4140 **Horn**, Pamela L. R. 'Old age and the Oxfordshire agricultural labourer 1870–1914.' *Oxoniensia*, XXXVIII (1973), 373–80.

4141 **Legge**, Karen. 'Obsolescence of people.' *Manage. Decis.*, XI (Spring 1973), 27–49.

4142 **Slater**, Robert. 'Age discrimination.' *New Soc.*, XXIV (10 May 1973), 301–2.

4143 **Slater**, Robert. 'The end of the road at forty?' *Pers. Manage.*, V, 5 (May 1973), 31–4.

4144 **Jacobson**, Dan. 'Rejection of the retiree role: a study of female industrial workers in their 50s.' *Hum. Relat.*, XXVII (May 1974), 477–92.

4145 **Prentice**, Gordon. '65 not out?' *Pers. Manage.*, VI, 6 (June 1974), 36–9.

4146 **Smith**, C. M. *Retirement: the organisation and the individual: a survey of current attitudes and company practice*. London: British Institute of Management, 1974. 55p. (B.I.M. management survey reports 23.)

4147 **Collins**, R. G. 'Age discrimination comes home to roost.' *Pers. Manage.*, VII, 4 (April 1975), 24–6.

4148 **Ekerdt**, D. J. 'Preferred age of retirement.' *J. Occup. Psychol.*, XLIX (1975), 161–9.

4149 **Fisher**, P. 'Labor force participation of the aged and the social security system in nine countries.' *Ind. Gerontol.*, II, 1 (Winter 1975), 1–13.

4150 **Wallis**, J. H. *Thinking about retirement*. London: Pergamon, 1975. ix, 110p.

4151 **Walker**, J. W. and **Price**, K. F. 'Retirement policy formation.' *Pers. Rev.*, VI, 1 (Winter

1976), 39–43.

4152 **Hedaa**, Laurids. 'Demotion: a step in the right direction?' *Pers. Manage.*, x, 10 (October 1978), 45–9.

4153 **Jolly**, J., **Mingay**, A. and **Creigh**, S. 'Age preferences of employers engaging professional and executive staff: an analysis of P.E.R. vacancy records.' *Dep. Employment Gaz.*, LXXXVI, 12 (December 1978), 1377–82.

4154 **Jolly**, James, **Mingay**, Alan and **Creigh**, Stephen. 'Age qualifications in job vacancies.' *Dep. Employment Gaz.*, LXXXVI, 2 (February 1978), 166–72.

4155 **Littlejohn**, Elizabeth. 'Planning for old age.' *Social Serv. Q.*, LII, 4 (December 1978), 60–61.

4156 **McGoldrick**, A. and **Cooper**, Cary L. 'Early retirement.' *Pers. Manage.*, x, 7 (July 1978), 25–9.

4157 **Jolly**, James, **Creigh**, Stephen and **Mingay**, Alan. 'Age as an influence on employment decisions.' *Pers. Manage.*, xi, 4 (April 1979), 29–32.

4158 **Tavernier**, Gerard. 'The age of discrimination.' *Int. Manage.*, XXXIV, 9 (September 1979), 18–21.

See also: 272; 380; 4361; 6400; 6401.

7. Employment of the Disabled

See also Part Seven, II, E; and Part Seven, VII, B, 3.

4159 **Grant**, G. W. B. *Some management problems of providing work for the mentally disordered, with particular reference to mental handicap.* 1971. (M.Sc. thesis, University of Manchester Institute of Science and Technology.)

4160 **Gretton**, John. 'Able to work.' *New Soc.*, XIX (24 February 1972), 394–6.

4161 **Hartmann**, Paul. 'A study of attitudes in industrial rehabilitation.' *Occup. Psychol.*, XLVI (1972), 87–97.

4162 **Department of Employment**. *Quota scheme for disabled people: a consultative document.* London: The Department, 1973. 39p.

4163 **Johnson**, Gillian S. and **Johnson**, Ralph H. 'Paraplegics in Scotland: a survey of employment and facilities.' *Br. J. Soc. Work*, III (Spring 1973), 19–38.

4164 **Lyth**, Margaret. 'Employers' attitudes to the employment of the disabled.' *Occup. Psychol.*, XLVII (1973), 67–70.

4165 **Tuckey**, L., **Parfit**, J. and **Tuckey**, B. *Handicapped school-leavers: their further education, training and employment.* London: NFER Publishing for the National Children's Bureau, 1973. 61p.

4166 **Jackson**, R. 'Job prospects for the educationally sub-normal.' *Careers Q.*, XXVI, 2 (1974), 11–15.

4167 **Dallos**, Rudi and **Winfield**, Ian. 'Instructional strategies in industrial training and rehabilitation.' *J. Occup. Psychol.*, XLVIII

(1975), 241–52.

4168 **Incomes Data Services**. *Employing disabled people.* London: I.D.S., 1975. 23p. (I.D.S. study 108.)

4169 **Kettle**, Melvyn. 'The disabled professional.' *Pers. Manage.*, VII, 11 (November 1975), 31–4.

4170 **Morton**, D. 'Employment of the disabled.' *Ind. Commer. Train.*, VII, 10 (October 1975), 419–20.

4171 **Green**, R. M. *The employment and visual ability of partially sighted school leavers and young adults.* 1977. (M.Phil. thesis, University of Aston in Birmingham.)

4172 **Sloan**, D. 'Jobs for the disabled – time for a re-think.' *Occup. Safe. Health*, VII, 9 (September 1977), 49–50.

4173 **Speake**, Barbara and **Whelan**, Edward. 'Work preparation courses are helping handicapped school leavers find permanent jobs.' *Dep. Employment Gaz.*, LXXXV, 8 (August 1977), 803–5.

4174 **Gennard**, John and **Wright**, Michael. 'A sheltered workshop.' *Dep. Employment Gaz.*, LXXXVI, 9 (September 1978), 1028–31.

4175 **Grant**, J. and **Orriss**, H. 'A helping hand for the disabled.' *Ind. Soc.*, LX, 4 (November–December 1978), 11–13.

4176 **Makeham**, Peter. 'The costs and benefits of sheltered employment.' *Dep. Employment Gaz.*, LXXXVI, 9 (September 1978), 1025–8.

4177 **MIND** [National Association for Mental Health]. *Nobody wants you: 40 cases of discrimination at work.* London: MIND, 1978. 51p.

4178 **Guest**, David, **Broadway**, Robin, **Gorman**, Rosanagh, **Gibas**, Sue, **Marshall**, Penny, **Moore**, Dennis and **Oliver**, Sarah. 'Failing to see past the disabled label.' *Pers. Manage.*, XI, 8 (August 1979), 41–5.

4179 **Hines**, John. 'Overcoming the obstacles to disabled employment.' *Pers. Manage.*, XI, 3 (March 1979), 40–43.

4180 **Jordan**, David. *A new employment programme wanted for disabled people.* London: Low Pay Unit, 1979. 55p. (Low pay pamphlets 10.)

4181 **Kettle**, Melvyn and **Papworth**, Carol. 'Let's quit the quota.' *New Soc.*, XXXV (31 May 1979), 514–5.

See also: 3619; 4321.

D. THE LEVEL AND STRUCTURE OF UNEMPLOYMENT

The literature on employment and unemployment overlaps considerably. Hence this section should be consulted in conjunction with Part Six, II, C; Part Six, IV, A, 3, d; and Part Seven, II, A – C. See also Part Three, II, E, 3; and Part Seven, VII, B, 1.

1. General

This section contains general works on the level and structure of unemployment. In particular, it contains works which are concerned with the causes and consequences of, and cures for, unemployment. But that literature which is primarily concerned with the consequences as they affect the conditions of the unemployed worker is classified at Part Six, IV, A, 3, d. And that literature which describes solutions which primarily involve action by the state is classified at Part Seven, II, B. The literature dealing with sit-ins and work-ins in response to the threat of factory closure is classified at Part Five, V, A and C. See also Part Six, II, C, 1; and Part Six, IV, A, 1.

4182 **Armstrong**, Noel. *Unemployment: the grim truth and the way out: food for thought: can Britain survive without redeployment of labour?* Norwich: The Author, 1971.

4183 **Miller**, Le Roy. 'The reserve labour hypothesis: some tests of its implications.' *Econ. J.*, LXXXI (March 1971), 17–35.

4184 **Anderson**, J. R. L. 'Has unemployment a future? Some heretical reflections.' *Encounter*, XXXIX (November 1972), 12–18.

4185 **General Federation of Trade Unions.** *Unemployment: an analysis and policy proposals.* London: The Federation, 1972. 28p.

4186 **MacKay**, Donald Iain. 'After the "shake-out".' *Oxf. Econ. Pap.*, XXIV, 1 (March 1972), 89–110.

4187 **MacKay**, Donald Iain and **Reid**, G. L. 'Redundancy, unemployment and manpower policy.' *Econ. J.*, LXXXII, 328 (December 1972), 1256–72.

4188 **Hill**, Michael J. 'Survey of unemployed men: first report.' *Br. J. Soc. Work*, III (Summer 1973), 257–61.

4189 **Holloway**, B. J. 'Does education create unemployment?' *Ind. Commer. Train.*, V, 6 (June 1973), 269–74.

4190 **Llewellyn**, D. T. and **Newbold**, P. 'Behaviour of unemployment and unfilled vacancies.' *Ind. Relat. J.*, IV, 1 (Spring 1973), 30–42.

4191 **Martin**, Roderick and **Fryer**, Robert H. *Redundancy and paternalist capitalism: a study in the sociology of work.* London: Allen & Unwin, 1973. 278p.

4192 **Mishan**, E. J. and **Anderson**, J. R. L. 'From Anderson to Vaizey: the unemployment controversy.' *Encounter*, XL (March 1973), 80–83.

4193 **Newsham**, Dorothy B. *Will to retrain: attitudes of redundant personnel to retraining for alternative employment.* Cambridge: University College, London, Industrial Training Research Unit, 1973. 17p. (Research paper SY1.)

4194 **Sinclair**, Betty. *Unemployment.* Dublin: Communist Party of Ireland, [1973?]. 18p.

4195 **Taylor**, Robert. 'The unemployed remain.' *New Soc.*, XXVI (6 December 1973), 582–5.

4196 **Aims of Industry.** *Mass unemployment: can it be halted?* London: The Authors, 1974. 9p.

4197 **Community Relations Commission.** *Un-

employment and homelessness: a report.* London: H.M.S.O., 1974. 73p.

4198 **Corry**, B. A. and **Roberts**, J. A. 'Activity rates and unemployment: the U.K. experience: some further results.' *Appl. Econ.*, VI, 1 (March 1974), 1–21.

4199 **Daniel**, William Wentworth. *A national survey of the unemployed.* London: Political and Economic Planning, 1974. 160p. (P.E.P. broadsheet 546.)

4200 **Daniel**, William Wentworth. 'The reality of unemployment.' *New Soc.*, XXIX (19 September 1974), 726–30.

4201 **Hampton**, Peter. *Unemployment: a weapon of the capitalists.* London: International Marxist Group, 1974, 16p.

4202 **Hill**, Michael J. 'Unstable employment in the histories of unemployed men.' *I.M.S. Monit.*, III, 2 (December 1974), 70–84.

4203 **Illersic**, Alfred Roman. *Unemployment: the wider issues.* London: Working Together Campaign, 1974. 15p.

4204 **Raven**, R. E. 'Redundancy.' *Work Study*, X, 3 (March 1974), 32–7.

4205 **Smith**, C. M. *Redundancy policies: a survey of current practice in companies.* London: British Institute of Management, 1974. 37p. (Management survey reports 20.)

4206 **Barclays Bank Review.** 'Unemployment in Great Britain: the issues behind the statistics.' *Barclays Bank Rev.*, L (November 1975), 76–9.

4207 **Harrison**, Roger. *Redundancy in Western Europe.* London: Institute of Personnel Management, 1975. 136p. (Information reports 20.)

4208 **Hunter**, Laurence Colvin. 'The no-growth economy and its impact on labour.' *Pers. Manage.*, VII, 6 (June 1975), 22–6.

4209 **Maki**, Dennis and **Spindler**, Z. A. 'The effect of unemployment compensation on the rate of unemployment in Great Britain.' *Oxf. Econ. Pap.*, XXVII (November 1975), 440–54.

4210 **Marsden**, Dennis and **Duff**, E. *Workless.* Harmondsworth: Penguin, 1975. 270p.

4211 **Mumford**, Peter. *Redundancy and security of employment.* Epping: Gower, 1975. ix, 166p.

4212 **Bowers**, John K. 'Some notes on current unemployment.' Worswick, G. (ed.). *The concept and measurement of involuntary unemployment.* 1976. p. 109–33.

4213 **Brown**, A. J. 'U. V. analysis.' Worswick, G. (ed.). *The concept and measurement of involuntary unemployment.* 1976. p. 134–45.

4214 **Counter Information Services.** *Who's next for the chop: the essential facts on unemployment.* London: The Services, 1976. 42p. (Anti-reports 14.)

4215 **Department of Employment Gazette.** 'The changed relationship between unemployment and vacancies.' *Dep. Employment Gaz.*, LXXXIV, 10 (October 1976), 1093–9.

4216 **Fisher**, Malcolm R. 'The new microeconomics of unemployment.' Worswick, G.

(ed.). *The concept and measurement of involuntary unemployment.* 1976. p. 35–57.

4217 **Hartley**, J. and **Cooper**, C. L. 'Redundancy: a psychological problem?' *Pers. Rev.*, v, 3 (Summer 1976), 44–8.

4218 **Incomes Data Services.** *Lay-offs and short time.* London: The Services, 1976. 78p. (I.D.S. handbook 3.)

4219 **Johnson**, P. S. and **Van Doorn**, J. 'Skill loss and unemployment: a note.' *Br. J. Ind. Relat.*, xiv, 2 (July 1976), 202–5.

4220 **Kahn**, Richard. 'Unemployment as seen by the Keynesians.' Worswick, G. (ed.). *The concept and measurement of involuntary unemployment.* 1976. p. 19–34.

4221 **Leicester**, Colin. 'The duration of unemployment and job search.' Worswick, G. (ed.). *The concept and measurement of involuntary unemployment.* 1976. p. 185–202.

4222 **Sinfield**, Adrian. 'Unemployment and social structure.' Worswick, G. (ed.). *The concept and measurement of involuntary unemployment.* 1976. p. 221–46.

4223 **Aldous**, Tony. 'Jobs in the depression.' *Town Ctry Plann.*, xlv (February 1977), 65–71.

4224 **Burghes**, Louis. 'Who are the unemployed?' Field, F. (ed.). *The conscript army.* 1977. p. 13–27.

4225 **Burghes**, Louis and **Field**, Frank. 'The cost of unemployment.' Field, F. (ed.). *The conscript army.* 1977. p. 78–90.

4226 **Daniel**, William Wentworth and **Stilgoe**, Elizabeth. *Where are they now? A follow-up study of the unemployed.* London: Political and Economic Planning, 1977. 99p. (P.E.P. broadsheet 572.)

4227 **Department of Employment Gazette.** 'Characteristics of the unemployed: sample survey, June 1976.' *Dep. Employment Gaz.*, lxxxv, 6 (June 1977), 559–74.

4228 **Field**, Frank (ed.). *The conscript army: a study of Britain's unemployed.* London: Routlege & Kegan Paul, 1977. xii, 160p.

4229 **Hannah**, Steve. 'Causes of unemployment.' Field, F. (ed.). *The conscript army.* 1977. p. 104–21.

4230 **Pond**, Chris. 'What price unemployment?' Field, F. (ed.). *The conscript army.* 1977. p. 91–103.

4231 **Barratt Brown**, Michael. 'International aspects.' Barratt Brown, M. and others (eds.). *Full employment.* 1978. p. 95–102.

4232 **Furth**, D., **Heertje**, A. and **van der Veen**, R. J. 'On Marx's theory of unemployment.' *Oxf. Econ. Pap.*, xxx (July 1978), 263–76.

4233 **Harris**, Ralph. 'Where does unemployment come from?' Addison, J. T. and others (eds.). *Job creation – or destruction?* 1978. p. 5–10.

4234 **Hughes**, John. 'A rake's progress.' Barratt Brown, M. and others (eds.). *Full employment.* 1978. p. 14–23.

4235 **Industrial Research and Information Services.** *Unemployment, the facts, the false trails, the remedies.* London: The Services, [1978]. 64p.

4236 **McGregor**, A. 'Unemployment duration and re-employment probability.' *Econ. J.*, lxxxviii (December 1978), 693–706.

4237 **Norris**, G. M. 'Unemployment, sub-employment and personal characteristics: job separation and work histories: the alternative approach.' *Sociol. Rev.*, xxvi (May 1978), 327–47.

4238 **Pond**, Chris. 'The tragedy of unemployment and the comedy of errors.' *Month*, xi (June 1978), 185–7.

4239 **Sinfield**, Adrian. 'The social meaning of unemployment.' Jones, K. (ed.). *Yearbook of Social Policy in Britain 1976.* London: Routledge & Kegan Paul, 1978. p. 61–78.

4240 **Townsend**, Peter. 'The problem: an overview.' Barratt Brown, M. and others (eds.). *Full employment.* 1978. p. 8–13.

4241 **Clarke**, Tom. 'Redundancy, worker resistance and the community.' Craig, G. and others (eds.). *Jobs and community action.* 1979. p. 80–99.

4242 **Field**, Brian. *The fixed-cost hypothesis and the behaviour of unemployment and unfilled vacancies.* London: Polytechnic of the South Bank, 1979. 92p.

4243 **Gain**, Geoffrey. *Britain works – OK.* London: Waterfront & Industrial Pioneer, 1979. 44p.

4244 **Hawkins**, Kevin H. *Unemployment.* Harmondsworth: Penguin, 1979. 143p.

4245 **Morley**, Samuel A. *Inflation and unemployment.* London: Dryden, 1979. 194p. Second edition.

4246 **Polemarchakis**, H. M. 'Implicit contracts and unemployment theory.' *Rev. Econ. Stud.*, xlvi (January 1979), 97–108.

4247 **Sawyer**, Malcolm C. 'The effects of unemployment compensation on the rate of unemployment in Great Britain: a comment.' *Oxf. Econ. Pap.*, xxxi (March 1979), 135–46.

4248 **Spindler**, Z. A. and **Maki**, Dennis. 'More on the effects of unemployment compensation on the rate of unemployment in Great Britain.' *Oxf. Econ. Pap.*, xxxi, 1 (March 1979), 147–64.

See also: 85; 455; 1486; 1767; 2909; 2911; 3880; 3888; 4401; 4415; 4446; 4499; 4508; 4512; 4543; 6357; 6417; 7074; 7076.

2. Types and Measurement

4249 **Brown**, Robert Leslie, **Cowley**, Athol Henderson and **Durbin**, J. *Seasonal adjustment of unemployment series.* London: Central Statistical Office, 1971. iii, 300p. (Studies in official statistics. Research series 4.)

4250 **Standing**, Guy. 'Hidden workless.' *New Soc.*, xviii (14 October 1971), 716–9.

4251 **Department of Employment.** *Unemployment statistics: report of an inter-departmental* *working party*. London: H.M.S.O., 1972. iv, 35p. (Cmnd. 5157.)

4252 **Metcalf**, David and **Richardson**, R. 'The nature and measurement of unemployment in the U.K.' *Three Banks Rev.*, XCIII (March 1972), 30–45.

4253 **Peston**, Maurice. 'Unemployment: why we need a new measurement.' *Lloyds Bank Rev.*, CIV (April 1972), 1–7.

4254 **Standing**, Guy. 'The distribution of concealed unemployment in Great Britain.' *Br. J. Ind. Relat.*, X, 2 (July 1972), 291–8.

4255 **Surrey**, M. J. C. 'The seasonal adjustment of unemployment statistics: a note.' *Oxf. Univ. Inst. Econ. Stat. Bull.*, XXXIV (May 1972), 241–7.

4256 **Bourlet**, Jim and **Bell**, Adrian J. *Unemployment and inflation: the need for a trustworthy unemployment indicator.* London: Economic Research Council, 1973.

4257 **Bowers**, John Kenneth. 'Unemployment statistics 1966–1970: a note.' *Br. J. Ind. Relat.*, IX, 2 (July 1973), 286–96.

4258 **Hughes**, James J. 'The use of vacancy statistics in classifying and measuring structural and frictional unemployment in Great Britain.' *Bull. Econ. Res.*, XXVI (May 1974), 12–33.

4259 **Thirlwall**, A. P. 'Types of unemployment in the regions of Great Britain.' *Manchr. Sch. Econ. Soc. Stud.*, XLII (December 1974), 325–39.

4260 **Department of Employment Gazette**. 'The unemployment statistics and their interpretation.' *Dep. Employment Gaz.*, LXXXIII, 3 (March 1975), 179–83.

4261 **Hughes**, James J. 'How should we measure unemployment?' *Br. J. Ind. Relat.*, XIII, 3 (November 1975), 317–33.

4262 **Wood**, John B. *How little unemployment? A micro-economic examination of the official statistics and their relationship to the 'natural' (or 'unnatural') rate of unemployment.* London: Institute of Economic Affairs, 1975. 72p. (Hobart paper 65.)

4263 **Woodfield**, Alan. 'Job search costs and the measurement of structural unemployment.' *Scott. J. Polit. Econ.*, XXII,1 (February 1975), 91–8.

4264 **Department of Employment Gazette**. 'Unemployment and notified vacancies: flow statistics.' *Dep. Employment Gaz.*, LXXXIV, 9 (September 1976), 976–9.

4265 **Department of Employment Gazette**. 'The unregistered unemployed in Great Britain.' *Dep. Employment Gaz.*, LXXXIV, 12 (December 1976), 1331–6.

4266 **Hill**, Michael J. 'Can we distinguish voluntary from involuntary unemployment?' Worswick, G. (ed.). *The concept and measurement of involuntary unemployment.* 1976. p. 168–84.

4267 **Maynard**, G. W. 'Keynes and unemployment today.' *Three Banks Rev.*, CXX (December 1976), 3–20.

4268 **Thatcher**, A. R. 'Statistics of unemployment in the United Kingdom.' Worswick, G. (ed.). *The concept and measurement of involuntary unemployment.* 1976. p. 83–94.

4269 **Worswick**, George David Norman (ed.). *The concept and measurement of involuntary unemployment.* London: Allen & Unwin, 1976. 327p.

Papers presented at a Royal Economic Society conference, 1974.

4270 **Cutler**, R. and **Rowles**, K. J. 'The unemployment statistics and government policy.' *J. Ind. Affairs*, IV, 2 (Spring 1977), 40–44.

4271 **Field**, Frank. 'Making sense of the unemployment figures.' Field, F. (ed.). *The conscript army.* 1977. p. 1–12.

4272 **Hildreth**, P. A. *The measurement of British unemployment: a study of the theory and empirical evidence relating to the recent criticism of the official unemployment statistics.* 1977. (M.Sc. thesis, University of Wales.)

4273 **Takagi**, Yasuoki. 'Surplus labour and disguised unemployment.' *Oxf. Econ. Pap.*, XXX (November 1978), 447–57.

4274 **Bosanquet**, Nicholas. '"Structuralism" and "structural unemployment".' *Br. J. Ind. Relat.*, XVII, 3 (November 1979), 299–313.
See also: 4310.

3. Unemployment and Technological Change

See also Part Two, IV; Part Five, II; and see Part Three, II, B for material on the Luddites.

4275 **Rooney**, A. G. *A study of the impact of economic and technological change on labour in the British aircraft manufacturing industry.* 1971. (M.Phil. thesis, University of Leicester.)

4276 **Department of Employment**. *Computers in offices 1972.* London: H.M.S.O., 1972. 80p. (Manpower studies 12.)

4277 **Jones**, Ken. *The human face of change: social responsibility and rationalization at British Steel.* London: Institute of Personnel Management, 1974. 71p.

4278 **Jenkins**, Clive and **Sherman**, Barrie. *Computers and the unions.* London: Longman, 1977. v, 135p.

4279 **Barratt Brown**, Michael. 'Technological unemployment.' Barratt Brown, M. and others (eds.). *Full employment.* 1978. p. 86–94.

4280 **Central Policy Review Staff**. *Social and employment implications of microelectronics.* London: The Authors, 1978. 24p.

4281 **Forester**, Tom. 'Society with chips and without jobs.' *New Soc.*, XXXIII (16 November 1978), 387–8.

4282 **Advisory Council for Applied Research and Development**. *Joining and assembly: the impact of robots and automation: report of a working group.* London: H.M.S.O., 1979. 44p.

4283 **Amalgamated Union of Engineering Workers**, Technical, Administrative and Supervisory Section. *Computer technology and employment: proceedings of a conference.* London: National Computing Centre, 1979. 167p.

4284 **Centre for Alternative Industrial and Technological Systems**. *Alternatives to unemployment: new approaches to work in industry and the community: papers presented at a conference.* London: The Centre, [1979]. 210p.

4285 **Hines**, Colin and **Searle**, Graham. *Automatic unemployment.* London: Earth Resources Research, 1979. ix, 77p.

4286 **Jenkins**, Clive and **Sherman**, Barrie. *The collapse of work.* London: Eyre Methuen, 1979. 182p.

4287 **Likieman**, A. 'The impact of microelectronics on employment.' *London Bus. School J.*, VII, 2 (Autumn 1979), 33–5.

4288 **Murray**, Lionel. 'The trades unions' view.' Washington, Derek (ed.). *Technological change and the future of work.* 1979. p. 39–52.

4289 **Sleigh**, Jonathan, **Boatwright**, Brian, **Irwin**, Peter and **Stanyon**, Roger. *The manpower implications of microelectronic technology.* London: H.M.S.O., 1979. x, 110p.

4290 **Stonier**, Tom. 'The impact of microprocessors on employment.' *Employee Relat.*, I, 4 (1979), 27–9.

4291 **Thornton**, Peter and **Wheelock**, Verner. 'What future for employment?' *Employee Relat.*, I, 1 (1979), 3–6.

4292 **Washington**, Derek (ed.). *Technological change and the future of work: proceedings of a conference arranged and presented by South East Forum in association with the Standing Conference on School's Science and Technology, 1979, University of Sussex.* Brighton: South East Forum, 1979. 80p.

See also: 517; 525; 4189.

4. Chronological Studies

This section contains works which are primarily concerned with describing or explaining the level and structure of unemployment prevailing in a specific period or the changes in these levels over time. Chronological studies with a primarily regional focus are classified at Part Six, II, D, 5; those with a primarily industrial or occupational focus at Part Six, II, D, 6; and those relating to particular aspects and groups are classified at Part Six, II, D, 7.

4293 **Brown**, Kenneth D. *Labour and unemployment, 1900–1914.* Newton Abbott: David & Charles, 1971. 219p.

4294 **Brown**, Kenneth D. 'The Labour Party and the unemployment question 1906–1910.' *Hist. J.*, XIV (September 1971), 599–616.

4295 **Baxter**, J. L. 'Long-term unemployment in Great Britain 1953–1971.' *Oxf. Univ. Inst.*

Econ. Stat. Bull., XXXIV, 4 (November 1972), 329–44.

4296 **Bowers**, J. K., **Cheshire**, P. C., **Webb**, A. F. and **Weeden**, R. 'Some aspects of unemployment and the labour market 1966–71.' *Natl. Inst. Econ. Rev.*, LXII (November 1972), 75–88.

4297 **Gujarati**, D. 'The behaviour of unemployment and unfilled vacancies: Great Britain 1958–1971.' *Econ. J.*, LXXXII, 325 (March 1972), 195–204.

4298 **Taylor**, J. 'The behaviour of unemployment and unfilled vacancies: Great Britain 1958–1971: an alternative view.' *Econ. J.*, LXXXII, 328 (December 1972), 1352–65.

4299 **Foster**, J. I. 'The relationship between unemployment and vacancies in Great Britain (1958–72): some further evidence.' Laidler, D.E.W. and Purdy, D.L. (eds.). *Inflation and labour markets.* 1973. p. 164–96.

4300 **Cripps**, T. F. and **Tarling**, Roger J. 'Analysis of the duration of male unemployment in Great Britain 1932–73.' *Econ. J.*, LXXXIV, 334 (June 1974), 289–316.

4301 **Booth**, Alan E. and **Glynn**, Sean. 'Unemployment in the inter-war period: a multiple problem.' *J. Contemp. Hist.*, X (October 1975), 611–36.

4302 **Taylor**, Jim. 'The unemployment gap in Britain's production sector, 1953–73.' Worswick, G. (ed.). *The concept and measurement of involuntary unemployment.* 1976. p. 146–67.

4303 **Evans**, Alan. 'Notes on the changing relationship between registered unemployment and notified vacancies: 1961–1966 and 1966–1971.' *Economica*, XLIV (May 1977), 179–96.

4304 **Crafts**, N.F.R. 'Enclosure and labour supply revisited.' *Explor. Econ. Hist.*, XV, 2 (April 1978), 172–83.

4305 **Fowkes**, A. S. *Structural unemployment and employers' labour requirements in Great Britain, 1952–1971.* 1978. (Ph.D. thesis, University of Leeds.)

4306 **Garraty**, John Arthur. *Unemployment in history: economic thought and public policy.* London: Harper & Row, 1978. 273p.

4307 **Benjamin**, Daniel K. and **Kochin**, Levis A. 'Searching for an explanation of unemployment in interwar Britain.' *J. Polit. Econ.*, LXXXVII, 3 (1979), 441–78.

4308 **Benjamin**, Daniel K. and **Kochin**, Levis A. 'Voluntary unemployment in interwar Britain.' *Banker*, CXXIX (February 1979), 33–6.

See also: 2871; 2899; 2900; 2909.

5. Regional Studies

See also Part Six, II, C, 2; Part Six, II, E, 4; and Part Seven, II, D, 3.

4309 **Cameron**, G. C. 'Economic analysis for a

declining urban economy.' *Scott. J. Polit. Econ.*, XVIII, 3 (November 1971), 315–45.

4310 **Taylor**, J. 'A regional analysis of hidden unemployment in Great Britain 1951–1966.' *Appl. Econ.*, III, 4 (December 1971), 291–303.

4311 **Brechling**, Frank P. R. *Wage inflation and the structure of regional unemployment.* Colchester: Essex University, Department of Economics, 1972. 76p. (Discussion paper 40.)

4312 **Daniel**, William Wentworth. *Whatever happened to the workers in Woolwich? A survey of redundancy in S.E. London.* London: Political and Economic Planning, 1972. 135p. (P.E.P. broadsheet 537.)

4313 **Herron**, F. 'Redundancy and redeployment from U.C.S. 1969–71.' *Scott. J. Pol. Econ.*, XIX (November 1972), 231–51.
Upper Clyde Shipbuilders.

4314 **Allan**, Charles Maitland. *Bullionfield: death of a paper mill: a study of redundancy.* Gartocharn: Famedram Publishers, [1973?]. 28p.

4315 **Cheshire**, Paul C. *Regional unemployment differences in Great Britain.* Cambridge: Cambridge U.P., 1973. 40p. (National Institute of Economic and Social Research regional papers 2.)

4316 **Hill**, Michael J., **Harrison**, R.M., **Sargeant**, A.V. and **Talbot**, V. *Men out of work: a study of unemployment in three English towns.* Cambridge: Cambridge U.P., 1973. xi, 194p.

4317 **Leslie**, Derek G. 'A note on the regional distribution of unemployment.' *Oxf. Univ. Inst. Econ. Stat. Bull.*, XXXV (August 1973), 233–7.

4318 **Pope**, R. *The unemployment problem in north-east Lancashire, 1920–1938.* 1974. (M.Litt. thesis, University of Lancaster.)

4319 **Vipond**, Joan. 'City size and unemployment.' *Urb. Stud.*, IX (February 1974), 39–46.

4320 **Webb**, A. E. *Unemployment, vacancies and the rate of change of earnings: a regional analysis.* Cambridge: Cambridge U.P., 1974. 49p.
Bound with Weeden, R. *Regional rates of growth of employment.*

4321 **Blake**, John. 'The Lomas report.' *Town Ctry Plann.*, XLIII (June 1975), 294–8.
London.

4322 **Brent**, C. E. 'Urban unemployment and population in Sussex between 1550 and 1660.' *Sx. Archaeol. Collect.*, CXIII (1975), 35–53.

4323 **Dixon**, R. J. and **Thirlwall**, Anthony Philip. *Regional growth and unemployment in the United Kingdom.* London: Macmillan, 1975. x, 251p.

4324 **Metcalf**, David. 'Urban unemployment in England.' *Econ. J.*, LXXXV, 339 (September 1975), 578–89.

4325 **Sewel**, John. *Colliery closure and social change:*
a study of a South Wales mining valley. Cardiff: University of Wales Press, 1975. ii, 81p.

4326 **Crompton**, D. *Employment decline in the engineering industries of the Manchester area: a case study.* 1976. (M.Sc. thesis, University of Salford.)

4327 **Metcalf**, David and **Richardson**, Ray. 'Unemployment in London.' Worswick, G. (ed.). *The concept and measurement of involuntary unemployment.* 1976. p. 203–20.

4328 **Armstrong**, K. and **Beynon**, Huw. *Hello are you working? Memories of the 30's in the North-East of England.* Whitley Bay: Strong Words Erdesdun Publications, 1977. 93p.

4329 **Dennehy**, Clare and **Sullivan**, Jill. 'Poverty and unemployment in Liverpool.' Field, F. (ed.). *The conscript army.* 1977. 56–77.

4330 **Whelan**, Brendan J. and **Walsh**, Brendan M. *Redundancy and re-employment in Ireland.* Dublin: Economic and Social Research Institute, 1977. 119p. (Institute papers 89.)

4331 **Community Development Project**. 'Decline in industry, decline in towns.' Coates, Ken (ed.). *The right to useful work.* 1978. p. 105–31.

4332 **Holtermann**, Sally. 'Unemployment in urban areas.' *Urb. Stud.*, XV (June 1978), 231–3.

4333 **Elias**, Peter B. 'Regional unemployment elasticities: migration or registration?' *Scott. J. Pol. Econ.*, XXVI (February 1979), 103–6.

4334 **Gordon**, Ian. 'Regional unemployment elasticities: the neglected role of migration.' *Scott. J. Pol. Econ.*, XXVI (February 1979), 97–101.

4335 **Greenwood**, John and **Pearson**, R. 'Redundancies and labour displacement: effects within a local labour market.' *Ind. Relat. J.*, X, 1 (Spring 1979), 22–9.

See also: 2291; 2298; 3920; 4259; 4341; 4345; 4362.

6. Occupational and Industrial Studies

See also Part Six, II, C, 3; and Part Seven, II, D, 3.

4336 **Lehmann**, P. J. *Unemployment and the opportunity cost of mining labour.* 1971. (D.Phil. thesis, University of Sussex.)

4337 **Scunthorpe Group**. *The threat to steel workers: a discussion pamphlet.* Nottingham: Institute for Workers' Control, [1971?]. 16p. (I.W.C. pamphlets 23.)

4338 **Bailey**, Dave. *Steel: the coming redundancies and how to fight them [including the confidential report on closures by the British Steel Corporation].* London: International Marxist Group, 1972. 54p.

4339 **Jones**, Ken. 'The company's responsibility in society.' *Pers. Manage.*, IV, 10 (October 1972), 22–5.
British Steel Corporation plant closures.

4340 **MacKay**, Donald I. 'Redundancy and re-engagement: a study of car-workers.'

Manchr. Sch. Econ. Soc. Stud., XL, 3 (September 1972), 295–312.

4341 **Slack**, Dorothy. 'Labour displacement in textiles and clothing in the North West.' *Advance*, XIII (December 1972), 23–8.

4342 **Scunthorpe Group.** 'The struggle in steel.' Barratt Brown, M. and Coates, K. (eds.). *Trade union register: 3.* 1973. p. 150–61.

4343 **Smith**, P. 'Seasonal fluctuations in the motor vehicle industry.' *J. Ind. Econ.*, XXI (April 1973), 184–6.

4344 **Thomas**, Brenda and **Madigan**, Chris. 'Strategy and job choice after redundancy: a case study in the aircraft industry.' *Sociol. Rev.*, XXII, 1 (February 1974), 83–102.

4345 **Herron**, Frank. *Labour market in crisis: redundancy of Upper Clyde Shipbuilders.* London: Macmillan, 1975. xii, 215p.

4346 **Mills**, Leif. 'Bank staff and the threat of redundancy.' *Banker*, CXXVI (April 1976), 361, 363–4.

4347 **Clarke**, Linda. 'Direct labour: goodbye to contractors.' Craig, G. and others (eds.). *Jobs and community action.* 1979. p. 146–60.

4348 **Coates**, Ken. 'The National Coal Board: what price consultation.' Craig, G. and others (eds.). *Jobs and community action.* 1979. p. 129–38.

4349 **Connolly**, John. 'Resisting the run-down of docklands.' Craig, G. and others (eds.). *Jobs and community action.* 1979. p. 139–45.

4350 **Davies**, Tom. 'Employment policy in one London borough.' Craig, G. and others (eds.). *Jobs and community action.* 1979. p. 217–27.

4351 **Fineman**, S. 'The stressless redundancy.' *Manage. Decis.*, XVI, 6 (1979), 331–7.

4352 **Hodgson**, Keith. 'Tate and Lyle: the campaign to save jobs.' Craig, G. and others (eds.). *Jobs and community action.* 1979. p. 60–79.

4353 **Ward**, Kevin. 'Leeds public transport: linking bus workers and community group.' Craig, G. and others (eds.). *Jobs and community action.* 1979. p. 176–97.

See also: 525; 3593; 4302; 4313; 4314; 6335; 6337.

7. Studies of Particular Aspects and Groups

This section includes works which discuss unemployment in relation to age and sex, as well as those dealing with juvenile unemployment, executive unemployment, and unemployment among women.

4354 **Fryer**, Robert H. 'Unemployment, myths and science.' *New Sci.* (16 December 1971), 165–8.

4355 **Genders**, J. E. 'How to cope with the obsolescent executive.' *Pers. Manage.*, III, 10 (October 1971), 26–8.

4356 **Monaghan**, W. *Redundancy: a study of its incidence, impact and causes, together with the reactions of some employers and trade unions to*

redundancy situations. 1971. (M.Sc. thesis, University of Strathclyde.)

4357 **British Institute of Management**. *Guidelines for the redundant manager.* London: Headley.
First edition. 1972. 27p.
Second edition. 1974. 30p.

4358 **British Institute of Management**. *Managerial mobility and redundancy: report of a B.I.M. working party set up in 1971 to examine the nature of the problems and to define those issues most urgently requiring attention.* London: B.I.M., 1972. 31p.

4359 **Institute of Careers Officers.** *About unemployed young people.* London: The Institute, 1972. 15p. (Icon series 3.)

4360 **Ahier**, V. 'The young unemployed: who are they and why?' *B.A.C.I.E. J.*, XXVII, 1 (March 1973), 8–14.

4361 **Harrison**, R. 'A strategy for helping redundant and retiring managers.' *Manage. Educ. Dev.*, IV, 2 (August 1973), 77–85.

4362 **Taylor**, J. H. 'High unemployment and coloured school leavers: the Tyneside pattern.' *New Community*, II (Winter 1972–3), 85–9.

4363 **Williams**, R. and **Sneath**, F. 'The redundant executive.' *Pers. Rev.*, III, 4 (Winter 1973), 52–60.

4364 **Bayliss**, Martin. 'School leavers on the scrap heap: time to stop the rot.' *Pers. Manage.*, VII, 8 (August 1975), 18–20.

4365 **Department of Employment Gazette**. 'Unemployment among workers from racial minority groups.' *Dep. Employment Gaz.*, LXXXIII, 9 (September 1975), 868–71.

4366 **Taylor**, Robert. 'Young and out of work.' *New Soc.*, XXXIII (28 August 1975), 462–5.

4367 **Allinson**, Chris, **Butterfield**, Michael, **Crace**, Nicholas, **Evanson**, Janet, **Falk**, Nicholas, **Harrison**, Jeremy, **Peston**, Maurice, **Roe**, William, and **Swain**, Graham. *Action against youth unemployment: approaches to young people and work, temporary jobs, permanent work, training opportunities, local planning.* London: Young Volunteer Force Foundation, 1976. 36p.

4368 **Garside**, William Redvers. 'Juvenile unemployment statistics between the wars.' *Soc. Study Labour Hist. Bull.*, XXXIII (Autumn 1976), 38–46.

4369 **Ball**, Colin. *Community service and the young unemployed.* London: National Youth Bureau, 1977. 16p.

4370 **Birmingham Community Development Project**. *Youth on the dole.* Birmingham: The Project, 1977. 46p.

4371 **Field**, Frank. *Unfair shares: the disabled and unemployment.* London: Low Pay Unit, 1977. 5p. (Low pay paper 20.)

4372 **Garside**, William Redvers. 'Juvenile unemployment and public policy between the wars.' *Econ. Hist. Rev.*, XXX (1977), 322–39.

4373 **Heap**, R. 'A.R.C. in community relations.'

Ind. Commer. Train., IX, 5 (May 1977), 187–9.
Action Resource Centre, Camden.

4374 **Department of Employment Gazette**. 'The young and out of work.' *Dep. Employment Gaz.*, LXXXVI, 8 (August 1978), 908–16.

4375 **Hughes**, John. 'Young workers.' Barratt Brown, M. and others (eds.). *Full employment*. 1978. p. 27–33.

4376 **Pahl**, R. E. 'Living without a job: how school leavers see the future.' *New Soc.*, XXXIV (2 November 1978), 259–62.

4377 **Benjamin**, Daniel K. and **Kochin**, Levis A. 'What went right with juvenile unemployment policy between the wars: a comment.' *Econ. Hist. Rev.*, XXXII, 4 (November 1979), 523–8.

4378 **Berthoud**, Richard. *Unemployed professionals and executives*. London: Policy Studies Institute, 1979. 121p. (Broadsheet 582.)

4379 **Department of Employment Gazette**. 'Age and redundancy: a view of the relationship between age and redundancies notified under the Redundancy Payments Act.' *Dep. Employment Gaz.*, LXXXVII, 9 (September 1979), 1032–9.

4380 **Garside**, William Redvers. 'Juvenile unemployment between the wars: a rejoinder.' *Econ. Hist. Rev.*, XXXI, 4 (November 1979), 529–32.

4381 **Grimond**, John (ed.). *Youth unemployment and the bridge from school to work*. London: Anglo-German Foundation for the Study of Industrial Society, 1979. 51p.

4382 **Morris**, Peter. 'Race, community and marginality: Spirolynx.' Craig, G. and others (eds.). *Jobs and community action*. 1979. p. 100–12.

4383 **Walker**, Derek H. 'Mid-career redundancy.' *Natl. Westminster Bank Q. Rev.*, (May 1979), 43–54.

See also: 4408; 5355; 6303; 6402.

E. LABOUR MOBILITY

1. General

In addition to including literature which covers more than one aspect of labour mobility, this section contains works dealing with the movement of labour between countries. It also includes the literature on job search. Literature on the movement of labour into the United Kingdom is classified at Part Six, II, E, 2 and that on the movement of labour from the United Kingdom is classified at Part Six, II, E, 3.

4384 **Böhning**, Wolf Rüdiger. *Problems and prospects of labour migration upon Britain's entry into the E.E.C.* Canterbury: University of Kent, Centre for Research in the Social Sciences, 1970. 18p.

4385 **Böhning**, Wolf Rüdiger. 'Britain, the E.E.C. and labour migration.' *New Community*, I, 1 (October 1971), 7–10.

4386 **Böhning**, Wolf Rüdiger and **Stephen**, David. *The EEC and the migration of workers: the EEC's system of free movement of labour and the implications of United Kingdom entry*. London: Runnymede Trust, 1971. 43p.

4387 **Cole**, W. A. 'Deane and Cole on industrialization and population change in the eighteenth century: rejoinder.' *Econ. Hist. Rev.*, XXIV, 4 (1971), 648–52.

4388 **Community Relations Commission**. 'Britain, Europe and migration.' *New Community*, I, 1 (October 1971), 3–51.

4389 **Livesy**, F. 'Occupational mobility and worker performance.' *Br. J. Ind. Relat.*, XI, 2 (July 1971), 234–50.

4390 **Neal**, Larry. 'Deane and Cole on industrialisation and population change in the eighteenth century.' *Econ. Hist. Rev.*, XXIV, 4 (1971), 643–7.

4391 **Böhning**, Wolf Rüdiger. 'Britain, the E.E.C. and labour migration.' Van Houte, H. and Melgert, W. (eds.). *Foreigners in our community*. 1972. p. 111–16.

4392 **Böhning**, Wolf Rüdiger. *The migration of workers in the United Kingdom and the European Community*. Oxford: Oxford U.P., 1972. xvi, 167p.

4393 **Incomes Data Services**. *Transfer between jobs*. Part 1. London: I.D.S., 1972. 16p. (I.D.S. study 37.)

4394 **Van Houte**, Hans and **Melgert**, Willy (eds.). *Foreigners in our community: a new European problem to be solved*. Amsterdam: Keesing, 1972. xii, 202p.

4395 **Webb**, Barbara and **Williams**, W. M. 'Mobility of general practitioners during the first few years in general practice: research note.' *Sociol. Rev.*, XX, 4 (November 1972), 591–600.

4396 **Incomes Data Services**. *Transfers between jobs*. Part 2. London: I.D.S., 1973. 20p. (I.D.S. study 54.)

4397 **International Catholic Migration Commission**. *A comparative study on the legal and social situation of E.E.C. and non-E.E.C. migrant workers in Denmark, Ireland and the United Kingdom*. Geneva: The Commission, 1973. 39p.

4398 **International Catholic Migration Commission**. *Migration in the Europe of nine*. Geneva: The Commission, 1973. 64p. (Migration informative series II.)

4399 **Klaasen**, Lev H. and **Drewe**, Paul. *Migration policy in Europe: a comparative study*. Lexington: Heath, 1973. vii, 134p.
See especially Chapter 2.4: 'Great Britain.' p. 75–7.

4400 **Kuhn**, Annette, **Poole**, Anne, **Sales**, Pauline and **Wynn**, H. P. 'An analysis of graduate job mobility.' *Br. J. Ind. Relat.*, XI, 1 (March 1973), 124–42.

Partly reprinted in Bartholomew, D.J. (ed.). *Manpower planning.* 1976. p. 279–99.

4401 **Salop**, S. C. 'Systematic job search and unemployment.' *Rev. Econ. Stud.*, XL (April 1983), 191–201.

4402 **Thomas**, Barry. *Migration and economic growth: a study of Great Britain and the Atlantic economy.* Cambridge: Cambridge U.P., 1973. xxxi, 498p.
Second edition.

4403 **Powell**, Maurice. 'Age and occupational change among coal miners.' *Occup. Psychol.*, XLVII, 1–2 (1974), 37–49.

4404 **Task Force on Interchange of Scientists.** *Report of the Task Force ...* London: Civil Service Department, 1974. iv, 35p.
Chairman: Herman Bondi.

4405 **Berger**, John and **Mohr**, Jean. *A seventh man: a book of images and words about the experience of migrant workers in Europe.* Harmondsworth: Penguin, 1975. 289p.

4406 **Braham**, Peter. 'Immigrant labour in Europe.' Esland, G. and others (eds.). *People and work.* 1975. p. 119–33.

4407 **Department of Employment Gazette.** 'The mobility of labour.' *Dep. Employment Gaz.*, LXXXIII, 12 (December 1975), 1264–8.

4408 **Lubbock**, Bill. *Finding another top job.* London: Institute of Personnel Management, 1975. 48p.

4409 **Newbury**, Colin. 'Labour migration in the imperial phase: an essay in interpretation.' *J. Imp. Commonw. Hist.*, III, 2 (January 1975), 234–56.

4410 **Sleeper**, R. D. 'Labour mobility over the life cycle.' *Br. J. Ind. Relat.*, XIII, 2 (July 1975), 194–214.

4411 **Underhill**, E. 'Living conditions and family life of migrants and their children in the main countries of Europe.' *Int. Child Welfare Rev.*, XXVI (September 1975), 28–36.

4412 **Ashtiany**, Sue. *Britain's migrant workers.* London: Fabian Society,1976. 24p. (Fabian tract 444.)

4413 **Hughes**, J. G. and **Walsh**, B. M. 'Migration flows between Ireland, the United Kingdom and the rest of the world, 1966–1971.' *Eur. Demogr. Inf. Bull.*, VII, 4 (1976), 125–49.

4414 **Incomes Data Services.** *Redeployment.* London: I.D.S., 1976. 16p. (I.D.S. study 124.)

4415 **Killingsworth**, M. R. *Labour supply, human capital and job search: analysis of the optimal intertemporal allocation of time.* 1977. (D.Phil. thesis, University of Oxford.)

4416 **Moore**, Robert. 'Migrants and the class structure of Western Europe.' Scase, R. (ed.). *Industrial society.* 1977. p. 136–49.

4417 **Rowe**, D. J. 'Population of 19th century Tyneside.' McCord, N. (ed.). *Essays in Tyneside labour history.* 1977. p. 1–24.

4418 **Carter**, A. R. 'Getting a better job.' *Work Study*, XIV, 3 (March 1978), 17–24.

4419 **Meyer**, Garry S. 'On the concept of maximum mobility.' *Popul. Stud.*, XXXII (July 1978), 355–66.

4420 **Dex**, Shirley. 'Job search methods and ethnic discrimination.' *New Community*, VII (Winter 1978–9), 85–91.

4421 **Edney**, P. 'Grouping skills for greater job mobility.' *Pers. Manage.*, XI, 10 (October 1979), 53–7.

4422 **Sykes**, Marjorie. 'The migrants.' *Hist. Today*, XXIX, 6 (June 1979), 401–7.

See also: 3462; 4000; 4182; 4220; 4263; 4358; 6317; 7014.

2. Immigration

This section includes works dealing with immigrants and the process of immigration. Material on the state regulation of immigration has generally been excluded. See also Part Three, II, E, 1; Part Six, IV, A, 3, c; and Part Seven, III, A, 1 for material on the legal aspects of the employment of immigrants.

4423 **Hepple**, Robert Alexander. 'The future protection of migrant workers.' *New Community*, I, 1 (October 1971), 47–51.

4424 **Cheetham**, Juliet. 'Immigration.' Halsey, A. H. (ed.). *Trends in British society since 1900.* London: Macmillan, 1972. p. 451–508.

4425 **MacDonald**, John Stuart and **MacDonald**, Leatrice D. *Invisible immigrants: a statistical survey of immigration into the United Kingdom of workers and dependants from Italy, Portugal and Spain.* London: Runnymede Industrial Unit, 1972. 62p.

4426 **Simmonds**, K. R. 'Immigration control and the free movement of labour: a problem of harmonisation.' *Int. Comp. Law Q.*, XXI, 2 (April 1972), 307–19.

4427 **Thomas**, M. and **Williams**, J. M. *Overseas nurses in Britain.* London: Political and Economic Planning, 1972. 54p. (P.E.P. broadsheet 539.)

4428 **Richmond**, A. H. *Migration and race relations in an English city: a study in Bristol.* Oxford: Oxford U.P., 1973. xiii, 344p.

4429 **Treble**, J. H. 'Irish navvies in the north of England 1830–50.' *J. Transp. Hist.*, VI (November 1973), 227–47.

4430 **Böhning**, Wolf Rüdiger and **Maillat**, D. *Effects of the employment of foreign workers.* Paris: O.E.C.D., 1974. 189p.

4431 **Kuepper**, W. G., **Lackey**, G. L. and **Swinerton**, E. N. *Ugandan Asians in Great Britain: forced migration and social absorption.* London: Croom Helm, 1975. 122p.

4432 **Foner**, Nancy. 'Women, work and migration: Jamaicans in London.' *New Community*, V, 1–2 (Summer 1976), 85–98.

4433 **Gwynne**, Terence and **Sill**, Michael. 'Census enumeration books: a study of mid-nineteenth century immigration.' *Local Historian*, XII, 2 (June 1976), 74–9.

4434 **O'Muircheartaigh**, Colm A. and **Rees**, Tom. 'Migrant/immigrant labour in Great Britain, France and Germany.' *New Community*, v (Autumn 1976), 280–91.

4435 **Fowler**, Bridget, **Littlewood**, Barbara and **Madigan**, Ruth. 'Immigrant school leavers and the search for work.' *Sociology*, XI, I (January 1977), 65–85.

4436 **MacDermott**, T. P. 'Irish workers on Tyneside in the 19th century.' McCord, N. (ed.). *Essays in Tyneside labour history*. 1977. p. 154–77.

4437 **Mayhew**, K. and **Rosewell**, B. 'Immigrants and occupational crowding in Great Britain.' *Oxf. Bull. Econ. Stat.*, XL (August 1978), 223–48.

4438 **Shah**, Samir. 'The immigrant community.' Barratt Brown, M. and others (eds.). *Full employment*. 1978. p. 42–58.

4439 **Wood**, Ian. 'Irish immigrants and Scottish radicalism, 1880–1906.' MacDougall, Ian (ed.). *Essays in Scottish labour history*. 1978. p. 65–89.

4440 **Allen**, Sheila. 'White migrants, black workers.' *New Community*, VII (Winter 1978–9), 11–18.

4441 **Collins**, B. 'Aspects of Irish immigration into two Scottish towns during the mid-nineteenth century.' *Ir. Econ. Soc. Hist.*, VI (1979), 71–3.

4442 **Lees**, Lynn Hollen. *Exiles of Erin: Irish migrants in Victorian London*. Manchester: Manchester U.P., 1979. 277p.

4443 **Peach**, Ceri. 'British unemployment cycles and West Indian immigration, 1955–1974.' *New Community*, VII (Winter 1978–9), 40–43.

3. Emigration

See also Part Six, II, E, I.

4444 **Gallaway**, Lowell E. and **Vedder**, Richard K. 'Emigration from the United Kingdom to the United States: 1860–1913.' *J. Econ. Hist.*, XXI, 4 (December 1971), 884–97.

4445 **Lewis**, Brian. *Overseas assignments: the treatment of expatriate staff*. London: Institute of Personnel Management, 1971. 39p.

4446 **Lockhart**, A. *Some aspects of emigration from Ireland to the North American colonies, 1660–1775*. 1971. (M.Litt. thesis, Trinity College, Dublin.)

4447 **Horn**, Pamela L. R. 'Agricultural trade unionism and emigration 1872–1881.' *Hist. J.*, xv (March 1972), 87–102.

4448 **Johnston**, H. J. M. *British emigration policy 1815–1830: shovelling out paupers*. Oxford: Oxford U.P., 1972. 216p.

4449 **Richardson**, H. W. 'British emigration and overseas investment, 1870–1914.' *Econ. Hist. Rev.*, XXV, I (1972), 99–113.

4450 **Hill**, Stan. 'From Brierley Hill to British Columbia: miners who emigrated in the nineteenth century.' *Blackcountryman*, VII (Spring 1974), 25–9.

4451 **Brown**, R. *Jobs and careers abroad: a directory of opportunities*. London: Vacation Work, 1975. x. 294p.

4452 **Bhagwati**, Jagdish Natwadal and **Partington**, Martin (eds.). *Taxing the brain drain: a proposal*. Amsterdam: North-Holland, 1976. xiii, 222p.
Proceedings of the Bellagiv Conference on the Brain Drain and Income Taxation, 1975.

4453 **Cameron**, Wendy. 'Selecting Peter Robinson's Irish emigrants.' *Hist. Soc.*, IX, 17 (May 1976), 29–46.
Emigration to Canada.

4454 **Lees**, Lynn H. 'Mid-Victorian migration and the Irish family economy.' *Vic. Stud.*, XX, I (Autumn 1976), 25–43.

4455 **Malchow**, H. L. 'Trade unions and emigration in late Victorian England: a national lobby for state aid.' *J. Br. Stud.*, XXV, 2 (Spring 1976), 92–116.

4456 **O'Farrell**, P. 'Emigrant attitudes and behaviour as a source for Irish history.' *Hist. Stud.*, X (1976), 109–31.

4457 **Synge**, Jane. 'Immigrant communities – British and continental European – in early twentieth century Hamilton, Canada.' *Oral Hist.*, IV, 2 (Autumn 1976), 38–51.

4458 **Williams**, G. *The desert and the dream*. Cardiff: University of Wales Press, 1976. 230p.
Welsh settlers in Patagonia 1865–1915.

4459 **Williams**, G. 'The structure and process of Welsh emigration to Patagonia.' *Welsh Hist. Rev.*, VIII, I (June 1976), 42–74.

4460 **Department of Employment Gazette**. 'Migration of managers from the U.K.: an analysis of recent information.' *Dep. Employment Gaz.*, LXXXV, 9 (September 1977), 903–5, 964.

4461 **Gottlieb**, Amy Zahl. 'The influence of British trade unionists on the regulation of the mining industry in Illinois, 1872.' *Labor Hist.*, XIX, 3 (Summer 1978), 397–415.

4462 **Souden**, D. 'Rogues, whores and vagabonds? Indentured servant emigrants to North America and the case of mid-seventeenth century Bristol.' *Soc. Hist.*, III, I (January 1978), 23–41.

4463 **Wareing**, John. 'The emigration of indentured servants from London, 1683–86.' *Genealogists' Mag.*, XIX (June 1978), 199–202.

4464 **Jones**, Huw R. 'Modern migration from Scotland to Canada.' *Scott. Geogr. Mag.*, XCV (April 1979), 4–12.

4465 **Kowallis**, Gay P. *To the Great Salt Lake from Litlington: based on the family records of a researcher from Utah*. Bassingbourn: Bassingbourn Village College, 1979. 4, 7p.

4466 **Parry**, Anne. *The Saddleworth–America connection*. Saddleworth: Saddleworth Festival of the Arts, 1979. 44p.

See also: 836.

4. Internal Migration

This section includes works dealing with inter-regional or inter-industrial migration of labour within the United Kingdom. The literature which emphasizes the movement of labour into and out of particular firms is classified at Part Six, II, E, 5. See also Part Six, II, C, 2; and Part Seven, II, D and E.

4467 **Birch**, Stephanie and **Macmillan**, B. *Managers on the move: a study of British managerial mobility.* London: British Institute of Management, 1971. 20p. (B.I.M. management survey report 7.)

4468 **Grant**, E. K. *Migration as an investment in human capital: the inter-regional case in Great Britain.* 1971. (Ph.D. thesis, University of Essex.)

4469 **Jack**, A. B. 'Inter-regional migration in Great Britain: some cross-sectional evidence.' *Scott. J. Polit. Econ.*, XVIII, 2 (June 1971), 147–60.

4470 **Sleeper**, R. D. *Inter-industry labour mobility in Britain since 1959.* 1971. (D.Phil. thesis, University of Oxford.)

4471 **Whalley**, A., **Thomas**, R. and **Pinder**, P. *Advertising overspill: can advertising prevent urban ghettos developing in Britain?* London: Political and Economic Planning, 1971. 48p. (Research studies in advertising 5.)

4472 **Hart**, R. A. 'The economic influence on internal labour force migration.' *Scott. J. Polit. Econ.*, XIX, 2 (June 1972), 151–73.

4473 **Hunt**, E. H. 'How mobile was labour in nineteenth century Britain?' Porter, J. (ed.). *Provincial labour history.* 1972. p. 29–51.

4474 **Thomas**, B. *Migration and urban development: a reappraisal of British and American long cycles.* London: Methuen, 1972. XVI, 259.

4475 **Bather**, Nicholas J. *Population movements in the Oxford sub-region: a test of some spatial models of migration.* Oxford: Oxford Polytechnic, Department of Town Planning, 1973. iii, 58p.

4476 **Burtenshaw**, David. 'Relocated wives.' *New Soc.*, XXIV (21 June 1973), 688–9.

4477 **Gasson**, Ruth. 'Industry and migration of farm workers.' *Oxf. Agrar. Stud.*, II, 2 (1973), 141–60.

4478 **Hart**, R. A. 'Economic expectations and the decision to migrate: an analysis by socio-economic group.' *Reg. Stud.*, VII, 3 (September 1973), 271–85.

4479 **Kasper**, H. 'Measuring the labour market costs of housing dislocation.' *Scott. J. Polit. Econ.*, XX (June 1973), 85–106.

4480 **Kuhn**, Annette, **Poole**, Anne, **Sales**, Pauline and **Wynn**, H. P. 'An analysis of graduate mobility.' *Br. J. Ind. Relat.*, XI, 1 (March 1973), 124–42.
    Partly reprinted in Bartholomew, D. J. (ed.). *Manpower planning.* 1976. p. 279–99.

4481 **Mann**, Michael. *Workers on the move: the sociology of relocation.* Cambridge: Cambridge U.P., 1973. ix, 265p.

4482 **Patten**, J. *Rural – urban migration in pre-industrial England.* Oxford: Oxford University School of Geography, 1973. 61p.

4483 **Roche**, D. J. D., **Birrell**, W. D., **Murie**, A. S. and **Hillyard**, P. A. R., 'Some determinants of labour mobility in Northern Ireland.' *Econ. Soc. Rev.*, V, 1 (October 1973), 59–73.

4484 **Weeden**, R. *Interregional migration models and their application to Great Britain.* Cambridge: Cambridge U.P., 1973. 67p.

4485 **Creedy**, John. 'Inter-regional mobility: a cross-section analysis.' *Scott. J. Polit. Econ.*, XXI, 1 (February 1974), 41–53.

4486 **Guest**, David, **Corby**, Susan, **Kov**, Angela and **Stirling**, Michael. 'Turn again Whittington: why people work in London.' *New Soc.*, XXVIII (16 May 1974), 374–6.

4487 **Hyman**, G. M. *Cumulative inertia and the problem of heterogeneity in the analysis of geographical mobility.* London: Centre for Environmental Studies, 1974. 17p. (Research paper 11.)

4488 **Johnson**, J. H., **Salt**, J. and **Wood**, P. A. *Housing and the migration of labour in England and Wales.* Westmead: Heath, 1974. xiv, 299p.

4489 **Jones**, Huw R. *New town: a case study of migration to a growth point in mid-Wales: report on 1973 survey.* Dundee: Dundee University, Department of Geography, 1974. 72p. (Occasional paper 2.)

4490 **Langley**, P. C. 'Spatial allocation of migrants in England and Wales 1961–6.' *Scott. J. Polit. Econ.*, XXI, 3 (November 1974), 259–77.

4491 **Pickett**, K. G. and **Boulton**, D. K. *Migration and social adjustment: Kirkby and Maghull.* Liverpool: Liverpool U.P., 1974. xiii, 179p.

4492 **Anderson**, Gregory L. 'The recruitment, apprenticeship and mobility of the mid-Victorian clerk: a study of the North and South Wales Bank 1850–75.' *Welsh Hist. Rev.*, VII, 3 (June 1975), 341–56.

4493 **Birrell**, W. D. *Some aspects of labour mobility in Northern Ireland.* Coleraine: New University of Ulster, 1975. 81p.

4494 **Evans**, D. G. *Miners on the move: an investigation relating to the transfer of miners into the Cannock Chase coalfield, with special reference to incomers from Northumberland and Durham.* 1975. (M.A. thesis, University of Keele.)

4495 **Gordon**, Ian. 'Employment and housing streams in British inter-regional migration.' *Scott. J. Polit. Econ.*, XXII, 2 (June 1975), 161–77.

4496 **Mackel**, C. J. *A study of some aspects of the movement of labour within Scottish agriculture.* 1975. (Ph.D. thesis, University of Edinburgh.)

4497 **Taylor**, Robert. 'Moving to jobs.' *New Soc.*, XXIX (20 November 1975), 425–6.

4498 **Beaumont**, Philip B. 'Assisted labour migration flows and Scotland.' *Scott. Geogr. Mag.*, XCII (December 1976), 161–71.

4499 **Beaumont**, Philip B. 'Moving the unemployed.' *Pers. Manage.*, VIII, 12 (December 1976), 30–31.

4500 **Beaumont**, Philip B. 'The problem of return migration under a policy of assisted labour mobility: an examination of some British evidence.' *Br. J. Ind. Relat.*, XIV, 1 (March 1976), 82–8.

4501 **Collins**, E. J. T. 'Migrant labour in British agriculture in the nineteenth century.' *Econ. Hist. Rev.*, XXIX (1976), 38–59.

4502 **Levine**, David. 'The demographic implications of rural industrialization: a family reconstruction study of Shepshed, Leicestershire, 1600–1851.' *Soc. Hist.*, II (May 1976), 177–218.

4503 **Pickles**, May F. 'Mid-Wharfedale 1721 –1812: economic and demographic change in a Pennine dale.' *Local Pop. Stud.*, XVI (Spring 1976), 12–44.

4504 **Redford**, Arthur. *Labour migration in England, 1800–1850.* Manchester: Manchester U.P., 1976. xvi, 209p. Third edition. Revised by W. H. Chaloner.

4505 **Beaumont**, Philip B. 'A further look at return migration rates under the employment transfer scheme in Britain.' *Br. J. Ind. Relat.*, XV, 1 (March 1977), 108–12.

4506 **Williams-Davies**, John. 'Merched y Geddi: a seasonal migration of female labour from rural Wales.' *Folklife*, XV (1977), 12–23.

4507 **British Institute of Management**. *Transferring employees: policy and practice in the UK.* London: The Institute, 1978. (Management survey report 43.)

4508 **Dahlberg**, Ake. 'Effects of migration on the incomes of unemployed people.' *Br. J. Ind. Relat.*, XVI, 1 (March 1978), 86–94.

4509 **Harkell**, Gina. 'The migration of mining families to the Kent coalfield between the wars.' *Oral Hist.*, VI, 1 (Spring 1978), 98 –113.

4510 **Lockhart**, Douglas G. 'Chartulary books: a source for migration in Scotland, 1740 –1850.' *Local Pop. Stud.*, XXI (Autumn 1978), 40–42.

4511 **Martin**, J. M. 'The rich, the poor and the migrant in eighteenth century Stratford-on-Avon.' *Local Pop. Stud.*, XX (Spring 1978), 38–48.

4512 **Palmer**, Derek and **Gleare**, David. 'Moving to find work.' *New Soc.*, XXX (31 August 1978), 454–5.

4513 **Townsend**, Christina and **Freshwater**, Michael. 'Manpower mobility and the grouping of skills.' *Pers. Manage.*, X, 6 (June 1978), 36–9.

4514 **Birks**, Stace and **Sewel**, John. 'A typology

of oil-stimulated movements in northern Scotland: implications for the future.' *Town Plann. Rev.*, L (January 1979), 94–101.

4515 **Devine**, T. M. 'Temporary migration and the Scottish highlands in the nineteenth century.' *Econ. Hist. Rev.*, XXXII, 3 (August 1979), 344–59.

4516 **Hey**, John D. and **McKenna**, Chris J. 'To move or not to move?' *Economica*, XLVI (May 1979), 175–85.

4517 **Lewis**, G. J. 'Mobility, locality and demographic change: the case of North Cardiganshire, 1851–71.' *Welsh Hist. Rev.*, IX (June 1979), 347–61.

4518 **McLure**, Peter. 'Patterns of migration in the late Middle Ages: the evidence of English place-name surnames.' *Econ. Hist. Rev.*, XXXII, 2 (May 1979), 167–82.

See also: 2; 3954; 4333; 4334.

5. Labour Turnover

This section includes works dealing with the movement of labour into and out of particular firms. The literature which emphasises the inter-regional and inter-industrial migration of labour within the United Kingdom is classified at Part Six, II, E, 4. Material on job search is classified at Part Six, II, E, 1. See also Part Two, III; and Part Seven, II, D, 2.

4519 **Bree**, D. S. 'Causal relationships within two variables in dynamic equilibrium: labour turnover and overtime.' *J. Manage. Stud.*, VIII, 1 (February 1971), 13–25.

4520 **Cope**, D. E. *Correlates of labour turnover in a clerical population.* 1971. (M.Phil. thesis, Birkbeck College, University of London.)

4521 **Dawson**, J. A. *The practicability of labour tenure.* 1971. (Ph.D. thesis, University of Bradford.)

4522 **Langrish**, S. V. *The effect of differences in induction and operative training upon labour turnover.* 1971. (M.Ed. thesis, University of Manchester.)

4523 **Owens**, D. *Labour turnover.* 1971. (M.A. thesis, University of Liverpool.)

4524 **Pettman**, Barrie Owen. *Determinants of labour turnover.* Bradford: Institute of Scientific Business, 1971. 100p. (Reports and surveys 5.)

4525 **Van der Merwe**, R. and **Miller**, Sylvia. 'The measurement of labour turnover: a critical appraisal and a suggested new approach.' *Hum. Relat.*, XXIV (June 1971), 233–53.

4526 **Elliston Research Associates**. *What the girls think! Report of the labour turnover attitude survey.* London: N.E.D.O., 1972. 28p.

4527 **Pettman**, Barrie Owen. 'Labour turnover.' *Ind. Soc.*, LIV, 11 (November 1972), 12–14.

4528 **Stoikov**, V. 'Quits and hires revisited.' *Br. J. Ind. Relat.*, X, 2 (July 1972), 298–9.

4529 **Wild**, Ray and **Dawson**, Alistair. *Labour*

turnover: theories and remedial action. Bradford: MCB Books, 1972. 28p.

4530 **Willis**, Kenneth George. *Geographical and labour mobility: electrical engineering, steel and woodworkers on Tyneside.* Newcastle-upon-Tyne: University of Newcastle-upon-Tyne, Department of Geography, 1972. 52p.

4531 **Elliston Research Associates**. *Employees' attitudes and their effect on labour turnover in the clothing industry.* London: N.E.D.O., 1973. 75p.

4532 **Industrial Society**. *Absence and labour turnover: survey.* London: The Society, 1973. 42p. (Survey and report series 182.)

4533 **Pettman**, Barrie Owen. 'Factors influencing labour turnover.' *Ind. Relat. J.*, IV, 3 (Autumn 1973), 43–61.

4534 **Ruskin College** (Oxford), Trade Union Research Unit. *Bitter lesson: teacher turnover and the London Allowance: a sample survey.* London: National Union of Teachers, 1973. 22p.

4535 **Wild**, Ray and **Gibb**, W. *Cost of labour turnover in the wool textile industry.* London: N.E.D.O., 1973. 16p.

4536 **Bramham**, John T. 'Staff succession.' *Pers. Rev.*, III, 4 (Winter 1974), 52–6.
Gas industry.

4537 **Gow**, John S., **Clark**, Alfred W. and **Dossett**, Graham S. 'A path analysis of variables influencing labour turnover.' *Hum. Relat.*, XXVII (September 1974), 703–19.

4538 **Moreton**, T. 'Labour turnover and job choice.' *Pers. Rev.*, III, 4 (Winter 1974), 12–22.

4539 **Lack**, C. D. *Labour turnover and retention in a local authority.* 1974–5. (M.Sc. thesis, University of Bath.)

4540 **Pettman**, Barrie Owen. *Labour turnover and retention.* Epping: Gower, 1975. XIX, 204p.

4541 **Van der Merwe**, R. and **Miller**, Sylvia. 'Inter-organizational labour turnover.' *J. Occup. Psychol.*, XLVIII, 3 (1975), 137–52.

4542 **Nickell**, S. J. 'Wage structures and quit rates.' *Int. Econ. Rev.*, XVII, 1 (February 1976), 191–203.

4543 **Prentice**, Gordon. 'Labour turnover and unemployment: what's the connection?' *Pers. Manage.*, VIII, 8 (August 1976), 33–7.

4544 **Price**, J. L. 'The measurement of turnover.' *Ind. Relat. J.*, VI, 4 (Winter 1975–6), 33–46.

4545 **Woodward**, N. 'Economic causes of labour turnover: a case study.' *Ind. Relat. J.*, VI, 4 (Winter 1975–6), 19–32.

4546 **Richardson**, Ray, **Robinson**, Chris and **Smith**, John. 'Quit rates and manpower policy.' *Dep. Employment Gaz.*, LXXXV, 1 (January 1977), 14–18.

4547 **Tüleyloğlu**, A. *A study of labour turnover in G.B. and U.S. manufacturing industries, 1958–73.* 1977. (Ph.D thesis, University of Lancaster.)

4548 **Wickens**, M. R. 'An econometric model of labour turnover in UK manufacturing industries 1956–73.' *Rev. Econ. Stud.*, XLV (October 1978), 469–77.

4549 **Zabalza**, Antoni. 'Internal labour mobility in the teaching profession.' *Econ. J.*, LXXXVIII (June 1978), 314–30.

4550 **Dillard**, J.F. and **Ferris**, K. R. 'Sources of professional staff turnover in public accounting firms.' *Account. Organ. Soc.*, IV, 3 (1979), 179–86.

4551 **Incomes Data Services**. *Labour turnover 1.* London: I.D.S., 1979. 14p. (I.D.S. study 199.)

4552 **Incomes Data Services**. *Labour turnover 2.* London: I.D.S., 1979. 21p. (I.D.S. study 201.)

4553 **Mercer**, Geoffrey. *The employment of nurses: nursing labour turnover in the NHS.* London: Croom Helm, 1979. 192p.

4554 **Williams**, Allan, **Levy**, Bryan, **Silverstone**, Rosalie and **Adams**, Paul. 'Factors associated with labour turnover.' *J. Occup. Psychol.*, LII, 1 (1979), 1–16.

See also: 27; 475; 510; 3542; 3949; 3978; 5351; 5680.

6. Private Labour Exchanges

See also Part Seven, II, D, 2.

4555 **Fulop**, Christina. *Markets for employment.* London: Institute of Economic Affairs, 1971. 114p.

4556 **Hayburn**, Ralph H. C. 'The Voluntary Occupational Centre Movement 1932–1939.' *J. Contemp. Hist.*, VI, 3 (1971), 156–71.

4557 **Bail**, David. 'Agency nursed.' *New Soc.*, XX (4 May 1972), 235–6.

4558 **Fulop**, Christina. 'The marketing of placement services.' *Eur. J. Mark.*, VI, 2 (Summer 1972), 87–97.

4559 **Campling**, Jo. 'Jobs and agencies.' *New Soc.*, XXVIII (23 May 1974), 445–6.

4560 **Bell**, E. G. *A study of private, fee-charging employment agencies in the office sector in Britain.* 1975. (M.Sc. thesis, University of Strathclyde.)

4561 **Federation of Personnel Services of Great Britain**. *Agency nurses: a national survey of attitudes, comments and statistics.* London: The Federation, 1975. iv, 27p.

4562 **Federation of Personnel Services of Great Britain**. *Private employment agencies: a survey of their services to permanent and temporary office workers.* London: The Federation, 1975. 32p.

4563 **Federation of Personnel Services of Great Britain**. *Temporary: a national survey of attitudes, comments and regional statistics.* London: The Federation, 1975. 35, xxip.

See also: 6277.

III. WAGES AND THE DISTRIBUTION OF INCOME

This section contains material which is primarily concerned with wages and salaries as opposed to other conditions of employment. Material relating to both wages and hours is generally classified here and is cross-referenced from Part Six, IV, B. See also the general note to Part Six. See also Part Seven, IV.

A. GENERAL

The literature on the economic effects of trade unions is classified here. Material on the relationship between unemployment and wages is classified at Part Six, I. See also Part Six, IV, A, 1.

4564 **Bechhoffer**, Frank. 'A sociological portrait: income.' *New Soc.*, XVIII (14 October 1971), 707–9.

4565 **Buckingham**, Graeme Lovell. 'Fact or fiction.' *Twentieth Century*, CLXXIX, 1046 (1971), 34–7.

4566 **Department of Employment.** *Labour costs in Great Britain 1968.* London: H.M.S.O., 1971. 71p.

4567 **Hartley**, Keith. 'Salary payments, age and learning.' *Bull. Econ. Res.*, XXIII, 1 (May 1971), 42–9.

4568 **Incomes Data Services.** *The pay of young workers: changes in the pattern of paying apprentices and manual workers.* London: I.D.S., 1971. 15p. (I.D.S. study 8.)

4569 **Pencavel**, John H. 'A note on the comparative predictive performance of wage inflation models of the British economy.' *Econ. J.*, LXXXI, 1 (March 1971), 113–9.

4570 **Phelps Brown**, Ernest Henry. 'The analysis of wage movements under full employment.' *Scott. J. Polit. Econ.*, XVIII, 3 (November 1971), 233–43.

4571 **Turner**, Herbert Arthur and **Wilkinson**, Frank. 'Real net incomes and the wage explosion.' *New Soc.*, XVII (25 February 1971), 309–10.

4572 **Burton**, John. *Wage inflation.* London: Macmillan, 1972. 94p.

4573 **Haberler**, Gottfried, **Parkin**, Michael and **Smith**, Henry. *Inflation and the unions: three studies in the effects of labour monopoly power on inflation in Britain and the US.* London: Institute of Economic Affairs, 1972. xii, 88p. (Readings in political economy 6.)

4574 **Incomes Data Services.** *Guide to pay statistics part 3.* London: I.D.S., 1972. 16p. (I.D.S. study 43.)

4575 **Jackson**, Dudley and **Turner**, Herbert A. 'Inflation, strato-inflation and social conflict.' Jackson, D. and others (eds.). *Do trade unions cause inflation?* 1972. p. 11–62.

4576 **Johnston**, J. 'A model of wage determination under bilateral monopoly.' *Econ. J.*, LXXXII, 327 (September 1972), 837–52.

Reprinted in Laidler, D. and Purdy, D. (eds.). *Inflation and labour markets.* 1973. p. 61–78.

4577 **Knight**, K. G. 'Strikes and wage inflation in British manufacturing industry 1950–1968.' *Oxf. Univ. Inst. Econ. Stat. Bull.*, XXXIV, 3 (August 1972), 281–94.

4578 **Smith**, Henry. 'The power of the unions.' Haberler, G., Parkin, M. and Smith, H. *Inflation and the unions.* 1972. p. 79–88.

4579 **Fogarty**, Michael Patrick. 'Fiscal measures and wage settlements.' *Br. J. Ind. Relat.*, XI, 1 (March 1973), 29–65.

4580 **Incomes Data Services.** *The pay of young workers.* London: I.D.S., 1973. 20p. (I.D.S. study 64.)

4581 **Institute of Manpower Studies.** 'Wage inflation in Britain.' *I.M.S. Monit.*, II, 1 (April 1973), 13–28; II, 2 (July 1973), 61–80.

4582 **Johnston**, J. and **Timbrell**, M. 'Empirical tests of a bargaining theory of wage rate determination.' *Manchr. Sch. Econ. Soc. Stud.*, XLI, 2 (July 1973), 141–67.

Reprinted in Laidler, D. and Purdy, D. (eds.). *Inflation and labour markets.* 1973. p. 79–108.

4583 **Jones**, Dewi-Davies. *Wages and employment in the E.E.C.* London: Kogan Page, 1973. 159p.

See especially Part 3: 'The effect on British employment and industrial relations of E.E.C. entry.' p. 137–46.

4584 **Mulvey**, Charles and **Trevithick**, J. A. 'Trade unions and wage inflation.' *Econ. Soc. Rev.*, IV, 2 (June 1973), 209–29.

4585 **Office of Manpower Economics.** *Wage drift: review of literature and research.* London: H.M.S.O., 1973. iv, 67p.

4586 **Purdy**, David L. and **Zis**, G. 'On the concept and measurement of union militancy.' Laidler, D.E.W. and Purdy, D.L. (eds.). *Inflation and labour markets.* 1973. p. 38–60.

4587 **Purdy**, David L. and **Zis**, G. 'Trade unions and wage inflation in the U.K.: a re-appraisal.' Laidler, D.E.W. and Purdy, D.L. (eds.). *Inflation and labour markets.* 1973. p. 1–37.

4588 **Rees**, Albert. *The economics of work and pay.* New York: Harper & Row.

First edition. 1973. 246p.

Second edition. 1979. xi, 228p.

4589 **Wilkinson**, R.K. and **Burkitt**, B. 'Wage determination and trade unions.' *Scott. J. Polit. Econ.*, XX, 2 (June 1973), 107–22.

4590 **Behrend**, Hilde. *Attitudes to price increases and pay claims.* London: N.E.D.O., 1974. v, 77p. (Monograph 4.)

4591 **Behrend**, Hilde. 'The impact of inflation on pay increase expectations and ideas of fair pay.' *Ind. Relat. J.*, v, 1 (Spring 1974), 5–10.

4592 **Burkitt**, Brian. 'Relationship between earnings and unionization in the inter-war years.' *Appl. Econ.*, VI, 2 (June 1974), 83–93.

4593 **Creedy**, John. 'Income changes over the life cycle.' *Oxf. Econ. Pap.*, XXVI (November 1974), 405–23.

4594 **Hyman**, Richard. 'Inequality, ideology and industrial relations.' *Br. J. Ind. Relat.*, XII, 2 (July 1974), 171–90.

4595 **Incomes Data Services.** *Cost of living arrangements.* London: I.D.S., 1974. 31p. (I.D.S. study 88.)

4596 **Lawson**, Nigel. 'New inflation, old obsession.' *Encounter*, XLIII (August 1974), 88–92.

4597 **Legge**, Karen and **Hilling**, S. 'Absence, overtime and the structure of the pay packet: some methodological points.' *J. Manage. Stud.*, XI, 3 (October 1974), 205–23; XII, 1 (February 1975), 45–65.

4598 **MacKay**, Donald I. and **Hart**, R. A. 'Wage inflation and the Phillips relationship.' *Manchr. Sch. Econ. Soc. Stud.*, XLII, 2 (June 1974), 136–61.

4599 **Pencavel**, John H. 'Relative wages and trade unions in the United Kingdom.' *Economica*, XLI, 162 (May 1974), 194–210.

4600 **Routh**, Guy G. C. 'Interpretations of pay structure.' *Int. J. Soc. Econ.*, I, 1 (1974), 13–39.

4601 **Stephen**, Frank H. 'Wage determination and trade unions: a comment.' *Scott. J. Polit. Econ.*, XXI, 2 (June 1974), 177–80.

4602 **Stephen**, Frank H. 'Wage determination and trade unions: a rejoinder.' *Scott. J. Polit. Econ.*, XXI, 3 (November 1974), 295–7.

4603 **Ward**, R. and **Zis**, G. 'Trade union militancy as an explanation of inflation: an international comparison.' *Manchr. Sch. Econ. Soc. Stud.*, XLII, 1 (March 1974), 46–65.

4604 **Wilkinson**, R. K. and **Burkitt**, Brian. 'Wage determination and trade unions: a reply.' *Scott. J. Polit. Econ.*, XXI (June 1974), 181-5.

4605 **Ashenfelter**, Orley and **Pencavel**, John H. 'Wage changes and the frequency of wage settlements.' *Economica*, XLII (May 1975), 168–70.

4606 **Burkitt**, Brian. *Trade unions and wages: implications for economic theory.* London: Granada, 1975. ix, 214p.

4607 **Department of Employment Gazette.** 'Wage drift: evidence from the New Earnings Survey.' *Dep. Employment Gaz.*, LXXXIII, 8 (August 1975), 754–6.

4608 **Husband**, Tom M. 'Management style and fair payment.' *Pers. Rev.*, IV, 4 (Autumn 1975), 23–6.

4609 **Hyman**, Richard and **Brough**, Ian. *Social values and industrial relations: a study of fairness and inequality.* Oxford: Blackwell, 1975. x, 277p. (Warwick studies in industrial relations.)

4610 **Incomes Data Services.** *The pay of young*

workers. London: I.D.S., 1975. 20p. (I.D.S. study 98.)

4611 **Incomes Data Services.** *Pay patterns and policies.* London: I.D.S., 1975. 20p. (I.D.S. study 90.)

4612 **Jackson**, Dudley and **Turner**, Herbert A. 'Inflation, strato-inflation and social conflict.' Jackson, D. and others (eds.). *Do trade unions cause inflation?* 1975. p. 11–62.

4613 **McCarthy**, William Edward John, **O'Brien**, J. F. and **Dowd**, V. G. *Wage inflation and wage leadership: a study of the role of key wage bargains in the Irish system of collective bargaining.* Dublin: Economic and Social Research Institute, 1975. 229p. (Papers 79.)

4614 **Norris**, W.K. 'Differentials in pay.' *Lloyds Bank Rev.*, CXVIII (October 1975), 27–39.

4615 **Paish**, F. W. 'Inflation, personal incomes and taxation.' *Lloyds Bank Rev.*, CXVI (April 1975), 1–20.

4616 **Tylecote**, Andrew B. 'Determinants of changes in the wage hierarchy in United Kingdom manufacturing industry 1954–70: a test of a new theory of wage determination under collective bargaining.' *Br. J. Ind. Relat.*, XIII, 1 (March 1975), 65–77.

4617 **Addison**, John T. 'Composition of manual worker wage earnings.' *Br. J. Ind. Relat.*, XIV, 1 (March 1976), 56–69,

4618 **Ashenfelter**, Orley and **Pencavel**, John H. 'A note on measuring the relationship between changes in earnings and changes in wage rates.' *Br. J. Ind. Relat.*, XIV, 1 (March 1976), 70–76.

4619 **Elliott**, R. F. 'The national wage round in the United Kingdom.' *Oxf. Univ. Inst. Econ. Stat. Bull.*, XXXVIII (August 1976), 179–201.

4620 **Hart**, P. E. 'The dynamics of earnings.' *Econ. J.*, LXXXVI (September 1976), 551–65.

4621 **Hawkesworth**, R. I. 'Private and public sector pay.' *Br. J. Ind. Relat.*, XIV, 2 (July 1976), 206–13.

4622 **Holden**, K. and **Peel**, D. A. 'The internal/external labour market and the rate of wage inflation in U.K. manufacturing industry.' *Manchr. Sch. Econ. Soc. Stud.*, XLIV (June 1976), 132–46.

4623 **Incomes Data Services.** *Young workers' pay.* London: I.D.S., 1976. 17p. (I.D.S. study 131.)

4624 **Kahn**, Richard Ferdinand. 'Thoughts on the behaviour of wages and monetarism.' *Lloyds Bank Rev.*, CXIX (January 1976), 1–11.

4625 **Metcalf**, David, **Nickell**, Stephen and **Richardson**, Ray. 'The structure of hours and earnings in British manufacturing industry.' *Oxf. Econ. Pap.*, XXVIII (July 1976), 284–303.

4626 **Mulvey**, Charles. 'Collective agreements and relative earnings in U.K. manufacturing in 1973.' *Economica*, XLIII (1976), 419–27.

4627 **Mulvey**, Charles and **Foster**, J. I. 'Occupational earnings in the U.K. and the effects of collective agreements.' *Manchr. Sch.*

Econ. Soc. Stud., XLIV, 3 (September 1976), 258–75.

4628 **Wootton**, Barbara. 'Must we be paid what we are paid?' Field, F. (ed.). *Are low wages inevitable?* 1976. p. 37–41.

4629 **Armstrong**, K. J., **Bowers**, David and **Burkitt**, Brian. 'The measurement of trade union bargaining power.' *Br. J. Ind. Relat.*, xv, 1 (March 1977), 91–100.

4630 **Copeland**, Laurence S. 'Wage-inflation, productivity and wage leadership.' *Manchr. Sch. Econ. Soc. Stud.*, XLV, 3 (September 1977), p. 258–69.

4631 **Incomes Data Services.** *Duration of agreements: the wage round and cost of living arrangements.* London: I.D.S., 1977. (I.D.S. study 158.)

4632 **Mulvey**, Charles and **Gregory**, Mary. 'The Hines wage inflation model.' *Manchr. Sch. Econ. Soc. Stud.*, XLV, 1 (March 1977), 29–40.

4633 **Scarth**, W. M. 'Expectations and the wage – price spiral in a simple monetary model.' *Manchr. Sch. Econ. Soc. Stud.*, XLV, 3 (September 1977), 208–20.

4634 **Zis**, George. 'On the role of strikes variables in U.K. wage equations.' *Scott. J. Polit. Econ.*, XXIV (February 1977), 43–53.

4635 **Addison**, John T. 'The balance of market advantage.' Institute of Economic Affairs. *Trade unions: public goods or public bads?* 1978. p. 34–7.

4636 **Burkitt**, Brian, **Bowers**, J. and **Armstrong**, K. J. 'The relationship between money wages and unionization: a re-appraisal.' *Bull. Econ. Res.*, XXX (November 1978), 95–107.

4637 **Clark**, Colin. 'Wages and profits.' *Oxf. Econ. Pap.*, XXX (November 1978), 388–408.

4638 **Demery**, D. and **McNabb**, R. 'The effect of demand on the union relative wage effect in the United Kingdom.' *Br. J. Ind. Relat.*, XVI, 3 (November 1978), 303–8.

4639 **Elliott**, Robert F. and **Dean**, A. J. H. 'The official wage rates index and the size of wage settlements.' *Oxf. Bull. Econ. Stat.*, XL (August 1978), 249–61.

4640 **Griffiths**, Brian. 'The economics of labour power: can trade unions raise real wages?' Institute of Economic Affairs. *Trade unions: public goods or public bads?* 1978. p. 101–11.

4641 **Grimond**, Jo. 'Trade unions harm the poor.' Institute of Economic Affairs. *Trade unions: public goods or public bads?* 1978. p. 129–32.

4642 **Hanson**, Charles G. 'Collective bargaining: the balance of market advantage.' Institute of Economic Affairs. *Trade unions: public goods or public bads?* 1978. p. 23–9.

4643 **Hartley**, Keith. 'Can trade unions raise real wages?' Institute of Economic Affairs. *Trade unions: public goods or public bads?* 1978. p. 114–16.

4644 **Holt**, D. H. *Empirical evidence on inflation and wage rate expectations: a disaggregated study based*

on qualitative data. 1978. (Ph.D. thesis, University of Strathclyde.)

4645 **Incomes Data Services.** *Relativities.* London: I.D.S., 1978. 20p. (I.D.S. study 172.)

4646 **Institute of Economic Affairs.** *Trade unions: public goods or public bads?* London: The Institute, 1978. xiv, 134p. (Readings 17.)
Report of a seminar, with an address by Lord Scarman.

4647 **Layard**, Roger, **Metcalf**, D. and **Nickell**, S. J. 'The effect of collective bargaining on relative and absolute wages.' *Br. J. Ind. Relat.*, XVI, 3 (November 1978), 287–302.

4648 **Mathias**, Peter. 'Economists, trade unions and wages.' Institute of Economic Affairs. *Trade unions: public goods or public bads?* 1978. p. 13–16.

4649 **Robbins**, *Lord.* 'Economists and trade unions, 1776–1977.' Institute of Economic Affairs. *Trade unions: public goods or public bads?* 1978. p. 5–12.

4650 **Smith**, Philip M. and **Wilton**, David A. 'Wage changes: the frequency of wage settlements, the variability of contract length and locked-in wage adjustments.' *Economica*, XLV (August 1978), 305–10.

4651 **Wabe**, John Stuart and **Leech**, Dennis. 'Relative earnings in UK manufacturing: a reconsideration of the evidence.' *Econ. J.*, LXXXVIII (June 1978), 296–313.

4652 **Wood**, Adrian. *A theory of pay.* Cambridge: Cambridge U.P., 1978. ix, 251p.

4653 **Artis**, M. J. and **Miller**, M. H. 'Inflation, real wages and the terms of trade.' Bowers, J. (ed.). *Inflation, development and integration.* 1979. p. 55–86.

4654 **Beenstock**, Michael and **Immanuel**, Harold. 'The market approach to pay comparability.' *Natl. Westminster Bank Q. Rev.* (November 1979), 26–41.

4655 **Brown**, William. 'Social determinants of pay.' Stephenson, G. and Brotherton, C. (eds.). *Industrial relations: a social psychological approach.* 1979. 115–30.

4656 **Confederation of British Industry.** *Pay: the choice ahead: CBI proposals for reforming pay determination.* London: C.B.I., 1979.

4657 **Turner**, Herbert A. 'The wages of fear.' *New Soc.*, XLVII (1 February 1979), 243–4.

4658 **Turnovsky**, Stephen J. 'Inflationary expectations in a two-sector model of wage – price determination.' *Oxf. Econ. Pap.*, XXXI (March 1979), 1–19.

See also: 334; 621; 694; 1145; 1171; 1172; 1672; 1673; 1674; 1675; 1700; 1701; 1725; 1878; 2136; 4542; 5007.

B. CHRONOLOGICAL STUDIES

This section contains works which are primarily concerned with describing or explaining the level of wages prevailing in a specific period or the changes in these levels over time. Chronological studies with a primarily regional focus are classified in Part Six, III, C and those with a primarily industrial or occupational focus in Part Six, III, D; those relating to women's wages are classified in Part Six, III, E. Some of the works on trade unionism in Part Three, II, B also contain material on wages and salaries.

4659 **Agarwala**, R. and **Goodson**, G. C. 'A study of earnings from employment in British industries 1958–1966.' *Bull. Econ. Res.*, XXIII, 1 (May 1971), 35–41.

4660 **Department of Employment.** *Prices and earnings in 1951–69: an econometric assessment.* London: H.M.S.O., 1971. 42p.

4661 **Levi**, L. *Wages and earnings of the working classes.* Shannon: Irish U.P., 1971. vii, 151p. Covers the period 1867–79.

4662 **Porter**, J. H. 'Wage determination by selling price sliding scales 1870–1914.' *Manchr. Sch. Econ. Soc. Stud.*, XXXIX, 1 (March 1971), 13–21.

4663 **Incomes Data Services.** *Guide to salary surveys 1972.* London: I.D.S., 1972. 40p. (I.D.S. study 23.)

4664 **Incomes Data Services.** *Guide to salary surveys 1973.* London: I.D.S., 1973. 35p. (I.D.S. study 63.)

4665 **Incomes Data Services.** *Panorama July 1973.* London: I.D.S., 1973. 103p. (I.D.S. study 57.)

4666 **Flinn**, M. W. 'Trends in real wages, 1750 –1850.' *Econ. Hist. Rev.*, XXVII, 3 (August 1974), 395–413.

4667 **Incomes Data Services.** *Guide to salary surveys 1974.* London: I.D.S., 1974. 37p. (I.D.S. study 89.)

4668 **Dowie**, J. A. '1919–20 is in need of attention.' *Econ. Hist. Rev.*, XXVIII, 3 (August 1975), 429–50.

4669 **Incomes Data Services.** *Guide to salary surveys 1975.* London: I.D.S., 1975. 40p. (I.D.S. study 112.)

4670 **Burkitt**, B. and **Bowers**, D. 'Wage inflation and union power in the United Kingdom: 1949–1967.' *Appl. Econ.*, VIII (1976), 289 –300.

4671 **Flinn**, M. W. 'Real wage trends in Britain, 1750–1850: a reply.' *Econ. Hist. Rev.*, XXIX, 1 (February 1976), 143–5.

4672 **Gourvish**, T. R. 'Flinn and real wage trends in Britain, 1750–1850: a comment.' *Econ. Hist. Rev.*, XXIX, 1 (February 1976), 136–42.

4673 **Mulvey**, Charles. 'Collective agreements and relative earnings in U.K. manufacturing in 1973.' *Economica*, XLIII (1976), 419–27.

4674 **Donnelly**, F. K. 'Documents: the value of labour in 1819.' *Soc. Study Labour Hist. Bull.*, XXXV (Autumn 1977), 33–4.

4675 **Incomes Data Services.** *Guide to salary surveys.* London: I.D.S., 1977. 32p. (I.D.S. study 137.)

4676 **Incomes Data Services.** *Review of settlements.* London: I.D.S., 1977. 22p. (I.D.S. study 146.)

4677 **Elliott**, R. F. and **Shelton**, H. C. 'A wage settlements index for the United Kingdom, 1950–1975.' *Oxf. Bull. Econ. Stat.*, XL (November 1978), 303–19.

4678 **Incomes Data Services.** *Guide to salary surveys 1977.* London: I.D.S., 1978. 37p. (I.D.S. study 161.)

4679 **Incomes Data Services.** *1978 review of settlements.* London: I.D.S., 1978. 17p. (I.D.S. study 177.)

4680 **Zis**, George. 'The 1969–70 wage explosion in the United Kingdom.' *Natl. Westminster Bank Q. Rev.* (February 1978), 55–64.

4681 **Incomes Data Services.** *Salary surveys 1978.* London: I.D.S., 1979. 33p. (I.D.S. study 185.)

4682 **Von Tunzelmann**, G. N. 'Trends in real wages 1750–1850 revisited.' *Econ. Hist. Rev.*, XXXII (February 1979), 33–49.

See also: 1725.

C. REGIONAL STUDIES

This section includes works with a primarily geographical orientation. Works comparing the United Kingdom as a whole with other countries are classified at Part Six, III, A. Many of the industrial and occupational studies in Part Six, III, D refer to a specific town or region. Some of the works on trade unionism in Part Three, II, C also contain material on wages and salaries.

4683 **Hunt**, E. H. *Regional wage variations in Britain, 1850–1914.* 1971. (Ph.D thesis, University of London.)

4684 **McGillivray**, A. *Regional differentials in the average earnings from employment in manufacturing industry.* 1971. (B.Phil. thesis, University of Dundee.)

4685 **Metcalf**, David. 'The determinants of earnings changes: a regional analysis for the V.F. 1960–1968.' *Int. Econ. Rev.*, XII, 2 (June 1971), 273–82.

4686 **Eversley**, D. E. C. 'Rising costs and static incomes: some economic consequences of regional planning in London.' *Urb. Stud.*, IX (October 1972), 347–68.

4687 **Hoch**, Irving. 'Income and city size.' *Urb. Stud.*, IX (October 1972), 299–328.

4688 **Schwarz**, L. D. 'Occupations and incomes in late eighteenth century East London.' *E. London Pap.*, XIV (December 1972), 87–100.

4689 **Corby**, Susan, **Kov**, Angela and **Stirling**, Michael. *Making allowances: a survey of attitudes towards London weightings.* London: London School of Economics, Personnel Management Department, 1973. 79p.

4690 **Hunt**, E. H. *Regional wage variations in Britain, 1850–1914.* Oxford: Clarendon Press, 1973. xii, 388p.

4691 **Sadler**, Peter, **Archer**, Brian and **Owen**, Christine. *Regional income multipliers: the*

Anglesey study. Bangor: University of Wales Press, 1973. 109p. (Bangor occasional papers in economics 10.)

4692 **Hare**, P. G. 'Regional investment criteria and shadow wage rates.' *Scott. J. Polit. Econ.,* XXII (November 1975), 305–20.

4693 **Mayhew**, K. 'Earnings dispersion in local labour markets: implications for search behaviour.' *Oxf. Bull. Econ. Stat.,* XXXIX, 2 (May 1977), 93–107.

4694 **Norris**, G. M. 'Industrial paternalist capitalism and local labour markets.' *Sociology,* XII, 3 (September 1978), 469–89.

4695 **Treble**, James H. 'The market for unskilled male labour in Glasgow, 1891–1914.' MacDougall, I. (ed.). *Essays in Scottish labour history.* 1978. p. 115–42.

See also: 1725; 3900; 4723; 4805; 4810; 5099.

D. OCCUPATIONAL AND INDUSTRIAL STUDIES

This section includes works with a primarily industrial or occupational orientation. Some of the works on trade unionism in Part Three, II, D, on collective bargaining in Part Five, IV, and on industrial conflict in Part Five, V, C also contain material on wages and salaries. See also Part Six, IV, A, 2.

4696 **Agricultural Wages Board for England and Wales.** *Guide to the agricultural wages structure in England and Wales.* London: Ministry of Agriculture, Fisheries and Food, 1971.

4697 **Architects' Journal.** 'Current wage rates, market prices and measured rates.' *Archit. J.,* CLIII (24 February 1971), 435–8.

4698 **Burkitt**, Brian. *A study of inter-industry wage determination: 1924–1938.* 1971. (Ph.D thesis, University of Leeds.)

4699 **Department of Education and Science.** *Survey of earnings of qualified manpower in England and Wales 1966–67.* London: H.M.S.O., 1971. viii, 43p. (Statistics of education, special series 3.)

4700 **Evans**, John. 'Salary patterns and the language of responsibility.' *Pers. Manage.,* III, 5 (May 1971), 25–8.

4701 **Incomes Data Services.** *Draughtsmen's pay: a survey of pay and gradings in the public sector.* London: I.D.S., 1971. 16p. (I.D.S. study 14.)

4702 **Institute for Workers' Control.** *Trade unions and rising prices: evidence of the IWC to the Court of Enquiry into Pay for Electricity Workers* ... Nottingham: The Institute, 1971. 24p. (I.W.C. pamphlet 24.)

4703 **Morgan**, V. 'Agricultural wage rates in late eighteenth century Scotland.' *Econ. Hist. Rev.,* XXIV, 2 (May 1971), 181–201.

4704 **RIBA Journal**. 'Architects' earnings: survey shows no improvement since 1967.' *RIBA J.,* LXXVIII (December 1971), 553–6.

4705 **Review Body on Doctors' and Dentists' Remuneration**. [*Report*] *1971.* London: H.M.S.O., 1971. 32p. (Cmnd. 4825.)
Chairman: The Earl of Halsbury.

4706 **Review Body on Top Salaries**. *First report: Ministers of the Crown and Members of Parliament.* London: H.M.S.O., 1971. 108p. (Cmnd. 4836.)
Chairman: Edward Boyle, Lord Boyle of Handsworth.

4707 **Battelle Memorial Institute**, Research Center. *Report on general service salary structure in London.* Geneva: The Institute, 1972. [224]p.
Office workers.

4708 **Bowey**, Angela M. *Salary structures for management careers.* London: Institute of Personnel Management, 1972. 31p.

4709 **Bowey**, Angela M. and **Lupton**, Tom. 'Job and pay comparisons in collective bargaining: a systematic procedure.' *Pers. Rev.,* I, 3 (Summer 1972), 74–84.

4710 **Department of Health and Social Security**, Committee on Nursing. *Report of the ... Committee.* London: H.M.S.O., 1972. x, 327p. (Cmnd. 5115.)
Chairman: Asa Briggs.

4711 **Ellery**, J. B. *Guide to grades and payscales in small scale computing.* Croydon: MSOR Ltd., 1972.

4712 **Farningham**, A. I. 'The electricity supply industry's work study data bank.' *Ind. Relat J.,* III, 1 (Spring 1972), 51–63.

4713 **Findlater**, Richard. 'What book writers earn.' *Author,* LXXXIII (Winter 1972), 147–55.

4714 **Hughes**, John and **Moore**, Roy (eds.). *A special case? Social justice and the miners.* Harmondsworth: Penguin, 1972. 164p.

4715 **Incomes Data Services.** *Drivers' pay.* Part 1. London: I.D.S., 1972. 16p. (I.D.S. study 25.)

4716 **Incomes Data Services.** *Drivers' pay.* Part 2. London: I.D.S., 1972. 16p. (I.D.S. study 38.)

4717 **Newby**, H. 'The low earnings of agricultural workers: a sociological approach.' *J. Agric. Econ.,* XXIII, 1 (January 1972), 15–24.

4718 **Pickard**, B. 'What's it worth?' *Ind. Soc.,* LIV, 4 (April 1972), 12–15.

4719 **Rawling**, Ian. 'Salaried architects want their own code.' *RIBA J.,* LXXIX (December 1972), 505–6.

4720 **Review Body on Doctors' and Dentists' Remuneration**. *Report 1972.* London: H.M.S.O., 1972. 80p. (Cmnd. 5010.)
Chairman: The Earl of Halsbury.

4721 **Review Body on Top Salaries**. *Report 2: interim report on top salaries.* London: H.M.S.O., 1972. 30p. (Cmnd. 5001.)
Chairman: Lord Boyle.

4722 **Scottish Education Department**, Arbitral Body of the Salaries of Teachers in Scotland.

Report of the Arbitral Body... London: H.M.S.O., 1972. 40p.
Chairman: Laurence Colvin Hunter.

4723 **Wood**, Oliver. 'A colliery payroll in 1802: Howgill Colliery, Cumberland.' *Cumberland & Westmorland Antiq. Archaeol. Soc. Trans.*, LXXII (1972), 303–19.

4724 **Young**, D. 'Executive remuneration and the Common Market.' *Pers. Manage.*, IV, 2 (February 1972), 26–9.

4725 **Bowey**, Angela M. and **Lupton**, Tom. *Job and pay comparisons: how to identify similar jobs in different companies and compare their rates of pay.* Epping: Gower, 1973. 96p.

4726 **Calvert**, C. J. and **Galton**, C. R. 'Controlled bank salary costs.' *Bankers' Mag.*, CCXV, 1546 (January 1973), 9–12.

4727 **Department of Employment**. *Report of an Inquiry into Remuneration of Electricians employed in the National Health Service.* London: H.M.S.O., 1973. 24p.
Chairman: W. A. Davidson.

4728 **Ellis**, Valerie. 'Civil Service pay: policy and principles.' *Pers. Manage.*, V, 4 (April 1973), 28–30.

4729 **Hughes**, Barry. 'Wages of the strong and the weak.' *J. Ind. Relat.*, XV, 1 (March 1973), 1–24.

4730 **Incomes Data Services**. *Canteen workers' pay.* London: I.D.S., 1973. 16p. (I.D.S. study 49.)

4731 **Incomes Data Services**. *Draughtsmen's pay.* Part 3. London: I.D.S., 1973. 16p. (I.D.S. study 45.)

4732 **Incomes Data Services**. *Drivers' pay.* London: I.D.S., 1973. 20p. (I.D.S. study 59.)

4733 **Incomes Data Services**. *Pay of laboratory technicians.* London: I.D.S., 1973. 16p. (I.D.S. study 53.)

4734 **McDougall**, Camilla. 'How well do you reward your managers?' *Pers. Manage.*, V, 3 (March 1973), 38–41.

4735 **Morgan**, Vernon. 'Civil Service pay: the role of the Pay Research Unit.' *Pers. Manage.*, V, 4 (April 1973), 26–7.

4736 **Pilcher**, R., **Jepson**, W.B., **Bayley**, L.G. and **Robinson**, C.K. *Building industry wage structure.* London: IPC Building and Contract Journals Ltd, 1973. 34p.

4737 **Review Body on Armed Forces Pay**. *Pay of service medical and dental officers.* London: H.M.S.O., 1973. 8p. (Cmnd. 5450.)
Chairman: H. W. Atcherley.

4738 **Review Body on Armed Forces Pay**. *2nd report 1973.* London: H.M.S.O., 1973. 68p. (Cmnd. 5336.)
Chairman: H. W. Atcherley.

4739 **Review Body on Doctors' and Dentists' Remuneration**. *3rd report 1973.* London: H.M.S.O., 1973. 28p. (Cmnd. 5353.)
With supplement. 12p. (Cmnd. 5377.)
Chairman: The Earl of Halsbury.

4740 **Review Body on Top Salaries**. *2nd interim report on top salaries.* London: H.M.S.O., 1973. 6p. (Cmnd. 5372.)
Chairman: Edward Boyle, Lord Boyle of Handsworth.

4741 **Roche**, Jim. 'Future trends in the clothing industry.' Barratt Brown, M. and Coates, K. (eds.). *Trade union register: 3.* 1973. p. 199–209.

4742 **Ruskin College** (Oxford), Trade Union Research Unit. *Bitter lesson no. 2: decline in teachers' pay.* London: National Union of Teachers, 1973. 16p.

4743 **Sawyer**, Malcolm C. 'The earnings of manual workers: a cross-section analysis.' *Scott. J. Polit. Econ.*, XX, 2 (June 1973), 141–57.

4744 **Scottish Education Department**. *Scottish teachers salaries memorandum 1973.* London: H.M.S.O., 1973. vii, 61p.

4745 **Searby**, Peter. '"Lists of prices" in the Coventry silk industry, 1800–1860.' *Soc. Study Labour Hist. Bull.*, XXVII (Autumn 1973), 39–53.

4746 **Thomas**, R. B. 'Post-war movements in teachers' salaries.' *Ind. Relat. J.*, IV, 3 (Autumn 1973), 12–26.

4747 **Watney**, A. 'Standards of translation.' *Campaign* (16 November 1973), 39–40.
Pay of translators.

4748 **Youds**, N. J. 'Bonus schemes in hospitals.' *Pers. Rev.*, III, 2 (Summer 1973), 62–72.

4749 **Alfred Marks Bureau**. *Survey of secretarial and clerical salaries, including right-hand women: a report on executive secretaries, their salaries, fringe benefits and job satisfactions.* London: The Bureau, 1974. 54p.

4750 **Department of Health and Social Security**, Committee of Inquiry into the Pay and Related Conditions of Service of Nurses and Midwives. *Report of the... Committee.* London: H.M.S.O., 1974. vii, 82p.
Chairman: J.A.H.G. Halsbury.

4751 **Fisher**, Malcolm Robertson. 'The human capital approach to occupational differentials.' *Int. J. Soc. Econ.*, I, 1 (1974), 40–62.

4752 **Fry**, Geoffrey K. 'Civil Service salaries in the post-Priestley era 1956–1972.' *Public Adm.*, LII (Autumn 1974), 319–33.

4753 **Hood**, W. and **Rees**, R. D. 'Inter-industry wage levels in United Kingdom manufacturing.' *Manchr. Sch. Econ. Soc. Stud.*, XLII, 2 (June 1974), 171–85.

4754 **Incomes Data Services**. *Cleaners' pay.* London: I.D.S., 1974. 16p. (I.D.S. study 72.)

4755 **Incomes Data Services**. *Clerical pay 1.* London: I.D.S., 1974. 20p. (I.D.S. study 75.)

4756 **Incomes Data Services**. *Draughtsmen's pay 1973.* London: I.D.S., 1974. 16p. (I.D.S. study 67.)

4757 **Incomes Data Services**. *Drivers' pay.*

London: I.D.S., 1974. 24p. (I.D.S. Study 87.)

4758 **Incomes Data Services**. *Executive salaries*. London: I.D.S., 1974. 16p. (I.D.S. study 80.)

4759 **Pay Board**. *Problems of pay relativities*. London: H.M.S.O., 1974. 30p. (Advisory report 2.)

4760 **Pay Board**. *Relative pay of mineworkers*. London: H.M.S.O., 1974. viii, 32p. (Cmnd. 5567.)

4761 **RIBA Journal**. 'Architects' earnings.' *RIBA J.*, LXXXI (June 1974), 16–29.

4762 **Remuneration Economics** and **British Institute of Management**. *National management salary survey 1974: remuneration in the U.K.* London: Remuneration Economics and the B.I.M., 1974. 2v.

4763 **Review Body on Armed Forces Pay**. *Pay of service medical and dental officers*. London: H.M.S.O., 1974. 10p. (Cmnd. 5729.)
Chairman: H.W. Atcherley.

4764 **Review Body on Armed Forces Pay**. *3rd report 1974*. London: H.M.S.O., 1974. 108p. (Cmnd. 5631.)
Chairman: H.W. Atcherley.

4765 **Review Body on Doctors' and Dentists' Remuneration**. *Fourth report*. London: H.M.S.O., 1974. vii, 51p. (Cmnd. 5644.)
Chairman: J.A.H.G. Halsbury.

4766 **Review Body on Top Salaries**. *Members of Parliament allowances*. London: H.M.S.O., 1974. 8p. (Cmnd. 5701.)
Chairman: Lord Boyle.

4767 **Review Body on Top Salaries**. *Report on top salaries*. London: H.M.S.O., 1974. v, 187p. (Report 6.)
Chairman: Lord Boyle.

4768 **Review Body on Top Salaries**. *3rd interim report on top salaries*. London: H.M.S.O., 1974. 8p. (Cmnd. 5595.)
Chairman: Lord Boyle.

4769 **British Institute of Management**. *Royal Commission on the Distribution of Income and Wealth, reference on higher incomes: first part of evidence submitted by the British Institute of Management*. London: The Institute, 1975.

4770 **Cosh**, Andrew. 'Remuneration of chief executives in the United Kingdom.' *Econ. J.*, LXXXV, 337 (March 1975), 75–94.

4771 **Department of Health and Social Security**, Committee of Inquiry into the Pay and Related Conditions of Service of the Professions Supplementary to Medicine and Speech Therapists. *Report of the ... Committee*. London: H.M.S.O., 1975. vii, 87p.
Chairman: J.A.H.G. Halsbury.

4772 **Grigg**, John and **Fenyo**, Andrew. 'Architects' earnings 1975: RIBA survey.' *Archit. J.*, CLXII (31 December 1975), 1332–5.

4773 **Handy**, L. J. 'Builders' pay.' *New Soc.*, XXXI (30 January 1975), 259–60.

4774 **Husband**, Tom M. 'Quantitative analyses of management salary differentials.' *J. Manage. Stud.*, XII, 3 (October 1975), 276–89.

4775 **Incomes Data Services**. *Clerical pay 2*. London: I.D.S., 1975. 20p. (I.D.S. study 93.)

4776 **Incomes Data Services**. *Draughtsmen's pay*. London: I.D.S., 1975. 20p. (I.D.S. study 91.)

4777 **Incomes Data Services**. *Drivers' pay*. London: I.D.S., 1975. 20p. (I.D.S. study 105.)

4778 **Incomes Data Services**. *Pay of maintenance craftsmen 1*. London: I.D.S., 1975. 16p. (I.D.S. study 107.)

4779 **Meeks**, Geoffrey. 'Directors' pay, growth and productivity.' *J. Ind. Relat.*, XXIV (September 1975), 1–14.

4780 **Newbould**, Gerald D. *Academic salaries: a personal application of managerial economics: inaugural lecture*. Bradford: University of Bradford, 1975. 14p.

4781 **Norris**, W. K. 'Differentials in pay.' *Lloyds Bank Rev.*, CXVIII (October 1975), 27–39.

4782 **Painter**, C. 'The Civil Service: post-Fulton malaise.' *Public Adm.*, LIII, 4 (Winter 1975), 427–41.

4783 **Review Body on Armed Forces Pay**. *4th report 1975*. London: H.M.S.O., 1975. 118p. (Cmnd. 6063.)
Chairman: H. W. Atcherley.

4784 **Review Body on Armed Forces Pay**. *London weighting and separation allowance*. London: H.M.S.O., 1975. 10p. (Cmnd. 5853.)
Chairman: H. W. Atcherley.

4785 **Review Body on Armed Forces Pay**. *Supplement to the 4th report: I. Service medical and dental officers. II. Officers of the non-regular permanent staffs of the Ulster Defence Regiment and the Territorial and Army Volunteer Reserve*. London: H.M.S.O., 1975. 20p. (Cmnd. 6146.)
Chairman: H. W. Atcherley.

4786 **Review Body on Doctors' and Dentists' Remuneration**. *5th report 1975*. London: H.M.S.O., 1975. 72p. (Cmnd. 6032.)
With supplement. 23p. (Cmnd. 6243.)
Chairman: Sir Ernest Woodroofe.

4787 **Review Body on Doctors' and Dentists' Remuneration**. *Supplement to 4th report 1974*. London: H.M.S.O., 1975. 16p. (Cmnd. 5849.)
Chairman: Sir Ernest Woodroofe.

4788 **Review Body on Top Salaries**. *Ministers of the Crown, Members of Parliament and the Peers' expenses allowance*. Part 1. London: H.M.S.O., 1975. 20p. (Cmnd. 6136.)
Chairman: Lord Boyle.

4789 **Swannack**, A. R. 'Small firm salary structures.' *Pers. Manage.*, VII, 1 (January 1975), 31–4.

4790 **Department of Employment Gazette**. 'Labour costs in the distributive trades, insurance and banking in Great Britain 1974.' *Dep. Employment Gaz.*, LXXXIV, 6 (June 1976), 596–604.

4791 **Greer**, W. R. and **Hawkins**, D. I. 'Sales force compensation, goal congruence and economic efficiency.' *Eur. J. Mark.*, X (1976), 28–33.

4792 **Hay-M.S.L. Limited.** *Analysis of managerial remuneration in the United Kingdom and overseas.* London: H.M.S.O., 1976. viii, 54p. (Royal Commission on the Distribution of Income and Wealth. Background paper 2.)

4793 **Holden**, K. and **Peel**, D. A. 'The internal – external labour market and the rate of wage inflation in U.K. manufacturing industry.' *Manchr. Sch. Econ. Soc. Stud.*, XLIV, 2 (June 1976), 132–46.

4794 **Husband**, Tom M. 'Equitable payment in the R & D function.' *R & D Manage.*, VI, 2 (1976), 51–8.

4795 **Incomes Data Services**. *Draughtsmen's pay.* London: I.D.S., 1976. 17p. (I.D.S. study 123.)

4796 **Incomes Data Services**. *Drivers' pay.* London: I.D.S., 1976. 16p. (I.D.S. study 136.)

4797 **Incomes Data Services**. *Pay in pharmaceuticals.* London: I.D.S., 1976. 18p. (I.D.S. study 117.)

4798 **Incomes Data Services**. *Pay in retail food outlets.* London: I.D.S., 1976. 22p. (I.D.S. study 113.)

4799 **Incomes Data Services**. *Pay of canteen workers.* London: I.D.S., 1976. 16p. (I.D.S. study 114.)

4800 **Incomes Data Services**. *Pay of laboratory technicians.* London: I.D.S., 1976. 21p. (I.D.S. study 125.)

4801 **Incomes Data Services**. *Pay of maintenance craftsmen 2.* London: I.D.S., 1976. 16p. (I.D.S. study 116.)

4802 **Incomes Data Services**. *Security Staff.* London: I.D.S., 1976. 22p. (I.D.S. study 122.)

4803 **Incomes Data Services**. *Top salaries £ 10,000 plus.* London: I.D.S., 1976. 20p. (I.D.S. study 121.)

4804 **Mayhew**, K. 'Plant size and earnings of manual workers in engineering.' *Oxf. Univ. Inst. Econ. Stat. Bull.*, XXXVIII (August 1976), 149–60.

4805 **Mayhew**, K. 'Regional variations of manual earnings in engineering.' *Oxf. Univ. Inst. Econ. Stat. Bull.*, XXXVIII (February 1976), 11–25.

4806 **Robinson**, Olive and **Wallace**, John. *Pay and employment in retailing.* London: Saxon, 1976. vi, 177p.

4807 **Wootton**, Barbara. 'Making differentials fair.' Field, F. (ed.). *Are low wages inevitable?* 1976. p. 118–24.

4808 **Bar Council**. *Survey of income at the bar 1974–75.* London: Inbucon/AIC Management Consultants, 1977. 49p.

4809 **Bosworth**, Derek L. and **Wilson**, Robert. 'The rate of return to highly qualified manpower.' *J. Ind. Affairs*, V, 1 (Autumn 1977), 8–14.

4810 **Duggett**, M. J. *A comparative study of the operation of the sliding scales in the coal-mining industry in Durham and South Wales, 1875–1900.* 1977. (Ph.D. thesis, University of Wales.)

4811 **Elliott**, R. F. 'Public sector wage movements 1950–1973.' *Scott. J. Polit. Econ.*, XXIV (June 1977), 133–51.

4812 **Incomes Data Services**. *Clerical pay.* London: I.D.S., 1977. 24p. (I.D.S. study 141.)

4813 **Incomes Data Services**. *Food manufacturing.* London: I.D.S., 1977. 26p. (I.D.S. study 142.)

4814 **Incomes Data Services**. *Manual workers' allowances.* London: I.D.S., 1977. 20p. (I.D.S. study 139.)

4815 **Incomes Data Services**. *Pay in engineering.* London: I.D.S., 1977. 20p. (I.D.S. study 153.)

4816 **Incomes Data Services**. *Pay of maintenance electricians.* London: I.D.S., 1977. 22p. (I.D.S. study 156.)

4817 **Incomes Data Services**. *Supervisors: pay and conditions for production supervisors.* London: I.D.S., 1977. 20p. (I.D.S. study 159.)

4818 **Incomes Data Services**. *Technicians' pay.* London: I.D.S., 1977. 24p. (I.D.S. study 148.)

4819 **McGregor**, Alan. 'Salary drift: the case of local government.' *Oxf. Bull. Econ. Stat.*, XXXIX, 3 (August 1977), 189–201.

4820 **Peach**, Len. 'Egalitarianism and the rewarding of management performance.' *Pers. Manage.*, IX, 4 (April 1977), 27–31.

4821 **Phelps Brown**, Ernest Henry. *The inequality of pay.* Oxford: Oxford U.P., 1977. xi, 360p.

4822 **Review Body on Armed Forces Pay**. *Report 6, 1977.* London: H.M.S.O., 1977. iv, 18p. (Cmnd. 6801.) Chairman: H.W. Atcherley.

4823 **Review Body on Doctors' and Dentists' Remuneration.** *Report 7, 1977.* London: H.M.S.O., 1977. vi, 74p. (Cmnd. 6800.) Chairman: Sir Ernest Woodroofe.

4824 **Review Body on Top Salaries**. *Ministers of the Crown and Members of Parliament and the Peers' expenses allowance.* Part 3. London: H.M.S.O., 1977. vi, 46p. (Cmnd. 6749.) Chairman: Lord Boyle.

4825 **Benson**, John. 'The thrift of the English coal-miners, 1860–95.' *Econ. Hist. Rev.*, XXI (August 1978), 410–18.

4826 **Hawkesworth**, R. I. 'The movement of skill differentials in the UK engineering industry.' *Br. J. Ind. Relat.*, XVI, 3 (November 1978), 277–86.

4827 **Incomes Data Services**. *Comparisons and cash limits: effects on public sector pay.* London: I.D.S., 1978. 16p. (I.D.S. study 183.)

4828 **Incomes Data Services**. *Computer staff pay*

and conditions. London: I.D.S., 1978. 21p. (I.D.S. study 174.)

4829 **Incomes Data Services**. *Drivers' pay.* London: I.D.S., 1978. 20p. (I.D.S. study 166.)

4830 **Incomes Data Services**. *Pay in the finance sector.* London: I.D.S., 1978. 20p. (I.D.S. study 180.)

4831 **Incomes Data Services**. *Pay of canteen workers.* London: I.D.S., 1978. 14p. (I.D.S. study 171.)

4832 **Incomes Data Services**. *Toolroom workers' pay.* London: I.D.S., 1978. 20p. (I.D.S. study 181.)

4833 **Incomes Data Services**. *Warehouse workers' pay.* London: I.D.S., 1978. 18p. (I.D.S. study 167.)

4834 **Review Body on Armed Forces Pay**. *Report 7, 1978.* London: H.M.S.O., 1978. iv, 40p. (Cmnd. 7177.)
With supplement. *Service medical and dental officers.* iv, 16p. (Cmnd. 7288.)
Chairman: *Sir* H. Atcherley.

4835 **Review Body on Doctors' and Dentists' Remuneration**. *Report 8, 1978.* London: H.M.S.O., 1978. vi, 96p. (Cmnd. 5176.)
Chairman: *Sir* Ernest Woodroofe.

4836 **Review Body on Top Salaries**. *Second report on top salaries.* London: H.M.S.O., 1978. vi, 130p. (Cmnd. 7253.)
Chairman: Edward Boyle, Lord Boyle of Handsworth.

4837 **Brown**, William A. 'Engineering wages and the Social Contract, 1975–1977.' *Oxf. Bull. Econ. Stat.*, XLI (1979), 51–61.

4838 **Delafield**, George L. 'Social comparisons and pay.' Stephenson, G. and Brotherton, C. (eds.). *Industrial relations: a social psychological approach.* 1979. p. 131–51.

4839 **Forester**, Tom. 'The bottom of the heap: public service workers.' *New Soc.*, XXXV (18 January 1979), 125–6.

4840 **Incomes Data Services**. *Apprentices' pay.* London: I.D.S., 1979. 18p. (I.D.S. study 198.)

4841 **Incomes Data Services**. *Clerical pay in London.* London: I.D.S., 1979. 18p. (I.D.S. study 197.)

4842 **Incomes Data Services**. *Drivers' pay and bargaining.* London: I.D.S., 1979. 20p. (I.D.S. study 193.)

4843 **Incomes Data Services**. *Manual workers' allowances: public sector.* London: I.D.S., 1979. 18p. (I.D.S. study 195.)

4844 **Incomes Data Services**. *Pay in heavy chemicals.* London: I.D.S., 1979. 20p. (I.D.S. study 208.)

4845 **Incomes Data Services**. *Qualified engineers' and scientists' pay.* London: I.D.S., 1979. 18p. (I.D.S. study 205.)

4846 **Incomes Data Services**. *Supervisors' pay.* London: I.D.S., 1979. 20p. (I.D.S. study 187.)

4847 **Incomes Data Services**. *Technicians' pay.*

London: I.D.S., 1979. 18p. (I.D.S. study 196.)

4848 **Incomes Data Services**. *Warehouse workers' pay 2.* London: I.D.S., 1979. 18p. (I.D.S. study 194.)

4849 **Review Body on Armed Forces Pay**. *Report 8, 1979.* London: H.M.S.O., 1979. iv, 28p.
With supplements 1: *Service medical and dental officers.* iv, 14p. (Cmnd. 7603.) 2.1: *Pay of university cadets and of medical and dental cadets.* 2.2: *London weighting.* 6p. (Cmnd. 7770.)
Chairman: *Sir* Harold W. Atcherley.

4850 **Review Body on Doctors' and Dentists' Remuneration**. *Report 9, 1979.* London: H.M.S.O., 1979. vi, 128p. (Cmnd. 7574.)
With supplement. iv, 10p. (Cmnd. 7723.)
Chairman: *Sir* Ernest Woodroofe.

4851 **Review Body on Top Salaries**. *Ministers of the Crown and Members of Parliament and the Peers' expenses allowance.* Part 1. London: H.M.S.O., 1979. vi, 74p. (Cmnd. 7598.)
Chairman: Lord Boyle.

4852 **Review Body on Top Salaries**. *Third report on top salaries.* London: H.M.S.O., 1979. vi, 36p. (Cmnd. 7576.)
Chairman: Lord Boyle.

4853 **Spooner**, Peter. 'Salesmen's rewards.' *Chief Exec.*, XII, 5 (May 1979), 22–4.

4854 **Standing Commission on Pay Comparability**. *Local authority and university manual workers, N.H.S. ancillary staffs and ambulancemen.* London: H.M.S.O., 1979. vi, 68p. (Cmnd. 7641.)
Supplement with statistical appendix. iv, 84p. (Cmnd. 7641–1.)

4855 **Standing Commission on Pay Comparability**. *University technicians.* London: H.M.S.O., 1979. vi, 28p. (Cmnd. 7640.)

See also: 1725; 1932; 1936; 1972; 1978; 1990; 2001; 2008; 2071; 3979; 4000; 4013; 4021; 4025; 4617; 4861; 4862; 4882; 4898; 4914; 4927; 4937; 4965; 4972; 4974; 4984; 4985; 4996; 5001; 5056; 5058; 5075; 5128; 5143; 6599; 6606; 6649; 6672; 6675; 6691; 6703; 6726; 6734; 6745; 6751; 6754; 6781.

E. WOMEN'S WAGES AND EQUAL PAY

See also Part Three, II, E, 2; Part Six, II, C, 4; Part Six, IV, A, 3, a; and Part Seven, IV, D.

4856 **Incomes Data Services**. *Women's pay: a progress report.* London: I.D.S., 1972. 15p. (I.D.S. study 32.)

4857 **Johnson**, P. R. 'The training officer and equal pay for women.' *Ind. Commer. Train.*, IV, 9 (September 1972), 443–5.

4858 **Buckingham**, Graeme Lovell. *What to do about equal pay for women.* Epping: Gower, 1973. xiii, 114p.

4859 **Incomes Data Services**. *Women's pay.*

London: I.D.S., 1973. 20p. (I.D.S. study 56.)

4860 **Mortimer**, James Edward. 'Progress towards equal pay.' *Pers. Manage.*, V, 1 (January 1973), 22–5.

4861 **Robinson**, Olive. 'Equal pay and implications for banking.' *Bankers' Mag.*, CCXV, 1549 (April 1973), 153–7.

4862 **Robinson**, Olive and **Wallace**, John. 'Equal pay in retailing.' *Retail Distrib. Manage.*, I, 6 (November–December 1973), 28–31.

4863 **Trades Union Congress**. *T.U.C. conference on equal pay, 1973*. London: T.U.C., 1973. 63p.

4864 **Chiplin**, Brian and **Sloane**, Peter J. 'Sexual discrimination in the labour market.' *Br. J. Ind. Relat.*, XII, 3 (November 1974), 371–402.

4865 **Dyer**, Barbara. *Implementing equal pay*. London: Industrial Society, 1974. iv, 24p.

4866 **Fyfe**, John and **Pettman**, Barrie Owen. *Equal pay and low pay*. Bradford: Institute of Scientific Business, 1974. 39p. (I.S.B. report and survey series 9.)

4867 **Hibbert, V.** 'Defecating the difference.' *Ind. Soc.*, LVI, 4 (April 1974), 15–17. Negotiations for equal pay in the tobacco industry.

4868 **Incomes Data Services**. *Women's pay*. London: I.D.S., 1974. 16p. (I.D.S. study 79.)

4869 **Mepham**, G. J. *Equal opportunity and equal pay: a review of objectives, problems and progress*. London: Institute of Personnel Management, 1974. 209p.

4870 **Pettman**, Barrie Owen and **Fyfe**, John. 'Equal pay and low pay in Britain.' *Int. J. Soc. Econ.*, I, 3 (1974), 268–79.

4871 **Addison**, John T. 'Sex discrimination: some comparative evidence.' *Br. J. Ind. Relat.*, XIII, 2 (July 1975), 263–5.

4872 **Cook**, Alice H. 'Equal pay: where is it?' *Ind. Relat.*, XIV, 2 (May 1975), 158–77.

4873 **Department of Employment Gazette**. 'Further progress towards equal pay.' *Dep. Employment Gaz.*, LXXXIII, 8 (August 1975), 747–53.

4874 **Fyfe**, John. 'Management for implementing equal pay.' *Manage. Decis.*, XIII, 1 (1975), 1–9.

4875 **Incomes Data Services**. *Women's pay and employment*. London: I.D.S., 1975. 50p. (I.D.S. study 100.)

4876 **Roberti**, Paolo. 'Did the U.K. trend towards equality really come to an end by 1957?' *Int. J. Soc. Econ.*, II, 1 (1975), 52–9.

4877 **Robinson**, Olive and **Wallace**, John. 'Equal pay and equality of opportunity.' *Int. J. Soc. Econ.*, II, 2 (1975), 87–105.

4878 **Seager**, A. 'Equal pay: an action plan.' *Ind. Commer. Train.*, VII, 8 (August 1975), 335–41.

4879 **Sullerot**, E. 'Equality of remuneration for men and women in the member states of the E.E.C.' *Int. Labour Rev.*, CXII, 2–3 (August–September 1975), 87–108.

4880 **Chapman**, Jane Roberts (ed.). *Economic independence for women: the Foundation for Equal Rights*. London: Sage, 1976. 285p.

4881 **Chiplin**, Brian and **Sloane**, Peter J. 'Male–female earnings differences: a further analysis.' *Br. J. Ind. Relat.*, XIV, 1 (March 1976), 77–81.

4882 **Chiplin**, Brian and **Sloane**, Peter J. 'Personal characteristics and sex differentials in professional employment.' *Econ. J.*, LXXXVI (December 1976), 729–45.

4883 **Department of Employment Gazette**. 'Teachers' pay: how and why men's and women's earnings differ.' *Dep. Employment Gaz.*, LXXXIV, 9 (September 1976), 963–8.

4884 **Glucklich**, P., **Hall**, C. R. J., **Povall**, M. and **Snell**, M. W. 'Equal pay experience in 25 firms.' *Dep. Employment Gaz.*, LXXXIV, 12 (December 1976), 1337–43.

4885 **Glucklich**, P., **Hall**, C. R. J., **Povall**, M. and **Snell**, M. W. 'Equal pay: time to go back to the drawing board.' *Pers. Manage.*, IX, 1 (January 1977), 16–21.

4886 **Robinson**, Olive and **Wallace**, John. 'National wage rates and earnings composition: a note on potential sources of sex discrimination in pay.' *Br. J. Ind. Relat.*, XV, 1 (March 1977), 101–7.

4887 **Coote**, Anna. *Equal at work? Women in men's jobs*. London: Collins, 1979. 128p.

F. PAYMENT SYSTEMS

In addition to the general literature on payment systems, this section includes material on wage and salary administration and the relationship between effort and remuneration. The technical literature on job evaluation has generally been excluded. Many of the industrial and occupational studies classified at Part Six, III, D contain information on wage systems. See Part Two, I and Part Two, II for the literature dealing with the psychological and sociological aspects of incentives at work and restriction of output. See Part Five, VI, C for material on profit-sharing and employee share ownership.

4888 **Addison**, John T. *The effect of productivity agreements on patterns of wages in a local labour market in the period 1960–1970*. 1971. (Ph.D. thesis, London School of Economics.)

4889 **Bean**, R. and **Garside**, D. A. 'Payment by results systems.' *Br. J. Ind. Relat.*, IX, 2 (July 1971), 182–97.

4890 **Brown**, Pamela. 'Jobs in the test tube.' *Pers. Manage.*, III, 1 (January 1971), 34–6.

4891 **Brown**, William A. 'Reforming wage systems.' Kessler, S. and Weekes, B. (eds.). *Conflict at work*. 1971. p. 94–104.

4892 **Clarke**, P. C. *Payment-by-results wage systems*

– the case for. 1971. (M.Litt. thesis, Trinity College, Dublin.)

4893 **Gotting**, D. A. 'The introduction of a wage grading and productivity plan in a large engineering factory.' *Br. J. Ind. Relat.*, IX, 3 (November 1971), 314–29.

4894 **Gray**, R. B. 'The Scanlon plan: a case study.' *Br. J. Ind. Relat.*, IX, 3 (November 1971), 291–323.

4895 **Harrison**, H. A. *Perceptions of pay: a study of hourly paid paper mill workers.* 1971. (M.Phil. thesis, Birkbeck College, University of London.)

4896 **Innes**, Irene. *Salary administration.* London: Industrial Society, 1971. 25p. (Notes for managers 17.)

4897 **Marriott**, Reginald. *Incentive payment systems: a review of research and opinion.* London: Staples, 1971. 317p. Fourth edition.

4898 **National Economic Development Committee**, Economic Development Committee for the Clothing Industry. *Work study in the clothing industry.* London: N.E.D.O., 1971. 35p.

4899 **Pickard**, B. *Job evaluation relative to a nationally negotiated wage structure within the building industry.* 1971. (M.Sc. thesis, University of Manchester Institute of Science and Technology.)

4900 **Richardson**, Roy. *Fair pay and work: an empirical study of fair pay perception and time span of discretion.* London: Heinemann, 1971. 125p.

4901 **Smith**, V. 'Making work study work.' *Work Study*, VII, 11 (November 1971), 43–50.

4902 **Smith**, V. 'The problem of work study.' *Work Study*, VII, 9 (September 1971), 51–5.

4903 **Whitmore**, Dennis A. *Measurement and control of indirect work.* London: Heinemann, 1971. 275p.

4904 **Work Study**. 'Work measurement in a maintenance department.' *Work Study*, VII, 12 (December 1971), 11–13.

4905 **Bishop**, Terry. 'Work study and where it can go wrong.' *Pers. Manage.*, IV, 1 (January 1972), 34–6.

4906 **Bowey**, Angela M. 'Tailor-made payment systems and employee motivation.' *Manage. Decis.*, X, 1 (Spring 1972), 82–92.

4907 **Bowley**, Arthur. *Salary structures for management careers.* London: Institute of Personnel Management, 1972. 31p.

4908 **Brown**, A. J. 'A case study illustration of the role of the wage payment scheme in the organizational system.' *Br. J. Ind. Relat.*, X, 1 (March 1972), 123–8.

4909 **Currie**, Russell Mackenzie. *Work study.* London: Pitman, 1972. xvi, 263p. Third edition. Revised by Joseph E. Faraday.

4910 **De Jong**, J. R. 'Job evaluation: history and trends.' Foundation for Business Responsibilities. *Some approaches to national job evaluation.* 1972. p. 7–18.

4911 **Engineering Employers' Federation**. *Business performance and industrial relations: added value as an instrument of management discipline.* London: Kogan Page, 1972.

4912 **Fisher**, Patrick. 'Job evaluation: a trade union assessment.' Foundation for Business Responsibilities. *Some approaches to national job evaluation.* 1972. p. 19–26.

4913 **Foundation for Business Responsibilities.** *Some approaches to national job evaluation: a symposium.* London: The Foundation, 1972. 43p.

4914 **Greenwood**, J. *Wage payment systems in the clothing industry.* London: N.E.D.O., 1972. 39p.

4915 **Henley**, J. S. 'Salary administration: a look to the future.' *Pers. Manage.*, IV, 4 (April 1972), 28–30.

4916 **Holden**, K. and **Wynn**, R. F. 'The incidence of payment by results systems: some results from further econometric analysis.' *Br. J. Ind. Relat.*, X, 3 (November 1972), 440–4.

4917 **Incomes Data Services.** *The guaranteed week part 1.* London: I.D.S., 1972. 16p. (I.D.S. study 20.)

4918 **Incomes Data Services.** *The guaranteed week part 2.* London: I.D.S., 1972. 16p. (I.D.S. study 22.)

4919 **Innes**, Irene. *Changing wage structures.* London: Industrial Society, 1972. 38p. (Notes for managers 20.)

4920 **Jaques**, Elliot. *Measurement of responsibility: a study of work, payment and individual capacity.* Chichester: John Wiley, 1972. xv, 144p.

4921 **Langton**, D. H. 'Methods of payment.' Torrington, Derek P. (ed.). *Handbook of industrial relations.* 1972. p. 159–78.

4922 **Lupton**, Tom (ed.). *Payment systems: selected readings.* Harmondsworth: Penguin, 1972. 381p.

4923 **Lupton**, Tom and **Gowler**, D. 'Wage payment systems: a review of current thinking.' *Pers. Manage.*, IV, 11 (November 1972), 25–8.

4924 **McTernan**, R. B. 'Control of clerical costs by work measurement.' *Work Study*, VIII, 4 (November 1972), 45–50.

4925 **Paterson**, Thomas Thomson. *Job evaluation.* London: Business Books, 1972. xii, 209p.

4926 **Phelps Brown**, Ernest Henry. 'Inter-industrial job evaluation and collective bargaining.' Foundation for Business Responsibilities. *Some approaches to national job evaluation.* 1972. p. 1–6.

4927 **Robinson**, Olive and **Wallace**, John. 'Pay in retail distribution: wage payment systems in department stores.' *Ind. Relat. J.*, III, 3 (Autumn 1972), 17–28.

4928 **Seymour**, A. C. 'Salary restructuring.' *Scott. Bankers' Mag.*, LXIII (February 1972), 205–10.

4929 **Thomas**, Raymond. 'National job evaluation:

a case against.' Foundation for Business Responsibilities. *Some approaches to national job evaluation.* 1972. p. 27–34.

4930 **Webb**, G. H. 'National job evaluation: a review of related issues and an approach.' Foundation for Business Responsibilities. *Some approaches to national job evaluation.* 1972. p. 35–43.

4931 **Woolf**, J. M. *Methods of payment of wages.* London: H.M.S.O., 1972. 85p.

4932 **Gillespie**, Alan. *The management of wage payment systems.* London: Kogan Page, 1973. 151p. (Engineering Employers' Federation research series 5.)

4933 **Jones**, Meurig Davies. *The make-up and payment of wages.* London: Working Together Campaign, [1973?]. 12p.

4934 **Office of Manpower Economics.** *Incremental payment systems: a report.* London: H.M.S.O., 1973. iii, 108p.

4935 **Office of Manpower Economics.** *Measured daywork: a report.* London: H.M.S.O., 1973. iii, 125p.

4936 **Schultz**, G. P. and **McKersie**, Robert B. 'Participation – achievement – reward systems.' *J. Manage. Stud.*, x, 2 (May 1973), 141–61.

4937 **Ward**, Derek. 'Job evaluation in local government.' *Pers. Manage.*, v, 7 (July 1973), 34–6.

4938 **Whitmore**, Dennis A. *Work study and related management services.* London: Heinemann, 1973. 336p.
       Third edition.

4939 **Armstrong**, Michael. *Principles and practice of salary administration.* London: Kogan Page, 1974. 331p.

4940 **Hughes**, John and **Gregory**, Denis. 'Richer jobs for workers?' *New Soc.*, xxvii (14 February 1974), 386–7.

4941 **Ibbetson**, J. F. R. *Remuneration: some discussion of the background, problems and practice, together with reference to pertinent related developments.* 1974. (M.Phil. thesis, University of Brunel.)

4942 **Incomes Data Services.** *The guaranteed week part 3.* London: I.D.S., 1974. 20p. (I.D.S. study 81.)

4943 **Incomes Data Services.** *Job evaluation.* London: I.D.S., 1974. 20p. (I.D.S. study 82.)

4944 **Lupton**, Tom and **Bowey**, Angela M. *Wages and salaries.* Harmondsworth: Penguin, 1974. 192p.

4945 **Pocock**, Pamela. 'London for love or money?' *Pers. Manage.*, vi, 7 (July 1974), 18–21.

4946 **Sharpe**, Peter. *Payment systems and incentives.* London: Working Together Campaign, [1974]. 12p.

4947 **Swannack**, A. R. 'The added value of men and materials.' *Pers. Manage.*, vi, 2 (February 1974), 26–31.

4948 **Thompson**, A. 'The value of added value.'

C.B.I. Rev. (Spring 1974), 26–34.

4949 **Andrews**, Richard E. 'Determining wage and salary policy.' Bowey, Angela M. (ed.). *Handbook of salary and wage systems.* 1975. p. 357–68.

4950 **Bowey**, Angela M. 'Facets of wage and salary administration.' Bowey, Angela M. (ed.). *Handbook of salary and wage systems.* 1975. p. 3–8.

4951 **Bowey**, Angela M. (ed.). *Handbook of salary and wage systems.* Epping: Gower, 1975. xxiii, 413p.
       Advisory editor: Tom Lupton.

4952 **Bowey**, Angela M. 'Installing salary and wage systems.' Bowey, Angela M. (ed.). *Handbook of salary and wage systems.* 1975. p. 19–26.

4953 **Bowey**, Angela M. 'Selecting a wage system.' Bowey, Angela M. (ed.). *Handbook of wage and salary systems.* 1975. p. 277–89.

4954 **Bowey**, Angela M. and **Lupton**, Tom. 'Job and pay comparisons.' Bowey, Angela M. (ed.). *Handbook of salary and wage systems.* 1975. p. 83–92.

4955 **Butterworth**, Jack. 'Relating wages to job evaluation and to work measurement.' Bowey, Angela M. (ed.). *Handbook of salary and wage systems.* 1975. p. 71–82.

4956 **Butterworth**, Jack. 'Techniques of job evaluation.' Bowey, Angela M. (ed.). *Handbook of salary and wage systems.* 1975. 41–54.

4957 **Fairburn**, Derek. 'Company-wide bonus schemes.' Bowey, Angela M. (ed.). *Handbook of salary and wage systems.* 1975. p. 263–76.

4958 **Gowler**, Dan and **Legge**, Karen. 'Status, effort and reward.' Bowey, Angela M. (ed.). *Handbook of salary and wage systems.* 1975. p. 253–62.

4959 **Gray**, R. B. *The Scanlon Plan: a study in participation.* 1975. (Ph.D. thesis, University of Strathclyde.)

4960 **Hamill**, Bernard J. *Clerical work measurement.* London: Institute of Chartered Accountants in England and Wales, 1975. 19p. (Accountants digests 18.)

4961 **Hopwood**, Anthony G. 'Budgetary control of salaries and wages.' Bowey, Angela M. (ed.). *Handbook of salary and wage systems.* 1975. p. 343–56.

4962 **Husband**, Tom M. 'Payment structures made to measure.' *Pers. Manage.*, vii, 4 (April 1975), 27–30.

4963 **Livy**, Bryan. *Job evaluation: a critical review.* London: Allen & Unwin, 1975. 192p.

4964 **Lupton**, Tom. 'The social context of work.' Bowey, Angela M. (ed.). *Handbook of salary and wage systems.* 1975. p. 9–18.

4965 **Mayhew**, K. 'The reversal of skill differentials under payment by results systems: the case of engineering.' *Oxf. Univ. Inst. Econ. Stat. Bull.*, xxxvii, 4 (November 1975), 251–67.

4966 **Naylor**, Peter G. D. 'Establishing salary

bands.' Bowey, Angela M. (ed.). *Handbook of salary and wage systems.* 1975. p. 151–62.

4967 **Percival**, John F. 'Operating, developing and adjusting reward systems.' Bowey, Angela M. (ed.). *Handbook of salary and wage systems.* 1975. p. 327–42.

4968 **Shaw**, Anne G. and **Pine**, D. Shaw. 'Payment by time systems.' Bowey, Angela M. (ed.). *Handbook of salary and wage systems.* 1975. p. 241–52.

4969 **Stewart**, Margaret. 'European payment systems.' Bowey, Angela M. (ed.). *Handbook of salary and wage systems.* 1975. p. 389–400.

4970 **Tabuteau**, Michael H. 'Salary progression curves.' Bowey, Angela M. (ed.). *Handbook of salary and wage systems.* 1975. p. 163–72.

4971 **Webb**, G. H. 'Payment by results systems.' Bowey, Angela M. (ed.). *Handbook of salary and wage systems.* 1975. 229–40.

4972 **White**, Michael. 'Incentive bonus schemes for managers.' Bowey, Angela M. (ed.). *Handbook of salary and wage systems.* 1975. p. 183–98.

4973 **White**, Michael. 'Selecting a salary system.' Bowey, Angela M. (ed.). *Handbook of salary and wage systems.* 1975. p. 209–26.

4974 **White**, Michael and **Shackleton**, V. 'Designing remuneration systems to match managers' preferences.' *Manage. Decis.*, XIII, 5 (1975), 348–59.

4975 **Whitmore**, Dennis A. *Work measurement.* London: Heinemann, 1975. xvi, 435p.

4976 **Williams**, H. 'A review of incentive schemes.' *Work Study Manage. Serv.* (March 1975), 91–5.

4977 **Wilson**, Frank. 'Salary reviews.' Bowey, Angela M. (ed.). *Handbook of salary and wage systems.* 1975. p. 199–205.

4978 **Wood**, E. G. 'Work study, method study and work measurement.' Bowey, Angela M. (ed.). *Handbook of salary and wage systems.* 1975. p. 55–68.

4979 **Younger**, W. F. 'The Hay-M.S.L. system.' Bowey, Angela M. (ed.). *Handbook of salary and wage systems.* 1975. p. 173–82.

4980 **Blain**, B. C. R. 'Financial incentives in construction.' *Work Study*, xii, 5 (May 1976), 18–20.

4981 **Bowey**, Angela M. 'Pay systems in perspective.' *Pers. Manage.*, VIII, 4 (April 1976), 28–32.

4982 **Clements**, L. 'Wage payment systems and work groups' frames of reference.' *Ind. Relat. J.*, VII, 1 (Spring 1976), 40–49.

4983 **Conboy**, Bill. *Pay at work: an introduction to wage payment schemes and wage structures.* London: Arrow, 1976. 93p. (Trade union industrial studies.)

4984 **Darmon**, R. Y. 'Salesmen's reactions to a new compensation scheme.' *Pers. Rev.*, v, 1 (Winter 1976), 25–31.

4985 **Dutton**, B. G. 'Job evaluation in libraries.' *Aslib Proc.*, XXVIII, 4 (April 1976), 144–60.

4986 **Husband**, Tom M. *Work analysis and pay structure.* London: McGraw-Hill, 1976. xii, 233p.

4987 **Husband**, Tom M. and **Schofield**, Alan P. 'The use of the Lorenz curve in pay structuring.' *J. Manage. Stud.*, XIII, 3 (October 1976), 288–96.

4988 **Husband**, Tom M. and **Schofield**, Alan P. 'The wage audit: a chance to check your pay bill.' *Pers. Manage.*, VIII, 2 (February 1976), 34–6.

4989 **Incomes Data Services.** *The guaranteed week.* London: I.D.S., 1976. 17p. (I.D.S. study 128.)

4990 **Lloyd**, Penelope A. *Incentive payment schemes: a review of current practice in 245 organisations.* London: British Institute of Management, 1976. 51p. (Management survey reports 34.)

4991 **Powell**, Jim and **Houlton**, Bob. *Work study.* London: Hutchinson, 1976. 87p. (Trade union industrial studies.)

4992 **Smallwood**, R. L. R. 'Open the minds with added value.' *Ind. Commer. Train.*, VIII, 8 (August 1976), 306–8.

4993 **Woods**, K. 'Job evaluation.' *Pers. Manage.*, VIII, 11 (November 1976), 27–30.

4994 **Armstrong**, Michael and **Murlis**, Helen. *Salary administration: a practical guide for the small and medium-sized organization.* London: British Institute of Management, 1977. 80p.

4995 **Bell**, D. Wallace. 'Incentive schemes compared.' *Ind. Participation*, DLX (1977), 23–7.

4996 **Boddy**, David. 'Salary payment and salary costs.' *Br. J. Ind. Relat.*, XV, 1 (March 1977), 18–28.

4997 **Davison**, J. 'Job evaluation using paired comparisons.' *Work Study*, XIII, 1 (January 1977), 42–6.

4998 **D'Sa**, R. *Wage system selection.* 1977. (M.Sc. thesis, University of Strathclyde.)

4999 **Edwards**, Ray and **Paul**, Stuart. *Job evaluation: a guide for trade unionists.* London: APEX, 1977. 26p.

5000 **Gill**, Colin, **Morris**, R. S. and **Eaton**, Jack. 'Job evaluation in a multi-site enterprise.' *Pers. Rev.*, VI, 4 (Autumn 1977), 51–7.

5001 **Haas**, J. M. 'Methods of wage payment in the royal dockyards, 1775–1865.' *Marit. Hist.*, v, 2 (Winter 1977), 99–115.

5002 **Ibbetson**, J. F. R. and **Whitmore**, Dennis A. *The management of motivation and remuneration.* London: Business Books, 1977. xvi, 230p.

5003 **Incomes Data Services.** *Incentive pay schemes 1.* London: I.D.S., 1977. 22p. (I.D.S. study 140.)

5004 **Incomes Data Services.** *Incentive pay schemes 2.* London: I.D.S., 1977. 18p. (I.D.S. study 143.)

5005 **Incomes Data Services.** *Salary increments.* London: I.D.S., 1977. 18p. (I.D.S. study 145.)

5006 **Jaques**, J. P. 'Rating – the sacred cow.' *Work Study*, XIII, 9 (September 1977), 28–34.

5007 **McCormick**, Brian Joseph. 'Methods of wage payment, wages structures and the influence of factor and product markets.' *Br. J. Ind. Relat.*, xv, 2 (July 1977), 246–64.

5008 **Marchington**, Mick P. 'Worker participation and incentive schemes.' *Pers. Rev.*, vii (Summer 1977), 35–8.

5009 **Pornschlegel**, H. 'Trends in job evaluation.' *Prod. Eng.*, lvi, 3 (March 1977), 21–4.

5010 **Advisory Conciliation and Arbitration Service.** *Job evaluation.* London: A.C.A.S., 1978. 12p. (ACAS guide 1.)

5011 **Flamholtz**, E. and **Wollman**, J. B. 'A stochastic rewards model.' *Pers. Rev.*, iii, 2 (Summer 1978), 20–32.

5012 **Incomes Data Services.** *Call out and standby payments.* London: I.D.S., 1978. 17p. (I.D.S. study 179.)

5013 **Incomes Data Services.** *Payment by results.* London: I.D.S., 1978. 18p. (I.D.S. study 170.)

5014 **White**, M. 'Pay methods: attitude survey, diagnosis and change.' *Pers. Rev.*, iii, 3 (Autumn 1978), 24–31.

5015 **Woodmansey**, Michael. *Added value: an introduction to productivity schemes.* London: British Institute of Management, 1978. 28p. (Management survey reports 40.)

5016 **Beacham**, R. H. S. *Pay systems: principles and techniques.* London: Heinemann, 1979. 108p.

5017 **Bradley**, Katherine. *Job evaluation: theory and practice.* London: British Institute of Management, 1979. iv, 51p.

5018 **Dastmalchian**, Ali and **Mansfield**, Roger. 'Payment systems in smaller companies: relationships with size and climate.' Colloquium on Management and Industrial Relations. *Proceedings.* 1979. p. 152–72.

5019 **Fonda**, Nickie, **Glucklich**, Pauline, **Maimon**, Zvi and **Ronen**, Simcha. 'Job evaluation without sex discrimination.' *Pers. Manage.*, xi, 2 (February 1979), 34–8.

5020 **Gale**, J. W. 'Freemans' staff productivity scheme.' *Ind. Participation*, dlxxviii (Summer 1979), 5–7.

5021 **Incomes Data Services.** *Added value schemes.* London: I.D.S., 1979. 20p. (I.D.S. study 189.)

5022 **Incomes Data Services.** *Cost of living arrangements.* London: I.D.S., 1979. 16p. (I.D.S Study 200.)

5023 **Incomes Data Services.** *Guide to job evaluation.* London: I.D.S., 1979. 70p.

5024 **Incomes Data Services.** *Shift and unsocial hours payments.* London: I.D.S., 1979. 21p. (I.D.S. study 207.)

5025 **Kenaghan**, Frank and **Redfearn**, Ann. *Determining company pay policy.* London: Institute of Personnel Management, 1979. 57p.

5026 **Wilde**, E. 'A new look at merit rating.' *Work Study*, xv, 10 (October 1979), 34–44.

5027 **Wilson**, Kevin. 'Payment systems in small companies: comments and replies.' Colloquium on Management and Industrial Relations. *Proceedings.* 1979. 173–5.

5028 **Yetton**, P. 'Piecework incentive payment schemes.' *J. Manage. Stud.*, xvi, 3 (October 1979), 253–69.

See also: 419; 477; 562; 1694; 1727; 1831; 1836; 1939; 1982; 1990; 2317; 3664; 3721; 4693; 4708; 4748; 6619; 6645; 6656; 6662; 6689; 6716; 6718.

G. LOW PAY AND POVERTY

See also Part Three, II, E, 3; Part Six, III, H; Part Six, IV, A, 3; Part Seven, IV; and Part Seven, VI.

5029 **Atkinson**, Anthony Barnes. 'Policies for poverty.' *Lloyds Bank Rev.*, c (April 1971), 17–28.

5030 **Bosanquet**, Nicholas. 'Jobs and the low-paid worker.' *Poverty*, xviii (Spring 1971), 2–6.
    Reprinted in Butterworth, E. and Weir, D. (eds.). *Social problems of modern Britain.* London: Fontana, 1972. p. 134–40.

5031 **Lawrence**, Susanne. 'Low pay: is there an answer?' *Pers. Manage.*, iii, 4 (April 1971), 18–22.

5032 **Vickers**, Jon. 'A trade without collective bargaining.' *Ind. Relat. J.*, ii, 3 (Autumn 1971), 46–51.
    Contract cleaning.

5033 **Bosanquet**, Nicholas and **Stephens**, R. J. 'Another look at low pay.' *J. Soc. Policy*, i, 3 (July 1972), 245–57.

5034 **Bradshaw**, J. and **Wakeman**, I. 'The poverty trap updated.' *Polit. Q.*, xlv, 4 (October–December 1972), 459–69.

5035 **Gretton**, John. 'A living wage.' *New Soc.*, xxii (14 December 1972), 633–5.

5036 **Hadden**, Tom. 'A policy for the lower paid.' *New Soc.*, xxii (12 October 1972), 82–4.

5037 **Hughes**, John. 'The low paid.' Townsend, P. and Bosanquet, N. (eds.). *Labour and inequality.* London: Fabian Society, 1972. p. 162–73.

5038 **Jackson**, D. *Poverty.* London: Macmillan, 1972. 96p.

5039 **Meade**, J. E. 'Poverty in the welfare state.' *Oxf. Econ. Pap.*, xxiv, 3 (November 1972), 289–326.

5040 **Atkinson**, Anthony B. 'Low pay and the cycle of poverty.' Field, F. (ed.). *Low pay.* 1973. p. 101–17.

5041 **Bosanquet**, Nicholas. 'The real low pay problem.' Field, F. (ed.). *Low pay.* 1973. p. 17–38.

5042 **Coates**, Ken and **Silburn**, Richard. *Poverty: the forgotten Englishmen.* Harmondsworth: Penguin, 1973.
    First published 1970. Re-issued with an introduction.

5043 **Field**, Frank. 'Action on low pay.' Field, F. (ed.). *Low pay.* 1973. p. 9–16.

5044 **Field**, Frank (ed.). *Low pay: Action Society Trust essays.* London: Arrow, 1973. 141p.

5045 **Field**, Frank. 'Low pay and social policy.' Field, F. (ed.). *Low pay.* 1973. p. 130–41.

5046 **Field**, Frank and **Winyard**, Stephen. 'Low pay in public employment and the wages council sector.' Field, F. (ed.). *Low pay.* 1973. p. 39–60.

5047 **Jordan**, B. *Paupers: the making of the new claiming class.* London: Routledge & Kegan Paul, 1973. 86p.

5048 **Layton**, David. 'Low pay and collective bargaining.' Field, F. (ed.). *Low pay.* 1973. p. 76–100.

5049 **Moore**, Roy. 'Low pay and fiscal policy.' Field, F. (ed.). *Low pay.* 1973. p. 118–30.

5050 **Stephen**, David. 'Immigrant workers and low pay.' Field, F. (ed.). *Low pay.* 1973. p. 61–75.

5051 **Townsend**, Peter. *The social minority.* London: Allen Lane, 1973. xiv, 319p.

5052 **Field**, Frank. *The rights of lower paid workers: a reply to the Employment Protection Bill consultative document.* London: Low Pay Unit, 1974. 13p. (Low pay papers 1.)

5053 **Fisher**, Alan and **Dix**, Bernard. *Low pay and how to end it: a union view.* London: Pitman, 1974. 117p.

5054 **Jordan**, B. *Poor parents: social policy and the cycle of deprivation.* London: Routledge & Kegan Paul, 1974. viii, 220p.

5055 **Le Noury**, Jim. *The national economic situation: implications for low growth – 30% lowest incomes.* London: Social Responsibility Council, 1974. 7p.

5056 **Robinson**, Olive and **Wallace**, John. 'Part-time employment and low pay in retail distribution in Britain.' *Ind. Relat. J.*, V, 1 (Spring 1974), 38–56.

5057 **Brown**, Marie and **Winyard**, Steve. *Low pay in hotels and catering.* London: Low Pay Unit, 1975. 37p. (Low pay pamphlets 2.)

5058 **Brown**, Marie and **Winyard**, Steve. *Low pay on the farm.* London: Low Pay Unit, 1975. 39p. (Low pay pamphlets 3.)

5059 **Le Noury**, Jim. *Low paid workers: some further evidence.* London: Social Responsibility Council, Industry and Work Committee, 1975. 8p.

5060 **Le Noury**, Jim. *Some suggested remedies for low pay.* London: Social Responsibility Council, 1975. 7p.

5061 **Lewis**, Paul, **Pond**, Chris, **Townsend**, Peter and **Walker**, Alan. *Inflation and low incomes.* London: Fabian Society, 1975. 33p. (Fabian research series 322.)

5062 **Bosanquet**, Nicholas. 'Can we protect the very low paid?' Field, F. (ed.). *Are low wages inevitable?* 1976. p. 125–35.

5063 **Edwards**, Peggy and **Flounders**, Eric. 'The lace outworkers of Nottingham.' Field, F. (ed.). *Are low wages inevitable?* 1976. p. 47–54.

5064 **Field**, Frank (ed.). *Are low wages inevitable?* Nottingham: Spokesman Books, 1976. 144p.

5065 **Field**, Frank. 'A strategy on low pay.' Field, F. (ed.). *Are low wages inevitable?* 1976. p. 136–41.

5066 **Field**, Frank. 'What is meant by low wages?' Field, F. (ed.). *Are low wages inevitable?* 1976. p. 11–16.

5067 **Hobbs**, May. 'Raising wages at a stroke: the night cleaners.' Field, F. (ed.). *Are low wages inevitable?* 1976. p. 42–6.

5068 **Moore**, Roy. 'Can't the trade unions do more?' Field, F. (ed.). *Are low wages inevitable?* 1976. p. 105–17.

5069 **Pond**, Chris. 'Inflation, incomes policy and the low paid.' *Month*, IX (January 1976), 4–7.

5070 **Pond**, Chris and **Winyard**, Steve. 'A profile of the low paid.' Field, F. (ed.). *Are low wages inevitable?* 1976. p. 17–34.

5071 **Pond**, Chris, **Field**, Frank and **Winyard**, Steve. *Trade unions and taxation.* London: W.E.A., 1976. 19p. (Studies for trade unionists II, 6.)

5072 **Field**, Frank. 'Unemployment and poverty.' Field, F. (ed.). *The conscript army.* 1977. p. 28–42.

5073 **Pond**, Chris. *For whom the pips squeak: differentials in the pay policy.* London: Low Pay Unit, 1977. 12p. (Low pay papers 15p.)

5074 **Pond**, Chris. *A jubilee year for the low paid?* London: Low Pay Unit, 1977. 8p. (Low pay papers 18.)

5075 **Pond**, Chris. *Trouble in store: a study of shopwork and low pay.* London: Low Pay Unit, 1977. 56p. (Low pay pamphlets 8.)

5076 **Pond**, Chris. *The wages free fall: a submission to the Chancellor and the TUC.* London: Low Pay Unit, 1977. 8p. (Low pay papers 14.)

5077 **Sullivan**, Jill. *The brush-off: a study of contract cleaning industry.* London: Low Pay Unit, 1977. 32p. (Low pay pamphlets 5.)

5078 **Winyard**, Steve. *From rags to rags: low pay in the clothing industry.* London: Low Pay Unit, 1977. 22p. (Low pay pamphlets 7.)

5079 **Field**, Frank. *Making companies accountable for low pay.* London: Low Pay Unit, 1978. 12p. (Low pay papers 24.)

5080 **Field**, Frank. 'The poor.' Barratt Brown, M. and others (eds.). *Full employment.* 1978. p. 34–41.

5081 **Hurstfield**, Jennifer. *The part-time trap: part-time workers in Britain today.* London: Low Pay Unit, 1978. 85p. (Low pay pamphlets 9.)

5082 **Jordan**, David. *Fleeced again: the Hairdressing Undertakings Wages Council's settlement under stage four of pay policy.* London: Low Pay Unit, 1978. 9p. (Low pay papers 27.)

5083 **Jordan**, David. *Low pay on a plate: a submission to the Licensed Residential and Licensed Restaurant Wages Council.* London: Low Pay Unit, 1978. 18p. (Low pay papers 26.)

5084 **Pond**, Chris. *Crumbs from the master's table? A checklist on the tax cuts.* London: Low Pay Unit, 1978. 8p. (Low pay papers 22.)

5085 **Rubery**, Jill. 'Structured labour markets,

worker organization and low pay.' *Camb. J. Econ.*, II, I (March 1978), 17–36.

5086 **Thomas**, Ceri and **Erlam**, Andy. *Unequal portions: a survey of pay in the hotel and catering industry.* London: Low Pay Unit, 1978. 18p. (Low pay papers 23.)

5087 **Cowell**, Frank A. 'Income and incentives for the working poor.' *Three Banks Rev.*, CXXII (June 1979), 32–48.

5088 **Crine**, Simon. *The hidden army.* London: Low Pay Unit, 1979. 28p. (Low pay pamphlets 11.)

5089 **Hyde**, Douglas. 'Plight of the low-paid workers.' *Month*, XII (April 1979), 116–17.

5090 **Jordan**, David. *A cut below the rest: submission to the Hairdressing Undertakings Wages Council.* London: Low Pay Unit, 1979. 6p. (Low pay papers 31.)

5091 **Kincaid**, Jim. 'Poverty in the welfare state.' Irvine, J. and others (eds.). *Demystifying social statistics.* 1979. p. 212–21.

5092 **Lansley**, Stewart. 'What hope for the poor?' *Lloyds Bank Rev.*, CXXXII (April 1979), 22–37.

5093 **Layard**, R., **Piachaud**, David and **Stewart**, M. 'The causes of poverty.' *Natl. Westminster Bank Q. Rev.* (February 1979), 30–42.

5094 **Policy Studies Institute**. *Social security research: the definition and measurement of poverty: papers and report of a seminar.* London: H.M.S.O., 1979. vi, 32p.
Chairman: Sir George Waller.

5095 **Townsend**, Peter. *Poverty in the United Kingdom: a survey of household resources and standards of living.* Harmondsworth: Penguin, 1979. 1216p.

See also: 2889; 4839; 4866; 4870; 6746; 6749; 6971; 6987; 7000; 7025.

H. INCOME DISTRIBUTION

This section contains material dealing with the share of wages and salaries in the national income as well as with the way in which income is distributed between different groups. See also Part Six, I; Part Six, III, A; Part Six, III, G; Part Six, IV, A, 1; and Part Seven, IV.

5096 **Atkinson**, Anthony Barnes. 'The distribution of wealth and the individual life-cycle.' *Oxf. Econ. Pap.*, XXIII (July 1971), 239–54.

5097 **Atkinson**, Anthony Barnes. 'The reform of wealth taxes in Britain.' *Polit. Q.*, XLII, I (January 1971), p. 45–54.

5098 **Pen**, J. *Income distribution.* Harmondsworth: Penguin, 1971. 424p.

5099 **Solton**, L. 'An index of the poor and rich of Scotland 1861–1961.' *Scott. J. Polit. Econ.*, XVIII, I (February 1971), 49–67.

5100 **Webb**, Adrian Leonard and **Sieve**, Jock E. B. *Income redistribution and the welfare state.* London: Bell, 1971. 125p. (Occasional papers on social administration 41.)

5101 **Wiles**, Peter John de la Fosse and

5102 **Markowski**, Stefan. 'Income distribution under communism and capitalism: some facts about Poland, the U.K., the U.S.A. and the U.S.S.R.: Poland and the U.K. compared.' *Sov. Stud.*, XXII (April 1971), 487–511.

5102 **Atkinson**, Anthony Barnes. *Unequal shares: wealth in Britain.* London: Allen Lane, 1972. xx, 279p.

5103 **Glyn**, A. and **Sutcliffe**, B. *British capitalism, workers and the profits squeeze.* Harmondsworth: Penguin, 1972. 286p.

5104 **Hahn**, F. H. *The share of wages in the national income: an inquiry into the theory of distribution.* London: Weidenfeld & Nicolson, 1972. 183p.

5105 **Nevitt**, D. A. *Hidden equalities and family incomes.* London: National Council for One Parent Families, 1972.

5106 **Stark**, Thomas. *The distribution of personal income in the United Kingdom 1949–1963.* Cambridge: Cambridge U. P., 1972. x, 192p.

5107 **Thirlwall**, A. P. 'Changes in industrial composition in the U.K. and U.S. and labour's share of national income 1948–69.' *Oxf. Univ. Inst. Econ. Stat. Bull.*, XXXIV, 4 (November 1972), 373–82.

5108 **Wesson**, John. 'On the distribution of personal incomes.' *Rev. Econ. Stud.*, XXXIX (January 1972), 77–86.

5109 **Atkinson**, Anthony Barnes. *The tax credit scheme and the redistribution of income.* London: Institute for Fiscal Studies, 1973. ix, 89p. (Publications 9.)

5110 **Atkinson**, Anthony Barnes (ed.). *Wealth, income and inequality: selected readings.* Harmondsworth: Penguin, 1973. 413p.

5111 **Bauer**, P. T. and **Prest**, Alan Richmond. 'Income difference and inequalities.' *Moor. Wall Street* (Autumn 1973), 22–43.

5112 **Baxter**, J. L. 'Inflation in the context of relative deprivation and social justice.' *Scott. J. Polit. Econ.*, XX (November 1973), 263–82.

5113 **Labour Party**. *Capital and equality: report of a Labour Party study group.* London: Labour Party, 1973. 45p.

5114 **Peters**, B. G. 'Income inequality in Sweden and the United Kingdom: a longitudinal analysis.' *Acta Sociol.*, XVI, 2 (1973), 108–20.

5115 **Atkinson**, Anthony Barnes and **Harrison**, A. J. 'Wealth distribution and investment income in Britain.' *Rev. Income Wealth*, XX, 2 (June 1974), 125–42.

5116 **Elks**, L. *The wage stop.* London: Child Poverty Action Group, 1974. 78p.

5117 **Piachaud**, D. *Do the poor pay more?* London: Child Poverty Action Group, 1974. 25p.

5118 **Polyani**, G. and **Wood**, J. B. *How much inequality? An inquiry into the evidence.* London: Institute of Economic Affairs, 1974. 85p. (Research monographs 31.)

5119 **Wiles**, Peter John de la Fosse. *Distribution of*

income: East and West. Amsterdam: North-Holland, 1974. xv, 136p.
UK – USSR comparison.

5120 **Atkinson**, Anthony Barnes. *The economics of inequality.* Oxford: Clarendon Press, 1975. x, 295p.

5121 **Atkinson**, Anthony Barnes. 'Income distribution and social change revisited.' *J. Soc. Policy*, IV, 1 (January 1975), 57–68.

5122 **Barr**, N. A. 'Negative income taxation and the redistribution of income.' *Oxf. Univ. Inst. Econ. Stat. Bull.*, XXXVII (February 1975), 29–48.

5123 **Harrison**, Alan. *The distribution of personal wealth in Scotland.* Glasgow: University of Strathclyde, Fraser of Allander Institute for Research on the Scottish Economy, 1975. (Research monographs 1.)

5124 **Lydall**, Harold. 'The economics of inequality.' *Lloyds Bank Rev.*, CXVII (July 1975), 32–47.

5125 **Royal Commission on the Distribution of Income and Wealth**. *Income from companies and its distribution.* London: H.M.S.O., 1975. xviii, 176p. (Report 2. Cmnd. 6172.)
Chairman: Lord Diamond.

5126 **Royal Commission on the Distribution of Income and Wealth**. *Initial report on the standing reference.* London: H.M.S.O., 1975. xiv, 250p. (Report 1. Cmnd. 6171.)
Chairman: Lord Diamond.

5127 **Sawyer**, Malcolm. *Income distribution in O. E. C. D. countries.* Paris: O.E.C.D., 1975. 36p.

5128 **Schofield**, J. A. 'Distribution of personal incomes at the regional level: an analysis for the period 1965–66 to 1970–71.' *Oxf. Univ. Inst. Econ. Stat. Bull.*, XXXVII (February 1975), 1–11.

5129 **Semple**, M. 'The effect of changes in household composition on the distribution of income 1961–73.' *Econ. Trends*, CCLXVI (December 1975), 99–105.

5130 **Wedderburn**, Dorothy (ed.). *Poverty, inequality and class structure.* Cambridge: Cambridge U.P., 1975. viii, 247p.

5131 **Wedderburn**, Dorothy and **Craig**, C. 'Relative deprivation in work.' Wedderburn, D. (ed.). *Poverty, inequality and class structure.* 1975. p. 141–64.

5132 **Berthoud**, Richard. *Disadvantages of inequality: a study of social deprivation.* London: Macdonald & Jane's, 1976. 207p.

5133 **Field**, Frank. *The new corporate interest.* London: Child Poverty Action Group, 1976. 27p. (Poverty pamphlet 23.)

5134 **Harbury**, C. D. 'Equality versus mobility in income and wealth distribution.' Jones, Aubrey (ed.). *Economics and equality.* 1976. p. 87–101.

5135 **Harrison**, Alan. 'Trends over time in the distribution of wealth.' Jones, Aubrey (ed.). *Economics and equality.* 1976. p. 66–86.

5136 **Hughes**, John (ed.). *Inequality: the evidence of*

the Transport & General Workers' Union to the Royal Commission on the Distribution of Income and Wealth. Nottingham: Spokesman, 1976. 183p.

5137 **Jones**, Aubrey (ed.). *Economics and equality.* London: Allan, 1976. xii, 165p.
Papers presented to Section F (Economics) at the 1975 Annual Meeting of the British Association for the Advancement of Science.

5138 **King**, John and **Regan**, Philip. *Relative income shares.* London: Macmillan, 1976. 87p.

5139 **Meeks**, Geoffrey and **Whittington**, Geoffrey. *The financing of quoted companies in the United Kingdom.* London: H.M.S.O., 1976. viii, 79p. (Royal Commission on the Distribution of Income and Wealth. Background paper 1.)
Chairman: Lord Diamond.

5140 **Royal Commission on the Distribution of Income and Wealth**. *High incomes from employment.* London: H.M.S.O., 1976. xvi, 244p. (Report 3. Cmnd. 6383.)
Chairman: Lord Diamond.

5141 **Royal Commission on the Distribution of Income and Wealth**. *Second report on the standing reference.* London: H.M.S.O., 1976. xv, 136p. (Report 4. Cmnd. 6626.)
Chairman: Lord Diamond.

5142 **Trades Union Congress**. *The distribution of income and wealth: a TUC digest of the first four reports of the Royal Commission on the Distribution of Income and Wealth.* London: T.U.C., 1976. 31p.

5143 **Willmott**, Peter (ed.). *Poverty report: sharing inflation?* London: Temple Smith, 1976. 200p.

5144 **Woodcock**, George. 'Trade unions and social equality.' Jones, Aubrey (ed.). *Economics and equality.* 1976. p. 122–33.

5145 **Cowell**, F. A. *Measuring inequality.* London: Philip Allan, 1977. 193p.

5146 **Dinwiddy**, Robert and **Reed**, Derek. *The effects of certain social and demographic changes on income distribution.* London: H.M.S.O., 1977. v, 168p. (Royal Commission on the Distribution of Income and Wealth. Background paper 3.)
Chairman: Lord Diamond.

5147 **Fiegehen**, Guy C., **Lansley**, P. S. and **Smith**, A. D. *Poverty and progress in Britain 1953–73.* Cambridge: Cambridge U.P., 1977. xiv, 173p.

5148 **Field**, Frank, **Meacher**, Molly and **Pond**, Chris. *To him who hath.* Harmondsworth: Penguin, 1977. 254p.

5149 **Royal Commission on the Distribution of Income and Wealth**. *Third report on the standing reference.* London: H.M.S.O., 1977. xxiii, 314p. (Report 5. Cmnd. 6999.)
Chairman: Lord Diamond.

5150 **Stark**, Thomas. *The distribution of income in eight countries.* London: H.M.S.O., 1977. viii, 249p. (Royal Commission on the

Distribution of Income and Wealth. Background paper 4.)
Chairman: Lord Diamond.

5151 **Williams**, Francis (ed.). *Why the poor pay more*. London: Macmillan, 1977. viii, 240p.

5152 **Atkinson**, Anthony Barnes and **Harrison**, A. J. *Distribution of personal wealth in Britain*. Cambridge: Cambridge U.P., 1978. xiv, 330p.

5153 **Creedy**, John. 'Negative income taxes and income redistribution.' *Oxf. Bull. Econ. Stat.*, XL (November 1978), 363–9.

5154 **Mushin**, J. D. 'Political structure, economic growth and the distribution of income.' *J. Ind. Affairs*, VI, 1 (Autumn 1978), 12–16.

5155 **Piachaud**, David. 'Inflation and income distribution.' Hirsch, F. and Goldthorpe, J. (eds.). *The political economy of inflation*. 1978. p. 88–116.

5156 **Pond**, Chris. 'How poverty gets taped.' *New Soc.*, XLIII (19 January 1978), 129–30.

5157 **Pond**, Chris. 'A 20-year poverty gap.' *New Soc.*, XLV (7 September 1978), 509–10.

5158 **Atkinson**, Anthony Barnes. 'Inequality under Labour.' *New Soc.*, XXXVI (26 April 1979), 194–5.

5159 **Field**, Frank (ed.). *The wealth report*. London: Routledge & Kegan Paul, 1979. xi, 196p.

5160 **Hird**, Christopher and **Irvine**, John. 'The poverty of wealth statistics.' Irvine, J. and others (eds.). *Demystifying social statistics*. 1979. p. 190–211.

5161 **Layard**, Richard and **Zabalza**, Antoni. 'Family income distribution: explanation and policy evaluation.' *J. Polit. Econ.*, LXXXVII, 5 (1979), 133–61.

5162 **Piachaud**, David. 'Inequality and social policy.' *New Soc.*, XXXVI (22 March 1979), 670–72.

5163 **Piachaud**, David. 'Who are the poor and what is the best way to help them?' *New Soc.*, XLVII (15 March 1979), 603–6.

5164 **Pond**, Chris. 'The poor and the pundits.' *New Soc.*, XLVII (29 March 1979), 740–41.

5165 **Sattinger**, Michael. 'Differential rents and the distribution of earnings.' *Oxf. Econ. Pap.*, XXXI (March 1979), 60–71.

5166 **Schwarz**, L. D. 'Income distribution and social structure in the late eighteenth century.' *Econ. Hist. Rev.*, XXXII (May 1979), 250–59.

5167 **Winegarden**, C. R. 'Schooling and income distribution: evidence from international data.' *Economica*, XLVI (February 1979), 83–7.

See also: 6711.

IV. CONDITIONS OF EMPLOYMENT

See also Parts Three and Five where many of the works on trade unionism and collective bargaining contain material on employment conditions.

A. GENERAL CONDITIONS OF WORK

This section includes material dealing with working conditions in general. Material relating primarily to wages is classified at Part Six, III; that relating to other specific conditions of employment is classified at Part Six, IV, B–D; and that on the more psychological and sociological aspects of the quality of working life is classified at Part Two, V. The emphasis here is on 'working' conditions as opposed to 'living' conditions. Material primarily concerned with the cost of living and such aspects of living conditions as food, clothing, and housing (except tied housing) has generally been excluded. Most general social and economic history texts contain material on working conditions, but it was not possible to analyse the contents of each of these volumes and include the relevant material here. The memoirs and autobiographies of workers also generally contain information on working conditions and these have been included here. See also Part Six, II, C; Part Six, III, G; Part Seven, III, A, 1; and Part Seven, VII, A.

1. General

5168 **Barnsby**, George J. 'The standard of living in the Black Country during the nineteenth century.' *Econ. Hist. Rev.*, XXIV, 2 (1971), 220–39.

5169 **Blackburn**, Elizabeth K. 'What it is like to work in a factory.' *Friends' Q.*, XVII (October 1971), 151–8.

5170 **Engels**, Frederick. *The condition of the working class in England*. Oxford: Blackwell, 1971. xxxv, 386p.
Second edition.
Translated and edited by W. O. Henderson and W. H. Chaloner.

5171 **Hopkins**, E. *The working classes of Stourbridge and district, 1815–1914*. 1971. (Ph.D. thesis, University of London.)

5172 **Vaughan**, Christopher. 'At work in Coventry.' *Month*, IV (December 1971), 173–5.

5173 *Conditions of work and living: the reawakening of the English conscience 1838–1844*. New York: Arno Press, 1972. (British labour struggles: contemporary pamphlets 1727–1850.)

5174 **Gourvish**, T. R. 'The cost of living in Glasgow in the early nineteenth century.' *Econ. Hist. Rev.*, XXV, 1 (February 1972), 65–80.

5175 **Hartwell**, R. M., **Mingay**, G. E. and **Boyson**, Rhodes. *The long debate on poverty: eight essays on industrialisation and 'the condition of England'*. London: Institute of Economic Affairs, 1972. xvi, 243p.

5176 **Macy**, Christopher. 'Job discrimination in Northern Ireland.' *Humanist*, LXXXVII (January 1972), 17–18.

5177 **Stewart**, Margaret. *Employment conditions in Europe.* Epping: Gower.
First edition. 1972. xviii, 206p. See especially Section 12: 'United Kingdom.' p. 165–86.
Second edition. 1976. xviii, 249p. See especially Section 11: 'United Kingdom.' p. 151–73.

5178 **Taylor**, J. *From self-help to glamour: the working man's club, 1860–1972.* Oxford: History Workshop, 1972. 94p.

5179 **Barnsby**, G. J. 'The standard of living in the Black Country in the nineteenth century: a rejoinder.' *Econ. Hist. Rev.*, XXVI, 3 (1973), 514–16.

5180 **Griffin**, Colin P. 'The standard of living in the Black Country in the nineteenth century: a comment.' *Econ. Hist. Rev.*, XXVI, 3 (1973), 510–13.

5181 **Huggett**, Frank Edward. *The past, present and future of factory life and work: a documentary inquiry.* London: Harrap, 1973. 125p.

5182 **Incomes Data Services**. *Part time work.* London: I.D.S., 1973. 20p. (I.D.S. study 62.)

5183 **Razzell**, P. E. and **Wainwright**, R. W. (eds.). *The Victorian working class: a selection from letters to the Morning Chronicle.* London: Frank Cass, 1973. xiii, 338p.

5184 **Sheehan**, James J. (ed.). *Industrialization and industrial labor in nineteenth century Europe.* New York: Wiley, 1973. 173p.

5185 **White**, David. 'Those who do the butt-end jobs.' *New Soc.*, XXIII (8 February 1973), 288–91.

5186 *The working classes in the Victorian age: debates on the issue from 19th century critical journals.* London: Gregg International, 1973. 4 v.
With an introduction by John Saville.

5187 **Worpole**, Ken. 'Working heroes: autobiographies of working class people.' *New Soc.*, XXIV (7 June 1973), 566–7.

5188 **Barnes**, Ron. *A licence to live: scenes from a post-war working life in Hackney.* London: Hackney Workers' Educational Association and Hackney Libraries Committee, 1974. 76p.

5189 **Burnett**, John (ed.). *Useful toil: autobiographies of working people from the 1820s to the 1920s.* Harmondsworth: Allen Lane, 1974. 364p.

5190 **Hopkins**, Eric. 'Working conditions in Victorian Stourbridge.' *Int. Rev. Soc. Hist.*, XIX, 3 (1974), 401–25.

5191 **Incomes Data Services**. *Temporary work.* London: I.D.S., 1974. 20p. (I.D.S. study 78.)

5192 **McCabe**, A. T. *The standard of living in Liverpool and Merseyside, 1850–1975.* 1974. (M. Litt. thesis, University of Lancaster.)

5193 **Marcus**, Steven. *Engels, Manchester and the working class.* London: Weidenfeld & Nicolson, 1974. xv, 271p.

5194 **Palmer**, Roy (ed.). *Poverty knock: a picture of industrial life in the nineteenth century through songs, ballads and contemporary accounts.* Cambridge: Cambridge U.P., 1974. 64p.

5195 **Thomis**, Malcolm I. *The town labourer and the industrial revolution.* London: Batsford, 1974. vi, 247p.

5196 **Cullen**, Michael J. 'The 1877 survey of the London working class.' *Int. Rev. of Soc. Hist.*, XX, 1 (1975), 48–60.

5197 **Cullen**, Michael J. *The statistical movement in early Victorian Britain.* Greenwood: Harvester, 1975. xii, 205p.

5198 **Hobsbawm**, Eric John. 'The standard of living debate.' Taylor, A. (ed.). *The standard of living in Britain in the industrial revolution.* 1975. p. 179–88.

5199 **Hopkins**, Eric. 'Small town aristocrats of labour and their standard of living 1840–1914.' *Econ. Hist. Rev.*, XXVIII, 2 (May 1975), 222–42.

5200 **Smith**, Lil. *The good old bad old days.* London: Centreprise, 1975. 9p.

5201 **Stearns**, Peter Nathaniel. *Lives of labour: work in a maturing industrial society.* London: Croom Helm, 1975. viii, 424p.

5202 **Taylor**, Arthur J. (ed.) *The standard of living in Britain in the industrial revolution.* London: Methuen, 1975. iv, 216p.

5203 **Todd**, F. A. *The condition of the working class in Preston, 1790–1855.* 1975. (M.Litt. thesis, University of Lancaster.)

5204 **Gennard**, John. *Economic and technological environments: key economic concepts and some technological considerations.* Milton Keynes: Open U.P., 1976. 44p. (PT 281 Unit 3.)

5205 **Pollard**, Sidney and **Holmes**, Colin (eds.). *Essays in the economic and social history of South Yorkshire.* Sheffield: South Yorkshire County Council, 1976. 308p.

5206 **Shergold**, P. R. *The standard of life of manual workers in the first decade of the twentieth century: a comparative study of Birmingham, U.K. and Pittsburgh, U.S.A.* 1976. (Ph.D. thesis, London School of Economics.)

5207 **Hackney Workers' Educational Association**. *Working lives: a people's autobiography of Hackney.* London: Centreprise Trust, 1976–7. 2 v.

5208 **Institute of Personnel Management**, National Committee on Payment and Employment Conditions. *Staff status for all.* London: The Institute, 1977. 70p.

5209 **Parsons**, S. R. *The standard of living of the working class in the south-west of England during the industrial revolution, 1750–1850, with special reference to the county of Devon.* 1977. (M.A. thesis, University of Exeter.)

5210 **Roberts**, Elizabeth. 'Working class standards of living in Barrow and Lancaster 1890–1914.' *Econ. Hist. Rev.*, XXX (May 1977), 306–21.

5211 **Butt**, John. 'Working-class housing in Glasgow, 1891–1914.' MacDougall, I. (ed.). *Essays in Scottish labour history*. 1978. p. 143–69.

5212 **Hammond**, John Lawrence Le Breton and **Hammond**, Lucy Barbara. *The village labourer*. London: Longman, 1978. 301p.
    Fourth edition.
    First published 1927. Reprinted with an introduction and bibliographical note by G. E. Mingay.

5213 **Seabrook**, Jeremy. *What went wrong? Working people and the ideals of the labour movement*. London: Gollancz, 1978. 286p.

5214 **Levitt**, Ian and **Smout**, Christopher. *The state of the Scottish working-class in 1843: a statistical and spatial enquiry based on the data from the Poor Law Commission Report of 1844*. Edinburgh: Scottish Academic Press, 1979. 284p.

See also: 6; 612; 1241.

2. Studies of Particular Occupations and Industries

Many of the general works in Part Six, IV, A also include material on particular industries. Works on the attitudes and behaviour of workers in particular occupations and industries are classified in Part Two. See also Part Three, II, D; Part Five, IV; Part Five, V, C; and Part Six, III, D.

a. AGRICULTURE, FORESTRY, AND FISHING

5215 **Coull**, James Reid. *Crofter-fishermen in Norway and Scotland*. Aberdeen: University of Aberdeen Department of Geography, 1971. 15p.

5216 **Gasson**, Ruth. 'Relative deprivation and attachment to farming.' *Sociol. Rev.*, XIX, 4 (November 1971), 557–83.

5217 **Goldie**, M. E. *The standard of living of the Scottish farm workers in selected areas at the time of the first two statistical accounts*. 1971. (M.Sc. thesis, University of Edinburgh.)

5218 **Huggett**, Frank Edward. *A day in the life of a Victorian farm worker*. London: Allen & Unwin, 1972. 88p.

5219 **Howell**, D. W. 'The agricultural labourer in 19th-century Wales.' *Welsh Hist. Rev.*, VI (1972–3), 262–87.

5220 **Godfrey**, Arthur. *Yorkshire fishing fleets: the story of Yorkshire's oldest and most dangerous industry*. Clapham: Dalesman, 1974. 72p.

5221 **Rushforth**, Louis. 'The Chipping Norton case: the story of the women of Ascott-under-Wychwood, May 1873.' Maynard, J. (ed.). *A hundred years of farmworkers' struggle*. 1974. p. 11–17.
    Tied cottages.

5222 **Van Es**, J. C. and **McGinty**, M. J. 'Relative deprivation and attachment to farming: some further considerations.' *Sociol. Rev.*, XXII, 2 (May 1974), 259–70.

5223 **Bowen**, Jack. 'Recollections of a farm worker.' *N. Yorks. County Record Office J.*, I (1975), 35–9.

5224 **Kitteringham**, Jennie. 'Country work girls in nineteenth century England.' Samuel, R. (ed.). *Village life and labour*. 1975. p. 73–138.

5225 **Morgan**, David H. 'The place of harvesters in nineteenth century village life.' Samuel, R. (ed.). *Village life and labour*. 1975. p. 27–72.

5226 **Samuel**, Raphael. 'Village labour.' Samuel, R. (ed.). *Village life and labour*. 1975. p. 1–26.

5227 **Samuel**, Raphael (ed.). *Village life and labour*. London: Routledge & Kegan Paul, 1975. 278p.

5228 **Brickell**, George E. *The north west Hampshire agricultural labourer 1867–1875*. Andover: Andover Local Archives Office, 1975. 30p.
    Bound with J. E. H. Spaul (ed.). *The north-west Hampshire agricultural labourer, 1846*.

5229 **Gasson**, Ruth. *Provision of tied cottages*. Cambridge: Cambridge University Department of Land Economy, 1975. 147p. (Occasional papers 4.)

5230 **Jones**, A. *Rural housing: the agricultural tied cottage*. London, Bell, 1975. 78p. (Social Administration Research Trust. Occasional papers on social administration 56.)

5231 **Kerr**, Barbara. *Bound to the soil: a social history of Dorset 1750–1918*. Wakefield: EP Publishing, 1975. 287p.

5232 **Olney**, R. J. (ed.). *Labouring life in the Lincolnshire Wolds: a study of Binbrook in the mid nineteenth century*. Sleaford: Society for Lincolnshire History and Archaeology, 1975. 39p.

5233 **Spaul**, J. E. H. (ed.). *The north-west Hampshire agricultural labourer, 1846, or the 'New Poor Law'*. Andover: Andover Local Archives Office, 1975. 30p.
    Bound with G. E. Brickell. *The north west Hampshire agricultural labourer 1867–1875*.

5234 **Frank**, Peter. 'Women's work in the Yorkshire inshore fishing industry.' *Oral Hist.*, IV, 1 (1976), 57–72.

5235 **Horn**, Pamela L. R. *Labouring life in the Victorian countryside*. Dublin: Gill & Macmillan, 1976. 292p.

5236 **Howkins**, Alun. 'The Norfolk farm labourer, 1900–23.' *Soc. Study Labour Hist. Bull.*, XXXIII (Autumn 1976), 7–9.

5237 **MacDonald**, Stuart. 'The diary of an agricultural apprentice in Northumberland, 1842.' *Local Historian*, XII, 3–4 (November 1976), 139–45.

5238 **Rule**, John. 'The smacksmen of the North Sea: labour recruitment and exploitation in British deep-sea fishing, 1850–90.' *Int. Rev. of Soc. Hist.*, XXI, 3 (1976), 383–411.

5239 **Smith-Powell**, Harry. *On the roads and in the fields: fifty years a Fowler driver, 1912–65*. Ilfracombe: Stockwell, 1976. 46p.

5240 **Darvill**, M. *I remember: the day's work in

Gloucestershire villages 1850–1950. Gloucester: Gloucester Community Council Local History Committee, 1977. 44p.

5241 **Lummis**, Trevor. 'The occupational community of East Anglian fishermen: an historical dimension through oral evidence.' *Br. J. Sociol.*, XXVIII, 1 (March 1977), 51–74.

5242 **Newby**, Howard. 'Tied cottage reform.' *Br. J. Law Soc.*, IV, 1 (Summer 1977), 94–102.

5243 **Seymour**, R. V. H. 'Toddington memories: men on the land.' *Beds. Mag.*, XVI (Summer 1978), 201–7.

5244 **Bochel**, Margaret. *The story of Nairn fisher girls at the gutting.* Edinburgh: National Museum of Antiquities of Scotland, 1979. 41p.

See also: 28; 276; 281; 312; 340; 374; 5209; 5409; 5899; 5922; 6458.

b. MINING AND QUARRYING

5245 **Griffin**, Alan Ramsay. *Mining in the East Midlands, 1550–1947.* London: Cass, 1971. xvi, 338p.

5246 **Rule**, John Graham. *The labouring miner in Cornwall, c1740–1870: a study in social history.* 1971. (Ph.D. thesis, University of Warwick.)

5247 **Davies**, W. H. *The right place, the right time: memories of boyhood days in a Welsh mining community.* Llandybie: Llyfrau'r Dryw, 1972. 240p.

5248 **Douglass**, Dave. *Pit life in County Durham: rank and file movements and workers' control.* London: History Workshop, 1972. iii, 92p. (Pamphlets 6.)

5249 **Northumberland Record Office**. *The Northumberland pitman: documents illustrating the coal-miner's life in the mid-nineteenth century.* Newcastle: The Office, 1972.

5250 **Paterson**, Barbara E. *The social and working condition of the Ayrshire mining population, 1840–1975.* Ayr: Ayrshire Archaeological and Natural History Society, 1972. 260p.

5251 **Paterson**, Barbara E. 'The social and working conditions of the Ayrshire mining population, 1840–1875.' *Ayrshire Collect.*, X (1970–72), 201–60.

5252 **Rieuwerts**, J. H. *Derbyshire's old lead mines and miners.* Leek: Moorland Publishing, 1972. 40p.

5253 **Douglass**, Dave. *Pit talk in County Durham: a glossary of miners' talk together with memories of Wardley Colliery, pit songs and piliking.* Oxford: Ruskin College, 1973. 78p. (History workshop pamphlets 10.)

5254 **Harris**, A. 'Colliery settlements in East Cumberland.' *Cumberland & Westmorland Antiq. Archaeol. Soc. Trans.*, LXXIV (1974), 118–46.

5255 **Kaijage**, F. J. *Labouring Barnsley, 1816–1856: a social and economic history.* 1975. (Ph.D. thesis, University of Warwick.)

5256 **Leister**, Ingeborg. *The sea coal mine and the Durham miner.* Durham: University of Durham, Department of Geography, 1975. 72p.

5257 **Samuel**, Raphael. 'Quarry roughs: life and labour in Headington Quarry, 1860–1920: an essay in oral history.' Samuel, R. (ed.). *Village life and labour.* 1975. p. 139–263.

5258 **Tracey**, James and **Thompson**, Norman. *Canary men and cobblers: the lives of two retired Northumberland miners told by themselves.* Whitley Bay: Erdesdun Poems, 1975. 15p.

5259 **Benson**, John and **Neville**, Robert G. (eds.). *Studies in the Yorkshire coal industry.* Manchester: Manchester U.P., 1976. xii, 180p.

5260 **Bullock**, Jim. *Bowers Row: recollections of a mining village.* London: EP Publishing, 1976. x, 230p.

5261 **Harris**, J. R. 'Skills, coal and British industry in the eighteenth century.' *History*, LXI, 202 (June 1976), 167–82.

5262 **Hughes**, Simon J. S. *Cardiganshire, its mines and miners.* Talybont: The Author, 1976. 49p.

5263 **John**, Angela V. 'The Lancashire pit-brow lasses.' *N. W. Labour Hist. Soc. Bull.*, III (1976), 1–5.

5264 **Colls**, Robert. *The collier's rant: song and culture in the industrial village.* London: Croom Helm, 1977. 224p.

5265 **Francis**, Hywel. 'The origins of the South Wales miners' library.' *Assist. Libr.*, LXX, 12 (December 1977), 186–90.

5266 **Benson**, John. 'The thrift of English coal miners, 1860–95.' *Econ. Hist. Rev.*, XXXI (1978), 410–18.

5267 **Bulmer**, Martin I. A. (ed.). *Mining and social change: Durham County in the twentieth century.* London: Croom Helm, 1978. 318p.

5268 **Howarth**, Ken. *Dark days: memories and reminiscences of the Lancashire and Cheshire coalmining industry up to nationalisation.* Manchester: The Author, 1978. ii, 127p.

5269 **Asquith**, Brian. 'Life's a picnic.' MacFarlane, J. (ed.). *Essays from the Yorkshire coalfield.* 1979. p. 37–40.

5270 **Bielby**, Fred. 'My working life.' MacFarlane, J. (ed.). *Essays from the Yorkshire coalfield.* 1979. p. 74–6.

5271 **Camm**, David. 'Progress.' MacFarlane, J. (ed.). *Essays from the Yorkshire coalfield.* 1979. p. 77–9.

5272 **Cooper**, Arthur. 'A tale of two cities.' MacFarlane, J. (ed.). *Essays from the Yorkshire coalfield.* 1979. p. 60–62.

5273 **Dodd**, Melvin. 'Born to be a miner.' MacFarlane, J. (ed.). *Essays from the Yorkshire coalfield.* 1979. p. 28–30.

5274 **Gosling**, Alan. 'South Yorkshire and the mining people.' MacFarlane, J. (ed.). *Essays from the Yorkshire coalfield.* 1979. p. 17–18.

5275 **Harrison**, Michael. 'The pride and the passion.' MacFarlane, J. (ed.). *Essays from the Yorkshire coalfield.* 1979. p. 70–73.

5276 **Hill**, Peter. 'From a Brumagem tupp to a Yorkshire tyke.' MacFarlane, J. (ed.). *Essays from the Yorkshire coalfield.* 1979. p. 44–50.

5277 **Kieno**, Henri. 'I remember.' MacFarlane, J. (ed.). *Essays from the Yorkshire coalfield*. 1979. p. 15–16.

5278 **McDevitt**, David. 'The first twenty years.' MacFarlane, J. (ed.). *Essays from the Yorkshire coalfield*. 1979. p. 31–2.

5279 **MacFarlane**, Jim (ed.). *Essays from the Yorkshire coalfield*. Sheffield: University of Sheffield, Division of Continuing Education, 1979. 94p.

5280 **Moore**, Michael. 'Life and working in a mining area.' MacFarlane, J. (ed.). *Essays from the Yorkshire coalfield*. 1979. p. 57–9.

5281 **Mountain**, Eric. 'A Yorkshire mining village.' MacFarlane, J. (ed.). *Essays from the Yorkshire coalfield*. 1979. p. 55–6.

5282 **O'Neill**, Patrick. 'Does childhood hide the real world?' MacFarlane, J. (ed.). *Essays from the Yorkshire coalfield*. 1979. p. 17–18.

5283 **Pearson**, Frank. 'A mining community: my fears for its future.' MacFarlane, J. (ed.). *Essays from the Yorkshire coalfield*. 1979. p. 51–2.

5284 **Pearson**, Ronald. 'In the beginning – and after.' MacFarlane, J. (ed.). *Essays from the Yorkshire coalfield*. 1979. p. 68–9.

5285 **Smith**, Frank. 'The early education of a militant.' MacFarlane, J. (ed.). *Essays from the Yorkshire coalfield*. 1979. p. 65–7.

5286 **Stevens**, Dennis. 'Childhood memories of a South Yorkshire miner.' MacFarlane, J. (ed.). *Essays from the Yorkshire coalfield*. 1979. p. 10–14.

5287 **Stevens**, Dennis. 'The degradation of work in the 20th century.' MacFarlane, J. (ed.). *Essays from the Yorkshire coalfield*. 1979. p. 89–94.

5288 **Thomas**, Peter. 'A glance at the past.' MacFarlane, J. (ed.). *Essays from the Yorkshire coalfield*. 1979. p. 41–3.

5289 **Thompson**, Selby. 'Childhood.' MacFarlane, J. (ed.). *Essays from the Yorkshire coalfield*. 1979. p. 33–6.

5290 **Wilkinson**, Alec. 'Dying communities.' MacFarlane, J. (ed.). *Essays from the Yorkshire coalfield*. 1979. p. 63–4.

5291 **Wroe**, Brian. 'Bare bones and me.' MacFarlane, J. (ed.). *Essays from the Yorkshire coalfield*. 1979. p. 7–9.

5292 **Wroe**, Brian. 'Starting work.' MacFarlane, J. (ed.). *Essays from the Yorkshire coalfield*. 1979. p. 26–7.

See also: 42; 471; 2289; 4825; 5410; 5441; 5870; 5907; 5913; 5915; 5919; 5920; 5925; 5939; 6160; 6573.

c. MANUFACTURING AND CONSTRUCTION

5293 **Gregory**, Denis Leslie and **Smyth**, Robert Leslie. *The worker and the pottery industry*. Keele: University of Keele, Department of Economics, 1971. 101p. (Studies on the British pottery industry 4.)

5294 **Webber**, Ronald. *The village blacksmith*. New-ton Abbott: Country Book Club, 1972.

5295 **Mitchell**, David C. *The darkest England match industry*. Camberley: British Matchbox Label and Booklet Society, 1973. 41p.

5296 **Elsegood**, A. 'A bit of a dead horse.' *Norfolk Ind. Archaeol. Soc. J.*, I, 7 (July 1974), 22–31. Shoemaking.

5297 **Newton**, Arthur. *Years of change: autobiography of a Hackney shoemaker*. London: Hackney Workers' Educational Association, 1974. 68p.

5298 **Bailey**, Jocelyn. *The village wheelwright and carpenter*. Aylesbury: Shire Publications, 1975. 33p.

5299 **Bede Gallery**, Jarrow. *Palmer's Yard and the town of Jarrow*. Jarrow: The Gallery, 1975. 87p. An exhibition compiled and organised by Vincent Rea.

5300 **Brooke**, D. 'Railway navvies on the Pennines, 1847–71.' *J. Transp. Hist.*, III, 1 (February 1975), 41–53.

5301 **Fletcher**, Harry. *A life on the Humber: keeling to shipbuilding*. London: Faber, 1975. 144p. With an introduction by L.T.C. Rolf.

5302 **Schmiechen**, James Andrew. *Sweated trades and sweated labor: a study of industrial disorganization and worker attitudes in the London clothing trades, 1867–1909*. 1975. (Ph.D. thesis, University of Illinois.)

5303 **Chapman**, S. D. 'Workers' housing in the cotton factory colonies, 1770–1850.' *Tex. Hist.*, VII (1976), 112–39.

5304 **Ercoloni**, R. *A furniture maker: his life, his work and his observations: an autobiography*. London: Benn, 1976. 182p.

5305 **Murray**, Norman. *A social history of the Scottish handloom weavers, 1790–1850*. 1976. (Ph.D. thesis, University of Strathclyde.)

5306 **Williams**, J. D. 'Richard Ward: an eighteenth-century bricklayer.' *Essex J.*, XI, 1–2 (Spring–Summer 1976), 39–45.

5307 **British Cast Iron Research Association.** *The working environment in iron foundries*. London: The Association, 1977. Papers presented at a conference, 1977, University of Warwick.

5308 **Burrett**, E. *Full point: a typographer remembers*. Esher: Penmiel Press, 1977. 33p.

5309 **Colman**, Sylvia. 'Diary of Thomas King of Thelnetham.' *Suffolk Rev.*, IV, 5 (Summer 1977), 215–36. Carpenter.

5310 **Davies**, G. M. 'Can you measure your working conditions?' British Cast Iron Research Association. *The working environment in iron foundries*. 1977. p. 11.1–11.7.

5311 **Hopkins**, Eric. 'The decline of the family work unit in Black Country nailing.' *Int. Rev. of Soc. Hist.*, XXII, 2 (1977), 184–97.

5312 **McCutcheon**, A. *Wheel and spindle: aspects of Irish industrial history*. Belfast: Blackstaff Press, 1977. 83p.

5313 **Murray**, Norman. *The Scottish handloom weavers, 1790–1850: a social history*. Edinburgh: Donald, 1978. 269p.

5314 **Sweetman**, W. 'A Wexford shipbuilder.' *Old Wexford Soc. J.*, VII (1978), 21–30.

5315 **Tibbott**, S. Minwel. 'Knitting stockings in Wales – a domestic craft.' *Folklife*, XVI (1978), 61–73.

5316 **Beynon**, Huw and **Wainwright**, Hilary. *The workers' report on Vickers: the Vickers Shop Stewards Combine Committee report on work, wages, rationalisation, closure and rank-and-file organisation in a multinational company.* London: Pluto, 1979. 102p.

5317 **Dickenson**, M. J. 'Fulling in the West Riding woollen cloth industry 1689–1770.' *Tex. Hist.*, x (1979), 127–41.

See also: 529; 543; 1098; 5459; 5571; 5800; 5805; 5900; 5903; 5905; 5906; 5908; 5910; 5911; 5921; 5923; 5931; 5940; 5941; 5944; 6557; 6560.

d. TRANSPORT, COMMUNICATIONS, AND DISTRIBUTION

5318 **Broadbridge**, S. R. 'Living conditions on Midland canal boats: some qualifications.' *Transp. Hist.*, III, 1 (March 1970), 36–51.

5319 **Jensen**, Vernon H. *Decasualization and modernization of dock work in London.* Ithaca, N.Y.: New York State School of Industrial and Labor Relations, 1971. vi, 101p.

5320 **Dixon**, C. 'The hard life and times of Henry Moffat, seaman.' *Mar. Mirror*, LIX (1973), 193–203.

5321 **Hanson**, H. 'Living conditions on Midland canal boats: some qualifications.' *Transp. Hist.*, VII, 1 (March 1974), 60–78.

5322 **Randell**, Arthur. *Fenland railwaymen.* London: Routledge & Kegan Paul, 1974. 94p.

5323 **Smith**, George. *Our canal population: a cry from the boat cabins, with a remedy.* Wakefield: EP Publishing, 1974.
Second edition. Reprinted with a new introduction by P.A.L. Vine.

5324 **Coles**, Arthur. 'Working the cut: reminiscences of a boatman.' *Cake and Cock Horse*, VI, 2 (Spring 1975), 19–29.

5325 **Elliot**, Bill. *Piano and herrings: autobiography of a Wolverhampton railway worker.* Milton Keynes: People's Press, 1975. 41p.

5326 **Ellis**, Harry. *London tramway memories: New Cross and Holloway depots, 1946–1952.* Farnborough: Light Railway Transport League, 1975. 16p.

5327 **Hollowell**, Peter. 'The remarkably constant fortunes of the British Railways locomotiveman.' Esland, G. and others (eds.). *People and work.* 1975. p. 230–40.

5328 **Huggett**, Frank Edward. *Past, present and future of life and work at sea: a documentary enquiry.* London: Harrap, 1975. 144p.

5329 **Mitchell**, William Reginald. *The railway shanties.* Settle: Settle & District Civic Society, Railway Centenary Committee, 1975. 17p.

5330 **Uglow**, Jim. *Sailorman: a barge-master's story.* Greenwich: Conway Maritime Press, 1975. 163p.

5331 **Bedale**, Len. *Station master: my lifetime's railway service in Yorkshire.* Sheffield: Turntable Publications, 1976. 80p.
As told to C.T. Goode.

5332 **Drayton**, John. *On the footplate: memories of a GWR engineman.* Truro: Barton, 1976. 111p.

5333 **Everitt**, Alan. 'Country carriers in the nineteenth century.' *J. Transp. Hist.*, III, 3 (February 1976), 179–202.

5334 **Gasson**, Harold. *Footplate days: more reminiscences of a Great Western fireman.* Oxford: Oxford U.P., 1976. 112p.

5335 **Postal, Telephone and Telephone International.** 'Conditions of work in the British Post Office.' *P.T.T.I. Stud.*, XI (Spring 1976), 3–52.

5336 **Press**, Jonathan P. *The merchant seamen of Bristol, 1747–1789.* Bristol: Bristol Branch of the Historical Association, 1976. 23p.

5337 **Broadbridge**, S. R. 'Living conditions on Midland canal boats: a rejoinder.' *Transp. Hist.*, VII, 1 (Spring 1977), 81–5.
This article was reprinted in volume VII, part 2 of the same journal, p. 141–6.

5338 **Collins**, S. *The wheels used to talk to us.* London: Tallis, 1977. 172p.
Tram driver's reminiscences, edited by T. Cooper.

5339 **Finch**, A. J. 'A signalman with the Great Western.' *Transp. Hist.*, VIII, 3 (Winter 1977), 217–28.

5340 **Roberts**, John Easter. *Northern Western enginemen: recollections of 34 years on the footplate.* Clapham: Dalesman, 1977. 88p.

5341 **Whiteside**, N. *The dock decasualisation issue, 1889–1924: public policy and port labour reform.* 1977. (Ph.D. thesis, University of Liverpool.)

5342 **Department of Trade**, Working Group on the Employment of Non-domiciled Seafarers. *Report of the Working Group ...* London: H.M.S.O., 1978. iv, 68p.
Chairman: J. N. Archer.

5343 **Kerrigan**, Colin. 'The coal heavers of East London.' *E. London Rec.*, 1 (1978), 2–12.

5344 **Meacher**, Charles. *LNER footplate memories: the story of twenty-five years on and off shed.* Truro: Barton, 1978. 150p.

5345 **Press**, Jonathan P. *The economic and social conditions of the merchant seamen of England, 1815–1854.* 1978. (Ph.D. thesis, University of Bristol.)

5346 **Wilkinson**, Albert. 'Mull, the son of Mull.' MacFarlane, J. (ed.). *Essays from the Yorkshire coalfields.* 1979. p. 53–4.
Railwaymen's conditions and unemployment.

See also: 468; 481; 945; 951; 1994; 4806; 5474; 5475; 5904.

e. WHITE-COLLAR AND PROFESSIONAL

5347 **Rook**, A. *Contracts of service for senior staff: a* *survey of current practice in 102 companies.* London: British Institute of Management, 1971. 53p. (Management survey reports 2.)

5348 **Benét**, Mary Kathleen. *Secretary: enquiry into the female ghetto.* London: Sidgwick & Jackson, 1972. 171p.

5349 **Powell**, Maurice. 'Occupational problems of professional men: dentists and pharmacists.' *Occup. Psychol.*, XLVI (1972), 53–67.

5350 **National Union of Teachers**. *Teachers talking: the growth of the teacher's job: a survey carried out by the National Union of Teachers for the Houghton inquiry into teachers' pay.* London: NUT, 1974. 26p.

5351 **Scott**, K. L. and **Deere**, M. L. *Office staff: holidays, turnover and other procedures.* London: Institute of Administrative Management, 1975. 84p.

5352 **Clark**, Leonard. *The inspector remembers: diary of one of Her Majesty's Inspectors of Schools 1936–70.* London: Dobson, 1976. 192p.

5353 **Horn**, Pamela L. R. 'Mid-Victorian elementary school teachers.' *Local Historian*, XII, 3–4 (November 1976), 161–6.

5354 **Gamarnikow**, Eva. 'Sexual division of labour: the case of nursing.' Kuhn, A. and Wolpe, A. (eds.). *Feminism and materialism.* 1978. p. 96–123.

5355 **Koutsoyiannis**, A. 'Managerial job security and the capital structure of firms.' *Manchr. Sch. Econ. Soc. Stud.*, XLVI (March 1978), 1979. 120p.

5356 **Delgado**, Alan. *The enormous file: a social history of the office.* London: John Murray, 1979. 120p.

5357 **Townsend**, Peter. 'Inequality at the workplace: how white-collar always wins.' *New Soc.*, L (18 October 1979), 120–23.

See also: 4021; 4749; 5435; 5472; 5473; 5591; 5593; 5634; 5635; 5874; 5878; 5882; 5884; 5893; 5902; 5917; 5928.

f. MISCELLANEOUS SERVICES

5358 **Davidoff**, L. 'Domestic service and the working-class life cycle.' *Soc. Study Labour Hist. Bull.*, XXVI (Spring 1973), 10–13.

5359 **Davidoff**, L. 'Mastered for life: servant and wife in Victorian and Edwardian England.' *Soc. Study Labour Hist. Bull.*, XXVII (Autumn 1973), 23–5.

5360 **Hobbs**, May. *Born to struggle.* London: Quartet Books, 1973. 164p.
Working conditions of female cleaners.

5361 **Brown**, Marie. *Sweated labour: a study of homework.* London: Low Pay Unit, 1974. 26p. (Low pay pamphlet 1.)

5362 **Franklin**, Jill. 'Troops of servants: labour and planning in the country house, 1840–1914.' *Vic. Stud.*, XIX. 2 (December 1975), 211–39.

5363 **Harrison**, Rosina. *Rose: my life in service.* London: Cassell, 1975. 268p.

5364 **Horn**, Pamela L. R. 'Domestic service in Northamptonshire 1830–1914.' *Northamps. Past Present*, V, 3 (1975), 267–75.

5365 **Horn**, Pamela L. R. *The rise and fall of the Victorian servant.* Dublin: Gill & Macmillan, 1975. 221p.

5366 **Davidoff**, Leonore and **Hawthorne**, Ruth. *A day in the life of a Victorian domestic servant.* London: Allen & Unwin, 1976. 94p.

5367 **Ebery**, Mark and **Preston**, Brian. *Domestic service in late Victorian and Edwardian England, 1871–1914.* Reading: University of Reading. Department of Geography, 1976. 117p.

5368 **McBride**, Theresa M. *The domestic revolution: the modernisation of household service in England and France, 1820–1920.* London: Croom Helm, 1976. 160p.

5369 **Huggett**, Frank Edward. *Life below stairs: domestic servants in England from Victorian times.* London: John Murray, 1977. 186p.

5370 **Taylor**, J. P. *Women domestic servants, 1919–1939: the final phase.* 1978. (M.A. thesis, University of Birmingham.)

5371 **Taylor**, Pam. 'Daughters and mothers: maids and mistresses: domestic service between the wars.' Clarke, J. and others (eds.). *Working class culture.* 1979. p. 121–39.

See also: 299; 389; 1018.

g. PUBLIC ADMINISTRATION

5372 **National Whitley Council**, Joint Committee on the Fulton Report. *Fulton: the reshaping of the Civil Service: developments during 1970.* London: The Council, 1971. vi, 36p.

5373 **Angus**, William S. 'University administrative staff.' *Public Adm.*, LI, 1 (Spring 1973), 17–39.

5374 **March**, Gerard. *Flames across the Tyne.* South Shields: E. F. Peterson, 1974. 127p.
Working lives of firemen.

5375 **Wilson**, David R. *Government dock-yard workers in Portsmouth, 1793–1815.* 1975. (Ph.D. thesis, University of Warwick.)

5376 **Rasor**, E. L. *Reform in the Royal Navy: a social history of the lower deck, 1850–1880.* Hamden, Connecticut: Anchor Books, 1977. 210p.

5377 **Winton**, J. *Hurrah for the life of a sailor! Life on the lower deck of the Victorian Navy.* London: Michael Joseph, 1977. 320p.

5378 **O'Broin**, Noirin and **Farrell**, Gillian. *The working and living conditions of civil service typists.* Dublin: Economic and Social Research Institute, 1978. 164p.

See also: 336; 416; 422; 437; 453; 474; 495; 528; 5461; 5596; 5601; 5916; 6127.

3. Particular Groups and Problems

a. WOMEN

Material on sweating and home work is classified here. Sociological and psychological material on women's attitudes to, and behaviour at, work is generally classified in Part Two. See also Part Three, II, E, 2; Part Six, II, C, 4; Part Six, II, D, 7; Part Six, III, E; Part Seven, II, C; and Part Seven, IV, D.

5379 **Dally**, Ann. 'Men and women at work.' *New Humanist*, LXXXVIII (November 1972), 285, 291.

5380 **Fogarty**, Michael Patrick. 'Women at work: the small child gap and other problems.' *Pers. Manage.*, IV, 2 (February 1972), 18–22.

5381 **Fogarty**, Michael Patrick, **Rapoport**, Rhona and **Rapoport**, Robert Norman. *Women and top jobs: the next move.* London: Political and Economic Planning, 1972. 91p. (P.E.P. broadsheet 535.)

5382 **Labour Party**. *Discrimination against women.* London: Labour Party, 1972. 45p.

5383 **Lloyd**, L. *Women workers in Britain.* London: Socialist Woman Publications, 1972. 46p.

5384 **Musgrave**, Beatrice and **Wheeler-Bennett**, Joan (eds.). *Women at work: combining family and a career, including Comeback: a directory to the professions.* London: Peter Owen, 1972. 156p.

5385 **Trades Union Congress**. *The roots of inequality.* London: T.U.C., 1972. 13p.

5386 **White**, David. 'Male backlash.' *New Soc.*, XXI (13 July 1972), 64–5.

5387 **Blackman**, Janet. 'Women's economic revolution.' Barratt Brown, M. and Coates, K. (eds.). *Trade union register: 3.* 1973. p. 89–97.

5388 **Boston**, S. 'Discrimination on grounds of sex.' *Ind. Soc.*, LV, 5 (May 1973), 6–10.

5389 **Holcombe**, Lee. *Victorian ladies at work: middle class working women in England and Wales 1850–1914.* Hamden, Connecticut: Anchor Books, 1973. x, 253p.

5390 **Wise**, Audrey. *Women and the struggle for workers' control.* Nottingham: Bertrand Russell Peace Foundation, 1973. 15p. (Spokesman pamphlets 33.)

5391 **Geary**, Robert Charles and **O'Muircheartaigh**, F. S. *Equalization of opportunity in Ireland: statistical aspects.* Dublin: Economic and Social Research Institute, 1974. 122p.

5392 **King**, J. S. *Women and work: sex differences and society.* London: H.M.S.O., 1974. 36p. (Department of Employment. Manpower paper 10.)

5393 **Oakley**, Ann. *Women's work: the housewife, past and present.* New York: Pantheon Press, 1974. 275p.

5394 **Workers' Educational Association**, Service Centre for Social Studies. *Equal opportunities for men and women.* London: W.E.A., 1974. 20p.

5395 **Addison**, John Thomas. 'Sex discrimination: some comparative evidence.' *Br. J. Ind. Relat.*, XIII, 2 (July 1975), 263–5.

5396 **Bolton**, Brian. *An end to homeworking?* London: Fabian Society, 1975. ii, 20p. (Fabian tract 436.)

5397 **Department of Employment**. *Women and*

work: a review. London: H.M.S.O., 1975. iii, 63p. (Manpower paper 11.)

5398 **Dorling**, Jenny. 'Making a start on training for women.' *Pers. Manage.*, VII 12 (December 1975), 18–21.

5399 **Granick**, D. *Equality of promotional opportunities in British industry.* London: Aims of Industry, 1975. 13p.

5400 **Helps**, Ian G. and **Skitmore**, P. M. 'Discrimination against women in employment.' *Long Range Plann.*, VIII, 1 (February 1975), 2–13.

5401 **Hunt**, Audrey. *Management attitudes and practices towards women at work: an employment policy survey.* London: H.M.S.O. for the Office of Population Censuses and Surveys, Social Survey Division, 1975. 221p.

5402 **Nandy**, Luise and **Nandy**, Dipak. 'Towards true equality for women.' *New Soc.*, XXXI (30 January 1975), 246–9.

5403 **Toner**, B. *Double shift: a practical guide to working mothers.* London: Arrow, 1975. 200p.

5404 **Adam**, R. *A woman's place, 1910–75.* London: Chatto & Windus, 1976. 224p.

5405 **Barker**, Diana Leonard and **Allen**, Sheila (eds.). *Dependence and exploitation in work and marriage.* London: Longman, 1976. viii, 265p. (Explorations in society, vol. 6.)

5406 **Barron**, R. and **Norris**, G. 'Sexual divisions and the dual labour market.' Barker, D. L. and Allen, S. (eds.). *Dependence and exploitation in work and marriage.* 1976. p. 47–69.

5407 **Dawes**, F. *A woman's place – women at work from 1830 to the present.* Hove: Wayland, 1976. 200p.

5408 **Fonda**, Nickie. 'Current entitlements and provisions: a critical review.' Fonda, N. and Moss, P. (eds.). *Mothers in employment.* 1976. p. 39–53.

5409 **Hostettler**, Eve. 'Women's work in the nineteenth century countryside.' *Soc. Study Labour Hist. Bull.*, XXXIII (Autumn 1976), 9–12.

5410 **John**, Angela V. *Women workers in British coal mines, 1840–90, with special reference to West Lancashire.* 1976. (Ph.D. thesis, University of Manchester.)

5411 **Mitchell**, Juliet and **Oakley**, Ann. *The rights and wrongs of women.* Harmondsworth: Penguin, 1976. 438p.

5412 **Nandy**, Luise and **Nandy**, Dipak. 'Towards true equality for women.' *New Community*, V, 1–2 (Summer 1976), 31–7.

5413 **Richbell**, Suzanne. 'De facto discrimination.' *Pers. Manage.*, VIII, 11 (November 1976), 30–33.

5414 **Counter Information Services**. *Women under attack.* London: The Services, 1977. 33p. (Anti-reports 15.)

5415 **Davies**, Margaret Llewelyn (ed.). *Life as we have known it, by cooperative working women.* London: Virago, 1977. xxxi, 141p.

First published in 1931 with an introductory letter by Virginia Woolf. Reprinted with a new introduction by Anna Davin.

5416 **Hollis**, Patricia. 'Working women.' *History*, LXII, 206 (October 1977), 439–45.

5417 **Incomes Data Services**. *Maternity schemes*. London: I.D.S., 1977. (I.D.S. study 150.)

5418 **Mackie**, Lindsay and **Patullo,** Polly. *Women at work*. London: Tavistock, 1977. 192p.

5419 **Badger**, Ethel. 'Lady clerk, 1918–1933.' *Blackcountryman*, XI (Autumn 1978), 14.

5420 **Beechey**, Veronica. 'Women and production: a critical analysis of some sociological theories of women's work.' Kuhn, A. and Wolpe, A. (eds.). *Feminism and materialism*. 1978. p. 155–97.

5421 **Bythell**, Duncan. *The sweated trades: outwork in nineteenth century Britain*. London: Batsford, 1978. 287p.

5422 **Daly**, M. E. 'Women, work and trade unionism.' MacCurtain, M. and O'Corrain, D. (eds.). *Women in Irish society: the historical dimension*. Dublin: Arlen House, 1978. p. 71–81.

5423 **Flynn**, Suzanne. 'Engineering management: one woman's approach.' *R. Soc. Arts J.*, CXXVI (August 1978), 541–51.

5424 **Kuhn**, Annette and **Wolpe**, Ann Marie (eds.). *Feminism and materialism: women and modes of production*. London: Routledge & Kegan Paul, 1978. xi, 328p.

5425 **McDonough**, Roisin and **Harrison**, Rachel. 'Patriarchy and relations of production.' Kuhn. A. and Wolpe, A. (eds.). *Feminism and materialism*. 1978. p. 11–41.

5426 **Thom**, Deborah. 'Women at the Woolwich Arsenal, 1915–19.' *Oral Hist.*, VI, 2 (Autumn 1978), 58–74.

5427 **Burman**, Sandra (ed.). *Fit work for women: papers from the interdisciplinary seminar organised at the University of Oxford, 1977–78*. London: Croom Helm in association with the Oxford University Women's Studies Committee, 1979. 201p.

5428 **Glew**, Jenny. *Woman at work: a handbook for the working woman*. London: Pitman, 1979. viii, 115p.

5429 **Glucklich**, Pauline and **Povall**, Margery. 'Equal opportunities: a case for action in default of the law.' *Pers. Manage.*, XI, 1 (January 1979), 28–31.

5430 **Hiley**, Michael. *Victorian working women: portraits from life*. London: Gordon Fraser, 1979. 142p.
Based on the papers of Arthur Joseph Mundy.

5431 **Incomes Data Services**. *Maternity cover and child care*. London: I.D.S., 1979. 17p. (I.D.S. study 191.)

5432 **Marsh**, Alan. *Women and shiftwork: the protective legislation survey*. London: H.M.S.O., for the Equal Opportunities Commission, 1979. vi, 130p.

5433 **Noble**, Joe. 'The London homeworking campaign.' Craig, G. and others (eds.). *Jobs and community action*. 1979. p. 113–27.

5434 **Pettman**, Barrie Owen. 'Women in work.' *Employee Relat.*, I, 1 (1979), 19–23.

5435 **Place**, Helen. 'A biographical profile of women in management.' *J. Occup. Psychol.*, LII (December 1979), 26–76.

5436 **Rickard**, John. 'The anti-sweating movement in Britain and Victoria: the politics of empire and social reform.' *Hist. Stud.*, XVIII, 73 (October 1979), 582–97.

See also: 125; 304; 439; 489; 502; 1098; 3495; 5234; 5302; 5751; 5753; 6251; 6573; 6576; 6998; 6999; 7058.

b. CHILDREN AND YOUTH

Sociological and psychological material on the industrial attitudes and behaviour of young persons is classified in Part Two. See also Part Six, II, A; Part Six, II, C, 5; Part Six, II, D, 7; and Part Seven, II, D, 2, b.

5437 **Evans**, Richard Meurig (comp.). *Children in the mines*. Cardiff: National Museum of Wales, 1972. 40p.

5438 **Oastler**, Richard. *Richard Oastler: king of factory children: six pamphlets, 1835–1861*. New York: Arno Press, 1972. (British labour struggles: contemporary pamphlets 1727–1850.)

5439 **Bushby**, D. W. 'Half-timers at Marston.' *Beds. Mag.*, XIV (Spring 1975), 340–44.

5440 **Horn**, Pamela L. R. 'The employment of children in Victorian Oxfordshire.' *Midl. Hist.*, IV, 1 (Spring 1977), 61–74.

5441 **Forster**, Eric. *The pit children*. Newcastle-upon-Tyne: Frank Graham, 1978. 48p. (Northern history booklet 83.)

5442 **Livingstone**, Sally. *A penny a boy: Norfolk children at work in Victorian days*. Ipswich: Boydell Press, 1978. 40p.

5443 **Challis**, James and **Elliman**, David. *Child workers today*. London: Quartermaine House, 1979. 170p.

See also: 4568.

c. ETHNIC GROUPS

See also Part Three, II, E, 1; Part Six, II, D, 7; Part Six, II, E, 2; and Part Seven, III, A, 1.

5444 **Wainwright**, David. *Race and employment: managing a multi-racial labour force*. London: Institute of Personnel Management, 1970. 88p.

5445 **Allen**, Sheila. 'Race and the economy: some aspects of the position of non-indigenous labour.' *Race*, XIII, 2 (October 1971), 165–78.

5446 **John**, G. and **Humphry**, D. *Because they're black*. Harmondsworth: Penguin, 1971. 204p.

5447 **Race Today**. 'Economy: GB.' *Race Today*, III, 4 (April 1971), 120–21.
Report of a conference paper on ethnic

groups at work and in the labour market.

5448 **Rees**, Tom. *Policy or drift? How three London firms handle racial integration in the workforce.* London: Runnymede Industrial Unit, 1971. 40p.

5449 **Stephen**, David. *Race and jobs: 71 questions answered on immigration, race relations and the Race Relations Act.* London: Runnymede Trust, 1971. [20]p.

5450 **Allen**, Sheila. 'Black workers in Great Britain.' Van Houte, H. and Melgert, W. (eds.). *Foreigners in our community.* 1972. p. 43–9.

5451 **Brooks**, D. U. and **Singh**, K. 'Does employment breed racialism?' *Race Today* (July 1972), 226–7.

5452 **Brooks**, D. U. and **Singh**, K. 'Race relations, industrial relations, and pluralism.' *New Community*, 1 (1972), 277–81.

5453 **Connelly**, T. J. 'Racial integration in employment.' Torrington, D. P. (ed.). *Handbook of industrial relations.* 1972. p. 193–206.

5454 **Department of Employment**. *Take 7: the report on a survey undertaken by the Department of Employment into immigrant labour relations at seven English firms.* London: H.M.S.O., 1972. 118p.

5455 **Lawrence**, Susanne. 'Working towards racial integration.' *Pers. Manage.*, IV, 7 (July 1972), 21–4.

5456 **Leppard**, J. W. and **Kaufman**, M. 'English for Asian immigrant workers.' *Ind. Comm. Train.*, IV, 9 (September 1972), 413–8.

5457 **Stephen**, David. *Racial discrimination in employment: will unemployment make things worse?* London: Runnymede Industrial Unit, 1972. [20]p.
Text of a lecture given to the Industrial Law Society.

5458 **Tinker**, Hugh. 'Manifestations of discrimination in Great Britain.' Van Houte, H. and Melgert, W. (eds.). *Foreigners in our community.* 1972. p. 66–70.

5459 **Williams**, Nerys. 'The new sweat shops.' *New Soc.*, XX (29 June 1972), 666–8.
Immigrants in the clothing industry.

5460 **Bagley**, Christopher. *Dutch plural society: a comparative study in race relations.* Oxford: Oxford U.P., 1973. xiv, 293p.
Comparison of Netherlands and U.K.

5461 **Bishop**, Terry. 'Immigrant labour in Britain's hospitals.' *Pers. Manage.*, V, 8 (August 1973), 25–7.

5462 **Bosanquet**, Nicholas. *Race and employment in Britain: a report.* London: Runnymede Trust, 1973. 16p.

5463 **Carter**, Mark Bonham. 'Employment in a multi-racial society.' *Careers Q.*, XXV, 4 (Autumn 1973), 24–31.

5464 **Castles**, Stephen and **Kosack**, Godula. *Immigrant workers and class structure in Western Europe.* Oxford: Oxford U.P., 1973. xiv, 514p.

5465 **Stewart**, Margaret. *A stitch in time: an employers' guide to equal opportunity in a multiracial workforce.* London: Runnymede Trust, 1973. 27p.

5466 **Wilson**, Sir Geoffrey. 'Race relations in industry.' *C.B.I. Rev.* (Winter 1973), 5–13.

5467 **Jupp**, Tom. 'Promotion and the immigrant.' *Pers. Manage.*, VI, 4 (April 1974), 34–7.

5468 **McIntosh**, N. and **Smith**, D. J. *The extent of racial discrimination.* London: Political and Economic Planning, 1974. 55p. (P.E.P. broadsheet 547.)

5469 **Power**, Jonathan. 'The new proletariat.' *Encounter*, XLIII (September 1974), 8–22.

5470 **Slater**, S. S. P., **Wilson**, A. T. M. and **Simonds**, K. *Employment of non-English speaking workers: what industry must do.* London: Community Relations Commission, 1974. 32p.

5471 **Smith**, David J. *Racial disadvantage in employment.* London: Political and Economic Planning, 1974. 107p. (P.E.P. broadsheet 544.)

5472 **Ballard**, Roger and **Holden**, Bronwen M. 'The employment of coloured graduates in Britain.' *New Community*, IV (Autumn 1975), 325–36.

5473 **Ballard**, Roger and **Holden**, Bronwen M. 'Racial discrimination: no room at the top: black graduates.' *New Soc.*, XXXII (17 April 1975), 133–5.

5474 **Brooks**, Dennis. 'Black and white on the buses.' *New Soc.*, XXXI (20 February 1975), 455–7.

5475 **Brooks**, Dennis. *Race and labour in London Transport.* Oxford: Oxford U.P., 1975. xxii, 389p.

5476 **Incomes Data Services**. *Race relations in employment.* London: I.D.S., 1975. 24p. (I.D.S. study 92.)

5477 **Lawrence**, Susanne. 'Racial discrimination: the poor relations.' *Pers. Manage.*, VII, 9 (September 1975), 22–6.

5478 **Morrison**, Lionel. 'A black journalist's experience of British journalism.' *New Community*, IV (Autumn 1975), 317–22.

5479 **Stewart**, Margaret. *Employment of minorities in Britain: an employers' guide.* London: Gower, 1975. xiii, 146p.

5480 **Deaton**, David R. 'The social mix of London Transport recruits.' *New Community*, V (1976), 316–9.

5481 **Ogden**, J. 'Finding out about the Sikhs.' *Ind. Soc.*, LVIII, 6 (November–December 1976), 14.

5482 **O'Muircheartaigh**, Colm A. and **Rees**, Tom. 'Immigrants at work: migrant–immigrant labour in Great Britain, France and Germany.' *New Community*, IV (Winter–Spring 1975–6), 493–500.

5483 **Pearn**, Michael A. 'Race relations legislation and the role of the occupational psychologist.' *Br. Psychol. Soc. Bull.*, XXIX (September 1976), 300–302.

5484 **Smith**, David John. *The facts of racial*

disadvantage: a national survey. London: Political and Economic Planning, 1976. xii, 257p.

5485 **Thakur**, Manab and **Williams**, Roger. 'Immigrants at work: hopeful travellers: a study of Asian graduates working in Britain.' *New Community*, IV (Winter–Spring 1975–6), 476–92.

5486 **Allen**, Sheila, **Bentley**, Stuart and **Bornat**, Joanna. *Work, race and immigration.* Bradford: University of Bradford, 1977. vi, 415p.

5487 **Sengupta**, Susan, **Williams**, Celia and **Pearn**, Michael. *Industrial training boards and race relations: a discussion paper.* London: Community Relations Commission and Runnymede Trust, 1977. 30p.

5488 **Rex**, John, **Tomlinson**, Sally, **Hearnden**, David and **Ratcliffe**, Peter. 'Housing and ethnic minorities: housing, employment and race relations in Birmingham.' *New Community*, VI (Winter 1977–8), 123–6.

5489 **Tavistock Institute of Human Relations**. *Application of race relations policy in the Civil Service.* London: H.M.S.O., 1978. vi, 276p.

5490 **Webb**, C. R. 'Some Irish poor in Lambeth, 1834–46.' *Ir. Ancestor*, X (1978), 108–15.

5491 **Brooks**, Dennis and **Singh**, Karamjit. 'Ethnic commitment versus structural reality: South Asian immigrant workers in Britain.' *New Community*, VII (1979), 19–30.

5492 **Brooks**, Dennis and **Singh**, Karamjit. 'Pivots and presents: Asian brokers in British foundries.' Wallman, S. (ed.). *Ethnicity at work.* 1979. p. 93–114.

5493 **Freeman**, Gary P. *Immigrant labor and racial conflict in industrial societies: the French and British experience, 1945–1975.* Princeton: Princeton U.P., 1979. xiv, 362p.

5494 **Khan**, Verity Saifullah. 'South Asian women in South London.' Wallman, S. (ed.). *Ethnicity at work.* 1979. p. 115–34.

5495 **Kosmin**, Barry. 'Exclusion and opportunity: traditions of work amongst British Jews.' Wallman, S. (ed.). *Ethnicity at work.* 1979. p. 37–70.

5496 **O'Brien**, John and **Gubbay**, Denise. 'Training to integrate: the multi-racial workforce.' *Pers. Manage.*, XI, 1 (January 1979), 20–23.

5497 **Okely**, Judith. 'Trading stereotypes: the case of English gypsies.' Wallman, S. (ed.). *Ethnicity at work.* 1979. p. 17–36.

5498 **Pearn**, Michael A. and **Ungerson**, Bernard. 'Ethnic recording for racial equality.' *Pers. Manage.*, XI, 3 (March 1979), 28–32.

5499 **Scottish Immigrant Labour Council**. *Working together for a multi-racial Scotland.* Edinburgh: The Council, 1979. [23]p.

5500 **Wallman**, Sandra (ed.). *Ethnicity at work.* London: Macmillan, 1979. xii, 252p.

See also: 181; 2138; 2985; 2990; 3469; 3492; 3603; 3965; 4362; 4420; 5576.

d. THE UNEMPLOYED: CONDITIONS AND RELIEF

Material on work sharing and the shorter working week as ways of relieving unemployment is classified at Part Six, IV, B. See also Part Three, II, E, 3; Part Six, II, D; Part Six, II, E, 3; Part Seven, II, B; Part Seven, II, D, 2; Part Seven, II, D, 4; Part Seven, VII, A; and Part Seven, VII, B, 1.

5501 **Gould**, Tony. 'Out of work: the experience.' *New Soc.*, XVII (20 May 1971), 859–61.

5502 **Ruskin College**, Oxford, Trade Union Research Unit. *Behind the dole queue: the facts about unemployment.* Nottingham: Bertrand Russell Peace Foundation, 1971. [7]p. (Spokesman pamphlet 23.)

5503 **Johns**, Stephen. *We demand the right to work.* London: J. Simmance, 1972. 64p.

5504 **Jones**, Mervyn. *Life on the dole.* London: Davis-Poynter, 1972. 142p.

5505 **Pocock**, P. 'Softening the blow of redundancy.' *Pers. Manage.*, IV, 6 (June 1972), 25–7.

5506 **Stewart**, Iain M. *Redundancy: the scrap heap or a new job opportunity?* Glasgow: Institution of Engineers and Shipbuilders in Scotland, 1972. 156p.

5507 **Martin**, Roderick and **Fryer**, Robert H. *Redundancy and paternalist capitalism: a study in the sociology of work.* London: Allen & Unwin, 1973. 278p.

5508 **Field**, Frank. *Unemployment: the facts.* London: Child Poverty Action Group, 1975. 32p. (Poverty pamphlet 20.)

5509 **Marsden**, Dennis and **Duff**, E. *Workless: some unemployed men and their families.* Harmondsworth: Penguin, 1975. 269p.

5510 **Newport and Gwent Industrial Mission**. *Redundant? A personal survival kit.* Newport: The Mission, 1975. 24p.

5511 **Parker**, Stanley. 'The effects of redundancy.' Esland, G. and others (ed.). *People and work.* 1975. p. 88–99.

5512 **Cox**, Sarah. *Down the road: unemployment and the fight for the right to work.* London: Writers and Readers Coop., 1976. 127p.

5513 **Harrison**, Richard. 'The demoralising experience of prolonged unemployment.' *Dep. Employment Gaz.*, LXXXIV, 4 (April 1976), 339–48.

5514 **National Federation of Claimants Unions**. *Unemployed: the fight to live: Claimants Union handbook.* London: The Federation, 1977. 57p.

5515 **Pope**, R. '"Dole schools": the North-East Lancashire experience, 1930–39.' *J. Educ. Adm. Hist.*, IX, 2 (July 1977), 26–33.

5516 **Roberts**, David. 'Before and after: redundancy, company policy and reality.' *Pers. Manage.*, IX, 7 (July 1977), 37–41.

5517 **Hill**, John. 'The psychological impact of unemployment.' *New Soc.*, XXXIII (19 January 1978), 118–20.

5518 **Craig**, Gary, **Mayo**, Marjorie and **Shar-**

man, Nick (eds.). *Jobs and community action.* London: Routledge & Kegan Paul, 1979. ix, 294p.

B. HOURS

Many of the general works contained in Part Six, IV, A also contain material on hours of work. Material on work sharing and the shorter working week is included here. Material on work and leisure is classified at Part Two, I.

1. General

5519 **Gretton**, John. 'The hours we work.' *New Soc.*, XVII (7 January 1971), 15–17.

5520 **Industrial Research and Information Services.** *Hours of work.* London: The Services, 1971. 18p.

5521 **Wilkinson**, Robert T. 'Hours of work and the twenty-four-hour cycle of rest and activity.' Warr, P. (ed.). *Psychology at work.* 1971. p. 31–54.

5522 *The battle for the ten hours day continues 1837–1843.* New York: Arno Press, 1972. (British labour struggles: contemporary pamphlets 1727–1850.)

5523 **Bienefeld**, Manfred A. *Working hours in British industry: an economic history.* London: Weidenfeld & Nicolson, 1972. 293p.

5524 *Demands for early closing hours 1843.* New York: Arno Press, 1972. (British labour struggles: contemporary pamphlets 1727–1850.)

5525 **Evans**, Archibald A. 'This short working life.' *Ind. Soc.*, LIV, 9 (September 1972), 21; LIV, 10 (October 1972), 8–10.

5526 **Mann**, Tom. *What a compulsory 8 hour working day means to the workers.* London: Pluto, 1972. 32p.
First published 1886. Reprinted with a new introduction by Richard Hyman.

5527 *Prelude to victory of the ten hours movement 1844.* New York: Arno Press, 1972. (British labour struggles: contemporary pamphlets 1727–1850.)

5528 *Sunday work: seven pamphlets 1794–1856.* New York: Arno Press, 1972. (British labour struggles: contemporary pamphlets 1727–1850.)

5529 *The ten hours movement in 1831 and 1832: six pamphlets and one broadside 1831–1832.* New York: Arno Press, 1972. (British labour struggles: contemporary pamphlets 1727–1850.)

5530 **Barry**, Anthony K. *Holidays and hours of work in the European Community.* London: Institute of Personnel Management, 1973. 74p.

5531 **Department of Employment.** *Hours of employment of women and young persons.* London: H.M.S.O., 1973. 28p. (Health and safety at work 23.)
Second edition.

5532 **Rainbow**, P. E. 'Work, working hours and leisure time.' *Work Study Manage. Serv.*, XI, 2 (February 1973), 84–9.

5533 **Williams**, R. *Tomorrow at work: essays on future patterns of work and leisure.* London: British Broadcasting Corporation, 1973. v, 53p.

5534 **Fincham**, Robin. 'Inequality and the three-day week.' *New Soc.*, XXIX (18 July 1974), 135–7.
Unequal effects on manual and white-collar workers.

5535 **Labour Research Department.** *Hours and holidays.* London: The Department, 1974. 16p.

5536 **Roberts**, K., **Clark**, S., **Cook**, F. G. and **Semeonoff**, E. 'How many hours in a week?' *Pers. Manage.*, VI, 6 (June 1974), 33–6.

5537 **Taylor**, Robert. 'Short-time view.' *New Soc.*, XXVII (24 January 1974), 181–2.
The three-day week.

5538 **Hodgson**, M. C. *The working day and the working week in Victorian Britain, 1840–1900.* 1975. (M.Phil. thesis, Birkbeck College, University of London.)

5539 **Hughes**, Barry and **Leslie**, Derek. 'Hours of work in British manufacturing industries.' *Scott. J. Polit. Econ.*, XXII (November 1975), 293–304.

5540 **Newton**, S. C. and **Parker**, S. R. 'Who are the temporary workers?' *Dep. Employment Gaz.*, LXXXIII, 6 (June 1975), 507–11.
Part-time work.

5541 **Sloane**, Peter James. *Changing patterns of working hours.* London: H.M.S.O., 1975. v, 45p. (Department of Employment. Manpower paper 13.)

5542 **Brown**, C. V., **Levin**, E. and **Ulph**, D. T. 'Estimates of labour hours supplied by married male workers in Great Britain.' *Scott. J. Polit. Econ.*, XXIII (November 1976), 261–77.

5543 **Incomes Data Services.** *Lay-offs and short time.* London: I.D.S., 1976. 78p. (I.D.S. handbook 3.)

5544 **Incomes Data Services.** *Part time work.* London: I.D.S., 1976. 18p. (I.D.S. study 118.)

5545 **Brown**, Mike, **Emerson**, Tony and **Griffiths**, David. 'Socially useful work.' Barratt Brown, M. and others (eds.). *Full employment.* 1978. p. 103–10.

5546 **Hughes**, John. 'The 35 hour week.' Barratt Brown, M. and others (eds.). *Full employment.* 1978. p. 113–24.

5547 **Taylor**, Robert. 'Work sharing and worklessness.' *New Soc.*, XXXIII (23 November 1978), 452–4.

5548 **Walsh**, B. 'More leisure–but when?' *Work Study*, XIV, 4 (April 1978), 15–19.

5549 **Evans**, Alastair. 'Measures to make the jobs go round.' *Pers. Manage.*, XI, 1 (January 1979), 32–5.

5550 **Incomes Data Services.** *Guaranteed week and*

lay-off. London: I.D.S., 1979. 18p. (I.D.S. study 192.)

5551 **Wainwright**, David. 'Shrinking the week and sharing the work.' *Pers. Manage.*, XI, 10 (October 1979), 48–52.

See also: 20; 335; 730; 3847; 3884; 3885; 4627; 4668; 5578.

2. Overtime

5552 **Brown**, William. 'The overtime habit.' *New Soc.*, XX (18 May 1972), 385–6.

5553 **Incomes Data Services**. *Overtime part 1*. London: I.D.S., 1972. 16p. (I.D.S. study 24.)

5554 **Incomes Data Services**. *Overtime part 2*. London: I.D.S., 1972. 16p. (I.D.S. study 28.)

5555 **Incomes Data Services**. *Overtime part 3*. London: I.D.S., 1972. 16p. (I.D.S. study 40.)

5556 **Hart**, R. A. 'The role of overtime working in the recent wage inflation process.' *Bull. Econ. Res.*, XXV, 1 (May 1973), 73–87.

5557 **Brown**, C. V. and **Levin**, E. 'The effect of income taxation on overtime: the results of a national survey.' *Econ. J.*, LXXXIV (December 1974), 833–48.

5558 **Incomes Data Services**. *Overtime part 4*. London: I.D.S., 1974. 16p. (I.D.S. study 68.)

5559 **Incomes Data Services**. *Overtime part 5*. London: I.D.S., 1975. 24p. (I.D.S. study 94.)

5560 **Industrial and Commercial Training.** 'Trade union studies: overtime.' *Ind. Commer. Train.*, VII, 12 (December 1975), 494–501.

5561 **Leslie**, Derek G. 'Hours and overtime in British and United States manufacturing industries: a comparison.' *Br. J. Ind. Relat.*, XIV, 2 (July 1976), 194–201.

5562 **Leslie**, Derek G. 'Overtime: the institution that will not die.' *Pers. Manage.*, IX, 7 (July 1977), 34–6.

5563 **Fishwick**, F. 'Overtime working: a matter for public concern.' *Employee Relat.*, I, 3 (1979), 2–6.

5564 **Incomes Data Services**. *Private sector overtime*. London: I.D.S., 1979. 19p. (I.D.S. study 190.)

See also: 4519; 4597.

3. Shift Work

5565 **Sergean**, Robert. *Managing shiftwork*. Epping: Gower, 1971. xiii, 242p.

5566 **Pocock**, S. J., **Sergean**, R. and **Taylor**, P. J. 'Absence of continuous three-shift workers.' *Occup. Psychol.*, XLVI, 1 (1972), 7–13.

5567 **Sergean**, R. 'Shiftwork.' Torrington, Derek P. (ed.). *Handbook of industrial relations*. 1972. p. 179–92.

5568 **Incomes Data Services**. *Shiftwork part 1*.

London: I.D.S., 1973. 16p. (I.D.S. study 44.)

5569 **Incomes Data Services**. *Shiftwork part 2*. London: I.D.S., 1973. 16p. (I.D.S. study 48.)

5570 **Incomes Data Services**. *Shiftwork part 3*. London: I.D.S., 1973. 20p. (I.D.S. study 65.)

5571 **Fishwick**, F. and **Harling**, C. J. *Shiftworking in the motor industry: detailed study and assessment*. London: National Economic Development Office, Economic Development Committee for the Motor Manufacturing Industry, 1974. vi, 177p.

5572 **Griffin**, M. and **Sergean**, Robert. 'Starting and living with shifts.' *Ind. Soc.*, LVI, 3 (March 1974), 7–11.

5573 **Incomes Data Services**. *Shiftwork 4*. London: I.D.S., 1975. 18p. (I.D.S. study 110.)

5574 **Telman**, N. *Shift-work in relation to accidents and errors*. 1975. (M.A. thesis, University of Manchester.)

5575 **Wedderburn**, Alexander. 'Waking up to shiftwork.' *Pers. Manage.*, VII, 2 (February 1975), 32–5, 47.

5576 **Ayatollahi**, A. *The implications of introducing shift work and flexible working hours into the clothing industry*. 1976. (Ph.D. thesis, University of Bradford.)

5577 **Brown**, D. 'Male shiftworkers: sociological implications.' *J. Occup. Psychol.*, XLVIII, 4 (1976), 231–40.

5578 **Hughes**, John. 'Shiftwork and shorter working week: two ways to make jobs.' *Pers. Manage.*, IX, 5 (May 1977), 18–20.

5579 **Incomes Data Services**. *Shiftwork 5*. London: I.D.S., 1977. (I.D.S. study 151.)

5580 **Bosworth**, D. L. and **Dawkins**, P. J. 'Shiftworking.' *Pers. Rev.*, III, 4 (Autumn 1978), 32–5.

5581 **Harrington**, J. M. *Shift work and health: a critical review of the literature*. London: H.M.S.O., 1978. 28p.

5582 **Nicholson**, Nigel, **Jackson**, Paul and **Howes**, Gillian. 'Shiftwork and absence.' *J. Occup. Psychol.*, LI, 2 (1978), 127–37.

5583 **Walker**, James. *Human aspects of shiftwork*. London: Institute of Personnel Management, 1978. x, 214p.

5584 **Wilson**, P. 'Night shift.' *Ind. Soc.*, LXI, 2 (March–April 1979), 11–12.

See also: 507.

4. Flexible Working Hours

Material on work sharing and the shorter working week is classified at Part Six, IV, B, 1.

5585 **Bolton**, J. Harvey. *Flexible working hours*. London: Anbar Publications, 1971. 54p.

5586 **Bishop**, Terry. 'Give and take in the working day.' *Pers. Manage.*, IV, 6 (June 1972), 33–6.

5587 **Hill**, J. M. *Flexible working hours*. London:

Institute of Personnel Management, 1972. 65p. (Information reports 12.)

5588 **Sheridan**, Geoffrey. 'Flexing time.' *New Soc.*, XXII (2 November 1972), 273–4.

5589 **Bartlett**, J. B. 'Attitudes to the changing week.' *Pers. Manage.*, V, 11 (November 1973), 36–8.

5590 **Baum**, Stephen J. and **Young**, W. McEwan. *A practical guide to flexible working hours.* London: Kogan Page, 1973. 186p.

5591 **Evans**, Martin G. 'Notes on the impact of flextime in a large insurance company: reactions of non-supervisory employees.' *Occup. Psychol.*, XLVII, 3–4 (1973), 237–40.

5592 **Galey**, G. 'Flexible hours experiments.' *Manage. Serv. Gov.*, XXVIII, 4 (November 1973), 182–7.

5593 **Partridge**, B. E. 'Notes on the impact of flextime in a large insurance company: reactions of supervisors and managers.' *Occup. Psychol.*, XLVII, 3–4 (1973), 241–2.

5594 **Rousham**, S. *Flexible working hours today: practices and experiences of over fifty British organisations.* London: British Institute of Management, 1973. ix, 58p. (Management survey reports 17.)

5595 **Wade**, Michael. *Flexible working hours in practice.* Epping: Gower, 1973. 112p.

5596 **Ward**, C. D. E. 'Flexible working hours in operation: the Cheshire County Council experiment.' *Adm. Manage.*, XXVII, 2 (Summer 1973), 38–43.

5597 **Incomes Data Services**. *Flexible working hours.* London: I.D.S., 1974. 16p. (I.D.S. study 84.)

5598 **Legge**, Karen. 'Flexible working hours: panacea or placebo?' *Manage. Decis.*, XII, 5 (1974), 264–80.

5599 **Summers**, Derek. *Flexible working hours: a case study.* London: Institute of Personnel Management, 1974. 52p.

5600 **Walsh**, B. 'Finding out about flexible working hours.' *Ind. Commer. Train.*, VI, 8 (August 1974), 368–70.

5601 **Drye**, E. S. 'Flexible working hours in D.H.S.S. offices.' *Manage. Serv. Gov.*, XXX, 1 (February 1975), 4–10.

5602 **Evans**, Martin G. 'Longitudinal analysis of the impact of flexible working hours.' *Stud. Pers. Psychol.*, VI, 2 (Spring 1975), 1–10.

5603 **Sloane**, Peter James. 'Flexible working hours.' *Dep. Employment Gaz.*, LXXXIII, 1 (January 1975), 3–5.

5604 **Incomes Data Services**. *Flexible working hours.* London: I.D.S., 1976. 16p. (I.D.S. study 119.)

5605 **Young**, W. M. 'Applying flexible working hours in production areas.' *Prod. Eng.*, LV, 4 (April 1976), 187–90.

5606 **Hesmondhaigh**, Sally. 'Can flexible working hours unjam the works?' *Pers. Manage.*, IX, 6 (June 1977), 30–33, 40–41.

5607 **Lee**, R. A. *Towards a contingency approach to work week structuring.* 1976–7. (M.Sc. thesis,

University of Loughborough.)

5608 **Young**, B. M. 'Goodbye nine-to-five.' *Ind. Soc.*, LIX (September–October 1977), 7–8.

5609 **Lee**, R. A. and **Young**, W. M. 'Discretion in a flexible work hour schedule.' *J. Manage. Stud.*, XV, 3 (1978), 265–84.

5610 **Tyler**, G. J. 'Flexible hours in a factory.' *Work Study*, XIV, 3 (March 1978), 29–32.

5611 **Young**, W. M. 'Flexible working hours in continuous production.' *Pers. Rev.*, III, 2 (Summer 1978), 12–19.

See also: 44; 5576.

C. FRINGE BENEFITS AND OTHER CONDITIONS

Works in this section deal with benefits provided by the employer, including the state when it is acting in its capacity as an employer. Material on benefits provided by the state to society as a whole is classified at Part Seven, VII. Material on staff status for manual workers is included here. Many of the general works in Part Six, IV, A also contain material on fringe benefits. Material on profit-sharing and employee share ownership is classified at Part Five, VI, C. See also Part Four, II, A.

1. General

5612 **Howard**, Carol A. and **Peat**, J. M. 'Perks and the pay package.' *Pers. Manage.*, III, 11 (November 1971), 36–8.

5613 **Ashall**, R. and **Child**, John. 'Employee services: people, profits or Parkinson?' *Pers. Manage.*, IV, 8 (August 1972), 18–22.

5614 **Incomes Data Services**. *Annual holidays part 1.* London: I.D.S., 1972. 20p. (I.D.S. study 29.)

5615 **Incomes Data Services**. *Annual holidays part 2.* London: I.D.S., 1972. 20p. (I.D.S. study 31.)

5616 **Incomes Data Services**. *Sick pay part 1.* London: I.D.S., 1972. 16p. (I.D.S. study 26.)

5617 **Incomes Data Services**. *Sick pay part 2.* London: I.D.S., 1972. 16p. (I.D.S. study 30.)

5618 **Incomes Data Service**. *White collar allowances.* London: I.D.S., 1972; 16p. (I.D.S. Study 42.)

5619 **Robinson**, Terry. *Staff status for manual workers.* London: Kogan Page, 1972. 116p.

5620 **Thompson**, R. 'A question of status.' *Ind. Soc.*, LIV, 12 (December 1972), 9–10.

5621 **Wedderburn**, Dorothy. 'Inequality at work.' Townsend, P. and Bosanquet, N. (eds.). *Labour and inequality.* London: Fabian Society, 1972. p. 174–86.

5622 **Hymans**, Clifford (ed.). *Handbook on pensions and employee benefits: their provision and administration.* London: Kluwer-Harrap, 1973.

5623 **Incomes Data Services**. *Holidays in 1973.* London: I.D.S., 1973. 16p. (I.D.S. study 52.)

5624 **Incomes Data Services**. *Manual workers' allowances*. London: I.D.S., 1973. 12p. (I.D.S. study 55.)

5625 **Incomes Data Services**. *Sick pay part 3*. London: I.D.S., 1973. 16p. (I.D.S. study 47.)

5626 **Incomes Data Services**. *Sick pay part 4*. London: I.D.S., 1973. 16p. (I.D.S. study 50.)

5627 **Moonman**, Jane. *The effectiveness of fringe benefits in industry, including a survey of current practice undertaken by an independent study group*. Epping: Gower, 1973. xii, 222p.

5628 **Hill**, J. M. *Special leave allowance*. London: Institute of Personnel Management, 1974. 36p. (Information reports 15.)

5629 **Incomes Data Services**. *Holidays 1974*. London: I.D.S., 1974. 20p. (I.D.S. study 85.)

5630 **Incomes Data Services**. *Housing assistance*. London: I.D.S., 1974. 20p. (I.D.S. study 83.)

5631 **Incomes Data Services**. *Staff status for manual workers part 1*. London: I.D.S., 1974. 16p. (I.D.S. study 73.)

5632 **Incomes Data Services**. *Staff status for manual workers part 2*. London: I.D.S., 1974. 16p. (I.D.S. study 77.)

5633 **Incomes Data Services**. *White collar allowances*. London: I.D.S., 1974. 20p. (I.D.S. study 74.)

5634 **Cockman**, Richard. 'Employee benefits for managers and executives.' Bowey, Angela M. (ed.). *Handbook of salary and wage systems*. 1975. p. 293–306.

5635 **Cockman**, Richard. 'Employee benefits for non-managerial staff.' Bowey, Angela M. (ed.). *Handbook of salary and wage systems*. 1975. p. 307–14.

5636 **Incomes Data Services**. *Call out payments*. London: I.D.S., 1975. 20p. (I.D.S. study 96.)

5637 **Incomes Data Services**. *Holidays 1975*. London: I.D.S., 1975. 20p. (I.D.S. study 109.)

5638 **Incomes Data Services**. *Living costs abroad*. London: I.D.S., 1975. 12p. (I.D.S. study 101.)

5639 **Incomes Data Services**. *Manual workers' allowances*. London: I.D.S., 1975. 21p. (I.D.S. study 102.)

5640 **Incomes Data Services**. *Sick pay 5*. London: I.D.S., 1975. 24p. (I.D.S. study 95.)

5641 **Martin**, Jean and **Morgan**, Margaret. *Prolonged sickness and the return to work*. London: H.M.S.O., 1975. 254p. (Office of Population Censuses and Surveys. Social Survey Division report SS1004.)

5642 **Wedderburn**, Dorothy and **Craig**, Christine. 'Relative deprivation in work.' Esland, G. and others (eds.). *People and work*. 1975. p. 59–69.

5643 **Bosworth**, P. 'Paying for personnel.' *Ind. Soc.*, LVIII, 2 (March–April 1976), 17–18. The hidden costs of fringe benefits.

5644 **Incomes Data Services**. *Child care at work*. London: I.D.S., 1976. 18p. (I.D.S. study 129.)

5645 **Incomes Data Services**. *Fringe benefits*. London: I.D.S., 1976. 11p. (I.D.S. study 127.)

5646 **Incomes Data Services**. *Holidays 1976*. London: I.D.S., 1976. 22p. (I.D.S. study 134.)

5647 **Incomes Data Services**. *Housing assistance*. London: I.D.S., 1976. 20p. (I.D.S. study 132.)

5648 **Incomes Data Services**. *Premium pay: public sector staff*. London: I.D.S., 1976. 20p. (I.D.S. study 133.)

5649 **Incomes Data Services**. *Staff status in 1976*. London: I.D.S., 1976. 20p. (I.D.S. study 130.)

5650 **Incomes Data Services**. *White collar allowances*. London: I.D.S., 1976. 20p. (I.D.S. study 115.)

5651 **Murlis**, H. and **Grist**, J. *Towards single status: current developments in conditions of employment for manual and non-manual employees*. London: British Institute of Management, 1976. 64p. (Management survey reports 30.)

5652 **Department of Health and Social Security**. *Report on a survey of occupational sick pay schemes*. London: H.M.S.O., 1977. xxii, 84p.

5653 **Incomes Data Services**. *Christmas closures*. London: I.D.S., 1977. (I.D.S. study 144.)

5654 **Incomes Data Services**. *Sick pay: company schemes*. London: I.D.S., 1977. (I.D.S. study 138.)

5655 **Incomes Data Services**. *Special leave*. London: I.D.S., 1977. (I.D.S. study 155.)

5656 **Incomes Data Services**. *Staff allowances: subsistence, travel, large town allowances*. London: I.D.S., 1977. 22p. (I.D.S. study 157.)

5657 **Incomes Data Services**. *Holidays 1978*. London: I.D.S., 1978. 20p. (I.D.S. study 168.)

5658 **Incomes Data Services**. *Long service conditions*. London: I.D.S., 1978. 18p. (I.D.S. study 164.)

5659 **Incomes Data Services**. *Sick pay changes*. London: I.D.S., 1978. 16p. (I.D.S. study 165.)

5660 **Incomes Data Services**. *Staff benefits*. London: I.D.S., 1978. 16p. (I.D.S. study 176.)

5661 **Incomes Data Services**. *Holidays 1979*. London: I.D.S., 1979. 20p. (I.D.S. study 206.)

5662 **Payne**, R. L. and **Arroba**, T. 'Managing illness at work.' *Pers. Rev.*, IV, 1 (Winter 1979), 31–9.

See also: 43.

2. Pensions

This section includes material on private pension schemes and on pensions provided by the state for its employees. Material on national pension funds is classified at Part Seven, VII, B, 4. Technical material relating to the actuarial aspects of pensions has generally been excluded. Some of the general material on worker participation in Part Five, VI, D, 1 also contains material on employee participation in the administration of pension schemes. See also Part Six, II, C, 6.

5663 **Ministry of Defence** and **Civil Service Department.** *Service pay and pensions.* London: H.M.S.O., 1969. vi, 48p. (Cmnd. 4157.)

5664 **Bandey**, Derek. 'Pensions: everyman's retirement right.' *Pers. Manage.*, III, 7 (July 1971), 35–9.

5665 **Department of Health and Social Security.** *Strategy for pensions: the future development of state and occupational provision.* London: H.M.S.O., 1971. iii, 39p. (Cmnd. 4755.)

5666 **Pilch**, Michael and **Wood**, V. *Company pension schemes.* London: Directors Bookshelf, 1971. xviii, 244p.
Second edition.

5667 **Schoff**, J. L. *The development of retirement pension schemes and their possible relation to the mobility of professional employees in the public sector.* 1971. (B.Phil. thesis, University of St Andrews.)

5668 **Chester**, Theodore Edward. 'Private pensions or state benefits.' *Natl. Westminster Bank Q. Rev.* (August 1971), 35–47.

5669 **Government Actuary.** *Occupational pension schemes 1971: fourth survey.* London: H.M.S.O., 1972. vi, 63p.

5670 **Lamey**, R. H. 'Talking about pensions.' *Ind. Soc.*, LIV, 7 (July 1972), 13–15.

5671 **Lewin**, C. G. 'Pensions and staff involvement.' *Ind. Soc.*, LIV, 8 (August 1972), 16–19.

5672 **National Whitley Council**, Joint Superannuation Committee. *Civil Service superannuation: report of the Civil Service Joint Superannuation Review Committee.* London: The Council, 1972. 47p.

5673 **Oldfield**, Maurice. 'Pension fund trustees.' *Ind. Soc.*, LIV, 9 (September 1972), 13–15.

5674 **Abbott**, R. W. 'Obtaining recognition.' *Pensions World*, II (November–December 1973), 369–72.

5675 **Byers**, Charles Frank. 'Company pensions: time for action.' *Pers. Manage.*, V, 12 (December 1973), 28–30.

5676 **Department of Education and Science.** *Allocation of pension under teachers' superannuation regulations.* London: H.M.S.O., 1973. iii, 27p.

5677 **Government Actuary.** *Report of the Government Actuary on the teachers' superannuation scheme (England and Wales) 1966–1971.* London: H.M.S.O., 1973. 22p.

5678 **Incomes Data Services.** *Occupational pensions part 1.* London: I.D.S., 1973. 20p. (I.D.S. study 66.)

5679 **Lynes**, Tony. 'A lottery of pensions.' *New Soc.*, XXVI (29 November 1973), 530–31.

5680 **Pilch**, Michael. 'Labour turnover and pension planning.' *Moor. Wall Street* (Autumn 1973), 64–77.

5681 **Wilson**, Thomas. 'Pensions, inflation and growth.' *Lloyds Bank Rev.*, CVIII (April 1973), 1–17.

5682 **Atkinson**, Anthony Barnes. 'Pensions leapfrog.' *New Soc.*, XXX (21 November 1974), 485–6.

5683 **Civil Service Department.** *Allocation of pension: explanatory memorandum, rules and tables prepared by the Government Actuary.* London: H.M.S.O., 1974. 34p.

5684 **Civil Service Department.** *Principal Civil Service Pension Scheme 1974: rules.* London: H.M.S.O., 1974.

5685 **Evans**, A. M. 'Industrial pensions and the manual worker.' *Pensions World*, III, 4 (July–August 1974), 159–61.

5686 **Fellows**, D. E. 'Life offices, pensions plans and industrial relations.' *Pensions World*, III, 5 (September–October 1974), 196–200.

5687 **Gilley**, D. F. 'Counting the cost of pensions.' *Pensions World*, III, 3 (May–June 1974), 103–7.

5688 **Gilling-Smith**, Dryden. *Manager's guide to pensions.* London: Institute of Personnel Management, 1974. 152p.

5689 **Incomes Data Services.** *Occupational pensions part 2.* London: I.D.S., 1974. 24p. (I.D.S. study 71.)

5690 **Incomes Data Services.** *Occupational pensions 3.* London: I.D.S., 1974. 24p. (I.D.S. study 86.)

5691 **Lyons**, J. S. W. 'Pensions and collective bargaining.' *Pensions World*, III, 3 (May–June 1974), 114–16.

5692 **Rosenthal**, Abraham and **Shand**, John. 'Pensions and the restraint of trade doctrine.' *Camb. Law J.*, XXXIII (November 1974), 293–306.

5693 **Smith**, K. G. 'Employee participation in pension planning.' *Ind. Participation*, DLIV (Spring 1974), 13–16.

5694 **Smith**, K. G. 'The public sector transfer club.' *Pensions World*, III, 4 (July–August 1974), 162–5.

5695 **Smith**, K. G. 'The scope for employee participation in pensions.' *Pensions World*, III, 2 (March–April 1974), 64–7.

5696 **Brunet**, E. 'Secure pensions: the long-term situation.' *Pensions World*, IV, 3 (May–June 1975), 104–7.

5697 **Byers**, Charles Frank. 'Pension pointers for the non-specialist.' *Pers. Manage.*, VII, 10 (October 1975), 41–4.

5698 **Chiene**, J. 'Measuring pension fund investment performance.' *Pensions World*, IV, 4 (July 1975), 12–14.

5699 **Civil Service Department.** *Principal Civil Service Pension Scheme (Amendment) Scheme 1975.* London: H.M.S.O., 1975. iii, 5p.

5700 **Cole**, K. 'Practical decisions facing pensions funds.' *Pensions World*, IV, 6 (September 1975), 74–8.

5701 **Hardiman**, J. L. 'Early retirement.' *Pensions World*, IV, 12 (December 1975), 181–4.

5702 **Jenkins**, Clive. 'Bargaining for better pensions rights.' *Pensions World*, IV, 3 (May–June 1975), 101–3.

5703 **Nottage**, R. *Financing public sector pensions.* London: Royal Institute of Public Administration, 1975. 38p.

5704 **Occupational Pensions Board.** *Report of the … Board on the questions of solvency, disclosure of information and member participation in occupational pension schemes.* London: H.M.S.O., 1975. 3v.
Chairman: *Sir* Phillip Allen.

5705 **Pilch**, Michael. 'Company pension schemes.' Bowey, Angela M. (ed.). *Handbook of salary and wage systems.* 1975. p. 315–24.

5706 **Pilch**, Michael. 'New trends in pension plan design.' *Pensions World*, IV, 2 (March–April 1975), 52–6.

5707 **Richardson**, R. 'How Unilever computerized its pension scheme.' *Pensions World*, IV, 1 (January–February 1975), 14–16.

5708 **Scholey**, J. K. 'The effects of inflation on pension funds.' *Pensions World*, IV, 8 (November 1975), 133–8.

5709 **Stuart**, C. F. 'Planning for pensions in inflation.' *Long Range Plann.*, VIII, 6 (December 1975), 13–19.

5710 **Webster**, A. R. and **Webster**, R. W. J. 'Phased retirement.' *Pensions World*, IV, 5 (August 1975), 41–2.

5711 **Young**, J. M. 'Accounting for pension funds.' *Pensions World*, IV, 6 (September 1975), 69; IV, 7 (October 1975), 100.

5712 **Civil Service Department.** *Civil Service pensions explained: a guide to the benefits of the principal civil service pension scheme and to the arrangements for increasing pensions under the Pensions (Increase) Act 1971.* London: H.M.S.O., 1976. 54p.

5713 **Colbran**, R. B. 'Contracting-out: what is the alternative?' *Pensions World*, V, 10 (October 1976), 279–81.

5714 **Gilley**, D. F. and **Coote**, B. 'Contracting out.' *Pensions World*, V, 1 (January 1976), 9–14.

5715 **Incomes Data Services.** *Occupational pensions.* London: I.D.S., 1976. 22p. (I.D.S. study 126.)

5716 **Kincaid**, James C. 'Recent developments in British pensions.' *Ind. Gerontol.*, III, 1 (Winter 1976), 41–56.

5717 **Lucas**, Harry. 'Pensions: a trade union view.' *Pensions World*, V, 6 (June 1976), 190–91.

5718 **Lucas**, Harry. 'Pensions and the role of trade unions.' *Pensions World*, V, 12 (December 1976), 351–6.

5719 **Occupational Pensions Board.** *Equal status for men and women in occupational pension schemes.* London: H.M.S.O., 1976. xvi, 232p. (Cmnd. 6599.)

5720 **Occupational Pensions Board.** *Occupational pension schemes: the role of members in the running of schemes.* London: H.M.S.O., 1976. 18p. (Cmnd. 6514.)

5721 **Pensions World.** 'Member participation in running pension schemes.' *Pensions World*, V, 9 (September 1976), 255–7.

5722 **Reardon**, G. 'Consultation and the pension fund manager.' *Pensions World*, V, 11 (November 1976), 316–21.

5723 **Smith**, K. G. 'Pensions in an inflationary economy.' *Pensions World*, V, 2 (February 1976), 44–7.

5724 **Trades Union Congress.** *Occupational pension schemes.* London: T.U.C., 1976. 103p.

5725 **Buckton**, Ray W. 'Occupational pensions and the unions.' *Pensions World*, VI, 1 (January 1977), 3–6.

5726 **Cleminson**, Paul. 'That pensions decision: a last-minute checklist.' *Pers. Manage.*, IX, 8 (August 1977), 31–3.

5727 **Department of Health and Social Security**, Occupational Pensions Board. *Occupational pension scheme cover for disabled people.* London: H.M.S.O., 1977. vi, 38p.

5728 **Greenwood**, P. 'Participation at Molins.' *Pensions World*, VI, 2 (February 1977), 35–7.

5729 **Hesmondhaigh**, Sally. 'Union participation in pension fund management.' *Pers. Manage.*, VIII, 9 (September 1977), 24–8.

5730 **Incomes Data Services.** *Early retirement.* London: I.D.S., 1977. 22p. (I.D.S. study 152.)

5731 **Lucas**, Harry. *Pensions and industrial relations: a practical guide for all involved in pensions.* London: Pergamon, 1977. xiv, 191p.

5732 **Lucas**, Harry and **Ward**, Sue. *Pensions bargaining.* London: Workers' Educational Association, 1977. 19p. (Studies for trade unionists, III, 10.)

5733 **McKelvey**, Roy K. Muir, **Round**, A.E.G. and **Arthur**, T. G. *Hosking's pension schemes and retirement benefits.* London: Sweet & Maxwell, 1977. ix, 372p.
Fourth edition.

5734 **Personnel Management.** 'Pensions: the facts 75–78.' *Pers. Manage.*, IX, 3 (March 1977), 5–9.

5735 **Incomes Data Services.** *Occupational pensions 1978.* London: I.D.S., 1978. 18p. (I.D.S. study 182.)

5736 **Lucas**, Harry. 'A union attitude to participation in pension funds.' *Pensions World*, VII, 1 (January 1978), 15–19.

5737 **Oldfield**, Maurice. 'The pension fund trustee.' *Pensions World*, VII, 1 (January 1978), 13–15.

5738 **Stewart**, C. S. 'Administration of contracted-out schemes.' *Pensions World*, VII, 6 (September 1978), 351–4.

5739 **Ward**, Sue. *Controlling pension schemes.* London: Workers' Educational Association, 1978. 26p. (Studies for trade unionists IV, 15.)

5740 **Genders**, P. 'Mobilizing the pensions package.' *Pers. Manage.*, XI, 8 (August 1979), 46–9.

5741 **Incomes Data Services.** *Public sector pen-*

sions. London: I.D.S., 1979. 26p. (I.D.S. study 188.)

5742 **Oldfield**, M. H. 'Pensions and personnel managers.' *Pensions World*, VII, 10 (January 1979), 14–16.

5743 **Pickering**, A. 'Union attitudes to pension management.' *Pensions World*, VII, 11 (February 1979), 66–8.

See also: 43; 1591; 1605; 5620; 6493; 7115; 7118.

3. Other

Material on holidays and vacations, sick pay, and health and welfare schemes is included here. See also Part Two, III for works on absenteeism, and Part Seven, VII, B, 2 for material on sickness benefit provided by the state.

5744 **Commission on Industrial Relations.** *Facilities afforded to shop stewards.* London: H.M.S.O., 1971. iv, 60p. (Report 17.)

5745 **Costello**, J. P. *Special leave allowance.* London: Institute of Personnel Management, 1971. 41p. (Information reports 9.)

5746 **Lunn**, J. A. *Occupational health 1970–71: review of the first year.* Harrow: Northwick Park Hospital, 1971. 8p.
Private in-house health scheme.

5747 **Pomeroy**, J. *Sick pay schemes.* London: Institute of Personnel Management, 1971. 100p. (Information reports 7.)

5748 **Balaam**, D. 'Personnel at its most personal.' *Ind. Soc.*, LV, 2 (February 1973), 12–14.
Industrial welfare.

5749 **Cullen**, P. 'Sporting event.' *Ind. Soc.*, LVI, 6 (June 1974), 13–15.

5750 **Cooke**, Peter N. C. *The company car: its allocation, acquisition and administration.* Epping: Gower. 1975. 128p.

5751 **Day**, Christine. *Company day nurseries.* London: Institute of Personnel Management, 1975. 61p. (Information reports 18.)

5752 **Swaffield**, L. 'Industry and the nurse.' *Occup. Saf. Health*, V, 11 (November 1975), 16–18.

5753 **Fonda**, Nickie. 'Managing maternity leave.' *Pers. Manage.*, VIII, 1 (January 1976), 25–9.

5754 **Pilch**, Michael. 'Employee benefits in an abnormal economic climate.' *Pensions World*, V, 2 (February 1976), 36–9.

5755 **Pimlott**, J. A. R. *The Englishman's holiday: a social history.* Hassocks: Harvester, 1976. 318p.
First published 1947.

5756 **Personnel Management.** 'Time off for trade union activities.' *Pers. Manage.*, IX, 3 (March 1977), 18–20.

5757 **Raistrick**, Arthur. *Two centuries of industrial welfare: the London (Quaker) Lead Company, 1692–1905: the social policy and work of the 'Governor and Company for smelting down lead with pit coal and sea coal', mainly in Alston Moor and the Pennines.* Buxton: Moorland Publishing, 1977.

Second edition.

5758 **Hesmondhaigh**, Sally. 'Controlling trade unionists' time off.' *Pers. Manage.*, X, 5 (May 1978), 26–30.

5759 **Mellish**, Michael. 'Time off for trade union duties and activities.' *Dep. Employment Gaz.*, LXXXVI, 3 (March 1978), 289–91.

5760 **Coppin**, M. 'An industrial health service.' *Occup. Saf. Health*, IX, 12 (December 1979), 40–41.

5761 **Incomes Data Services.** *Guide to sick pay and absence.* London: I.D.S., 1979. 87p.

5762 **Incomes Data Services.** *Holidays 1979.* London: I.D.S., 1979. 20p. (I.D.S. study 206.)

5763 **Incomes Data Services.** *Manual workers' allowances: public sector.* London: I.D.S., 1979. 18p. (I.D.S. study 195.)

5764 **Incomes Data Services.** *Maternity cover and child care.* London: I.D.S., 1979. 17p. (I.D.S. study 191.)

5765 **Jago**, Alison. *Sick pay schemes.* London: Institute of Personnel Management, 1979. 47p. (Information reports 26.)

See also: 1257; 1258; 5351; 5530; 5535.

D. SAFETY, HEALTH, AND WELFARE

This section contains works describing the general state of safety, health, and welfare in industry. Works dealing with the techniques of medical practice or of accident prevention have generally been excluded. Many of the general works contained in Part Six, IV, A also contain material on safety, health, and welfare. See Part Six, IV, C, 3 for material dealing with the provision of health and welfare schemes by employers. See also Part Two, III; Part Seven, III, B; and Part Seven, VII, B, 3.

1. General

5766 **Ball**, David. 'Shop floor health.' *New Soc.*, XVII (18 March 1971), 440–41.

5767 **Bishop**, Terry. 'Hazards, health and hygiene.' *Pers. Manage.*, III, 9 (September 1971), 37–9.

5768 **Kay**, Harry. 'Accidents: some facts and theories.' Warr, P. (ed.). *Psychology at work.* 1971. p. 121–45.

5769 **Powell**, P. and **Hale**, M. *2,000 accidents: a shop floor study of their causes based on 42 months' continuous observation.* London: National Institute of Industrial Psychology, 1971. 189p. (Reports 21.)

5770 **Tye**, J. and **Ullyett**, K. *Safety uncensored: an alarming account of industrial accidents in Great Britain today.* London: Corgi, 1971. 159p.

5771 **Bishop**, Terry. 'Putting safety to the test.' *Pers. Manage.*, IV, 5 (May 1972), 37–9.
Testing procedures at the National Engineering Laboratory.

5772 **Freeman**, N. T. 'Creative safety incentive schemes.' *Occup. Saf. Health*, II, 5 (May 1972), 22–6.

5773 **Furniss**, R. P. 'Safety begins in the boardroom.' *Occup. Saf. Health*, II, I (January 1972), 18–21.

5774 **King**, W. A. 'Implementing an award scheme.' *Occup. Saf. Health*, II, 8 (August 1972), 22–4.

5775 **Shipp**, P. J. and **Sutton**, A. S. *Study of the statistics relating to safety and health at work.* London: H.M.S.O., 1972. 47p.

5776 **Sinclair**, Craig, **Marstrand**, Pauline and **Newick**, Pamela. *Innovation and human risk: the evaluation of human life and safety in relation to technical change.* London: Centre for the Study of Industrial Innovation, 1972. 36p.

5777 **Sinclair**, T. C. and **Eisner**, H. S. 'Safety research and development.' *Occup. Saf. Health*, II, 9 (September 1972), 16–21.

5778 **Elliott**, D. and **Beishon**, J. *Industrial safety systems.* Milton Keynes: Open University Press, 1973. 124p. (Open University. Systems Behaviour Course. Module 3.)

5779 **Kinnersly**, Patrick. *The hazards of work: how to fight them.* London: Pluto, 1973. 394p. (Workers' handbooks 1.)

5780 **Nichols**, Theo and **Armstrong**, Pete. *Safety or profit: industrial accidents and the conventional wisdom.* Bristol: Falling Wall Press, 1973. 32p.

5781 **Trevithick**, R. A. *Environmental and industrial health hazards: a practical guide.* London: Heinemann, 1973. 211p.

5782 **Carr**, C. F. 'Accidents in factories.' *Occup. Saf. Health*, IV, I (January 1974), 9–10.

5783 **Hewitt**, Patricia and **Mackie**, L. *Danger – women at work: report of a conference.* London: National Council for Civil Liberties, 1974. iii, 54p.

5784 **McKinnon**, Robert. 'Against accidents.' *Occup. Saf. Health*, IV, 10 (October 1974), 12–13.

5785 **Manning**, D. P. 'An accident model.' *Occup. Saf. Health*, IV, I (January 1974), 14–16.

5786 **Atherley**, G. R. C. 'Health and safety strategies.' *Prod. Eng.*, LIV, I (January 1975), 49–55.

5787 **Briggs**, J. H. and **Murray**, Robert. *Responsibilities of industry in the field of health.* London: Foundation for Business Responsibilities, 1975. 16p.

5788 **Gregory**, Denis and **McCarty**, Joe. *The shop steward's guide to workplace health and safety: a critical analysis of industry's health and safety problems and the Health and Safety at Work Act 1974.* Nottingham: Spokesman, 1975. 69p.

5789 **Hines**, John. 'The psychology of safety.' *Ind. Soc.*, LVII, I (January–February 1975), 13–14.

5790 **Incomes Data Services.** *Accidents: pay and prevention.* London: I.D.S., 1975. 21p. (I.D.S. study 103.)

5791 **Kenny**, T. P. 'Stating the case for welfare.' *Pers. Manage.*, VII, 9 (September 1975), 18–21, 35.

5792 **McKinnon**, Robert. 'A new management status for safety.' *Occup. Saf. Health*, V, 8 (August 1975), 10–12.

5793 **Nichols**, Theo. 'The sociology of accidents and the social production of industrial injury.' Esland, G. and others (eds.). *People and work.* 1975. p. 217–29.

5794 **Topham**, Tony. *Health and safety: a question of workers' control.* Nottingham: Institute for Workers' Control, 1975. 14p. (IWC pamphlets 39.)

5795 **Child**, P. F. 'Safety and management services.' *Work Study*, XII, 8 (August 1976), 19–23.

5796 **Department of Employment Gazette.** 'Improving firms' safety performance.' *Dep. Employment Gaz.*, LXXXIV, I (January 1976), 16–18.

5797 **Freeman**, N. T. 'Safety responsibilities.' *Occup. Saf. Health*, VI, 5 (May 1976), 14–6.

5798 **Freudenberger**, Herman and **Cummins**, Gaylord. 'Health, work and leisure before the industrial revolution.' *Explor. Econ. Hist.*, XIII, I (January 1976), 1–12.

5799 **Gill**, J. and **Martin**, E. 'Safety management: reconciling rules with reality.' *Pers. Manage.*, VIII, 6 (June 1976), 36–9.

5800 **Atherley**, G. R. C. 'Specialist advisers in health and safety: are they needed in the foundry industry?' British Cast Iron Research Association. *The working environment in iron foundries.* 1977. p. 10.1–10.8.

5801 **Hale**, A. R. and **Perusée**, M. 'Attitudes to safety: facts and assumptions.' Phillips, Jennifer (ed.). *Safety at work.* 1977. p. 73–86.

5802 **McKinnon**, Robert. 'Job enrichment: implications for safety.' *Occup. Saf. Health*, VII, 10 (October 1977), 8–10.

5803 **Oi**, Walter Y. 'On socially acceptable risks.' Phillips, Jennifer (ed.). *Safety at work.* 1977. p. 35–72.

5804 **Phillips**, Jennifer (ed.). *Safety at work: recent research into the causes and prevention of industrial accidents.* Oxford: Wolfson College, 1977. 86p.

Papers presented to a conference, Oxford, 1977.

5805 **Prince**, W. 'The role of the trade unions in health and safety at work in the foundry industry.' British Cast Iron Research Association. *The working environment in iron foundries.* 1977. p. 3.1–3.10.

5806 **Ross**, D. S. 'Medical aspects of health and safety at work.' *Occup. Saf. Health*, VII, 4 (April 1977), 22–3.

5807 **Turner**, Barry A. 'The origins of disaster.' Phillips, Jennifer (ed.). *Safety at work.* 1977. p. 1–18.

5808 **Adams**, N. L. and **Hartwell**, N. M. 'Accident reporting.' *J. Occup. Psych.*, L, 4 (1978), 285–98.

5809 **Duffy**, K. J. and **Haines**, B. W. 'Risk management and safety.' *Occup. Saf. Health*, VIII, 9 (September 1978), 8–12.

5810 **O'Neill**, Hugh. 'Safety is everybody's business,' *Occup. Saf. Health*, VIII, 6 (June 1978), 31–2.

5811 **Wright**, T. G. 'The confidentiality of safety information.' *Occup. Saf. Health*, VIII, 7 (July 1978), 11; VIII, 8 (August 1978), 22.

5812 **Bamber**, L. 'Accident prevention: the economic argument.' *Occup. Saf. Health*, IX, 6 (June 1979), 18–21.

5813 **Brookes**, Keith and **Hartley**, Ted. 'Conflict and consensus on health and safety.' *Employee Relat.* I, 3 (1979), 26–7.

5814 **Douglas**, R. 'Information as a stimulus to safety.' *Occup. Saf. Health*, IX, 10 (October 1979), 14–16.

5815 **Incomes Data Services.** *Health and safety: private sector.* London: I.D.S., 1979. 18p. (I.D.S. study 202.)

5816 **Stuttard**, Geoffrey. 'Health, safety and industrial democracy.' *Employee Relat.*, I, 3 (1979), 23–5.

5817 **Walsh**, B. 'Safety by objectives.' *Occup. Saf. Health*, IX, 12 (December 1979), 20–22.

2. Safety Education and Training

5818 **Furniss**, R. P. 'The T.U.C. Centenary Institute of Occupational Health.' *Occup. Saf. Health*, I, 12 (December 1971), 12–15.

5819 **Walsh**, B. 'New ideas in safety training.' *Ind. Commer. Train.*, III, 11 (November 1971), 521–3.

5820 **Walsh**, B. 'A safe place of work.' *Ind. Commer. Train.*, III, 8 (August 1971), 355–7.

5821 **Wigglesworth**, E. C. 'Educating the safety specialist.' *Occup. Saf. Health*, I, 10 (October 1971), 12–17.

5822 **Department of Employment**. *Safety training needs and facilities in one industry.* London: H.M.S.O., 1973. 76p.

5823 **Freeman**, N. T. 'Programmed learning in safety training.' *Occup. Saf. Health*, IV, 2 (February 1974), 15–17.

5824 **Freeman**, N. T. 'Safety and the new employee.' *Occup. Saf. Health*, IV, 5 (May 1974), 20–21.

5825 **Ross**, D. S. 'Safety talk for safety action.' *Occup. Saf. Health*, IV, 6 (June 1974), 20–21.

5826 **White**, S. 'A measure of safety.' *Ind. Soc.*, LVI, 6 (November–December 1974), 17–18.

5827 **Food, Drink and Tobacco Industry Training Board**. *Training for health and safety at work.* London: The Board, 1975. 40p.

5828 **Hesmondhaigh**, Sally. 'Safety training from top to bottom.' *Pers. Manage.*, VIII, 12 (December 1976), 32–5.

5829 **Hill**, C. 'Publicizing safety.' *Occup. Saf. Health*, VI, 4 (April 1976), 6–7.

5830 **Pirani**, M. and **Reynolds**, G. 'Gearing up for safety.' *Pers. Manage.*, VIII, 2 (February 1976), 25–9.

5831 **Freeman**, N. T. 'In-company safety training.' *Occup. Saf. Health*, VII, 4 (April 1977), 16–18.

5832 **Hazzlewood**, John. 'Site and sound: safety training for building managers.' *Pers. Manage.*, X, 11 (November 1978), 38–41.

5833 **Kletz**, T. A. 'Making safety intrinsic.' *Occup. Saf. Health*, VIII, 11 (November 1978), 8–11.

5834 **Black**, P. 'A training structure for safety skills.' *Occup. Saf. Health*, IX, 8 (August 1979), 26–9.

5835 **Jordan**, D. 'Training for safety at sea.' *Ind. Soc.*, LXI, 2 (March–April 1979), 15–16.

See also: 5842.

3. Safety Officers and Representatives

5836 **Freeman**, N. T. 'Joint consultation on safety.' *Occup. Saf. Health*, III, 9 (September 1973), 10–12.

5837 **Howells**, Richard W. L. and **Lewis**, D. 'Worker participation in safety.' *Ind. Law J.*, III, 2 (June 1974), 87–104.

5838 **Prentice**, Gordon. 'The safety rep: his roots and role.' *Pers. Manage.*, VI, 11 (November 1974), 36–9.

5839 **Atherley**, G. R. C., **Booth**, T. T. and **Kelly**, Michael J. 'Workers' involvement in occupational health and safety in Britain.' *Int. Labour Rev.*, CXI, 6 (June 1975), 469–82.

5840 **Smith**, S. 'The safety officer of the future.' *Occup. Saf. Health*, V, 1 (January 1975), 9–11.

5841 **Health and Safety Executive**. *Health and safety at work: safety representatives and safety committees.* London: H.M.S.O., 1976. 48p.

5842 **Glendon**, A. Ian. 'The role and training of safety representatives.' *Occup. Saf. Health*, VII, 11 (November 1977), 35–6; VII, 12 (December 1977), 37–8.

5843 **Health and Safety Commission**. *Safety representatives and safety committees: approved version.* London: H.M.S.O., 1977. 48p.

5844 **Health and Safety Commission**. *Time off for training of safety representatives: consultative document.* London: H.M.S.O., 1977. 4p.

5845 **Kletz**, T. A. 'The safety officer – past and future.' *Occup. Saf. Health*, VII (July 1977), 10–12.

5846 **Broadhurst**, V. A. 'Safety representatives.' *Works Manage.*, XXIX, 8 (August 1978), 30–33.

5847 **Cunningham**, Michael. *Safety representatives: shop floor organisation for health and safety.* London: Workers' Educational Association, 1978. 30p. (Studies for trade unionists IV, 13.)

5848 **Egan**, Bowes. *The manual of safety representation.* London: New Commercial Publishing Company. (New law guidance series 2.) Part I. *Appointment and functions of safety representatives.* 1978. 30p.

5849 **Webster**, Bryan. 'Paving the way for safety representatives: the Singer story.' *Pers. Manage.*, X, 6 (June 1978), 30–32, 43.

5850 **Abell**, D. 'Industrial relations and safety representatives.' *Pers. Rev.*, IX (Summer 1979), 30–33.

5851 **Egan**, Bowes. *Safety policies.* London: New Commercial Publishing Company, 1979. 268p. (New law guidance series 11.)

5852 **Hamilton**, M. 'Safety policies.' *Occup. Saf. Health*, IX, 6 (June 1979), 10–14.

See also: 6541; 6556; 6562.

4. Particular Hazards and Problems

5853 **Poulton**, E. Christopher. 'Skilled performance and stress.' Warr, P. (ed.). *Psychology at work.* 1971. p. 55–75.

5854 **Rolfe**, J. M. 'Multiple task performance: operator overload.' *Occup. Psychol.*, XLV (1971), 125–32.

5855 **Department of Employment**. *Noise and the worker.* London: H.M.S.O., 1973. 18p. Third edition.

5856 **Industrial Injuries Advisory Council**. *Occupational deafness: report of the ... in accordance with section 62 of the National Insurance (Industrial Injuries) Act 1965 on the question whether there are degrees of hearing loss due to noise which satisfy the conditions for prescription under the Act.* London: H.M.S.O., 1973. 54p. (Cmnd. 5461.)

5857 **Industrial Injuries Advisory Council**. *Pneumoconiosis and Byssinosis: report of the ... in accordance with section 62 of the National Insurance (Industrial Injuries) Act 1965 on Pneumoconiosis and Byssinosis.* London: H.M.S.O., 1973. 95p. (Cmnd. 5443.)

5858 **Industrial Society**. 'The environment at work: noise.' *Ind. Soc.*, LV, 1 (January 1973), 20–22.

5859 **Buzzard**, Richard Bethune. 'A practical look at industrial stress.' *Occup. Psychol.*, XLVII, 1–2 (1974), 51–61.

5860 **Department of Employment**. *Drilling machines: guarding of spindles and attachments.* London: H.M.S.O., 1974. 31p. (Health and safety at work series 20.) Second edition.

5861 **Department of Employment**. *Safety in the use of guillotines and shears.* London: H.M.S.O., 1974. 33p. (Health and safety at work series 33.)

5862 **Hines**, John. 'Mental illness in industry.' *Pers. Manage.*, VI, 4 (April 1974), 38–40.

5863 **Kenyon**, W. H. 'The alcoholic at work.' *Pers. Manage.*, VI, 7 (July 1974), 33–6.

5864 **Muir**, G. D. 'Dealing with laboratory dangers.' *Occup. Saf. Health*, IV, 11 (November 1974), 10–13.

5865 **Cooper**, Cary L. and **Marshall**, Judi. 'The management of stress.' *Pers. Rev.*, IV, 4 (Autumn 1975), 27–31.

5866 **Department of Employment**. *Flixborough disaster: report of the Court of Inquiry.* London: H.M.S.O., 1975. 64p.

5867 **Gowler**, Dan and **Legge**, Karen (eds.). *Managerial stress.* Epping: Gower, 1975. xiv, 236p.

5868 **Morgan**, W. K. C. and **Seaton**, A. *Occupa-tional lung diseases.* London: W. B. Saunders, 1975. xiii, 391p.

5869 **Wright**, H. B. *Executive ease and disease.* Epping: Gower, 1975. xii, 195p.

5870 **Carver**, J. 'Impact of legal requirements on safety and health in mines and quarries.' *Medicoleg. J.*, XLIV, 3 (1976), 85–96.

5871 **Cooper**, Cary L. and **Marshall**, Judi. 'Occupational sources of stress: a review of the literature relating to coronary heart diseases and mental ill health.' *J. Occup. Psychol.*, XLIX (1976), 11–28.

5872 **Health and Safety Commission**, Advisory Committee on Major Hazards. *Report 1.* London: H.M.S.O., 1976. 28p.

5873 **McKinnon**, Robert. 'Beating asbestosis.' *Occup. Saf. Health*, VI, 3 (March 1976), 8–11.

5874 **Nelson**, T. M. and **Ladan**, C. J. 'Patterns of correlates of fatigue among office workers.' *J. Occup. Psychol.*, XLIX, 2 (June 1976), 65–74.

5875 **Hamilton**, M. 'Radiological protection.' *Occup. Saf. Health*, VII, 7 (July 1977), 14–16.

5876 **Hill**, C. 'Alcoholism.' *Occup. Saf. Health*, VII, 3 (March 1977), 20–21.

5877 **Kenyon**, D. 'Unlocking silence.' *Ind. Soc.*, LIX, 4 (July–August 1977), 14–15.

5878 **Norfolk**, Donald. *Executive stress: strategies for survival.* London: Associated Business Programmes, 1977. 186p.

5879 **Ross**, D. S. 'Pre-empting occupational deafness.' *Occup. Saf. Health*, VII, 3 (March 1977), 50–51.

5880 **Torrington**, Derek P. and **Cooper**, Cary L. 'The management of stress.' *Pers. Rev.*, VII (Summer 1977), 48–54.

5881 **Bennett**, David. *Safety representatives' guide to fire precautions.* London: Workers' Educational Association, 1978. 31p. (Studies for trade unionists IV, 16.)

5882 **Cherry**, Nicola. 'Stress, anxiety and work: a longitudinal study.' *J. Occup. Psychol.*, LI (September 1978), 259–70.

5883 **Cooper**, Cary L., **Mallinger**, Mark and **Kahn**, Richard. 'Identifying sources of occupational stress among dentists.' *J. Occup. Psychol.*, LI (September 1978), 227–34.

5884 **Cooper**, Cary L. and **Marshall**, Judi. *Understanding executive stress.* London: Macmillan, 1978. xi, 132p.

5885 **Humphrey**, Michael and **Oddy**, Michael. 'The social costs of head injuries.' *New Soc.*, XXXV (31 August 1978), 452–3.

5886 **Industrial Injuries Advisory Council**. *Occupational deafness: report: on the operation of the provisions for occupational deafness and on other processes with severe noise levels.* London: H.M.S.O., 1978. 36p. (Cmnd. 7266.)

5887 **Keenan**, A. and **McBain**, G. D. M. 'Consequences of role stress.' *Pers. Rev.*, III, 3 (Summer 1978), 41–4.

5888 **Price**, Bill. 'Mental illness: a case for company concern.' *Pers. Manage.*, X, 12 (December 1978), 39–43.

5889 **Rousell**, D. F. 'Lung protection.' *Occup. Saf. Health*, VIII, 4 (April 1978), 8–10.

5890 **Bennett**, David. *Fighting chemical hazards at work*. London: Workers' Educational Association, 1979. 48p. (Studies for trade unionists, v, 18.)

5891 **Blacklaws**, A. 'Tackling alcoholism.' *Ind. Soc.*, LXI, 4 (November–December 1979), 14–15.

5892 **Fineman**, Stephen. 'A psycho-social model of stress and its application to management unemployment.' *Hum. Relat.*, XXXII, 4 (April 1979), 323–45.

5893 **Fletcher**, Ben, **Gowler**, Dan and **Payne**, Roy. 'Exploding the myth of executive stress.' *Pers. Manage.*, XI, 5 (May 1979), 30–34.

5894 **Martin**, A. 'Tuning in to hearing hazards.' *Pers. Manage.*, XI, 11 (November 1979), 42–6.

5895 **May**, J. 'Noise in industry.' *Occup. Saf. Health*, IX, 2 (February 1979), 16–19.

5896 **Plant**, Martin A. *Drinking careers: occupations, drinking habits and drinking problems*. London: Tavistock, 1979. xiv, 167p.

5897 **Sim**, David. 'The day I will never forget.' MacFarlane, J. (ed.). *Essays from the Yorkshire coalfield*. 1979. p. 80–83.
Coal mine accident.

5898 **Wilkinson**, Alec. 'Houghton Main.' Mac-Farlane, J. (ed.). *Essays from the Yorkshire coalfield*. 1979. p. 84–5.
See also: 3576; 6524; 6535; 6539; 6565; 6566; 6569; 6571; 6574; 6579; 6582.

5. Studies of Particular Occupations and Industries

5899 **Committee of Inquiry into Trawler Safety.** *Trawler safety: final report of the Committee* .... London: H.M.S.O., 1969. x, 166p. (Cmnd. 4114.)
Chairman: *Sir* Deric Holland-Martin.

5900 **Joint Standing Committee on Health, Safety and Welfare in the Wool Textile Industry.** *Wool textile industry: developments in safety, health and welfare 1948–1968: report of the* .... London H.M.S.O., 1970. VIII, 32p.

5901 **Construction Industry Training Board.** *Safety manual for mechanical plant construction.* London: The Board, 1971. 42p.

5902 **Felstein**, I. *Snakes and ladders: medical and social aspects of modern management*. London: Constable, 1971. 197p.
Managers.

5903 **Pocock**, Pamela. 'Choc tactics: how safety is practised at Bournville.' *Pers. Manage.*, III, 5 (May 1971), 44–5.

5904 **Butcher**, John and **De Boo**, Arie. *Safety at sea*. London: Conservative Political Centre, 1973. 36p.

5905 **Department of Employment.** *Safety in construction work: demolition.* London: H.M.S.O., 1973. 61p. (Health and safety at work series 6E.)

5906 **Department of Employment.** *Safety training needs and facilities in one industry: an accident prevention survey ... carried out in the paper and boardmaking industry by the Industrial Training Service.* London: H.M.S.O., 1973. 75p.

5907 **Duckham**, H. and **Duckham**, B. *Great pit disasters: 1700 to the present day*. Newton Abbot: David & Charles, 1973. 227p.

5908 **Department of Employment.** *Safety in the cotton and allied fibres industry: opening processes.* London: H.M.S.O., 1974. 28p. (Health and safety at work series 49A.)

5909 **Gowing**, M. and **Arnold**, L. 'Health and safety in Britain's nuclear programme.' *New Sci.*, LXIV, 925 (28 November 1974), 659–61.

5910 **Joint Standing Committee on Health and Welfare in the Cotton and Allied Fibres Industry.** *Towards a healthy working environment: first report of the* .... London: H.M.S.O., 1974. 34p.

5911 **McKinnon**, Robert and **Gregory**, Denis. 'Safety from above.' *Occup. Saf. Health*, IV, 9 (September 1974), 20–23.
Unilever.

5912 **Occupational Safety and Health.** 'Safety a-brewing.' *Occup. Saf. Health*, IV, 1 (January 1974), 6–8.

5913 **Vitek**, Jan. 'Reducing the price in human lives we pay for our coal.' *Contemp. Rev.*, CCXXIV (April 1974), 173–5.

5914 **British Medical Association**, Scottish Council. *Medical implications of oil-related industries: a Scottish Council report*. Edinburgh: The Council, 1975. iv, 26p.

5915 **Bryan**, *Sir* Andrew. *The evolution of health and safety in mines*. London: Ashire Publishing, 1975. 192p.

5916 **Fraser**, *Sir* Ian. 'Safety in hospital.' *Hosp. Health Serv. Rev.*, LXXI, 10 (October 1975), 389–92.

5917 **McKinnon**, Robert. 'Safety in a research environment.' *Occup. Saf. Health*, V, 10 (October 1975), 18–20.

5918 **Macquiban**, Tim and **Ackers**, Norma (eds.). *Mining disasters in the Leigh area*. Leigh: Leigh History Society, 1975. 24p.

5919 **Wilkinson**, Alec. 'Houghton Main, June 1975.' *Soc. Study Labour Hist. Bull.*, XXXI (Autumn 1975), 93–5.

5920 **Woodhead**, John. 'The Bentley Colliery disaster.' *Soc. Study Labour Hist. Bull.*, XXXI (Autumn 1975), 66–90.

5921 **McKinnon**, Robert. 'Accident prevention in construction.' *Occup. Saf. Health*, VI, 1 (January 1976), 23–5.

5922 **Neville**, Robert G. 'The martyrdom of the mine, by Edward Allen Rymer (document).' *Hist. Workshop*, 1 (Spring 1976), 220–44.

5923 **Blayloch**, S. S. 'Provisions of health services for the smaller foundry.' British Cast Iron Research Association. *The working environment in iron foundries*. 1977. p. 9.1–9.5.

5924 **H.M. Factory Inspectorate.** *The explosion at*

the Dow Chemical factory Kings Lynn, June 27, 1976. London: H.M.S.O., 1977. 20p.

5925 **Hoole**, Roger. 'An appalling colliery accident: Steer's Meadow Colliery, Wednesbury.' *Blackcountryman*, x (Spring 1977), 55–6.

5926 **Wright**, Beric. *Executive ease and disease.* London: Pan, 1977. 90, 254p.

5927 **Burke**, Gillian and **Richardson**, Peter. 'The profits of death: a comparative study of miners' phthisis in Cornwall and the Transvaal, 1876–1918.' *J. South Afr. Stud.*, IV (April 1978), 147–71.

5928 **Civil Service Department** and **Health and Safety Executive.** *Is my office safe? A handbook for supervisors.* London: H.M.S.O., 1978. vi, 22p.

5929 **Department of Trade.** *Code of safe working practices for merchant seamen.* London: H.M.S.O., 1978. viii, 190p.

5930 **Department of Trade**, Steering Committee on the Safety of Merchant Seamen at Work. *Safety of seamen at work.* London: H.M.S.O., 1978. 54p.

5931 **H.M. Factory Inspectorate.** *Safety in the cotton and allied fibres industry: fabric production.* London: H.M.S.O., 1978. 60p.

5932 **Locke**, J. H., **Dunster**, H. J. and **Pittom**, L. A. *Canvey: an investigation of potential hazards from operations in the Canvey Island/Thurrock area.* London: H.M.S.O. for the Health and Safety Executive, 1978. viii, 192p.

5933 **Smith**, A. 'Safety prescription from Du Pont.' *Occup. Saf. Health*, VIII, 12 (December 1978), 8–10.

5934 **Agricultural Health and Safety Inspectorate.** *Health and safety: agriculture, 1977.* London: H.M.S.O., 1979. 24p.

5935 **Department of Trade.** *Recommended code of safety for fishermen.* London: H.M.S.O., 1979. 64p.

5936 **Department of Trade**, Working Group on the Occupational Safety of Fishermen. *Report of the Working Group ...* London: H.M.S.O., 1979. 22p.
Chairman: M. J. Service.

5937 **H.M. Factory Inspectorate.** *The fire and explosion at Braehead container depot, Renfrew, January 4, 1977.* London: H.M.S.O., 1979. 28p.

5938 **H.M. Inspectorate of Mines and Quarries.** *The accident at Bentley Colliery, South Yorkshire, November 21, 1978.* London: H.M.S.O., 1979. 18p.

5939 **H.M. Inspectorate of Mines and Quarries.** *The explosion at Golborne Colliery, Greater Manchester County, March 18, 1979.* London: H.M.S.O., 1979. VI, 16p.

5940 **Hamilton**, M. 'Machine shop safety priorities.' *Occup. Saf. Health*, IX, 7 (July 1979), 42–3.

5941 **Health and Safety Executive.** *Ceramics: health and safety, 1971–77.* London: H.M.S.O., 1979. 16p.

5942 **Health and Safety Executive.** *Construction: health and safety, 1977–78.* London: H.M.S.O., 1979. 48p.

5943 **Healy**, Geraldine. 'Health and safety.' Bosanquet, N. (ed.). *Industrial relations in the N.H.S.* 1979. p. 97–124.

5944 **Ord**, R. 'A safer way to build.' *Train. Off.* (August 1979), 234–7.

5945 **Purdon**, Gavin (comp.). *The Sacriston mine disaster.* Stanley, Co. Durham: The Author, 1979. 56p.

See also: 1; 1202; 1204; 5864; 5870; 5874; 5878; 5882; 5884; 5893; 6520; 6547; 6568; 6573; 6580.

PART SEVEN

THE STATE AND ITS AGENCIES

I. GENERAL

This section includes general works on such topics as labour law, trade unions and the state, and government policy. Material on the Bullock Report and the White Paper on industrial democracy is classified at Part Five, VI, D, 2. See also Part One, III; Part Three, II, A; Part Five, I; and Part Five, V, A–B.

5946 **Schmidman**, John. *British unions and economic planning.* University Park, Pa.: Pennsylvania State University Press, 1969. v, 104p. (Penn State studies 27.)

5947 **Hawkins**, Kevin. 'Industrial relations reform: some neglected issues.' *Manage. Decis.*, IV (Winter 1970). 5–7.

5948 **Miller**, Isaac Pritchard. *Industrial law in Scotland.* Edinburgh: Green, 1970. xlviii, 461p.

5949 **Pritt**, Denis N. *Law, class and society.* London: Lawrence & Wishart.
Vol. 1. *Employers, workers and trade unions.* 1970. 174p.

5950 **Trades Union Congress.** *Reason: the case against the Government's proposals on industrial relations.* London: T.U.C., 1970. 29p.

5951 **Campbell**, Alan. *The Industrial Relations Act: an introduction.* London: Longman, 1971. xx, 421p.

5952 **Catherwood**, *Sir* Frederick. 'Government industry dialogue: an aspect of economic strategy.' *Manchr. Stat. Soc. Trans.* (1970–71), 1–12.

5953 **Chomet**, S. (ed.). *Industrial Relations Bill: a basis for agreement?* London: Transcriptor, 1971. 227, 188p.

5954 **Coates**, Ken. *Can we kill that bill? An appeal to trade unionists to defend democracy.* Nottingham: Bertrand Russell Peace Foundation, 1971. 6p. (Spokesman pamphlets 16.)

5955 **Confederation of British Industry.** *Guidance to employers on the Industrial Relations Bill: report of a working party.* London: C.B.I., 1971. 51p.

5956 **Crabtree**, Cyril. *The Industrial Relations Act: a comprehensive guide.* London: Charles Knight, 1971. 241p.

5957 **Department of Employment.** *Code of industrial relations practice: consultative document.* London: H.M.S.O., 1971. 30p.

5958 **Department of Employment.** *Industrial relations: a guide to the Industrial Relations Act 1971.* London: The Department, 1971. 84p.

5959 **Department of Employment.** *Industrial Relations Act.* London: The Department, 1971. 17p. (Background briefing 4.)

5960 **Department of Employment Gazette.** 'Code of industrial relations practice.' *Dep. Employment Gaz.*, LXXIX, 6 (June 1971), 522–9.

5961 **Elliott**, John. *Industrial relations: the new Act.* London: Financial Times, 1971. 43p.

5962 **Fleeman**, Robert Keith, **Cooper**, F. R. and **Selwyn**, N. W. *Outline of the Industrial Relations Act.* Sutton Coldfield: Fleeman Cooper, 1971. 23p.

5963 **Gordon-Brown**, Ian. 'The code of practice.' *Co-partnership*, DXLV (July 1971), 7–8.

5964 **Gunther**, K. 'Special complaint procedures concerning discrimination in employment.' *Int. Labour Rev.*, CIV, 5 (November 1971), 351–65.

5965 **Hanna**, Vincent. 'The code in practice.' *Pers. Manage.*, III, 9 (September 1971), 20–23.

5966 **Hanson**, Charles Goring. *The development of trade unionism and trade union law, with special reference to the Royal Commission of 1867.* 1971. (Ph.D. thesis, University of Newcastle upon Tyne.)

5967 **Harrison**, Royden. 'The War Emergency Workers' National Committee.' Briggs, A. and Saville, J. (eds.). *Essays in labour history, 1886–1923.* 1971. p. 211–59.

5968 **Harvey**, R. J. 'The Industrial Relations Act 1971.' *New Law J.*, CXXI (1971), 896–8.

5969 **Heath**, Christopher George. *A guide to the Industrial Relations Act 1971.* London: Sweet & Maxwell, 1971. xx, 256p.

5970 **Henderson**, Joan. *A guide to the Industrial Relations Bill.* London: Industrial Society, 1971. 19p.

5971 **Henderson**, Joan. *The Industrial Relations Act at work.* London: Industrial Society, 1971. 28p.

5972 **Hepple**, Robert Alexander and **O'Higgins**, Paul. *Public employee trade unionism in the*

United Kingdom: the legal framework. Ann Arbor: University of Michigan – Wayne State University, Institute of Labor and Industrial Relations, 1971. 221p.

5973 **Institute of Directors.** *Understanding the Industrial Relations Bill.* London: The Institute, 1971. 9p.

5974 **Labour Research Department.** *Industrial Relations Act 1971: trade unionist's guide.* London: L.R.D., 1971. 39p.
Second edition. 1972. 39p.

5975 **Local Authorities Conditions of Service Advisory Board.** *Guide to the Industrial Relations Act, 1971.* London: L.A.C.S.A.B., 1971. 31, ivp.

5976 **Meston**, Dougall, Baron Meston. *Shaw's guide to the Industrial Relations Act, 1971.* London: Shaw, 1971. 287p.
Includes Text of Act.

5977 **Milligan**, Stephen. *Industrial relations: Britain's battle for reform.* London: Economist, 1971. 24p.

5978 **Mitchell**, Ewan. *The employer's lawyer.* London: Business Books, 1971. 485p.

5979 **Neal**, *Sir* Leonard Francis. *Guidance to employers on the Industrial Relations Bill: Report of a working party.* London: Confederation of British Industry, 1971. 51p.

5980 **Parsons**, O. H. *Tory war on the unions: an analysis of the Industrial Relations Bill.* London: Labour Research Department, 1971. 31p.

5981 **Paterson**, Peter. *An employers' guide to the Industrial Relations Act.* London: Kogan Page, 1971. 135p.

5982 **Paulden**, S. 'Lessons from Fairfields.' *Pers. Manage.*, III, 11 (November 1971), 22–5.

5983 **Phelps Brown**, Ernest Henry. 'Effects of the Industrial Relations Bill.' *Banker*, CXXI (April 1971), 352–7.

5984 **Phelps Brown**, Ernest Henry. 'Industrial relations and the law: lessons of Australian experience.' *Three Banks Rev.*, LXXXIX (March 1971), 3–29.

5985 **Price**, Norman. 'The code: an I.P.M. view.' *Pers. Manage.*, III, 10 (October 1971), 39–42.

5986 **Radice**, Giles and **Vickers**, Jon. *Divide and rule: the Industrial Relations Bill.* London: Fabian Society, 1971. 20p. (Fabian tracts 406.)

5987 **Rideout**, Roger William. 'The Industrial Relations Act 1971.' *Mod. Law Rev.*, XXXIV (November 1971), 655–75.

5988 **Rideout**, Roger William. 'The Industrial Relations Bill.' *Curr. Leg. Probl.*, XXIV (1971), 18–35.

5989 **Sapper**, Laurie. *A guide to the Industrial Relations Act, 1971.* London: Barry Rose, 1971. 24p.

5990 **Thornton**, Alan Henry. *The Industrial Relations Bill: for and against.* Nottingham: University of Nottingham Department of Adult Education, 1971. 36p.

5991 **Timperley**, Stuart R. and **Woodcock**, G.

L. 'Shop floor attitudes to industrial relations change.' *Ind. Relat. J.*, II, 4 (Winter 1971), 22–33.

5992 **Trades Union Congress.** *Industrial Relations Bill: report of the special Trades Union Congress, 1971.* London: T.U.C., 1971. 99p.

5993 **Wedderburn**, Kenneth William, Lord Wedderburn of Charlton. *Professor Wedderburn on the Industrial Relations Bill.* London: Trades Union Congress, 1971. 7p.

5994 **Wedderburn**, Kenneth William, Lord Wedderburn of Charlton. 'The small print in Carr's bill.' *New Soc.*, XVII (21 January 1971), 106–7.

5995 **Wedderburn**, Kenneth William, Lord Wedderburn of Charlton. *The worker and the law.* Harmondsworth: Penguin, 1971. 587p.
Second edition.

5996 **Whittingham**, T. G. and **Towers**, Brian. 'The British Industrial Relations Bill: an analysis.' *Relat. Industrielles*, XXVI, 3 (August 1971), 620–41.

5997 **Wood**, John Crossley. 'After the bill.' *New Soc.*, XVII (11 February 1971), 233–4.

5998 **Wood**, John Crossley. *The Industrial Relations Act: an introduction for personnel managers.* London: Institute of Personnel Management, 1971. 43p.

5999 **Woodcock**, G. L. *A study of the influences of shop floor opinions in a period of industrial relations change.* 1971. (M.A. thesis, University of Liverpool.)

6000 **Cookson**, J. L. 'The Industrial Relations Act 1971.' Torrington, Derek P. (ed.). *Handbook of industrial relations.* 1972. p. 29–48.

6001 **Department of Employment.** *Industrial Relations Act 1971: agency shop agreements.* London: The Department, 1972. 14p.

6002 **Department of Employment.** *Industrial Relations Act 1971: rights of the individual.* London: The Department, 1972. 18p.

6003 **Department of Employment.** *Industrial relations code of practice.* London: H.M.S.O., 1972. 31p.

6004 **Fridman**, Gerald Henry Louis. *The modern law of employment.* London: Stevens.
Third supplement. 1972.

6005 **Hall**, D. J. *Industrial relations problems and the Industrial Relations Act.* London: Kogan Page, 1972. 208p.

6006 **Harrison**, Royden. 'A bloody liberty.' *New Soc.*, XX (22 June 1972), 631–2.
Intervention of the Official Solicitor.

6007 **Harvey**, Richard John Stanley. *Industrial relations, including the Industrial Relations Act 1971.* London: Butterworths, 1971–2. 2 v.

6008 **Hogg**, George. 'A dose of the code.' *Scott. Bankers' Mag.*, LXIV (May 1972), 36–41.

6009 **Industrial Research and Information Services.** *The public interest.* London: The Services, 1972. 34p.

6010 **Institute of Personnel Management,** National Committee on Employee Relations. *A practical guide to the Industrial Relations*

Act, based on a working seminar. London: The Institute, 1972. 115p.

6011 **Kahn-Freund**, Sir Otto. *Labour and the law.* London: Stevens.
First edition. 1972. xii, 270p.
Second edition. 1977. xxxii, 295p.

6012 **Macbeath**, Innis. *Times guide to the Industrial Relations Act: workers, managers and the law in Britain.* London: Times Newspapers, 1972. 146p.

6013 **Martin**, Andrew. 'Organized labor and the shaping of economic policy in Western Europe.' Industrial Relations Research Association. *Proceedings of the twenty-fourth annual winter meeting, New Orleans, December 27–28, 1971.* Chicago: I.R.R.A., 1972. p. 176–85.

6014 **Mitchell**, Ewan. *Letters of industrial law: the executive's practical guide to the Industrial Relations Act.* London: Business Books, 1972. 293p.

6015 **Naylor**, Rachel. 'Central government services in industrial relations.' Torrington, Derek P. (ed.). *Handbook of industrial relations.* 1972. p. 65–79.

6016 **Pain**, Peter. 'The Industrial Court: a missed opportunity.' *Ind. Law J.*, I, 1 (March 1972), 5–11.

6017 **Pardoe**, Alan. *A practical guide for employer and employee to the Industrial Relations Act, 1971.* Bristol: Jordan, 1972. 319p.

6018 **Parsons**, Owen Henry and **Henderson**, Norman. *The Industrial Relations Act 1971.* London: Law Society, 1972. 30p.

6019 **Phelps**, Edmund Strother. *Inflation policy and unemployment theory: the cost-benefit approach to monetary planning.* London: Macmillan, 1972. 322p.

6020 **Rideout**, Roger William. *Principles of labour law.* London: Sweet and Maxwell.
First edition. 1972. 422p.
Second edition. 1976. 457p.
Third edition. 1979. li, 464p.

6021 **Ringrone Newspapers**. *Government v. unions: Britain faces the crunch.* Cheltenham: The Authors, 1972. 33p.

6022 **Ritson**, John. *Case studies in industrial law and relations.* London: Knight, 1972. viii, 223p.

6023 **Rose**, Frank W. *Personnel management law.* Epping: Gower, 1972. 539p.

6024 **Selwyn**, Norman Mordecai. *Selected questions and answers on the Industrial Relations Act, 1971.* Sutton Coldfield: Fleeman Cooper, 1972. 25p.

6025 **Steel**, David. 'Industrial relations: the liberal view.' *Contemp. Rev.*, CCXX (February 1972), 63–5.

6026 **Trades Union Congress**. *T.U.C. handbook on the Industrial Relations Act.* London: T.U.C., 1972. 77p.

6027 **United States**, Bureau of Labor Statistics. *Labor law and practice in Great Britain.* Washington: U.S.G.P.O., 1972. viii, 89p.

6028 **Wedderburn**, Kenneth William, Lord Wedderburn of Charlton. 'Labour law and labour relations in Britain.' *Br. J. Ind. Relat.*, X, 2 (July 1972), 270–90.

6029 **Wedderburn**, Kenneth William, Lord Wedderburn of Charlton. 'Multinational enterprise and national labour law.' *Ind. Law. J.*, I, 1 (March 1972), 12–19.

6030 **Whittingham**, T. G. and **Towers**, Brian. 'The code of industrial relations practice: some implications.' *Ind. Relat. J.*, III, 2 (Summer 1972), 2–7.

6031 **Armstrong**, Eric George Abbott. *Straitjacket or framework? The implications for management of the Industrial Relations Act.* London: Business Books, 1973. xii, 195p.

6032 **Balfour**, Campbell. *Unions and the law.* Farnborough: Heath, 1973. vii, 141p.

6033 **Brown**, Wilfred Banks Duncan, Baron Brown. *Earnings conflict: proposals for tackling the emerging crisis of industrial relations, unemployment, and wage inflation.* London: Heinemann, 1973. 128p.
Also published by Penguin, 1973.

6034 **Burchardt**, Andrew. 'The machine tool industry.' Barratt Brown, M. and Coates, K. (eds.). *Trade union register: 3.* 1973. p. 210–18.

6035 **Donaldson**, Sir John. 'Life at court.' *Ind. Participation*, DLIII (Autumn–Winter 1973), 3–7.

6036 **Drake**, Charles Dominic. *Labour law.* London: Sweet & Maxwell, 1973. xxix, 358p.
Second edition.

6037 **Ellis**, I. G. and **Greenhaigh**, R. 'Rethinking the Industrial Relations Act.' *Pers. Manage.*, V, 4 (April 1973), 18–21.

6038 **Garbarino**, J. W. 'The British experiment with industrial relations reform.' *Ind. Labor Relat. Rev.*, XXVI, 2 (January 1973), 793–804.

6039 **Hanson**, Charles Goring. *Trade unions: a century of privilege? An historical explanation of the 1971 Industrial Relations Act and the perennial issues of trade union power and the law.* London: Institute of Economic Affairs, 1973. 34p. (Occasional papers 38.)

6040 **Hawkins**, Kevin. 'Company policy and the Industrial Relations Act.' Cuthbert, N. and Hawkins, K. (eds.). *Company industrial relations policies.* 1973. p. 62–88.

6041 **Hepple**, Robert Alexander. 'The reform of the Industrial Relations Act.' *New Soc.*, XXIV (3 May 1973), 239–40.

6042 **Hepple**, Robert Alexander and **O'Higgins**, Paul. *Encyclopaedia of labour relations law.* London: Sweet & Maxwell, 1973. 2 v.

6043 **Hills**, D. H. 'National Industrial Relations Court: a personal history.' *Br. J. Ind. Relat.*, XI, 2 (July 1973), 259–85.

6044 **Hooberman**, Ben. 'Recent developments in labour relations law in Britain 1971/2.' *Univ. Leuven Inst. Labour Relat. Bull.*, IV (1973), 235–43.

6045 **Industrial Society**. *Legal problems of employment*. London: The Society, 1973. 88p. Fifth edition.

6046 *Law and order on the shop floor?* Coventry: Workshop Books, 1973. 18p.

6047 **Lewis**, Norman. 'The National Industrial Relations Court.' Barratt Brown, M. and Coates, K. (eds.). *Trade union register: 3*. 1973. p. 60–73.

6048 **McCarthy**, William Edward John and **Ellis**, Norman D. *Management by agreement: an alternative to the Industrial Relations Act*. London: Hutchinson, 1973. 209p.

6049 **Rideout**, Roger William. *Practice and procedure of the National Industrial Relations Court*. London: Sweet & Maxwell, 1973. xvi, 94p.

6050 **Roberts**, Benjamin Charles. 'Industrial relations and the European Economic Community.' Industrial Relations Research Association. *Proceedings of the spring meeting, Jamaica, May 3–6, 1973*. Chicago: I.R.R.A., 1973. p. 484–90.

6051 **Selwyn**, Norman. 'The British Industrial Relations Act of 1971.' Parkinson, C. N. (ed.). *Industrial disruption*. 1973. p. 48–63.

6052 **Simpson**, Robert Cecil and **Wood**, John Crossley. *Industrial relations and the 1971 Act*. London: Pitman, 1973. viii, 393p.

6053 **Chapman**, Robert. 'The industrial tribunal system.' *J. Ind. Affairs*, I, 2 (March 1974), 37–42.

6054 **Commission on Industrial Relations**. *Small firms and the code of industrial relations practice*. London: H.M.S.O., 1974. 52p. (Report 69.)

6055 **Davies**, Paul Lyndon. 'The end of an Act.' *New Soc.*, XXVIII (9 May 1974), 318–19.

6056 **Department of Employment**. *Employment Protection Bill: consultative document*. London: H.M.S.O., 1974. 27p.

6057 **Engleman**, Stephen R. and **Thomson**, Andrew William John. 'Experience under the British Industrial Relations Act.' *Ind. Relat.*, XIII, 2 (May 1974), 130–55.

6058 **Flanders**, Allan. 'The tradition of voluntarism.' *Br. J. Ind. Relat.*, XII, 3 (November 1974), 352–70.
    Reprinted in Barrett, B. and others (eds.). *Industrial relations and the wider society*. 1975. p. 374–84.

6059 **Goldthorpe**, John H. 'Industrial relations in Great Britain: a critique of reformism.' *Polit. Soc.*, IV, 4 (1974). 419–50.
    Reprinted in Clarke, T. and Clements, L. (eds.). *Trade unions under capitalism*. 1977. p. 184–224.

6060 **Henderson**, Joan. *Guide to the Trade Union and Labour Relations Act 1974*. London: Industrial Society, 1974. ii, 30p.

6061 **Henderson**, Joan. *New law on industrial relations: a practical guide to the Trade Union and Labour Relations Bill and future industrial relations legislation*. London: Industrial Society, 1974. 20p.

6062 **Incomes Data Services**. *The EEC social action programme*. London: I.D.S., 1974. 24p. (I.D.S. study 69.)

6063 **Jackson**, James. *Labour relations: the new law*. London: Commercial Publishing Company, 1974. 273p.

6064 **James**, Bernard and **Clifton**, R. 'Labour relations in the firm: the impact of the Industrial Relations Act.' *Ind. Relat. J.*, V, 1 (Spring 1974), 11–26.

6065 **Kahn-Freund**, Sir Otto. 'Industrial Relations Act 1971: some retrospective reflections.' *Ind. Law J.*, III. 4 (December 1974), 186–200.

6066 **Kahn-Freund**, Sir Otto. 'Reflections on labour law in Britain.' *Univ. Leuven Inst. Labour Relat. Bull.*, V (1974), 251–63.

6067 **Lewis**, Norman. 'Con-Mech: showdown for the N.I.R.C.' *Ind. Law J.*, III, 4 (December 1974), 201–14.

6068 **Local Authorities Conditions of Service Advisory Board**. *Handbook on the Trade Union and Labour Relations Act 1974*. London: L.A.C.S.A.B., 1974. 61p.

6069 **Lowe**, Rodney. 'Ministry of Labour 1916–1924: a graveyard of social reform?' *Public Adm.*, LII (Winter 1974), 415–38.

6070 **Rear**, J. 'British labour law in a colonial environment: the Hong Kong experience.' *Ind. Law J.*, III, 3 (September 1974), 138–51.

6071 **Rubenstein**, Michael. 'Labour law: lessons from the past and predictions for the future.' *Pers. Manage.*, VI, 10 (October 1974), 38–9, 48.

6072 **Schmidt**, F. 'On social contracts in the making of labour law.' *Ind. Law J.*, III, 2 (June 1974), 69–78.

6073 **Widmer**, Gary K. 'Is the Industrial Relations Court jeopardising your rights?' *J. Ind. Affairs*, I, 2 (March 1974), 43–6.

6074 **Aikin**, Olga. 'Employment protection: the legal machinery.' *Pers. Manage.*, VII, 12 (December 1975), 30–33.

6075 **Aims of Industry**. *Trade Union and Labour Relations (Amendment) Bill: the right to work, the right to write*. London: The Authors, 1975. 13p.

6076 **Anderman**, Steven Daniel. 'Employment and labour relations: the salient points of law.' *Pers. Manage.*, VII, 5 (May 1975), 28–9, 41.

6077 **Carby-Hall**, Joseph Roger. *Labour relations and the law*. Bradford: MCB Books, 1975. 40p.

6078 **Donaldson**, Sir John. 'Lessons from the Industrial Court.' *Law Q. Rev.*, XCI (April 1975), 181–92.

6079 **Donaldson**, Sir John. 'The role of labour courts.' *Ind. Law J.*, IV, 2 (June 1975), 63–8.

6080 **Eaton**, John, **Barratt Brown**, Michael and **Coates**, Ken. *An alternative economic strategy for the labour movement*. Nottingham: Institute for Workers' Control, 1975. 12p. (Spokesman pamphlet 47.)

6081 **Eldridge**, John E. T. 'Industrial relations and industrial capitalism.' Esland, G. and others (eds.). *People and work.* 1975. p. 306–24.

6082 **Harries**, John V. *Employment protection: the 1975 Act explained.* London: Oyez Publishing, 1975. xix, 194p.

6083 **Industrial Society**. *Improving industrial relations: implementing the code of practice.* London: The Society, 1975. 83p. (Survey and report series 188.)

6084 **Ionescu**, Ghita. *Centripetal politics: government and the new centres of power.* London: Hart-Davis/McGibbon, 1975. x, 231p.

6085 **National Economic Development Committee**, Economic Development Committee for the Distributive Trades. *Impact of the Employment Protection Act on part-time employment in retailing.* London: N.E.D.C., 1975.

6086 **Perrins**, B. *Labour relations law now.* London: Butterworth, 1975. xiii, 157p.

6087 **Rubenstein**, Michael. *A practical guide to the Employment Protection Bill.* London: Institute of Personnel Management and Industrial Relations Review and Report, 1975. 40p.

6088 **Smith**, N. A. 'Government versus trade unions in Britain.' *Polit. Q.*, XLVI (July–September 1975), 293–303.

6089 **Thomson**, Andrew William John and **Engleman**, Stephen R. *The Industrial Relations Act: a review and analysis.* London: Martin Robertson, 1975. vii, 185p. (Glasgow social and economic research studies 20.)

6090 **Weekes**, Brian, **Mellish**, Michael, **Dickens**, Linda and **Lloyd**, John. *Industrial relations and the limits of law: the industrial effects of the Industrial Relations Act, 1971.* Oxford: Blackwell, 1975. xvii, 344p. (Warwick studies in industrial relations.)

6091 **Weerasinghe**, D. P. A. 'The role of government in industrial relations: a comparative study of the industrial relations systems in Great Britain and Sri Lanka.' *Sri Lanka Labour Gaz.*, XXVI, 6 (June 1975), 315–22.

6092 **Witcher**, M. J. 'Preparing for the Employment Protection Act.' *Ind. Soc.*, LVII, 6 (November–December 1975), 9–10.

6093 **Anderman**, Steven Daniel. *Employment protection: a new legal framework.* London: Butterworth, 1976. xvii, 310p.

6094 **Beazley**, D. Nigel and **Wood**, Duncan H. *Employment legislation: the requirements and implications of 1975–1976's unique flood of legislation.* London: Institute of Chartered Accountants, 1976. (Accountants' digests 36.)

6095 **Benedictus**, Roger. 'Employment protection: new institutions and trade union rights.' *Ind. Law J.*, v, 1 (March 1976), 12–23.

6096 **Bescoby**, John H. and **Hanson**, Charles Goring. 'Continuity and change in recent labour law.' *Natl. Westminster Bank Q. Rev.* (May 1976), 7–19.

6097 **Carby-Hall**, Joseph Roger (ed.). *Studies in*

labour law. Bradford: MCB Books, 1976. 283p.

6098 **Carpenter**, L. P. 'Corporatism in Britain, 1930–45.' *J. Contemp. Hist.*, XI, 1 (January 1976), 3-25.

6099 **Clemitson**, Ivor. *A workers' guide to the Employment Protection Act.* Nottingham: Bertrand Russell Foundation, 1976. 61p. (Practical guides to industrial relations 21.)

6100 **Derbyshire**, J. D. *The Royal Commission on Trade Unions and Employers' Associations, 1965–1968: an analysis of a Royal Commission as an instrument for public policy making.* 1976. (Ph.D. thesis, University of London.)

6101 **Drake**, Charles D. 'The Trade Union and Labour Relations (Amendment) Bill.' *Ind. Law J.*, v, 1 (March 1976), 2–11.

6102 **Hay**, Roy. 'Government policy towards labour in Britain, 1900–1914: some further issues.' *Scott. Labour Hist. Soc. J.*, x (June 1976), 41–9.

6103 **Hepple**, Robert Alexander. 'Recent developments in British labour relations law 1974–1975.' *Univ. Leuven Inst. Labour Relat. Bull.*, VII (1976), 13–21.

6104 **Hillard**, John. *Institutions and political and legal environments.* Milton Keynes: Open University Press, 1976. 68p. (Industrial relations unit 13.)

6105 **Hillard**, John. *Political and legal environments: an introduction.* Milton Keynes: Open University Press, 1976. 33p. (PT 281 Unit 8B.)
Bound with Loveridge, R. *Socio-cultural environment.*

6106 **Hillard**, John. *Political and legal factors and regulation.* Milton Keynes: Open University Press, 1976. 52p. (PT 281 Unit 14.)

6107 **Jackson**, James. *Employment protection: the new law.* London: Commercial Publishing Company, 1976. 273p.

6108 **Kahn-Freund**, Sir Otto. 'The impact of constitutions on labour law.' *Camb. Law J.*, XXXV (November 1976), 240–71.

6109 **King**, J. E. 'Penal clauses in labour relations legislation: the case of the British Industrial Relations Act, 1971–74.' *J. Ind. Relat.*, XVIII, 2 (June 1976), 142–55.

6110 **Kloss**, Diana. 'Industrial relations and the law.' *Manchr. Lit. Philos. Soc. Proc.*, CXVIII (1975–6), 39–54.

6111 **Lewis**, Norman. 'The solar plexus.' Carby-Hall, J. R. (ed.). *Studies in labour law.* 1976. p. 35–109.
Sections 96–8 of the Industrial Relations Act.

6112 **Lewis**, Roy. 'The historical development of labour law.' *Br. J. Ind. Relat.*, XIV, 1 (March 1976), 1–17.

6113 **Ritson**, John. 'The Employment Protection Act, 1975.' *J. Ind. Affairs*, III, 2 (Spring 1976), 168–74.

6114 **Selwyn**, Norman Mordecai. *Law of employment.* London: Butterworth, 1976. 236p.

6115 **Tinnion**, John. 'The Industry Act 1975 and

industrial strategy.' *Ind. Law J.*, v, 2 (June 1976), 80–89.

6116 **Wigham**, Eric. '80 years of ministering to industrial relations.' *Dep. Employment Gaz.*, LXXXIV, 3 (March 1976), 235–41.

6117 **Workers' Fight**. *The Industrial Relations Act and the fight for a general strike: articles from Workers' Fight*. London: Workers' Fight, 1976. [56]p. (Phoenix pamphlets 4.)

6118 **Crouch**, Colin. *Class conflict and the industrial relations crisis: compromise and corporatism in the policies of the British state*. London: Heinemann, 1977. xvii, 302p.

6119 **Griffith**, J. A. G. *The politics of the judiciary*. London: Fontana/Collins, 1977. 224p.

6120 **Incomes Data Services**. *The E.E.C. and the U.K. employer*. London: I.D.S., 1977. 120p. (I.D.S. handbook 7.)

6121 **Larman Associates**. *Concise guide to employment law*. London: The Authors, 1977. 281p.

6122 **Moran**, Michael J. *The politics of industrial relations: the origins, life and death of the 1971 Industrial Relations Act*. London: Macmillan, 1977. 195p.

6123 **Napier**, Brian. 'Judicial attitudes towards the employment relationship: some recent developments.' *Ind. Law J.*, VI, 1 (March 1977), 1–18.

6124 **Wallington**, Peter (ed.). *Labour law statutes*. London: Butterworth, 1977.

6125 **Wigham**, Eric. 'A diamond year for the department.' *Dep. Employment Gaz.*, LXXXV, 1 (January 1977), 3–5.

6126 **Winkler**, J. T. 'The corporatist economy: theory and administration.' Scase, R. (ed.). *Industrial society*. 1977. p. 43–58.

6127 **Beaumont**, Philip B. 'The obligation of the British government as an employer in the British civil service.' *Public Adm.*, LVI (Spring 1978), 13–24.

6128 **Coates**, Ken. 'Planning by the people.' Coates, Ken (ed.). *The right to useful work*. 1978. p. 11–22.

6129 **Coates**, Ken (ed.). *The right to useful work: planning by the people*. Nottingham: Spokesman, 1978. 287p.

6130 **Crouch**, Colin. 'The changing role of the state in industrial relations in Western Europe.' Crouch, Colin and Pizzorno, Alessandro (eds.). *The resurgence of class conflict in Western Europe since 1968*. London: Macmillan. Vol. 2. *Comparative analyses*. 1978. p. 197–220.

6131 **Crouch**, Colin. 'Inflation and the political organization of economic interests.' Hirsch, F. and Goldthorpe, J. (eds.). *The political economy of inflation*. 1978. p. 217–39.

6132 **Daniel**, William Wentworth and **Stilgoe**, Elizabeth. *The impact of employment protection laws*. London: Policy Studies Institute, 1978. (Broadsheets 577.)

6133 **Davidson**, Roger. 'The Board of Trade and industrial relations, 1896–1914.' *Hist. J.*, XXI, 3 (September 1978), 571–91.

6134 **Grunfeld**, Cyril. 'Union law and power: current issues.' Institute of Economic Affairs. *Trade unions: public goods or public bads?* 1978. p. 79–89.

6135 **Lowe**, Rodney. 'The erosion of state intervention in Britain, 1917–24.' *Econ. Hist. Rev.*, XXXI (May 1978), 270–86.

6136 **Lowe**, Rodney. 'The failure of consensus in Britain: the National Industrial Conference, 1919–1921.' *Hist. J.*, XXI (September 1978), 649–75.

6137 **McMullen**, Jeremy. *Rights at work: a workers' guide to employment law*. London: Pluto, 1978. xii, 423p.

6138 **Perrins**, B. *Industrial relations and employment law*. 1978. (Ph.D. thesis, University of Birmingham.)

6139 **Prentice**, Reg. 'The issues in public policy.' Institute of Economic Affairs. *Trade unions: public goods or public bads?* 1978. p. 126–8.

6140 **Scarman**, Lord. 'Individual v. corporate freedom before the law.' Institute of Economic Affairs. *Trade unions: public goods or public bads?* 1978. p. 65–74.

6141 **Upex**, Robert V. *Employment protection legislation*. London: Oyez, 1978. 249p.

6142 **White**, P. J. 'Is voluntarism in decline?' *Ind. Relat. J.*, IX, 3 (Autumn 1978), 34–43.

6143 **Brown**, William A., **Weekes**, Brian C.M. and **Hart**, Moira. 'T.U.C. – government "concordat".' *Ind. Law J.*, VIII, 2 (June 1979), 114–17.

6144 **Butler**, Francis. 'Government policy in Great Britain and the social psychology of industrial relations.' Stephenson, G. and Brotherton, C. (eds.). *Industrial relations: a social psychological approach*. 1979. p. 339–60.

6145 **Crouch**, Colin. *The politics of industrial relations*. Manchester: Fontana/Collins and Manchester University Press, 1979. 223p.

6146 **Crouch**, Colin (ed.). *State and economy in contemporary capitalism*. London: Croom Helm, 1979. 264p.

6147 **Crouch**, Colin. 'The state, capital and liberal democracy.' Crouch, C. (ed.). *State and economy in contemporary capitalism*. 1979. p. 13–54.

6148 **Davies**, Paul Lyndon and **Freedland**, Mark B. *Labour law: text and materials*. London: Weidenfeld & Nicolson, 1979. xliv, 766p.

6149 **Dickens**, Linda, **Hart**, Moira, **Jones**, Michael and **Weekes**, Brian C.M. 'Law reform proposals: the government's working papers on employment protection legislation.' *Ind. Law J.*, VIII, 4 (December 1979), 246–8.

6150 **Dorfman**, Gerald A. *Government versus trade unionism in British politics since 1968*. London: Macmillan, 1979. vii, 179p.

6151 **Fox**, Alan. 'The growth of the social services. Labour in a new era of law.' *New Soc.*, XXXV (1 March 1979), 480–83.

6152 **Fox**, Alan. 'The growth of the social services: labour law between two wars. How did the system we now know develop?' *New Soc.*, XXXV (22 February 1979), 419–21.

6153 **Hamwee**, John. 'Worker cooperatives.' *Ind. Law J.*, VIII, I (March 1979), 19–31.
State assistance.

6154 **Harkin**, Guy. 'Government control of work.' Purcell, J. and Smith, R. (eds.). *The control of work.* 1979. p. 77–99.

6155 **Hayhoe**, Barney. 'Conservative Party plans for industrial relations reform.' *Pers. Manage.*, XI, 2 (February 1979), 26–9, 42.

6156 **Hepple**, Robert Alexander. *Hepple and O'Higgins' employment law.* London: Sweet & Maxwell, 1979. xlvii, 396p.
Third edition.

6157 **Jenkins**, Glen. 'The Webbs and corporatism: a critique.' Colloquium on Management and Industrial Relations, 1979. *Proceedings.* 1979. p. 55–66.

6158 **Kahn-Freund**, *Sir* Otto. 'The study of labour law: some reflections.' *Ind. Law J.*, VIII, 4 (December 1979), 197–201.

6159 **Keenoy**, Tom. 'Industrial relations and the law: from the Webbs to corporatism.' Colloquium on Management and Industrial Relations, 1979. *Proceedings.* 1979. p. 23–54.

6160 **Kirby**, M. W. 'The politics of state coercion in inter-war Britain: the Mines Department of the Board of Trade, 1920–1942.' *Hist. J.*, XXII (June 1979), 373–96.

6161 **Lewis**, Roy. 'Kahn-Freund and labour law: an outline critique.' *Ind. Law J.*, VIII, 4 (December 1979), 202–21.

6162 **Middlemas**, Robert Keith. *Politics in industrial society: the experience of the British system since 1911.* London: Deutsch, 1979. 512p.

6163 **Moran**, Michael. 'Citizens and workers.' *Polit. Q.*, L, I (January–March 1979), 59–70.

6164 **Strinati**, Dominic. 'Capitalism, the state and industrial relations.' Crouch, C. (ed.). *State and economy in contemporary capitalism.* 1979. p. 191–236.

6165 **Sweet & Maxwell Ltd**. *Sweet and Maxwell's labour relations statutes and materials.* London: Sweet & Maxwell, 1979. 675p.
Advisory editors: B.A. Hepple, Paul O'Higgins and *Lord* Wedderburn.

6166 **Trades Union Congress**. *The economy, the government and trade union responsibilities: joint statement by the TUC and the government.* London: T.U.C., 1979. 12p.

6167 **Wrigley**, Chris. *The government and industrial relations in Britain 1910–1921.* Loughborough: Loughborough University, Department of Economics, 1979. 20p.

See also: 38; 45; 121; 134; 135; 189; 206; 732; 777; 787; 1304; 1307; 1474; 1475; 1753; 1785; 1850; 2117; 2185; 2218; 2348; 2443; 2472; 2565; 2624; 2631; 2784; 6431; 6473.

II. REGULATION OF MANPOWER

A. GENERAL

See also Part Six, II, C – D.

6168 **Evans**, Erick Wyn. 'Manpower policy in the seventies.' *Bankers' Mag.*, CCXII (December 1971), 268–73.

6169 **Bayliss**, Frederick Joseph. 'U.K. national manpower forecasting.' *B.A.C.I.E. J.*, XXV, 6 (June 1972), 76–80.

6170 **Graham**, Ken. 'The TUC's view on manpower policy.' *Pers. Manage.*, IV, 9 (September 1972), 36–9.

6171 **Institute of Personnel Management.** *The need for a national manpower commission.* London: The Institute, 1972. 7p.

6172 **Thirlwall**, A. P. 'Government manpower policies in Great Britain: their rationale and benefits.' *Br. J. Ind. Relat.*, X, 2 (July 1972), 165–79.

6173 **Lawrence**, John. *The Manpower Services Commission: expectation and realisation.* London: Institute of Manpower Studies, 1973. 6p.

6174 **Mukherjee**, Santosh. 'Manpower services: the quiet revolution.' *Pers. Manage.*, V, 8 (August 1973), 22–5.

6175 **Barnes**, *Sir* Denis. 'The work of the Manpower Services Commission.' *Ind. Commer. Train.*, VI, 3 (March 1974), 112–18.

6176 **Organisation for Economic Cooperation and Development.** *Manpower policy in Ireland.* Paris: O.E.C.D., 1974. 68p. (Reviews of manpower and social policies 15.)

6177 **Campling**, Jo. 'Manpower Services: the new approach.' *Contemp. Rev.*, CCXXVII (November 1975), 231–4.

6178 **Pringle**, Robin. 'Employment policy: time for a change of fashion.' *Banker*, CXXV (September 1975), 1031–3.

6179 **Schmiechen**, James Andrew. 'State reform and the local economy: an aspect of industrialization in late Victorian and early Edwardian London.' *Econ. Hist. Rev.*, XXVIII (August 1975), 413–28.

6180 **Barnes**, C. 'Reorganisation of manpower services in Great Britain.' *Int. Labour Rev.*, CXIII, I (January–February 1976), 97–114.

6181 **Department of Employment Gazette.** 'Elephant jobs: how a community workshop is being set up under the job creation programme in south London.' *Dep. Employment Gaz.*, LXXXIV, 7 (July 1976), 707–9.

6182 **Manpower Services Commission.** *Towards a comprehensive manpower policy.* London: The Commission, 1976. 43p.

6183 **Mukherjee**, Santosh. *Governments and labour markets: aspects of policies in Britain, France, Germany, Netherlands and Italy.* London: Political & Economic Planning, 1976. 77p. (Broadsheet 566.)

6184 **Perry**, Peter John Charles. *The evolution of British manpower policy: from the Statute of Artificers 1563 to the Industrial Training Act, 1964.* London: British Association for Commercial and Industrial Education, 1976. 329p.

6185 **Craven**, Peter. 'Where there's muck there's brass: how the job creation programme helped the Oxfam Wastesaver project in Huddersfield.' *Dep. Employment Gaz.*, LXXXV, 2 (February 1977), 128–8.

6186 **Department of Employment Gazette.** 'M.S.C. evaluates job creation.' *Dep. Employment Gaz.*, LXXXV, 3 (March 1977), 211–17.

6187 **Duysens**, Daniel. 'Work permits: Department of Employment control of the labour market.' *Ind. Law J.*, VI, 2 (June 1977), 85–98.

6188 **Manpower Services Commission.** *M.S.C. review and plan 1977.* London: The Commission, 1977. 89p.

6189 **Von Beyme**, Klaus and **Ionescu**, Ghita. 'The politics of employment policy in Germany and Great Britain.' *Gov. Oppos.*, XII (Winter 1977), 88–107.

6190 **Central Office of Information.** *Manpower and employment in Britain: the role of government.* London: H.M.S.O., 1978. ii, 28p. (Reference pamphlet 152.)

6191 **Manpower Services Commission.** *M.S.C. review and plan 1978.* London: The Commission, 1978. 47p.

6192 **Loney**, Martin. 'The politics of job creation.' Craig, G. and others (eds.). *Jobs and community action.* 1979. p. 228–41.

6193 **Manpower Services Commission.** *Research 1977–78.* London: H.M.S.O., 1979. vi, 82p.
See also: 939.

B. GENERAL LEVEL OF EMPLOYMENT

This section includes works dealing with employment and unemployment as a problem of public policy. See also Part Three, II, E, 3; Part Six, II, C–D; Part Six, IV, A, 3, d; Part Seven, II, D, 2–3; and Part Seven, II, E.

6194 **Powell**, J. Enoch. 'Ritual remedies.' *Twentieth Century*, CLXXIX (1971), 39–41.

6195 **Tilney**, R. H. *Aids to reducing unemployment in Great Britain between 1957 and 1967.* 1971. (M.Phil. thesis, University of Nottingham.)

6196 **Bosanquet**, Nicholas and **Standing**, G. 'Government and unemployment 1966–1970; a study of policy and evidence.' *Br. J. Ind. Relat.*, X, 2 (July 1972), 180–92.

6197 **Harris**, Jose. *Unemployment and politics: a study in English social policy 1886–1914.* Oxford: Clarendon Press, 1972. x, 411p.

6198 **Raison**, Timothy. *Prospects for employment: a Tory view.* London: Conservative Political Centre, 1972. 118p.

6199 **Sopariwala**, Dorab. 'Towards the greatest relief of unemployment: a forecasting method.' *Manage. Decis.*, X (Winter 1972), 283–92.

6200 **Wood**, John B. *How much unemployment? The methods and measures dissected.* London: Institute of Economic Affairs, 1972. 68p. (Research monographs 28.)

6201 **Brittan**, Samuel. 'Jobs, money and policies.' *New Soc.*, XXX (3 October 1974), 37–8.

6202 **Mukherjee**, Santosh. *There's work to be done: unemployment and manpower policies.* London: Manpower Services Commission, 1974. 101p.

6203 **Brittan**, Samuel. *Second thoughts on full employment policy.* London: Barry Rose, 1965. 132p.

6204 **Hayek**, Friedrich August von. *Full employment at any price?* London: Institute of Economic Affairs, 1975. 52p. (Occasional papers 45.)

6205 **Blackaby**, Frank T. 'The target rate of unemployment.' Worswick, G. (ed.). *The concept and measurement of involuntary unemployment.* 1976. p. 279–304.

6206 **Brittan**, Samuel. 'Full employment policy: a reappraisal.' Worswick, G. (ed.). *The concept and measurement of involuntary unemployment.* 1976. p. 249–78.

6207 **Broadway**, Frank Edward. *Upper Clyde shipbuilders: a study of government intervention in industry: the way the money goes.* London: Centre for Policy Studies, 1976. 58p.

6208 **Ganeson**, S. *Employment generation through investments in housing and construction.* 1976. (Ph.D. thesis, University College, London.)

6209 **Miller**, Frederic M. 'The unemployment policy of the National Government, 1931–6.' *Hist. J.*, XIX, 2 (June 1976), 453–76.

6210 **Rifflet**, R. 'Employment policy prospects in the European Communities.' *Int. Labour Rev.*, CXIII, 2 (March–April 1976), 139–58.

6211 **Sharp**, R. *Whose right to work?* London: Oxfam, 1976. 49p. (Public Affairs Unit. Report 2.)

6212 **Burton**, John, 'Employment subsidies: the case for and against.' *Natl. Westminster Bank Q. Rev.* (February 1977), 33–43.

6213 **Department of Employment Gazette.** 'Surveys carried out into special employment schemes.' *Dep. Employment Gaz.*, LXXXV, 7 (July 1977), 692–6.

6214 **Field**, Frank, 'The return to full employment.' Field, F. (ed.). *The conscript army.* 1977. p. 138–52.

6215 **Field**, Frank and **Winyard**, Stephen. 'Government action against unemployment.' Field, F. (ed.). *The conscript army.* 1977. p. 125–37.

6216 **Holden**, K. and **Peel**, D. A. 'Manipulating money to cut the dole queue.' *Pers. Manage.*, IX, 4 (April 1977), 32–5, 43.

6217 **Manpower Services Commission.** *The new special programmes for unemployed people: the next steps.* London: The Commission, 1977. 17p.

6218 **Robinson**, Joan and **Wilkinson**, Frank.

'What has become of employment policy?' *Camb. J. Econ.*, I, I (1977), 5–14.

6219 **Addison**, John Thomas. 'Does job creation work?' Addison, J. T. and others. *Job creation – or destruction?* 1978. p. 13–29.

6220 **Addison**, John Thomas, **Watrin**, Christian, **Fisher**, Malcolm R., **Rees**, Albert, **Okono**, Yukihide, **Okabe**, Mitsuaki and **Eltis**, Walter. *Job creation – or destruction? Six essays on the effects of government intervention in the labour market.* London: Institute of Economic Affairs, 1978. xiii, 146p. (Readings in political economy 20.)
   With an introductory essay by Ralph Harris.

6221 **Barratt Brown**, Michael, **Coates**, Ken, **Fleet**, Ken and **Hughes**, John (eds.). *Full employment.* Nottingham: Spokesman Books, 1978. 144p.

6222 **Basnett**, David. 'North Sea oil: a chance to tackle unemployment.' *Lloyds Bank Rev.*, CXXX (October 1978), 1–17.

6223 **Booth**, Alan E. 'An administrative experiment in unemployment policy in the thirties.' *Public Adm.*, LVI (Summer 1978), 139–57.

6224 **Coates**, Ken. 'The abandonment of full employment.' Barratt Brown, M. and others (eds.). *Full employment.* 1978. p. 3–7.

6225 **Coates**, Ken. 'What, then, must we do next?' Barratt Brown, M. and others (eds.). *Full employment.* 1978. p. 137–42.

6226 **Cripps**, Francis and **Wilkinson**, Frank. 'Economic conditions.' Barratt Brown, M. and others (eds.). *Full employment.* 1978. p. 81–5.

6227 **Department of Employment Gazette.** 'Small firms employment subsidy: an evaluation of its effectiveness.' *Dep. Employment Gaz.*, LXXXVI, 5 (May 1978), 549–54.

6228 **Eltis**, Walter. 'Public policy.' Addison, J. T. and others. *Job creation – or destruction?* 1978. p. 117–23.

6229 **Gulland**, Douglas and **Zaklukiewicz**, Stefan. *No cosmetic exercise: an account of the job creation projects sponsored by the Colleges of Education in Scotland.* Edinburgh: Scottish Council for Research in Education and Scottish Community Education Centre, 1978. 60p.

6230 **Hannington**, Walter. *Ten lean years: an examination of the record of the National Government in the field of unemployment.* London: E.P. Publishing, 1978. 287p.
   First published 1940. Reprinted with a new introduction by Chris Jones and Tony Novak.

6231 **Holland**, Stuart. 'An alternative economic strategy.' Barratt Brown, M. and others (eds.). *Full employment.* 1978. p. 133–6.

6232 **Hughes**, John. 'Three modest proposals.' Barratt Brown, M. and others (eds.). *Full employment.* 1978. p. 125–32.

6233 **Hunter**, Laurence Colvin and **Beaumont**,

Philip B. *Labour shortages and manpower policy.* London: H.M.S.O. for the Manpower Services Commission, 1978. 103p. (Manpower studies 1978–2.)

6234 **Incomes Data Services.** *Subsidising jobs.* London: I.D.S., 1978. 21p. (I.D.S. study 173.)

6235 **Joseph,** *Sir* Keith. *Conditions for fuller employment.* London: Centre for Policy Studies, 1978. 20p.

6236 **Neary**, J. Peter. 'Capital subsidies and employment in an open economy.' *Oxf. Econ. Pap.*, XXX, 3 (November 1978), 334–56.

6237 **Philip**, Alan Butt. *Creating new jobs: a report on long-term job creation in Britain and Sweden.* London: Policy Studies Institute, 1978. 63p. (Broadsheet 576.)

6238 **Pocock**, Carmichael Charles Peter. *More jobs: a small cure for a big problem.* Berkhamsted: Ashridge Management College, 1978. 12p.
   Ashridge lecture, 1977.

6239 **Scott**, Maurice Fitzgerald and **Laslett**, Robert A. *Can we get back to full employment?* London: Macmillan, 1978. 164p.

6240 **Sedgemore**, Brian. 'The stages of sin.' Barratt Brown, M. and others (eds.). *Full employment.* 1978. p. 61–9.

6241 **Tomlinson**, J. D. 'Unemployment and government policy between the wars: a note.' *J. Contemp. Hist.*, XIII, 1 (January 1978), 65–78.

6242 **Deacon**, Alan. 'Towards 1931: unemployment and the Labour Party in the 1920s.' Wrigley, C. (ed.). *The British labour movement in the decade after the First World War.* 1979. p. 36–54.

6243 **Employment Think Tank.** *Unemployment: a new approach for the 80's: a report.* London: Employment Think Tank, 1979. 23p.

6244 **Evans**, A. J. 'Measures to make the jobs go round.' *Pers. Manage.*, XI, 1 (January 1979), 32–5.

6245 **Jackson**, Michael P. and **Hanby**, Victor J. B. (eds.). *Work creation: international experiences.* London: Saxon House, 1979. 168p.
   Proceedings of the International Conference on Work Creation, University of Stirling, 1979.

6246 **Manpower Services Commission.** *Review of the first year of special programmes.* London: The Commission, 1979. 56p.

See also: 4294; 4306.

C. WAR AND RECONSTRUCTION

See also Part Six, II, C, 4.

6247 **Hinton**, James. 'The Clyde Workers' Committee and the dilution struggle.' Briggs, A. and Saville, J. (eds.). *Essays in labour history, 1886–1923.* 1971. p. 152–84.

6248 **McCalman**, Janet. 'The impact of the First World War on female employment in England.' *Labour Hist.*, XXI (November 1971), 36–47.

6249 **Angell**, *Sir* Norman. *War and the workers.* New York: Garland, 1972. 13, 63, xivp.
First published by the National Labour Press, 1916.

6250 **Gowing**, Margaret. 'The organisation of manpower in Britain during the Second World War.' *J. Contemp. Hist.*, VII (January–April 1972), 147–67.

6251 **Marwick**, Arthur. *Women at war 1914–1918.* London: Croom Helm, 1977. 176p.

6252 **Rubin**, G. R. 'The Munitions Appeal Reports 1916–1920: a neglected episode in modern legal history.' *Juridical Rev.*, XXII (December 1977), 211–37.

6253 **Rubin**, G. R. 'The origins of industrial tribunals: munitions tribunals during the First World War.' *Ind. Law J.*, VI, 3 (September 1977), 149–64.

6254 **Hamilton**, *Lady* Peggy. *Three years or the duration: the memoirs of a munition worker, 1914–1918.* London: Owen, 1978. 125p.

See also: 4093; 5426.

D. LABOUR MOBILITY

See also Part Six, II, E.

1. Vocational Guidance Services

There is a vast literature on vocational guidance but most of it is outside the scope of this bibliography. The section only includes material which is concerned with describing the nature and development of vocational guidance services. The more psychological literature on the techniques of vocational guidance is specifically excluded. See also Part Six, II, A; and Part Seven, II, D, 2, b.

6255 **Hayes**, J. and **Hopson**, B. *Careers guidance: the role of the school in vocational development.* London: Heinemann Educational, 1972, 259p.

6256 **Schools Council**, Working Party on the Transition from School to Work. *Careers education in the 1970s: a report.* London: Methuen, 1972. 117p. (Working paper 40.)

6257 **Department of Education and Science.** *Careers education in secondary schools.* London: H.M.S.O., 1973. 90p. (Education survey 18.)

6258 **Greenaway**, Harriet. 'The changing role of careers advisory services.' Greenaway, H. and Williams, G. (eds.). *Patterns of change in graduate employment.* 1973. p. 77–84.

6259 **Hough**, P. 'Careering ahead.' *Ind. Soc.*, LV, 1 (January 1973), 11–13.

6260 **Merton**, B. 'Community care for school leavers.' *Ind. Commer. Train.*, V, 8 (August 1973), 385–90.

6261 **Engineering Industry Training Board.** *Outline of secondary and further education, training and vocational guidance in the United Kingdom.*

London: The Board, 1974. 35p. (Research planning and statistics internal reference paper 5.)

6262 **B.A.C.I.E. Journal.** 'Vocational preparation for young people.' *B.A.C.I.E. J.*, XXIX, 9 (September 1975), 121–2.

6263 **Department of Employment Gazette.** 'Occupational guidance service.' *Dep. Employment Gaz.*, LXXXIII, 10 (October 1975), 992–4.

6264 **Griffiths**, R. D. P. 'Vocational guidance conducted with psychiatric patients.' *Br. Psychol. Soc. Bull.*, XXVIII (November 1975), 427–36.

6265 **Teasdale**, J. R. 'The Employment Service Agency Psychological Services.' *Br. Psychol. Soc. Bull.*, XXVIII (April 1975), 156–8.

6266 **Training Services Agency.** *Grouping of skills: a first report of an investigation into a possible basis for a unified vocational preparation system: a document for discussion.* London: The Agency, 1975. ii, 61p.

6267 **Training Services Agency.** *Vocational preparation for young people: a discussion paper.* London: The Agency, 1975. 38p.

6268 **Marsh**, C. and **Winstanley**, P. 'Closing the careers gap.' *Ind. Soc.*, LX, 4 (July–August 1978), 15–16.

2. Employment Services

See also Part Six, II, E, 6; and Part Six, IV, A, 3, d.

a. GENERAL

6269 **British Psychological Society Bulletin**. 'Report on the future of the employment service.' *Br. Psychol. Soc. Bull.*, XXIV (April 1971), 137–8.

6270 **Department of Employment**. *People and jobs: a modern employment service.* London: H.M.S.O., 1971. 27p.

6271 **Department of Employment**. *Into action: plan for a modern employment service.* London: H.M.S.O., 1972. 27p.

6272 **Hartley**, Keith. 'A programme for labour mobility.' *New Soc.*, XXII (9 November 1972), 327–9.

6273 **Jones**, Richard Merfyn. 'The role of public employment agencies in the labour market.' *Ind. Relat. J.*, III, 4 (Winter 1972), 43–50.

6274 **Rees**, D. 'Top jobs, top people.' *Pers. Manage.*, IV, 10 (October 1972), 26–9.

6275 **Showler**, Brian. *Employment service and management.* Bradford: Institute of Scientific Business, 1972. 41p. (Reports and surveys 6.)

6276 **Showler**, Brian. 'Manpower policy and employment.' *Pers. Manage.*, IV, 7 (July 1972), 29–31.

6277 **Campling**, P. J. 'Nathaniel Cohen and the beginnings of the Labour Exchange Movement in Great Britain.' *Surrey Archaeol. Collect.*, LXIX (1973), 155–67.

6278 **House of Commons**, Expenditure Committee. *Employment services and training: seventh report.* London: H.M.S.O., 1973. 3v.

6279 **Showler**, Brian. *Onto a comprehensive employment service.* London: Fabian Society, 1973. 28p. (Research series 309.)

6280 **Employment Service Agency.** *Employment service: plans and programmes.* London: The Agency, 1974. 50p.

6281 **Department of Employment Gazette.** 'Employers, recruitment and the employment service.' *Dep. Employment Gaz.*, LXXXIII, 12 (December 1975), 1251–7.

6282 **Employment Service Agency.** 'Agency's performance in the manpower market.' *Dep. Employment Gaz.*, LXXXIV, 10 (October 1976), 1083–91.

6283 **Showler**, Brian. *The public employment service.* London: Longman, 1976. 101p.

6284 **Manpower Services Commission.** *MSC review and plan 1977.* London: The Commission, 1977. 87p.

6285 **Beaumont**, Philip B. 'The public employment service and employers.' *Ind. Relat. J.*, IX, 1 (Spring 1978), 4–11.

6286 **Campling**, Jo. 'Centres for layabouts.' *New Soc.*, XXXIII (27 April 1978), 196–7.

6287 **Harding**, John. *Employment and the probation and after-care service.* London: Barry Rose, 1978. 40p.

6288 **McGregor**, A. 'The placement activity of the Employment Service Agency.' *Br. J. Ind. Relat.*, XVI, 3 (November 1978), 309–19.

6289 **Bell**, D. and **Evans**, A. 'Judgement on jobcentres.' *Pers. Manage.*, XI, 9 (September 1979), 36–9.

6290 **Cornwell**, David. 'How job centres do their job.' *New Soc.*, XXXV (15 March 1979), 615–16.

6291 **Efstratoglon**, C. B. *An appraisal of the Employment Service policy in Great Britain, 1909–1978: the case of the E.S.A. jobcentres.* 1979. (M.Phil. thesis, University of York.)

b. YOUTH EMPLOYMENT SERVICE
AND POLICY

See also Part Six, II, A; Part Six, II, B, 3, a; Part Six, II, C, 5; Part Six, II, D, 7; and Part Six, IV, A, 3, b.

6292 **National Youth Employment Council.** *The work of the youth employment service 1968–1971: a report.* London: H.M.S.O., 1971. xi, 56p.

6293 **Roberts**, K. *From school to work: a study of the Youth Employment Service.* Newton Abbott: David & Charles, 1971. 168p.

6294 **Ewen**, J. *Towards a youth policy.* Manchester: M.B.S. Publications, 1972. 61p.

6295 **Higginbotham**, H. 'Occupational classification in the Birmingham Youth Employment Service.' *Occup. Psychol.*, XLVII (1973), 111–20.

6296 **House of Commons**, Expenditure Committee. *Youth employment services: fourth report.* London: H.M.S.O., 1973. xxii, 217p.
With part of the minutes of the evidence taken before the Employment and Social Services Sub-Committee in sessions 1971–2 and 1972–3 and appendices.

6297 **Christie**, R. P. 'The future of the youth employment service.' *Careers Q.*, XXVI, 1 (1974), 28–31.

6298 **Department of Employment.** *Government observations on the reports of youth employment services, the employment of women, and employment services and training.* London: H.M.S.O., 1974. 34p. (Cmnd. 5536.)

6299 **National Youth Employment Council.** *Final triennial report.* London: H.M.S.O., 1974. ix, 67p.

6300 **Black**, D. 'Work experience: a systematic approach.' *Br. J. Guid. Couns.*, IV, 1 (January 1976), 88–97.

6301 **Campling**, Jo. 'Jobs for new boys.' *New Soc.*, XXXVI (3 June 1976), 528–9.

6302 **Newell**, David. 'An employment project in Loughborough: the future role of Community Relations Councils.' *New Community*, IV (Winter–Spring 1975–76), 436–42.

6303 **Garside**, William Redvers. 'Juvenile unemployment and public policy between the wars.' *Econ. Hist. Rev.*, XXX (May 1977), 322–39.

6304 **Manpower Services Commission.** *Young people and work: report on the feasibility of a new programme of opportunities for unemployed young people.* London: The Commission, 1977. 63p.

6305 **Atkinson**, Frank. 'A report on job creation in museums 1976 to 1978.' *Mus. J.*, LXXVII (March 1978), 158–60.

6306 **Manpower Services Commission.** *Young people and work.* London: H.M.S.O., 1978. 80p. (Manpower studies 1978–1.)

6307 **Rolfe**, W. D. Ian. 'Special Temporary Employment (STEP) and Youth Opportunity Programmes (YOP) in museums.' *Mus. J.*, LXXXVIII (December 1978), 132–3.

6308 **Smith**, A. J. and **Thompson**, D. J. 'Work experience.' *B.A.C.I.E. J.*, XXXIII, 6 (June 1979), 100–101.
See also: 3555.

3. Industrial and Regional Manpower Planning

See also Part Six, II, B, 3; Part Six, II, C, 2–3; Part Six, II, D, 5–6; Part Seven, II, C; and Part Seven, II, E.

6309 **Farmer**, T. J. *The provisions of new job opportunities in areas of South Wales affected by colliery closures.* 1971. (M.Sc. thesis, University of Bath.)

6310 **Pellegrini**, J. G. *The effects of the selective employment tax on British manufacturing indus-*

tries. 1971. (Ph.D. thesis, London School of Economics.)

6311 **Gee**, F. A. *Homes and jobs for Londoners in new and expanding towns: a survey of Industrial Selection Scheme registrants.* London: H.M.S.O., 1972. vii, 111p.

6312 **Holmes**, R. C. *Employment in Wandsworth: a policy paper presented to Wandsworth Borough Council on behalf of the Planning Committee.* London: Wandsworth Borough Council, 1972. 33p.

6313 **MacKay**, R. R. 'Employment creation in the development areas.' *Scott. J. Polit. Econ.*, XIX, 3 (November 1972), 287–96.

6314 **Moxon**, J. W. J. 'The Industrial Development Certificate system and employment creation.' *Urb. Stud.*, IX (July 1972), 229–33.

6315 **Sleeper**, Robert D. 'S.E.T. and the shake-out: a note on the productivity effects of the Selective Employment Tax.' *Oxf. Econ. Pap.*, XXIX, 2 (July 1972), 197–211.

6316 **Hart**, R. A. 'Employment creation in the development areas: reply.' *Scott. J. Polit. Econ.*, XX (June 1973), 171–3.

6317 **MacKay**, R. R. 'Employment creation: a resurrection.' *Scott. J. Polit. Econ.*, XX (June 1973), 175–7.

6318 **Mukherjee**, Santosh. *Strathclyde employment and development agency: a proposal for discussion.* Glasgow: Scottish International Education Trust, 1973.

6319 **Reddaway**, W. B., **Glynn**, D. R. and **Sugden**, J. D. *Effects of Selective Employment Tax: final report.* Cambridge: Cambridge University Press, 1973. xv, 275p. (Cambridge University. Department of Applied Economics. Occasional papers 32.)

6320 **Böhning**, Wolf Rüdiger. 'Migration of workers as an element in employment policy.' *New Community*, II (Winter–Spring 1974), 6–25.

6321 **Camina**, Margaret M. 'Local authorities and the attraction of new employment: experience in East Anglia.' *Plann.*, LX (February 1974), 553–8.

6322 **Eversley**, David. 'Employment planning and income maintenance.' *Town Ctry Plann.*, XLIII (April 1975), 206–9.

6323 **Beaumont**, Philip B. *The operation of assisted labour mobility policy in a high unemployment region.* 1976. (Ph.D. thesis, University of Glasgow.)

6324 **Gripaios**, Peter. 'A new employment policy for London?' *Natl. Westminster Bank Q. Rev.* (August 1976), 37–45.

6325 **Holden**, K. and **Peel**, D. A. 'The "shake-out" hypothesis: a note.' *Oxf. Univ. Inst. Econ. Stat. Bull.*, XXXVIII (May 1976), 141–6.

6326 **Hughes**, John. *Industrial restructuring: some manpower aspects.* London: National Economic Development Office, 1976. iv, 62p. (Discussion papers 4.)

6327 **Manners**, Gerald. 'Regional policy rethink.' *Town City Plann.*, XLIV (April 1976), 208–14.

6328 **Beaumont**, Philip B. 'An assessment of subsidized relocation of worker policy in Britain.' *J. Ind. Relat.*, XIX, 1 (March 1977), 24–33.

6329 **Bowers**, J. K. and **Gunawardena**, A. 'Industrial Development Certificates and regional policy.' *Bull. Econ. Res.*, XXIX (November 1977), 112–22; XXX (May 1978), 3–13.

6330 **Allen**, Kevin and **Yuill**, Douglas. *Small area employment forecasting: data and problems.* London: Saxon House, 1978. 248p.

6331 **Lean**, Bill. 'Employment policies for inner London.' *Greater London Intell. J.*, XLI (1978), 19–23.

6332 **Campbell**, R. H. 'The Scottish Office and the special areas in the 1930's.' *Hist. J.*, XXII (March 1979), 167–83.

6333 **Dey**, E. M. *A study of the formulation and implementation of policies relating to redundancy and unemployment in Bristol 1970–72.* 1979. (Ph.D. thesis, University of Bristol.)

6334 **Ross**, Michael and **Walsh**, B. M. *Regional policy and the full employment target.* Dublin: Economic and Social Research Institute, 1979. ix, 53p.

See also: 3924; 3927; 4498; 4500; 6200; 6367.

4. Redundancy Payments

See also Part Six, II, D, 7; Part Six, IV, A, 3, d; Part Seven, II, E; and Part Seven, III, A.

6335 **Bulmer**, Martin I. A. 'Mining redundancy: a case study of the working of the Redundancy Payments Act in the Durham coalfield.' *Ind. Relat. J.*, II, 4 (Winter 1971), 3–21.

6336 **Department of Employment**. *The redundancy payments scheme.* London: H.M.S.O., 1971. 47p.

6337 **Farndale**, William Arthur James and **Cooper**, A. J. *The law on redundancy payments, with special reference to the National Health Service.* London: Ravenswood Publications, 1971. 111p.

6338 **Grunfeld**, Cyril. *The law of redundancy.* London: Sweet & Maxwell, 1971. xxiv, 279p.

6339 **Parker**, Stanley Robert, **Thomas**, C. G., **Ellis**, N. D. and **McCarthy**, William Edward John. *The effects of the Redundancy Payments Act.* London: H.M.S.O., 1971. ix, 225p. (Office of Population Censuses and Surveys. Social Surveys Division reports 438.)

6340 **Incomes Data Services**. *Redundancy part 3.* London: I.D.S., 1972. 16p. (I.D.S. study 36.)

6341 **Incomes Data Services**. *Redundancy part 4.* London: I.D.S., 1972. 16p. (I.D.S. study 41.)

6342 **Fryer**, Robert H. 'Myths of the Redundancy Payments Act.' *Ind. Law J.*, II, 1 (March 1973), 1–16.

6343 **Fryer**, Robert H. 'Redundancy values and public policy.' *Ind. Relat. J.*, IV, 2 (Summer 1973), 2–19.

6344 **Incomes Data Services**. *Redundancy part 5.* London: I.D.S., 1973. 16p. (I.D.S. study 61.)

6345 **Mukherjee**, Santosh. *Through no fault of their own: systems for handling redundancy in Britain, France and Germany.* London: Macdonald for Political & Economic Planning, 1973. 284p.

6346 **Aikin**, Olga. 'Short time problems.' *Pers. Manage.*, VI, 2 (February 1974), 48–50.

6347 **Harley**, Douglas. 'The basic facts of redundancy.' *J. Ind. Affairs*, I, 2 (March 1974), 47–8.

6348 **Cowan**, Nick. 'New rights for the redundant.' *Pers. Manage.*, VII, 10 (October 1975), 28–32.

6349 **Incomes Data Services**. *Redundancy 6.* London: I.D.S., 1975. 19p. (I.D.S. study 99.)

6350 **Daniel**, William Wentworth. 'The high price of redundancy payments.' *Pers. Manage.*, VIII, 9 (September 1976), 16–19.

6351 **Department of Employment**. *Employment Protection Act, 1975: procedure for handling redundancies.* London: The Department, 1976. 14p.

6352 **Freedland**, M. R. 'Employment protection: redundancy procedures and the E.E.C.' *Ind. Law J.*, V, 1 (March 1976), 24–34.

6353 **Incomes Data Services**. *Redundancy.* London: I.D.S., 1976. 21p. (I.D.S. study 120.)

6354 **Incomes Data Services**. *Redundancy source book.* London: I.D.S., 1977. 123p. (I.D.S. handbook 6.)

6355 **Incomes Data Services**. *Redundancy practice.* London: I.D.S., 1978. 20p. (I.D.S. study 178.)

6356 **Incomes Data Services**. *Redundancy schemes.* London: I.D.S., 1978. 21p. (I.D.S. study 175.)

6357 **Sampson**, A. A. 'Optimal redundancy compensation.' *Rev. Econ. Stud.*, XLV (October 1978), 447–52.

See also: 6415; 6417; 6420; 6441.

E. TRAINING AND RETRAINING

This section includes material on government support for vocational and industrial training narrowly defined, and on the retraining of disabled workers. It generally excludes material on education more broadly defined, the educational system and planning, and non-industrially based adult and worker education. Many popular management and professional journals also include material on training but this has generally been excluded. See also Part Three, II, K; Part Six, II, B, 3; Part Six, II, C, 7; Part Six, IV, D, 2; Part Seven, II, D, 3; and Part Seven, VII, B, 3.

6358 **Edwards**, M. *Industrial rehabilitation units: studies of two organisations.* 1971. (Ph.D. thesis, University of Loughborough.)

6359 **Garbutt**, D. 'A systems approach to the Industrial Training Act.' *Account. Bus. Res.*, II, 4 (Winter 1971), 60–66.

6360 **Hartley**, K. and **Mancini**, P. 'Budgeting and the training boards.' *Pers. Manage.*, III, 5 (May 1971), 38–42.

6361 **Johnson**, P. S. 'The economics of training and the industrial training boards.' *Moor. Wall Street* (Autumn 1971), 51–63.

6362 **Metcalfe**, Frank. *The idea of a training board.* London: Industrial, Educational and Research Foundation. [1971]. 12p. (Discussion paper 4.)

6363 **Perrigo**, A. E. B. *The Industrial Training Act and management training, with particular reference to the needs of the small firms.* 1971. (Ph.D. thesis, University of Aston.)

6364 **Pettman**, Barrie Owen. *Attitudes of engineering firms towards the E.I.T.B.'s previous levy-grant schemes.* Bradford: Institute of Scientific Business, 1971. 8, [2]p.

6365 **Pettman**, Barrie Owen. *A comparison of attitudes of engineering firms to the importance of the Industrial Training Act, 1964 for the country and their firm.* Bradford: Institute of Scientific Business, 1971. 33p.

6366 **Pettman**, Barrie Owen. *The Industrial Training Act and the industrial training boards: history, machinery, progress and criticisms.* Bradford: Institute of Scientific Business, 1971. 114p.

6367 **Price**, J. B. *The role of government training centres, with special reference to North Wales.* 1971. (M.A. thesis, University of Liverpool.)

6368 **Stewart**, J. G. 'Adult retraining: the government's role.' *B.A.C.I.E. J.*, XXV, 4 (December 1971), 112–16.

6369 **Day**, N. L. *Further education and employment: a case study of technical education and industrial employment.* London: Society for Research into Higher Education, 1972. 91p.

6370 **Department of Employment**. *Training for the future: a plan for discussion.* London: The Department, 1972. 80p.

6371 **Engineering Industry Training Board**. *The government's proposals for industrial training.* London: The Board, 1972. 8p. (Information papers 31.)

6372 *The Factory Education Bill of 1843.* New York: Arno, 1972. (British labour struggles: contemporary pamphlets 1727–1850.) First published 1843.

6373 **Hughes**, James J. 'The role of manpower retraining programmes: a critical look at retraining in the United Kingdom.' *Br. J. Ind. Relat.*, X, 2 (July 1972), 206–23.

6374 **Hunt**, A., **Fox**, J. and **Bradley**, M. *Post-training careers of government training centre trainees: an enquiry carried out in 1968 and 1969.* London: H.M.S.O., 1972. iii, 291p.

6375 **Institute of Personnel Management**. *Training for the future: statement by the I.P.M. on the government's consultative document.* London: I.P.M., 1972. 13p.

6376 **Johnson**, P. S. 'Industrial training boards

in the U.K.: model for Australia?' *J. Ind. Relat.*, xiv, 2 (June 1972), 101–12.

6377 **Malm**, F. T. 'Britain's Training Act: a manpower revolution.' *Ind. Relat.*, xi, 2 (May 1972), 245–59.

6378 **Pettman**, Barrie Owen. 'In partial defence of the industrial training boards: some criticisms examined.' *Br. J. Ind. Relat.*, x, 2 (July 1972), 224–39.

6379 **Pettman**, Barrie Owen. 'Some managerial attitudes in the context of the Industrial Training Act.' *Ind. Relat. J.*, iii, 3 (Autumn 1972), 60–65.

6380 **Road Transport Industry Training Board.** *Manpower in the seventies: a manpower plan for the road transport industry.* London: The Board, 1972. 144p.

6381 **Salford University.** *Unemployment and occupational training.* Salford: The University, 1972. 63p.

6382 **Broadhurst**, Alison. 'Disabled persons and the law.' *Ind. Commer. Train.*, v, 12 (December 1973), 578–81.

6383 **Department of Employment.** *Employment and training: government proposals.* London: H.M.S.O., 1973. 13p. (Cmnd. 5250.)

6384 **Evans**, E. W. 'The National Training Agency and manpower policy.' Pettman, B. (ed.). *Training and retraining.* 1973. p. 55–60.

6385 **Fyfe**, John. 'The government's proposals on training for the future.' Pettman, B. (ed.). *Training and retraining.* 1973. p. 29–32.

6386 **Hartley**, K. and **Mancini**, P. 'The Industrial Training Act and the hotel and catering industry: a case study.' *Ind. Relat. J.*, iv, 2 (Summer 1973), 37–44.

6387 **Hughes**, James J. 'Britain's Training Act: a manpower revolution?' *Ind. Relat.*, xii, 3 (October 1973), 352–3.

6388 **Hughes**, James J. 'In defence of the Industrial Training Act.' *J. Ind. Relat.*, xxi, 2 (April 1973), 126–4.

6389 **Pettman**, Barrie Owen (ed.). *Training and retraining: a basis for the future.* London: Transcriptor, 1973. 135p.

6390 **Rees**, A. M. 'Trade union officials and government training centres.' *Br. J. Ind. Relat.*, xi, 2 (July 1973), 229–41.

6391 **Showler**, Brian. 'The training needs of individuals and the Training Opportunities Scheme.' Pettman, B. (ed.). *Training and retraining.* 1973. p. 45–54.

6392 **Walsh**, B. 'Training managers to take account of recent legislation.' *Ind. Commer. Train.*, v, 3 (March 1973), 119–34.

6393 **Wellens**, John. 'The Employment and Training Bill.' *Ind. Commer. Train.*, v, 4 (April 1973), 162–6.

6394 **Ziderman**, Adrian and **Driver**, C. 'A Markov chain model of the benefits of participating in government training schemes.' *Manchr. Sch. Econ. Soc. Stud.*, xli (December 1973), 401–17.

6395 **Cassels**, J. 'The work of the Training Services Agency.' *Ind. Commer. Train.*, vi, 4

(April 1974), 154–9.

6396 **Industrial and Commercial Training.** 'Training Services Agency: a five year plan.' *Ind. Commer. Train.*, vi, 6 (June 1974), 270–84.

6397 **Manpower Services Commission.** *The Training Services Agency: a five-year plan.* London: H.M.S.O., 1974. vi, 38p.

6398 **Pettman**, Barrie Owen and **Showler**, Brian. 'Government vocational training schemes in Great Britain.' *Int. J. Soc. Econ.*, i, 2 (1974), 184–96.

6399 **Sharpa**, P. H. 'The Training Services Agency and exception criteria: formula for success or failure?' *Train. Off.*, x, 3 (March 1974), 63–9.

6400 **Smith**, J. M. 'Age and retraining.' *Occup. Psychol.*, xlvii, 3–4 (1974), 141–7.

6401 **Smith**, J. M. 'Older workers retrained.' *New Soc.*, xxix (4 July 1974), 16–17.

6402 **Soothill**, K. *Prisoner's release: a study of the employment of ex-prisoners.* London: Allen & Unwin, 1974. 319p.

6403 **Taylor**, Robert. 'A normal job: training for disabled and mentally handicapped school leavers.' *New Soc.*, xxix (4 July 1974), 19–20.

6404 **Webster**, Pat. *Redeployment and re-training.* London: Working Together Campaign, 1974. 16p.

6405 **Woodhall**, Maureen. 'Investment in industrial training: effects of the Industrial Training Act on the volume and costs of training.' *Br. J. Ind. Relat.*, xii, 1 (March 1974), 71–90.

6406 **Brennan**, E. J. T. *Education for national efficiency: the contribution of Sidney and Beatrice Webb.* London: Athlone, 1975. 208p.

6407 **Department of Employment Gazette.** 'Employment rehabilitation, 1974–75.' *Dep. Employment Gaz.*, lxxxiii, 11 (November 1975), 1120–22.

6408 **Hall**, Kenneth and **Miller**, Isobel. *Retraining and tradition: the skilled worker in an era of change.* London: Allen & Unwin, 1975. 175p.

6409 **Ziderman**, Adrian. 'Costs and benefits of manpower training programmes in Great Britain.' *Br. J. Ind. Relat.*, xiii, 2 (July 1975), 223–44.

6410 **Ziderman**, Adrian and **Walder**, A. 'Trade unions and the acceptability of G.T.C. trainees: some survey results.' *Br. J. Ind. Relat.*, xiii, 1 (March 1975), 78–85.

6411 **British Association for Commercial and Industrial Education.** *Industrial training boards: progress report seven.* London: B.A.C.I.E., 1976. 23p.

6412 **Incomes Data Services.** *Training.* London: I.D.S., 1976. 17p. (I.D.S. study 136.)

6413 **Perry**, Peter John Charles. *The Industrial Training Act, 1964: its origins, purposes, provisions and effects.* 1976. (Ph.D. thesis, Birkbeck College, University of London.)

6414 **Thorne**, Paul and **Bolton**, Mac. 'New skills for redundant steel workers.' *Dep. Employment Gaz.*, lxxxiv, 1 (January 1976), 13–15.

6415 **Warr**, Peter Bryan. 'Redundancy, retraining and reincarnation.' *Pers. Manage.*, VIII, 11 (November 1976), 23–6.

6416 **Jarvis**, B. 'What should we do with the ITBs?' *J. Eur. Ind. Train.*, I, 6 (June 1977), 2–7.

6417 **Warr**, Peter Bryan and **Lovatt**, J. 'Retraining after redundancy.' *J. Occup. Psychol.*, L, 2 (1977), 67–84.

6418 **Berthoud**, Richard. 'Tapping the talents of skillcentre trainees.' *Pers. Manage.*, X, 7 (July 1978), 33–6.

6419 **Berthoud**, Richard. *Training adults for skilled jobs: skill centre training and local labour markets.* London: Policy Studies Institute, 1978. 121p. (Broadsheet 575.)

6420 **Dagger**, G. 'Helping small engineering firms.' *Ind. Commerc. Train.*, X, 3 (March 1978), 120–23.

6421 **Department of Employment Gazette**. 'The Employment Rehabilitation Centres.' *Dep. Employment Gaz.*, LXXXVI, 1 (January 1978), 34–6.

6422 **Lasko**, Roger. 'The Work Experience Programme.' *Dep. Employment Gaz.*, LXXXVI, 3 (March 1978), 294–7.

6423 **Smith**, Sheila and **Lasko**, Roger. 'After the Work Experience Programme: following their progress.' *Dep. Employment Gaz.*, LXXXVI, 8 (August 1978), 901–7.

6424 **Manpower Services Commission**, Training Services Division. *T.O.P.S. review 1978.* London: The Commission, 1979. 60p.

See also: 13; 237; 3399; 3422; 5487.

III. REGULATION OF TERMS AND CONDITIONS OF EMPLOYMENT

A. INDIVIDUAL EMPLOYEE–EMPLOYER RELATIONSHIP

1. General

This section includes general works on such topics as the law surrounding the contract of employment and the payment of wages. More specialised references relating to discipline and dismissal are included in Part Seven, III, A, 2; those dealing with redundancy payments are in Part Seven, II, D, 4; and those dealing with the employer's liability for industrial injury are in Part Seven, VII, B, 3. See also Part Six, IV, A, 1.

6425 **Flanders**, Allan. 'Terms of employment regulated by legislation in the United Kingdom.' Conference on Labour Law in Europe with Special Reference to the Common Market, 1962, London. *Report.* London: Stevens for the British Institute of International and Comparative Law, 1962. p. 13–16.

6426 **Aikin**, Olga and **Reid**, Judith. *Employment, welfare and safety at work.* Harmondsworth: Penguin, 1971. 416p. (Penguin labour law 1.)

6427 **Hepple**, Robert Alexander and **O'Higgins**, Paul. *Individual employment law: an introduction.* London: Sweet & Maxwell, 1971. xxiii, 203p.

6428 **Whitesides**, K. R. *The industrial tribunals: a study in the applications of administrative law and justice.* 1971. (M.Phil. thesis, University of Nottingham.)

6429 **Burney**, E. and **Wainwright**, D. *After four years: a practical guide to the Race Relations Act after four years: what it says and what it means.* London: Runnymede Trust, 1972. 11p.

6430 **Department of Employment**. *Contracts of Employment Act 1963: a revised guide incorporating changes arising from the Industrial Relations Act 1971.* London: The Department, 1972. 28p.

6431 **Dix**, D. K. and **Crump**, D. W. *Dix on contracts of employment with special reference to the Contracts of Employment, Redundancy Payments and Industrial Relations Acts.* London: Butterworth, 1972. xli, 643p. Fourth edition.

6432 **Lawrence**, Susanne. 'Civil rights in employment.' *Pers. Manage.*, IV, 12 (December 1972), 30–32, 36.

6433 **Lester**, A. and **Bindman**, G. *Race and law.* Harmondsworth: Penguin, 1972. 491p.

6434 **Reid**, R. 'Industrial tribunals and the law.' *Juridical Rev.* (April 1972), 32–49.

6435 **Schofield**, Peter. 'Liability for "misinformation" and the consultant employee.' *Ind. Law J.*, I, 2 (June 1972), 84–94.

6436 **Greenhaigh**, R. M. *Industrial tribunals: a practical guide.* London: Institute of Personnel Management, 1973. 219p.

6437 **Industrial Society**. *Security of earnings and employment.* London: The Society, 1973. 22p. (Survey and reports 183.)

6438 **Lambert**, P. 'The code of practice and the foundry industry.' *Pers. Rev.*, III, 4 (Winter 1973), 36–50.

6439 **Miller**, *Sir* Bernard. 'Company law: the position of employees.' *Ind. Participation*, DLI (Spring 1973), 9–12.

6440 **Broadhurst**, Alison. 'Fair employment legislation.' *Ind. Commer. Train.*, VI, 5 (May 1974), 212–15.

6441 **Hillier**, Andrew. *Contracts of employment: engagement, termination and redundancy.* Harrow: Training for Business Ltd., 1974. iii, 80p. With supplement, 1976. 29p.

6442 **Weekes**, Brian C. M. and **Mellish**, Michael. 'Industrial employment rights.' *Soc. Comment.*, XXXIII, 9 (September 1974), 10–11.

6443 **Brooks**, Dennis. 'Migrants, work and the law: railways, railwaymen and race.' *New Community*, IV (Winter–Spring 1974–5), 37–45.

6444 **Carter**, Mark Bonham. 'Migrants, work and the law: race, sex and the law.' *New Community*, IV (Winter–Spring 1974–5), 1–4.

6445 **Kohler**, David. 'Migrants, work and the law: a ballot on race laws.' *New Community*, IV (Winter–Spring 1974–5), 62–4.

6446 **Roots**, Paul J. 'Keeping up with employee rights.' *Pers. Manage.*, VII, 9 (September 1975), 31–5.

6447 **Smith**, David J. 'Migrants, work and the law: job discrimination and the function of law.' *New Community*, IV (Winter–Spring 1974–5), 55–61.

6448 **Stewart**, Margaret. *Employment of minorities in Britain: an employer's guide*. Epping: Gower, 1975. xiii, 146p.

6449 **Whitesides**, Keith Robert and **Hawker**, Geoffrey. *Industrial tribunals*. London: Sweet & Maxwell, 1975. xvi, 118p.

6450 **Baker**, C. D. 'Employment protection: individual rights.' *Ind. Law J.*, V, 2 (June 1976), 65–79.

6451 **Freedland**, M. R. *Contract of employment*. Oxford: Clarendon Press, 1976. xliii, 398p.

6452 **Greenhaigh**, Roger. 'Tribunals at work.' *Pers. Manage.*, VIII, 5 (May 1976), 26–9.

6453 **Hepple**, Robert Alexander. 'Workers' rights in mergers and takeovers: the E.E.C. proposals.' *Ind. Law J.*, V, 4 (December 1976), 197–210.

6454 **Hepple**, Robert Alexander and **O'Higgins**, Paul. *Employment law*. London: Sweet & Maxwell, 1976. 337p.
       Second edition of *Individual employment law*.

6455 **Incomes Data Services**. *Employment contracts*. London: I.D.S., 1976. 119p. (I.D.S. handbook 2.)

6456 **Incomes Data Services**. *The new race law and employment*. London: I.D.S., 1976. 92p. (I.D.S. handbook 4.)

6457 **Leighton**, P. and **Dumville**, S. 'The employment contract.' *Pers. Manage.*, VIII, 12 (December 1976), 23–5.

6458 **Napier**, B. W. 'Individual employment law within the British fishing industry.' *Juridical Rev.*, XXI (December 1976), 189–209.

6459 **O'Higgins**, Paul. *Workers' rights*. London: Arrow, 1976. 96p. (Trade union industrial studies.)

6460 **Carby**, Keith and **Thakur**, Manab. *No problems here? Management and the multi-racial workforce including a guide to the Race Relations Act, 1976*. London: Institute of Personnel Management, 1977. 156p.

6461 **Carnell**, Reg. *Employment law progress report*. London: Workers' Educational Association, 1977. 13p. (Studies for trade unionists III, 12.)

6462 **Janner**, Greville. 'Service contract: a shield against the shake-out.' *Pers. Manage.*, IX, 9 (September 1977), 32–4.

6463 **Leighton**, P. E. and **Dumville**, S. M. 'From statement to contract: some effects of the Contracts of Employment Act 1972.' *Ind. Law J.*, VI, 3 (September 1977), 133–48.

6464 **Lustgarten**, Lawrence. 'Problems of proof in employment discrimination cases.' *Ind. Law J.*, VI, 4 (December 1977), 212–28.

6465 **Marsh**, G. Barrie. 'Employment contracts today.' *Natl. Westminster Bank Q. Rev.* (November 1977), 56–68.

6466 **Rose**, F. D. 'Liability for an employee's assaults.' *Mod. Law Rev.*, XXX, 4 (July 1977), 420–39.

6467 **Best**, S. 'Industrial tribunals.' *Ind. Soc.*, XIV, 2 (March–April 1978), 18–20.

6468 **Egan**, Bowes. *The industrial tribunals handbook*. London: New Commercial Publishing Co., 1978. 368p.

6469 **Forde**, M. 'Transnational employment and employment protection.' *Ind. Law J.*, VII, 4 (December 1978), 228–38.

6470 **Hepple**, B. A. and **Napier**, B. W. 'Temporary workers and the law.' *Ind. Law J.*, VII, 2 (June 1978), 84–99.

6471 **Incomes Data Services**. *Employee rights: the money side*. London: I.D.S., 1978. 99p. (I.D.S. handbook 10.)

6472 **Ingman**, Terence. 'The rise and fall of the doctrine of common employment.' *Juridical Rev.*, XXIII (August 1978), 106–25.

6473 **Phillips**, the Hon. Mr Justice. 'Some notes on the Employment Appeal Tribunal.' *Ind. Law J.*, VII, 3 (September 1978), 137–42.

6474 **Capstick**, J. B. 'Industrial tribunals.' *Pers. Manage.*, XI, 12 (December 1979), 29–32.

6475 **Hewitt**, Patricia. *Your rights at work: a practical guide*. London: National Council for Civil Liberties, 1979. 84p.

See also: 1079; 2512; 3064; 5692; 6252; 6253; 6842; 6856.

2. Discipline and Dismissal

6476 **Connelly**, Tom. 'Dismissals and the Industrial Relations Act 1971.' *New Community*, I (October 1971), 75–6.

6477 **Shahaf**, E. *Disciplinary provisions governing seamen employed in the Merchant Marine in England and in Israel*. 1971. (M.Phil. thesis, University of Southampton.)

6478 **Anderman**, Steven Daniel. *Voluntary dismissal procedure and the Industrial Relations Act*. London: Political & Economic Planning, 1972. 151p. (Broadsheet 538.)

6479 **Freedland**, M. R. 'The burden of proof in claims of unfair dismissal.' *Ind. Law J.*, I, 1 (March 1972), 20–28.

6480 **Walsh**, B. 'The avoidance of unfair dismissals.' *Ind. Commer. Train.*, IV, 8 (August 1972), 400–403.

6481 **Anderman**, Steven Daniel. *Unfair dismissals*

and the law. London: Institute of Personnel Management, 1973. 184p.

6482 **Ashdown**, R. T. and **Baker**, K. H. *In working order: a study of industrial discipline.* London: H.M.S.O., 1973. vii, 68p. (Department of Employment. Manpower papers 6.)

6483 **Baker**, K. H. and **Ashdown**, R. T. 'Disciplinary procedures: practice and law.' *Dep. Employment Gaz.*, LXXXI, 7 (July 1973), 643–8.

6484 **MacKie**, Anne and **Blair**, Jon. 'Europe, Britain and collective dismissals.' *Pers. Manage.*, V, 10 (October 1973), 32–5.

6485 **Williams**, Kevin. *Remedies on dismissal.* 1973. (LL.M. thesis, University of Warwick.)

6486 **Williams**, Kevin. 'Sacked unfairly.' *New Soc.*, XXV (2 August 1973), 275–7.

6487 **Aikin**, Olga. 'A question of unfair dismissal.' *Pers. Manage.*, VI, 1 (January 1974), 20–24.

6488 **Cockerill**, Alan J. and **Hodkinson**, Christopher. *A guide to unfair dismissal.* Liverpool: Christopher James, 1974. 131p.

6489 **Department of Employment**. *Unfair dismissal: a guide to the unfair dismissal provisions of the [Trade Union and Labour Relations] Act.* London: The Department, 1974. 22p.

6490 **Long**, G. 'Dismissals in Europe.' *Pers. Manage.*, VI, 2 (February 1974), 38–9, 43.

6491 **Department of Trade**. *Discipline in the fishing industry: report of the Working Group.* London: H.M.S.O., 1975. 45p. Chairman: M. J. Service.

6492 **Department of Trade**. *Discipline in the Merchant Navy: report of the Working Group.* London: H.M.S.O., 1975. 41p. Chairman: L. F. Standen.

6493 **Jackson**, Dudley. 'Compensation for loss of pension rights in cases of unfair dismissal.' *Ind. Law J.*, IV, 1 (March 1975), 24–33.

6494 **Jackson**, Dudley. *Unfair dismissal: how and why the law works.* Cambridge: Cambridge U.P., 1975. viii, 92p. (Cambridge University. Department of Applied Economics. Papers in industrial relations and labour 1.)

6495 **Lambert**, W. R. 'Drink and work – discipline in industrial South Wales c.1800–1870.' *Welsh Hist. Rev.*, VII, 3 (June 1975), 289–306.

6496 **Williams**, Kevin. 'Job security and unfair dismissal.' *Mod. Law Rev.*, XXXVIII (May 1975), 292–310.

6497 **Carby-Hall**, Joseph Roger. 'A study in three termination aspects of modern employment.' Carby-Hall, J. R. (ed.). *Studies in labour law.* 1976. p. 202–80.

6498 **Daru**, C. C. *The problem of reinstatement of employees in public corporations in India and the United Kingdom.* 1976. (LL.M. thesis, University of Keele.)

6499 **Department of Employment Gazette**. 'Unfair dismissal applications in 1975.' *Dep. Employment Gaz.*, LXXXIV, 6 (June 1976), 590–94.

6500 **Gill**, R. W. T. and **Taylor**, D.S. 'Discipline and grievance interviews.' *J. Eur. Train.*, V (1976), 217–27.

6501 **Incomes Data Services**. *Unfair dismissal.* London: Unwin, 1976. 119p. (I.D.S. handbook 1.)

6502 **McGlyne**, John E. *Unfair dismissal cases.* London: Butterworth. First edition. 1976. xix, 279p. Second edition. 1979. xxxii, 362p.

6503 **Mellish**, Michael and **Collis-Squires**, N. 'Legal and social norms in discipline and dismissal.' *Ind. Law J.*, V, 3 (September 1976), 164–77.

6504 **Advisory Conciliation and Arbitration Service**. *Disciplinary practice and procedures in employment.* London: A.C.A.S., 1977. 5p. (A.C.A.S. codes of practice 1.)

6505 **Egan**, Bowes. *Dismissals: the complete practical guide incorporating the encyclopaedia of dismissals rules and practice.* London: New Commercial Publishing Co., 1977. 383p.

6506 **Foxen**, Trevor. *Effective discipline.* London: Industrial Society, 1977. 30p. (Notes for managers 27.)

6507 **Kelway**, John. *An employers' guide to fair dismissal and the maternity provisions.* London: Kogan Page, 1977. 28p.

6508 **Anderman**, Steven Daniel. *The law of unfair dismissal.* London: Butterworth. 1978. xxxvii, 378p. With appendices on procedure by John H. Angel.

6509 **Bagust-Chang**, M. *Dismissal and misconduct: a study of the legal concept of employees' misconduct.* 1978. (LL.M. thesis, University of Edinburgh.)

6510 **Elias**, Patrick. 'Unravelling the concept of dismissal.' *Ind. Law J.*, VII, 1 (March 1978), 16–29; VII, 2 (June 1978), 100–112.

6511 **Incomes Data Services**. *Unfair dismissal updated.* London: I.D.S., 1978. 199p. (I.D.S. handbook 12.)

6512 **Kloss**, Diana. 'Criminals at work.' *Crim. Law Rev.*, XXV, 5 (May 1978), 280–86.

6513 **Warburton**, John. *Open and positive: an account of how John Warburton came out at school and the consequences.* London: Gay Teachers' Group, 1978. 71p.

6514 **Dickens**, Linda. 'Unfair dismissal applications and the industrial tribunal system.' *Ind. Relat. J.*, IX, 4 (Winter 1978), 4–18.

6515 **Dickens**, Linda. 'Unfair dismissal applications and the industrial tribunal system.' *Dep. Employment Gaz.*, LXXXVII, 3 (March 1979), 233–5.

6516 **Eccles**, G. W. *Unfair dismissal.* London: Institute of Chartered Accountants in England and Wales, 1979. 28p. (Accountants digests 83.)

6517 **Incomes Data Services**. *Handling dismissals.* London: I.D.S., 1979. 80p. (I.D.S. handbook 15.)

6518 **Institute of Personnel Management**. *Dis-*

ciplinary procedures and practice. London: The Institute, 1979. 161p. (Information reports 28.)

6519 **Whincup**, Michael. 'Discipline and dismissal: legal aspects.' Bosanquet, N. (ed.). *Industrial relations in the N.H.S.* 1979. p. 23–54.

See also: 1575; 1652; 2165.

B. SAFETY, HEALTH, AND WELFARE

This section includes the literature relating to the governmental regulation of safety, health, and welfare. Literature describing the conditions of safety, health, and welfare is classified in Part Six, IV, D; and that on the effect of length of working hours on safety and health in Part Six, IV, B. See also Part Seven, VII, B, 3.

6520 **Department of Trade and Industry** and **Ministry of Technology.** *The law relating to safety and health in mines and quarries.* London: H.M.S.O., 1970–72. 4v.

6521 **Henriques**, Ursula Ruth Quixano. *The early factory acts and their enforcement.* London: Historical Association, 1971. 22p. (Appreciations in history 1.)

6522 **Samuels**, Harry and **Stewart-Pearson**, Neville. *The Offices, Shops and Railway Premises Act 1963.* London: Knight, 1971. xviii, 219p. Second edition.

6523 **Vandore**, Peter K. 'The mischief of the section.' *Juridical Rev.*, XVI (April 1971), 20–58. Factory law.

6524 **Atherley**, G. R. C. 'Action on occupational deafness in the United Kingdom.' *Int. Labour Rev.*, CV, 5 (May 1972), 463–74.

6525 **Broadhurst**, Alison. 'Robens: a missed opportunity?' *Ind. Commer. Train.*, IV, 12 (December 1972), 595–7.

6526 **Department of Employment**, Committee on Safety and Health at Work. *Safety and health at work: report of the Committee … 1970–72.* London: H.M.S.O., 1972. 2v. (Cmnd. 5034.) Chairman: Lord Robens.

6527 *The Factory Act of 1818–1819.* New York: Arno, 1972. (British labour struggles: contemporary pamphlets 1727–1850.)

6528 *The Factory Act of 1833: 1833–1834.* New York: Arno, 1972. (British labour struggles: contemporary pamphlets 1727–1850.)

6529 **Fife**, I. and **Machin**, E. A. *Redgrave's Factory Acts.* London: Butterworth, 1972. lxvi, 1537p. Twenty-second edition.

6530 **Howells**, R. W. L. 'The Robens report.' *Ind. Law J.*, I, 4 (December 1972), 185–96.

6531 *Improving the lot of the chimney sweeps 1785–1840.* New York: Arno, 1972. (British labour struggles: contemporary pamphlets 1727–1850.)

6532 **Powell**, Philip I. and **Slater**, Doreen. 'What is a safe system of work?' *Ind. Law J.*, I, 3

(September 1972), 135–42.

6533 **Broadhurst**, Alison. 'A neo-classical safety bill?' *Ind. Commer. Train.*, V, 9 (September 1973), 425–8.

6534 **Denyer**, Roderick Lawrence. *Industrial law and its application in the factory.* London: Macmillan for the Institution of Works Managers, 1973. 79p.

6535 **Department of Employment.** *Code of practice for reducing the exposure of employed persons to noise.* London: H.M.S.O., 1973. 33p.

6536 **Department of Employment.** *Proposals for a Safety and Health at Work Bill.* London: The Department, 1973. 35p.

6537 **Factory Inspectorate.** *Lead: code of practice for health precautions.* London: H.M.S.O., 1979. 50p.

6538 **Fife**, Ian and **Machin**, Edward Anthony. *Redgrave's offices and shops, together with agricultural, railway and offshore installation safety.* London: Butterworth, 1973. lxvii, 619p. Second edition.

6539 **Samuels**, Alec. 'Liability for noise at work.' *Ind. Law J.*, II, 2 (June 1973), 78–87.

6540 **Woolf**, Anthony D. 'Robens report: the wrong approach?' *Ind. Law J.*, II, 2 (June 1973), 88–95.

6541 **Howells**, R. W. L. 'Worker participation in safety I: the development of legal rights.' *Ind. Law J.*, III, 2 (June 1974), 87–95.

6542 **Jackson**, James. *Health and safety: the new law.* London: Commercial Publishing Co., 1974. 108p.

6543 **Kinnersly**, Pat. 'The politics of safety.' *Occup. Saf. Health*, IV, 6 (June 1974), 8–11.

6544 **Lewis**, David. 'Worker participation in safety II: an industrial relations approach.' *Ind. Law. J.*, III, 2 (June 1974), 96–104.

6545 **Ritson**, John. 'Safety and health at work.' *J. Ind. Affairs*, I, 2 (March 1974), 56–9.

6546 **Coles**, R. R. A. 'The medico-legal aspects of noise hazards to hearing.' *Medicoleg. J.*, III, 1 (1975), 3–19.

6547 **Grime**, R. P. *Law of noise-induced hearing loss and its compensation.* Southampton: University of Southampton, Institute of Sound and Vibration Research, Wolfson Unit for Noise and Vibration Control, 1975. 21p.

6548 **Howells**, Richard W. L. and **Barrett**, Brenda. *The Health and Safety at Work Act: a guide for managers.* London: Institute of Personnel Management, 1975. 117p.

6549 **Lewis**, Norman. 'Health and Safety at Work Act 1974.' *Mod. Law Rev.*, XXXVIII (July 1975), 442–8.

6550 **Mitchell**, Ewan. *Employer's guide to the law on health, safety and welfare at work.* London: Business Books, 1975. xvii, 394p. Second edition. 1978. 471p.

6551 **Wrigglesworth**, Frank E. B. and **Earl**, Barry. *Guide to the Health and Safety at Work Act.* London: Industrial Society, 1975. 31p.

6552 **Locke**, J. H. 'Information from the Health and Safety Executive.' *Aslib Proc.*, XXVIII, 1 (January 1976), 8–16.

6553 **McKown**, R. and **Parris**, J. *Comprehensive guide to factory law: a classified guide to the requirements of the Factories Act and other legislation affecting factories and allied premises including construction sites, docks and offices.* London: George Godwin, 1976. ix, 176p.
Sixth edition.

6554 **Rose**, Paul. 'Surveying the new safety structure.' *Pers. Manage.*, VIII, 11 (November 1976), 34–7.

6555 **Wood**, J. C. 'Health and safety at work.' Carby-Hall, J. R. (ed.). *Studies in labour law.* 1976. p. 11–34.

6556 **Barrett**, Brenda. 'Safety representatives, industrial relations and hard times.' *Ind. Law J.*, VI, 3 (September 1977), 165–78.

6557 **Grant**, S. 'Implementation and enforcement of the law.' British Cast Iron Research Association. *The working environment in iron foundries.* 1977. p. 2.1–2.11.

6558 **Hamilton**, D. 'Reacting positively to HASWA.' *Occup. Saf. Health*, VII, 3 (March 1977), 46–8.

6559 **Health and Safety Commission.** *Proposals for the notification of accidents and dangerous occurrences: consultation document.* London: H.M.S.O., 1977. ii, 6p.

6560 **Kelly**, M. J. 'The law as it applies to working conditions in iron foundries in the UK.' British Cast Iron Research Association. *The working environment in iron foundries.* 1977. p. 1.1–1.7.

6561 **Kitchen**, Jonathan. *Labour law and off-shore oil.* London: Croom Helm, 1977. 261p.

6562 **Lewis**, David. 'The Health and Safety at Work Act 1974: new opportunities for worker participation.' Phillips, Jennifer (ed.). *Safety at work.* 1977. p. 19–34.

6563 **Broadhurst**, Alison. *The Health and Safety at Work Act in practice.* London: Heyden, 1978. 245p.

6564 **Broadhurst**, Alison. 'Health and safety legislation.' *Works Manage.*, XXIX, 10 (October 1978), 73–4.

6565 **Guest**, K. 'Meeting the code on noise.' *Occup. Saf. Health*, VIII (April 1978), 16–18.

6566 **Health and Safety Commission.** *Control of lead at work: draft regulations and draft approved code of practice.* London: H.M.S.O., 1978, vi, 36p.

6567 **Health and Safety Commission.** *Genetic manipulation: regulations and guidance notes.* London: H.M.S.O., 1978. 14p.

6568 **Health and Safety Commission.** *Health and safety at work (diving operations) regulations.* London: H.M.S.O., 1978. 20p.

6569 **Health and Safety Commission.** *Ionising radiations: proposals for provisions on radiological protection.* London: H.M.S.O., 1978. 36p.

6570 **Health and Safety Commission.** *Notification of occupational ill health.* London: H.M.S.O., 1978. 10p.

6571 **Health and Safety Commission**, Advisory Committee on Asbestos. *Asbestos: measuring and monitoring of asbestos in air.* London: H.M.S.O., 1978. 30p.

6572 **H.M. Factory Inspectorate.** *Lighting in offices, shops and railway premises.* London: H.M.S.O., 1978. 32p.

6573 **John**, Angela V. 'Colliery legislation and its consequences: 1842 and the women miners of Lancashire.' *Bull. John Rylands Univ. Lib. Manchr.*, LXI, 1 (Autumn 1978), 78–114.

6574 **Lewis**, Roy. 'Nuclear power and employment rights.' *Ind. Law J.*, VII, 1 (March 1978), 1–15.

6575 **Beaumont**, Philip B. *Safety legislation: the trade union response.* Leeds: Universities of Leeds and Nottingham/Institute of Personnel Management, 1979. 32p.

6576 **Equal Opportunities Commission.** *Health and safety legislation: should we distinguish between men and women?* London: The Commission, 1979. 261p.

6577 **Health and Safety Commission.** *Proposals for dangerous substances (conveyance by road) regulations.* London: H.M.S.O., 1979. 76p.

6578 **Health and Safety Commission.** *Proposals for notification of accidents, dangerous occurrences and ill health regulations and guidance notes.* London: H.M.S.O., 1979. ii, 24p.

6579 **Health and Safety Commission.** *Work with asbestos insulation and sprayed coatings: draft approved code of practice and draft guidance notes.* London: H.M.S.O., 1979. 30p.

6580 **Health and Safety Executive.** *A guide to agricultural legislation.* London: H.M.S.O., 1979. iv, 50p.

6581 **Health and Safety Executive.** *A guide to the 1963 OSRP Act.* London: H.M.S.O., 1979. vi, 38p.

6582 **Health and Safety Executive.** *Molten metal and water explosions.* London: H.M.S.O., 1979. 24p.

6583 **Health and Safety Executive.** *Packaging and labelling of dangerous substances: regulations and guidance notes.* London: H.M.S.O., 1979. iv, 24p.

6584 **Whiteside**, Noelle. 'Welfare insurance and casual labour: a study of administrative intervention in industrial employment, 1906–26.' *Econ. Hist. Rev.*, XXXII, 4 (November 1979), 507–22.

See also: 5753; 5788; 5870; 5886.

IV. REGULATION OF WAGES AND SALARIES

A. INCOMES POLICIES

This section includes works dealing with the state's attempts to regulate wages. All reports of the National Board for Prices and Incomes were included in G. S. Bain and G. B. Woolven, *A Bibliography of British Industrial Relations*, 1979. The more general reports of official bodies such as the

Pay Board have been classified here; those dealing with specific industries, occupations, and topics have generally been classified at Part Six, III. See also Part Six, I; and Part Six, III, A.

6585 **Allen**, Rodney. 'Concerning incomes policy.' *Moor. Wall Street* (Spring 1971), 4–23.

6586 **Bell**, G. 'Incomes policy: the British experience.' *Bus. Econ.*, VI, 1 (January 1971), 18–22.

6587 **Blackaby**, Frank Thomas. 'Incomes policies and inflation.' *Natl. Inst. Econ. Rev.*, LVIII (November 1971), 34–53.

6588 **Clegg**, Hugh Armstrong. *How to run an incomes policy, and why we made such a mess of the last one.* London: Heinemann, 1971. 88p.

6589 **Hines**, A. G. 'The determinants of the rate of change of money wage rates and the effectiveness of incomes policy.' Johnson, H. G. and Nobay, A.R. (eds.). *The current inflation.* London: Macmillan, 1971. p. 143–75.

6590 **Molhuysen**, P. C. 'Wage decisions of the British National Board for Prices and Incomes 1965–1969.' *J. Ind. Relat.*, XIII, 2 (June 1971), 117–29.

6591 **Mortimer**, James Edward. 'The rise and fall of the P.I.B.' *Pers. Manage.*, III, 2 (February 1971), 20–24.

6592 **Paish**, Frank Walter. *Rise and fall of incomes policy.* London: Institute of Economic Affairs, 1971. 64p. (Hobart papers 47.) Second edition.

6593 **Pickering**, J. F. 'The Prices and Incomes Board and private sector prices: a survey.' *Econ. J.*, LXXXI (June 1971), 225–41.

6594 **Robinson**, Derek. *Incomes policy: report of a conference at Ditchley Park, 1971.* Enstone: Ditchley Foundation, 1971. (Ditchley paper 38.)

6595 **Schiff**, E. *Incomes policies abroad.* Washington: American Enterprise Board for Public Policy Research, 1971. 42p. (Special analysis 3.)
See especially chapter on United Kingdom, p. 3–14.

6596 **Ulman**, Lloyd and **Flanagan**, Robert J. *Wage restraint: a study of incomes policies in Western Europe.* Berkeley: University of California Press, 1971. x, 257p.

6597 **Wallis**, Kenneth F. 'Wages, prices and incomes policies: some comments.' *Economica*, XXXVIII (August 1971), 304–10.

6598 **Weintraub**, Sidney. 'An incomes policy to stop inflation.' *Lloyds Bank Rev.*, XCIX (January 1971), 1–12.

6599 **Balfour**, Campbell. *Incomes policy and the public sector.* London: Routledge & Kegan Paul, 1972. xiii, 276p.

6600 **Behrend**, Hilde. 'Public acceptability and a workable incomes policy.' Blackaby, F. (ed.). *An incomes policy for Britain.* 1972. p. 187–216.

6601 **Blackaby**, Frank Thomas. 'Incomes policies: background paper.' Blackaby, F. (ed.). *An incomes policy for Britain.* 1972. p. 217–36.

6602 **Blackaby**, Frank Thomas: 'Incomes policy: a longer view.' *New Soc.*, XXII (9 November 1972), 329–31.

6603 **Blackaby**, Frank Thomas (ed.). *An incomes policy for Britain: policy proposals and research needs.* London: Heinemann, 1972. viii, 250p.

6604 **Burrows**, Paul and **Hitiris**, Theodore. 'Estimating the impact of incomes policy.' *Bull. Econ. Res.*, XXIV (May 1972), 42–51.

6605 **Clegg**, Hugh Armstrong. 'A workable incomes policy for Britain.' Blackaby, F. (ed.). *An incomes policy for Britain.* 1972. p. 47–65.

6606 **Daly**, J. 'The salary syndrome.' *Ind. Soc.*, LIV 9 (September 1972), 9–12.

6607 **Derrick**, Paul. 'Socialist incomes policy.' *Polit. Q.*, XLIII, 4 (October–December 1972), 437–47.

6608 **Fels**, A. *The British Prices and Incomes Board.* Cambridge: Cambridge University Press, 1972. xi, 298p. (Cambridge University. Department of Applied Economics. Occasional papers 29.)

6609 **Haberler**, Gottfried. 'Incomes policies and inflation.' Haberler, G., Parkin, M. and Smith, H. (eds.). *Inflation and the unions.* 1972. p. 1–62.

6610 **Hein**, J. *Aspects of incomes policies abroad.* New York: Conference Board, 1972. v, 57p. (Conference Board reports 563.)
See especially p. 28–32.

6611 **Industrial Research and Information Services**. *Incomes policy.* London: I.R.I.S., 1972. 33p.

6612 **Institute of Economic Affairs**. *Inflation: economy and society: twelve papers by economists, businessmen and politicians on causes, consequences, cures.* London: I.E.A., 1972. ix, 136p. (Readings in political economy 8.)

6613 **Jarratt**, Alex A., **Phelps Brown**, Ernest Henry, **Clegg**, Hugh Armstrong and **Corina**, John. 'A workable incomes policy for Britain.' Blackaby, F. (ed.). *An incomes policy for Britain.* 1972. p. 25–88.

6614 **Jones**, Aubrey. 'A policy for prices and incomes now.' *Lloyds Bank Rev.*, CIII (January 1972), 1–11.

6615 **Lewis**, Russell and **Brown**, Wilfred Banks Duncan. *Incomes policy? Against and for.* London: Industrial, Educational and Research Foundation, 1972. 12p.

6616 **Liddle**, R. J. and **McCarthy**, William Edward John. 'The impact of the Prices and Incomes Board on the reform of collective bargaining.' *Br. J. Ind. Relat.*, X, 3 (November 1972), 412–39.

6617 **Minchinton**, W. E. (ed.). *Wage regulation in pre-industrial England.* Newton Abbot: David & Charles, 1972. 263p.
Including works by R. H. Tawney and R. Keith Kelsall.

6618 **Mitchell**, Joan. *The National Board for Prices and Incomes.* London: Secker & Warburg, 1972. xii, 294p.

6619 **Parkin**, Michael and **Sumner**, M. J. *Incomes*

policy and inflation. Manchester: Manchester University Press, 1972. xii, 283p.

6620 **Phelps Brown**, Ernest Henry, **de Jong**, J. R., **Fisher**, Patrick, **Thomas**, R. E. and **Webb**, George. *Some approaches to national job evaluation: a symposium.* London: Foundation for Business Responsibilities, 1972. 43p.

6621 **Radice**, Giles and **Lipsey**, David. 'A trade union view of a workable incomes policy.' Blackaby, F. (ed.). *An incomes policy for Britain.* 1972. p. 175–86.

6622 **Robinson**, Derek. 'Prices and incomes: is there a workable policy?' *Pers. Manage.*, IV, 10 (October 1972), 18–21.

6623 **Saunders**, C. T. 'Lessons for Britain from European experience.' Blackaby, F. (ed.). *An incomes policy for Britain.* 1972. p. 89–98.

6624 **Treasury**. *A programme for controlling inflation: the first stage.* London: H.M.S.O., 1972. 8p. (Cmnd. 5125.)

6625 **Turvey**, R. 'If we had an incomes policy, should we have a prices policy too?' Blackaby, F. (ed.). *An incomes policy for Britain.* 1972. p. 163–74.

6626 **Aims of Industry**. *Phase 2 and after.* London: Aims, [1973].

6627 **Behrend**, Hilde. *Incomes policy, equity and pay increase differentials: an analysis of employee attitudes towards pay increases in Ireland and the implications for incomes policy in Britain.* Edinburgh: Scottish Academic Press, 1973. 79p.

6628 **Bracewell-Milnes**, John Barry. *Pay and price control guide.* London: Butterworth, 1973. vi, 218p.

6629 **Cairncross**, *Sir* Alec K. 'Incomes policy: retrospect and prospect.' *Three Banks Rev.*, C (December 1973), 8–28.

6630 **Chancellor of the Exchequer**. *Price and pay code: a consultative document.* London: H.M.S.O., 1973. ii, 26p. (Cmnd. 5247.)

6631 **Chancellor of the Exchequer.** *Programme for controlling inflation: the second stage.* London: H.M.S.O., 1973. 18p. (Cmnd. 5205.)

6632 **Daniel**, William Wentworth and **McIntosh**, Neil. *Incomes policy and collective bargaining at the workplace: a study of the productivity criterion cases.* London: Political & Economic Planning, 1973. iii, 73p. (Broadsheet 541.)

6633 **Deadman**, W. B. and **Hockey**, P. J. *Prices and pay codes with a commentary on the 1973 Finance Bill.* London: Farringdon, 1973. 54p.

6634 **Derrick**, Paul. *The incomes problem.* Nottingham: Institute for Workers' Control, 1973. 19p. (I.W.C. pamphlet 34.)

6635 **Derrick**, Paul. 'Is a voluntary incomes policy possible?' *Contemp. Rev.*, XXII (May 1973), 248–53.

6636 **Dorfman**, Gerald Allen. *Wage politics in Britain, 1945–1967: government vs. the TUC.* Ames: Iowa State University Press, 1973. x, 180p.

6637 **Field**, Frank. *An incomes policy for poor families.* London: Child Poverty Action Group, 1973. 12p.

6638 **Griffiths**, Brian. 'Phase III: expansion and less inflation?' *Banker*, CXXIII (November 1973), 1253, 1255–6.

6639 **Handy**, L. J. 'Threshold agreements.' *New Soc.*, XXV (26 July 1973), 213–14.

6640 **Hunter**, Laurence Colvin. 'Some lessons from the failure of British incomes policies.' Galenson, Walter (ed.). *Incomes policy: what can we learn from Europe?* Ithaca, N.Y.: New York State School of Industrial & Labor Relations, 1973. p. 1–40.

6641 **Isaac**, J. E. 'Incomes policy: unnecessary? Undesirable? Impracticable?' *Aust. Econ. Rev.*, XXI (January–March 1973), 41–50.

6642 **Jones**, Aubrey. *The new inflation: the politics of prices and incomes.* London: Penguin/Deutsch, 1973. xi, 228p.

6643 **Locke**, John. 'Counter inflation policies in Britain.' Industrial Relations Research Association. *Proceedings of the spring meeting, Jamaica, May 3–6, 1973.* Chicago: I.R.R.A., 1973. p. 526–32.

6644 **Mailer**, C. 'Steps to a threshold agreement.' *Ind. Soc.*, LV, 2 (February 1973), 8–10.

6645 **North Paul & Associates Limited**. *Report on the study of some aspects of national job evaluation.* London: Working Together Campaign, 1973. 18p.

6646 **Pay Board**. *Anomalies arising out of the pay stand-still of November 1972.* London: H.M.S.O., 1973. viii, 18p. (Advisory report 1. Cmnd. 5429.)

6647 **Pay Board**. *Pay Board: a guide to its work.* London: Central Office of Information, 1973. 28p.

6648 **Pay Board**. *Pay Board: a guide to its work in Stage 3.* London: Pay Board, 1973. 36p.

6649 **Robinson**, Derek. 'Differentials and incomes policy.' *Ind. Relat. J.*, IV, 1 (Spring 1973), 4–20.

6650 **Robinson**, Derek. 'Flexibility and Phase Three.' *Pers. Manage.*, V, 9 (September 1973), 24–7.

6651 **Robinson**, Derek. *Incomes policy and capital sharing in Europe.* London: Croom Helm, 1973. 223p.

6652 **Taylor**, Robert. 'Pay adrift.' *New Soc.*, XXIII (22 March 1973), 646–7.

6653 **Treasury**. *Counter inflation programme: operation of Stage 2.* London: H.M.S.O., 1973. 56p. (Cmnd. 5267.)

6654 **Treasury**. *The price and pay code for Stage 3: a consultative document.* London: H.M.S.O., 1973. 56p. (Cmnd. 5444.)

6655 **Ulman**, Lloyd. 'Phase II in context: towards an incomes policy for Conservatives.' Galenson, W. (ed.). *Incomes policy: what can we learn from Europe?* Ithaca, N.Y.: New York State School of Industrial & Labor Relations, 1973. p. 80–103.

6656 **Webb**, G. H. 'National job evaluation in the current climate.' *Pers. Manage.*, V, 10 (October 1973), 29–33.

6657 **Wood**, Duncan. 'Phase III.' *Pers. Manage.*, v, 12 (December 1973), 20–23.

6658 **Basnett**, David. 'Policies for fair pay.' *Pers. Manage.*, vi, 5 (May 1974), 24–6.

6659 **Brown**, Wilfrid. 'The basis of a new social contract.' *Month*, vii (May 1974), 583–4.

6660 **Corina**, John and **Meyrick**, A. J. *Incomes policy in crisis: an overview 1973–4.* Oxford: Oxford University Incomes Policy Evaluation Programme and University of Manchester Institute of Science and Technology, 1974. 51p.

6661 **Counter Information Services**. *Three phase trick: a handbook on inflation and phase three.* London: The Services, 1974. 32p. (Anti-report 6.)

6662 **Fores**, Michael. 'Job evaluation and incomes policy.' *Lloyds Bank Rev.*, cxiv (October 1974), 38–48.

6663 **Fosh**, Patricia and **Jackson**, Dudley. 'Pay policy and inflation: what Britain thinks.' *New Soc.*, xxvii (7 February 1974), 311–17.

6664 **Gibbins**, Michael E. S., **Conran**, C. C. and **Vaughan**, David B. *Counter inflation: the operation of stage IV.* London: Institute of Chartered Accountants in England and Wales, 1974. 43p.

6665 **Goldthorpe**, John H. 'Political consensus, social inequality and pay policy.' *New Soc.*, xxvii (10 January 1974), 55–8.

6666 **Gore**, T. 'Trade unions and the social contract: British and Swedish style.' *Ind. Commer. Train.*, vi, 12 (December 1974), 561–6.

6667 **Hughes**, James J. 'Are threshold agreements inflationary?' *Banker*, cxxiv (October 1974), 1191–4.

6668 **Hughes**, James J. 'Cost of living, threshold bargaining and incomes policy.' *Ind. Relat. J.*, iv, 4 (Winter 1973–4), 23–33.

6669 **Lall**, Sanjaya. 'A proposal for index-linking in Britain.' *Natl. Westminster Bank Q. Rev.* (November 1974), 6–14.

6670 **Mitchell**, W. 'Index-related wages and threshold syndrome.' *Pers. Manage.*, vi, 10 (October 1974), 30–34.

6671 **Parkin**, Michael. 'Indexation and inflation.' *New Soc.*, xxx (12 December 1974), 678–80.

6672 **Pay Board**. *Criteria and methods for determining the pay of the science group in the Civil Service.* London: H.M.S.O., 1974. vi, 16p. (Advisory report 3.)

6673 **Pay Board**. *Experience of operating a statutory incomes policy.* London: Pay Board, 1974. 49p.

6674 **Pay Board**. *London weighting.* London: H.M.S.O., 1974. ix, 115p. (Advisory report 4.)

6675 **Pay Board**. *Problems of pay relativities.* London: Pay Board, 1974. viii, 30p. (Advisory report 2.)

6676 **Pocock**, P. 'Learning from the Pay Board legacy.' *Pers. Manage.*, vi, 9 (September 1974), 30–31.

6677 **Stankiewicz**, W. J. 'Is the social contract obsolete?' *Polit. Sci.*, xxvi (December 1974), 57–62.

6678 **Trades Union Congress**. *Collective bargaining and the social contract.* London: T.U.C., 1974. 11p.

6679 **Wootton**, Barbara Frances, Baroness Wootton of Abinger. *Fair pay, relativities and a policy for incomes.* Southampton: University of Southampton, 1974. 21p. (Fawley Foundation lecture.)

6680 **Wootton**, Barbara Frances, Baroness Wootton of Abinger. *Incomes policy: an inquest and a proposal.* London: Davis-Poynter, 1974. 177p.

6681 **Zaidi**, Mahmood A. 'Inflation, employment and incomes policies.' *Int. J. Soc. Econ.*, i, 2 (1974), 124–45.

6682 **Blackaby**, Frank Thomas and **Dean**, Andrew. 'The dismal history of the "social contract" '. *New Soc.*, xxxi (13 February 1975), 375–8.

6683 **Braun**, A. R. 'Role of incomes policy in industrial countries since World War 2.' *Int. Monetary Fund Staff Pap.*, xxii, 1 (March 1975), 1–36.

6684 **Cabinet Office**. *The attack on inflation.* London: H.M.S.O., 1975. 13p. (Cmnd. 6151.)

6685 **Carr**, Lord. 'Incomes policy.' *Polit. Q.*, xlvi (October–December 1975), 403–10.

6686 **Cliff**, Tony. *Crisis: social contract or socialism?* London: Pluto, 1975. 192p.

6687 **Cohen**, C. D. 'The social contract and the standard of living.' *Natl. Westminster Bank Q. Rev.* (August 1975), 44–56.

6688 **Daniel**, William Wentworth. *The PEP survey on inflation.* London: Political & Economic Planning, 1975. xi, 60p. (Broadsheet 553.)

6689 **Donaldson**, John and **Lupton**, Tom. 'The effect of government policy on payment systems.' Bowey, Angela M. (ed.). *Handbook of salary and wage systems.* 1975. p. 377–88.

6690 **Glendon**, A. Ian, **Tweedie**, D. P. and **Behrend**, Hilde. 'Pay negotiations and incomes policy: a comparison of views of managers and trade union lay negotiators.' *Ind. Relat. J.*, vi, 3 (Autumn 1975), 3–19.

6691 **Hawkins**, Kevin H. 'Miners and incomes policy 1972–1975.' *Ind. Relat. J.*, vi, 2 (Summer 1975), 2–22.

6692 **Hunter**, Laurence Colvin. 'British incomes policy 1972–1974.' *Ind. Labor Relat. Rev.*, xxix, 1 (October 1975), 67–84.

6693 **Kahn**, Richard. 'Monetarism and incomes policy.' *Banker*, cxxv (October 1975), 1167, 1169–70.

6694 **McLachlan**, Hugh. 'The "social contract" '. *Parliamentary Aff.*, xxviii (Summer 1975), 293–8.

6695 **Organisation for Economic Cooperation and Development**. *Socially responsible wage policies and inflation: a review of four countries' experience.* Paris: O.E.C.D., 1975. 68p.
   See especially Chapter IIId.: 'United Kingdom'.

6696 **Panitch**, Leo V. *The Labour Party and the trade unions: a study of incomes policy since 1945, with special reference to 1964–1970.* 1975. (Ph.D. thesis, London School of Economics.)

6697 **Rein**, M. and **Marris**, P. 'Equality, inflation and wage control.' *Challenge*, XVIII, 1 (March–April 1975), 42–50.

6698 **Roberts**, K. 'Unfair or unfounded? Pay differentials and incomes policy.' *Pers. Manage.*, VII, 8 (August 1975), 29–32.

6699 **Stokes**, Richard S. 'Ineffective incomes policies: the great British obsession.' *Pers. Manage.*, VII, 9 (September 1975), 14–17.

6700 **Tylecote**, Andrew B. 'The effect of monetary policy on wage inflation.' *Oxf. Econ. Pap.*, XXVII (July 1975), 240–44.

6701 **Wagstaff**, Peter. 'A Benthamite wages policy.' *Rev. Econ. Stud.*, XLII (October 1975), 571–80.

6702 **Brittan**, Samuel and **Lilley**, Peter. *The delusion of incomes policy.* London: Temple Smith, 1976. 254p.

6703 **Brown**, William A. 'Incomes policy and pay differentials.' *Oxf. Bull. Econ. Stat.*, XXXVII (February 1976), 27–49.

6704 **Brown**, William A. 'Options for incomes policy.' *Social. Comment.*, XXXV, 9 (September 1976), 15–16.

6705 **Brown**, William A. and **Sisson**, Keith. *A positive incomes policy.* London: Fabian Society, 1976. 18p. (Fabian tract 442.)

6706 **Confederation of British Industry**. *The counter-inflation policy: pay – the second year, 1 August 1976 to 31 July 1977, practical guidance.* London: C.B.I., 1976. 12p.

6707 **Daniel**, William Wentworth. *The next stage of incomes policy.* London: Political & Economic Planning, 1976. 35p. (Broadsheet 568.)

6708 **Gennard**, John. 'Incomes policy: problems and a proposal.' *Three Banks Rev.*, CX (June 1976), 21–39.

6709 **Hughes**, James J. 'Incomes policy: the case for a third phase.' *Banker*, CXXVI (November 1976), 1215–19.

6710 **Hughes**, John. 'Seeking a successor for the £6 pay policy.' *Pers. Manage.*, VIII, 1 (January 1976), 16–19.

6711 **Lea**, David. 'Income distribution and the social contract.' *Pers. Manage.*, VIII, 10 (October 1976), 16–20.

6712 **Panitch**, Leo V. *Social democracy and industrial militancy: the Labour Party, the trade unions and incomes policy, 1945–74.* Cambridge: Cambridge U.P., 1976. 318p.

6713 **Pond**, Chris. *The attack on inflation: who pays? A reply to the White Paper on the pay policy.* London: Low Pay Unit, 1976. 16p. (Low pay papers 12.)

6714 **Trinder**, Chris. 'The role of incomes policies since 1960.' Field, F. (ed.). *Are low wages inevitable?* 1976. p. 77–86.

6715 **Vaughan**, Christopher. 'In defence of the social contract.' *Month*, IX (November 1976), 365–7.

6716 **Bushell**, R. *Nationwide job evaluation as an adjunct to a government policy for incomes and the relevance of the experience of the Netherlands to the current situation in the United Kingdom.* 1977. (M.A. thesis, University of Sussex.)

6717 **Counter Information Services**. *Paying for the crisis.* London: The Services, 1977. 46p. (Anti-reports 18.)

6718 **Craig**, C. 'Towards national job evaluation.' *Ind. Relat. J.*, IX, 1 (Spring 1977), 23–36.

6719 **Johnston**, T. L. *Incomes policy: the long view and the short.* Glasgow: Fraser of Allander Institute, 1977. 20p. (Speculative papers 6.)

6720 **Treasury**. *The attack on inflation after July 31, 1977.* London: H.M.S.O., 1977. 8p.

6721 **Vaughan**, D. B., **Conran**, C. C. and **Beresford**, C. C. H. *Counter inflation: the operation of the 1977 legislation.* London: Institute of Chartered Accountants in England and Wales, 1977. 31p.

6722 **Blackwell**, Norman R. and **Santomero**, Anthony M. 'Incomes policy and tax rates: an innovative policy attempt in the United Kingdom.' *Economica*, XLV (May 1978), 153–64.

6723 **Boon**, G. T. 'Incomes policy: a cautionary note.' *Scott. J. Polit. Econ.*, XXV (June 1978), 201–9.

6724 **Forester**, Tom and **Mack**, Joanna. 'Whose pay policy?' *New Soc.*, XLVI (12 October 1978), 76–7.

6725 **Glynn**, Dermot. 'The last 14 years of incomes policy: a CBI perspective.' *Natl. Westminster Bank Q. Rev.* (November 1978), 23–34.

6726 **Gradish**, S. F. 'Wages and manning: the Navy Act of 1758.' *Engl. Hist. Rev.*, XCIII, 3666 (January 1978), 46–67.

6727 **Incomes Data Services**. *Pay policy and stage four rules.* London: I.D.S., 1978. 20p. (I.D.S. study 184.)

6728 **Jones**, Peter. 'Incomes policy and the public sector: ten year turmoil.' *Pers. Manage.*, X, 2 (February 1978), 38–43.

6729 **National Union of Public Employees**. 'The social contract.' Barratt Brown, M. and others (eds.). *Full employment.* 1978. p. 70–78.

6730 **Political Quarterly**. 'Incomes policy fit for the future.' *Polit. Q.*, XLIX, 2 (April–June 1978), 136–58.

6731 **Southern Region Trade Union Information Unit**. *Incomes policy: the alternative.* Brighton: The Unit, 1978. 12p.

6732 **Towers**, Brian. *British incomes policy.* London: University of Leeds and University of Nottingham in association with the Institute of Personnel Management, 1978. iv, 44p. (Occasional papers in industrial relations 3.)

6733 **Brown**, William A. 'Antipodean contrasts in incomes policy.' Bowers, J. K. (ed.).

Inflation, development and integration. 1979. p. 101–18.

6734 **Brown**, William A. 'Engineering wages and the social contract, 1975–1977.' *Oxf. Bull. Econ. Stat.*, XLI (February 1979), 51–61.

6735 **Fox**, Andrew. 'Collective bargaining in the United Kingdom: whither income restraint.' *Berclays Bank Rev.*, LIV (May 1979), 30–34.

6736 **Routledge**, Paul. 'Will the concordat contribute to IR reform?' *Pers. Manage.*, XI, 4 (April 1979), 24–8.

6737 **Wootton**, Barbara Frances, Baroness Wootton of Abinger. 'Towards a rational pay policy.' *New Soc.*, XLVII (29 March 1979), 735–7.

See also: 182; 1309; 1727; 1759; 1786; 1838; 1892; 1987; 2117; 2281; 2710; 4590; 4591; 4929; 4930; 5069; 6749; 6759; 6762; 6918.

B. WAGES COUNCILS AND MINIMUM WAGE LEGISLATION

See also Part Six, III, D and Part Six, IV, A, 2 for particular industries and groups. See also Part Six, III, E; Part Six, III, G; and Part Six, IV, A, 3, a.

6738 **Greenwood**, J. A. 'On the abolition of wages councils.' *Ind. Relat. J.*, III, 4 (Winter 1972), 30–42.

6739 **Armstrong**, Eric George Abbott. 'Taking the sweat out of wages councils.' *Pers. Manage.*, VI, 12 (December 1974), 20–21.

6740 **Field**, Frank and **Winyard**, Steve. *Low wages councils.* Nottingham: Spokesman Books, 1975. 11p. (Spokesman pamphlets 49.)

6741 **Advisory Conciliation and Arbitration Service**. *Inquiry into the future of the Road Haulage Wages Council.* London: A.C.A.S., 1976. 63p. (Report 6.)

6742 **Department of Employment**, Commission of Inquiry on the Draft Order to Abolish the Industrial and Staff Canteen Undertakings Wages Council. *Report of the Commission ....* London: H.M.S.O., 1976. 32p.
Chairman: Hugh Armstrong Clegg.

6743 **Field**, Frank and **Winyard**, Steve. 'The effects of the Trade Boards Act.' Field, F. (ed.). *Are low wages inevitable?* 1976. p. 57–66.

6744 **Hughes**, John. 'What part can a minimum wage play?' Field, F. (ed.). *Are low wages inevitable?* 1976. p. 89–104.

6745 **Winyard**, Steve. *Nine into two equals progress: an examination of the merging of the retail wages councils.* London: Low Pay Unit, 1976. 14p. (Low pay papers 10.)

6746 **Winyard**, Steve. *Policing low wages: a study of the Wages Inspectorate.* London: Low Pay Unit, 1976. 38p. (Low pay pamphlets 4.)

6747 **Winyard**, Steve. *The weak arm of the law? An assessment of the new strategy of minimum wage*

enforcement. London: Low Pay Unit, 1976. 16p. (Low pay papers 13.)

6748 **Department of Employment Gazette**. 'The wages inspector cometh.' *Dep. Employment Gaz.*, LXXXV, 2 (February 1977), 107–10.

6749 **Jordan**, David. *Short measures for the poor: wages council increases under pay policy, 1975–77.* London: Low Pay Unit, 1977. 9p. (Low pay papers 17.)

6750 **Jordan**, David. *The wages of uncertainty: a critique of wages council orders.* London: Low Pay Unit, 1977. 60p. (Low pay pamphlets 6.)

6751 **Thomas**, Ceri. *Short back and sides for the poor: a memorandum to the Hairdressing Undertakings Wages Council.* London: Low Pay Unit, 1977. 7p. (Low pay papers 19.)

6752 **Sharp**, Hugh. 'Wages councils: a way forward?' *Dep. Employment Gaz.*, LXXXVI, 9 (September 1978), 1044–6.

6753 **Sharp**, Hugh. 'Working in a wages council industry.' *Dep. Emloyment Gaz.*, LXXXVI, 11 (November 1978), 1259–62.

6754 **Thomas**, Ceri. *The charge of the wages brigade: an assessment of the enforcement of minimum wages.* London: Low Pay Unit, 1978. 14p. (Low pay papers 21.)

6755 **Jordan**, David. *Complexity itself: the simplification of wages council orders.* London: Low Pay Unit, 1979. 28p. (Low pay papers 30.)

6756 **Jordan**, David. *A cut below the rest: submission to the Hairdressing Undertakings Wages Council.* London: Low Pay Unit, 1979. 12p. (Low pay papers 31.)

6757 **Jordan**, David. *Meagre rations: submission to the Licensed Residential and Licensed Restaurant Wages Council.* London: Low Pay Unit, 1979. 16p. (Low pay papers 29.)

See also: 1969.

C. FAIR WAGES RESOLUTIONS

6758 **Skinner**, J. *Fair wages and public sector contracts.* London: Fabian Society, 1973. 20p. (Fabian research series 310.)

6759 **Bercusson**, Brian. 'The new fair wages policy: Schedule 11 to the Employment Protection Act.' *Ind. Law J.*, V, 3 (September 1976), 129–47.

6760 **Beaumont**, Philip B. 'The use of fair wages clauses in government contracts in Britain.' *Labor Law J.*, XXVIII, 3 (March 1977), 147–60.

6761 **Bercusson**, Brian. *Fair wages resolutions.* London: Mansell, 1978. xxvii, 538p.

6762 **Wood**, Penny. 'The Central Arbitration Committee's approach to Schedule 11 to the Employment Protection Act 1975 and the Fair Wages Resolution 1946.' *Ind. Law J.*, VI, 2 (June 1978), 65–83.

See also: 6918; 6927.

D. EQUAL PAY AND OPPORTUNITY FOR WOMEN

See also Part Three, II, E, 2; Part Six, II, C, 4; Part Six, III, E; Part Six, IV, A, 3, a; and Part Seven, II, C.

6763 **Barrett**, Brenda. 'Equal Pay Act 1970.' *Mod. Law Rev.*, XXXIV (May 1971), 308–12.

6764 **Industrial Society**. *Survey on the implementation of the Equal Pay Act 1970.* London: The Society, 1971. 42p. (Survey and report series 174.)

6765 **Larsen**, C. A. 'Equal pay for women in the United Kingdom.' *Int. Labour Rev.*, CIII, 1 (January 1971), 1–11.

6766 **Seear**, Beatrice Nancy, *Baroness*. 'The Equal Pay Act 1970.' *Mod. Law Rev.*, XXXIV (May 1971), 312–16.

6767 **Naylor**, Rachel. 'Women and equality.' Torrington, Derek P. (ed.). *Handbook of industrial relations.* 1972. p. 207–20.

6768 **Office of Manpower Economics**. *Equal pay: first report on the implementation of the Equal Pay Act 1970.* London: H.M.S.O., 1972. iii, 106p.

6769 **Paterson**, Peter and **Armstrong**, Michael. *An employers guide to equal pay.* London: Kogan Page, 1972. 143p.

6770 **Broadhurst**, Alison. 'Equal pay: the discriminating Act.' *Ind. Commer. Train.*, V, 1 (January 1973), 35–8.

6771 **Department of Employment**. *Equal pay: what are you doing about it?* London: The Department, 1973. 10p.

6772 **Department of Employment, Department of Education and Science** and **Home Office**. *Equal opportunities for men and women: governmental proposals for legislation.* London: H.M.S.O., 1973. 31p.

6773 **Industrial Society**. *Survey on the implementation of the Equal Pay Act, 1970.* London: The Society, 1973. 40p. (Survey and report series 184.)

6774 **Lester**, K. *Equal opportunity for men and women: government proposals for legislation: observations on the consultative document.* London: Runnymede Trust, 1973. 38p.

6775 **National Council for Civil Liberties**. *Women's rights: comments on the government's proposals for an anti-discrimination law.* London: The Council, 1973. 10p.

6776 **Trades Union Congress**. *Special report by the Women's Advisory Committee on the anti-discrimination Bill: appendix to the 43rd T.U.C. Women's Congress report... 1973.* London: T.U.C., 1973. 26p.

6777 **Boothman**, F. J. 'Whatever happened to the Equal Pay Act?' *J. Ind. Affairs*, I, 2 (March 1974), 52–5.

6778 **Coote**, Anna and **Gill**, Tess. *Women's rights: a practical guide.* Harmondsworth: Penguin, 1974. 349p.

6779 **Home Office**. *Equality for women.* London:

H.M.S.O., 1974. 26p. (Cmnd. 5724.)

6780 **Institute of Personnel Management**. 'Equality for women: IPM statement on government proposals prepared by the Institute's working party on equal pay and opportunity.' *Train. Off.*, X, 12 (December 1974), 360–63.

6781 **Robinson**, Olive and **Wallace**, John. 'Prospects for equal pay in Britain: retail distribution and the Equal Pay Act 1970.' *Int. J. Soc. Econ.*, I, 3 (1974), 243–60.

6782 **Creighton**, W. B. 'Whatever happened to the Sex Disqualification (Removal) Act?' *Ind. Law J.*, IV, 3 (September 1975), 155–67.

6783 **Department of Employment Gazette**. 'Further progress towards equal pay.' *Dep. Employment Gaz.*, LXXXIII, 8 (August 1975), 747–53.

6784 **Nash**, M. *Sex Discrimination Act: a guide for managers.* London: Institute of Personnel Management, 1975. 46p.

6785 **Pettman**, Barrie Owen and **Fyfe**, John (eds.). *Equal pay for women: progress and problems in seven countries.* Bradford: MCB Books, 1975. ix, 173p.

6786 **Thornton**, L. H. F. *The legal right to equal pay, with special reference to European Community law.* 1975. (LL.M. thesis, University of Manchester.)

6787 **Barrett**, Ian. 'Sex Discrimination Act 1975.' *J. Ind. Affairs*, III, 2 (Spring 1976), 185–8.

6788 **Blackstone**, Tessa. 'The limits of legislating for equality for women.' *New Community*, V, 1–2 (Summer 1976), 22–9.

6789 **Coussins**, Jean. *The equality report: one year of the Equal Pay Act, the Sex Discrimination Act, the Equal Opportunities Commission.* London: National Council for Civil Liberties, 1976. 123p.

6790 **Creighton**, W. B. 'Enforcing the Sex Discrimination Act.' *Ind. Law J.*, V, 1 (March 1976), 42–53.

6791 **Hewitt**, Patricia. 'Women's rights in law and practice.' *New Community*, V, 1–2 (Summer 1976), 19–21.

6792 **Mayhew**, Judith. 'Women, work and the law.' *New Community*, V, 1–2 (Summer 1976), 39–44.

6793 **Mitchell**, Alison. 'The consequences of the Equal Pay Act.' Field, F. (ed.). *Are low wages inevitable?* 1976. p. 67–76.

6794 **Richards**, Margaret A. 'The Sex Discrimination Act: equality for women?' *Ind. Law J.*, V, 1 (March 1976), 35–41.

6795 **Rubenstein**, Michael and **Frost**, Yvonne. 'The Equal Pay Act: the E.A.T. to the rescue.' *Pers. Manage.*, IX, 2 (February 1977), 6–9.

6796 **Seear**, Beatrice Nancy, *Baroness*. 'Equal opportunity?' *Ind. Soc.*, LIX, 5 (September–October 1977), 10–11.

6797 **Smith**, Pat. 'The straight facts about red circling.' *Pers. Manage.*, IX, 8 (August 1977), 28–30.

Differential maintenance vs. Equal Pay Act, the role of the Employment Appeal Tribunal.

6798 **Bateson**, P. L. 'The status of female labour and the law in Northern Ireland.' *Univ. Leuven Inst. Labour Relat. Bull.*, IX (1978), 177–204.

6799 **Silverstone**, Rosalie. 'How the law put an end to the dolly bird ads.' *Pers. Manage.*, X, 8 (August 1978), 25–7, 35.

6800 **Wallington**, Peter. 'Discrimination, equal pay and the living, changing law.' *Pers. Manage.*, X, 1 (January 1978), 28–31.

6801 **Creighton**, W. B. *Working women and the law.* London: Mansell, 1979. xii, 292p.

6802 **Glucklich**, P. and **Povall**, M. 'Equal opportunities.' *Pers. Manage.*, XI, 1 (January 1979), 28–31.

6803 **Snell**, Mandy. 'The Equal Pay and Sex Discrimination Acts: their impact in the workplace.' *Feminist Rev.*, 1 (1979), 37–57.

See also: 4080; 4869; 4877; 4887; 5429; 6444; 7119.

V. REGULATION OF TRADE UNIONS

Material relating to the Combination Acts and their repeal is included here, but more general material on the Tolpuddle Martyrs is classified at Part Three, II, B. Material on the powers of professional bodies to discipline their members is generally classified at Part Three, II, D, 6. See also Part Three, II; Part Seven, I; and Part Seven, VI.

6804 **Department of Employment**. *Industrial Relations Act, 1971: registration.* London: The Department, 1971. 15p.

6805 **Hepple**, Robert Alexander and **O'Higgins**, Paul. *Public employee trade unionism in the United Kingdom: the legal framework.* Ann Arbor: University of Michigan and Wayne State University. Institute of Labor and Industrial Relations, 1971. 221p.

6806 **Industrial Research and Information Services**. *Trade union rules and the Registrar.* London: The Services, 1971. [22]p.

6807 **Jones**, Bill, **Nicholson**, Brian and **Fleet**, Ken. *An open letter to the true (anti-registration) trade union delegates to the TUC.* Nottingham: Bertrand Russell Peace Foundation, [1971]. 4p.

6808 **Sherman**, Barrie. *The Immigration Bill and the Industrial Relations Bill – a combined threat to trade unions: a discussion paper.* London: National Council for Civil Liberties, 1971. 18p.

6809 **Britten**, S. 'Trade unions and the law: a background.' *Marxism Today*, XVI (1972), 260–66.

6810 **Hepple**, Robert Alexander. 'Union responsibility for shop stewards.' *Ind. Law J.*, I, 4 (December 1972), 197–211.

6811 **McCarthy**, William Edward John. 'Principles and possibilities in British trade union law.' McCarthy, W. (ed.). *Trade unions.* 1972. p. 345–65.

6812 *Repeal of the Combination Acts 1825.* New York: Arno, 1972. (British labour struggles: contemporary pamphlets 1727–1850.)

6813 *Trade unions under the Combination Act: five pamphlets 1799–1823.* New York: Arno, 1972. 142p. (British labour struggles: contemporary pamphlets 1727–1850.)

6814 **Elias**, Patrick. 'Trade union amalgamations: patterns and procedures.' *Ind. Law J.*, II, 3 (September 1973), 125–36.

6815 **Hanson**, Charles Goring. *Trade unions: a century of privilege? An historical explanation of the 1971 Industrial Relations Act and the perennial issues of trade union power and law.* London: Institute of Economic Affairs, 1973. 34p. (Occasional paper 38.)

6816 **Kidner**, Richard. 'The right to be a candidate for union office.' *Ind. Law J.*, II, 2 (June 1973), 65–77.

6817 **Rideout**, Roger William. *Trade unions and the law.* London: Allen & Unwin, 1973. 276p.

6818 **Aims of Industry**. *'Always to be shielded': must we move towards unionocracy?* London: The Authors, 1974. 9p.

6819 **Berry**, Alan P. 'A sober look at Schedule 10.' *Pers. Manage.*, VII, 11 (November 1975), 29–41.

6820 **Dickens**, Linda. 'Staff associations and the Industrial Relations Act: the effect on union growth.' *Ind. Relat. J.*, VI, 3 (Autumn 1975), 29–41.

6821 **Elias**, P. *The legal regulation of trade union democracy and members' rights.* 1975. (Ph.D. thesis, University of Cambridge.)

6822 **Hanson**, Charles Goring. 'Craft unions, welfare benefits and the case of trade union law reform 1867–75.' *Econ. Hist. Rev.*, XXVIII, 2 (May 1975), 243–59.

6823 **Kidner**, Richard. 'The individual and the collective interest in trade union law.' *Ind. Law J.*, V, 2 (June 1976), 90–106.

6824 **Lustgarten**, Laurence. *Common law crimes and trade union activities.* London: Workers' Educational Association, 1976. 10p. (Studies for trade unionists II, 5.)

6825 **Weekes**, Brian. 'Law and the practice of the closed shop.' *Ind. Law J.*, V, 4 (December 1976), 211–22.

6826 **Bercusson**, Brian. 'One hundred years of conspiracy and protection of property: time for a change.' *Mod. Law Rev.*, XXXX, 3 (May 1977), 268–92.

6827 **Department of Employment Gazette**. 'Certification Office: the first year.' *Dep. Employment Gaz.*, LXXXV, 5 (May 1977), 439–42.

6828 **Prentice**, Gordon. 'What is an independent trade union?' *Pers. Manage.*, IX, 1 (January 1977), 27–30.

6829 **Rideout**, Roger William. 'Ferrybridge and

the future: the law on closed shop exemption.' *Pers. Manage.*, IX, 4 (April 1977), 18–21, 43.

6830 **Weekes**, Brian. 'Collective rights and individual liberty.' *Pers. Manage.*, X, 8 (August 1978), 18–21.

6831 **Benedictus**, Roger. 'Closed shop exemptions and their wording.' *Ind. Law J.*, VIII, 3 (September 1979), 160–71.

6832 **Kidner**, Richard. *Trade union law.* London: Stevens, 1979. xxxiv, 343p.

6833 **Roberts**, Benjamin Charles. 'The government's challenge to the unions.' *Three Banks Rev.*, CXXIV (December 1979), 3–26.

6834 **Taylor**, Robert. 'Unions above the law?' *New Soc.*, XXXV (18 January 1979), 131–2.

See also: 87; 100; 750; 769; 782; 1192; 1203; 1205; 1206; 1207; 2278.

VI. REGULATION OF COLLECTIVE BARGAINING AND INDUSTRIAL CONFLICT

Material on the legal aspects of trade union recognition is included here, but that on the more general aspects of union recognition by employers is classified at Part Five, I, and that on recognition disputes at Part Five, V, C. Works on conciliation and arbitration by the state are included here, but those on private conciliation and arbitration are classified at Part Five, V, A and C.

6835 **Khan**, M. A. *The right to organise and to strike in Great Britain and the Islamic Republic of Pakistan.* Birmingham: University of Aston in Birmingham, 1970. [164]p.

6836 **Brown**, R. 'The *Temperton v. Russell* case: the beginning of the legal offensive against the unions.' *Bull. Econ. Res.*, XXIII (May 1971), 50–66.

6837 **Commission on Industrial Relations.** *British Home Stores.* London: H.M.S.O., 1971. iv, 32p. (Report 24. Cmnd. 4791.)

6838 **Commission on Industrial Relations.** *Electrolux Ltd.* London: H.M.S.O., 1971. 45p. (Report 18. Cmnd. 4697.)

6839 **Commission on Industrial Relations.** *Scottish Stamping and Engineering Company Limited.* London: H.M.S.O., 1971. 39p. (Report 19. Cmnd. 4702.)

6840 **Commission on Industrial Relations.** *Second general report.* London: H.M.S.O., 1971. vi, 31p. (Report 25. Cmnd. 4803.)

6841 **Desmarais**, Ralph H. 'The British government's strike breaking organization and Black Friday.' *J. Contemp. Hist.*, VI, 2 (1971), 112–27.

6842 **Foster**, Ken. 'Strikes and employment contracts.' *Mod. Law Rev.*, XXXIV (May 1971), 275–87.

6843 **James**, Bernard. *The right to strike: a concept to legitimise the disruption of industrial relationships by the withdrawal of labour.* 1971. (Ph.D. thesis, London School of Economics.)

6844 **McCarthy**, William Edward John. 'The role of third parties in resolving industrial conflict.' *Co-partnership*, DXLV (November 1971), 15–24.

6845 **Aaron**, Benjamin. 'Methods of industrial action: courts, administrative agencies, and legislatures.' Aaron, B. and Wedderburn, K. (eds.). *Industrial conflict.* 1972. p. 70–174.

6846 **Aaron**, Benjamin and **Wedderburn**, Kenneth William. *Industrial conflict: a comparative legal survey.* London: Longman, 1972. xv, 396p.

6847 **Acton**, Harry Burrows. *The right to work and the right to strike.* London: Aims of Industry, 1972. 12p.

6848 **Blanc-Jouvan**, Xavier. 'The effect of industrial action on the status of the individual employee.' Aaron, B. and Wedderburn, K. (eds.). *Industrial conflict.* 1972. p. 176–253.

6849 **Commission on Industrial Relations.** *C. A. Parsons & Co. Limited and associated companies.* London: H.M.S.O., 1972, vi, 32p. (Report 32.)

6850 **Commission on Industrial Relations.** *Disclosure of information.* London: H.M.S.O., 1972. v, 57p. (Report 31.)

6851 **Drake**, Charles D. 'The right to picket peacefully: section 134.' *Ind. Law J.*, I, 4 (December 1972), 212–18.

6852 **Incomes Data Services.** *Conciliation and arbitration.* London: I.D.S., 1972. 36p. (I.D.S. study 35.)

6853 **Kahn-Freund**, Sir Otto and **Hepple**, Robert. *Law against strikes.* London: Fabian Society, 1972. 60p. (International comparisons in social policy 1.)

6854 **Labour Research Department.** *Picketing: a trade unionist's guide.* London: The Department, 1972. 8p.

6855 **Mellish**, Michael and **Dickens**, Linda. 'Recognition problems under the Industrial Relations Act.' *Ind. Law J.*, I, 4 (December 1972), 229–41.

6856 **Napier**, Brian. 'Working to rule: a breach of the contract of employment?' *Ind. Law J.*, I, 3 (September 1972), 125–34.

6857 **Paynter**, Will. 'Is there a future for conciliation and arbitration?' *Pers. Manage.*, IV, 12 (December 1972), 18–21.

6858 **Ramm**, Thilo. 'The legality of industrial actions and methods of settlement procedure.' Aaron, B. and Wedderburn, K. (eds.). *Industrial conflict.* 1972. p. 256–318.

6859 **Schmidt**, Folke. 'Industrial action: the role of trade unions and employers' associations.' Aaron, B. and Wedderburn, K. (eds.). *Industrial conflict.* 1972. p. 2–63.
   See especially p. 2–15.

6860 *The Spitalfields Acts of 1818–1828.* New York:

Arno, 1972. (British labour struggles: contemporary pamphlets 1727–1850.)

6861 **Wallington**, Peter. 'The case of the Longannet miners and the criminal liability of pickets.' *Ind. Law J.*, I, 4 (December 1972), 219–28.

6862 **Wedderburn**, Kenneth William, *Lord Wedderburn of Charlton.* 'Industrial action, the state and the public interest.' Aaron, B. and Wedderburn, K. (eds.). *Industrial conflict.* 1972. p. 320–83.

6863 **Casey**, James. 'Collective agreements: some Scottish footnotes.' *Juridical Rev.*, XVIII (April 1973), 22–42.

6864 **Commission on Industrial Relations**. *Allied Breweries (UK) Limited.* London: H.M.S.O., 1973. vi, 30p. (Report 38.)

6865 **Commission on Industrial Relations**. *Annual report for 1972.* London: H.M.S.O., 1973, v, 39p. (Report 37.)

6866 **Commission on Industrial Relations**. *Con Mech (Engineers) Limited.* London: H.M.S.O., 1973. v, 8p. (Report 53.)

6867 **Commission on Industrial Relations**. *Connor and Forbes Limited.* London: H.M.S.O., 1973. v, 15p. (Report 44.)

6868 **Commission on Industrial Relations**. *Coventry Economic Building Society.* London: H.M.S.O., 1973. v, 21p. (Report 42.)

6869 **Commission on Industrial Relations**. *Edinburgh Corporation Transport Department.* London: H.M.S.O., 1973. v, 13p. (Report 56.)

6870 **Commission on Industrial Relations**. *G. Clancey Limited.* London: H.M.S.O., 1973. v, 25p. (Report 54.)

6871 **Commission on Industrial Relations**. *General Accident Fire and Life Assurance Corporation Limited (second report).* London: H.M.S.O., 1973. v, 47p. (Report 52.)

6872 **Commission on Industrial Relations**. *Horizon Holidays Limited and associated companies.* London: H.M.S.O., 1973. vi, 28p. (Report 43.)

6873 **Commission on Industrial Relations**. *The hotel and catering industry part III: public houses, clubs and other sectors.* London: H.M.S.O., 1973. v, 70p. (Report 36.)

6874 **Commission on Industrial Relations**. *National Coal Board bulk terminal, Immingham.* London: H.M.S.O., 1973. iv, 12p. (Report 41.)

6875 **Commission on Industrial Relations**. *Pan American World Airways Incorporated.* London: H.M.S.O., 1973. vi, 21p. (Report 55.)

6876 **Commission on Industrial Relations**. *Williams and Glyn's Bank Limited.* London: H.M.S.O., 1973. v, 26p. (Report 35.)

6877 **Davies**, P. L. and **Anderman**, S. D. 'Injunction procedure in labour disputes I.' *Ind. Law J.*, II, 4 (December 1973), 213–28.

6878 **Desmarais**, Ralph H. 'Strikebreaking and the Labour Government of 1924.' *J. Contemp. Hist.*, VIII (October 1973), 165–75.

6879 **Foster**, Ken. 'Strike notices: section 147.' *Ind. Law J.*, II, 1 (March 1973), 28–33.

6880 **Lewis**, Norman. 'Railroading the workers: one way or-another.' Barratt Brown, M. and Coates, K. (eds.). *Trade union register: 3.* 1973. p. 74–88.

6881 **Mulholland**, John. 'In support of arbitration.' *Pers. Manage.*, v, 9 (September 1973), 38–41.

6882 **O'Higgins**, Paul. 'Strike notices: another approach.' *Ind. Law J.*, II, 3 (September 1973), 152–7.

6883 **Rubin**, G. R. 'Strengths and weaknesses of the picketing law.' *Ind. Relat. J.*, IV, 2 (Summer 1973), 57–64.

6884 **Selwyn**, Norman. 'The law in Britain.' Parkinson, C. N. (ed.). *Industrial disruption.* 1973. p. 18–31.

6885 **Stern**, James L. 'Arbitration of wage disputes in the British non-industrial civil service.' Industrial Relations Research Association. *Proceedings of the spring meeting, Jamaica, May 3–6, 1973.* Chicago: I.R.R.A., 1973. p. 491–500.
The proceedings of the meeting were reprinted in full in the *Labor Law Journal*, XXIV, 8 (August 1973). This paper was also reprinted as a monograph by the I.R.R.A. in 1973.

6886 **Anderman**, S. D. and **Davies**, P. L. 'Injunction procedure in labour disputes: II.' *Ind. Law J.*, III, 1 (March 1974), 30–45.

6887 **Askwith**, George Ranken. *Industrial problems and disputes.* Brighton: Harvester, 1974. xviii, x, 494p.
First published 1920. New edition with an introduction by Roger Davidson.

6888 **Commission on Industrial Relations**. *Airline Engineering Limited.* London: H.M.S.O., 1974. v, 16p. (Report 66.)

6889 **Commission on Industrial Relations**. *Anglia Building Society.* London: H.M.S.O., 1974. v, 22p. (Report 79.)

6890 **Commission on Industrial Relations**. *Annual report for 1973.* London: H.M.S.O., 1974. v, 76p. (Report 65.)

6891 **Commission on Industrial Relations**. *The Associated Octel Company Limited (second report).* London: H.M.S.O., 1974. v, 7p. (Report 68.)

6892 **Commission on Industrial Relations**. *Ballots and union recognition: a guide for employers.* London: H.M.S.O., 1974. 14p.

6893 **Commission on Industrial Relations**. *Barclays Bank International Limited.* London: H.M.S.O., 1974. v, 25p. (Report 58.)

6894 **Commission on Industrial Relations**. *The Bridgwater Building Society.* London: H.M.S.O., 1974. iii, 16p. (Report 57.)

6895 **Commission on Industrial Relations**. *Colvern Limited.* London: H.M.S.O., 1974. vi, 12p. (Report 67.)

6896 **Commission on Industrial Relations**. *Davenports Brewery (Holdings Limited).* London: H.M.S.O., 1974. v, 20p. (Report 70.)

6897 **Commission on Industrial Relations.** *Final report.* London: H.M.S.O., 1974. v, 66p. (Report 90.)

6898 **Commission on Industrial Relations.** *Hector Macdonald Limited.* London: H.M.S.O., 1974. v, 8p. (Report 81.)

6899 **Commission on Industrial Relations.** *John Joyce Limited.* London: H.M.S.O., 1974. v, 8p. (Report 71.)

6900 **Commission on Industrial Relations.** *Ken Hails Limited.* London: H.M.S.O., 1974. v, 7p. (Report 72.)

6901 **Commission on Industrial Relations.** *Ken Munden (Turf Accountant) Limited; Ken Munden (Racing) Limited.* London: H.M.S.O., 1974. v, 11p. (Report 74.)

6902 **Commission on Industrial Relations.** *Lesney Products and Co. Limited.* London: H.M.S.O., 1974. vi, 20p. (Report 62.)

6903 **Commission on Industrial Relations.** *Lloyds Bank Limited.* London: H.M.S.O., 1974. v, 18p. (Report 78.)

6904 **Commission on Industrial Relations.** *Lombard North Central Limited.* London: H.M.S.O., 1974. v, 3p. (Report 84.)

6905 **Commission on Industrial Relations.** *Mansfield Hosiery Mills Limited.* London: H.M.S.O., 1974. v, 62p. (Report 76.)

6906 **Commission on Industrial Relations.** *Messrs. Gordon Nunns.* London: H.M.S.O., 1974. v, 3p. (Report 59.)

6907 **Commission on Industrial Relations.** *Messrs. Roland Jones.* London: H.M.S.O., 1974. v, 4p. (Report 73.)

6908 **Commission on Industrial Relations.** *Navy, Army and Air Force Institutes (NAAFI).* London: H.M.S.O., 1974. iv, 9p. (Report 60.)

6909 **Commission on Industrial Relations.** *Norwich Union Insurance Group.* London: H.M.S.O., 1974. v, 40p. (Report 82.)

6910 **Commission on Industrial Relations.** *Pfizer Limited.* London: H.M.S.O., 1974. iv, 9p. (Report 61.)

6911 **Commission on Industrial Relations.** *Professional football.* London: H.M.S.O., 1974. vi, 113p. (Report 87.)

6912 **Commission on Industrial Relations.** *Rubery Owen and Company Limited and associated companies.* London: H.M.S.O., 1974. vi, 64p. (Report 80.)

6913 **Commission on Industrial Relations.** *Seymour and Story Group.* London: H.M.S.O., 1974. v, 10p. (Report 64.)

6914 **Commission on Industrial Relations.** *Small firms and the code of industrial relations practice.* London: H.M.S.O., 1974. v, 52p. (Report 69.)

6915 **Commission on Industrial Relations.** *Temperance Permanent Building Society.* London: H.M.S.O., 1974. v, 18p. (Report 75.)

6916 **Commission on Industrial Relations.** *William Hill Organization.* London: H.M.S.O., 1974. v, 17p. (Report 63.)

6917 **Harker**, John. 'The case for C.A.S.: a Canadian view.' *Pers. Manage.*, VI, 9 (September 1974), 37–40.

6918 **Latta**, Geoff. 'The legal extension of collective bargaining: a study of section 8 of the Terms and Conditions of Employment Act 1959.' *Ind. Law J.*, III, 4 (December 1974), 215–33.

6919 **Lindsay**, Robert. 'Picket law: look back in anger.' *Contemp. Rev.*, CCXXXV (September 1974), 150–53.

6920 **Anderman**, S. D. 'The "status quo" issue and industrial disputes procedures: some implications for labour law.' *Ind. Law. J.*, IV, 3 (September 1975), 131–54.

6921 **Boothman**, F. J. 'The Advisory, Conciliation and Arbitration Service: a D.I.Y. facility.' *J. Ind. Affairs*, III, 1 (December 1975), 133–5.

6922 **Department of Employment Gazette.** 'ACAS: the (almost) silent service.' *Dep. Employment Gaz.*, LXXXIII, 4 (April 1975), 313–17.

6923 **Desmarais**, Ralph H. 'Lloyd George and the development of the British government's strikebreaking organization.' *Int. Rev. Soc. Hist.*, XX (1975), 1–15.

6924 **Dickens**, Linda. 'Is arbitration the answer?' *New Soc.*, XXXIV (23 October 1975), 205–7.

6925 **Gill**, W. H. *Law of arbitration.* London: Sweet & Maxwell, 1975. xxx, 139p.
Second edition.

6926 **Hann**, P. 'A. C. A. S. uses its loaf.' *Ind. Soc.*, LVII, 3 (May–June 1975), 15–16.

6927 **Hunter**, R. L. C. 'Collective agreements, fair wages clauses and the employment relationship in Scots law.' *Juridical Rev.*, XX (April 1975), 47–63.

6928 **Kay**, Maurice. 'Strikes: law and the community interests.' Preston, R. (ed.). *Perspectives on strikes.* 1975. p. 94–113.

6929 **Kidner**, Richard. 'Picketing in perspective: 1. Picketing and the criminal law.' *Crim. Law Rev.*, XXII, 5 (May 1975), 256–70.

6930 **Mortimer**, James Edward. 'Collective bargaining: the key to C. A. S.' *Pers. Manage.*, VII, 1 (January 1975), 27–30, 38.

6931 **Trice**, J. E. 'Picketing in perspective: 2. Methods of and attitudes to picketing.' *Crim. Law Rev.*, XXII, 5 (May 1975), 271–82.

6932 **Wallington**, Peter. 'Criminal conspiracy and industrial conflict.' *Ind. Law J.*, IV, 2 (June 1975), 69–88.

6933 **Bragg**, Richard J. 'Recognition and legal procedures.' Carby-Hall, J. R. (ed.). *Studies in labour law.* 1976. p. 119–59.

6934 **Holt**, James. 'The political origins of compulsory arbitration in New Zealand: a comparison with Great Britain.' *J. New Zealand Hist.*, X (October 1976), 99–111.

6935 **O'Higgins**, Paul. 'Picketing and the law.' Coker, E. and Stuttard, G. (eds.). *Industrial studies 2.* 1976. p. 246–60.

6936 **O'Higgins**, Paul. 'The right to strike: some

international reflections.' Carby-Hall, J. R. (ed.). *Studies in labour law.* 1976. p. 110–18.

6937 **Wigham**, Eric Leonard. *Strikes and the government, 1893–1974.* London: Macmillan, 1976. viii, 206p.

6938 **Advisory, Conciliation and Arbitration Service.** *Disclosure of information to trade unions for collective bargaining purposes.* London: A. C. A. S., 1977. 5p. (Code of practice 2.)

6939 **Davies**, Paul and **Wedderburn**, K. W., *Lord Wedderburn of Charlton.* 'The land of industrial democracy.' *Ind. Law J.*, VI, 4 (December 1977), 197–211.

6940 **Department of Employment.** *Report of a Court of Inquiry into a Dispute between Grunwick Processing Laboratories Ltd. and Members of the Association of Professional, Executive, Clerical and Computer Staff.* London: H.M.S.O., 1977. ii, 26p. (Cmnd. 6922.)
Chairman: *Sir* Leslie Scarman.

6941 **Incomes Data Services.** *Central Arbitration Committee awards 1976.* London: I.D.S., 1977. 168p. (I.D.S. handbook 5.)

6942 **James**, Bernard. 'Third party intervention in recognition disputes: the role of the Commission on Industrial Relations.' *Ind. Relat. J.*, VIII, 2 (Summer 1977), 29–40.

6943 **Kahn-Freund**, *Sir* Otto. 'Industrial democracy.' *Ind. Law J.*, VI, 2 (June 1977), 65–84.

6944 **Ralph**, Chris. *The picket and the law.* London: Fabian Society, 1977. 21p. (Fabian research series 331.)

6945 **Simpson**, Robert Cecil. '"Trade dispute" and "industrial dispute" in British labour law.' *Mod. Law Rev.*, XL (January 1977), 16–30.

6946 **Thomson**, J. M. 'The effect of a strike on the contract of employment.' *Juridical Rev.*, XXII (December 1977), 187–99.

6947 **Concannon**, H. M. G. 'The growth of arbitration work in ACAS.' *Ind. Relat. J.*, IX, 1 (Spring 1978), 12–18.

6948 **Dickens**, Linda. 'A.C.A.S. and the union recognition procedure.' *Ind. Law J.*, VII, 3 (September 1978), 160–77.

6949 **Hart**, Moira. 'Grunwick: has America got the answer?' *New Soc.*, XXXIV (16 February 1978), 361–2.

6950 **Hart**, Moira. 'Trade union recognition in America: the legislative snare.' *Ind. Law J.*, VII, 4 (December 1978), 201–15.

6951 **Incomes Data Services**. *Central Arbitration Committee awards 1977.* London: I.D.S., 1978. 107p. (I.D.S. handbook 9.)

6952 **James**, Bernard. 'Trade union recognition after Grunwick.' *Pers. Manage.*, X, 7 (July 1978), 20–25.

6953 **Lees**, Dennis. 'Economic logic and legal rules.' Institute of Economic Affairs. *Trade unions: public goods or public bads?* 1978.
p. 94–6.

6954 **Morris**, G. S. *A study of the protection of public and essential services in labour disputes, 1920–1976.* 1978. (Ph.D. thesis, University of Cambridge.)

6955 **Weekes**, Brian C. M. 'Collective rights and individual liberty: a recognition job for the judges.' *Pers. Manage.*, X, 8 (August 1978), 18–20, 33.

6956 **Wood**, John. 'Shedding light on Schedule 11.' *Pers. Manage.*, X, 10 (October 1978), 30–32.

6957 **Beaumont**, Philip B. 'Arbitration and the extension of terms in Britain.' *Arbit. J.*, XXXIV, 2 (June 1979), 32–6.

6958 **Bourn**, Colin. 'Statutory exemptions for collective agreements.' *Ind. Law J.*, VIII, 2 (June 1979), 85–99.

6959 **Brown**, William A. 'Comparability.' *Ind. Law J.*, VIII, 4 (December 1979), 242–4.

6960 **Dickens**, Linda. 'Conciliation, mediation and arbitration in British industrial relations.' Stephenson, G. and Brotherton, C. (eds.). *Industrial relations: a social psychological approach.* 1979. p. 289–307.

6961 **Ewing**, Keith. 'The Golden Formula: some recent developments.' *Ind. Law J.*, VIII, 3 (September 1979), 133–46.

6962 **Incomes Data Services**. *Central Arbitration Committee awards 1978.* London: I.D.S., 1979. 91p. (I.D.S. handbook 13.)

6963 **Lewis**, Roy. 'Collective agreements: the Kahn-Freund legacy.' *Mod. Law Rev.*, XLII, 6 (November 1979), 613–22.

6964 **Lockyer**, John. *Industrial arbitration in Great Britain: everyman's guide.* London: Institute of Personnel Management, 1979. 158p.

6965 **McIlroy**, John. *Trade union recognition: the limitations of law.* London: Workers' Educational Association, 1979. 33p. (Studies for trade unionists V, 17.)

6966 **Simpson**, Robert Cecil. 'Judicial control of A.C.A.S.' *Ind. Law J.*, VIII, 2 (June 1979), 69–84.

6967 **Webb**, Janette. 'Behavioural studies of third-party intervention.' Stephenson, G. and Brotherton, C. (eds.). *Industrial relations: a social psychological approach.* 1979. p. 309–31.

6968 **Weekes**, Brian. 'A.C.A.S.: an alternative to law?' *Ind. Law J.*, VIII, 3 (September 1979), 147–59.

6969 **Whelan**, Christopher J. 'Military intervention in industrial disputes.' *Ind. Law J.*, VIII, 4 (December 1979), 222–34.

See also: 132; 1257; 1258; 1285; 1677; 1678; 1703; 1737; 1751; 1752; 1753; 1764; 1780; 1782; 1796; 1898; 1954; 1960; 1969; 1992; 2018; 2023; 2099; 2163; 2314; 2327; 2342; 2361; 2362; 2363; 2364; 2366; 6252; 6253; 6759; 6762.

VII. EMPLOYMENT AND SOCIAL SECURITY

A. GENERAL

In addition to general works, this section includes historical accounts of the Poor Law and the development of the welfare state, as well as textbooks on social administration. Material on the relationship between strikes and social security benefits is classified at Part Five, V, A. See also Part Six, IV, A, 3, d.

6970 **Barratt Brown**, Michael. 'The welfare state in Britain.' *Social. Reg.* (1971), 185–225.

6971 **Boyson**, Rhodes. *Down with the poor: an analysis of the 'welfare state' and a plan to end poverty.* London: Churchill, 1971. vi, 137p.

6972 **Chandler**, D. *Pressure groups and the reform of social security in England and Wales 1919–1925.* 1971. (M.Phil. thesis, University of Nottingham.)

6973 **Christmas**, E. A. *The administration of the Poor Law in some Gloucestershire unions, 1815–1847.* 1971. (M.Litt. thesis, University of Bristol.)

6974 **Forder**, Anthony (ed.). *Penelope Hall's social services of England and Wales.* London: Routledge & Kegan Paul, 1971. xxv, 357p.
Eighth edition. Ninth edition, edited by J. B. Mays and others, published 1975.

6975 **Hindle**, G. B. *Provision for the relief of the poor in Manchester, 1754–1826.* 1971. (M.A. thesis, University of Manchester.)

6976 **Kincaid**, James C. 'The decline of the welfare state.' Harris, Nigel and Palmer, John (eds.). *World crisis.* London: Hutchinson, 1971. p. 35–75.

6977 **Land**, Hilary. 'Women, work and social security.' *Soc. Econ. Adm.*, v, 3 (July 1971), 183–92.

6978 **Mawson**, P. *Poor Law administration in South Shields, 1830–1930.* 1971. (M.A. thesis, University of Newcastle upon Tyne.)

6979 **O'Neill**, T. P. *The state, poverty and distress in Ireland, 1815–45.* 1971. (Ph.D. thesis, University of Ireland.)

6980 **Palmer**, W. N. 'The administration of the Poor Law in East Sussex.' *Battle Dist. Hist. Soc. Trans.*, xxi (1971), 5–10.

6981 **Parker**, D. R. *The Poor Law in the area of the Eastbourne and Steyning Poor Law unions, 1790–1840.* 1971. (M.A. thesis, University of Sussex.)

6982 **Smith**, N. *Social reform in Edwardian Liberalism: the genesis of the policies of national insurance and old age pensions, 1906–1911.* 1971. (M.A. thesis, University of Durham.)

6983 **Brundage**, Anthony. 'The landed interest and the New Poor Law: a reappraisal of the revolution in government.' *Engl. Hist. Rev.*, LXXXVII (1972), 27–48.

6984 **Courtenay**, W. J. 'Token coinage and the administration of poor relief during the Middle Ages.' *J. Interdisciplinary Hist.*, III (1972), 275–95.

6985 **Department of Health and Social Security.** *1972 review of social security benefits and associated changes.* London: H.M.S.O., 1972. 19p. (Cmnd. 4958.)

6986 **Department of Health and Social Security.** 'Social security in Great Britain.' *Int. Soc. Secur. Rev.*, xxv, 3 (1972), 145–73.

6987 **Piven**, Frances F. and **Cloward**, Richard A. *Regulating the poor: the functions of public welfare.* London: Tavistock, 1972. xvii, 389p.

6988 **Rose**, Michael Edward. *The relief of poverty: 1834–1914.* London: Macmillan, 1972. 64p.

6989 **Walley**, J. *Social security: another British failure?* London: Charles Knight, 1972. ix, 289p.

6990 **Brockman**, J. S. L. and **Nilsson**, P. C. *The law relating to family allowances and national insurance: the statutes, regulations and orders as now in force annotated and indexed.* London: H.M.S.O., 1973. 2v.

6991 **Bruce**, Maurice. *The rise of the welfare state: English social policy 1601–1971.* London: Weidenfeld & Nicolson, 1973. xxvii, 299p.

6992 **Canadian Council on Social Development.** 'Work incentives and welfare reform in Britain and the United States.' *Guaranteed annual income: an integrated approach.* Ottawa: The Council, 1973. p. 175–216.

6993 **Central Office of Information.** *Social security in Britain.* London: H.M.S.O., 1973. 47p. (Reference pamphlets 90.)
Second edition.

6994 **Dunkley**, P. 'The landed interest and the New Poor Law: a critical note.' *Engl. Hist. Rev.*, LXXXVIII (1973), 836–41.

6995 **Fraser**, Derek. *The evolution of the British welfare state: a history of social policy since the industrial revolution.* London: Macmillan, 1973. xviii, 299p.

6996 **George**, V. *Social security and society.* London: Routledge & Kegan Paul, 1973. 154p.

6997 **Harris**, Jose. *The welfare state.* London: Batsford, 1973. 95p.

6998 **Hoskins**, D. and **Bixby**, L. E. *Women and social security: law and policy in five countries.* Washington U.S.G.P.O., 1973. v, 95p. (United States. Social Security Administration. Office of Research and Statistics. Research reports 42.)

6999 **International Social Security Association.** 'Women and social security: study of the situation in five countries: Belgium, France, Federal Republic of Germany, Great Britain, United States of America.' *Int. Soc. Secur. Rev.*, xxvi, 1–2 (1973). 73–133.

7000 **Kincaid**, James C. *Poverty and equality in Britain: a study of social security and taxation.* Harmondsworth: Penguin, 1973. 278p.

7001 **McCloskey**, Donald N. 'New perspectives

on the Old Poor Law.' *Explor. Econ. Hist.*, x, 4 (Summer 1973), 419–36.

7002 **Maynard**, A.'Survey of social security in the U.K.' *Soc. Econ. Adm.*, VII, 1 (January 1973), 39–57.

7003 **Misha**, Ramesh. 'Welfare and industrial man: a study of welfare in Western industrial societies in relation to a hypothesis of convergence.' *Sociol. Rev.*, XXI, 4 (November 1973), 535–60.

7004 **Willmott**, Peter. *Public social services: a handbook of information.* London: Bedford Square Press, 1973. 201p.

7005 **Government Actuary**. *Social Security Amendment Bill 1974: reports on the financial provisions of the Bill.* London: H.M.S.O., 1974. 14p. (Cmnd. 5652.)

7006 **Longmate**, Norman. *Workhouse.* London: Temple Smith, 1974. 320p.

7007 **Morrill**, Sylvia A. 'Poor Law in Hereford 1836–1851.' *Woolhope Nat. Field Club Trans.*, XLI (1974), 239–52.

7008 **Baugh**, D. A. 'The cost of poor relief in SE England 1790–1834.' *Econ. Hist. Rev.*, XXVIII, 1 (February 1975), 50–68.

7009 **Brown**, R. G. S. *The management of welfare: a study of British social service administration.* London: Fontana/Collins, 1975. 317p.

7010 **Cage**, R. A. and **Mitchison**, R. 'The making of the old Scottish Poor Law.' *Past & Present*, LXIX (November 1975), 113–21.

7011 **Callund**, David. *Employee benefits in Europe: an international survey of state and private schemes in 16 countries.* Epping: Gower, 1975. xxii, 260p.

7012 **Davis**, R. H. 'Leeds Friends and the Lancashire cotton districts relief fund, 1862–1866., *Friends Hist. Soc. J.*, V, 3 (1974, *i.e.* 1975), 260–62.

7013 **Digby**, A. 'The labour market and the continuity of social policy after 1834: the case of the eastern counties.' *Econ. Hist. Rev.*, XXVIII, 1 (February 1975), 69–83.

7014 **Fyfe**, John. 'Social security systems and benefits and migrants in the E.E.C.' *Int. J. Soc. Econ.*, II, 1 (1975), 60–64.

7015 **Gutchen**, Robert M. 'Paupers in union workhouses: computer analysis of admissions and discharges.' *Local History*, XI (November 1975), 452–6.

7016 **Humphreys**, V. E. *Social security for migrant workers in the European Community.* 1975. (LL.M. thesis, University of Wales, Aberystwyth.)

7017 **Lawson**, R. and **Reed**, B. *Social security in the European Community.* London: Political & Economic Planning, 1975. 75p. (European series 23.)
See especially Chapter II: 'Social security and medical care in Britain.' p. 10–17.

7018 **Lindsay**, Jean. *The Scottish Poor Law: its operation in the North East from 1745 to 1845.* Ilfracombe: Stockwell, 1975. 265p.

7019 **Lister**, Ruth. *Social security: the case for reform.* London: Child Poverty Action Group, 1975. 72p. (Poverty pamphlets 22.)

7020 **Mays**, John Barron, **Forder**, Anthony and **Keidan**, Olive (eds.). *Penelope Hall's social services of England and Wales.* London: Routledge & Kegan Paul, 1975. xxviii, 339p.
Ninth edition. Eighth edition, edited by Forder, published 1971.

7021 **Thane**, Pat. 'The working class and state "welfare" 1880–1914.' *Soc. Study Labour Hist. Bull.*, XXXI (Autumn 1975), 6–8.

7022 **Tucker**, G. S. L. 'The old Poor Law revisited.' *Explor. Econ. Hist.*, XII, 3 (July 1975), 233–52.

7023 **Wood**, P. A. *The activities of the Sunderland Poor Law Union, 1834–1930.* 1975. (M.Litt. thesis, University of Newcastle upon Tyne.)

7024 **Ashforth**, David. 'The urban Poor Law.' Fraser, D. (ed.). *The New Poor Law in the nineteenth century.* 1976. p. 128–48.

7025 **Coats**, A. W. 'The relief of poverty, attitudes to labour, and economic change, 1660–1782.' *Int. Rev. of Soc. Hist.*, XXI, 1 (1976), 98–115.

7026 **Digby**, Anne. 'The rural Poor Law.' Fraser, D. (ed.). *The New Poor Law in the nineteenth century.* 1976. p. 149–70.

7027 **Flinn**, M. W. 'Medical services under the New Poor Law.' Fraser, D. (ed.). *The New Poor Law in the nineteenth century.* 1976. p. 45–66.

7028 **Fraser**, Derek (ed.). *The New Poor Law in the nineteenth century.* London: Macmillan, 1976. 218p.

7029 **Fraser**, Derek. 'The Poor Law as a political institution.' Fraser, D. (ed.). *The New Poor Law in the nineteenth century.* 1976. p. 111–27.

7030 **Hill**, Michael. *The state, administration and the individual.* London: Fontana/Collins, 1976. 256p.

7031 **McCord**, Norman. 'The Poor Law and philanthropy.' Fraser, D. (ed.). *The New Poor Law in the nineteenth century.* 1976. p. 87–110.

7032 **Mosley**, J. V. *Poor Law administration in England and Wales, 1834–1850, with special reference to the problem of able-bodied pauperism.* 1976. (Ph.D. thesis, University of London.)

7033 **Paterson**, Audrey. 'The Poor Law in nineteenth century Scotland.' Fraser, D. (ed.). *The New Poor Law in the nineteenth century.* 1976. p. 171–93.

7034 **Reid**, Judith. 'New social security legislation.' *Ind. Law J.*, V, 1 (March 1976), 54–61.

7035 **Rogers**, B. *Cross-national studies of social service systems: United Kingdom reports.* New York: Columbia University, School of Social Work, 1976. 2v.

7036 **Rose**, Michael E. 'Settlement, removal and the New Poor Law.' Fraser, D. (ed.). *The New Poor Law in the nineteenth century.* 1976. p. 25–44.

7037 **Stein**, Bruno. *Work and welfare in Britain and the USA.* London: Macmillan, 1976. xiii, 112p.

7038 **Thompson**, R. N. *The New Poor Law in Cumberland and Westmorland (1834–1871).* 1976. (Ph.D. thesis, University of Newcastle upon Tyne.)

7039 **Chester**, T. E. 'Social security, work and poverty.' *Natl. Westminster Bank Q. Rev.* (November 1977), 38–46.

7040 **Cowherd**, Raymond G. *Political economists and the English Poor Laws: a historical study of the influence of classical economics on the formation of social welfare policy.* Ohio: Ohio University Press, 1977. 300p.

7041 **Davies**, Alun C. 'The Old Poor Law in an industrializing parish: Aberdare, 1818–36.' *Welsh Hist. Rev.*, VIII, 3 (June 1977), 285–311.

7042 **Digby**, Anne. 'Recent developments in the study of the English Poor Law.' *Local Historian*, XII, 5 (February 1977), 206–11.

7043 **McCracken**, Alex. 'Some poor's-house correspondence.' *Dumfriesshire & Galloway Nat. Hist. Antiq. Soc. Trans.*, LII (1976–7), 158–64.

7044 **Searby**, Peter. 'The relief of the poor in Coventry, 1830–1863.' *Hist. J.*, XX, 2 (June 1977), 345–61.

7045 **Thomson**, Pamela. 'South Shields Poor Law Union in the 19th century.' McCord, N. (ed.). *Essays in Tyneside labour history.* 1977. p. 47–61.

7046 **Vorspan**, Rachel. 'Vagrancy and the New Poor Law in later Victorian and Edwardian England.' *Econ. Hist. Rev.*, XCII, 362 (January 1977), 59–81.

7047 **Woodroofe**, Kathleen. 'The Royal Commission on the Poor Laws, 1905–09.' *Int. Rev. of Soc. Hist.*, XXII, 2 (1977), 137–64.

7048 **Anderson**, P. W. *The Leeds workhouse under the Old Poor Law, 1726–1844.* 1978. (M.Phil. thesis, University of Leeds.)

7049 **Batley**, Richard. 'From Poor Law to positive discrimination.' *J. Soc. Policy*, VII, 3 (July 1978), 305–28.

7050 **Brundage**, Anthony. *The making of the New Poor Law: the politics of inquiry, enactment and implementation 1832–39.* London: Hutchinson, 1978. 204p.

7051 **Caplan**, Maurice. 'The New Poor Law and the struggle for union chargeability.' *Int. Rev. of Soc. Hist.*, XXIII, 2 (1978), 267–300.

7052 **Evans**, Eric J. *Social policy, 1830–1914: individualism, collectivism and the origins of the welfare state.* London: Routledge & Kegan Paul, 1978. 318p.

7053 **Farrell**, Michael. *The Poor Law and the workhouse in Belfast, 1838–1948.* Belfast: Public Record Office of Northern Ireland, 1978. 111p.

7054 **Hastings**, R. P. *Poverty and treatment of poverty in the North Riding of Yorkshire c1780–c1847.* 1978. (D.Phil. thesis, University of York.)

7055 **Hay**, J. R. *The development of the British welfare state.* London: Edward Arnold, 1978. x, 116p.

7056 **Henriques**, Ursula Ruth Quixano. *Before the welfare state: social administration in early industrial Britain.* London: Longmans, 1978. 348p.

7057 **Thane**, Pat (ed.). *The origins of British social policy.* London: Croom Helm, 1978. 209p.

7058 **Thane**, Pat. 'Women and the Poor Law in Victorian and Edwardian England.' *Hist. Workshop*, VI (Autumn 1978), 29–51.

7059 **Burditt**, J. E. *Philanthropy and the Poor Law: a study of the relief of poverty in the Romford Union, 1795–1914.* 1979. (M.Phil. thesis, Birkbeck College, University of London.)

7060 **Harris**, Jose. 'The growth of the social services. From cradle to grave: the rise of the welfare state.' *New Soc.*, XXXV (18 January 1979), 127–31.

7061 **Harris**, Jose. 'The growth of the social services: what happened after Beveridge.' *New Soc.*, XXXV (25 January 1979), 190–92.

7062 **Townsend**, Peter. 'Social policy in conditions of scarcity.' *New Soc.*, XXXVI (10 May 1979), 320–23.

See also: 8; 48; 1241; 1884; 3378; 5039; 7066; 7073; 7108.

B. PARTICULAR ASPECTS

Many of the works included in Part Seven, VII, A also contain material on the particular aspects of social security classified below. See also Part Three, I; and Part Three, II, F, 5.

1. Unemployment Benefit

See also Part Three, II, E, 3; Part Six, II, D; Part Six, IV, A, 3, d; and Part Seven, II, B.

7063 **Miller**, Frederic M. 'National assistance or unemployment assistance? The British Cabinet and relief policy, 1932–33.' *J. Contemp. Hist.*, IX (April 1974), 163–84.

7064 **Moore**, P. *Unemployed workers and strikers guide to social security.* London: Child Poverty Action Group, 1974. 48p. Second edition.

7065 **Deacon**, Alan. 'Labour and the unemployed: the administration of insurance in the twenties.' *Soc. Study Labour Hist. Bull.*, XXXI (Autumn 1975), 10–11.

7066 **Fulbrook**, J. G. H. *Relief for the unemployed: some aspects of the development and present administration of the law relating to unemployment insurance and supplementary benefits.* 1975. (Ph.D. thesis, University of Cambridge.)

7067 **Ogus**, A. I. 'Unemployment benefit for workers on short time.' *Ind. Law J.*, IV, 1 (March 1975), 12–23.

7068 **Deacon**, Alan. *In search of the scrounger: the administration of unemployment insurance in Britain, 1920–31.* London: Bell, 1976. 110p.

7069 **Mesher**, John. *Compensation for unemployment.* London: Sweet & Maxwell, 1976. xvii, 138p.

7070 **Mukherjee**, Santosh. *Unemployment costs.*

London: Political & Economic Planning, 1976. 20p. (Broadsheet 561.)

7071 **Deacon**, Alan. 'Concession and coercion: the politics of unemployment insurance in the twenties.' Briggs, A. and Saville, J. (eds.). *Essays in labour history 1918–1939.* 1977. p. 9–35.

7072 **Field**, Frank. 'Control measures against abuse.' Field, F. (ed.). *The conscript army.* 1977. p. 43–55.

7073 **Novak**, T. *Poverty and the state: a study of unemployment and social security in Britain.* 1978. (Ph.D. thesis, University of Durham.)

7074 **Smee**, Clive H. and **Stern**, Jon. *The unemployed in a period of high unemployment: some notes on characteristics and benefit status.* London: Department of Health and Social Security, 1978. 30p. (Government Economic Service working papers 11.)

7075 **Miller**, Frederic M. 'The British Unemployment Assistance crisis in 1935.' *J. Contemp. Hist.,* XIV (April 1979), 329–52.

7076 **Nickell**, S. J. 'The effect of unemployment and related benefits on the duration of unemployment.' *Econ. J.,* LXXXIX (March 1979), 34–49.

See also: 4209.

2. Sickness Benefit

This section includes works primarily concerned with state benefits for the sick. More general works relating to the administration and functioning of the National Health Service are excluded.

7077 **Mardon**, P. 'Long-term sickness benefits.' *Ind. Soc.,* LV, 8 (August 1973), 18–20.

7078 **Martin**, J. and **Morgan**, M. *Prolonged sickness and the return to work: an enquiry carried out in 1972–73 for the Department of Health and Social Security of the circumstances of people who have received incapacity benefits for between a month and a year, and the factors affecting their return to work.* London: H.M.S.O. for the Office of Population Censuses and Surveys. Social Survey Division, 1975. viii, 247p.

7079 **Doherty**, N. A. 'National Insurance and absence from work.' *Econ. J.,* LXXXIX (March 1979), 50–65.

See also: 509.

3. Industrial Injury and Workmen's Compensation

This section includes material not only on workmen's compensation but also on the employer's responsibilities to employees injured at work. Many of the general works in Part Seven, III, A, 1 on the individual employee – employer relationship also contain material on the employer's liability for industrial injury. See Part Seven, II, E for material on the training of the disabled. See also Part Six, II, C, 7; Part Six, IV, D; and Part Seven, III, B.

7080 **Poole**, T. 'Where safety slips.' *Bus. Manage.,* C, 7 (July 1970), 42–3, 59–63.

7081 **Munkman**, John. *Employer's liability at common law.* London: Butterworth.
Seventh edition. 1971. lxxxi, 637p.
Eighth edition. 1975. lxxvii, 683p.
Ninth edition. 1979. xlix, 653p.

7082 **Lees**, Dennis and **Doherty**, Neil. 'Compensation for personal injury.' *Lloyds Bank Rev.,* CVIII (April 1973), 18–32.

7083 **O'Connell**, Jeffrey. 'No-fault insurance for Great Britain.' *Ind. Law J.,* II, 4 (December 1973), 187–96.

7084 **Carmichael**, J. A. G. 'Medical aspects of the Industrial Injuries Act: some illustrative case studies.' *Medicoleg. J.,* XLII, 2 (1974), 44–55.

7085 **Hasson**, R. A. 'Employers' Liability (Compulsory Insurance) Act 1969: a broken reed.' *Ind. Law J.,* III, 2 (June 1974), 79–86.

7086 **Parsons**, O. H. 'A no-fault system? Not proven.' *Ind. Law J.,* III, 3 (September 1974), 129–37.

7087 **Society of Labour Lawyers.** *Accidents at work: compensation for all: evidence to the Royal Commission on Civil Liability and Compensation for Personal Injury.* London: The Society, 1974. 15p.
By Bruce Douglas Mann, Peter Weitzman and Tony Gasson.

7088 **Williams**, David. 'State-financed benefits in personal injury cases.' *Mod. Law Rev.,* XXXVII (May 1974), 281–96.

7089 **Atiyah**, P. S. 'Accident prevention and variable premium rates for work-connected accidents.' *Ind. Law J.,* IV, 1 (March 1975), 1–11; IV, 2 (June 1975), 89–105.

7090 **Hasson**, R. A. and **Mesher**, J. 'No-fault: private or social insurance?' *Ind. Law J.,* IV, 3 (September 1975), 168–80.

7091 **Industrial Law Society**. 'Compensation for industrial injury: memorandum of evidence submitted to the Royal Commission on Civil Liability and Compensation for Personal Injury.' *Ind. Law J.,* IV, 4 (December 1975), 195–217.

7092 **Lewis**, Roy and **Latta**, Geoff. 'Compensation for industrial injury and disease.' *J. Soc. Policy,* IV, 1 (January 1975), 25–55.

7093 **Phillips**, Jenny. 'Economic deterrence and the prevention of industrial accidents.' *Ind. Law J.,* V, 3 (September 1976), 148–63.

7094 **Ogus**, A. I., **Corfield**, P. and **Harris**, D. R. 'Pearson: principled reform or political compromise?' *Ind. Law J.,* VII, 3 (September 1978), 143–59.

7095 **Smith**, Peter. *Industrial injuries benefits.* London: Oyez, 1978. xxv, 183p.

7096 **Fagelson**, Ian. 'The last bastion of fault? Contributory negligence in actions for employers' liability.' *Mod. Law Rev.,* XXXXII, 6 (November 1979), 646–66.

4. Pensions

This section includes material on the economic, social, and political aspects of national pension funds. Material on private pension funds and on pensions provided by the state for its employees is classified at Part Six, IV, C, 2. Material on the actuarial basis of pension funds and their administration is generally excluded. See also Part Six, II, C, 6.

7097 **Heclo**, Hugh. 'Pensions politics.' *New Soc.*, XVIII (23 September 1971), 566–8.

7098 **Kaim-Candle**, Peter Robert and **Byrne**, J. G. *Irish pension scheme, 1969.* Dublin: Economic and Social Research Institute, 1971. viii, 41p. (Broadsheet 5.)

7099 **Prime Minister**. *Explanatory memorandum on the Pensions (Increase) Bill 1971.* London: H.M.S.O., 1971. 15p. (Cmnd. 4657.)

7100 **Fryd**, J. 'The government's pension strategy.' *Ind. Law J.*, I, 2 (June 1972), 61–73.

7101 **Bosscher**, A. E. 'An E. E. C. Commission view on pensions.' *Pensions World*, II (August 1973), 268–74.

7102 **Gilling-Smith**, Dryden. 'Occupational pensions and the Social Security Act 1973.' *Ind. Law J.*, II, 4 (December 1973), 197–212.

7103 **Government Actuary.** *Pensioners' payments and the National Insurance Bill 1973: reports on the financial provisions affecting the National Insurance and Industrial Injuries Fund.* London: H.M.S.O., 1973. 10p. (Cmnd. 5449.)

7104 **Government Actuary.** *Social Security Bill 1972: report by the Government Actuary on the financial provisions of the Bill relating to Northern Ireland.* London: H.M.S.O., 1973. 23p. (Cmnd. 5269.)

7105 **Pilch**, Michael. 'New policies for pensions.' *Pers. Manage.*, V, 1 (January 1973), 37–9.

7106 **Walley**, Sir John. 'Social security through occupational pensions: the government's strategy.' *Polit. Q.*, XLIV (April–June 1973), 167–82.

7107 **Department of Health and Social Security.** *Better pensions fully protected against inflation: proposals for a new pensions scheme.* London: H.M.S.O., 1974. v, 29p. (Cmnd. 5713.)

7108 **Department of Health and Social Security.** *Family benefits and pensions.* London: H.M.S.O., 1974. iv, 43p.

7109 **Allen**, Sir Phillip. 'The role of the Occupational Pension Board.' *Pensions World*, IV, 6 (September 1975), 79–82.

7110 **Department of Health and Social Security.** *Explanatory memorandum on the Social Security Pensions Bill 1975.* London: H.M.S.O., 1975. 20p. (Cmnd. 5929.)

7111 **Department of Health and Social Security.** *Order by Her Majesty concerning pensions and other grants in respect of disablement or death due to service in the air forces.* London: H.M.S.O., 1975. 16p. (Cmnd. 6246.)

7112 **Department of Health and Social Security.** *Order in Council dated 17th September 1975 concerning pensions and other grants in respect of disablement or death due to service in the naval forces.* London: H.M.S.O., 1975. 15p.

7113 **Department of Health and Social Security.** *Royal warrant concerning pensions and other grants in respect of disablement or death due to service in the military forces.* London: H.M.S.O., 1975. 15p. (Cmnd. 6247.)

7114 **Government Actuary.** *Social Security Pensions Bill 1975: report by the Government Actuary on the financial provisions of the Bill.* London: H.M.S.O., 1975. 20p. (Cmnd. 5928.)

7115 **Occupational Pensions Board.** *Report of the ... in accordance with Section 66 of the Social Security Act 1973, on the questions of solvency, disclosure of information and member participation in occupational pension schemes.* London: H.M.S.O., 1975. 3v. (Cmnd. 5904.)

7116 **Blakely**, Brian L. 'Pensions and professionalism: the Colonial Governors (Pensions) Acts and the British Colonial Service 1865–1911.' *J. Imp. Commonw. Hist.*, IV (January 1976), 138–53.

7117 **Fogarty**, Michael Patrick. 'Pensions, politics and the economy.' *Month*, IX (October 1976), 343–9.

7118 **Lucas**, Harry. 'Employee representation and contracting in or out.' *Pensions World*, V, 3 (March 1976), 72–5.

7119 **Occupational Pensions Board**. *Equal status for men and women in occupational pension schemes: a report of the ... in accordance with Section 66 of the Social Security Act 1973.* London: H.M.S.O., 1976. xvi, 231p. (Cmnd. 6599.)

7120 **Bolton**, L. J. 'Pensions: administration and the DHSS.' *Pensions World*, VI, 12 (December 1977), 404–6.

7121 **Arthur**, T. G. 'Pensions: the role of the state.' *Natl. Westminster Bank Q. Rev.* (August 1978), 36–46.

7122 **Hemming**, Richard. 'State pensions and personal savings.' *Scott. J. Polit. Econ.*, XXV (June 1978), 135–47.

7123 **Kincaid**, James C. 'The politics of pensions.' *New Soc.*, XXXIV (16 February 1978), 369–70.

7124 **Marshall**, G. P. 'The UK retirement pension and negative taxation.' *Bull. Econ. Res.*, XXX (May 1978), 33–8.

See also: 5665; 6493.

INDEX

An asterisk (*) denotes that the work indicated appears twice in the bibliography.

Aaron, Benjamin, 6845; 6846; 6848; 6858; 6859; 6862
Aarons, H., 3689
Abbott, Lewis F., 532
Abbott, R. W., 5674
Abbott, Stephen, 1144
Abell, D., 5850
Abell, Peter, 430; 1732; 2728
Abrams, Philip, 381
Abrines, Sam, 2291
Ackers, Norma, 5918
Ackroyd, Stephen, 307; 348
Acton, Harry Burrows, 6847
Adam, R., 5404
Adams, Kenneth, 2590
Adams, N. L., 5808
Adams, Paul, 4554
Adams, Rex, 2729
Adams, Roy Joseph, 996; 997; 1139; 1152
Adamson, Campbell, 3403
Adamson, H., 3239
Addison, John Thomas, 1725; 1856; 1864; 2940; 2951; 4233; 4617; 4635; 4871; 4888; 5395; 6219; 6220; 6228
Adelman, Paul, 1297
Adeney, Martin, 1161
Advisory Conciliation and Arbitration Service, 1967; 2009; 2010; 2011; 2039; 2320; 2321; 2351; 5010; 6504; 6741; 6938
Advisory Council for Applied Research and Development, 4282
Advisory Panel on Hospital Administration, 421
The aftermath of the 'last labourers' revolt', 2265
Agarwala, R., 4659
Ager, M. E., 3113
Agnew, W. M., 3822
Agricultural Health and Safety Inspectorate, 5934
Agricultural Wages Board for England and Wales, 4696
Ahier, V., 4360
Aikin, Olga, 1691; 6074; 6346; 6426; 6487
Aims for Freedom and Enterprise, 1170
Aims of Industry, 1347; 2560; 4196; 6075; 6626; 6818
Air Transport and Travel Industry Training Board, 3596
Alden, Jeremy D., 3874; 3878; 3898
Alderman, Geoffrey, 778; 944
Aldington, *Lord*, 2000

Aldous, Tony, 4223
Aldrich, J., 2667
Aldridge, Alan, 1874
Alexander, Kenneth John Wilson, 2306; 2591
Alford, T. J., 3787
Alfred Marks Bureau, 4749
Allan, Charles Maitland, 4314
Allan, David R., 2561
Allan, J. Murray, 2435
Allard, R., 1798
Allen, A., 1589
Allen, E., 2292
Allen, Keith R., 3098; 3124; 3221; 3234; 3245
Allen, Kevin, 6330
Allen, *Sir* Phillip, 5704; 7109
Allen, Rodney, 6585
Allen, Roger, 3210
Allen, Sheila, 2972; 4440; 5405; 5406; 5445; 5450; 5486
Allen, Victor Leonard, 101; 152; 1535
Allinson, Chris, 4367
Allner, D., 3522
Almond, J. M., 492
Al-Nuami, A. T. O., 3099
Amalgamated Union of Engineering Workers, Technical, Administrative and Supervisory Section, 4283
Amos, R., 3626
Anderman, Steven Daniel, 6076; 6093; 6478; 6481; 6508; 6877; 6886; 6920
Anderson, Geoff, 1165
Anderson, Gregory L., 1031; 1032; 1042; 4492
Anderson, John Richard Lane, 1228; 4184; 4192
Anderson, M. F., 1593
Anderson, Malcolm, 2937
Anderson, N., 3679
Anderson, N. J., 3683
Anderson, Nels, 308
Anderson, P. W., 7048
Anderson, Raoul R., 3848
Anderson, T., 3373
Anderson, W. T., 3468
Andrews, Peter, 4137
Andrews, Richard E., 4949
Angel, John H., 6508
Angell, *Sir* Norman, 6249
Angus, William S., 5373
Anstey, Edgar, 1566; 3222; 3298; 3299; 3314; 3339; 3340; 3690

Clinton, Geoffrey S., 2636
Close, Tony, 1995
Cloward, Richard A., 6987
Coates, Christine, 73
Coates, David, 974
Coates, J., 1785
Coates, J. A. G., 2517
Coates, Jack, 1455
Coates, Ken, 167; 709; 1916; 1921; 2080; 2296;
    2307; 2335; 2348; 2416; 2417; 2418; 2419; 2420;
    2421; 2422; 2423; 2424; 2444; 2445; 2453; 2459;
    2472; 2519; 2528; 2558; 2674; 2706; 2707; 2715;
    2725; 2814; 2893; 4331; 4342; 4348; 4741; 5042;
    5387; 5954; 6034; 6047; 6080; 6128; 6129; 6221;
    6224; 6225; 6880
Coates, R. D., 1014
Coats, A. W., 7025
Cockburn, Claude, 1147
Cockerill, Alan J., 6488
Cockman, Richard, 5634; 5635
Cockroft, Laurence, 2675
Codd, F. A., 605
Cohen, C. D., 6687
Cohen, H., 2994
Cohen, Jack, 2213
Cohen, Stanley, 2060
Coker, Ed, 39; 1275; 1402; 1403; 1408; 1599; 1746;
    1747; 1750; 1752; 1753; 1754; 1756; 1875; 2137;
    6935
Colbeck, Logan, 3283
Colbran, R. B., 5713
Colclough, Julia A., 1556
Coldrick, A. P., 731
Coldrick, Percy, 2601
Cole, George Douglas Howard, 695; 2446
Cole, K., 5700
Cole, Margaret, 2372; 2375; 2376; 2377;
    2391; 2441
Cole, W. A., 4387
Cole, W. J., 2323
Coleman, Bruce P., 3140
Coles, Arthur, 5324
Coles, R. R. A., 6546
Colledge, Maureen, 4127; 4128
The Collier, 1860
Collier, A. S., 1703
Collier, P. C., 3889
Collins, B., 4441
Collins, E. J. T., 3951; 4501
Collins, J. T. E., 1231
Collins, R., 3602
Collins, R. G., 132; 4147
Collins, S., 5338
Collis-Squires, N., 6503
Colloquium on Management and Industrial Rela-
    tions (1979), 204; 210; 1008; 1065; 1066; 5018;
    5027; 6157; 6159
Colls, Robert, 5264
Colman, Sylvia, 5309
Colquhoun, J. C., 3461; 3499
Commission of Inquiry into Industrial and Com-
    mercial Representation, 1420
Commission on Industrial Relations, 1208; 1210;
    1421; 1479; 1693; 1713; 1714; 1715; 1837; 1940;

1941; 1942; 1948; 1949; 1950; 1951; 1960; 1961;
1964; 1985; 1999; 2017; 2028; 2568; 3800; 3805;
5744; 6054; 6837; 6838; 6839; 6840; 6849; 6850;
6864; 6865; 6866; 6867; 6868; 6869; 6870; 6871;
6872; 6873; 6874; 6875; 6876; 6888; 6889; 6890;
6891; 6892; 6893; 6894; 6895; 6896; 6897; 6898;
6899; 6900; 6901; 6902; 6903; 6904; 6905; 6906;
6907; 6908; 6909; 6910; 6911; 6912; 6913; 6914;
6915; 6916
Committee of Inquiry into Trawler Safety, 5899
Committee of Inquiry on Industrial Democracy,
    2817
Community Development Project, 4331
Community Relations Commission, 4197; 4388
Conboy, Bill, 4983
Concannon, H. M. G., 6947
Conditions of work and living, 5173
Confederation of British Industry, 1420; 1595;
    1610; 1759; 1786; 1910; 2501; 2569; 2637;
    2638; 2815; 3409; 4656; 5955; 6706
Conference on Human Resources and the Train-
    ing Plan, 3577
Conference on Research in the Field of Further
    Education, 3478
Conference on Sociology, Health and Illness,
    1976, 1001
Congdon, R. A., 3554
Congdon, Tim, 2602
Connelly, T. J., 5453
Connelly, Tom, 6476
Connock, Steve L., 1609; 3836; 3839
Connolly, D. J., 517
Connolly, James, 1244; 1245; 1254
Connolly, John, 4349
Connor, Danny, 2691
Conran, C. C., 6664; 6721
Construction Industry Training Board, 3744; 5901
Conway, Eddie, 59; 133
Cook, Alice H., 4872
Cook, F. G., 353, 378, 5536
Cook, Frederick G., 680; 1006
Cook, Stephen, 3386
Cooke, A. J., 1246; 1248; 2437
Cooke, P. J. D., 1435
Cooke, Peter N. C., 5750
Cookson, J. L., 6000
Cooley, Michael J. E., 623; 2473; 2707
Coombs, Rod, 384
Cooper, A., 1603
Cooper, A. J., 6337
Cooper, Arthur, 5272
Cooper, Bruce M., 186; 2139
Cooper, Cary L., 479; 659; 3480; 3515; 3768; 3769;
    4156; 4217; 5865; 5871; 5880; 5883; 5884
Cooper, F. R., 1801; 5962
Cooper, John, *Baron Cooper of Stockton Heath*, 153
Cooper, K. R., 1480
Cooper, N. J., 2736
Cooper, Neville, 1657
Cooper, Robert, 265; 431; 432; 443
Cooper, T., 5338
Cooperation and the working class, 2393
Cooperative communities, 2394
Cooperative Union Library, 36